*The
Savannah
River
Chiefdoms*

The
Savannah River
Chiefdoms

Political Change in the Late Prehistoric Southeast

DAVID G. ANDERSON

The University of Alabama Press
Tuscaloosa and London

Library of Congress Cataloging-in-Publication Data

Anderson, David G., 1949–
The Savannah River chiefdoms: political change in the late
prehistoric Southeast / David G. Anderson.
p. cm.
Originally presented as author's dissertation (doctoral—University of
Michigan, 1990).
Includes bibliographical references and index.
ISBN 0-8173-0725-7 (alk. paper)
1. Mississippian culture—Savannah River Watershed (Ga. and S.C.)
2. Chiefdoms—Savannah River Watershed (Ga. and S.C.) 3. Indians of
North America—Savannah River Watershed (Ga. and S.C.)—
Politics and government. 4. Indians of North America—Savannah
River Watershed (Ga. and S.C.)—Antiquities. 5. Savannah River
Watershed (Ga. and S.C.)—Antiquities. I. Title.
E99.M6815A53 1994
975.8'101—dc20   93-48393

British Library Cataloguing-in-Publication Data Available

For Jenalee, and our parents,
And all the others who helped along the way

Contents

Figures and Tables

TABLES

Acknowledgments

The support and encouragement of a great many people made the completion of this research possible and remind me that exploring the past is a truly cooperative venture. First and foremost, I would like to thank my doctoral committee at the University of Michigan, Richard I. Ford (Chair), William R. Farrand, John D. Speth, and Henry T. Wright, who channeled my energies into the exploration of a challenging research topic. David W. Stahle and Malcolm K. Cleaveland of the Tree Ring Laboratory, Department of Geography, University of Arkansas, provided primary data on their bald cypress dendrochronological investigations in Georgia and South Carolina, as well as advice about analysis and interpretation. Sergei Kan of Dartmouth College provided detailed instruction in the use of documentary evidence, shaping the ethnohistoric research.

Specific interpretations of the southeastern archaeological and ethnohistoric literature were facilitated by the kindness of a number of scholars associated with the University of Georgia. Charles M. Hudson provided me with copies of his published and ongoing works, most importantly the successive drafts of *The Juan Pardo Expeditions: Exploration of the Carolinas and Tennessee, 1566–1568* (1990). This effort was also greatly assisted by Chester B. DePratter and Marvin T. Smith, whose recent doctoral dissertations, respectively, *Late Prehistoric and Early Historic Chiefdoms in the Southeastern United States* (1983, 1991a) and *Archaeology of Aboriginal Culture Change in the Interior Southeast: Depopulation during the Early Historic Period* (1984, 1987) should, with Hudson's book on the Pardo expeditions, be read by any archaeologist or ethnologist seriously examining Mississippian culture. Mark Williams and David J. Hally served as guides to the intricacies of Georgia archaeology (and archaeologists), easing my work with the record and artifact collections in Athens.

At the South Carolina Institute of Archaeology and Anthropology (SCIAA), Tommy Charles, Chester B. DePratter, Keith Derting, Albert C. Goodyear, Jonathan M. Leader, Sharon Pekrul, Nena Powell, Bruce E. Rippeteau, and Steven D. Smith provided access to archaeological materials from South Carolina. Their continual support and encouragement have made SCIAA something of a second archaeological home for me for many years. In the summer of 1985 and from 1988 to 1990, I was at SCIAA much of the time, participating in a residency supported by Dr. Bruce Rippeteau, South Carolina state archaeologist, and by Glen T. Hanson, Mark J. Brooks, and Richard D. Brooks, the program managers of SCIAA's Savannah River Archaeological Research Project (SRARP) laboratory on the Department of Energy's Savannah River Site near Augusta. A generous stipend provided by the Oak Ridge Associated Universities (ORAU) graduate fellowship program enabled me to write at SRARP in relative comfort. Kenneth E.

Sassaman, who was also writing his doctoral dissertation at SRARP at the same time I was preparing this manuscript, was a particularly valued source of advice and criticism; his research on the Late Archaic occupations of the Savannah River valley (1993) is itself now a University of Alabama Press book and is an excellent synthesis of life during this period. Finally, the good-natured humor of SRARP technician George S. Lewis helped reduce the tension associated with writing a dissertation.

Other material assistance in the preparation of this manuscript was provided by the staff of the National Park Service's Interagency Archaeological Services division in Atlanta (IAS), where I worked in 1988 prior to accepting the ORAU fellowship and where I returned in the spring of 1990, after having been granted educational leave. The support of my IAS colleagues, John Jameson, Harry Scheele, and, above all, John E. Ehrenhard, my supervisor and mentor in government service, has enabled me to mix research and public careers.

Also greatly facilitating my research was the staff of Mound State Monument, Moundville, Alabama, where the records and collections from the Russell Reservoir investigations along the upper Savannah River are stored. Carey Oakley, director, and Eugene Futato, associate director, were particularly helpful in locating artifacts and camera-ready original graphics, providing housing, and giving technical advice about the directions of the research. Thanks to the hospitality of Eugene Futato, who put me up during visits, my research in Alabama was both professionally rewarding and personally enjoyable. In addition to a fine archaeological library, Eugene's science fiction collection is the only one I have encountered that exceeds my own; our conversations thus ranged widely over both time and space.

Readers providing technical commentary on portions of this manuscript included Alex Barker, Jim Bates, Elizabeth M. Brumfiel, John E. Clark, Malcolm K. Cleaveland, Chester B. DePratter, Timothy K. Earle, William R. Farrand, Richard I. Ford, Joan M. Gero, Sergei Kan, David J. Hally, Glen T. Hanson, Charles M. Hudson, Stephen A. Kowalewski, Clark Spencer Larsen, Janet E. Levy, Charles H. McNutt, George R. Milner, Timothy R. Pauketat, Kenneth E. Sassaman, John F. Scarry, Marvin T. Smith, John D. Speth, David W. Stahle, Paul D. Welch, J. Mark Williams, Henry T. Wright, and various anonymous press reviewers. Many of those individuals made primary data or advance copies of research manuscripts available, and all have offered important advice. Any good ideas in the pages that follow are in large measure due to the positive research atmosphere created by these colleagues. The illustrations that appear in this study were produced by Julie Barnes Smith, to whom I owe great thanks both for advice about formatting and for superb technical skills. I appreciate the assistance of Judith Knight, Malcolm M. MacDonald, and the staff of the University of Alabama Press, including Suzette Griffith and particularly Trinket Shaw, the copy editor.

The dissertation on which this study is based was completed in 1990 and was revised for publication from 1991 to early 1993. An early discussion of the theoretical arguments reported in this volume, a prospectus for my doctoral research, in fact, was published in 1990 in Mark Williams and Gary Shapiro's University of Alabama Press volume, *Lamar Archaeology: Mississippian Chiefdoms in the Deep South* (see Anderson 1990a, 1990b). Readers will now have the opportunity to see how my approach to examining political change in chiefdom societies has evolved, and how the theoretical framework advanced in that paper was meshed with the regional archaeological record. Minor portions of chapters 3, 4, 5, and 7 have appeared, in somewhat different form, in papers published by the Archaeological Society of South Carolina, the Florida Anthropological Society, Cambridge University Press, and the Society for American Archaeology (Anderson 1985a, 1990c, 1993; Anderson et al. n.d.). I thank these organizations for providing permission to publish this material, enabling me to put essentially all my research to date on the Savannah River chiefdoms in one place. I also wish to thank the Smithsonian Institution Press, and particularly Daniel R. Goodwin, for permission to reprint the accounts of early archaeological investigations conducted in and near the Savannah River valley, which appear in appendix A.

Finally, it must be said that this manuscript would never have been produced were it not for the continued love and encouragement provided by my wife, Jenalee Muse. Cooperation and support, I have found, are as important in marriage as they are in research.

*The
Savannah
River
Chiefdoms*

1

Political Evolution and Cycling

The question of how organizational and administrative structures emerged and evolved over time has been a subject of considerable interest to anthropologists since the beginnings of the discipline. Subsumed under this topic is the question of cycling behavior, the focus of this study. Why is it that organizational structures appear to fluctuate, or cycle, back and forth between specified levels of sociopolitical complexity in some societies, while in others they move seemingly uninterruptedly to ever-higher levels? Why, for example, have societies in some parts of the world remained at approximately the same level of complexity for hundreds or perhaps thousands of years, such as that observed among the tribes and chiefdoms in New Guinea, lowland South and Central America, (Bronze Age) Europe, and central Africa, while in other regions more complex societies emerged fairly quickly? Why, furthermore, should large, complex, and seemingly successful societies fall apart, only to have similar forms appear a century or two later? Cycling behavior, it will be demonstrated, is particularly characteristic of chiefdom societies. Exploring this process should not only advance our understanding of how chiefdoms operate but should also shed light on their emergence and, in some cases, evolutionary transformation into state-level societies or their collapse into simpler organizational forms.

While anthropologists and historians alike have advanced the notion that cyclicity appears to characterize aspects of human history, analysis of this proposition is in its infancy. In this study, what I call cycling refers to a fluctuation in administrative or decision-making levels within designated upper and lower limits. More specifically, it encompasses the social transformations that occur when administrative or decision-making levels within chiefdom-level societies in a given region fluctuate between one and two levels above the local community. As such, the process subsumes transitions between simple and complex chiefdoms. Such transitions are generally assumed to fall under the scope of cultural evolution. It is argued here, to the contrary, however, that cycling is an inherent aspect of chiefdoms, a process that occurs within this form of sociopolitical organization. This is not to say that cycling cannot have evolutionary effects. As we shall see, cycling can lead, over time, to pronounced changes in chiefly authority structures. Its study can thus lead us to a better understanding of what we mean by the chiefdom form of sociopolitical structure, as well as how evolutionary transformations occurred in the organization of human society.

The pervasiveness of cycling in chiefdom societies is a matter of particular interest, since evidence for the process does not appear restricted to isolated dramatic or enigmatic cases. Evidence for cycling is present wherever chiefdoms have been examined archaeologically or ethnographically in any detail. However, exactly what happens during the cycling process, which encompasses phenomena as disparate as regional population shifts and localized renewal ceremonies, is not well understood at the present. Even less certain are the reasons *why* such changes occurred. The purpose of this study is to remedy this situation to some extent, by exploring through a wide range of data what cycling is and how it operates. Awareness of the process of cycling, it is argued, is critical to understanding the archaeological and ethnographic record of the world's chiefdoms.

To understand how and why cycling occurs, factors promoting both stability and change in chiefdom political organization are examined in the pages that follow. While addressing a question of relevance to the study of chiefdoms worldwide, the research is directed to a specific region, the southeastern United States, with particular attention to the Mississippian societies that existed in the Savannah River valley from circa A.D. 1000 to 1600. There are a number of reasons for this narrowing of focus.

First, while the development of a general descriptive and explanatory model of cycling in chiefdoms is the objective of this research, such a formulation must be evaluated with real-world data. The archaeological record from the Southeast is particularly well suited to this task. During the final millennium before European contact, simple and complex chiefdoms arose throughout the region. Their emergence and development have fascinated archaeologists for over a century and have resulted in the production of a massive data base. Even though research directions have changed, from concerns about the origin of the "mound builders" to an interest in material culture and chronology and, most recently, to questions about the operation and evolution of these societies, basic data have continued to accumulate. Tens of thousands of Mississippian period sites have been recorded over the region, and hundreds have been excavated. Thanks largely to cultural resource management projects, fieldwork has been increasingly directed to documenting the universe of possible site types, including mound centers, villages, hamlets, and limited-activity loci. In many areas, furthermore, chronological resolution on the order of 100-year intervals or less is now possible, permitting fine-grained areally extensive diachronic analyses of settlement patterning, land use, and social change.

Second, an extensive historic record exists describing southeastern chiefdoms from the period of early European contact. Regional political geography, particularly social relations within and between Mississippian societies, has become a productive area for research, and early contact accounts have been used in conjunction with archaeological data to examine the location, extent, internal organization, operation, and evolution of Mississippian societies across the region.

Third, the Southeast has seen considerable paleoenvironmental research in recent years, directed to the reconstruction of past vegetational communities, fluvial dynamics, and climatic conditions. Much of this research, encompassing the disciplines of geoarchaeology, geomorphology, palynology, and dendrochronology, can be profitably employed in the examination of late prehistoric social evolution.

Fourth, the primary geographic focus of this study, the South Appalachian Mississippian area, comprising Georgia, South Carolina, and contiguous portions of adjoining states (Ferguson 1971; Griffin 1967; Holmes 1903:130), has a long history of archaeological research. The Mississippian societies occupying the Savannah, Oconee, Coosa, Tennessee, and Santee/Wateree river basins, in fact, have been the object of appreciable research by both archaeologists and ethnohistorians in recent years. As a result, the archaeological and historic data from this part of the Southeast are among the most extensive available anywhere in the world for the study of chiefdom political change.

Finally, the selection of the Savannah River basin was dictated, in no small measure, by the occurrence of dramatic examples of cycling in the archaeological record; the fact that I had extensive archaeological experience in this area was, of course, also a major consideration. In brief, evidence accumulated to date and summarized in the present study indicates that a number of chiefdoms rose and fell along the Savannah River from circa 1100 to 1450. After 1450, however, virtually the entire basin, which was densely occupied throughout much of prehistory, and by progressively more complex chiefdoms from circa 1200 to 1450, was precipitously abandoned. Only after circa 1650, some 200 years later, did native groups return to the area. Understanding why the earlier pattern of cycling occurred as well as why the basin was ultimately abandoned were primary objectives of this study. The research summarized in this volume was thus prompted by a particularly intriguing case from an area where, fortunately, a considerable body of evidence existed.

The late prehistoric and early contact-era Mississippian chiefdoms of the southeastern United States, I believe, offer an incomparable opportunity for the study of social and political change. The archaeological record from the region is replete with evidence for the emergence, expansion, collapse, and reemergence or replacement of simple and complex chiefdoms. Some of these societies existed for centuries, while others lasted only a generation or two. At ceremonial centers throughout the region, major construction and rebuilding episodes are documented, specifically the replacement of buildings and fortifications and the addition of new mounds or mound stages. This activity appears directly linked to changes in leadership positions, organizational structures, and physical centers of power. On a larger geographic scale, southeastern archaeologists have long been intrigued by the emergence, growth, and collapse of major regional polities such as those centered at Cahokia, Moundville, Spiro, or Etowah, as well as by the disappearance of Mississippian societies from large areas, occupational hiatuses that in some cases lasted centuries. The "vacant quarter" hypothesis advanced by Stephen Williams (1982, 1990), that much of the central Mississippi alluvial valley was abandoned circa 1400, following the collapse of Cahokia, is perhaps the most dramatic example of this latter process known from the Eastern Woodlands.

While this volume thus explores the emergence, expansion, and fragmentation of Mississippian polities in the Savannah River basin and immediately adjoining areas, events elsewhere in the Eastern Woodlands are also considered. Major conclusions of this study are that understanding the political and social histories of individual chiefdoms requires the adoption of broad geographic and temporal perspectives, and that organizational change in chiefdoms must be examined from regional as well as local levels, using information drawn from both synchronic and diachronic frameworks.

The Relationship of Cycling to the Chiefdom Concept

A primary goal of this research is to make a contribution to our understanding of how and why complex societies emerge and evolve. Cycling, it is argued, is an integral part of chiefdom society, a process that tends to preserve rather than eliminate chiefly structures in the short term (i.e., on a scale of decades to centuries), although it can also lead to dramatic consequences in the long run (i.e., on a scale of centuries to millennia). By focusing on patterns and processes of internal organizational change, however, chiefdoms may be seen in their own terms and not merely as a developmental stage between societies of lesser and greater complexity.

Understanding the causes of organizational stability in chiefdoms is crucial to understanding the cycling process. Stability is here taken to mean the maintenance of a given level of organizational or administrative complexity, as measured by the number of decision-making levels in place. Organizational instability, in contrast, refers to fluctuations in decision-making levels and hence to the cycling process itself. Factors promoting organizational stability in chiefdoms thus tend to limit the possibility of change or cycling, while factors promoting organizational instability tend to promote its likelihood. That the study of processes shaping chiefdom organizational structures can inform more general evolutionary questions, such as the origins of social inequality or the emergence or collapse of state-level societies, is understood but is not a primary focus of this work. Evolution between societal forms or stages defers, in this study, to developmental processes operating within a given organizational form, the chiefdom (although as we shall see, cycling can have evolutionary consequences).

The causes of cycling behavior in chiefdoms, I argue in chapter 2, are complex and multivariate, requiring the evaluation of a wide range of data and the adoption of a research strategy employing a number of lines of evidence. Central to this approach is a concern for hypothesis falsification in the evaluation of alternative explanations, a process that forms the core of the scientific method. While the incorporation of a number of causal mechanisms in the explanation of cycling that is advanced here may be less aesthetically pleasing than an argument based on one or a few "prime movers," I have no doubt that it provides a more accurate picture of the forces in play.

To understand cycling we must first specify what we mean by a chiefdom. A number of definitions of what is meant by a chiefdom have appeared in the literature, most of which emphasize the nature of leadership and organizational structures. To Service (1971:134, 144–45, 159), chiefdoms are "redistributional societies with a permanent central agency of coordination. . . . . The most distinctive characteristic of chiefdoms as opposed to tribes and bands is . . . the pervasive inequality of persons and groups in the society. It begins with the status of the chief as he functions in the system of redistribution. Persons are then ranked above others according to their genealogical nearness to him. Concepts involving prescriptions, proscriptions, sumptuary laws, marriage rules and customs, genealogical conceptions, and etiquette in general combine to create and perpetuate this sociopolitical ordering. . . . [T]he rise of broad strata as well as particular social positions, all of unequal rank, are characteristic of chiefdoms." Service's observation that chiefdoms are predicated on genealogically sanctioned leadership structures appears valid and, as we shall see, is critical to understanding why cycling occurs. His views on the importance of redistribution, however, are no longer widely held. Most communities in these kind of societies appear to be economically self-sufficient, particularly in subsistence production. Instead of the collection and generalized redistribution of a wide range of subsistence and other goods, tribute mobilization and the limited redistribution of sumptuary goods to lesser elites in a deliberate effort to obtain their support appear to be hallmarks of chiefdom political economy (Earle 1977:225–27, 1978:181, 1987:292; Peebles and Kus 1977:425–26; Spencer 1987:369; Steponaitis 1978:428; Welch 1991; Wright 1984:45). Chiefs, in this view, exacted tribute to fuel their own ambitions, which were usually centered on the maintenance or extension of their prestige and power, rather than for the benefit of society as a whole. Redistribution of subsistence goods appears to have been rare and typically occurred only during periods of severe societal stress, when it would have been designed to maintain the well-being and hence labor resources of commoner populations.

Fried's (1967:109, 116, 126) arguments about social status and its relation to leadership structures in what he calls rank societies are also instructive and complement Service's views on the importance of genealogical relationships. In rank societies, "positions of valued status are somehow limited so that not all those of sufficient talent to occupy such statuses actually achieve them. Such a society may or may not be stratified. . . . One of the major developments is the emergence of a clearly distinguished descent principle requiring demonstration of relationship. The basic technique of accomplishing this is the specific genealogy which, at least in theory, specifies all consanguinal ties and many affinal ones. . . . Given such forms of grouping and the device of the genealogy, it is possible to develop a hierarchical arrangement of kin such that, for example, proximity or distance to a particular ancestor becomes significant. . . . It might be better to say that what must be known is the distance of relationship between any member and the highest ranking person of his generation." Stratified societies are those "in which members of the same sex and equivalent age status do not have equal access to the basic resources that sustain life" (186). Chiefdoms can thus be viewed as rank societies with essentially two social strata, chiefly elites and commoners. The differences between these strata in individual chiefdoms vary considerably and appear to be scale dependent, that is, related to the size and complexity of the society in question (Feinman and Neitzel 1984:57). Within the elite strata, genealogical distance from an apical ancestor or, as Fried would have it, the current ruler, has a great deal to do with determining an individual's chances of succeeding to the chieftainship. How these kinship and successional relationships are structured markedly affects organizational stability in these societies. Where many individuals can potentially succeed to power and institutions regulating succession are weak, competition for chiefly authority is likely to be widespread. This competition between elites for power is, I shall argue, a major force driving organizational change in chiefdoms.

To return to our review of what constitutes a chiefdom, the coordination of activities in two or more communities may be perhaps the single most important responsibility facing chiefly elites (and in many cases may subsume the control of rivals). According to Carneiro (1981:37–38), for example, the emergence of chiefdom societies represents "the first transcending of local autonomy in human history. With chiefdoms, multicommunity political units emerged for the first time. . . . The emergence of chiefdoms was a qualitative step. Everything that followed, including the rise of states and empires, was, in a sense, merely quantitative." A similar view is held by Earle (1987:288), who has focused on the nature and scale of leadership roles in these societies. Thus chiefdoms are "regionally organized societies with a centralized decision-making hierarchy coordinating activities among several village communities. Polities vary in size from simple chiefdoms integrating populations of perhaps a thousand to complex chiefdoms with populations in the tens of thousands." Chiefdoms are thus multicommunity political units under the control of a hereditary decision-making group or elite. Given this, it should be possible to measure the power and authority of a chief through reference to the number of communities under his direct or indirect control.

Care must be taken, however, to avoid reifying the chiefdom category or imposing too narrow an interpretation on the concept. Recent analyses have shown the vulnerability of monolithic definitions predicated on factors such as redistribution, population size, or degree of stratification and have documented the considerable variability that characterizes these systems. Uncritical use of evolutionary stage formulations, furthermore, has been shown to constrain analyses of variability, directing research into typological cul-de-sacs and away from evolutionary or processual concerns (as forcefully noted by Earle 1978:227, 1987; Feinman and Neitzel 1984:40–45; Friedman and Rowlands 1977:201–6; Price and Brown 1985:4– 5; Renfrew 1974:72–73; Spencer 1987:379–83, 1990:2–4; Steponaitis 1981:320–21; Upham 1987:346–48; Wenke 1981:84–87; Wright 1984:41–42). The chiefdom concept is currently seen as a useful if somewhat overdrawn heuristic device, indicating the general kind of society under investigation and providing a framework within which information and research can be organized. When working with particular societies, however, care must be taken to document their characteristics; classifications are useful only if they are viewed as a beginning rather than the end point of research.

Some of the most recent definitions of the chiefdom have combined organizational and scalar measures. To Henry Wright, the emergence of chiefdoms represents the development of hereditary elites maintaining control apparatuses extending over a series of communities and the widespread emergence of groups of people having unequal access to resources. In Wright's (1984:42–43) view, chiefdoms are characterized by "one generalized kind of political control. . . . Simple chiefdoms are those in which such control is exercised by figures drawn from an ascribed elite subgroup; these chiefdoms characteristically have only one level of control above the level of the local community. . . . Complex chiefdoms characteristically cycle between one and two levels of control hierarchy above the level of the local community . . . [and are characterized by] a chiefly class or nobility, members of which control generalized, polity wide decision making." This approach offers a typology of chiefdoms—simple and complex—and incorporates cycling, specifically shifts between levels in an idealized information-processing and management control hierarchy, as a basic characteristic of chiefdoms. The concept of control hierarchies in relation to changes in organizational complexity has seen considerable investigation (Flannery 1972:409–11; Johnson 1973:1–12, 1978, 1982; Wright 1969, 1977:381–2, 1984:42–44; Wright and Johnson 1975), although most of this work has been directed to understanding processes behind the emergence and evolution of state societies, with somewhat less emphasis on the actual operation of chiefdoms themselves.

Further clarification is necessary as to what is meant by an administrative or decision-making level, the basic element of a control hierarchy. Following Johnson (1978:89), and using terminology derived from information theory, each level may be defined as a vertical control unit, specifically "an organizational unit specialized in providing integration among sources or lower-level vertical control units. . . . [Sources are] the minimal organizational unit under consideration. Types of source units may include territorial units, population units, residence units, activity units, etc." Individual communities represent the basic source units employed in the analyses of chiefdom political evolution conducted in this study (figure 1). Thus a chiefdom with a single-level control hierarchy, or one decision-making/administrative level, is characterized by one level of control above the village or hamlet level. This pattern is typical of simple chiefdoms, while complex chiefdoms or hierarchies are societies with two levels of control above the basic community (Steponaitis 1978:420; Wright 1984:42–43; Pauketat 1991:9–10). These control apparatuses are assumed to be amenable to detection through traditional archaeological settlement hierarchy analyses.

Kent Flannery's (1972:409–11) classic description of the operation of social control apparatuses also warrants mention in this context:

> A simple human ecosystem . . . consists of a series of subsystems arranged hierarchically, from lowest and most specific to highest and most general. Each subsystem is regulated by a control apparatus whose job is to keep all the variables in the subsystem within appropriate goal ranges— ranges which maintain homeostasis and do not threaten the survival of the system. . . . Normally, higher-order controls regulate only the output of lower-order subsystems, and not the variables kept in range by the latter. But should a lower-order control fail to keep its relevant variables within their ranges (as in the case of socio-environmental stress), the control apparatus on the next higher level of the hierarchy may be called into operation as a "back-up." Should all controls on the levels fail, the system is in trouble; it needs a new regulatory institution, and unless one evolves the system may collapse, or "devolve" to a lower level of integration. If a system is buffered in such a way that deviant variables in one subsystem take a long time to affect other subsystems, it is likely to be stable.

Explanations for cycling behavior, namely the failure of society to evolve more efficient higher-level regulatory or control units, or buffer deviant variables, are subsumed in this argument. Administrative levels

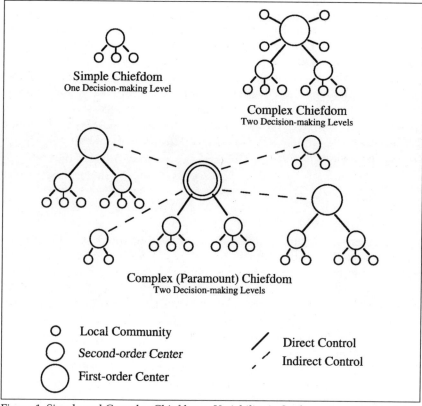

Figure 1 Simple and Complex Chiefdoms: Variability in Settlement and Control Hierarchies.

are thus seen as vertical control or integrative units that coordinate activity at the community level or in lower administrative levels in complex multicommunity societies, such as chiefdoms or states. The definition of cycling used in this study is drawn from this foundation.

A Definition of Cycling

Cycling encompasses the transformations that occur when administrative or decision-making levels within the chiefdom societies occupying a given region fluctuate between one and two levels above the local community. Cycling is thus the recurrent process of the emergence, expansion, and fragmentation of complex chiefdoms amid a regional backdrop of simple chiefdoms. The adoption of a regional perspective is critical to the investigation of this process, since changes in the number of decision-making levels in the chiefdoms within a given region are rarely concurrent. That is, chiefdoms rarely form or collapse in precisely the same location or with the same periodicity; instead, these societies typically expand or contract at the expense of or because of the actions of other chiefdoms. Centers of power shift or rotate over the landscape, as first one community and then another assumes prominence. It is this regional pattern of emergence and decline of complex chiefdoms that is of interest and represents what is meant by cycling behavior, necessitating a broad geographical perspective (see also Carneiro 1991:185–86; Drennan 1991a:129; Earle 1991:13–14; Nassaney 1992a; and Pauketat 1991:28 for recent discussions of this process).

Why Explore Cycling?

The most important reason to examine cycling behavior is because its study can yield important clues about how chiefdoms operate. At a more general level, examining the process can give us new insights into how and why human beings organize societies the way they do, and how changes in sociopolitical structure come about. Inspection of the global anthropological literature yields numerous examples of the rise and decline of chiefdoms, including the fluctuations between simple and complex chiefdoms that meet the definition of cycling used in this study. This same literature documents the regional scale at which the process operates, as centers of power shift back and forth over the landscape. The best evidence for the process tends to come from archaeological and ethnohistoric research, however, rather than from ethnographies, since the latter rarely have sufficient temporal or geographic scope.

Prestate developmental trajectories in areas where state formation occurred have been the subject of intensive examination by a number of scholars, and evidence for cycling behavior in the chiefdoms of these regions has been widely noted (e.g., Adams 1966:9–33, 1981; Blanton et al. 1981, 1982; Flannery 1976; Flannery and Marcus 1983:53–64; Johnson 1973:87–101, 1987; Kowalewski 1990; Kowalewski et al. 1989; Parsons et al. 1982:316–31; Pollock 1983; Wilson 1987; Wright and Johnson 1975). In what is unquestionably the broadest examination of the general topic of sociopolitical evolution and its relationship to cycling behavior, Wright (1986) examined the fluctuations in control hierarchies that occurred prior to and during the period of primary state formation in four areas of the world: in Greater Mesopotamia, the Indus River valley, central Mexico, and Peru. He found that simple and complex chiefdoms persisted for centuries in these areas prior to state emergence, "with intense competition and much replacement of centers and no doubt of paramounts, but with little or no increase in sociopolitical complexity" (357). State emergence eventually occurred in each area, and typically fairly abruptly, but only after a lengthy period of increasing competition and conflict between closely spaced complex chiefdoms. The process of state emergence thus appears to be closely tied to cycling (see also reviews by Carneiro 1981; Earle 1987, 1991; Kohl 1987; Tainter 1988; Wright 1977, 1986).

Archaeological analyses documenting cycling in chiefdoms in areas where primary states did not form are also common, however, and include studies from settings as diverse as Central and South America, Africa, Polynesia, and Western Europe (e.g., Champion and Champion 1986; Champion et al. 1984; Cordy 1981; Drennan 1991a, 1991b; Drennan and Uribe 1987; Helms 1979; Kirch 1984, 1986; Renfrew 1973, 1974, 1986; Renfrew and Shennan 1982; Shennan 1987; D. Taylor 1975). Understanding why cycling persisted (and state formation did not occur) in these areas is, I believe, as important as understanding why cycling led to state emergence in other areas. Ethnohistorical evidence for the kinds of activities leading to or subsumed under chiefly cycling, importantly, is available from some of these same regions, primarily because chiefdoms in these areas survived until comparatively recently and because that evidence is not shrouded by the activities of several millennia of subsequent states and empires (e.g., Firth 1961; Goldman 1970; Helms 1979:38–69; Sahlins 1958, 1981; Steward 1946–1950; Steward and Faron 1959). Particularly classic examples of ethnographic studies documenting events that can be subsumed under the process of cycling include Leach's (1954) analysis of Kachin social structural variability, Turner's (1957) examination of the causes of fissioning in Ndembu society, and Petersen's (1982) analysis of fissioning in a Ponapean chiefdom. Exploring and evaluating the causes of cycling is, I believe, an important subject for anthropological research, and the process itself is one that plays a major role in human political evolution.

2

The Causes of Cycling

The emergence and collapse of complex chiefdoms amid a regional land-scape of simple chiefdoms, or cycling, it is argued, is caused by a wide array of factors, the most important of which are examined in the pages that follow. To understand why organizational change occurs in complex societies, we must move beyond explanations based on the actions of isolated factors or "prime movers" such as climate or social competition and look to a more realistic matrix approach that incorporates a range of variables. This chapter focuses primarily on ethnographic evidence for cycling to illustrate its widespread occurrence and to explore some of the factors that bring it about.

Developmental Trajectories

The developmental histories of chiefly societies determine patterns of social ranking, sanctifying ideologies, and authority structures, which in turn predispose responses to changes in the natural and cultural land-scape, matters that affect organizational stability and propensity for cycling. As we shall see, the process by which chiefdoms emerged in a given region is also important to the study of cycling. Some of the causal mechanisms that have been advanced to explain the emergence of chiefdoms include warfare, competition among elites for power and prestige, increased information processing demands, and subsistence uncertainty (e.g., Carneiro 1981:54–65; Flannery 1972:402–18; Fried 1967:191–223; Sahlins 1958; Service 1971:134–43; Wright 1984:41–51).

As noted in chapter 1, managerial stress arguments linking the emergence of hereditary social inequality and ranking to increased decision-making demands upon society have become popular in recent years. A direct relationship between organizational size and complexity and number of decision-making levels has, in fact, been documented cross-cultur-ally (Johnson 1973:10–11, 1978; see also Carneiro 1967; Feinman and Neitzel 1984). Johnson (1978:101–2) has suggested that the "development of ranking systems may be associated with increment in the number of information sources integrated on a societal level," while Earle (1987:289) has argued that increased information-processing requirements can lead to the creation of new social groups: "As polity scale increases, the number of decisions required by any node increases until it exceeds an individual's personal capacity to make decisions and requires an expansion in the hierarchy of decision-makers." The emergence of ascribed or hereditary social statuses may thus be seen as a solution to the problem of defining, recruiting, and training a decision-making group.

While increased decision-making demands upon a society may well necessitate the development of patterns of social ranking, this does not tell us why these demands arose in the first place. Traditional materialist explanations for the emergence of social hierarchies have emphasized efforts by early societies (driven perhaps by one or more stressors such as population pressure, environmental change or uncertainty, or social circumscription) to increase labor/subsistence productivity (*sensu* Childe 1952; Wittfogel 1957). Increased information-processing demands, in these constructs, arose from a need by the affected populations to develop and maintain irrigation networks and/or large cleared field systems, or to control agricultural production or trade over large areas, or to defend against enemies.

These kinds of explanation have been viewed with increasing dissatisfaction in recent years, with the primary criticism brought against them being that they tend to ignore social or political (i.e., agent-centered) forces driving organizational change (e.g., Bender 1985, 1989; Brumfiel and Fox 1994; Clark 1987; Clark and Blake 1994; Helms 1979, 1988; Marquardt 1986, 1988, 1989, 1992; Nassaney 1992a, 1992b; Pauketat 1991:8–9, 1992; Shryock 1987). Increased information-processing demands are now seen as arising, at least in part, from competition among individuals for followers (i.e., in order to control their labor) and, once elites were in place, from a need to maintain the loyalty and subordinate position of these followers. Managerial stress arguments, accordingly, have been modified in recent years to accommodate patterns of elite competition and interaction, with the most viable frameworks (in my opinion) also incorporating underlying materialistic/ecological factors. To understand the formation of hereditary decision-making groups, a developmental process that I argue markedly shapes subsequent organizational stability and hence cycling, we must thus explore how and why individuals sought, obtained, and then maintained power.

One compelling explanation as to how competition between elites can lead to patterns of social ranking has been offered by Ross Cordy (1981:220–21; see also Clark and Blake 1994). Chiefly largesse in rewarding relatives, official overseers, and other assistants and retainers, quite simply, creates a group of people with a vested interest in the successful continuation of the system. These family, friends, and hangers-on are equated with the decision maker and come to assume the same trappings of status. The formation of a new decision-making level can thus lead to the creation of a new social rank echelon. Simple chiefdoms, in this view, may be seen as those with two rank echelons, commoners (dispersed throughout the chiefdom) and elites (located primarily at the chiefly center), while complex chiefdoms are those with three or more rank echelons, encompassing commoners (again, dispersed throughout the chiefdom), lesser elites (located primarily at local centers), and apical elites (located primarily at the paramount center) (Cordy 1981:3–4). Fluctuation in the numbers of decision-making/administrative levels in a region's chiefdoms, or cycling, parenthetically, would thus be accompanied by pronounced changes in the number of rank echelons present (i.e., in patterns of social ranking), although the rate at which these changes occurred would likely vary appreciably from case to case.

Changes in administrative level leading to the formation or dissolution of rank echelons are also typically accompanied by changes in behavioral patterns between the members of these echelons. Social differentiation can occur when higher-level decision makers and their associates are increasingly physically and symbolically isolated from lower-level decision makers or commoners, as part of a conscious strategy to emphasize and reinforce their authority. In simple chiefdoms, interaction between social groups is frequent and relatively unconstrained, while in complex chiefdoms there is greater social distancing, and access to resources such as food, clothing, housing, or luxury goods is more unequal. The formation of new administrative levels and their associated rank echelons, or the abandonment of levels and rank echelons already in place, is thus subsumed in the definition of cycling employed in the present study. The establishment or loss of political hegemony thus encompasses change in a wide array of behavior.

Mechanisms for the emergence of chiefly elites, as noted, tend to emphasize competition among individuals for control over labor, strategic resources, or prestige items, which in turn can be used to increase status or form alliances or to reduce subsistence or conflict risk (e.g., Bender 1985:58–59; D. Braun and Plog 1982:507; Fried 1967:186; Helms 1979, 1987:67–70; Shennan 1982; Wright 1984:69). The development of an ideology of power or chiefly sanctity manifested in both objects and behavior is widely regarded as a critical aspect to the development of social inequality (e.g., Bender 1985:59; Wright 1984:69). The strength of this rationalizing idiom or appeal to sacred authority (which is potentially able to legitimize or promote an acceptance of social inequality among all segments of a population), I shall argue, is directly related to societal stability.

Mary Helms, in a series of perceptive essays, has described how prestige goods (i.e., objects manifesting chiefly sanctity) function to maintain the social order. In Helms's (1987:67, 69, 70) view, these items "are imbued with complex, multifaceted symbolism and thereby become exquisitely succinct encapsulations of social, political and ideological constructs. . . . Consideration of the particular qualities and characteristics of symbolically relevant natural objects can help cast light on the existential and cosmological assumptions that validate so much cultural activity. . . . [Prestige goods are] representative of the special qualities and activities of the elite, and [thus function in] . . . active and passive expressions of rank and associated prerogatives" (see also Helms 1979, 1988, 1992). Iconography and ancestor worship additionally combine to symbolize and legitimize the positions and aspirations of the participants in major sectors of chiefdom societies (see particularly Rappaport 1971, 1979a, 1979b for extended discussion of this point). The diverse symbolism, furthermore, served to accentuate and simultaneously to mediate tensions in these nonegalitarian societies. Potential planes of social cleavage, centered around areas of greatest social tension, occur not only between elites and commoners in chiefdoms, however, but also between different factions among the elites themselves. Chiefdom stability thus depended on the ways social tensions could be mediated, and how this occurred is something explicitly shaped by historical trajectories.

Resource control, alliance, and exchange networks and supporting ideologies did not spring into existence overnight but emerged slowly and were already in place in some form well before chiefdom organizational and control structures emerged. This pattern has been documented in the archaeological record of the Eastern Woodlands of North America, across Western Europe, and in wide areas of Central and South America. In all of these areas, the existence of prestige goods–based exchange networks preceded the emergence of recognizable chiefdoms by several millennia (e.g., Brose 1979; Byrd 1991; Champion et al. 1984; Clark and Blake 1994; Flannery 1976; Flannery and Marcus 1983; Griffin 1967; Renfrew and Shennan 1982; C. Webb 1977; Winters 1968). Braun and Plog (1982) have suggested that such exchange and alliance networks emerged in tribal societies as risk-minimization strategies. The emergence of these networks, they argue, was directly linked to the emergence of sanctifying ideologies, which formed an essential underpinning of initial chiefdom authority structures (see also J. Brown, Kerber, and Winters 1990; Friedman and Rowlands 1977; Wright 1984). Successful practitioners of strategies that led to long-term enhancement of group living conditions, in this view, might be accorded a measure of sanctity and undoubtedly were more secure in their positions than less successful individuals. Degree of control over exchange thus came to be tied, in some cases, to the relative stability of authority structures. A pattern of gradual emergence thus characterizes pristine chiefdoms and distinguishes them from secondary chiefly polities, which typically formed quickly in response to the existence and/or encroachment of other chiefdoms or more complex systems (Carneiro 1981:66; Sanders and Price 1968:132; Webster 1975:467). As a result, the presence of entrenched ideological mechanisms assisting in the maintenance of elite power particularly characterizes pristine chiefdoms. Such mechanisms may not be present or may not be as effective in secondary chiefdoms, which form as a reactionary process and follow different developmental trajectories.

The formation of authority structures in pristine chiefdoms warrants further consideration, since the stability of these structures is closely tied with that of society in general. Wright (1984:69) has suggested that the development of sanctifying ideologies came about through patterns of elite competition: "continued competition for alliance and offices among local ranking groups would weld such groups into a region-wide chiefly or noble class. . . . [S]uch a process of competition should generate an ideology of chiefly sanctity." Friedman and Rowlands (1977:209–11) have discussed how this process might operate in some detail, focusing on the competitive exchange of valuables as a mechanism behind the development of rank differentiation. In their view, surplus extraction and wealth accumulation is transformed into personal status and power through redistributive activities such as feasting, which leads to the recruitment of supporters. The manipulation of marital alliances is coupled with this, creating asymmetrical dependency relationships among various groups or lineages, which translates into relative rank (see also Sahlins 1968:86–89). The group or lineage dominating "feast giving and affinal exchange [by virtue of its success] becomes identified with the direct descendant of the territorial deity" (Friedman and Rowlands 1977:211). As other lineages define their position in relation to this primary lineage, what were asymmetrical and temporary dependency relationships soon become permanent status differences.

As the members of the primary lineage assume increasing (direct as well as ideological) responsibility for the maintenance of community welfare, they also warrant increased gifts from the community, typically in the form of labor or surplus food. What begins as a moral obligation, however, eventually becomes tribute given under threat of sanction, as the dominant lineage consolidates its position through the legitimized use of secular power. The dictation of what constitutes appropriate tribute leads to increasing control over primary production and the appropriation of surplus. Extralocal exchange of prestige goods, whose production is sponsored by subsistence surplus, soon comes under the same kind of control, as dominant elites make use of extralocal materials and social relationships to legitimize their positions of rank and sanctity. Centers of power controlling both production and exchange thus expand at the expense of those precluded from access to these networks (see also Helms 1979:31–32, 67ff).

In spite of these arguments, it is still difficult to understand how extended success at wealth accumulation and redistribution and favorable marital alliance formation can translate into hereditary patterns of inequality between lineages. In many ways, these theories represent little more than an extension of the strategy whereby "big-men" (*sensu* Sahlins

1963) rise to power, differing only in suggesting that long-term success legitimizes the transformation of individually achieved status into hereditary or ascribed status. That the long-term result of competition would be the establishment of hereditary patterns of inequality was certainly not foreseen by the participants (Clark and Blake 1994; Pauketat 1991:16, 23). Why, therefore, should individuals and lineages compete with each other, participating in a process that eventually leads to marked patterns of social inequality? Lenski (1966:210–11), although referring to patterns of competition in simple states, has described the reasons for competition for positions of authority in terms of personal self-interest: "because of the great powers vested in it, it [i.e., leadership] was the supreme prize for all who coveted power, privilege, and prestige. To win control . . . was to win control of the most powerful instrument of self-aggrandizement found in agrarian societies. . . . [S]truggles for power . . . were usually between individuals and groups concerned far more with their own partisan advantage than with either the principles of distributive justice or the common good, except in those cases where private advantage and the common good happened to coincide. . . . [T]hey were struggles between opposing factions of the privileged class, each seeking its own special advantage, or, occasionally, a small segment of the common people seeking political advantage and preferment for themselves." The tangible rewards of belonging to the elite or minimally obtaining recognition and prestige from them thus served as the means by which members of society competed with and in some cases suppressed each other.

However, reliance on coercive authority and the playing off or co-opting of rivals, while often necessary, are not in and of themselves effective ways of maintaining power, because of the time and energy that must be spent keeping the population under control and extracting surplus from it. Newly emergent elites are thus likely to devote considerable energy to legitimizing their rule, that is, to the creation of "an ideology which provides a moral justification for the regime's exercise of power" (Lenski 1966:51–54; see also Bender 1989 and Pauketat 1991 for extended discussion of this point). In pristine chiefdoms, presumably characterized by a gradual process of emergence and the close equation of elite authority with sanctity, such an ideology is likely already to be in place. The maintenance of ideological structures by social elites, it should be stressed, while unquestionably self-serving, was also something thought by exploiters and exploited alike to be essential to the material well-being of society.

Degree of public support for and participation in ritual activity, I believe, appears to be an effective measure of the strength of a society's ideological structures and, ultimately, its stability. Ritual is a routinizing social mechanism which, by virtue of stressing norms of behavior and the importance of group unity, exposes the abnormality of disruptive forces and, ideally, leads to their dissipation (Rappaport 1979a). The strategy works effectively only in groups where long-established ties are already present, however, and are hence amenable to reinforcement through traditional behavior (V. Turner 1957:195, 316). Where ritual behavior was strongly supported, society itself tended to be stable. Legitimizing ideologies thus take time to develop but, once in place, can provide strong support to chiefly decision-making hierarchies. While something of a truism, sociopolitical stability in *any* society ultimately depends on the nature of and public support for organizational structures.

To conclude this section, it can thus be argued that the stability of chiefdom societies, at least in part, is directly related to the nature of their emergence and subsequent development, particularly the process by which the elite arrive at and maintain their positions of authority. Significant differences, in this view, should be evident in the developmental trajectories, social hierarchies, and legitimizing ideologies and hence in the stability of the organizational structures of pristine as opposed to secondary chiefdoms. The relatively rapid emergence of secondary chiefdom societies, quite simply, means that there is little time for a rationalizing idiom, an ideology of chiefly sanctity, to develop. Chiefly authority in these cases may be more likely to reside in coercive or cooperative measures. That is, political authority in secondary chiefdoms, at least initially, might have to be maintained through the overt use of secular power or force, probably to a greater extent than in pristine chiefdoms, or it might have to rest on cooperative agreements between the participating constituents. As such, these authority structures may be fairly fragile and of short duration, unless they manage to survive until a legitimizing ideology can be set in place. Finally, leadership positions in secondary chiefdoms may have been less likely (initially) to be hereditary, since prowess in warfare or decision making, rather than membership in a sanctified elite, may have been the most important criterion for social advancement.

Several characteristics are thus postulated for pristine chiefdom societies, which serve to differentiate them from secondary chiefdoms: a slow pattern of emergence; well-established and widely accepted ideological structures; the presence of well-established, genealogically sanctioned authority structures and patterns of succession; and a system of social advancement restricted to hereditary elites. Secondary chiefdoms, in contrast, are characterized by: rapid emergence; weakly developed legitimizing ideologies; weakly sanctioned and (in some cases) nonkin-based authority structures; and a more open system of advancement, where authority is probably based to a fair degree on personal ability. To the extent that the presence of pristine and secondary chiefdoms can be identified, the viability of these characteristics should be examined. Coupled with this should be an examination of changes in the nature and strength of ideological structures over time. Examining the emergence and expansion of chiefdoms is important to understanding the arena in which cycling is played out.

Mechanisms Maintaining Elite Authority Structures

As shown, the stability of chiefdom societies, and particularly the nature and intensity of political competition in a given region, is closely tied to the nature and effectiveness of ideological and secular mechanisms used to maintain and legitimize elite authority structures. These factors appear to be directly related to both the size and time depth of chiefdoms in a region. The relationship and importance of "sacred" (i.e., consensual, ideologically based) as opposed to "secular" (i.e., coercive authority, use of force) mechanisms for maintaining power in these societies, for example, has been shown to be scale dependent by Marshall Sahlins in his classic study *Social Stratification in Polynesia* (1958:11–12). In Polynesia, appeal to sacred authority as a means of maintaining power was associated with fairly simple chiefdoms (i.e., Sahlins's type IIb or III societies, such as Tikopia, Marquesas, Pukapuka, Ontong Java). The ability of chiefly elites in such societies to initiate warfare or take other strong action in defense of their own position, specifically to subordinate rivals, was severely restricted or at least subject to public consensus. In contrast, authority in more complex chiefdoms (i.e., Sahlins's type I or IIa societies, such as Hawaii, Tonga, Samoa, Mangareva) was largely based on secular power, specifically the use of force, regardless of the underlying ideological framework. In these societies, the use of force as a means of maintaining elite prerogatives and controlling rival factions was more prevalent.

Comparable relationships are inferred by Goldman (1970:20–27) in his tripartite classification of Polynesian chiefdoms as traditional, open, and stratified. In traditional chiefdoms, which are typically very small in size and complexity (i.e., simple chiefdoms), chiefly authority is ideologically based, and while succession tends to be secure and factional competition minimal, leaders themselves are quite weak. In more complex open chiefdoms, in contrast, secular power relationships predominate, and factional competition for chiefly positions is intense, creating an unstable social landscape. Finally, in stratified (or paramount) chiefdoms, status and power relationships tend to be fairly evenly balanced, leading to more stable conditions. In evolutionary terms, the first Polynesian chiefdoms are assumed to resemble traditional societies, with open or stratified chiefdoms later evolving from this type. Shifts between these forms were common, particularly between open and stratified societies among the more complex Polynesian chiefdoms.

Similar scale-dependent relationships between various measures of chiefly power and authority and group population size have been noted by Feinman and Neitzel (1984:67) in a cross-cultural analysis of 63 New World prestate sedentary societies. In their study, they observed not only a moderate correlation between elite authority, measured as the number of functions under chiefly control, and maximal community size, but also a strong correlation between the number of elite status markers and total group population (69). Strong chiefly leaders exerting direct control over a number of societal functions occurred almost exclusively in large, complex chiefdoms that were typically characterized by two administrative levels above the local community. Weak leaders, in contrast, occurred in smaller, less complex societies typically characterized by fewer administrative levels.

Recognizing the ideological and secular bases of chiefly authority and the diachronic or evolutionary trends within these authority structures is thus an important aspect of any analysis of cycling behavior. Following Sahlins and Goldman, I suggest that, in the first chiefdoms in a region or in fairly simple chiefly societies at any time, appeals to sacred authority as a means of justifying elite prerogatives will be more important than the use of force or the imposition of secular authority. Factional competition in these societies is likely to be minimal and succession fairly peaceful. The opposite pattern is suggested in more complex chiefly societies or in regions where chiefdoms have been in place for some time. In these societies, factional competition is likely to be intense and succession violent.

Attributes of the cycling process follow directly from this. Changes in the number of decision-making levels in a chiefdom should be accompanied by changes in ideological and secular authority structures, with one sphere likely increasing or decreasing in importance at the expense of the other. In the southeastern United States, a decline in the sacred/ideological spheres is indicated over the course of the Mississippian and may reflect such a trend. Major mound-building activity and the highly developed mortuary ceremonialism and iconography typified by the Southeastern Ceremonial Complex, for example, peaked by the 13th century and declined thereafter throughout the region. This may reflect a change in authority structures, from societies where elite power was based in large measure on appeals to sacred authority, to societies where secular authority was pervasive (see chapter 4).

Tribute Mobilization and Control of Surplus

A labor force for producing an exploitable surplus and a system for its efficient collection and storage are also critical to the maintenance of stable chiefly authority structures. While elites competed with each other for followers, the ultimate purpose of this competition was to obtain control over societal wealth, which was typically defined in terms of surplus

production. In chiefdom societies, surplus production was almost invariably defined in terms of subsistence products. Food surpluses produced
by commoner populations, beyond providing for the subsistence needs of
the elite, also fueled the prestige goods production and exchange networks that legitimized their power and authority (e.g., Earle 1978: 225–27;
Flannery 1972; Lenski 1966:44–45; Orans 1966; Peebles and Kus 1977;
Steponaitis 1978, 1981; Welch 1991). The stability of elite administrative
structures thus directly depended on the regular production of surplus
food and other goods, the efficiency by which these goods were collected
or "mobilized" by the elite for their own uses, and the storage technology
and other mechanisms in place to overcome production shortfalls or other
types of losses.

Degree of control over surplus (and the labor producing it) is thus one
method of defining power and status relations in chiefdoms, and the
competition and conflicts engendered by rival elites seeking such control
are a primary cause of organizational instability. Lenski (1966:44–45) has
described the linkage between power, prestige, and surplus by noting that
the generation of surplus "will give rise to struggles aimed at its control
. . . [and that] power will determine the distribution of nearly all of the
surplus possessed by a society. . . . Prestige is largely, though not solely, a
function of power and privilege, at least in those societies where there is a
substantial surplus." Such a pattern is evident in the ethnographies and
histories of chiefdoms from around the world. Control of surplus productivity was widely perceived by members of these societies as the way to
achieve both prestige and power. Tribute mobilization for the maintenance
of chiefly prestige and power characterized Hawaiian society (Earle
1978:195; Kirch 1984:260), for example, and a comparable strategy was
found to operate in Panama, where chiefs extracted tribute for their own
political ends, rather than for the benefit of society as a whole (Helms
1979). The extent of control an elite has over societal surplus and prestige
goods may thus be viewed as a direct measure of their power and prestige
and of social stratification itself.

Organizational stability not only depended on the extent to which
elites could successfully create and then appropriate surplus production,
but also on how well or effectively they put this surplus to work enhancing
their positions. Where elite authority was weak, care had to be taken to
avoid alienating producers. If unusually high levels of surplus production
were appropriated with little or no recompense, even if only in the form of
temporarily conferred prestige, commoners might be left with little or no
incentive to produce and might actively encourage or support the rebel-
lious activity of rival elites. Among the Lozi, a complex chiefdom or simple
kin-based state in Barotselande, Zimbabwe, a reputation for generosity
rather than despotism was the mark of a successful chief (Gluckman
1951:14). This has been widely noted throughout sub-Saharan Africa and
in chiefdom societies in general and appears to have been an essential

strategy if a chief was to maintain power. A reputation for generosity was thus an effective way of maintaining power while simultaneously checking the ambitions of potential rivals. Where elite authority was securely grounded, particularly where the chief wielded strong coercive power, however, surplus extraction was likely much greater and concern with alienating producers less important.

While tribute in simple chiefdoms was probably perceived as a social duty and was freely given, in more complex chiefdoms, it was often viewed as a burden and in some cases was ruthlessly exacted. In Tikopia, where chiefly authority was quite limited, an unpopular chief might find his tribute cut off (Firth 1936:341), while among the 19th-century Lunda, a complex central African society, "wars of extermination" against "recalcitrant tributaries" are reported (Capello and Ivens cited in V. Turner 1957:5). Tribute mobilization in complex chiefdoms was a primary task of the lesser elites, who could raise the threat of divine sanction or secular punishment, or both, to assist them in their efforts. These same elites could take advantage of their position to advance their own goals. To avoid this possibility, redistributional mechanisms for rewarding supporters were in place. Much of the surplus appropriated by elites, in fact, was used to provide subsistence and prestige goods to the chief's principal supporters.

The extent of an individual elite's power was thus measured, to some degree, by his position in the surplus appropriation network. Tribute or surplus mobilization in chiefdoms typically takes the form of a flow of goods such as foodstuffs, raw materials, or craft products toward a center and an outward flow of services such as religious or ceremonial products, together with a lesser flow of essential or desired commodities (Lenski 1966:206). The flow in both directions was created, maintained, and manipulated by the elites to further their own personal and political agendas. Tribute was sometimes viewed as something of a property right, an obligation between individuals or groups that might be passed on from generation to generation.

Redistribution of tribute was typically according to rank and kinship and was a visible method by which the chief affirmed the relative status of his supporters. Chiefly redistribution of sumptuary goods was thus a mechanism regulating the tributary economy and maintaining the prestige of elites at all levels. Redistributional failure, brought about through internal factors (i.e., declining surplus production or rebellion) or external factors (i.e., warfare or the collapse of interregional exchange networks), sometimes led to organizational change that might be marked by violence. Reorganization, if accompanied by a change in administrative or decision-making levels, would constitute an example of chiefdom cycling behavior. This is thought to have happened in Formative Oaxaca, where a decline in imported obsidian occurred prior to an episode of destruction at Fabrica San Jose, a local chiefly center (Wright 1984:46). A similar set of circumstances is documented at the site of La Libertad in Chiapas, a Middle

Preclassic chiefdom that collapsed after falling out of a long-distance trade/prestige goods network (Clark 1987, 1988:197–200).

Patterns of Population Growth

The stability of chiefdom societies and hence the propensity for cycling behavior also appears to be closely tied to demographic processes of population growth and decline. Once a chiefdom (primary or secondary) formed in an area, it should have tended to grow, if for no other reason than because of the adaptive advantage that belonging to such a society likely conferred upon its members. Carneiro (1970, 1981, 1990) has described this process of expansion in militaristic (conflict theory) terms, with warfare and conquest the posited mechanisms behind the reproduction and spread of chiefdom organizational structures. Biological (i.e., reproductive) success is implicit in his argument: "Once chiefdoms begin to form in a region, the process proceeds rapidly. The military advantage that size alone confers on a society means that even a minimal chiefdom will have a significant edge over its neighbors if they are still independent villages. As a result, it will not be long before autonomous villages as such will cease to exist. Either they will be defeated by and incorporated into one of the existing chiefdoms or they will join forces with other such villages in a defensive alliance, which will itself tend to become a chiefdom" (1981:66). Chiefdom social organization, in this view, spread either through conquest (i.e., was imposed from outside) or in self-defense (i.e., reorganization occurred in response to a perceived external threat). Although this perspective tells us little about the process by which chiefdoms emerged, it does support the idea that, once the form appeared, it spread quickly. Interaction theories of chiefdom emergence, such as those centered on regional patterns of elite competition directed to the use of external goods to increase local or internal prestige, likewise posit chiefdoms emerging contemporaneously over large areas, albeit for much different reasons (e.g., Clark and Blake 1994; Renfrew and Cherry 1986). However, the appearance of chiefdoms in a region, for whatever reason, is likely to have had a considerable impact on population distributions and growth rates.

Once a regional backdrop of simple chiefdoms was in place, the stage was set for cycling behavior. Competition between elites within and between differing polities would have likely led to the repeated formation and fragmentation of complex chiefdoms. As rival elites competed with one another for followers, dramatic population shifts might have occurred, with people relocating (voluntarily or otherwise) from less successful to more successful leaders. Population nucleation around central communities may have also occurred, as elites sought to keep both commoners and potential rivals under their direct control, as well as to appropriate more readily any surplus they might produce. While the emergence of chiefdoms over a region is thus likely to have prompted considerable population growth—assuming the advantages of successful chiefly decision making translated into greater relative reproductive success—the long-term effects of chiefly cycling on regional population levels are currently poorly documented.

How were population levels maintained in chiefdom societies? This question has two parts, focusing on how people were distributed over the landscape and how reproductive rates were controlled within these groups. Relationships between organizational complexity and population size and distribution receive further attention below. Reproductive behavior in chiefdom societies is somewhat more difficult to address. Within these societies, were population policies or control mechanisms in place and, if so, how did they operate (see examples in Betzig 1986, 1988b; Dickemann 1979; Nag 1962)? Were differing reproductive strategies in use among commoner and elite subgroups, for example, and what were the long-term implications of these strategies? Chiefly prerogatives may have been jealously guarded, for example, to the point where reproductive strategies designed to minimize the potential number of competitors or to maintain elite/commoner population levels within certain parameters may have been in operation. This might have been implemented via restrictions on polygyny or through deliberate strategies of infanticide or murder. Alternatively, little or no formal population control mechanisms may have been in place.

Elite population growth, in the absence of culturally mediated leveling mechanisms or population policies constraining growth, may have been a primary cause of expansion in chiefdom societies. There is little doubt that reproductive advantage accrued to elite members of most human societies (e.g., Betzig 1982, 1986; Betzig, Mulder, and Turke 1988; Boone 1988; Chagnon and Irons 1979; Turke and Betzig 1985). Elite polygyny, often in conjunction with a pattern of (typically) monogamous marriage among commoners, is frequently noted in chiefdoms (Betzig 1986; Clignet 1970; Murdock 1967). Elites in these societies, having greater access to resources, including food, would have typically enjoyed greater reproductive success than commoners. That is, given better nutrition and a more protective and healthy social environment, children of elites would have enjoyed a higher survival rate than the children of commoners, other things being equal. This proposition is well documented in the ethnographic and historic record (e.g., Betzig 1986; Boone 1988; Chagnon and Irons 1979) and undoubtedly occurred in prehistoric societies as well. Paleoanthropological and mortuary analyses of skeletal series from such societies should be able to confirm this and, importantly, the magnitude of differential reproductive success.

The very success of elites in wielding power, when translated into greater reproductive success, would have led to increasing numbers of competitors for power over time. Elite population growth is thus likely to have been a cause of both expansion and instability in chiefdoms. The children of elites, innocuous while young, would grow up to be contenders for power and would promote either political instability or expansion. Dispersing these possible rivals, through conquest (i.e., imposing them as administrators/elites over conquered groups) or through advantageous marital alliances, would be one way to reduce their potentially destabilizing influence. Patterns of geographic expansion within chiefdoms, and of resulting competition among chiefdoms, may have been brought about by a need to disperse potential chiefly contenders and maintain the prerogatives of elite lineages.

The proportion of elites in a given population may prove to be an effective indicator of overall societal stability. Undercontrol or overcontrol of society, prompted by the presence of too few or too many elites, in this view, is likely to be destabilizing (an inference that has lessons for modern societies as well as chiefdoms). Unfortunately, paleodemographic studies of elite/commoner population trends in chiefdoms and their relationship to societal stability are rare; demographic analyses are more typically directed to resolving overall population levels, that is, the proportions of people in centers as opposed to outlying communities (e.g., Butzer 1980; Drennan 1987; Hassan 1981:231–57; Upham 1983:232). The governing/ elite class in historic and modern states rarely exceeded 2% of the total population and may have been closer to 1% (Lenski 1966:219). Whether comparable figures apply to chiefdom societies remains unknown but is beginning to be explored.

In a classic study, Steponaitis (1981) found that as much as 20% of the total population of complex Mesoamerican chiefdoms was apparently supported by tribute mobilization (i.e., of subsistence goods). That all of these people belonged to the elite is doubtful; many people were probably employed in nonsubsistence tasks (i.e., craft production, goods exchange). Peebles (1987a:27–28), in an analysis of grave goods from burials at Moundville in west-central Alabama, argued that elite population levels grew from approximately 1% of the total population early in the history of the chiefdom, during the Moundville I phase, to around 5% during the Moundville II phase two centuries later. In a third case, this time from the Southwest, Upham (1983:232) found that graves with extensive prestige goods at Nuvaqueotaka pueblo made up 2% of the total sample, with another 5% containing lesser quantities of these same materials (see also Lightfoot 1987:45). Elites thus may have made up from 2% to 7% of this population. Whether there is an upper limit to the proportion of elites a chiefdom society can have and remain stable is unknown, but there is unquestionably an upper limit to the number of nonfood producers in any society.

In addition to society-wide demographic patterns, the stability of a chief's position was closely linked to demographic patterns within specific communities. The ratio of primary and affinal kin of a headman or chief to nonkin in a community typically defined that administrator's power base and hence influence, barring an ability to draw on external support (V. Turner 1957:61–62). Among the matrilineal Ndembu, a simple chiefdom in sub-Saharan Africa, for example, uterine siblings tend to relocate to their native villages following divorce from or the death of a spouse, and "there is a constant tendency . . . for the matricentric family to reconstitute itself as a local unit" (76). In long-established communities among the Ndembu, as a result, primary kin came either to outnumber classificatory kin and nonkin or else to represent a dominant plurality of the village population (63, 74). Leadership was most stable in those communities where numerous supporters, in this case kin, were on hand to help reinforce authority. In general, chiefly authority structures also tended to be most stable in newly formed communities (which were often formed by the fission and relocation of a like-minded uterine kin group to begin with) or in communities with some time depth, which Turner defined as having at least three successive village headmen (74). Instability, manifested in challenges to chiefly authority, is most common when a community begins to grow and is most likely if nonkin (i.e., members of other lineages) achieve numerical dominance. The Ndembu case suggests that, in chiefdom societies in general, the relocation of rival elites to a central community or the incorporation of other lineages had to be done with great care, to ensure that they did not build up too large a following. Successfully expanding chiefdoms, by incorporating large numbers of nonkin into their communities, including possible rivals, may thus have been sowing the seeds of their later destruction.

For an ambitious individual to create and maintain a power base in a chiefdom, it probably helped to belong to a large extended family capable of generating a large following and support base, both through sheer numbers and via marriage alliances. Individuals from small kin groups, lacking such a support base, might not be able to achieve power or, if achieving it, might not be able to maintain it long. As Turner put it, "Happy is the ambitious man who has many sisters and unambitious younger brothers with children of their own" (199). When a society was expanding rapidly, the tendency toward recruitment of proximate kin for leadership positions would probably have been relaxed, to ensure that administrative posts were filled with effective personnel, to facilitate alliances, and to co-opt former defeated elites.

Population change may have played a role in organizational cycling. If population levels grew or declined dramatically within individual societies or over a region, organizational changes would likely have occurred as well, in response to the changing administrative needs of these societies. Whether overall population levels actually rose in areas dominated by complex chiefdoms or fell after their fragmentation, however, remains unknown. There is little doubt that dramatic population change did sometimes occur at specific centers or in particular areas, as records of abandonment make clear. Whether the people declined in number or died out, continued at their present level in a more dispersed settlement system (i.e., less hierarchically organized and hence possibly less visible archaeologically), or were absorbed into other societies, however, should be determined on a case-by-case basis.

Fairly strong relationships have been noted between overall population size and degree of sociopolitical complexity over a wide range of societies (Carneiro 1962, 1967, 1968; Naroll 1956; Tatje and Naroll 1973) and among chiefdom societies in particular (Feinman and Neitzel 1984; D. Taylor 1975). As noted previously, some authors have suggested that population growth or decline led directly to changes in the number of decision-making levels within the societies occupying a given region. Building upon arguments developed by Johnson (1973, 1978), Cordy (1981:229–30), for example, has described these relationships as scalar in nature: "If societal territorial and population size increase and cross an upper threshold, a new echelon in the hierarchical structure will appear. . . . If societal territorial and population size decrease and cross a lower threshold, an echelon in the hierarchical structure will disappear (sometimes instantly, sometimes given time)." Research to date has shown that organizational complexity and population/territorial measures strongly covary. It has not been possible, however, to demonstrate the existence of critical demographic thresholds where organizational change *invariably* occurs, only the existence of population levels (i.e., where community size is greater than 500 people or total societal population is greater than 10,000 people) where the potential for hierarchy formation is likely (Carneiro 1967; Feinman and Neitzel 1984:69; Naroll 1956; Orans 1966:30; Tatje and Naroll 1973; see particularly Upham 1990:101, 112).

Circumscription was also a potential cause of organizational instability. Large populations undoubtedly served as highly visible indicators of elite power and provided the labor resources necessary to advance their agendas. A primary arena of elite competition was over followers, since supporting populations could have been used for public works, tribute or craft goods production, and defense. Some expansionist tendencies in chiefdom societies were linked to a desire to increase the labor force; the capture of prisoners to work chiefly estates or to produce craft goods is sometimes reported, usually from more complex chiefdoms (e.g., Carneiro 1990:194; DePratter 1983:61, 1991a:52; Feinman and Neitzel 1984:58–59). When societal population levels declined, for whatever reason, the ability of the elites to finance their social agendas also likewise probably declined, contributing to organizational instability.

When complex chiefdoms were forming, it is suggested, localized increases in population likely occurred, as emergent centers attracted support populations. When these societies collapsed, localized population declines also likely occurred. Population decline would be expected, in fact, as populations relocated to or were incorporated into more successful polities. However, if most communities were indeed largely self-sufficient in terms of subsistence production (an inference that should itself be carefully tested), it is difficult to argue that localized population decline occurred because the simplified organizational structures were unable to meet the subsistence needs of the (former paramount) population. Great care must be taken when exploring population change, since the same demographic picture could conceivably be the result of the operation of any of a number of factors (i.e., the incorporation of outside groups, modification of settlement patterning, population movement or relocation to more successful elites, losses due to warfare, etc.).

Warfare

Warfare has been described as a primary factor behind the spread of the chiefdom form of sociopolitical organization by some scholars (Carneiro 1981, 1990, 1991; Sanders and Price 1968:132; Webster 1975:467). Carneiro (1981:66), for example, has argued that warfare leading to the incorporation of defeated enemies can result in the elaboration of organizational structures in chiefdoms. In this view, a change in organizational structure, specifically the development of intermediate leadership positions, would have to occur if rival chiefdoms were to be effectively absorbed as a complex chiefdom emerged and spread. This reorganization, from a perspective emphasizing cycling behavior, would have entailed the replacement of a single decision-making level (characteristic of a simple chiefdom) by a two-level decision-making hierarchy composed of ruling and lesser elites (characteristic of a complex chiefdom). Unless the ruling elite in the emergent two-level political hierarchy took steps to suppress rival factions, however, fragmentation could quickly occur, particularly since conquest would bring new potential challengers into the competitive arena. The global ethnohistoric and archaeological record suggests that complex chiefdoms were fragile, with internal dissension, typically competition for positions of power, a primary cause of organizational stress. Cycling in chiefdoms, from the perspective of conflict theory, thus comes about through patterns of conquest, expansion, and, ultimately, overextension, leading to a collapse or fragmentation back to simpler organizational forms, from which the process begins anew.

The military advantage conferred by chiefdom political organization suggests that while individual polities may cycle between higher and lower levels of sociopolitical complexity, chiefdoms as a category are unlikely to disappear completely from a region, barring their incorporation into state-level societies. Furthermore, because of the competitive nature of these societies, the fragmentation of one complex chiefdom is likely to trigger the emergence of one or more others. This comes about as regional elites vie with one another to fill the power vacuum. Complex chiefdoms might also emerge as a secondary or reactionary process. Changes in the regional social environment, specifically the emergence of complex chiefdoms in other areas or the presence of increasing numbers of complex societies in the landscape, may necessitate political reorganization if local elites are to retain a measure of autonomy. In a sample of 23 advanced horticultural societies from sub-Saharan Africa, for example, Lenski (1966:163) noted a weak positive correlation between the level of external threat and degree of sociopolitical complexity. These data suggest that reorganization to a higher level of political complexity may have typically only occurred when military threats were greatest, although, as we shall see, it might also occur when prestige-based elite competition was pronounced. Over the same sample, a high correlation was found between level of technology and degree of sociopolitical complexity, indicating that differences in technology or technological innovations also played a major role in societal development and stability (162–63).

Factional Competition

Competition between elites is an intrinsic aspect of chiefdom societies and is particularly pronounced among complex chiefdoms, promoting general instability and the likelihood of change in organizational/administrative structures (e.g., Brumfiel and Fox 1994; Earle 1987:294; Pauketat 1991:25–27). The advantages that accrued to successful elite competitors, such as a high standard of living, personal power and prestige, and possibly greater relative reproductive success, as we have seen, all appear to have been motivating factors. Helms (1979, 1987) has examined how patterns of elite competition, once established, maintain themselves. Leaders in chiefdoms "must on the one hand continue to evidence their commonality with the general population and on the other strive for the individual distinctiveness of high rank, generally acquired and held by a mixture of inheritance and personal attributes. Chiefly elites are, therefore, particularly prone to rivalries among themselves. To be effective as political-religious leaders they must be active and in an atmosphere of rivalry make visible to other contending elites and to the general populace their skills and activities as leaders in (external) warfare, as specialists in long-distance exchange, [and] as experts in communication with the cosmic powers that must be understood and controlled for the proper functioning of society" (1987:77). Control of esoteric knowledge was often tied to subsistence production, thus creating a linkage of chiefly ability and sanctity with the economic well-being of society in general.

Competition between elites for followers, typically other elites and their retinues (including commoners), was thus the basis of chiefly power. Because power in chiefdom societies was kin based, however, this limited its scope and effectiveness and necessitated a continual effort on the part of the dominant elites to maintain and legitimize their authority. Rivals and claimants were often the chief's closest male relatives or advisers (e.g., Gluckman 1951:23; Lenski 1966:171–73; Pauketat 1991:38; Schapera 1956:157–72). In such circumstances, the power of the chief often depended on the skill by which he maintained control of and subordinated these people. *The fact that a chief's principal supporters were also typically his most likely successors, and hence potentially his greatest rivals, meant that factional competition was universal in these societies.* This is a primary cause of organizational instability in chiefdoms and a dilemma facing elites. Webster (1975:465–66) has stated these concerns perhaps best of all. According to him:

> Chiefs in such societies tread the fine line between receipt of gifts due to senior kinsmen on the one hand (with the expectation of reciprocity), and outright coercive mobilization of labor and taxation on the other. Here is a source of instability in such systems, since the (usually) insufficient coercive force at the disposal of the chief is unable to counteract fissioning tendencies produced when he overreaches himself in his demands.
>
> Another fundamental weakness of ranked societies is that withdrawal of support [by commoners or lesser elites] results in increased authority of competing individuals or factions. Because the status of the chief is highly desirable, it is coveted by others. . . . [P]recisely because there are other members of the society of near equivalent rank (and because genealogies can be so easily manipulated), other individuals can usurp the chief's position, and enjoy his prerogatives provided the force at their disposal is superior. . . . [Chiefdoms] often appear to be more political arenas than political entities.

Only through the replacement of these fragile kin-based leadership structures by more stable secular and ideally nonkin-based structures, such as formalized administrative classes or bureaucracies, could more complex, state-level societies arise.

Factional competition, interestingly, while disruptive, may have been actively encouraged by ruling elites. A particularly effective method of dissipating the frustrations and resentments of differing groups would have been consciously or otherwise to set their members into competition with one another and then co-opt or eliminate the most successful practitioners. Such competitions were typically the kind that directly or indirectly enhanced the ruling elite's position, such as skill in warfare or tribute extraction. In the process, though, co-opted lesser elites acquired the knowledge necessary to run the chiefdom themselves and hence were a potential source of rebellion. Elites and not commoners were the usual source of rebellions in these societies, since they alone possessed the knowledge and the support base necessary to pull off a successful challenge to a chief's authority. Given the way it was carried out, elite competition was potentially extremely divisive (unless ruthlessly controlled), since elites tended to involve not only themselves but also their retinues in their struggles with other elites. Thus factional competition between elites could produce society-wide conflict and promote organizational instability, which could lead to cycling.

Succession to Chiefdomship

Mechanisms by which chiefdoms dealt with matters of succession or changes in leadership were of critical importance to the long-term stability of these societies and represented the stage on which factional competition and, ultimately, cycling operated. Among more complex societies, internal power struggles tended to be common where rules of succession were ambiguous or weak—"without an institutionalized pattern of succession" (Lenski 1966:196–97). Where rules of succession were poorly defined or subject to challenge, the death of a paramount might trigger widespread social upheaval until a successor could consolidate his (or sometimes her) grasp on authority. Competition between rival elites is widely recognized as a primary factor contributing to the instability of chiefdom political systems, and ethnographic accounts from these societies are filled with tales of rebellion, treachery, and warfare directed toward obtaining authority (e.g., Burling 1974; Goldman 1970; Helms 1979:24; Kirch 1984; Marquardt 1992:123; Sahlins 1958:176–96; Wright 1984). The personal abilities of the chief were often critical to the outcome of events surrounding a particular successional crisis and thus to the developmental history of a given society (V. Turner 1957:200).

The possibility of chiefly cycling was thus to some extent dependent upon how clearly and formally succession was defined (i.e., whether it was regular and secure, or uncertain and insecure) and upon whether or not the replacement of leaders was likely to lead to shifts in the number of decision-making levels. Care must be taken to differentiate successional events that led to a change in the number of administrative levels (i.e., cycling) from events that merely resulted in the replacement of one individual by another. Rebellions typically tended to be against the person of the chief and not against the structure of the system itself. Struggles between elites usually resulted in little change in the commoners' way of life. Changes in organizational structure were most likely when leaders of markedly different capabilities succeeded one another. The succession of a poor leader to the office of chief could cause a complex chiefdom to fragment, while the succession of a strong leader might lead a simple chiefdom to a position of dominance over a number of its neighbors, resulting in the development of a complex chiefdom. Competition between elites in different polities might lead to one center emerging or declining at the expense of another; this competition may have intensified when one chief within a center replaced another.

Competition for the position of the chief appears to have been greatest, and most violent, when the material rewards associated with the position were greatest. Among the Ndembu, for example, this was the case during the period of the slave trade, when the chief and his senior headmen exercised considerable control over a highly profitable external exchange network. In weakly structured chiefdoms, in contrast, succession tended to shift between lineages or communities fairly readily, with much lower levels of accompanying violence (V. Turner 1957:104). Successional crises did not invariably come about for materialistic reasons (although this was undoubtedly an underlying motivating factor promoting patterns of rivalry and competition). Sometimes relatively minor events could trigger social unrest, such as quarrels over the relative rank or position of members of the elite (Gluckman 1951:42–43).

Although generally referring to events in more complex social systems, Lenski (1966:59) has argued that events following successional crises tend to exhibit a consistent format: "As a reading of human history makes clear, there has usually been a more or less cyclical alternation in human societies. . . . Each cycle begins with the forcible seizure of power by a new elite and involves an initial phase of violence during which organized resistance is either destroyed or suppressed. The next phase is one in which the regime strives to reduce its dependence on naked force and to increase its legitimate authority. . . . [U]nless there is a steady succession of challenges the long term trend involves a reduction in the active role of force and coercion and an increase in the role of persuasion and incentive until finally the cycle comes to an end when the regime is overthrown." Elites in chiefdoms had to devote considerable attention to preventing their own replacement, since defeat was likely to result in death or, at the very least, considerable reduction in status and privilege. Instilling patterns of competition among lesser elites and playing them off against each other (as noted in the discussion of factional competition) is one way of dealing with this problem, which has been observed in many chiefdom societies. By stressing prowess in warfare as a method of achieving honored social status, for example, and rewarding successful warriors with prestige and luxury goods, chiefly elites could co-opt potential rivals and in the process likely gain strong supporters.

In societies where force is viewed as a basis of authority, it is almost axiomatic that if a leader's "coercive authority is weak, challenges inevitably occur, and the system is eventually destroyed and replaced by another based more firmly on force" (Lenski 1966:51). Where succession was particularly violent, the victor was likely to be both strong and ruthless, able to eliminate immediate rivals as well as suppress subsequent challengers. This, interestingly, would have likely translated into a (typically temporary) period of relative peace and stability, at least until new challengers arose. It could also, however, have evolutionary consequences. The result of a pattern of repeated challenges to chiefly authority in an area where such authority was initially weak could be the emergence of ever-stronger institutions, increasingly based on secular power. Changes in political organization observed over the course of the Mississippian period in the Southeast may be related to such an evolutionary process.

Specific rules governing succession could also have a marked effect on overall societal stability. Where a chief's brothers sequentially inherit power (adelphic succession), there may be a fairly rapid turnover in officeholders, since "a number of aged office-holders will succeed one another, few of whom will live long" (V. Turner 1957:88). When inheritance passes between generations, from a chief to his sister's son (nepotic succession), turnover may be much less frequent. Among the Ndembu, where adelphic succession occurs, sisters' sons tend to grow impatient waiting for all the members of a senior generation to die off and may either revolt or relocate to found a new community. If chiefly succession is likely to remain within a well-populated lineage, the possibility of community fissioning or challenge by rivals may be increased, since their chances for legitimate succession are drastically reduced. A particularly critical period in societies where adelphic succession or regencies are present occurs when succession passes from the last living member of one generation to the next adjacent generation; these transitions tend to be characterized by unusual tension, since power is typically passing from a well-established and experienced individual/cohort into the hands of a much younger individual, with less experience and potentially a number of living rivals.

How societies with fairly rigid rules of succession dealt with incompetent heirs also affected their overall stability. Among the Yao of southern Nyasaland, succession to village headmanship was typically matrilineal, passing from the headman to his sister's first son, unless that person was judged unfit, in which case another was chosen (J. Mitchell 1951:339–40). Other examples in which succession bypasses a designated heir because of that individual's inability have been noted over a range of tribal as well as more complex societies, such as the Jivaro of South America (Stirling 1938:40–41) and the Kuma of New Guinea (Reay 1959:114; see also Lenski 1966:132). Substitution is common in many South American groups if "the customary successor is deemed unfit" (Lowie 1946:346). Where the choice of alternative heirs was ambiguous, the potential for conflict between possible successors may have been increased.

Cordy (1981:207, 217) has compiled data on successional crises from Hawaiian oral histories, illustrating the kinds of things that could occur. Four successful revolts against chiefly authority, for example, took place over the course of 16 generations of chiefly leaders on the island of Oahu, averaging about one a century. The sources of rebellion were often the chief's closest allies or relatives. One successful revolt was by a paramount's younger brother, who overthrew and killed his older brother and later his younger brother as well when the latter's district court (i.e., power base) began to rival his own. Another successful revolt was by lesser chiefs in reaction to the excessive greed of the paramount. The lesser chiefs killed the paramount, replacing one chiefly line with another, colateral line. The third successful revolt occurred upon the succession of a child. Shortly thereafter, the appointed regent, the dead chief's brother, usurped power. In the fourth example, a paramount was replaced in a bloodless removal when he proved incompetent.

The oral tradition from the main island of Hawaii offers a similar picture of revolts by younger brothers, usually supported by factions within the lesser nobility, that is, high or district chiefs (Cordy 1981:210–14). From circa 1550 on, revolts occurred in almost every generation until contact, resulting in the rapid fragmentation, reunification, and refragmentation of the island's paramountcy. Similar turbulence surrounding chiefly succession is also reported from Kaua'i (Earle 1978:174–80). Successful revolts frequently resulted in the breakup of a complex chiefdom rather than the replacement of one paramount by another, particularly if the challenger's goal was to achieve autonomy rather than increase his power base; often, however, once the first goal was achieved, the successful elite often attempted to obtain paramount status (Cordy 1981:216). The Hawaiian accounts thus document that, at least in this setting, acts of rebellion and treachery against high chiefs were common. They also indicate, however, that such revolts were only rarely successful, something probably due to the strong power base the paramount commanded and the skill with which he manipulated his underlings.

Rules of succession thus play a major role in determining the stability of chiefdom societies and affect matters such as the incidence, intensity, and geographic scale of factional competition and how long power was maintained at particular centers. How succession was specifically determined—either matrilineally, patrilineally, or by some other procedure—coupled with postmarital residence rules, could also affect the stability of these societies or at least centers of power. These matters are discussed in greater detail, with specific reference to southeastern Mississippian societies, in ensuing chapters.

Environmental Constraints

A range of environmental factors shape the evolution of chiefdoms, of which the most important are regional physiographic structure, resource productivity, and climate. Regional physiographic structure greatly influences the possible social landscape by constraining the location and spacing of individual settlements, centers, and polities (Blake and Clark n.d.; Carneiro 1970:734–35; Hodder and Orton 1976:224–36; Johnson 1977:488–94; J. Scarry and Payne 1986; Steponaitis 1978). Physiographic structure also dictates communication and trade arteries and, as a result, the kinds of interaction that could occur between communities. The availability and incidence of specific resources such as agricultural soils, game, plant communities, and knappable stone have a similar effect. Competition between chiefly elites for control of agricultural land, hunting territories, raw materials, or trading networks, for example, has been variously suggested as the cause of at least some of the organizational fluctuations observed in these societies (Gramly 1977; L. Larson 1972; E. Turner and Santley 1979; Wright 1984). Finally, climatic factors such as short- and long-term rainfall, frost, sunlight, and other patterns play a major role in shaping local and regional biotic communities and agricultural production and even influence areas chosen for habitation (Butzer 1982; Dincauze 1987; Gladfelter 1981).

Arguments about the relationships among sociopolitical complexity, regional physiographic conditions, and environmental resource productivity have had a long history in anthropology (e.g., Kroeber 1939; Wissler 1917). Sahlins (1958:107–35, 201–17), in a continuation of the argument mentioned previously, suggested that the degree of social stratification and the occurrence of specific organizational structures on Polynesian islands were related to the variability and distribution of natural resources on these islands (i.e., indirect measures of their subsistence productivity and potential for surplus). He observed that ramages or conical clans— "internally stratified, unilineal . . . descent [groups where] . . . distance from the senior line of descent from the common ancestor is the criterion of stratification" (Sahlins 1958:140; see also Kirchoff 1955)—were most likely in rich, diversified environments (Sahlins 1958:203). Simpler unilineal descent systems, in contrast, were more typically found in less productive or more uniform environments. Although the accuracy of Sahlins's ethnohistoric analyses has seen severe challenge, his primary thesis—that sociopolitical complexity and organizational form are closely linked to resource structure and potential subsistence productivity—has remained essentially intact (Cordy 1981:33–44).

The reason environmental constraints are of critical importance to the organizational stability of chiefdom societies is because, quite simply, elite authority structures depend upon surplus production and its efficient mobilization for their continued existence. Relationships between culture and environment are not precise, however, as many authorities have demonstrated. While it has been suggested that among relatively simple societies "the richer the environment, the larger the surplus and the greater the importance of power in the distributive process" and that "the degree of inequality in distributive systems will vary directly with the size of a society's surplus" (Lenski 1966:48), I believe these kinds of arguments are overdrawn. Although a relationship admittedly exists between the amount of surplus that can be produced in a given environment and the level of sociopolitical complexity that may emerge, no exact correlation is evident. Resource structure and productivity and fluctuations in carrying capacity only indicate the potential of a given area, not the actual outcome of sociopolitical evolution.

Regional physiographic structure also constrains travel time and transportation costs and directly determines the location of communication arteries (Johnson 1977:485–87). The presence of efficient internal communication networks' linking centers and subsidiary communities was essential to the development of sociopolitical complexity, since they would facilitate tribute mobilization as well as the movement of people and information. Lenski (1966:160–62) has noted that few complex societies in sub-Saharan Africa were located in rain forests, something he attributed, in part, to transportation difficulties in these areas. Helms (1979), in an examination of chiefdom development in Panama and Colombia, demonstrated that a community's size and importance were directly determined by its position in regional exchange networks. Chiefly centers located along major river systems or near major physiographic ecotones, that is, along favored transportation arteries or near important resources, typically expanded at the expense of centers located farther away from these locations. This same phenomenon has been observed among southeastern Mississippian societies by a number of scholars (e.g., Fowler 1974; Hally 1989; L. Larson 1971a; Steponaitis 1991).

The development of complex chiefdoms may have been possible only in certain areas and thus precluded or hindered in other regions. As Blake and Clark (n.d.) have elegantly demonstrated, variation in interaction potential, measured in terms of the number of communities or polities with which a given community is in regular interaction, is directly linked to regional physiographic structure. Interaction potential is greatest in open, homogeneous, or otherwise unrestricted environments and is lowest in circumscribed, patchy, and restricted environments. The emergence and maintenance of social complexity, they argue, is directly related to the shape of the interaction networks that can form in a given area and the ease by which these interactions occur. Environments permitting extensive interaction, such as open plains or areas of extensive braided watercourses, would facilitate the development and maintenance of (ideally hexagonal) lattices of interacting polities as well as multipolity aggregates, while in restricted or patchy environments, interaction would be more difficult, constraining the emergence of complex or stable political structures. Fundamental to this argument, of course, is the realization that the nature of environmental restrictedness and interaction potential is dependent on the scale or geographic extent of the polities in question (Blake and Clark n.d.; Clark and Blake 1994). What might be an unrestricted environment at the scale of simple chiefdoms may be a restricted environment at the level of complex or paramount chiefdoms.

Intensity of factional competition also appears to have been related to regional political geography. In areas where few chiefdoms were present and there was room to expand, rival elites might be intentionally relocated to subsidiary/support positions in other communities or might move to new areas on their own. Where the landscape was packed with chiefdoms and movement was more constrained, making the dispersal or relocation of rival elites unfeasible, however, greater violence (i.e., elimination of rivals) might attend factional competition.

The size, spacing, and stability of the chiefdom societies that arose in the southeastern United States were unquestionably shaped, at least in part, by the widely separated linear riverine systems characteristic of much of the region. In most areas of the Southeast, information flow between polities located in differing river systems would have been difficult, restricting political development primarily to individual drainages. Similar geographical arguments have been advanced to help explain the development of complex societies in some parts of the world and their absence in other areas (Adams 1974; Carneiro 1970; Johnson 1987:115ff).

Political relationships within as well as among the chiefdoms occupying a given region were constrained, to some extent, by the relative proximity of communities to one another. Whether or not a community participated in a rebellion against chiefly authority, for example, was frequently determined by its position within the landscape, specifically its distance from the center. Among the Lozi, "men supported one or the other claimant to the throne according to which was nearest to them at the time or what line was taken by prominent men among them. Adjacent villages frequently took opposite sides. But in the outer provinces tribes tended to take sides as wholes. These outer provinces were not administered by princes sent out to establish capitals among them as is usual in Bantu kingdoms. They were left under their own chiefs, where they had them" (Gluckman 1951:17). Typically, the potential for rebellion was greatest in the most distant reaches of a chiefdom, since these areas tended to have the greatest autonomy. Distance, it should be emphasized, is usually measured in reference to travel time between communities rather than straight lines. The extent of area under the direct control of a center was usually a factor of ease of transportation (and hence communication), which was directly shaped by physiographic conditions. In many early societies, this was usually no more than one or two days' travel time, or a radius of about 20 to 40 kilometers (Hally 1987; Hally, Smith, and Langford 1990:130; Johnson 1987:115–16; Renfrew 1975, 1984:97; J. Scarry and Payne 1986:83–84; Spencer 1987).

Regional physiographic conditions thus combine with more localized patterns of resource occurrence to shape settlement systems and organizational structures, as well as to place parameters on the stability of these systems. This is not altogether surprising, since the distribution and density of plant and animal populations have long been known to shape human settlement. In the Eastern Woodlands, for example, the absence of a reliable (i.e., domesticated) source of animal protein is thought to have had a great deal to do with the spacing of populations on the landscape;

each group had to have enough hunting territory to ensure an adequate supply of protein or, alternatively, hides (Gramly 1977; Bruce Smith 1974a, 1975; E. Turner and Santley 1979).

The production of crop surpluses and the maintenance of these surpluses through storage are particularly important factors affecting the stability of chiefdom organizational structures. Agricultural surpluses had to occur at levels necessary to maintain elite prerogatives, or in the event of production shortfalls, resources had to be present in storage in sufficient quantity to maintain the system until restocking could occur (Burns 1983:186–87). The number and diversity of plant species in cultivation or the number of harvests possible per year all affect crop yields and hence the extent of possible surpluses. Different crop species likewise had different storage requirements, which in turn determined the length of time surpluses could be used to advance organizational goals. Effective risk minimization strategies may have included the dispersal of fields and storage facilities, specifically either the scattering of fields over fairly large areas and in a number of microenvironmental zones or the placement of storage facilities in a number of communities (Chmurny 1973; DeBoer 1988; Ford 1980; Gluckman 1951:9–10). Changes in agricultural production and storage strategies also appear closely tied to patterns of interaction at a regional or subregional scale. The scattering of fields or granaries, for example, or the hiding of storage facilities appears to be a typical response to increased warfare and raiding activity.

Climatic conditions, specifically short- and long-term perturbations in critical variables such as summer rainfall or the length of the growing season, are particularly important factors to consider when examining the stability of chiefdom societies (figure 2). Crop failures brought about by localized or widespread droughts, flooding, or other catastrophes, for example, would have threatened the stability of agricultural chiefdoms by reducing the productive surplus the elites needed to maintain their authority. It might have led also to a reduction in support population if people (subsidiary elites and commoners alike) physically relocated to more favored areas or polities or, in extreme cases, if population decline occurred as a result of famine or warfare triggered by subsistence stress. Extended crop or hunting failures would have also led to a weakening of chiefly authority by posing direct questions about the sacred position and intermediary role of the elite. In societies where chiefly sanctity was strongly accepted, climatic perturbations would probably have to be severe before challenges to leadership or changes in organization occurred. Where legitimizing ideologies were weakly developed, however, such stresses might have brought about rapid social collapse or reorganization.

Another means by which chiefdoms might attempt to deal with periodic crop failure or production shortfalls may have been the development of larger or more complex organizational networks, permitting the allevia-

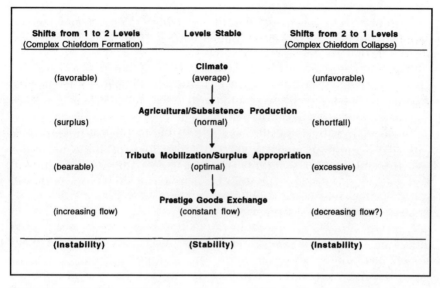

Shifts from 1 to 2 Levels (Complex Chiefdom Formation)	Levels Stable	Shifts from 2 to 1 Levels (Complex Chiefdom Collapse)
	Climate	
(favorable)	(average)	(unfavorable)
	↓	
	Agricultural/Subsistence Production	
(surplus)	(normal)	(shortfall)
	↓	
	Tribute Mobilization/Surplus Appropriation	
(bearable)	(optimal)	(excessive)
	↓	
	Prestige Goods Exchange	
(increasing flow)	(constant flow)	(decreasing flow?)
(Instability)	**(Stability)**	**(Instability)**

Figure 2   The Relationship between Climate and Chiefly Cycling Behavior.

tion of resource shortages in one area by the distribution of stored surpluses from other localities. Adoption of such a strategy may have helped rationalize or legitimize the growth of large chiefdoms and, concomitantly, powerful elite authority structures. The extent to which this kind of redistribution actually occurred, however, has been challenged in recent years. If redistribution-based "buffering" systems were indeed present, it is probable that surpluses were directed first to the elite and only secondarily to commoner populations during periods of stress. This appears to be the way things work in normal times in chiefdoms (e.g., see Betzig 1988a), and it is unlikely that elites would be less favored during periods of stress.

Territorial Boundary Maintenance

The ethnographic and ethnohistoric literature from around the world indicates that at least some chiefdoms occupied well-defined territories surrounded by and separated from other such societies by depopulated or underpopulated areas, variously described as buffer zones, hunting territories, or no-man's lands. There is some suggestion, furthermore, that intensity of territorial behavior—the maintenance or defense of exclusive patterns of land use or what were perceived as critical resources (Dyson-Hudson and Smith 1978:22)—was directly related to level of sociopolitical complexity, although the ethnographic literature on this subject is characterized by considerable ambiguity (e.g., D. Taylor 1975:33–34). Intensive and small-scale warfare was a primary method by which chiefdoms maintained territories and boundaries. Intensive warfare, which included either population relocation or extermination, is sometimes reported among more complex chiefdoms (Carneiro 1990; Milner 1993; Vayda 1960, 1961). Such behavior would have been a direct and unequivocal means of defining territory or settling boundary disputes and would likely leave pronounced archaeological signatures.

Small-scale warfare appears to have been more common, however, and may have profoundly affected regional settlement distributions, hunting patterns, and other resource procurement activities (DeBoer 1981; Durham 1976; Gage 1979; Gross 1975; Harner 1972:56; Hickerson 1965). This type of warfare, which may be difficult to recognize archaeologically, was characterized by skirmishes between small parties and typically occurred when task groups strayed too far from population centers and encountered individuals or parties from other polities. Areas closest to permanent settlements came to be viewed as the safest for hunting and other activities, while increasing danger obtained the farther one went out from this zone. A direct result of a regional pattern of low-intensity warfare would be that group boundaries would come to be defined by the unoccupied zones between polities, areas that were only infrequently visited. An ecological consequence of this, interestingly, was that buffer zones served as prey reservoirs from which game animal populations depleted closer to settlements might replenish themselves (Hickerson 1965; Mech 1977). The maintenance of buffer zones, whether intended or not, helped these societies avoid potentially serious resource shortages.

Some evidence suggests that the existence and extent of buffer zones were related to user-group population size or density, and that the successful functioning of these buffers was essential to the maintenance of organizational stability. Population apparently strongly covaried with territorial extent (core territory and outlying buffers) in precontact Hawaiian chiefdoms (Cordy 1981:216), and similar relationships have been noted in other complex societies (Lenski 1966:194). Given this, organizational change might be as likely to ensue from a long-term pattern of low-intensity conflict that resulted in resource shortfalls as from outright attacks on settlements. Continuing low-level subsistence stress or population attrition might be as devastating, in the long run, as intensive warfare (e.g., Milner, Smith, and Anderson 1991).

The existence of geographically extensive buffer zones may be inferred when ethnographic accounts or archaeological distribution maps are examined, although a range of variables, such as survey coverage bias, population measures, and the accuracy of temporal indicators, needs to be carefully considered. One result of analyses directed to the creation of phase distribution maps encompassing the Eastern Woodlands, in fact, has been the identification of buffer zones over large areas (Anderson 1990a:240–48, 1991; Milner, Anderson, and Smith 1992). Other procedures that have been used to reconstruct territorial extent include: (1) examining the distribution of artifact styles or raw materials; (2) using locational analysis or central place theory to determine the distribution of centers and associated outlying communities; and (3) examining the occurrence of center or boundary features such as cairns, megaliths, mounds, fortifications, cemeteries, or other kinds of features reflecting considerable labor investment (Cordy 1981:94; Hodder 1978; Renfrew 1976, 1984). A procedure that classifies "temples (a political artifact) along stylistic lines and then [plots] their distribution in space and time" (Cordy 1981:95) has been employed in Hawaii, and similar analyses, based on mound size and number, have been conducted in the southeastern United States (Ferguson 1975; Hally 1987; Hally and Rudolph 1986).

Buffer zones, to offer another example, were "the only consistent archaeological pattern marking community borders" in a study of political evolution undertaken in precontact Hawaii by Cordy (1981:172). No cairns, boundary markers, or other special site types were found in these areas. On the main island of Hawaii, the disappearance of buffer zones was linked with rapid settlement expansion, the emergence of a paramount chief, and the development of a multidistrict society replacing several formerly autonomous, simpler chiefdoms (179–83). A similar pattern was observed on Maui, which was occupied by two complex chiefdoms separated by a large unoccupied buffer until circa 1600, when the island was unified and the buffer occupied (198–200). The presence and size of buffer zones in these Hawaiian cases thus appear to be directly related to the complexity of the political apparatus. The existence of these buffers, furthermore, was apparently for sociological (i.e., to maintain separation of autonomous political units) as well as ecological reasons (i.e., to ensure an adequate supply of protein, hides, firewood, etc.). While care must be taken when transferring observations from circumscribed island societies to those on more open continental land masses, such inferences are worth exploring.

How chiefdom societies defined and maintained their boundaries and buffers and thus helped shape the regional social landscape, I believe, was critical to the maintenance of organizational stability. Understanding cycling thus necessitates the analysis of not only areas where people lived (i.e., centers and other settlements), but also the areas they avoided or used infrequently. It also necessitates a consideration of areas large enough to encompass many chiefdoms, and not merely the area around one or a few societies. Comparative analyses of buffer zones can provide clues about the population size, political complexity, and stability of the chiefdoms creating these social landscapes.

Information Management

The stability of chiefdom societies also appears to be related to the effectiveness of the procedures by which elites receive and process information and then make decisions, an observation derived from the managerial theories of chiefdom formation and organization noted previously (e.g., Earle 1987:292–93; Johnson 1973, 1978; Peebles and Kus 1977:427–31; Tainter 1977; Wright 1969, 1977, 1984; Wright and Johnson 1975). According to this functionalist perspective, chiefly decision-making structures arose, at least in part, to deal with pressing social problems (i.e., perhaps brought on by population pressure or resource shortages). Chiefly elites as decision makers typically controlled (or managed at some level) societal food production, public construction activity (e.g., irrigation networks and monuments), warfare and military activity, long-distance trade, patterns of interpolity and intrapolity social and political interaction, ritual, and access to sacred or esoteric knowledge. As the geographic scale of chiefdom societies increased, however, information management became increasingly difficult, particularly as the number of discrete, interacting locales requiring administrative coordination and management increased (see Johnson 1982 for an extended discussion of this problem facing elites). As the elite's administrative burden increased, so too did the possibility of information overload and system collapse, barring the emergence of more effective or efficient decision-making apparatus.

Cycling in chiefdoms can thus also be viewed, in part, as an alternation of successful and unsuccessful responses to information-processing demands; that is, social stability is maintained as long as processing capability is not exceeded. As information-processing capacity is approached, however, stress increases. Once a critical threshold is reached, reorganization must occur or system collapse will follow. The addition or removal of a decision-making level would yield a hierarchical or steplike developmental profile, while reorganization within an existing administrative level would not. The pattern has been described as steplike, because the levels are clear-cut, and change is typically rapid from one level to the next (Cordy 1981:231; Johnson 1978:97).

Deriving effective measures of the information load chiefly elites had to address is crucial to examining the relationship between information processing and cycling behavior. One suggested scalar measure of information load is the number of communities under a given administrative level, or its span of control (Johnson 1982:410). The span of control of a center would thus indicate the information load on its elites and would provide a measure of the potential stability of that particular political system. Such information is sometimes inferred from archaeological settlement pattern analyses where direct relationships between site size classes and administrative levels are assumed to exist.

There is appreciable evidence to support such an approach. Feinman and Neitzel (1984:67–74), using a sample of 63 New World prestate sedentary societies, for example, have shown that a strong relationship exists between a society's total population and the number of administrative levels in place. A weaker positive relationship was found between maximal community size and the number of administrative levels. Interestingly, the span of control of the paramount or chiefly center only rarely exceeded seven subsidiary communities, suggesting possible upper limits on the size of these polities. Ethnographic and ethnohistoric accounts provide excellent information from which to examine relationships between information management and organization structure, and fortunately, the latter exist from the southeastern United States (chapter 4).

Control over information was also important to the maintenance of chiefly authority structures. Among the patrilineal Azande of equatorial Africa, where successional strife was common, paramounts are reported to have maintained careful control over the location of both settlements and trails, to maximize information flow to their center and to minimize its flow between potential rivals. This has been described by DeSchlippe (1956:12):

> Chief's villages were connected by paths with subchiefs' villages and these again with homesteads of the elders. From the homestead of an elder a path used to run along a contour, parallel to a stream, on which individual family homesteads of the ordinary Azande were dispersed like beads. No path was allowed to connect the homesteads of two Azande owing allegiance to different elders, not the homesteads of two elders, without it passing through their respective subchiefs. Even the homesteads of two subchiefs may not be connected without the path passing first through the chief's place. Whenever, among paths radiating from the chief's village, one was leading for a certain distance towards two different subchiefs, a sentinel was placed at the fork to watch any possible direct communications between the two subchiefs. Jealousy of power, suspicion, and political intrigue underlie this system.

It is possible that the example is overstated, although an emphasis on information control is clearly indicated. This same example also indicates how the very structure of the landscape may either facilitate or hinder information flow (as well as other kinds of interaction) and hence organizational developments. Lenski (1966:154, 162, 235) has argued that the stability and complexity of many sub-Saharan African political systems were directly related to the efficiency of their internal communication and transportation systems. Where transportation and information flow was poor, chiefly control over outlying groups was difficult, and rebellions from this quarter were common. This relationship was shown to be scale dependent; that is, the larger the society and the poorer the internal information and transportation facilities, the greater the likelihood of internal dissension.

The kind of information controlled by decision makers was as important as how effectively information was transmitted. Information essential to the maintenance of elite control would have encompassed areas as diverse as subsistence (knowledge of planting strategies, harvest results, and amounts of stored surplus), politics (procedures for co-opting rivals and retaining supporters and for maintaining an awareness of the activities of rival elites in immediate and outlying communities), tribute mobilization (strategies for exacting goods and labor from supporters or information about the flow of these goods), "foreign affairs" (knowledge about the operation and current status of alliance and exchange networks between polities), warfare (knowledge of current hostilities and the organization of responses to potential threats), and public ceremony and ritual (knowledge about the content and coordination of public ceremony and strategies for maintaining and increasing esoteric information). It would be a mistake to assume, however, that chiefly elites controlled or dictated all aspects of life. Local communities or subsidiary polities in chiefdom societies, and the individuals within them, typically had considerable or complete autonomy over many aspects of their existence.

Control of esoteric or sacred knowledge was important to elite legitimization, and its role should not be underestimated. Helms (1987:80) has described "sacred wisdom and esoteric knowledge" as the "essence of eliteness." Esoteric knowledge included information about remote people and places, something that could be generated as a consequence of elite participation in regional prestige goods exchange networks (see also Helms 1979, 1988). Efficient decision making was dependent, in part, on the strength and importance attached to ideologies of chiefly sanctity; where the chief was held sacred, so too were his decisions.

Control of knowledge as the prerogative of the elite could have a disastrous effect on the organizational hierarchy as well as throughout the total population if poor decisions jeopardized the successful functioning of the subsistence economy or other critical areas of society. The loss of one or a few key individuals with the personal skills and knowledge necessary to manage crop dispersal practices, to maintain surplus appropriation, tribute appropriation, or prestige goods networks, or to lead in warfare might bring about an organizational failure. That is, the loss of a particularly effective administrator and his replacement by a less-skilled individual could bring about stress and ultimate collapse if sufficient checks were not built into the system. Both the historical and ethnographic literature is replete with examples of incompetent rulers who dissipated the accomplishments of their predecessors.

One final measure of the degree of stability of a decision-making level appears to be the number of offices or administrative positions in place supporting or assisting elite decision making. Where counsel or consensus was tolerated, greater breadth of knowledge could be brought to bear on decisions, and individual action could be moderated. Incompetent or underage rulers were more likely to be tolerated in political systems where supporting elites/administrators were present and capable of performing essential societal functions in the ruler's place. There was always the likely possibility, however, that these supporting elites would usurp power, given the emphasis placed on personal ability in determining succession and the competitive nature of the kinship/status system.

Population Movement

Extensive population movement is a hallmark of chiefly cycling behavior. We have seen that chiefdom societies are predisposed to a fair degree of instability by the nature of their basic social structure. Population movement was one mechanism for resolving this social tension, and the movement or relocation of groups or whole societies over moderate distances, the ethnographic record indicates, was commonplace. Resolving the causes of observed population movement is critical, since individuals, villages, and centers may move for a variety of reasons unrelated to cycling behavior. Exhaustion of local soil, game, or firewood resources has been variously advanced to explain community movement, as well as the deterioration of buildings under the impact of climate and fauna. When this kind of population movement occurred within existing social configurations and territorial boundaries, it likely posed little threat to chiefly authority structures.

Intrasocietal population movement by individuals or small groups of related kin is particularly well documented in the ethnographic record. It was common, for example, between local communities among the matrilineal Lozi of Zimbabwe. These movements were often prompted by quarrels, accusations of sorcery, divorce, or resource stress and were exemplified by the saying "If you live badly at your father's you have a right to seek a home at your mother's" (Gluckman 1951:68). The ideal situation, however, was to remain in or near one's home village, "where it was proper for a man to die" (69). Frequent movement also characterized the membership of Yao and Plateau Tonga villages, less complex simple or nonchiefdom matrilineal societies of southwestern Africa. As among the Lozi, population movement was often prompted by personal quarrels that got out of hand (Colson 1951:135, 139; J. Mitchell 1951:337–38). Among some chiefdom societies, individual movement, while tolerated, required chiefly sanction. Among the patrilineal Azande, who practiced shifting cultivation, for example, individual moves prompted by soil exhaustion usually required the permission of the headman, who usually gave it, in part to avoid jeopardizing his own power base (DeSchlippe 1956:192–94). In more complex chiefdoms, however, individual movement, particularly that of commoners, was often strictly controlled. Cordy (1981:18), for example, has noted that in complex Hawaiian chiefdoms commoners "spent their lives within the sphere of their own community." The paramount had control over the building of villages among the Lozi and could order the relocation of people to new communities (Gluckman 1951:62).

Community or societal fissioning leading to the establishment of independent communities and authority structures is directly tied to organizational stability and hence cycling (see also Lillios 1991:100–115). Fissioning has been defined as "the division of a village community along lines of structural cleavage so that one section maintains continuity, usually symbolized by the retention of its name, with the original undivided village; and the other section or sections, named after their leading elders, seek to establish themselves as independent villages" (V. Turner 1957:169). Turner further noted that fissioning was a form of social drama marked by four stages: a breach of social norms and relationships; a period of increasing crisis; attempts to correct the situation; and reintegration of the differing factions, or schism and societal fissioning (91–92). Incidence of societal fissioning appears to be inversely related to the degree of political centralization present in a region. Where central authority was weak and a chief exerted little control over the movement of communities and individuals, fissioning tended to occur much more often than when chiefly authority was strong. Among the Ndembu, for example, fissioning has increased markedly during the recent historic period, apparently because chiefly authority had been superseded by colonial administration (49–50). Among the Yao, another African group where chiefly authority has weakened considerably in recent years, more important headmen sometimes "launched out and became independent leaders" (J. Mitchell 1951:348). That is, where chiefly authority structures were strong, successful fissioning, or the breaking away of dissident groups, tended to be difficult or unnecessary.

Where chiefly authority was weakly defined, community fissioning was more common, since relocation elsewhere was a viable option. Dissatisfied subjects in weakly organized chiefdoms may have been more likely and able to vote with their feet than those in strong chiefdoms. Where chiefly leadership and inheritance were secure, fissioning and out-migration may have been the only option available to impatient rivals. Their movement may have even been encouraged by the paramount as a means of reducing the likelihood that they would challenge his authority. Ironically, the longer a strong leader was in power, the more frustrated his rivals, including his heirs, might become. Fissioning would diffuse potential rivals, by removing them from central arenas of power, while simultaneously facilitating societal expansion (e.g., Pauketat 1991:35).

Kinship relationships were critical to defining fission units. Groups of related males and their dependents tend to be the primary units forming new communities. In chiefdoms, these fission groups tended to be members of junior elite lineages outside of the direct line of inheritance, or else they were members of the ruling lineage but either outside of the direct line of succession or in lower (descendant) generations. These elites, their families, and associated commoners formed the basic fission units. In matrilineal societies such as those presumed common in the southeastern

United States in the late prehistoric era, uterine kinship groups (i.e., groups of related women and their brothers) are likely to have been the basic unit of fission. The power of the uterine sibling group is suggested in ethnohistoric accounts, notably by the position of women in societies such as the Natchez and at Cofitachequi and Guatari and by the affection reported between the chief of Coosa and his sister (Ranjel in Bourne 1904, 2:116) (see chapter 3).

Fissioning can rapidly lead to selective amnesia about a group's origin and ties with other groups; the deliberate revision of genealogical charters is a common strategy setting groups apart from or over other groups in chiefdoms as well as in more complex societies (Ogilvie 1971:12–13; Sahlins 1958:146; V. Turner 1957:86). Memories of a common origin fade within a few generations after fissioning among Ndembu communities (V. Turner 1957:175–76). This is related, in part, to the weak chiefly authority structure and shallow lineages present in this particular society, but it is also related to the necessity of focusing on the origins, charter, and autonomy of the present leadership. Ties are remembered but are not emphasized and are weak on detail. Equation of a leader's title with the name of the polity is also a fairly common practice in chiefdom societies and tends to occur in older, more established polities or communities (e.g., V. Turner 1957:105).

The likelihood of community fissioning in Ndembu society was based on a wide range of factors, including "the length of establishment of the settlement, the fertility of women and men, the strength of marital ties, the reputation and astuteness of the headman and of candidates for headmanship, the age and experience of these candidates, the local numerical strength of sibling groups and minimal lineages, and so on" (V. Turner 1957:226–27). As community size increased, so too did the possibility for conflict leading to rebellion or fissioning, following scalar stress arguments developed by Johnson (1982). Villages among the Ndembu typically consisted of 12 or 13 huts and under 50 people and rarely had more than 20 huts. When the upper end of this scale was reached, "powerful social tensions" were present, and fissioning was described as inevitable (V. Turner 1957:37–39, 43, 58, 215). In the absence of effective social controls, the greater the number of people in close proximity to one another, the greater the likelihood that society-rending disputes would occur.

The geographic scale of population movement after fissioning was related to the underlying causes of the split and to regional political relationships (V. Turner 1957:177, 206–7). If ties between local communities in a given area were fairly strong, then fissioning populations might have to move fairly appreciable distances. That is, where close relations or alliance networks existed between many communities, relocation over short distances may not have been feasible, and movement might have had to be to an area completely outside of this alliance network. Where fissioning was between close kin, particularly where violent conflict occurred between these kin, the fissioning group typically relocated at a considerably greater distance than if the breaches were between more distant groups or nonkin and were characterized by fairly minimal violence. Where events leading to fissioning were acrimonious or bloody, population relocation might be over considerable distances, to ensure the separation of the rival factions. Generally, the greater the intensity of conflict, the farther the movement upon fissioning.

Fission units were often unstable, particularly if they did not have enough members to sustain viable community replication. Their lack of appreciable time depth might hinder the development of support for the new elite authority structures, much less communal loyalty. These groups also had to be able to use existing technology where they relocated, prompting movement to areas and environmental zones comparable to those left behind (Anthony 1990). The spread of the Mississippian adaptation in the Southeast, wherever direct population movement was involved, would have been constrained by factors such as these. While some evidence for population movement has been documented archaeologically (e.g., Morse 1977, Morse and Morse 1980), the process has been downplayed by some authorities to the point where it is only rarely considered (e.g., Bruce Smith 1984; but see M. Williams and Smith 1989 for an alternate view).

Conclusions

Cycling refers to changes in administrative levels in the chiefdom societies occupying a region. These fluctuations have been described as cyclical because they tend to follow a recurrent pattern rather than directional change to greater or lesser sociopolitical complexity. Furthermore, the process characterizes chiefdom political organization rather than stands as exceptional or aberrant behavior.

The study of cycling, we have seen, necessitates the consideration of a wide range of topics, including factors as diverse as the developmental histories of the societies in question, their basic social and economic organization, and their placement in regional patterns of geography and climate. Figure 3 lists factors shown to be linked to chiefly cycling in this chapter, specifically by promoting organizational stability or instability. Since stability is defined as stasis in the number of administrative or decision-making levels, cycling can only occur under conditions of organizational instability, with the result of either an expansion or contraction in the number of levels. Figure 3 indicates the general circumstances under which this happens, illustrating each variable state when the system is stable, when shifts from one to two decision-making levels occur (i.e., when complex chiefdoms form), and when shifts from two to one decision-making levels occur (i.e, when complex chiefdoms fragment into

Increases in Complexity (decision-making levels stable or increasing)		Decreases in Complexity (decision-making levels unstable or decreasing)
homogeneous	**Regional Physiographic Structure**	irregular
favorable	**Climate**	unfavorable
predictable/even	**Resource Structure**	unpredictable/irregular
surplus	**Agricultural/Subsistence Production**	shortfall
present/extensive capability	**Storage Technology**	absent/minor capability
bearable	**Tribute Mobilization**	excessive
constant/increasing flow	**Prestige Goods Exchange**	decreasing/interrupted flow
strong	**Alliance Network**	weak
regular	**Information Flow**	erratic
aggressive	**Territorial Boundary Maintenance**	passive
increasing	**Population Change**	decreasing
sanctioned	**Population Movement**	unsanctioned
strongly supported	**Ritual Institutions**	weakly supported
strong	**Authority Structures**	weak
minor/channeled	**Factional Competition**	major/uncontrolled
regular/insitutionalized	**Nature of Succession**	uncertain/weakly institutionalized

Complex Chiefdom Formation   **Complex Chiefdom Collapse**

Figure 3 Factors Promoting Organizational Change in Chiefdom Societies.

simple chiefdoms).

Causal links are evident between many of these variables, something indicated by their relative placement in the figure. Thus regional physiographic structure, climate, and resource structure are listed at the top, since these factors constrain or predispose the limits of many subsequent variables (see also figure 2). Similar groupings of interrelated variables include agriculture/subsistence production, tribute mobilization/surplus appropriation, and storage technology, which in turn shape developments within prestige goods exchange and intrapolity and interpolity alliance and information flow networks. Less precise relationships and linkages are evident with factors further down on the list, such as the nature and strength of elite authority structures, how succession is determined, or the intensity of factional competition, although the importance of these variables, we have seen, cannot be understated. The relationships among these variables generating chiefly cycling are complex and multivariate, and changes in one variable do not necessarily produce changes in other variables down the column in a linear fashion. Accordingly, figure 3 should be viewed as a highly simplified, partial representation of the forces shaping an extremely complex process.

However, the underlying causes of cycling, that is, why the process occurs, are more basic. Competition for prestige and power between rival elites, it is argued, is what initiates and drives cycling in chiefdom societies. The process is cyclical because this very pattern of competition precludes the development of stable organizational structures capable of maintaining a two-level decision-making hierarchy indefinitely. That elites in chiefdom societies compete with one another for followers and for control over commoner populations is well documented. Within a simple chiefdom, this process typically results in the replacement of one leader by another, with no change in organizational structure. When elites in one chiefdom sought domination over those in another, however, a complex chiefdom might form and expand, necessitating a change in organizational hierarchy from one to two levels. The formation of a complex chiefdom greatly enlarged the arena of elite competition and changed the potential outcome of the competitive process. Replacement of leaders in complex chiefdoms may have occurred with minimal alteration to existing organizational structures, as when one elite within a paramount center succeeded another. Given repeated challenges, however, sooner or later power would either shift to another center (in which case the two-level organizational hierarchy continues, albeit in a different setting) or the chiefdom would fragment. It is this process of shifting power relations, and particularly the fragmentation of complex chiefdoms over a landscape into parts from which expansion begins anew, that constitutes cycling.

To elaborate, simple chiefdoms are essentially autonomous economic and sociopolitical units. Complex chiefdoms, formed from a number of

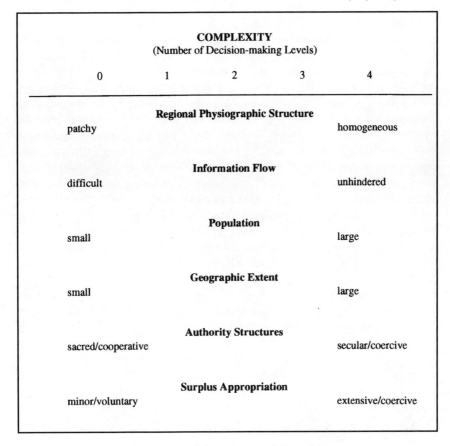

COMPLEXITY
(Number of Decision-making Levels)

0	1	2	3	4

Regional Physiographic Structure

patchy — homogeneous

Information Flow

difficult — unhindered

Population

small — large

Geographic Extent

small — large

Authority Structures

sacred/cooperative — secular/coercive

Surplus Appropriation

minor/voluntary — extensive/coercive

Figure 4   Factors Related to Level of Organizational Complexity.

simple chiefdoms, are thus made up of entities perfectly capable, if given the chance, of usurping the role of the paramount center or, alternatively, operating autonomously. Accordingly, complex chiefdoms existed only as long as their elites could maintain political control over similar yet subsidiary elites in other centers. Struggles for political control in these societies were typically between paramount and lesser elites and their retinues and only rarely encompassed entire populations. Commoners appear to have had very little power or influence in shaping chiefdom organizational structures, except through weight of numbers. Maintaining the support of fellow and lesser elites was, therefore, crucial to the stability of a chiefdom.

Elite support was fragile, however, since the elites living within the constituent parts of a complex chiefdom were fully capable of operating on their own. Obtaining the cooperation of fellow elites was thus an essential prerequisite and primary means by which paramount elites emerged and retained their positions as leaders/rulers of complex chiefdoms. Lesser elites were, in effect, responsible for the allegiance of the constituent parts or simple chiefdoms making up the larger whole. Both the lesser elite as well as the paramount's own kin were dangerous, though, since they were typically genealogically close in rank to the paramount and since some were rulers of chiefdoms themselves and operated from positions of considerable power. Because of these legitimate successors to power, challenges to chiefly leadership were inevitable, given human ambition and opportunity. The outcome of these leadership struggles in complex chiefdoms, as noted, almost invariably took one of three courses. Either the office of the paramount chief and its associated rank echelon continued at the original center, or it rotated or relocated to a new center, or it disappeared altogether, as the paramount chiefdom fragmented back into a series of simple chiefdoms and the process began anew.

Notably, many of the factors promoting organizational stability or instability and hence leading to chiefly cycling also operate to shape or constrain the development of organizational *complexity* (figure 4). Maintaining a distinction between these processes is important, because factors promoting organizational complexity may have little effect on the stability of the resulting organizational structures. In the next two chapters, the ethnohistoric and archaeological record from the southeastern United States is examined, to see whether the causes of cycling behavior identified in this chapter are present and amenable to study. Chapters 3 and 4 thus serve as an introduction to the chiefdom societies that occupied this region, while simultaneously providing a review of evidence available for the study of cycling.

3

Mississippian Political Change
Evidence from Ethnohistoric Accounts

This chapter examines documentary evidence for cycling behavior and its causes within the Mississippian chiefdoms present in the Southeast at the time of initial European contact in the 16th century. Historic accounts from across the region are used, with an emphasis on descriptions of native societies in the South Appalachian area, the focus of subsequent archaeological investigations. The earliest 16th-century accounts, from the period before the native chiefdoms collapsed from contact-induced depopulation and warfare, contain valuable descriptions of political, genealogical, and settlement hierarchies, social stratification, tributary and alliance relationships, fortifications and warfare, labor mobilization, decision-making organizations, sumptuary ritual and mortuary behavior, and individual and chiefly wealth (e.g., Anderson 1985a; DePratter 1983, 1991a; Dye 1990; Hoffman 1993; Hudson 1976, 1986, 1990; Hudson, Smith, and DePratter 1984; Hudson, Worth, and DePratter 1990; Hudson et al. 1985, 1987; Knight 1990; M. Smith 1987; M. Smith and Hally 1992). This documentary evidence is of considerable value in the examination of late prehistoric and early contact-era archaeological materials from the region. Through a combination of archaeological and ethnohistoric analysis, it is possible to produce a detailed picture of the location, size, and operation of southeastern chiefly societies.

The value of ethnohistoric information for the study of cultural evolution lies, in part, in the effectiveness with which its rich synchronic detail about economic, social, and political organization can be linked with diachronic archaeological data from the precontact past of the societies under investigation. Drennan and Uribe (1987:viii), in a classic volume entitled *Chiefdoms in the Americas,* have presented several cautionary notes about the use of ethnohistoric data. First, only the earliest accounts are likely to provide accurate data on the form and operation of these societies, given their rapid alteration upon contact. Second, ethnohistoric observations are, for the most part, synchronic pictures, often of political systems in great distress, providing an incomplete or partial perspective from which to study long-term trends. Finally, as the authors note, "we clearly cannot base our whole idea of processes of change in chiefdoms, and especially not our notions of their initial development on information about their sometimes cataclysmic ends" (viii).

Although researchers continually lament the limited nature of the southeastern ethnohistoric record, excellent regionally oriented syntheses of the anthropological data contained within it have been produced, most notably by Swanton (1911, 1946), Hudson (1976), and DePratter (1991a). In the South Appalachian area, ethnohistoric research has had great success in documenting both the routes of early explorers and the location and general nature of the native societies with which they interacted (Baker 1974, 1975; DePratter 1987a, 1989; DePratter, Hudson, and Smith 1983; Hudson 1987, 1990; Hudson, Smith, and DePratter 1984; Hudson, Worth, and DePratter 1990; Hudson et al. 1985, 1987; Levy, May, and Moore 1990; Waddell 1980). The present examination of cycling, which proceeds by resolving explicit linkages between the observations about contact-era southeastern chiefdom societies recorded in these early accounts and the processes shaping the patterns of chiefly cycling observed in the regional archaeological record, is a direct beneficiary of this research. The ethnohistoric record, by providing a highly detailed if essentially synchronic picture of native life, thus complements the diachronic and coarser-grained perspective available from archaeological analyses. Prior to addressing the ethnohistoric record directly, I shall introduce the primary source materials, in order to document how they were created, what they contain, and their reliability.

The Nature of the Documentary Data Base

Sixteenth-century materials form the primary ethnohistoric data base employed in the present study, although references to a few later sources are provided when these illustrate details lacking in earlier documents. Almost all of the documentary sources are in Spanish, French, or English, with most in Spanish, reflecting the extent of exploration and settlement by these three nations during this period. Two reasons explain a documentary focus on the 16th century. First, during this century, comparatively "pristine" chiefdoms were encountered in the Southeast, although even then dramatic and destabilizing changes occurred within fairly short periods as a result of the effects of disease and conquest (Ramenofsky 1987, 1990; M. Smith 1987). Second, the most extensive sources date from the first half of the initial one and a half centuries of European exploration and settlement, from circa 1520 to 1580. This corresponds to the greatest period of Spanish interest in and exploration of the Southeast, encompassing the explorations of Pánfilo de Narváez, Hernando de Soto, Tristan de Luna, and Juan Pardo and the efforts to colonize La Florida at Santa Elena and St. Augustine (figure 5).

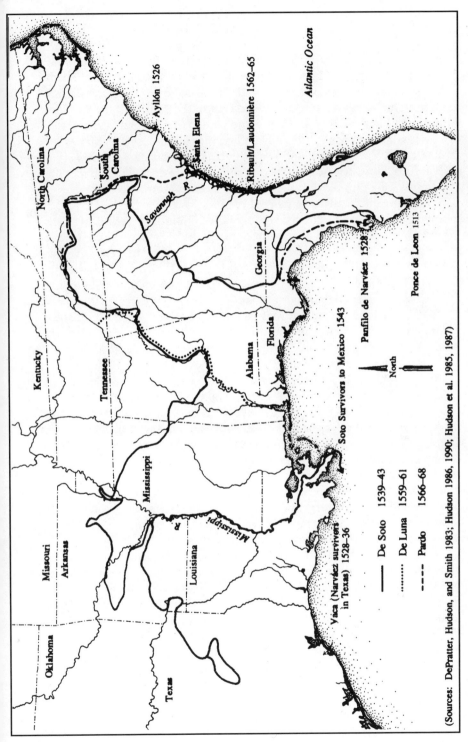

(Sources: DePratter, Hudson, and Smith 1983; Hudson 1986, 1990; Hudson et al. 1985, 1987)

Figure 5   Sixteenth-century European Exploration in the Southeastern United States.

Initial Contact (circa 1500 to 1539)

The first European exploration of the interior Southeast is traditionally assumed to begin in 1513 with Ponce de Léon's "discovery" of Florida. From 1500 onward, however, Spanish ships were at least occasionally touching and were sometimes wrecked upon the southeastern Gulf and Atlantic coasts of what later became the United States. Léon's encounters were with the Calusa, a southern Florida group (C. Lewis 1978; Marquardt 1987, 1988, 1992; Widmer 1988). The extent of European contact even at this early date is indicated by the fact that the Indians Ponce de Léon met had apparently encountered Spanish previously (Swanton 1946:101).

Following initial settlement in the West Indies, the Spanish had quickly mounted search and discovery ventures throughout the Caribbean, looking for land, slaves, and other sources of wealth. The earliest well-documented Spanish venture in the general South Appalachian area took place in 1521 under the direction of Lucas Vásquez de Ayllón, one of the auditors of Santo Domingo, who sent a caravel under the direction of Francisco Gordillo to explore the northern coast of Florida, as the North American continent was then described. Ayllón, who was interested in establishing a settlement in the region, was at this point conducting advance exploration. On 24 June 1521, Gordillo and a second captain, Pedro de Quexó, made landfall at the mouth of a large river they named the St. Johns. The location, 33°30' north latitude, corresponds to that of Winyah Bay, where the Pee Dee River and several lesser drainages enter the Atlantic, or possibly the Santee River (Hudson 1990:6). After brief explorations, they seized some 70 of the local natives and carried them back to Santo Domingo for sale as slaves. From this unfortunate record of initial contact emerged what the great early 20th-century ethnohistorian John R. Swanton (1946:36) has called "the longest description of any tribe in North America which can claim such an early date of record." This account, a lengthy description of the history and customs of the country by one of the captured natives, Francisco of Chicora, was recorded firsthand by the Spanish historian Pietro Martiere d'Anghiera (1457–1526).

Francisco, who was apparently a remarkable individual, was attached to Ayllón's household in Santo Domingo, where he learned Spanish. It was there that he met Anghiera, who was a chronicler for the Royal Council of the Indies and who summarized the stories he heard from Francisco in the next to last of his decades in *De Orbe Novo* (Anghiera in MacNutt 1912, 2:259–69). Francisco's account contains numerous details about native life in the Carolinas, although seemingly fanciful items such as the herding and milking of deer caused Anghiera to remark "these fables and other similar nonsense have been handed down to the natives by their parents. . . . Such is the story told to me, and I repeat it for what it is worth. Your excellency may believe it or not" (261, 268). It is perhaps because of this skepticism that Francisco's account is of particular interest, for Anghiera's wording implies an effort to give a faithful rendition. Aside from somewhat improbable heaven/hell imagery that may have been slyly added by Francisco to please Anghiera, who had been a chaplain to the court of Ferdinand II and Isabella, the account is of considerable value, as it presents the first detailed description of southeastern chiefdom societies, specifically those along the coast and in the interior of South Carolina (Baker 1974:59–74).

Francisco described a ranked, hierarchical society with settlements over large areas owing allegiance and tribute to specific communities and leaders. These rulers received deferential treatment from the commoners; dressed, lived, and ate better than their subjects; were carried about on litters; and resided in combination temple/dwelling areas. Substantial ritual activity associated with the planting and harvesting of crops was described, as was burial/mortuary ceremonialism and a passionate interest in ball games. Specific details included mention of feather mantles, stone idols in temples, cathartic beverages (the black drink?), and the weaving of fiber mats and clothes. Swanton, while curiously dismissing "tales of subjection and tribute," was so impressed with Francisco's account that he began an exegesis of it with the comment "in this narrative there appears to be very little not based on fact" (Swanton 1946:47).

Few references describing native groups in the general South Appalachian area date from the period 1521 to 1539, not because attempts at exploration and colonization were lacking, but because contact with local populations was either minimal or else few survived to tell of it. A brief account by Giovanni da Verrazzano opens the period, describing events conducted in 1524 while in the service of France, when he sailed along the eastern coast of the United States. At his initial landfall at about 34° north latitude, possibly at or near the mouth of the Cape Fear River, Verrazzano met some natives, whose animal skin and bird feather robes he briefly described in a subsequent letter to Francis I (Verrazzano 1600). The major events of this period, however, were the catastrophic Spanish attempts at colonization by Ayllón and Narváez.

In the summer of 1526, Ayllón and a party of 600 settlers attempted to establish a colony, named San Miguel de Gualdape, somewhere on the southern Atlantic coast. Although opinions about the location of this colony vary considerably—from the central Georgia to northern South Carolina coast (Hoffman 1990; Hudson 1990:7; Quattlebaum 1956)—discoveries by the De Soto expedition (see below) suggest that the probable location was somewhere in coastal South Carolina, possibly near the mouth of the Santee River. Shipwreck, disease, and the subsequent factionalization of the survivors brought the colony to a disastrous end. Barely one-quarter of the party that left Santo Domingo in July made it back in early 1527, when the colony was abandoned. Descriptions of local Indian groups are minimal, since most contemporary records were absorbed with the magnitude of the tragedy that had occurred (Oviedo 1855,

3:626–30). Large communal houses were reported in use among the native groups living in the vicinity of the colony, however, as well as a brief description of ceremonial facilities where the bodies of important individuals were maintained (630). Ayllón's interpreters, including Francisco, had, in fact, deserted almost immediately upon landfall, precluding serious communication.

The Ayllón colony is noteworthy for the study of southeastern political organization because Spanish remains from it quickly found their way to the main temple of the province of Cofitachequi, located some 200 kilometers inland from the coast. During De Soto's visit in 1540:

> In that town were found a dagger and some beads of Christians, whom the Indians said had been in the port two days' journey thence . . . many years since . . . (Elvas in Robertson 1993:84; see also Bourne 1904, 1:67).

> This same day the Governor [De Soto] and Rodrigo Ranjel entered the temple or oratory of these idolatrous people, and . . . found . . . beads of glass and rosaries with their crosses. They also found Biscayan axes of iron, by which they recognized that they were in the district or land where the licenciado Lucas Vásquez de Ayllón was lost (Ranjel in Worth 1993a:279; see also Bourne 1904, 1:100).

> Here we found buried two Castilian axes for cutting wood, and a rosary of beads of jet and some *margaraitas* [trade beads] of the kind that they carry from here [Spain] to barter with the Indians. All this we believed they had obtained from barter with those who went with the licenciado Ayllón. According to the information that we had from the Indians, the sea was up to thirty leagues from there (Biedma in Worth 1993b:231; see also Bourne 1904, 2:14).

The logical port two days' canoe travel (?) distant from Cofitachequi, which is now thought to have been located near the modern city of Camden, South Carolina, would be downstream at or near the mouth of the Santee, or possibly on Winyah Bay just to the north. This is in approximate agreement with Biedma's (1904, 2:14) figure of 30 leagues or 103.5 miles (166.5 kilometers), using a figure of 3.45 miles (5.55 kilometers) per league (after Hudson, Smith, and DePratter 1984:66). Ayllón's colony remains undiscovered to this day, although finding it is a major goal of local archaeologists (e.g., Michie 1990:25, 1992; R. Stephenson 1975:95–96). The occurrence of artifacts from the Ayllón colony in a paramount center located a considerable distance away indicates the extent of tributary or trading networks operating in the region (see also DePratter and Smith 1980). Other evidence, notably references to the tributary roles of the Escamacu and Sanapa, coastal South Carolina groups, suggests the sway of Cofitachequi extended to the Sea Islands (Hudson 1990:78–83).

In 1528, a second attempt to settle the Southeast also ended disastrously. That year Pánfilo de Narváez landed near Tampa, Florida, with a force of several hundred men and proceeded to march inland to the north

(Marrinan, Scarry, and Majors 1990). Routed by continual sniping and skirmishing by warriors from Apalachee, a complex chiefdom occupying the region of the Florida panhandle, the expedition was forced to retreat to the sea somewhere near Pensacola Bay. Here they built a number of vessels and put to sea, attempting to follow the Gulf coastline to Mexico. The fleet was wrecked on the Texas coast, and only four members of the expedition, after suffering incredible hardships, survived to reach Mexico some eight years later in 1536. A narrative of this expedition by one of the four, Alvar Núñez Cabeza de Vaca, provides primary ethnohistoric detail on the Indians of coastal Texas. In an attempt to recoup his fortunes, Cabeza de Vaca tried to join De Soto's planned expedition and, dissembling about the condition of Florida, "gave them to understand that it was the richest country in the world" (Elvas in Bourne 1904, 1:6; see also Robertson 1993:48). The two quarreled, however, and only De Soto ultimately returned to Florida. Had De Soto known the conditions Cabeza de Vaca had actually encountered, and had he chosen to seek new fortunes elsewhere, our knowledge of southeastern Mississippian life would be appreciably poorer.

The De Soto Entrada (1539 to 1543)

The De Soto expedition has been justly described by Swanton (1946:38) as "the most impressive of all Spanish attempts to conquer and settle the territory" of the interior southeastern United States. De Soto, a former second in command to the Pizarros in the conquest of the almost unimaginable riches of the Inca empire in Peru, sought to find new riches in the northern continent. The magnitude of this expedition was immense: 600 men, over 200 horses, 100 or more servants and camp followers, and a large quantity of supplies and equipment, including trade goods, hogs, mules, and dogs. Landing near Tampa Bay in May of 1539, the expedition proceeded into the interior, where it spent the next four years visiting the complex Mississippian chiefdoms of Apalachee, Ocute, Cofitachequi, Coosa, Tastaluca, and Chicaca to the east of the Mississippi and Casqui, Pacaha (or Capaha, depending on the account), and many other societies to the west. The route the expedition took through the region has been the subject of extensive research (e.g., Swanton 1939) and has been masterfully reconstructed in recent years through a combination of ethnohistoric and archaeological research (figure 5) (DePratter 1987a; DePratter, Hudson, and Smith 1983; Hudson 1987, 1990; Hudson, Smith, and DePratter 1984; Hudson et al. 1985, 1987). De Soto died in Arkansas on 21 May 1542, and it was not until September 1543 that the survivors of the expedition, some 300 men, finally reached northern Mexico after traveling by boat down the Mississippi and along the Gulf coast. Having vanished completely and been given up as lost, the survivors were received with great acclaim, in spite of the relative lack of success of the expedition. Their tenacity, in fact, led to invidious comparisons and criticism of the comparably equipped Coronado expedition, which had made a relatively brief foray into the Southwest shortly before, in 1540–41 (Vega in Shelby 1993:543; see also Varner and Varner 1951:622).

The members of the De Soto entrada spent over four years in the interior of the Southeast, and the surviving accounts of the expedition form the earliest and, some would argue, the only detailed record of precontact or protocontact southeastern chiefdoms. As Swanton (1932:570) accurately, if somewhat romantically, noted, "much of the territory penetrated by De Soto was practically unvisited for a hundred and fifty years afterward, and to Englishmen and Frenchmen the country and its people had sunk into obscurity and the story of the enterprise itself had become semi-legendary." Native societies throughout the interior underwent precipitous organizational changes in the years immediately following this initial contact (M. Smith 1987). In the vicinity of Georgia and the Carolinas, for example, the groups documented in the later historic era, specifically the tribes and confederacies present at the time of the English settlement of Charles Town in 1670, were pale reflections of the complex chiefdoms encountered by De Soto and his men. The earliest accounts are thus invaluable sources of information on the organization and operation of these societies and hence about behavior relevant to the study of cycling.

The importance of these documentary resources cannot be emphasized strongly enough. Charles M. Hudson (1990:4) has gone so far as to state that "the documents of the Soto and Luna expeditions, together with those of the Pardo expeditions, contain most of the information we are ever likely to ever possess on the history of the sixteenth-century southeastern Indians of the interior." Although the utility of 16th-century documents for the reconstruction of native political organization and evolution has been questioned (e.g., Boyd and Schroedl 1987; Sturtevant 1983), the impact that studies based on them have had, I believe, discredits such notions. Any serious student of the Mississippian archaeological record, in fact, would be well advised to read these early accounts, starting with those from the De Soto and Pardo expeditions.

Four major documentary accounts of the De Soto entrada have survived to the present day (Clayton, Knight, and Moore 1993). These are, in order of publication or appearance, the narratives of: Rodrigo Ranjel (1904/1993), written during the expedition and finalized some time before August 1546; Luis Hernández de Biedma (1904/1993), written in 1544; the Gentleman of Elvas (1904/1993), first published in 1557 and hence written some time before this; and Garcilaso de la Vega (1951/1993), completed in the late 1580s or early 1590s and first published in 1601. These accounts are briefly discussed in turn, but first it should be noted that one letter from De Soto himself survived the expedition. This document, written on 9 July 1539, is instructive, for it gives De Soto's own opinion on the accuracy of native sources: "for what these Indians say I believe nothing but what I see" (De Soto in Bourne 1904, 1:162; see also Clayton, Knight, and Moore 1993, 1:376). For a similar reason the three eyewitness accounts of the expedition, written soon after the fact, tend to be more highly regarded by modern scholars than the fourth, written almost half a century later (Galloway 1990, 1991, 1992, n.d.; Henige 1986; Hoffman 1993:14).

The first of the four accounts to have been produced, at least in large measure, was that by Ranjel, De Soto's private secretary. This account is actually a diary of the events of the entrada, recorded either daily or at brief intervals. This account, covering the period from May 1539 through September 1541, was transcribed by Oviedo in Santo Domingo some time after Ranjel's return to the island but prior to August 1546, when Oviedo left for Spain (Ranjel in Bourne 1904, 2:48). Because it is a diary of events set down as they happened, this account is considered "the most reliable of all the accounts of the famous undertaking" (Swanton 1932:571; similar commentary appears in Bourne 1904, 1:xv, and Hudson, Smith, and DePratter 1984:65). So detailed was Ranjel's account that Oviedo (in Bourne 1904, 2:47; see also Worth 1993a:277) felt compelled to offer the following remarks: "let not the reader marvel that the historian goes over, in exact detail, the days marches and rivers and crossings that this Commander encountered . . . because among those gentlemen who were with the army there was one named Rodrigo Ranjel . . . who . . . wrote down day by day at the end of his labors, every thing that happened." While presenting valuable detail on the native societies in the region, the account additionally offers an instructive example of the insidious kind of bias that can occur in historic accounts: the deliberate falsification or distortion of information. In his last communication with Cuba, for example, De Soto ordered that "even though he might not find good land, he should write good news, in order to inspire the men" (Ranjel in Worth 1993a:258; see also Bourne 1904, 2:62).

The second account of the De Soto expedition to be prepared was that by Biedma, completed in 1544, shortly after the surviving members of the entrada reached Mexico. Luis Hernández de Biedma was the king's factor, and the narrative that he prepared was an official account of the expedition submitted to the Spanish crown. The shortest of all the accounts, the narrative is highly compressed and offers little that was not mentioned in the other accounts in the way of detail about the native societies. Although in broad agreement with the Ranjel and Elvas accounts, because it is an obvious summary prepared up to several years after the events in question, it is generally considered unreliable as a source of specific information about the chronology of the entrada or the terrain that it passed over.

The third source, and the first of the De Soto accounts actually published, appeared in 1557 (Elvas in Bourne 1904, 1:1–223; see also Robertson 1993). Written by an unidentified "Gentleman from Elvas" who accompanied De Soto, the account provides a wealth of detail about the expedition and the peoples it encountered. Although this record had long been considered less reliable than Vega's narrative, the discovery of the Ranjel and Biedma accounts in the mid-19th century provided "triumphant support" for its accuracy (Swanton 1932:571; see similar commentary in Bourne 1904, 1:viii). In spite of this, portions of the Elvas account have tended to be undervalued, particularly the numerous speeches attributed to various native rulers, such as those by Achese, Patofa, the Lady of Cofitachequi, Chiaha, Tali, Coosa, and Tastaluca. While unquestionably literary devices, the speeches nonetheless contain important references to customs, such as tributary relationships and the matrilineal succession of chiefly leaders (Elvas in Bourne 1904, 1:58, 64, 73–74; see also Robertson 1993:77–78, 82, 87–88), that suggest they are authentic in general content.

The fourth account of the De Soto entrada is Garcilaso de la Vega's *La Florida del Inca*, which was written between circa 1587 and 1591 (based on internal evidence) and published in Lisbon in 1605 (Bourne 1904, 1:viii). Vega, who was born in 1537 and was hence a child at the time of the entrada, was the son of a Spanish officer and the sister of the last Inca. As a boy growing up in Peru, Vega met some of the survivors of the De Soto expedition, and upon moving to Spain in 1560, he met several additional members. His manuscript was based on the memories of at least three of these survivors, of whom the cavalier Gonzalo Silvestre is assumed to be his principal informant, given his prominent role in (only) this account (viii–ix). The most extensive document describing the entrada, it is also regarded as the least reliable, primarily because it was written long after the events described (Galloway 1990, 1991, 1992, n.d.; Henige 1986; Hudson, Smith, and DePratter 1984:655; Swanton 1932:571). *La Florida* thus diverges wildly from the other three accounts in specific detail, notably in matters of chronology, distance, travel time, and casualty figures. Thus while Elvas records that 700 bearers accompanied De Soto from Ocute to Cofitachequi (Robertson 1993:80; see also Bourne 1904, 1:60), Vega puts the figure at 4,000 (Shelby 1993:272; see also Varner and Varner 1951:282). At the battle of Mauvila, both Elvas and Ranjel put the Indians' casualties at between 2,500 and 3,000 (Robertson 1993:104; Worth 1993a:294; see also Bourne 1904, 1:97; 2: 128), while Vega puts the figures at around 11,000 (Shelby 1993:351; see also Varner and Varner 1951:379).

Much has been made of Vega's inaccuracies, but this should not be used to discredit the source, since it stands as virtually the only sympathetic, detailed Spanish account of the southeastern Indians produced during the 16th century, by someone justifiably and admittedly proud of his dual Spanish/Indian heritage. Furthermore, Vega's preface contains a lengthy discussion of both his methods and sources and how he resolved discrepancies between conflicting accounts. Above all, he fully acknowledged the potential for error in his work, particularly the problems arising from his use of informants' dated memories and limited written accounts: "It is true that in their proceedings they have no regard for chronology, unless it be at the beginning, nor for order in the events they recount, because they put some too soon and others too late, nor do they name provinces, except for a few scattered ones. They simply tell the most important things that they saw as they happen to remember them" (Vega in Shelby 1993:55–56; see also Varner and Varner 1951:xl–xli).

Only recently have ethnohistoric reconstructions been prefaced with the kind of honesty shown by Vega in *La Florida del Inca*. Swanton (1932:751) himself noted that "the tales which his aged soldier informants related to him were inexact, often exaggerated, but they were not the results of a deliberate intention to deceive. They represent the attempts of old men, unassisted by diaries, letters, notes, or other aids to the memory to recall the events in which they had participated so many years before. In so far as I have been able to check this material it appears to me that the quantitative and associational elements have suffered, while the qualitative elements have survived." While subject to exaggeration, the Vega account is the richest in recounting details of southeastern native life and hence is a source to be used, albeit with caution.

Later 16th-Century Accounts

Following the De Soto entrada, Spanish exploration in the Southeast again paused for nearly a generation, as it did in the interval after the Ayllón and Narváez attempts at colonization in the mid-1520s. Interest in the area continued, however, particularly as Spanish vessels were occasionally shipwrecked along the Atlantic or Gulf coasts, often with considerable loss of life and treasure (Barcia in Priestley 1928:xxi). In the late 1550s, the Spanish crown decided to establish colonies in the lower Southeast to further Spanish expansion in North America, check potential advances of other European powers, and protect their shipping. On 11 June 1559, under the direction of Tristrán de Luna y Arellano, an expedition of approximately 1,000 colonists, 500 soldiers, and 240 horses sailed from Mexico, arriving in the area of Mobile Bay in mid-July. The area between Mobile and Pensacola bays was explored and a settlement established in the latter area. Unfortunately, a hurricane wrecked several ships and destroyed most of the food reserves in August, and by early 1560, the expedition was in great distress. Attempts to live off the countryside failed, and the colony had to be abandoned in early 1561.

An extensive documentary record exists from the De Luna expedition, much of it in the form of letters and petitions by the colonists to De Luna demanding their removal. Other documents that survive are records to and from exploring parties in the interior and official reports to Santo Domingo and Spain. The accounts of the expedition are of interest here for their descriptions of native groups, some of which had been contacted previously by De Soto. A major expedition of 200 men and 50 horses spent several months in the interior in 1560, reaching the principal town of the province of Coosa, now tentatively identified as at the Little Egypt site along the Coosawattee River in northwestern Georgia (Hally and Langford 1988; Hally, Smith, and Langford 1990; Hudson et al. 1985:732). Recent archaeological and ethnohistoric research (Hudson et al. 1989) has provided a possible reconstruction of the movements of De Luna's parties in the interior. The descriptions of Coosa indicate that this powerful chiefdom was much reduced in size and power compared to its position in 1540, supporting the cautionary note presented at the start of this chapter that only the very earliest accounts are likely to be reliable guides to conditions at and just prior to contact.

Although abandoning their venture on the Gulf coast, the Spanish continued plans for settlement on the Atlantic coast in the early 1560s. In 1561, a Spanish fleet under Villafañe briefly explored the lower Atlantic coastline, entering the area later settled as Santa Elena. Before settlements could be established, though, a series of three French expeditions occurred, directly challenging Spanish claim to the area. The expeditions were by Ribault in 1562, Laudonnière in 1564–65, and again by Ribault in 1565 (Bennett 1975:xiii–xxii). Several accounts survive from these expeditions, the most useful of which, from an anthropological perspective, are the narratives of René Laudonnière, first published in 1586, and the illustrations of Jacques Le Moyne de Morgues, which appeared in 1591. A wealth of detail about the Indians of the Florida, Georgia, and South Carolina coast and their relations with groups in the interior was presented, prompting Swanton (1946:62) to state that "to the Laudonnière expedition . . . we owe more of our knowledge of the ancient inhabitants of Florida than to the sum total of the Spanish sources." This statement is greatly overdrawn, particularly in light of the information that has been extracted from the De Soto, De Luna, and Pardo accounts in recent years, and indicates that care must be taken to avoid placing too much faith in some accounts and not enough in others.

The initial French expedition, under Jean Ribault, touched along the Florida to South Carolina coast from April through June 1562. In Port Royal Sound, somewhere near the modern town of Beaufort, South Carolina, Ribault, prior to departing for France, left a colony of 28 men in a fortification christened Charlesfort. Because of religious conflicts in France, he was unable to return immediately to relieve the colony. After almost a year of waiting, the men at Charlesfort, with native help, built a small boat and attempted to sail back to Spain with tragic results—many starved to death en route before being picked up by friendly ships. The primary accounts of this first expedition were by Laudonnière (1975) and Ribault (1927). Ribault's account, written in England after fleeing the religious struggles he encountered immediately upon his return to France, was published in English in 1563. This account, *The Whole and True Discovery of Terra Florida*, contains a number of descriptions of the coastal Indians. Comparable detail is also found in Laudonnière's account, including a reference to the ruler of "Chiquola [Chicora, probably Cofitachequi], the great lord of that territory" (Laudonnière in Bennett 1975:28), indicating the extent of influence interior groups may have had on the coastal groups. Parenthetically, the location of Charlesfort is currently uncertain, in spite of major survey efforts directed to its detection, and it is possible that it has since eroded away (DePratter and South 1990:63; but see DePratter and South 1993 for a new interpretation placing Charlesfort's location within the area of the slightly later Santa Elena colony).

Laudonnière himself commanded the second French expedition, sent out in 1564 to reestablish a French colony in the southeastern region. Landing along the Florida coast, they established a settlement named Fort Caroline near the mouth of the St. John's River. In the meantime, in mid-1565, a Spanish expedition to the same area was initiated, under the direction of Pedro Menéndez de Avilés, to colonize and to counter French activity in Florida. In August 1565, Ribault arrived with a third expedition to relieve Laudonnière, running into Avilés's fleet, which had arrived a few days earlier, almost upon landfall. The subsequent battle was inconclusive, but the French fleet was subsequently wrecked in a storm. Most of the French forces, including Ribault himself, were killed by Avilés after surrendering. Avilés then attacked and destroyed Fort Caroline on 20 September 1565, but fortunately for the study of southeastern Indian life, Laudonnière and a number of colonists escaped in one of the surviving vessels.

The accounts of the survivors of this 1564–65 French colony, describing native groups in the lower Southeast, provide the most detailed information currently available from the 16th century from non-Spanish sources. Laudonnière, who was a participant in the events of all three expeditions, prepared extended descriptions on the coastal Indians, accounts that have been judged to be "exceedingly well-recorded geography and anthropology" (Bennett 1975:xix) and that prompted Swanton's enthusiastic tribute noted previously. Jacques le Moyne de Morgue's account and illustrations are noteworthy because of the detailed drawings of coastal Florida Indian life. The only comparable illustrations from the Southeast dating from this period are those published in 1590 by John White depicting the coastal Algonkian groups of North Carolina and Virginia, groups encountered by the English expedition of Sir Richard Grenville in 1585 (J. White 1972).

With the destruction of the French, the Spanish under Avilés established two principal settlements along the Atlantic coast, at St. Augustine in 1565 and at Santa Elena in 1566. Detailed Spanish records of Indian life in the South Appalachian area, both along the coast and well into the interior, come from Santa Elena. This colony was maintained from 1566 to 1576, when the local Indians rose up and destroyed it, and from 1577, when it was reestablished, to 1587, when it was permanently abandoned. The site of Santa Elena was relocated on Parris Island, South Carolina, in the late 1970s by Stanley South (1979, 1980, 1991) and has been the subject of near-continuous archaeological investigation since that time. Two major expeditions that were sent into the interior from Santa Elena in 1566 and 1567, under the direction of Captain Juan Pardo, have provided invaluable records of the location and description of native groups in South Carolina, central and western North Carolina, eastern Tennessee, and northern Georgia (Hudson 1990). This is because the areas visited by Pardo can be accurately determined from the accounts of these expeditions, which covered many of the towns and provinces visited by De Soto a quarter of a century earlier (DePratter, Hudson, and Smith 1983; Hudson 1990). This has led to major revisions in the traditional route of the De Soto expedition as formulated by Swanton (1939), with the result that many of the towns and provinces visited by De Soto in 1540 can finally be identified with a fair degree of certainty (figure 6). This research has had important ramifications for archaeologists throughout the region, as documented in subsequent sections of this study.

There are four primary accounts of the Pardo expeditions (three are presented in Ketchem 1954 and DePratter 1987a, and all four are presented and analyzed in Hudson 1990). Three of these, by Pardo, Francisco Martinez, and Juan de la Bandera, were fairly brief, while a second much longer Bandera document (Bandera II), only recently published (Hoffman 1990:205–96), contained detailed figures on the direction and distance Pardo traveled each day, which permitted DePratter and his colleagues (1983) to reconstruct the path of the expeditions. Pardo's account, a summary of both expeditions, was an official report prepared for Avilés in late 1567. Pardo "appears to have [been] a bluff and occasionally tough-minded soldier. His story is severely factual, and will remind some readers of Caesar, others of Xenophon. He admits that he forgets names and he may well oversimplify the diplomatic and religious results of his mission" (Ketchem 1954:68). His account contains place names and brief descriptive information for many Indian towns in the interior, including information about the number of chiefs met at each and in some cases their relations with other towns. This information, duplicated in greater detail in the other accounts, particularly Bandera II, is of particular value for delimiting political relationships over the region.

The second account, by Francisco Martinez, a soldier accompanying Pardo, covers only the second expedition and was prepared in Santa Elena on 11 July 1567, at the request of Avilés. This statement, much briefer than Pardo's, is also more suspect, emphasizing as it does the bounty of the land and the military exploits of a Sergeant Boyano, whom Pardo had left in the interior with 30 men during his first expedition. According to Martinez, Boyano had killed some 2,500 Indians in two towns by the time Pardo arrived with the second expedition, a statement widely regarded as "a patent exaggeration" (Swanton 1946:655). Pardo's account, in contrast, notes only that Boyano had managed to get himself surrounded and cut off by the local Indians (Pardo in Ketchem 1954:72).

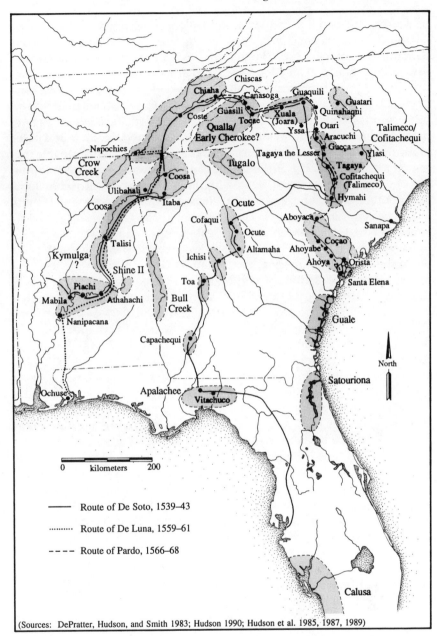

Figure 6 European Explorations and Native Societies in the Carolinas and Georgia.
(Reprinted from Anderson 1994, courtesy Cambridge University Press)

The third document, by Juan de la Bandera (Bandera I), is described by its translator, Ketchem (1954:78), as "a very brief abstract of the extensive Banderas Document" (i.e., Bandera II). This document was prepared at Santa Elena on 23 January 1569 and is a markedly compressed account of the second expedition, skipping numerous events mentioned in the Pardo account. The manuscript contains greater detail on Indian life than the two other short accounts. The fourth account, Bandera II, contains greater detail on the Pardo route and the peoples encountered than is found in the other three accounts. This information has proved to be invaluable, not only for revolutionizing our knowledge of the routes of the early explorers, but also for its contribution to our understanding of native life in the 16th century (DePratter and Smith 1980; DePratter, Hudson, and Smith 1983; Hudson 1987, 1990).

Following the abandonment of Santa Elena in 1587 (see chapter 7), Spanish activity north of Florida was restricted to missions established along the coast. Missionary activity contracted southward after this time and was largely restricted to Georgia and Florida after 1600. Major Spanish accounts after this period detailing native life include Vera's account of Governor Pedro Ibarra's visit to coastal Georgia in 1604 (Serrano y Sanz 1912) and the accounts of two voyages by Francisco Fernandez de Ecija along the South Carolina coast in 1605 and 1609 (Ecija in Waddell 1980:222–32). With the collapse of Spanish interest in the exploration of the Southeast in the late 16th century, it is not until almost a century later, with the English settlement of the Carolinas and the French settlement of Louisiana, that fairly extensive documentation of native groups in the interior reappears. By this time, however, the collapse and reorganization of the native chiefdoms into different and less complex societies had occurred, under the combined effects of disease and depopulation, exposure to European trade goods, missionization efforts along the coast, and the emerging slave and deerskin trade (Dobyns 1983; Ramenofsky 1987; M. Smith 1987). While documents dating to the late 17th century and after describing native life are extensive, they should be used to extrapolate earlier conditions only with great care.

Contributions from Ethnohistoric Research: Understanding Mississippian Political Change

Regional Political Structure

In recent years, ethnohistorical investigations have made significant contributions to our understanding of the late prehistoric and protohistoric periods in the South Appalachian area, particularly to the area encompassing the Savannah River valley, the archaeological test case employed in the present analysis. Two major developments have been: the synthesis of a large body of information on coastal Georgia and South Carolina contact-period populations (e.g., G. Jones 1978; Waddell 1980); and the identification of many of the early contact-period sites in the interior visited by the early Spanish De Soto, De Luna, and Pardo expeditions, providing a linkage between the extant archaeological record from these sites and areas and the historic accounts of the complex chiefdoms, such as Ocute, Coosa, and Cofitachequi, described in these areas (DePratter 1989; DePratter, Hudson, and Smith 1983; Hudson 1990; Hudson, Smith, and DePratter 1984; Hudson, Worth, and DePratter 1990; Hudson et al. 1985, 1987).

Ethnohistoric examination of southern Atlantic coastal groups has included Waddell's (1980) work summarizing much of the early historic literature on the native inhabitants of the South Carolina Sea Island zone. These people practiced intensive agriculture and had an organizational structure similar to that in simple chiefdoms and, as such, were apparently employing a Mississippian way of life. A high degree of seasonal mobility was documented among some of the coastal South Carolina groups, who were aggregated in central towns only over a fairly limited portion of the year. A description of the movements of the Orista (for which Edisto Island and the Edisto River are named) by Fray Jean Rogel (in Waddell 1980:147–51) in 1570 gives some indication of the extent of this movement: "At this season [summer] they were congregated together [to plant and tend crops], but when the acorns ripened they left me quite alone, all going to the forests, each one to his own quarter, and only met together for certain festivals, which occurred every two months, and this is not always in the same spot. . . . [T]he inhabitants of these twenty houses [at the main village of Orista] scattered themselves in twelve or thirteen different villages, some twenty, some ten, some six, and some four. Only two families remained. . . . [F]or nine out of the twelve months they wander without any fixed abode" (see also Le Moyne 1875:12). A Jesuit with degrees in arts and medicine, Rogel, while based out of Santa Elena, had spent 14 months as a missionary living with the coastal South Carolina Indians and had learned their language. His statement suggests that seasonal population dispersal, a possibility only rarely considered in Mississippian settlement models, may have been common in at least some areas, particularly in coastal areas or perhaps during times of stress (see chapter 7). Evidence for sedentary village life in South Appalachian Mississippian societies, this account indicates, should be considered a proposition to be confirmed and not a given, as is commonly assumed.

In a comparable fashion, Grant Jones (1978) and other researchers have summarized historic information on coastal Georgia native groups, many of whom were incorporated into the Spanish mission system that was active in the Sea Island area throughout the latter half of the 16th and well into the 17th century (see also L. Larson 1978, 1980a). However, many of these records date to the late 16th century or later, well after initial contact, and tend to focus on events at or around mission sites. While providing a valuable perspective on the process of acculturation and occasionally containing useful information on native conditions, their utility for reconstructing precontact native political conditions and lifeways is fairly limited when compared with the records available from the South Carolina coastal zone.

Recent ethnohistoric research has also led to the identification of specific communities visited by early explorers, permitting the use of early accounts in the archaeological reconstruction of life at these sites and in these societies. The primary accounts of the 1539–43 De Soto entrada provide fairly detailed descriptions of the central towns of the chiefdom-level societies or provinces the Spaniards encountered, and some of these societies were later revisited by the De Luna (1560–61) and Pardo (1566–68) expeditions (figures 5 and 6). Three geographically extensive, complex chiefdoms described in the South Appalachian area at the time of initial European contact, which are of particular relevance to the analysis of late prehistoric populations in the Savannah River valley, include the province of Coosa, centered on northwestern Georgia and extending from east-central Alabama into eastern Tennessee; the province of Ocute and a series of lesser chiefdoms in central Georgia; and the province of Cofitachequi, extending from central South Carolina into central North Carolina (DePratter, Hudson, and Smith 1983; Hally, Smith, and Langford 1990; Hudson 1990; Hudson et al. 1985, 1987).

The 16th-century accounts provide considerable detail on the political organization and tributary relationships within these societies. Provinces such as Cofitachequi and Coosa were complex, paramount chiefdoms characterized by two administrative levels with large areas, including many communities and lesser (quasi-autonomous) chiefdoms, ruled from a central town. These polities were geographically extensive, covered tens of thousands of square kilometers, and encompassed many subsidiary towns and lesser chiefdoms bound together by alliance networks and the use or threat of force. The De Soto entrada provides a direct record of the extent and power of these chiefdoms and the degree to which these leaders were obeyed, situations that the expedition was quick to exploit. Upon leaving the principal towns of both Cofitachequi and Coosa, for example, De Soto forced the principal chiefs to accompany him. The Gentleman of Elvas's account noted that by taking the Lady of Cofitachequi, "in all the towns through which the governor passed, the cacica ordered the Indians to come and carry the loads from one town to another. We traversed her lands for a hundred leagues, in which, as we saw, she was very well obeyed, for all the Indians did with great efficiency and diligence what she ordered of them. . . . her lands reached [as far as Guaxule]" (Elvas in Robertson 1993:85–86; see also Bourne 1904, 1:70). Guaxule (Guasili) has been placed on the extreme upper reaches of the Catawba River, some 240 kilometers to the north of Cofitachequi, indicating the distances over which contact-era paramount chiefdoms exerted influence (figure 6).

The identification of the central towns of Cofitachequi with the mound complexes near the modern city of Camden on the Wateree River in central South Carolina by DePratter, Hudson, and Smith (1983) is a particularly important contribution of recent research and is one of direct relevance to the present study, which focuses on Mississippian developments in the Savannah River valley. Earlier investigators, most notably Swanton (1939), had been nearly unanimous in placing Cofitachequi along the Savannah River. Prior to the 1980s, only Baker (1974) had presented extended evidence placing Cofitachequi on the Wateree River, and his placement was somewhat to the south of its currently accepted location. One of the contributions of the extensive collections analysis associated with the present research is the demonstration that the central and lower Savannah River basin was largely depopulated at the time of the De Soto entrada (see chapter 6), making it an unlikely candidate for the location of Cofitachequi and supporting the recent reconstructions of the De Soto and Pardo routes.

The extent and power of the chief and territories of Coosa (Coca) is described in comparable terms. Upon leaving Chiaha, a town subject to Coosa in eastern Tennessee, Elvas (in Robertson 1993:92–93; see also Bourne 1904, 1:81–83) noted:

> The governor [De Soto] marched for six days, passing through many towns subject to the cacique of Coca, and as he entered his lands, many Indians daily came to him on the way on the part of the cacique with messages, some going, others coming.
>
> He reached Coça, on Friday, July 16 [1540]. The cacique came out to welcome him two crossbow flights from the town in a carrying chair borne on the shoulders of his principal men, seated on a cushion, and covered with a robe of marten skins of the form and size of a woman's shawl. He wore a crown of feathers on his head; and around him were many Indians playing and singing.
>
> . . . He ordered his Indians to move out of their dwellings, in which the governor and his men were lodged. In the barbacoas and fields there was a great quantity of maize and beans. The land was very populous and had many large towns and planted fields which reached from one town to the other. It was a charming and fertile land, with good cultivated fields stretching along the rivers.
>
> . . . The governor was accustomed to place a guard over the caciques so that they might not go away, and took them along with him until leaving their land; for by taking them, the people would await in their towns and they would give a guide and Indians as carriers.

A similar summary is provided by Ranjel (in Worth 1993a:284–85; see also Bourne 1904, 1:112–13): "[Coosa] is a great cacique with much land, and one of the best and most abundant [provinces] that they found in Florida; and the cacique came forth to receive the Governor on a litter, covered with white blankets of the land. Sixty or seventy of his principal Indians carried the litter on their shoulders, and none was an Indian of the plebeians or commoners, and those that carried him took turns from time to time, with great ceremony in their manner . . . so that the land would not rise in revolt nor deny them supplies they took him with them." The effectiveness of the Spaniard's strategy of seizing chiefly elites, which was employed at both Cofitachequi and Coosa, illustrates the authority and power these individuals commanded. The province of Coosa has been the subject of extensive archaeological and ethnohistoric research in recent years (Hally and Langford 1988; Hally, Smith, and Langford 1990; Hudson et al. 1985, 1987).

The third principal chiefdom encountered by the Spanish in the interior South Appalachian area was Ocute, one of several polities occupying the central Georgia area. The descriptions of this chiefdom suggest that it was less complex and extensive than either Coosa or Cofitachequi. Although Ocute appears to have been the most powerful polity in central Georgia, other autonomous "provinces" or polities were reported nearby, including Cofaqui and Patofa. The latter is described as being "at peace with the chief of Ocute and the other lords round about" (Elvas in Robertson 1993:77; see also Bourne 1904, 1:57). Although the nature of the relationship between these centers is unclear, there is no report of a dominance relationship like that noted between Coosa or Cofitachequi and other towns. The central Georgia chiefdoms, given their small areal extent and relative autonomy from one another, may reflect simple chiefdoms in the "collapse" or nonintegrated phase of regional chiefly cycling, while complex chiefdoms such as Coosa and Cofitachequi represent the "integrated" phase of such a process (Henry T. Wright, personal communication, 1986).

The ethnographic accounts of these and other southeastern chiefdoms, which were visited at various times in the 16th century, provide an explicit historical record of cycling, by illustrating changing levels of organizational complexity within these societies (figure 7). The fortunes of the Coosa, for example, fluctuated between the time of De Soto's visit in 1540, when it was a complex chiefdom and a regional power, to the time of the De Luna expedition in 1560, when the chiefdom had apparently fragmented and nearby towns were refusing tribute. By the time of the Pardo expeditions, however, Coosa had apparently regained its preeminence (Hudson 1990:106; see below). The chiefdom(s) of Ocute, visited only during the De Soto expedition, in contrast, appears to have declined thereafter (Hudson 1986, 1990; M. Williams and Shapiro 1987). Cofitachequi, which was unquestionably a paramount chiefdom early in the 16th century, may have fragmented by the time of the Pardo expeditions (Hudson 1990:83). This is a controversial inference, however, since DePratter (1989), using the same sources, has argued that the chiefdom maintained its preeminence throughout the 16th century.

During the early historic period, it must be cautioned, the effects of contact and particularly disease on chiefdom organizational structures

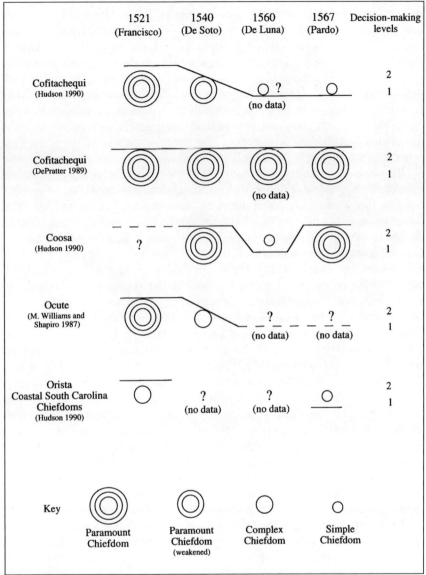

Figure 7 Cycling in the South Appalachian Area: Evidence from Ethnohistoric and Archaeological Sources.

need to be taken into consideration (M. Smith 1987). These effects do not need to be considered, of course, when analyses are directed to unambiguous prehistoric cases. When greater time depth is added through archaeological analyses of the immediately preceding Mississippian societies in the region, though, the political changes observed in the early contact era, at least during the first two-thirds of the 16th century, do not appear all that unusual. Throughout the preceding half millennium, paramount centers had emerged and declined throughout the region, and organizational structures had fluctuated between less complex and more complex systems, albeit, at least in part, for different reasons.

The evidence about the geographic extent of southeastern paramount chiefdoms that is emerging from the ethnohistoric data is almost revolutionary. Previous estimates of the size of these societies have tended to be much smaller. Peebles (1978:375), for example, estimated that the extent of the Moundville phase, centered on the second largest Mississippian mound group in the Eastern Woodlands, was on the order of 120 river kilometers in length. Hally (1987, 1993; Hally, Smith, and Langford 1990:130) has recently suggested an even smaller average size, on the order of approximately 40 kilometers, or two days' travel time from the center, was the maximum dimension of most chiefly polities in the Southeast. Parallels with more complex polities of comparable scale are sometimes cited in these analyses, with Renfrew's (1975) concept of an "early state module" cited most frequently. While these figures may accurately reflect distances to communities under the direct control of a center, they do not in any way correspond to the areas dominated by the region's paramount chiefdoms. The early contact-era provinces of Coosa and Cofitachequi, based on the locations of towns reported by the Spanish as aligned with or subject to the domination of these centers, for example, extended over areas hundreds of kilometers in linear extent. Major centers undoubtedly exercised indirect control over societies at great distances, with power relationships likely acknowledged through tribute mobilization and presentation and uneven alliance structures (see also King and Freer 1992; McKivergan 1992; Peregrine 1992a, 1992b). It is thus becoming evident that the complex chiefdoms of the early contact-era Southeast were composed of a number of subsidiary chiefdoms linked together in alliance, conquest, or tributary relations. While the size of these constituent units may cluster around distinctive modes, variation resulting from local environmental (i.e., physiographic or resource structure) or political conditions will probably need to be considered on a case-by-case basis.

Settlement Hierarchies and Tributary Networks

The early sources provide a number of specific details about the operation of southeastern chiefdoms, including information about settlement hierarchies and tributary and exchange networks. Large numbers of towns were tied together in the more complex, areally extensive polities such as Coosa or Cofitachequi, which were characterized by at least two administrative/decision-making levels consisting of primary chiefs and their retinues and lesser chiefs and their retinues. Commoners had little direct contribution to decision making in these societies. A three-level settlement hierarchy, consisting of major ceremonial and political centers, larger villages/small centers, and scattered small hamlets or villages, is, in fact, documented for both Coosa and Cofitachequi in the De Soto accounts. Evidence about Ocute is more ambiguous, but the presence of "cabins" scattered along streams between major centers suggests a two-level settlement hierarchy and a single decision-making level consisting of chiefs and their retinues over the commoner population (Ranjel in Bourne 1904, 2:89–90; see also Worth 1993a:272). This matches the pattern of dispersed hamlets away from centers observed archaeologically (Kowalewski and Hatch 1991; M. Smith and Kowalewski 1980).

The Pardo expedition documents are particularly valuable sources on the nature of political relationships within and between chiefdoms in the South Appalachian area, in this case between the inhabitants of Cofitachequi and those of related communities to the north along the Catawba/Yadkin River. The existence of a noble elite distinguished from the commoners in dress, and hence readily recognizable to Pardo (in Ketchem 1954:70–72), is clearly indicated "at the said Canos [Cofitachequi] . . . I found a great number of chiefs and Indians. . . . From there I left for Tagaya, where I brought together the Indians and chiefs. . . . I went to Tagaya the Lesser and had all the Indians and the chief brought together. . . . From there I went to Ysa, who is a great chief; there I found many chiefs and a great quantity of Indians. . . . From there I went to an outlying district of the said Ysa, and brought together the Indians." It is interesting to note that the number of "chiefs" or elites the Spanish encountered varied considerably from community to community. In at least some cases, the number of "chiefs" present likely indicated the size and importance of a particular community. This interpretation must be made with caution, however, since considerable visiting between communities appears to have occurred. Curiosity as well as the possibility of gifts drew elites to meet with the Spanish, in some cases from appreciable distances.

The subsidiary elites supported and reinforced the status of the chief. They ruled in outlying communities and served as something of a privy council as necessary. Decisions were typically made by the chief, although often after discussion with his principal supporters (e.g., Elvas in Robertson 1993:89; see also Bourne 1904, 1:75; Laudonnière in Bennett 1975:14). While the power of a chief might have been considerable, the stability and permanence of the position ultimately depended upon public acceptance of this power, and particularly the support of other elites. Swanton (1946:650), who tended to minimize the authority of southeastern chiefs, interpreted the Natchez accounts to indicate their power was dependent, to a fair measure, on the good will and support of other chiefly elites: "it is plain that in practice the absolutism of the Great Sun depended upon his age and personal abilities, and that his power was considerably curtailed by the other members of the Sun caste, particularly the other town chiefs, back of whom again lay that great body of usage and prejudice which no sovereign can indefinitely override." Membership in the elite appears at least partially the result of ascribed, or inherited, social position, although ability was sometimes recognized, particularly in the case of men who had distinguished themselves in warfare (Gibson 1974:132).

The elite in some cases lived in close physical proximity to the chief, as evidenced by statements such as that by Le Moyne (1875:12; also in Swanton 1922:352), who, referring to Indians on the southern Atlantic coast, noted that "the chief's dwelling stands in the middle of the town. . . . Around this are the houses of the principal men." This appears to be a common strategy used by chiefs worldwide. Among the matrilineal Lunda, for example, a chief's close kinsmen (paternal and uterine kin) lived around him and were trusted, while relatives or persons from other lineages were located at a greater distance (V. Turner 1957:322–23). From this same elite could come possible successors to the position of paramount, through legitimate succession or through conquest or rebellion. Usually, however, the status of the elite relative to the chief was clearly indicated by dress or deed. By serving as litter, awning, or fan bearers, for example, as documented by De Soto at Cofitachequi, Coosa, and Tastaluca (Elvas in Robertson 1993:82, 92; see also Bourne 1904, 1:65, 81), the noble class demonstrated their subservience to the chief and at the same time their close proximity both physically and socially.

The chief's residence was often set apart from the homes of commoners and sometimes served as a combination house, elite council room, and temple. The accounts contain explicit references to mound building and use. Thus, the dwelling of Tastaluca was described as "on an elevated place" (Elvas in Robertson 1993:95; see also Bourne 1904, 1:87), while Biedma (in Worth 1993b:239; see also Bourne 1904, 2:28), describing Casqui, noted that "the caiques there were accustomed to have, next to the houses where they live, some very high mounds, made by hand, and that others have their houses on the mounds themselves." Ranjel (in Worth 1993a:280; see also Bourne 1904, 2:101) described the temple of Talimeco at Cofitachequi as "on a high mound." The chief was also set apart in death, and extensive mortuary rituals frequently accompanied his or her death. Among coastal groups, this included the burning of his house (Laudonnière in Bennett 1975:14–15). The bodies of the dead were maintained in elaborate mortuary structures, of which the temple of Talimeco in Cofitachequi has provided the fullest description, albeit one that is to some extent exaggerated (Vega in Shelby 1993:298–304; see also Varner and Varner 1951:315–22, Biedma in Bourne 1904, 2:14, and Swanton 1932; this temple was visited by De Soto and was located near the central town of the province of Cofitachequi in South Carolina).

Tributary arrangements within southeastern chiefdoms are particularly well documented (DePratter 1983:170–78; 1991a:132–38; M. Smith and Hally 1992). Within the major provincial-level polities, for example, lesser elites submitted tribute to those higher in the hierarchy. Tribute thus served to help define and formalize social relationships in these societies, particularly those concerned with status positions, alliances, and trade. Tribute included both foodstuffs and luxury goods, both of which were stored in large quantity:

> They have barbacoas in which they keep their maize. This is a house raised up on four posts, timbered like a loft and the floor of cane. . . . [Around] the houses of the lords or principal men . . . [are] many large barbacoas in which they gather together the tribute paid them by their Indians, which consists of maize and deerskins and native blankets resembling shawls, some being made of the inner bark of trees and some from a plant like daffodils which when pounded remains like flax. (Elvas in Robertson 1993:75; see also Bourne 1904, 1:53)

> In the barbacoas of the towns there was considerable amount of clothing—blankets made of thread from the bark of trees and feather mantles (white, gray, vermilion, and yellow), made according to their custom, elegant and suitable for winter. There were also many deerskins, well tanned and colored, with designs drawn on them and made into [trousers, leggings], and shoes. (Elvas in Robertson 1993:83; see also Bourne 1904, 1:66)

The early sources indicate that chiefs maintained barbacoas filled with food in outlying settlements and could call on these stores when they wished. De Soto's strategy of capturing and carrying along native leaders wherever possible, as noted previously, was predicated upon this fact. When De Soto's army arrived at Ilapi, a town some three days to the northeast of Cofitachequi, they found "seven barbacoas of corn that they said were there, which were a deposit of the cacica" (Ranjel in Worth 1993a:279; see also Bourne 1904, 2:100). Food reserves in storage in many of the southeastern societies encountered by De Soto were reported as extensive. Thus the entrada, consisting of over 600 men, was able to spend the winters of 1539 and 1540 at Apalachee and Coosa, respectively, drawing on the food reserves of those complex chiefdoms. In discussing the Apalachee case, DePratter (1983:165) notes that De Soto's entire army was provisioned for five months from stores in or near the central town.

Tribute served to acknowledge power relations within and between chiefdoms. DePratter (1983:176, 1991a:132–38) cites a number of examples of tribute collection by subject chiefs for submission to a paramount. Tribute could be paid voluntarily or collected through the threat or use of force. Withholding tribute was considered an act of rebellion and could trigger punitive expeditions and warfare, and in Cofitachequi, seizing tribute was considered a capital offense (Elvas in Robertson 1993:86, 106, 134; see also Bourne 1904, 1:70, 101, 154). Luxury goods such as bark blankets, deer and marten skins, and other valuables appear to have constituted tribute between elites and are commonly mentioned as goods sealing alliances or acknowledging power relationships; bulk foodstuffs, in contrast, do not appear to have moved over great distances or served a similar role (Elvas in Robertson 1993:83, 121; Ranjel in Worth 1993a:270, 278; see also Bourne 1904, 1:65, 129; 2:86, 99).

Hudson (1990:110), noting that Pardo observed Indians distinguishing tribute in the form of food from tribute in the form of deerskins, has suggested that tribute from towns closest to centers probably included a great deal of corn and other foodstuffs, while communities located farther away probably submitted more readily transported luxury goods. Bulk transport probably was most effective between communities along navigable watercourses. Use of watercraft by native groups is well documented in the 16th-century accounts, and their use to transport corn, albeit by the Spanish, is specifically mentioned in the Pardo accounts (Hudson 1990:132–34). These same accounts also note that Pardo ordered native leaders from a number of communities to transport bulk foodstuffs over considerable distances to Cofitachequi, indicating that the Spanish, at least, considered such movement feasible.

Among elites, the exchange of prestige goods appears to have been a way of sealing or maintaining alliances and of acknowledging the power or position of another elite or community. Throughout the entrada, for example, De Soto was welcomed by native chiefs offering gifts of blankets, deer and marten skins, and other valuables, in addition to food and housing. These were precisely the kinds of items accounted as tribute by the natives themselves, and it is probable that the gifts were an attempt to placate an unknown and potentially dangerous enemy, while simultaneously attempting to enter into a reciprocal alliance relationship with him. The act of presenting tribute, therefore, was an acknowledgement of power and a statement of relationship. The giving of gifts was not merely one way, from subject to ruler, but was also a method by which the paramount could demonstrate his own power and prestige. It thus served as an important form of competitive display. Thus the chiefs of Pacaha and Casqui in northeastern Arkansas, whom De Soto later met in the entrada, each "tried to see which of them could perform the greater services" to De Soto (Elvas in Robertson 1993:121; see also Bourne 1904, 1:129), although in this case each undoubtedly also hoped to use the favor they gained with De Soto to the other's disadvantage.

While foodstuffs were apparently typically dispersed to storage facilities scattered throughout the chiefdom, luxury or prestige goods tended to be maintained in the temples in the central towns of these societies (DePratter 1983:138, 1991a:108). This suggests that while prestige goods distribution was limited to the elite, food products may have been more widely redistributed, to elites and commoners alike, or at least may have been held in reserve to accommodate periods of crop failure or harvest shortfall. The centralized control of wealth by the elite appears to have been closely linked to their maintenance of power. The distribution of luxury goods and captives to followers is well documented and appears to have been a successful method of maintaining supporters among the lower ranks (e.g., Laudonnière in Bennett 1975:15). Given this, disruptions in prestige goods exchange or distribution networks would have a profound impact and, as noted in chapter 2, could signal organizational instability and shifting power relationships within a chiefdom or a region.

Ideological and Secular Authority Structures

Iconographic representations and the veneration of chiefly ancestors can be interpreted as devices to legitimize and reinforce the ideology of sacred chiefly power that permeated and gave structure to early southeastern Mississippian life. James Brown (1976:126, 1985) and Knight (1986) have defined three roughly similar foci of this socially defining sacred power. According to Brown (1985:102–29), these were: the temple/mortuary-based ancestor cults; the chiefly elites, with a warrior cult subsumed or co-opted under this sphere; and communal earth or fertility cults. The first two spheres were the domain of the elite and functioned to reinforce their prestige and status. The third, in contrast, encompassed all sectors of society. Knight's (1986:680–81) perspective is essentially the same, with Mississippian religion consisting of three interacting cult institutions, each with its own complex imagery and iconography, including: a warfare/cosmogony complex subsuming chiefly elites; a communal earth and fertility cult co-opted by commoners and symbolized by mound construction; and a more or less organized priesthood responsible for elite temple/mortuary maintenance and community ritual, hence possibly serving to mediate tensions between the elite and commoner constituents of the other two institutions. The stability of elite authority and hence of individual Mississippian polities, it is argued, was directly related to the strength or importance attached to these ideological structures.

The cult surrounding the veneration of chiefly/elite ancestors appears to have been the central focus of the Mississippian ideological sphere. Major sites throughout the Southeast are characterized by the presence of temple/mortuary complexes where the bodies of the elite were maintained in honored status in shrines that were often physically, and hence symbolically, elevated above and maintained apart from the surrounding populace. Objects of wealth, sumptuary devices, weapons, statuary, fetishes, and sacred relics—what Brown (1985:106) has called "condensed symbols of sacred ancestral power"—were held within these temple-shrines in addition to the remains of the noble dead (see also Knight 1986:679). An extended description of one such shrine, the temple of Talimeco, where the sacred wealth and chiefly elite of Cofitachequi were placed, was recorded in Garcilaso de la Vega's account of the De Soto entrada (Shelby 1993:298–306; see also Varner and Varner 1951:315–25). This location may well be that of the Adamson mound group near Camden, South Carolina (DePratter, Hudson, and Smith 1983).

Ties to ancestral territories and to the actual bodies of ancestors, rather than to ceremonial facilities such as mounds and earthworks, appears to have been a particularly important aspect of Mississippian ideology (Brown 1985:104; Knight 1986). There is convincing ethnohistoric evidence that these shrines were the ideological centers of individual polities. Desecration of a rival society's temple, specifically its ancestral burials, was considered the ultimate insult and a primary goal in warfare. There are numerous examples from the De Soto entrada supporting this inference. Vega's description of the sacking of the principal town of Capaha (Pacaha) by Casqui is particularly graphic:

> After the Casquines ascertained that there was no one in the pueblo [village] to oppose them, they showed well the hatred and rancor that they felt against its inhabitants, for they killed the men on whom they could lay hands. . . . They sacked the whole pueblo, particularly robbing the lord's houses with more satisfaction and enjoyment than any of the others, because they were his. They captured many boys, children, and women, and among them two very beautiful young women who were among the many wives of Capaha.
>
> . . . Not content with having pillaged the curaca's house and robbed the pueblo, and killed and taken as many prisoners as they could, the Casquines went to the temple, which was on a large plaza that the pueblo contained, which was the burial place of all the former lords of that province: the father, grandfathers, and ancestors of Capaha. Those temples and burial places, as has already been told elsewhere, are the most esteemed and venerated possessions that these Indians of La Florida have. . . . The Casquines, summoning one another so that all could enjoy the triumph, went to this temple. Since they understood how much Capaha (being arrogant and haughty because he had not hitherto been attacked by them) would feel it that his enemies had the boldness to enter his temple and burial place contemptuously, they not only entered it, but committed all the ignominious and offensive affronts that they could, because they pillaged everything that the temple contained in the way of riches, ornaments, spoils, and trophies that had been gathered at the expense of their own ancestors.
>
> They knocked down on the ground all the wooden chests that served as sepulchers, and for their own satisfaction and revenge and to affront their enemies, they threw out on the ground the bones and dead bodies that were in the chests. Not content with throwing them on the ground, they stamped

and kicked them in an excess of contempt and disdain. (Shelby 1993:397–98; see also Varner and Varner 1951:437–38)

This was not an isolated incident during the entrada. Comparable desecration occurred when the Indians of Ocute first reached Cofitachequi in South Carolina, and when the Guachoyas entered Anilco, probably in northern Louisiana. Undermining an elite faction's authority by striking at a source and inspiration for its power would be one way a rival faction could co-opt or bring about the relocation of retinues or commoner labor forces. Permanent site abandonment might follow such desecration; the attached dishonor might have been such to preclude any reuse, regardless of the extent of the facilities in place, although Capaha (Pacaha) himself appears to have set his temple back in order.

Further evidence from the early Spanish accounts supports the inference that towns or centers might be abandoned by their own populations upon desecration or defeat in warfare. The town of Vitachuco in Florida was destroyed by its inhabitants upon their defeat by the Spanish under De Soto. A Spanish troop, returning to the town some time after its warriors were routed in battle, "found it entirely burned and destroyed and the walls leveled to the ground; and the bodies of the Indians who died on the day of the battle . . . were all heaped together in the fields, no one having desired to bury them. The Indians said later that they abandoned and destroyed the pueblo because it was founded on an unlucky and unfortunate site; and the dead Indians, as ill-fated men who had not carried out their pretensions, they left unburied as food for birds and wild beasts, for among them this was a very infamous punishment and was given to those who were unlucky and unfortunate in arms" (Shelby 1993:207–8; see also Varner and Varner 1951:198). Equation of ancestor cult with land ownership/holding is fairly common among more complex societies (Fortes 1945); hence the desecration of an ancestral shrine is a challenge not only to a chief's authority per se but also specifically to his right to hold and control territory.

This may help to explain why major Mississippian centers, once abandoned, were not invariably reoccupied. Elites in newly ascendant Mississippian polities, quite simply, were ideologically bound to remain about their place of origin. Relocation to previously dominant centers where elaborate ceremonial facilities were already in place does not appear to have invariably or even typically occurred. For example, the central town of the 16th-century province of Coosa, apparently at the Little Egypt site, was characterized by only small mounds. This suggests that, even given a probable decline in mound building at this time (see chapter 4), this center was just emerging and perhaps had fairly shallow time depth. Its physical appearance, with mounds less than 4 meters high, was certainly far less imposing than the nearby Etowah site, which was characterized by mounds up to 18 meters high. By the early 16th century, however, Etowah had lost its former regional preeminence and was apparently a tributary town to Coosa (Hudson et al. 1985:728). Occupying former centers of power, even those with impressive physical facilities, does not, therefore, appear to have been a prerequisite for claiming or maintaining leadership in some southeastern chiefdom societies. The size and number of mounds on a site, furthermore, does not invariably equate with its position in the local political hierarchy.

The iconography of the elite chiefs and powerful warriors, the second of our three major foci of Mississippian ideology, was expressed by three themes, according to James Brown (1985): the chiefly litter, the chunky player, and the falcon warrior. A number of archaeological traces of this iconography can tell us something of the nature and strength of local legitimizing ideologies. Emblems of office—badges of chiefly power or elite status—included the columella pendant and a heart-shaped apron. Specific emblems may have been used by the elite of particular polities. The distribution in time and space of the distinctive entwined rattlesnake design known as the Citico-style gorget, for example, appears to be coextensive with the polity of Coosa (Hudson et al. 1985, figure 7; M. Smith and Smith 1989), although in this case the emblem occurs almost exclusively with young women and appears to reflect an age-grade (Hatch 1975:133). Chiefly litters, described in De Soto's encounter with the caciques of Coosa, Cofitachequi, and other southeastern polities, were found in mound 72 at Cahokia and are sometimes depicted or suggested on gorget and pottery motifs. Chunky players are also sometimes depicted on gorgets, and chunky stones are a fairly common item on southeastern Mississippian sites. The game is thought to have been a mechanism for integrating the population through the play of individuals or teams, just as during the historic period (Hudson 1976:421–25).

The third major symbol of the chiefly elite was the falcon warrior, perhaps the single most distinctive of all Mississippian symbols. The falcon warrior is typically shown brandishing a club in one hand and carrying a severed head or head-shaped rattle in the other (J. Brown 1985, figures 19–21). Perhaps the most famous representation is that on a copper plate from Etowah (figure 8 in this text); one of the elite burials from that site appears to have been similarly costumed (L. Larson 1971b). The falcon warrior is thought to have been the primary symbol of a major military cult dominated by the elites, but in all probability co-opting especially brave or talented commoners. Other probable military cult symbols include monolithic axes and ceremonial daggers, which are assumed to have been nonfunctional high-status items. In Mississippian society, warriors stood midway between the chiefly elite and commoners. The ubiquity of warrior symbols indicates that warfare was quite common and probably served as a mechanism for mediating social tension by providing commoners a means for increasing their personal status (J. Brown 1985:140; see also Gibson 1974). Peaceful conditions, interestingly, may have created a source of societal instability.

(Source: Phillips and Brown 1978:Figure 243; J. Brown 1985:100)

Figure 8 Elite Iconography from the Southeastern United States: The Falcon Warrior. Drawing of Rogan No. 1, one of two outstanding repoussé copper plates from Mound C, Etowah, Georgia. Figure 243 from Philip Phillips and James A. Brown, *Pre-Columbian Shell Engravings from the Craig Mound at Spiro, Oklahoma*, Paperback Edition Part 1, Peabody Museum Press, Copyright 1978 by the President and Fellows of Harvard College. Figure 243 was drawn from photograph in the collection of U.S. National Museum (National Museum of Natural History), Smithsonian Institution, Washington, D.C.

In Knight's (1986:680) view, the warfare/cosmogony complex served to legitimize social inequality by providing for an elite monopoly of "two critically important kinds of esoteric knowledge and ritual manipulation: first, that associated with mythological beings, and second, that associated with the supernatural aspects of success in warfare." Warfare iconography, consisting of elaborate, labor-intensive, and essentially nonutilitarian elements, such as copper-covered celts, monolithic axes, or flint swords, served to link membership in the elite with societal success in warfare. In a similar fashion, cosmogonic imagery, which Knight (677) describes as "representational art with mythic content," specifically the occurrence of imaginary composite human/animal creatures, further served to accentuate the nature of the supernatural world and the elite's close ties with this domain. Thus to Knight (685), religion provided "the context to Mississippian political power" rather than something set apart from it.

The third major foci of Mississippian ideology encompassed communal earth/fertility beliefs (J. Brown 1985:123–29; Knight 1986:678, 680–81). These were closely linked to maize agriculture, the success of which was, of course, of great importance to local Mississippian societies. Earth/fertility iconography and beliefs were identified, to some extent, with the position of the chief, although all parts of society appear to have shared in them (Brown 1985; Knight 1986; Waring 1968a:51–53; Waring and Holder 1945). To Knight (1985, 1986:678), platform mounds were the principal symbol of Mississippian community and social identity to both commoner and elite populations and hence of these cults. Because commoners participated in mound construction as part of periodic rites of intensification, these structures served as a focus for the communal earth/fertility cults. Since the strength and well-being of society were thought to be bound up in the condition of the temple/mortuary complex, maintenance of these facilities was as important to commoners as to elites, resulting in their incorporation and active participation in renewal/rebuilding ceremonies.

Fertility cults, elite iconography, and ancestor worship thus combined to symbolize and legitimize the positions and aspirations of the participants in major sectors of southeastern Mississippian societies. The diverse symbolism, furthermore, served to accentuate and simultaneously mediate social tension between elites and commoners, and between rival elites, in these nonegalitarian societies. Chiefdom organizational stability was tied to the strength of these institutions and to the success with which elites were able to address these potentially divisive forces.

Succession to the Chieftainship

Chiefly succession appears to have been matrilineal in most southeastern Mississippian polities; that is, succession passed from a chief to his sister's son, or nephew (DePratter 1983:100–110, 1991a:79–87; Hudson

1976:185–95). Direct evidence for this pattern was observed by members of the De Soto entrada in the South Appalachian area. At Chiaha, for example, the young cacique noted that "an uncle of mine . . . is governing these lands for me until I am of proper age" (Elvas in Robertson 1993:89; see also Bourne 1904, 1:76), while at Cofaqui, where the chief was an old man, "a nephew of his governed for him" (Ranjel in Worth 1993a:273; see also Bourne 1904, 2:91). While succession was theoretically based on kinship and was typically matrilineal, whether it was secure in these societies is highly debatable. DePratter (1983:108, 110, 1991a:85, 87), taking a somewhat extreme position, has argued that succession was a routine matter, in part because the institution of regency was reported in several societies: "Apparently the order of succession in the southeastern chiefdoms was strongly enough enforced that this [where children succeeded to the chiefdomship before they were old enough to handle the job] was not a major problem, but simply one to be dealt with in turn. . . . In short, succession served to maintain continuity within the southeastern chiefdoms, and those chiefdoms were able to last through time in part because they had strong rules governing succession to the office of chief." A considerable body of evidence from these same historic records, as well as supporting archaeological and ethnographic data both from the Southeast and from other parts of the world where chiefdoms existed, indicates that uninterrupted or unchallenged succession was far from typical (see chapter 2). DePratter (personal communication, 1993) has since indicated that succession in southeastern chiefdoms probably took a range of forms depending on the local situation.

Strict adherence to rules of inheritance for dictating succession appears to have been unlikely where obvious differences in power bases or ability existed between the designated heir and rival elites. Lawson (1967:205), although referring to groups in the Carolinas at a much later date, circa 1700, noted that violence sometimes accompanied succession to the chieftainship: "The succession falls not to the king's son, but to his sister's son, which is a sure way to prevent imposters in the succession. Sometimes they poison the heir to make way for another, which is not seldom done, when they do not approve of the youth that is to succeed them. The king himself is commonly chief Dr. in that cure." The chief himself, or other principal elites close to him, might thus do away with potential heirs that did not meet expected leadership standards. While genealogical ranking was unquestionably important in succession, so too was secular power, as illustrated by an exchange recorded between the rival chiefs of Pacaha and Casqui in northeastern Arkansas: "there was great contention about which of them would seat himself at the right hand of the Governor. Pacaha told Casqui: 'You know well that I am a greater lord than you and of more honored parents and grandparents, and that to me belongs a better place than to you.' Casqui responded thus: 'It is true that you are a greater lord than I, and your ancestors were greater than mine. . . . notwithstanding, you know well that I am older and more than a match for you, and I confine you in your palisade whenever I want, and you have never seen my land" (Ranjel in Worth 1993a:303; see also Bourne 1904, 2:143–44). The size and stability of rival elite power bases, as well as their genealogical position, were undoubtedly important considerations when power passed from one leader to another.

In a classic example of elite competition for the office of chief, Marquardt (1987:104–8; 1988:179–84) has summarized historic accounts describing the events associated with the succession of paramounts in the 16th-century nonagricultural Calusa chiefdom of southern Florida. Accession to office in the Calusa chiefdom at this time was marked by severe social disruption, something in all probability brought on, at least in part, by recent European contact, the effects of disease, and the appearance of new sources of wealth. Adoptions and marriages were arranged among allied factions to ensure and legitimize the eventual succession of a particular candidate, and factions apparently planned or encouraged incidents damaging to the authority of principal rivals. As Marquardt (1988:187) has noted: "an ostensibly orderly, supernaturally sanctioned succession to the seat of power was in fact beset by rivalry, jealousy, and tension." Power was consolidated following one succession by the execution of some 15 town chiefs suspected of treachery, defined as suspected allegiance to other factions or leaders. One Spanish account, by the Jesuit priest Juan Rogel, described the chief of the Calusa as "dancing about with the heads of four chiefs whom he had been informed intended to rebel and go over to his enemies with their people. For this he had them slain" (Vargas Ugarte in Marquardt 1988:180). While competition for chiefly office unquestionably existed in southeastern chiefdoms, the Calusa example suggests that extreme competition and violence may have been common during periods of instability and, indeed, were characteristic of such periods. This same example also indicates that chiefs could deal with threats of rebellion quickly and harshly.

Succession may have followed more regular lines in larger and more stable polities. The importance of the principle of orderly matrilineal succession may be reinforced by the presence of female chiefs at Cofitachequi at the time of the De Soto entrada and at Guatari at the time of the Pardo expeditions. Hudson (1990:66–67), noting that no evidence exists for the presence of female chiefs elsewhere in the Southeast at this time (although others are observed later, in 17th-century Virginia), has suggested that these women may have held their position because there were no surviving males in the ruling matriline. Cofitachequi is reported to have recently undergone severe disease-induced depopulation at the time of the De Soto entrada, to the point where the chroniclers referred to abandoned towns near the center (Elvas in Robertson 1993:83; see also Bourne 1904, 1:66). The woman ruler of Cofitachequi was described as a widow by Vega (in Shelby 1993:289; see also Varner and Varner 1951:304), prompting Hudson (1990:67) to remark that "if succession was matrilineal, as seems likely, the truth may be that she lacked a brother rather than a husband" (but see Trocolli 1993 for another viewpoint). It is likely that the chiefdom of Guatari underwent similar stress. Both of these cases may document southeastern chiefdoms striving to maintain an orderly process of matrilineal succession during an era of severe societal upheaval, with the woman chief's male children perhaps expected to succeed to the chiefdomship.

Resolving archaeological evidence for the succession of elites is difficult because of the short time scales involved, although ethnohistoric data support the inference that the death of a chief may have been marked by the construction of new mound stages in many southeastern chiefdoms. This possibility is clearly indicated among the Natchez, although the account documenting this process dates to well after initial contact, to the early 18th century: "When the great chief dies they demolish his cabin and then raise a new mound, on which they build the cabin of him who is to replace him in this dignity, for he never lodges in that of his predecessor. The old men prescribe the laws for the rest of the people, and one of their principles is to have a sovereign respect for the great chief as being the brother of the sun and the master of the temple" (Le Petit in Swanton 1911:103). Accounts of burials of chiefly elites in mounds also exist about this time from among the Chitimacha of the Mississippi delta area and among the Choctaw (Swanton 1946:726, 729). In the Choctaw case, communal charnel houses were covered over with earth once full, and there is a suggestion that a new charnel house was then built on that location and the process repeated.

Marriage and Postmarital Residence

Mechanisms dictating permissible marriage ties, along with postmarital residence patterns, can have an affect on the stability of chiefdom organizational structures. Southeastern Mississippian societies were composed of exogamous clans, which, during the period when chiefdoms were present, were apparently ranked in relation to one another (Knight 1990). Postmarital residence in the Southeast was typically matrilocal (Murdock 1967:114), although most of the cases for which good data exist date to well after contact. Accordingly, men would relocate to their wives' homes or communities upon marriage. To reduce the influence of males' marrying women in the chiefly lineage and hence relocating in close physical proximity to the center of chiefly power, specific rules were in place in some southeastern chiefdoms to suppress these individuals and any political ambitions they might have. Thus, among the Natchez, "the princesses of the blood never espouse any but men of obscure family, and they have but one husband, but they have the right of dismissing him whenever it pleases them, and of choosing another among those of the nation, provided he has not made any other alliance among them. If the husband has been guilty of an infidelity, the princess may have his head cut off in an instant; but she is not herself subject to the same law, for she may have as many lovers as she pleases without the husband having any power to complain. In the presence of his wife he acts with the most profound respect, never eats with her, and salutes her with howls as is done by her servants" (Le Petit in Swanton 1911:103). The marriage of the chief's sister to an "obscure" commoner and the keeping of him in a subservient position would ensure that potentially destabilizing rivals did not move too close to the center of power. This example shows that at least some of the social rules in place in southeastern chiefdoms had the effect of minimizing factional conflict.

A pattern of matrilocal residence indicates that heirs to succession would have stayed within individual communities, at least until marriage. Upon reaching maturity, however, given the prevailing postmarital residence rules, chiefly heirs might be required to marry outside the local community. These practices would have dramatically reduced the possibility of chiefly succession continuing within a given community unless rules granting exceptions were in play. This appears to have been the case. Commoners in most southeastern chiefdoms appear to have been monogamous, while elite polygyny is well documented among the early accounts (Swanton 1946:701–9). Typically, wives either relocated to the chief's house or remained in their own home. Among the Natchez, men could "have as many wives as they chose. Nevertheless, the common people generally have but one or two. This, however, is not the case with the chiefs. . . . Although they have many wives, they keep but one or two in their cabins; the rest remain at the houses of their parents, where they go to see them when they wish" (Le Petit in Swanton 1911:97). Chiefly elites thus appear to have been exempt from matrilocal postmarital residence rules. How this process operated warrants further discussion, since organizational stability in these societies undoubtedly depended upon continuity in leadership within specific communities. Where marriages were unstable, furthermore, alliances based upon marriage were also likely to be unstable (Gluckman 1950; Radcliffe-Brown 1952).

Polygyny and other elite marriage arrangements were important mechanisms by which status and power relations were acknowledged, alliances were sealed, and administrative structures filled in southeastern chiefdoms. Although ethnohistoric accounts indicate that polygyny and the out-marriage of high-status females was common among elites in Mississippian chiefdoms (Hudson 1976:199ff), how these rules were followed appears to depend upon the relative status of the participants. Given the importance of the chief's sister in producing his successor and the presence of mechanisms such as commoner marriage, alliances by marriage in dominant southeastern societies were probably sealed through the position of the chief rather than through his sister. That is, elite female out-marriage in complex Mississippian chiefdoms below the level of the ruling lineage was probably unidirectional, from lesser to more dominant elites. While the highest female elites (as far as we can determine) had to marry commoners, lesser female elites, particularly those from other communities, could have married upward. Such a strategy would cement alliances as well as acknowledge power relationships. Marriage between elites of roughly equal status may have occurred to foster alliances. In subservient communities or polities, alliance with higher centers may well have been sealed through the female line, with either the relocation of women to the center or the marriage of one of the chief's relatives or supporters to a female elite in the outlying community.

Adherence to a pattern of matrilocal postmarital residence (except for the chief) would be an effective method of dispersing brothers or other close male relatives, thus building up a regional power base while minimizing the potential threats that might arise from their close proximity (figure 9). At a center, the presence of a number of close kin in positions immediately below the chief in authority could have prompted conflict upon the death or perceived weakening of this individual. Evidence from the 16th-century accounts indicates that vassal chiefs administering outlying centers were often the direct kin of the paramount and were probably appointed by him (DePratter 1983:25–28, 1991a:19–25). Thus Satouriona, a paramount occupying the region of the St John's River in Florida, was described by Laudonnière as having "thirty vassal chiefs under him, of whom ten were his brothers" (Bennett 1975:76), and comparable situations were described during the De Soto entrada. The strategy of dispersing near-kin through marital alliances, while initially stabilizing, would create problems later on, as these elites built up their own power bases and as questions arose about how their successors would be chosen (figure 10). A critical question would be whether the children of relocated elites (in the matriline they married into) would succeed to power in these centers, or whether new elites/administrators would be imposed from above, from the paramount center.

Another important question would be how the children of male elites, who were born to wealth and power, would accept reduced social status as required by prevailing patterns of descent and inheritance. Knight (1990:13), in a solution derived from an examination of the ethnohistoric literature, has suggested that limited noble elite or status was also transmitted through the male line, although it quickly deteriorated "to commoner status beyond specified degrees of genealogical distance from the royal line." Matrilineal succession coupled with matrilocal residence, when linked with clan exogamy and markedly different patterns of inheritance in the male and female line, thus formed a structurally ingrained, potentially destabilizing characteristic of southeastern Mississippian society.

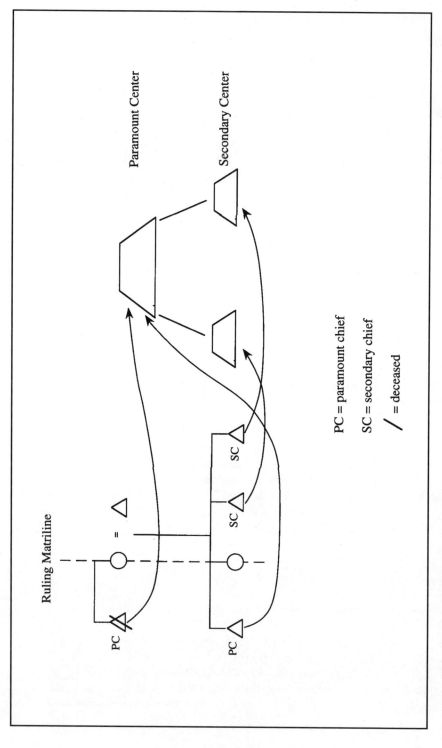

Figure 9 Dispersion of Chiefly Elites in Southeastern Mississippian Chiefdoms: Advantages of Matrilocal Postmarital Residence Patterns. (Reprinted from Anderson 1994, courtesy Cambridge University Press)

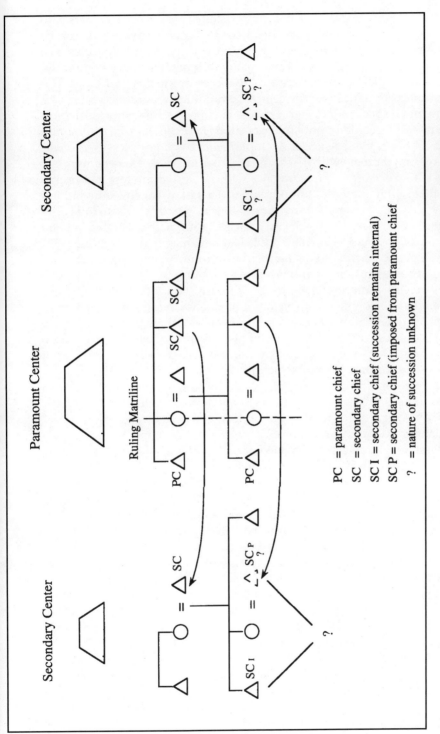

Figure 10 Dispersion of Chiefly Elites in Southeastern Mississippian Chiefdoms: Sources of Instability in Later Generations. (Reprinted from Anderson 1994, courtesy Cambridge University Press)

Fortunately, effective mechanisms existed to keep heirs at centers or to relocate them there upon the death of the chief, reducing the social tensions potentially created by the existence of special marital rules. The presence of ceremonial facilities, notably temple/mortuary complexes, would ideologically predispose an elite succeeding to the chiefdomship to remain near or relocate to the central community. Where succession was interrupted, specifically when a rival seized power, this same ideological predisposition could prompt the relocation of the center to the community where the new chief's ancestral temple/mortuary complex was located.

Another problem with matrilocal postmarital residence systems is that they tend to create groups of males with no vested interest in working together within individual communities. That is, males linked by propinquity may not cooperate with one another as readily as those linked by kinship (V. Turner 1957:76–77). In a society with matrilineal descent and matrilocal postmarital residence, this had advantages and disadvantages for a chief. His core male kinsmen tend to out-marry, reducing his primary support base, while males in-marrying, being unrelated, might raise challenges to his position. Given their numerical minority, this is unlikely, although a wise chief would undoubtedly try either to co-opt or to eliminate potential rivals. As a Yao chief expressed this situation to a newly installed headman, "Beware how you treat the men who have married into the village. They have it in their power to break the village" (J. Mitchell 1951:328). Opposed arcs of structures or discrete clusters of structures within a community, for example, might indicate groups of people with allied interests, who could form potential fission groups (V. Turner 1957:80). Community reorganization to accommodate increasing social tension may occur prior to actual disruption or fissioning. Such reorganization should be detectable archaeologically, although delimiting its cause is likely to be considerably more difficult.

The kinds of problems besetting matrilineal kin groupings in general have been aptly summarized by Turner (1957:225): "Male members of such a sibling group are opposed to their own children who belong to a different sibling group, belong potentially to a different village, and belong actually to a different genealogical generation. . . . Female members of a uterine sibling group are opposed through marriage to their brothers. . . . They are opposed to their brother's children if they live in the same village; for their brothers tend to favor their own children with food and attention rather than sisters' children, who will ultimately oust brother's children from the village. Sisters are united with their brothers as members of the same genealogical generation, and with their other male and female classificatory matrilineal kin, against all members of the adjacent generations." Matrilineal succession thus emphasizes the bond between brothers and sisters at the expense of the bond between husbands and wives (Radcliffe-Brown 1952:42). The pattern of limited agnathic inheritance inferred to exist in Mississippian society would, however, help to counter these divisive forces, by giving the husbands and wives of elites (and their children) lesser elite status and hence (by weaning them from privilege gradually) a stake in maintaining the system. Matrilineal principles of descent coupled with matrilocal postmarital residence patterns do, however, tend to result in the development of lineages with considerable residential stability and time depth. These social rules also create cadres of related and cooperating women, groups that may be very important in societies such as those documented in the late prehistoric Southeast, where women played a major role in agricultural food production.

Williams and Shapiro (1987, 1990a) have noted that a number of Mississippian centers in central Georgia were characterized by alternate periods of occupation and abandonment, in some cases up to several generations. While ecological reasons for such abandonment, such as soil or firewood depletion, have been advanced, from the arguments just raised it is equally probable that social mechanisms delimiting inheritance and land tenure may have been a factor, something the authors acknowledge. The occupation, abandonment, and relocation of centers in the late prehistoric Southeast, I suggest, was probably related as much to social as to ecological factors.

The Identification of Territories and Boundaries

In the South Appalachian area, increasing evidence suggests that political change in Mississippian societies can be addressed, at least in part, by examining patterns of variation over time in the spatial extent and contexts of archaeologically identified Mississippian phases. Given the success that Hudson and his colleagues have had equating 16th-century archaeological phases with ethnohistorically documented aboriginal polities, equation of prehistoric Mississippian phases with similar kinds of sociopolitical entities appears to be a viable research option, albeit one that should be approached with great caution. Following just such a strategy, the existence and developmental trajectories of a number of probable local prehistoric Mississippian societies have been examined, and evidence for cycling behavior, specifically the movement of centers over the landscape, has been widely noted (e.g., Anderson, Hally, and Rudolph 1986; Hally 1986a, 1987, 1993; Hally, Hudson, and DePratter 1985; Hally, Smith, and Langford 1990; Rudolph and Blanton 1980; Shapiro 1983; M. Smith and Kowalewski 1980; M. Williams and Shapiro 1987, 1990a).

Contacts between major polities in the South Appalachian area, which tended to be widely separated from one another, appear to have been minimal during the 16th century. The central towns of the three principal polities of Ocute, Cofitachequi, and Coosa were separated by distances on the order of 250 kilometers, and even the outlying communities on the margins of these chiefdoms were isolated from the towns in the next major polity by appreciable distances. These distributions are unquestionably caused by regional physiographic structure, specifically the wide stretches separating major river systems in the South Appalachian area. A result of this geographic separation, perhaps in combination with Mississippian hunting and warfare patterns, was the creation of extensive buffer zones between these polities.

DePratter (1983:34–36, 1991a:30–33), who has conducted the most intensive examination of these features to date, compiled references for 27 "deserts" or probable buffer zones encountered by the De Soto entrada as it passed through the Southeast. These ranged in size from between two and ten days' travel time, tended to be linguistic as well as cultural or political boundaries, and were frequently characterized by fortified settlements at their peripheries. DePratter (1983:32–33, 37–38, 1991a:28–29, 33–35) noted the relationship between skirmish warfare and the maintenance of these buffer zones and argued that the process was a deliberate effort to produce well-defined boundaries between polities in areas where natural boundaries, such as extensive upland areas between major rivers, were absent. He (1983:39–42, 1991a:35) also observed that because the De Soto expedition continually caught native societies unaware, the permeability of these buffers was minimal: "For Soto and his large force to arrive unannounced anywhere in the Southeast, it means that the isolation brought about by the combination of warring political units, linguistic differences, and separation of chiefdoms by uninhabited buffers must have been extreme." While long-distance trade is known to have existed, it appears to have been decidedly uncommon (Swanton 1946:736–42). Upon reaching Apalachee, the De Soto expedition met a youth who had visited Cofitachequi in the company of traders, but this was some years previously (Vega in Shelby 1993:248; see also Varner and Varner 1951:253). The infrequency of trade is suggested by the fact that this youth proceeded to get the expedition lost once it passed beyond Ocute (see below). Production of salt for exchange is documented from several areas, although the dynamics of the exchange process are not well understood (I. Brown 1980; J. Brown, Kerber, and Winters 1990). No other accounts from the early historic period exist to document traders' operating over comparable distances, which suggests long-distance trade was uncommon. This may reflect increasingly hostile political relations within the region at and shortly before European contact, since some evidence suggests that trade was more widespread and polities more open in the centuries immediately prior to circa 1400 (see chapter 4).

Although the Indians of Ocute and Patofa were eager to make war on their apparent enemies in Cofitachequi and hence accompanied De Soto as he marched there, it became obvious that they had little direct contact with them: the caciques of "Ocute and Cofaqui . . . told us that if we wished to go to make war on the lady of Cofitachique, they would give us all that we might want for the journey. They told us there was no road by which to go, since they had no dealings with one another because they were at war; sometimes when they came to make war on one another, they passed through hidden and secret places where they could not be detected" (Biedma in Worth 1993b:229; see also Bourne 1904, 1:11). Between Ocute and Cofitachequi, the Spanish were told, was "an uninhabited region of nine or ten days' journey" (Ranjel in Worth 1993a:273; see also Bourne 1904, 2:91). The De Soto entrada, including several hundred bearers from Ocute and Patofa, became thoroughly lost in this wilderness attempting to find Cofitachequi.

Upon leaving the town of Cofaqui in central Georgia, the entrada moved eastward through "the large uninhabited region that lies between the two provinces of Cofaqui and Cofachiqui" (Vega in Shelby 1993:272; see also Varner and Varner 1951:283). The expedition followed a major pathway for the first seven days of their journey, a trail that Hudson and his colleagues have interpreted as following the later, 18th-century Hightower Trail (Hudson, Smith, and DePratter 1984:71). The countryside was described as pleasant and easily traversed. The entrada apparently crossed the Savannah River on the fifth day and the Congaree two days later, apparently near the confluence of the Broad and Saluda rivers at Columbia. It was here that both the "Indians and Spaniards found themselves in great confusion, because the road that they had been following up to that time, which appeared to be a very wide public highway, came to an end, and many narrow paths that led through the woods in every direction were lost after they had followed them for a short distance. Thus after making many efforts, they found themselves closed up in that wilderness without knowing how to get out of it, and the woods were different from the former ones because they were taller and denser, and they could travel through them only with difficulty" (Vega in Shelby 1993:274; see also Varner and Varner 1951:283–84). At this point, the expedition, having run out of food, was in real trouble and endured considerable hardship for several days until food was found in an outlying town of Cofitachequi. These accounts, when coupled with archaeological analyses such as those presented herein (chapters 6–8), have led to the recent recognition that the central Savannah, rather than the center of the major province of Cofitachequi, was actually an unoccupied buffer zone during the 16th century (e.g., Anderson, Hally, and Rudolph 1986; DePratter 1989; Hudson, Smith, and DePratter 1984:71–72; Hudson et al. 1987:846, 1990).

Ethnohistoric evidence also suggests that Mississippian buffer zones not only existed but were aggressively maintained throughout the region (DePratter 1983:20–43, 1991a:19–38). Individuals from other polities found in these areas were typically subject to attack. Patofa, a war leader from Ocute, described the nature of this interaction in the Georgia–South Carolina area in general terms to De Soto during the Spanish army's march to Cofitachequi in 1540: "the wars these two provinces had waged had never been open battle between two forces, one taking an army to the territory of the other, but only at the fisheries on those two rivers and the other streams that they had left behind them and at the hunting grounds, between the parties that both sent out through the woods and uninhabited districts that they had passed. Meeting at these hunting grounds and fisheries, they killed and captured one another as enemies, and because those of Cofachiqui had been superior to his and had always gained many advantages over them in the fights that they had thus had, his Indians were intimidated and submissive, not daring to go any distance or leave their own boundaries" (Vega in Shelby 1993:274; see also Varner and Varner 1951:284). The operation of these societal boundaries was also forcefully illustrated during the Pardo expeditions, when the leaders of mountain Cherokee groups were described as studiously avoiding any contact with towns or individuals aligned with Coosa (Hudson 1990:97–102). The absence of readily identifiable major chiefs, or *micos*, among the mountain Cherokee at the time of Pardo's visit is taken by Hudson (101) to indicate these were relatively simple societies compared to the chiefdoms around them. DePratter (1983:44–67, 1991a:39–56) has provided convincing evidence that small-scale skirmishing was not the only form of warfare practiced during the initial contact era. During the De Soto entrada, for example, the expedition was repeatedly attacked by large, well-organized, and well-coordinated groups of Indians, indicating both small-scale skirmishing and more extensive warfare were practiced. Group territories, while perhaps most commonly maintained by indirect or small-scale warfare, could also have been more aggressively defended or expanded, through larger-scale conflict.

Information Management and Decision-making Hierarchies

The presence of three administrative offices in the 16th-century chiefdoms of the South Appalachian area has been documented by Hudson (1990:61), based on his work with the Pardo documents. These offices corresponded to village headmen responsible for one or a few small communities (*oratas*), chiefs over a fairly appreciable number of subsidiary communities (*micos*), and paramount chiefs ruling over extensive territories (*caciques grandes*). There is a strong possibility that other administrative/leadership groups were also present in these societies, since the same accounts also specify the existence of war leaders and village magistrate-like figures. At a number of sites, in fact, the accounts report large numbers of elites, presumably more than would be required to handle routine decision making (Anderson 1990a:115–18). These individuals, members of what Cordy (1981) described as a rank echelon, could, however, help those actually wielding power to maintain their positions. The presence of officials at villages and centers in simple chiefdoms and of officials at the villages, secondary centers, and the primary center in complex and paramount chiefdoms is clearly documented in the contact-era Mississippian Southeast.

Oratas typically administered activities in one community, although in a few cases oratas who held authority over several towns were described (Hudson 1990:62). These were lesser elites who, acting on behalf of the chief, supervised the production and mobilization of tribute and the organization of corvee labor as required. While Pardo met a great many oratas, with at least one apparently present at every community he encountered, he met only three micos, who ruled over the chiefdoms of Guatari, Joara, and Chiaha, and he heard of only one cacique grande, at Coosa. Hudson (63) notes that there was no specific term for the position of the paramount, suggesting that the institution was either new in the region or else was so strongly identified with the chief at the polity that held it that additional formal terminology was unnecessary. It is also possible that the institution was not perceived as sufficiently different from the chiefdoms ruled by micos (which may have been viewed as differing only in scale) to warrant the creation of additional titles. The absence of precise terminology describing leadership positions in complex southeastern chiefdoms, if not an artifact of Spanish recording, may be a further indication of the fragility of these entities.

The Bandera II account gives the numbers, names, and social position (i.e., orata, mico, cacique grande) of many of the chiefly elites Pardo met in each town, many of whom were visitors from subsidiary or nearby communities. This level of historical detail permitted Hudson (1990) to reconstruct the probable importance of the communities in the regional settlement hierarchy. The kinds of status positions represented in a given town and the number of elites residing or visiting there were seen as a possible measure of that community's relative position in the administrative hierarchy. Thus when Pardo visited Canos, Ysa, Juada, and Guatari, to cite a few examples, he encountered many chiefs, suggesting that these towns were extensive and probably powerful, while at other communities, such as Tagaya the Lessor and one "whose name I do not remember," only a single chief (orata) was mentioned (Pardo in Ketchem 1954:70–71). Care must be taken to avoid reading too much into the Pardo accounts, however, since some of the elites Pardo met were visitors who had traveled considerable distances to meet him.

Comparison of the De Soto and Pardo documents indicates the kinds of political changes that had occurred over the region in the roughly 25 years separating these two expeditions (Hudson 1990:64ff; see also figure 7 in this text). Collapse of administrative hierarchy is evident in some societies, while others appear to have been expanding. The paramount or complex chiefdom of Cofitachequi, for example, may have fragmented into a number of autonomous lesser simple chiefdoms, of which Joara and Guatari were the most prominent, a view held by Hudson (1990; but see DePratter 1989 for an alternative interpretation, that there was no immediate post–De Soto disintegration of Cofitachequi). There is some indication from the Pardo documents that, by the 1560s, Joara and Guatari were expanding and competing with each other, probably in hopes of attaining the status of a paramount chiefdom (Hudson 1990:89–93). The absence of archaeological reports of mounds in the area of the Guatari towns on the upper Yadkin led Hudson to suggest that either it was a relatively young chiefdom or that its ability to coerce labor from subsidiary communities was still in doubt. Coosa, reported in steep decline during the De Luna expedition (see below), appears to have rebounded by the time of the Pardo expedition, since its ruler was described as a cacique grande.

Warfare

Two kinds of warfare are documented in the early historic accounts: an almost continual pattern of small-scale raiding and skirmishing; and a more infrequent pattern of massive, well-coordinated campaigns closer to the traditional European view of warfare (DePratter 1983:44–67, 1991a:39–56). Southeastern warfare is described in considerable detail in the accounts of the De Soto expedition:

> . . . nearly all the provinces that these Spaniards traversed were at war with one another. . . . It must be known, then, that this was not a war of one power against another with armies drawn up and general engagements, except on very rare occasions. Nor was it a war of greed and ambition on the part of some lords to take away the states of others.
>
> The warfare that they waged consisted of ambushes and stratagems, making surprise attacks on the fisheries, hunting grounds, cultivated fields, and roads, wherever they could find their adversaries off guard. Those whom they captured in such assaults were held as slaves, some in perpetual captivity with one foot disabled, as we have seen in some of the provinces, and others as prisoners for ransom, to be exchanged for others.
>
> The enmity among them extended only to inflicting injury on their persons, with death or wounds or imprisonment, without attempting to take away one another's states, and if the war sometimes became general, it would lead to the burning of pueblos [villages] and laying waste the fields. But as soon as the victors had done as much damage as they wished, they went back to their own country without attempting to take possession of that of others.
>
> . . . This kind of warfare has now become second nature to them and is the cause of their going about, wherever they may be, with their weapons constantly in readiness, because they are nowhere safe from their enemies. . . . [A] cacique did not carry on this warfare with only one of his neighbors, but with all those whose boundaries touched his . . . (Vega in Shelby 1993:438–39; see also Varner and Varner 1951:487–88).

While this statement is exaggerated—alliances were possible, ensuring relative peace within fairly large areas—the accounts do indicate considerable competition and conflict was occurring between elites. Warfare had its functions, including the creation and maintenance of territorial buffers and boundaries. A pattern of continual warfare and hostility could promote group solidarity by promoting a concern for mutual self-interest and defense. It would also reinforce the position of the elite since, given the possibility of hostile reception elsewhere, commoner populations would have to stay in their place.

Clear examples of military circumscription, the expansion of one chiefdom at the expense of another, are also documented in the early historic record. The rivalry between the chiefdoms of Capaha (Pacaha) and Casqui in northeastern Arkansas, noted previously, is described in detail in the accounts of the De Soto entrada. It is evident that Capaha was expanding at the expense of Casqui: ". . . this cacique Casquin and his parents, grandparents, and ancestors for many centuries previously had war with the lord and lords of another province, called Capaha, which bordered on his own. These latter, because they were more-powerful lords of lands and vassals, had hemmed in Casquin, and were continuing to do so, having almost overcome him. He dared not take up arms for fear of angering Capaha and irritating him lest he [Capaha] do him [Casquin] the harm that he could do, being so powerful. He [Casquin] remained quiet, content only with guarding his boundaries, and not leaving them or giving occasion for being attacked . . . " (Vega in Shelby 1993:394; see also Varner and Varner 1951:434–435). The same pattern is also noted in the South Appalachian region, where the province of Cofitachequi in central South Carolina appears to have been expanding at the expense of its neighbors to the west, as documented in the exchange between De Soto and Patofa cited previously. The long-term effects of this kind of behavior would be the collapse of the losing chiefdom, with effects including possible population relocation or their subjugation into tributary relationships. This appears to have occurred quite often during the Mississippian period in the Southeast.

Warfare may not have been as extreme in the area occupied by Ocute and Cofitachequi, which were separated by extensive buffers, as it was in other parts of the Southeast. It was not until the De Soto expedition arrived at Chiaha in eastern Tennessee in the province of Coosa, for example, that "these Spaniards first found the towns palisaded" (Ranjel in Worth 1993a:283; see also Bourne 1904, 2:108); Biedma makes the same observation (in Worth 1993b:232; see also Bourne 1904, 2:15). Mississippian chiefdoms in the South Appalachian area were typically widely separated from one another, a distribution that may have rendered hostilities difficult. Fortifications were infrequent in this area, and contact between these societies appears to have been minimal. Chiefdoms in the central Mississippi River valley encountered later in the De Soto entrada, in contrast, were more closely packed together, something that appears to have prompted increased conflict. The accounts indicate that towns were typically fortified in this area and that warfare between neighboring chiefdoms was common (Dye 1990; Vega in Shelby 1993:394–419, 438; see also Varner and Varner 1951:434–36, 487).

The absence of obvious fortifications in the territories the Spanish encountered prior to reaching Chiaha does suggest a reduced level of hostilities or, alternatively, that these chiefdoms were secure without them. Towns in the central portions of complex chiefdoms throughout the Southeast were apparently more secure than those in outlying areas, particularly towns on borders facing rival polities, which were frequently described as strongly fortified (e.g., Ranjel in Worth 1993a:283; see also Bourne 1904, 2:108; Vega in Shelby 1993:325, 331, 395; Varner and Varner 1951:346, 353, 436; Steinen 1992). Interestingly, the ethnohistoric accounts hint that the appearance of fortifications may actually be indicative of a chiefdom in a weakened state. Thus, among the Natchez, "when a nation is too weak to sustain the war, it endeavors to build a fort in order to protect itself," with the fortifications "of a size proportional to the number of warriors and the remainder of the nation" (Du Pratz in Swanton 1911:133). The absence of major fortifications over much of the South Appalachian area, besides a manifestation of the great distance separating the polities occupying the area, may have also been due to the apparent absence of comparable complex societies to the east or northeast along the Atlantic seaboard. The native societies that were present in these areas simply may not have been perceived as threats.

Reasons for warfare between polities are sometimes provided in the early historic accounts. Elite competition for power and prestige appears to have been responsible for at least some of the observed conflict. For example, in the case from Arkansas, cited previously, warfare occurred within a framework of a long-standing rivalry between the elites of adjoining polities. The hostilities between Casqui and Capaha (Pacaha), while ostensibly brought about by Capaha's territorial expansion, were explicitly couched in terms of a jockeying for status and prestige (Vega in Shelby 1993:394–406; see also Varner and Varner 1951:434–49; P. Morse 1990:126–33). Casqui's desecration of Capaha's ancestral sepulchres, his wives, and his subjects and his later insistence on a place of honor by De Soto when meeting with Capaha were all tactics designed to reinforce his status relative to the other and to delegitimize the authority of his traditional enemy (Casqui was able to accomplish these victories against his more powerful neighbor by enlisting the aid of De Soto).

The same pattern of interpolity elite competition is also noted in the South Appalachian region, where during the 14th and 15th centuries the provinces of Ocute in central Georgia and Cofitachequi in central South Carolina, as we shall see (chapters 6–8), were apparently expanding at the expense of chiefdoms in the Savannah River valley (Anderson, Hally, and

Rudolph 1986; DePratter 1989). The long-term effects of this kind of expansion could result in the death or relocation of the losing populations or, more likely, the subjugation of their elites into tributary relationships. De Soto was told that the low-intensity conflict existing between the provinces of Ocute and Cofitachequi had existed from time immemorial, with little or no contact between the elites of these polities. No memory apparently remained of the Savannah River chiefdoms that had existed between these two chiefdoms only a century or so before.

While underlying ecological factors may have prompted southeastern warfare, such as competition for hunting territory or agricultural land or for control of unusual resources or access to trading networks (e.g., Gramly 1977; L. Larson 1972; E. Turner and Santley 1979), little actual documentation supports such inferences. Laudonnière (Bennett 1975:77), in one of the few applicable references, recorded one example of warfare in Florida that had occurred over control of knappable stone sources; how unusual this was is unknown. Investment in facilities, such as cleared agricultural fields, is also thought to have prompted the aggressive defense of these areas, although, again, documentary evidence for this is lacking (DePratter 1983:44, 1991a:39ff; L. Larson 1972). DePratter (1983:24–28, 1991a:23–25) has cited ethnohistoric evidence to suggest that southeastern chiefdoms grew by conquest, through advantageous marital alliances, and through the shared defensive needs of cooperating communities. The capture of slaves may have been another motive for warfare. While men were often killed outright or subsequently tortured, in some cases men as well as women and children are reported to have been taken alive. The economic importance of native southeastern slavery was illustrated by the practice of hamstringing male captives put to work in the fields; this ensured their value over the long-term by preventing them from running away (Vega in Shelby 1993:400, 439; see also Varner and Varner 1951:439, 488). The labor production of these individuals, both in agriculture and the manufacture of tributary goods, would have increased the wealth of their elite owners (DePratter 1983:61, 1991a:52; see also Carneiro 1991:176–78).

What *is* well documented is that, in the 16th-century Southeast, *warfare was a mechanism for establishing and enforcing tributary relationships* (Anderson 1987a; DePratter 1983; Dye 1990; see Elvas in Robertson 1993:106 for an explicit account from the De Soto expedition). When the De Luna expedition visited Coosa in 1560, for example, it was enlisted in a military expedition to exact restitution from the rival town of Napochies, which had refused to submit tribute (DePratter 1983:57–58, 173–74, 1991a:49, 134–35; Hudson 1988, 1990:13, 104). The Napochies, apparently a subsidiary polity in the Coosa province 20 years earlier when De Soto came through, had taken advantage of the weakened state of the paramount following European contact to break away. The process of the decline of Coosa at the expense of its rival, Napochies, is clearly outlined in the De

Luna accounts: "In ancient times the Napochies were tributaries of the Coza people, because this place (Coza) was always recognized as head of the kingdom and its lord was considered to stand above the one of the Napochies. Then the people from Coza began to decrease while the Napochies were increasing until they refuse to be their vassals, finding themselves strong enough to maintain their liberty which they abused. Then those of Coza took to arms to reduce the rebels to their former servitude, but the most victories were on the side of the Napochies. Those from Coza remained greatly affronted as well from seeing their ancient tribute broken off, as because they found themselves without strength to restore it. On that account they had lately stopped their fights . . . [and] had not gone into the battlefield, for fear lest they return vanquished, as before" (Padilla in Swanton 1922:231–39). The Spanish were enlisted on the side of Coosa and quickly defeated the Napochies. This appears to have reversed the fortunes of this particular chiefdom, for by the time of the Pardo expeditions in 1566 and 1567, Coosa was again reported to be a powerful chiefdom. The second Pardo expedition, in fact, turned back toward Santa Elena when word came that a powerful alliance headed by the chief of Coosa was waiting to attack the Spanish once they crossed the mountains (DePratter, Hudson, and Smith 1983:148).

The 1560 Coosa-Napochies rivalry documents the cycling process in operation, detailing specific events that could have ultimately led to the replacement of one regional center/complex chiefdom by another. Population decline at a paramount center, perhaps brought about through reverses in warfare, famine, or emigration could lead to the loss of a numerical advantage in manpower (i.e., warriors) held by that community over its neighbors. As the strength of neighboring societies relative to that of the paramount grew, challenges to leadership would arise. Refusal to acknowledge or submit to the authority of the paramount would be the first step in this process and would typically take the form of an indirect challenge rather than outright warfare, although this often quickly followed. Refusal to submit tribute, actively hampering the formation of alliances by the paramount with other communities, or refusal to cooperate in communal ceremonial or construction activities were the means by which such a challenge was raised, as documented in the regional ethnohistoric record. Archaeological correlates of this process would include evidence for population decline, a change in the regional flow of luxury/prestige goods, and, of course, evidence for the decline, destruction, or abandonment of one center at the same time another in the area was expanding.

Factional Competition

Early 16th-century European explorers in the Southeast, such as Cabeza de Vaca, Hernando de Soto, Tristan de Luna, Juan Pardo, René

Laudonnière, John White, and others, saw complex Mississippian chiefdoms before they disintegrated under contact. These early explorers were certainly familiar with the processes and effects of factional competition. Many of the great nation states of the day had themselves only just emerged from intense periods of factional competition, as exemplified by struggles such as the War of the Roses in England or the events leading to the political unification of the Iberian peninsula. Well-schooled in these processes—this was the period, after all, when Machiavelli wrote his classic work *The Prince*—these early explorers made use of them in their conquests. Native factions were pitted against each other whenever possible, and descriptions of this process survive in the ethnohistoric record (Anderson 1994).

Factional competition between elites within a given polity or between nearby polities is described in some detail in the early accounts. Internecine warfare, commonly over succession to chiefly office, appears to have been rife. In the example cited previously detailing the rivalry of Pacaha and Casqui in Arkansas, factional competition occurred within a framework of long-standing sparring for absolute power between two adjoining polities. Sometimes rivalries between polities were for the loyalties of elites in subject communities, as documented during the De Soto entrada, when the expedition reached the town of Talise (or Talisi) at the southwestern margin of Coosa: "This pueblo Talise was not wholly obedient to its lord Coza, because of its double-dealing with another lord, named Tascaluca, whose state bordered upon that of Coca, and he was not a safe neighbor or a true friend. Although the two were not openly at war, Tascaluca was a haughty and belligerent man, very cunning and deceitful . . . and as such had stirred up this pueblo to disobedience to its lord" (Vega in Shelby 1993:325–26; see also Varner and Varner 1951:346). Communities near the boundaries of a chiefdom, given their distance from the center, probably exercised considerable autonomy. The activities of rival factions in these communities would, accordingly, have been difficult for a paramount to address. Accounts of outright revolts by subsidiary elites within particular societies also exist from the early Southeast, such as the Napochies rebellion described by the De Luna expedition in 1560. The Napochies example illustrates one mechanism by which chiefly authority might be challenged by a rival faction, specifically the withholding of tribute. This would only occur as part of a bid for local autonomy, since warfare was an almost certain outcome of such a refusal.

The effects of factional competition can be seen in the circumscription of chiefly polities and in the relocation of political centers over the southeastern landscape, typified in the archaeological record by the abandonment of sites or areas, often with evidence of destruction. Outright threats or actual violence, refusal to pay tribute or obey commands, and the appropriation of a chief's stores or personnel (including his allies or wives) were all reported methods by which chiefly authority was challenged.

Relationships between local and regional ruling elites were thus often delicate in southeastern chiefdoms. For this reason, some scholars have suggested that cooperation between elites was essential to the maintenance of regional power relationships, and that jockeying for power occurred within a larger framework constraining elite competition to within certain bounds (e.g., McKivergan 1992). While this was unquestionably true, the rapidity with which elites in several parts of the Southeast discarded traditional patterns of interaction when De Soto provided them with the opportunity to subordinate their rivals suggests that self-interest remained a basic force driving elite competition in these societies.

The Importance of Early Southeastern Accounts to the Study of Mississippian Political Change

From this brief review, a number of generalizations can be made about the nature and operation of the chiefdom societies present in the Southeast and in the South Appalachian area at the time of initial European contact and, by inference, during the century or so immediately prior to this time. First, it is evident that these societies were true chiefdoms characterized by a "pervasive inequality of persons and groups" (Service 1971:145) and widely varying levels of size and complexity—from simple chiefdoms occupying small areas and controlling a few towns, to complex chiefdoms covering massive areas and incorporating many subsidiary communities and chiefdoms. Some of the largest of these paramount chiefdoms exerted sway over tens of thousands of square kilometers and over appreciable numbers of lesser chiefdoms, the elites of which were either replaced or forced into subsidiary roles.

Within complex southeastern chiefdoms, three institutionalized social rank echelons were present, consisting of the chief and his associates (i.e., micos or cacique grandes), lesser elites and their associates (oratas), and commoners. Commoners had little political influence or power, although it is probable that some care had to be taken by the elites to avoid their complete alienation. Elite power in southeastern chiefdoms was derived from both sanctified and secular sources, such as genealogical proximity to chiefly clans and lineages, public acceptance of their sacred position and abilities, and real or implied coercive powers. In the more complex southeastern chiefdoms, the ruling elites were set apart from the great mass of people by distinctive modes of dress and compulsory sumptuary and ritualistic behavior. A physical separation was also enforced, with the elites occupying special (i.e., larger, better-quality) residential areas. This separation included mortuary behavior, with "the noble dead . . . isolated in death, as they were in life, close to the areas of major ritual display" (Wright 1984:44). This separation was evident at all levels of the settlement hierarchy above the level of the individual household. Members of the

ruling elite were present at primary and secondary centers in some numbers, with smaller numbers in outlying villages, where they administered
tribute collection and the maintenance of public granaries.

The chiefly elite was a geographically extensive group linked through
marriage and other, predominantly kin-based alliances. This elite had the
responsibility for coordinating collective ritual behavior as well as directing the polity-wide tributary economy, in which goods inevitably flowed
from lower to higher levels in the status and settlement hierarchy. This
tributary economy operated on two levels, one concerned with subsistence items and the other with luxury goods. Foodstuffs tended to be
stored at or near where they were produced, although their use was under
the control of the elite. Storage facilities thus tended to be widely scattered
in these societies, with concentrations at primary centers. In contrast,
luxury goods, many of which were produced in the smaller communities
(i.e, blankets, skins, river pearls), invariably gravitated toward the centers,
into the hands of the chiefly elite, who had undoubtedly encouraged and,
where necessary, coerced their production.

In simple chiefdoms, one decision-making level was present, and
society was essentially subdivided into two classes or rank echelons, elites
and commoners. In complex chiefdoms, an additional administrative level
was present, with three rank echelons consisting of elites, lesser elites, and
commoners. Secondary centers were occupied by lesser elites allied with,
related to, or under the control of elites at the paramount center. These
secondary communities may have had considerable autonomy, but ultimate allegiance to the paramount was required and was demonstrated
through the periodic submission of tribute. Food may or may not have
been periodically submitted to the paramount center, depending upon the
distances between the centers and whether bulk transportation using
watercraft was feasible. The paramount would, however, have been able
to call upon the resources of the secondary center at any time.

The attention of the elites in complex southeastern chiefdoms was
directed inward for the most part, toward intrapolity political, social, and
ceremonial matters. Little evidence suggests regular contact between
distinct polities, at least in the South Appalachian area, where chiefdoms
were widely separated. In the central Mississippi River valley, in contrast,
given the seemingly greater packing of the landscape, more attention to
external affairs appears to have been required of the elites (see chapter 4).
All across the region, warfare appears to have been rigorously controlled
and directed externally (i.e., against other polities). Conflict typically took
the form of isolated skirmishes and sneak attacks on small parties or
settlements, although larger attacks sometimes occurred as well. The
enhancement of personal status, the recovery of captives (particularly
women), and the maintenance of territorial boundaries all figured into
warfare. Over time this would have contributed, of course, to the
redisposition of people and polities over the landscape.

The present study makes use of early contact-period accounts to work backward into the past, toward the reconstruction of the record and causes of political change in the prehistoric Mississippian chiefdoms we observe archaeologically. Critical to such an analysis, of course, is the reliability of the descriptions of native life provided by these early accounts. Do they indeed describe pristine societies, or had significant changes already occurred by the time the first explorers entered the interior? When De Soto arrived at Cofitachequi in 1540, we have seen that he found artifacts presumably from the 1526 Ayllón colony in the temples and was told that there had been disease in the land, depopulating whole towns and villages (Elvas in Robertson 1993:83; see also Bourne 1904, 1:66). Furthermore, when the De Luna expedition reached Coosa in 1560, the powerful chiefdom De Soto had encountered was much reduced in size and was having trouble exacting tribute from its neighbors.

The effects of contact and introduced diseases upon native populations in the Southeast have received considerable attention in recent years (e.g., Dobyns 1983; Milner 1980; Ramenofsky 1987, 1990; M. Smith 1987). That marked social and demographic change occurred following contact is widely accepted, although the rate at which this change occurred remains the subject of contentious debate. Marvin Smith (1987:143–47) has shown that pronounced depopulation and organizational change were occurring among the Mississippian chiefdoms of the interior Southeast as early as 1540 to 1565, although the greatest changes, including the collapse of chiefdom-level political structures, appear to have occurred from 1565 to 1600 and certainly by 1600 to 1630. Thus even the earliest accounts of the region's chiefdoms, particularly of societies near coastal areas, such as Cofitachequi and Apalachee, undoubtedly reflect, to some unknown extent, the effects of contact. These effects do not appear to have been pronounced during the first few decades of contact, however, and polities in the interior Southeast may have remained more or less unchanged for up to a half-century following initial European landfall in the early 1500s. Polities such as Coosa and Casqui, which were encountered during the De Soto expedition, may, therefore, reflect near-pristine Mississippian societies, perhaps the best descriptions of such societies we are ever likely to have. By the time of the subsequent De Luna and Pardo expeditions in the 1560s, however, it is clear that marked changes had occurred throughout the region, and accounts from this point onward must be viewed with suspicion.

In spite of these difficulties, early historic accounts of chiefdoms in the southeastern United States can, when interpreted with care, tell us a great deal about life in these societies, as well as provide clues to patterns and processes of change. The ethnohistoric record, above all, shows that our theoretical expectations about both the existence and causes of cycling in the region's chiefdoms are sustained. The early historic records thus contain observations that can be used to help refine and evaluate this as well as other models of chiefdom development. While providing rich detail about life in these societies, the ethnohistoric record also highlights the importance of archaeological research. This is because the existing ethnohistoric accounts are, with few exceptions, essentially synchronic. While the foundations of political authority are indicated and individual episodes of change sometimes described in graphic detail, long-term processes and consequences are only suggested. The examination of cycling in these societies, both during the prehistoric and early historic eras, accordingly, *must* proceed using both ethnohistoric and archaeological evidence, the strategy that comprises the remainder of this study. Clues to understanding the concept of cycling derived from ethnohistoric research are important guides; however, we must now turn to the archaeological record to evaluate evidence for political change and cycling in the late prehistoric southeastern United States.

4

Mississippian Political Change

Evidence from Archaeological Research

During the interval from circa A.D. 900 to 1600, a complex and changing constellation of chiefdom-level societies occupied much of the southeastern United States. Called the Mississippian culture, after the central Mississippi River valley, where extensive remains from this culture were identified in the 19th century, this way of life was characterized by sedentary communities, intensive maize agriculture, platform mounds, and a ranked hierarchical society. The subsistence economy was based on the intensive utilization of both cultigens and wild plant and animal resources, and major settlements were located, for the most part, on the terraces and levees of major drainages.

The Mississippian archaeological record exhibits numerous examples of the emergence, expansion, and decline of chiefly polities, in a complex mosaic of shifting power relationships. As a result, the late prehistoric and early historic archaeological record from the region forms, as one researcher has put it, "one of the world's major observational laboratories for the study of pristine evolution . . . of complex societies" (House 1982:37). In this chapter, archaeological evidence for cycling in Mississippian societies is examined, along with the procedures by which the process may be investigated. Critical to such research is understanding how chiefdom societies and patterns of organizational change in these societies are recognized archaeologically.

Definitions of Mississippian Culture

In recent years, definitions of Mississippian culture have appeared that have come to be widely accepted by researchers working with these societies. According to Griffin (1967:189), Mississippian "is used to refer to the wide variety of adaptations made by societies which developed a dependence upon agriculture for their basic, storable food supply." While the degree of dependence upon agriculture varies markedly over the region, there is little doubt that intensive, agriculturally based food production was present in most of the societies identified as Mississippian. The emphasis on subsistence that characterizes this definition, however, was soon found to be unsatisfactory (Griffin 1978). During the late prehistoric period a number of societies present in the Eastern Woodlands, such as the Iroquois, had intensive agriculture yet lacked many of the attributes traditionally assigned to the Mississippian, such as social stratification, mound building, or, in some cases, the use of shell-tempered pottery. Other societies with some or all of these Mississippian attributes, in contrast, have produced little evidence for a reliance on intensive agriculture. This is particularly true in coastal settings, where marine resources appear to have been quite important (e.g., Pearson 1978; Widmer 1988).

In an attempt to address these concerns, Bruce Smith (1978:486, 488) proposed a somewhat more specific definition of Mississippian, encompassing populations with:

> A ranked form of social organization, and [who] had developed a specific complex adaptation to linear, environmentally circumscribed floodplain habitat zones. . . . The location of almost any Mississippian settlement within a floodplain habitat zone can, to a great extent, be generally explained as a result of two energy-capture factors:
>
> 1. The availability of well-drained, easily tilled, energy-subsidized natural levee soils suitable for horticultural garden plots.
> 2. Easy access to the rich protein resources of fish and waterfowl in channel-remnant oxbow lakes.

While less monolithic a definition than Griffin's, the definition was again directed primarily to subsistence concerns, excepting only the qualification that these societies were characterized by a rank form of social organization (after Fried 1967:109ff). More seriously, objections were raised by researchers working with what appeared to be Mississippian societies occupying areas outside of circumscribed oxbow floodplain microenvironments, such as the Apalachee, some of the Caddo, and many of the societies along the lower Atlantic and Gulf coasts, as seen in figure 11 (Shapiro 1986).

To accommodate this problem and in recognition of the considerable variability that existed within these societies, Griffin (1985:63) revised and considerably expanded his definition of Mississippian to encompass those societies within the Eastern Woodlands that:

1. Developed many cultural innovations over much of the culturally defined Southeast between A.D. 700 and 900.
2. Added these disparate innovations to local cultural inventories by contact between neighboring and distant groups.
3. Increased in population, resulting from an augmented energy input from a more efficient agronomy.
4. Constructed planned permanent towns and ceremonial centers, villages, and subsidiary support hamlets, farmsteads, and other extractive camps.

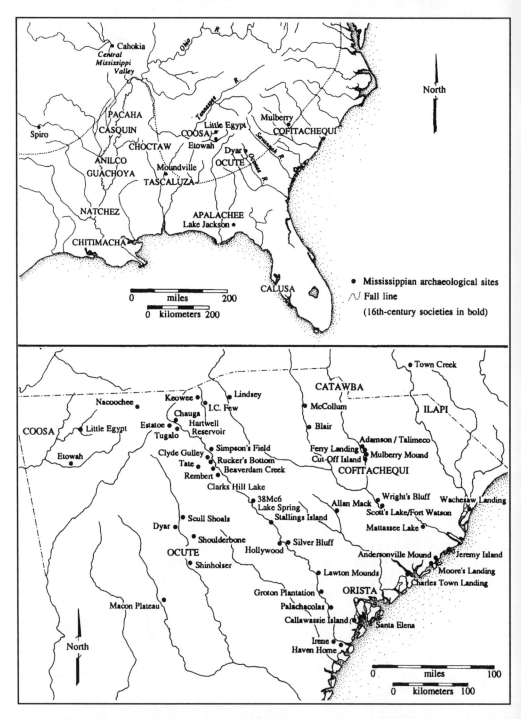

Figure 11 Mississippian Archaeological Sites and 16th-century Societies in the Southeastern United States and in the Vicinity of Georgia and the Carolinas. (Top, reprinted from Anderson 1994, courtesy Cambridge University Press)

5. Had regional and temporal variations of a hierarchical social, political, and religious structure.

6. Participated in an area-wide belief system that integrated and empha- sized the complex interaction of the spirit world and man, and ritualized these concepts in an elaborate symbolic iconography on marine shells, copper, ceramics, and stone.

7. Had an extensive trade network of rivers and trails, over which manu- factured symbolic and mundane items and raw materials were moved either to neighboring or distant societies.

8. Reached an area-wide cultural crest between 1200 and 1500, and slowly receded to less formally organized and controlled groups of the post- 1700 colonial period.

While minor disagreement may exist on specific points, such as the prevalence of long-distance trade or the importance of shared religious beliefs, Griffin's definition reflects a general consensus among scholars working within the region about what constitutes Mississippian culture. This definition, however, while certainly accurate and appropriate, is quite general in scope. To accommodate the interests of the present re- search, which focuses on the organizational properties of these societies, some reformulation and narrowing of the definition is proposed. Accept- ing the regional context and subsuming the criteria advanced by Griffin, this study considers Mississippian societies to be multicommunity polities characterized by one or two decision-making levels above the local com- munity and administered by hereditary elites. This also serves as a useful definition of chiefdom societies in general.

The Archaeological Recognition of Chiefdoms

To examine cycling in chiefdoms archaeologically, the methods by which these kinds of societies are identified warrant consideration. This is because many of the attributes used to identify chiefdoms are also those that must be considered when studying organizational change. A number of authors have advanced specific attributes and archaeological correlates of chiefdoms (e.g., Creamer and Haas 1985:742–43; Earle 1987; Peebles and Kus 1977; Renfrew 1973; Wright 1984). How these criteria have been used in the southeastern United States is instructive. Peebles and Kus (1977:431– 33), for example, have proposed five attributes of chiefdoms, which they examined using data from the Moundville chiefdom of west-central Ala- bama. These attributes, encompassing aspects of mortuary behavior, settlement hierarchy, subsistence production, craft specialization, long- distance prestige goods exchange, and organizational responses to exter- nal stimuli, are listed in table 1, along with a brief discussion of methods advanced for their investigation.

Table 1. Attributes of Chiefdom Societies (Adopted from Peebles and Kus 1977:431–33)

---

(1) *The presence of ascribed social ranking.* This is identified by differentiating ascribed or superordinate status dimensions from achieved or subordinate status. The former is social position that is genealogically determined; the latter, social position earned through personal accomplishment, and generally dependent upon age, sex, and individual capabilities. These status dimensions are resolvable through analyses of mortuary behavior, Peebles and Kus argued, with specific archaeological correlates for the presence of a system of social ranking, including (a) markedly different and distinctive energy expenditures associated with interments of different ranks, (b) overlap in the occurrence of items marking achieved status, but little or no overlap in the occurrence of markers of ascribed status, and (c) a marked drop in the number of individuals occupying successively higher social ranks.

(2) *The presence of "a hierarchy of settlement types and sizes," with the corollary that "the position of a settlement in the hierarchy should reflect its position in the regulatory and ritual network."* Resolution of settlement hierarchies would entail analyses of site type and size, geographic dispersion, and relation to ceremonial facilities. Specific archaeological correlates advanced included the presence of a multilevel site hierarchy, with clusters of lower-order sites located within fixed territories around higher-order civic/ceremonial centers.

(3) *The location of settlements in areas that ensure "a high degree of local subsistence autonomy," ostensibly to reduce administrative burden.* Choice of this attribute followed from a rejection of Service's (1971) hypothesis that extensive redistribution of subsistence goods was a hallmark of chiefdoms. This necessitated revision of the perspective that individual communities within chiefdoms were highly interdependent. The resolution of subsistence autonomy, it was suggested, could be addressed through the careful examination of the resource potential of both sites and territories. No specific archaeological correlates were advanced, although tabulating the number and diversity of resource zones within individual site territories was one method suggested to indicate how the subject might be approached (e.g., Renfrew 1973; Sanders and Marino 1970; Sanders and Price 1968).

(4) *The presence of organized productive activities that "transcend the basic household group," specifically monumental construction and "part-time craft specialization, usually coupled with intersocietal trade."* Specific archaeological correlates advanced included the presence of monumental architecture and evidence for the manufacture and distribution of craft goods from a limited number of locations, and on an interhousehold or intercommunity level rather than at the level of an individual household or craftsperson.

(5) *Evidence for a direct relationship between chiefly organizational complexity and the strength and variety of environmental (cultural and natural) perturbations requiring administrative attention.* Specific archaeological correlates included evidence for society-wide change in social organization, settlement pattern, trading relationships, warfare, and food production and storage, which could be associated with changes in climate, regional political structure, or regional trade networks. The greater the frequency, amplitude, and duration of the perturbation, the greater the response.

To accommodate research directed to resolving organizational properties of chiefdoms, particularly the recognition of decision-making apparatus in the more complex of these social forms, something incompletely
developed by Peebles and Kus, Wright (1984:43–44) proposed three additional archaeological correlates of complex chiefdoms:

1. Settlement hierarchy: The center of each polity in a network of interacting complex chiefdoms, usually the seat of the paramount, will become
   both larger than and architecturally differentiated from ordinary chiefly
   centers, both physically accommodating the paramount's following and
   providing a focus for major social rituals. There will thus be two levels
   of settlement hierarchy above the level of producer communities. . . .

2. Residential segregation: While architecturally differentiated housing,
   albeit without vastly greater labor inputs, characterizes all societies with
   ascriptively higher-ranking domestic units, in complex chiefdoms with
   a discrete noble class there will be segregation by neighborhoods or in
   special communities of elite residences. We do not, however, expect
   palaces, built with mass labor inputs and providing spaces for specialized administrative activity.

3. Mortuary segregation: In addition to the more complex burial programs
   afforded ascriptively ranked individuals in simpler chiefdoms, we can
   expect that the noble dead will be isolated in death, as they were in life,
   close to areas of major ritual display.

Although Wright's associated analyses were directed to the complex
prestate polities of the Deh Luran and Susiana plains of southwestern Iran,
his emphasis on the archaeological recognition of decision-making levels
has been widely adopted by archaeologists working with chiefdom societies in the southeastern United States.

The Archaeological Analysis of Political Change
in the Late Prehistoric Southeast

Once chiefdoms have been recognized in the archaeological record, the
next step in the study of cycling is the analysis of change in their organizational structures over time. As described in chapter 3, an extensive body of
ethnohistoric data exists documenting the existence of a number of geographically extensive, complex chiefdoms in the Southeast at the time of
initial European contact during the 16th century. This information serves
as a benchmark for archaeological analyses of earlier, precontact Mississippian societies in the region, a procedure much like the direct historical
approach used by earlier generations of anthropologists (Steward 1942). In
the following sections methods are reviewed by which political organization and long-term change have been examined archaeologically in the
late prehistoric Southeast, with particular attention to work in Georgia and
the Carolinas.

Regional Political Structure

Attempts to delimit cultural and political structure across the South-east using archaeological evidence date back to the turn of the century, when Holmes (1903:130–33) first defined the South Appalachian tradition. Throughout the 1880s and 1890s, Holmes examined the ceramic artifacts recovered from throughout the Eastern Woodlands by the excavations of the Mound Division, and in 1903, his monumental synthesis of these remains, entitled *Aboriginal Pottery of the Eastern United States,* appeared as the 20th Annual Report of the Bureau of American Ethnology. In it Holmes appraised the ceramics from the general Georgia–South Carolina area with those recovered from elsewhere in the East. A major contribution was the recognition that many of the ceramics from this "South Appalachian" area were characterized by a distinctive, stamped exterior finish, which in turn suggested a common background: "A culture of somewhat greater marked characteristics comprises the states of Georgia, South Carolina, and contiguous portions of Alabama, Florida, North Carolina, and Tennes-see. . . . [T]he ceramic phenomena of this province include one great group of products to which has been given the name South Appalachian stamped ware. . . . [T]his stamped pottery is obtained from mounds, graves of several classes, village sites, and shell heaps. . . . [T]he remarkable style of decoration, more than other features, characterizes this pottery. Elabo-rately figured stamps were rarely used elsewhere" (130–33). Holmes's recognition of a South Appalachian cultural province characterized by a distinctive ceramic tradition stands as a major step toward the under-standing of the later prehistory of the region. It was not until 1967, in a synthesis of eastern North American prehistory, however, that Griffin (1967:185) formally noted the existence of a South Appalachian geo-graphic variant of Mississippian. Soon thereafter, Ferguson (1971) pro-duced a synthesis of the Mississippian research undertaken to that time in the South Appalachian area, and again similarities in assemblages were noted. In recent years, it has been recognized that these similarities reflect a long history of interaction among the societies in this area, albeit at varying levels of intensity.

Recognition of geographic and temporal variants within the South Appalachian Mississippian tradition dates from the WPA-sponsored work of the late 1930s, when major site/ceramic complexes such as Etowah, Savannah, and Lamar were recognized in Georgia, assemblages corre-sponding roughly in time with the Early, Middle, and Late Mississippian periods, which in this area range from circa A.D. 1000 to 1200, 1200 to 1400, and 1400 to 1600, respectively (Caldwell and Waring 1939a, 1939b; Fairbanks 1950; Wauchope 1948, 1950). In the early 1950s, Caldwell (1974a:88), in a discussion of ceramics from the Mulberry mound group near Camden, South Carolina, which had been partially examined by Caldwell and Kelly in 1952, noted that "the Lamaroid sequence in South

Carolina is sufficiently different from the various Lamar sequences of Georgia to be considered a separate ceramic tradition." In a refinement of this observation, Reid (1965, 1967) noted close similarities in Mississippian ceramic assemblages over the South Carolina area, based on an inspection of materials from the widely separated Town Creek, Hollywood, and Irene sites. This tradition was equated with the Pee Dee series, originally defined at Town Creek site in Piedmont North Carolina (Coe 1952; Reid 1967).

In the early 1970s, South (1973) posited the existence of a distinctive Chicora ceramic horizon in the Carolinas and extreme eastern Georgia, encompassing centers such as Town Creek, Charles Town Landing, Fort Watson, Hollywood, Mulberry, and Irene. Reed punctations, nodes and pellets placed below the vessel lip, and classic Pee Dee series rim decorations were the key ceramic attributes defining this horizon. No broad-scale comparative analyses of Mississippian ceramics have been conducted in South Carolina in recent years prior to the present study, although some work has appeared directed to the resolution of ceramic sequences for the upper Wateree and lower Santee River valleys (e.g., Anderson 1982; DePratter and Judge 1990:56–58). In Georgia, in contrast, under the leadership of David Hally, detailed comparative analyses of ceramic assemblages from large numbers of Mississippian sites have occurred, with the result that distinctive, tightly dated phases can be recognized in many areas (Hally and Rudolph 1986; Hally and Langford 1988). In some cases, the assemblage differences that have been recognized do appear to reflect the extent or influence of specific prehistoric societies (e.g., see particularly Hally, Smith, and Langford 1990).

Locational analyses have proved an effective alternative means of examining regional political structure. The distribution of Mississippian mound centers over the region has been extensively examined, and these sites are commonly found to occur in particular settings and at regular distances from one another. Ferguson (1975), who was the first to explore mound spacing in the South Appalachian area, examined the distances between the then-known Mississippian mound sites in eastern Georgia and the Carolinas, finding several clusters of centers that were inferred to reflect closely related societies (figure 12). Interestingly, ties between the mound sites along the central Oconee and central Savannah rivers, which flow in close proximity to each other in the Piedmont, were suggested by this analysis. Mississippian populations along the Savannah River may have moved into the Oconee River basin during the 15th century (see chapter 8), a relocation that would have been facilitated by possible relationships between these societies, as hinted in the spacing of the centers.

In a subsequent, now classic study, M. Smith and Kowalewski (1980) examined the distribution of mound centers along the upper Oconee River in Georgia and found that all were between 41 and 47 kilometers apart.

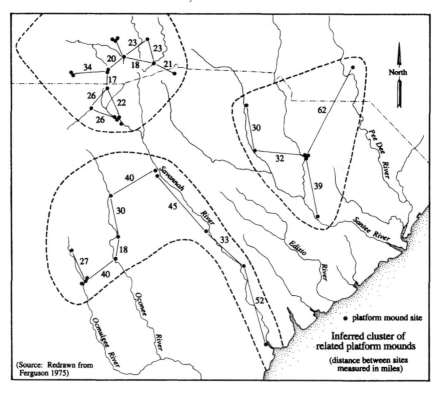

Figure 12   Nearest Neighbor Analysis of Mississippian Mound Centers in Eastern Georgia and the Carolinas. (Courtesy Leland G. Ferguson)

This striking distributional patterning was used to infer the existence of a complex Mississippian chiefdom or province in the area, an inference that received resounding support a few years later when the area was shown to be the probable location of the province of Ocute encountered by De Soto in the mid-16th century (DePratter, Hudson, and Smith 1983; Hudson, Smith, and DePratter 1984). Although the mound centers of the upper Oconee have since been shown to have been intermittently occupied over the course of the Mississippian, this differential occupation does appear to reflect shifting power relationships within a larger, periodically integrated province-level settlement and political system (M. Williams and Shapiro 1987). Most recently, in another classic study, Hally (1987, 1993; Hally and Langford 1988; Hally, Smith, and Langford 1990) has shown that Mississippian centers in northwestern Georgia were separated from one another by fairly regular intervals, and that subsidiary communities around the centers themselves were typically at distances of no more than 10 to 15 kilometers (see discussion of the Coosa polity, below).

As these examples indicate, some of the most exciting work directed to the resolution of regional political structure has come from the linkage of ethnohistory and archaeology. In recent years, a concerted effort has been made in the South Appalachian area to equate archaeological sites and assemblages with locations and events described in early historic accounts, notably those of the De Soto, De Luna, and Pardo expeditions. Hally and his colleagues have been examining archaeological evidence from the province of Coosa (in Hally and Rudolph 1986:77–78; Hally and Langford 1988; Hally, Smith, and Langford 1990; Hudson et al. 1985:726–32), and DePratter and Judge (1990; see also DePratter 1989 and Judge 1987) have made similar efforts with materials from sites linked to Cofitachequi. A number of scholars have also been examining the archaeological record in the area of Ocute (e.g., Kowalewski and Hatch 1991; Kowalewski and Williams 1989; M. Williams 1983, 1988, 1990a, 1990b; M. Williams and Shapiro 1986, 1987, 1990a).

Settlement and Decision-making Hierarchies

The resolution of Mississippian settlement patterns using archaeological data was a major focus for research across the Eastern Woodlands throughout the 1970s (e.g., Bruce Smith 1978). This subject has seen renewed attention in recent years, in part because of attempts to equate Late Mississippian archaeological sites across the region with towns and provinces identified in early historic accounts (e.g., Hally, Smith, and Langford 1990; Levy, May, and Moore 1990; P. Morse and Morse 1990). Archaeological settlement studies have typically been directed to the creation of settlement hierarchies based on measures of site size or complexity, such as surface area, number and size of mounds, or assemblage density or diversity. Locational and environmental analyses sometimes accompany these efforts, in an attempt to predict site occurrence in the landscape (e.g., Brose and Percy 1978; Davis, Kimball, and Baden 1982; Pearson 1978). The existence of settlement hierarchies is sometimes then used to infer not only political relationships, such as primary and secondary centers in complex chiefdoms, but also the status and relative contribution of individual sites in tributary economies (e.g., Peebles 1978; Steponaitis 1978, 1981).

The most common methods used by Mississippian researchers to demonstrate the presence of settlement hierarchies typically focus on the overall incidence and geographic distribution of sites by size class. When site areas are plotted using rank size analyses, marked changes or points of inflection in the curve may indicate differing functional categories of settlements. Site categories, once defined, may then be illustrated using simple histograms giving the number of sites per defined size class (e.g., Johnson 1977, 1980; Lundmark 1984; P. Morse 1981). In an early analysis from the upper Oconee River valley, Lee (1977, 1978) used surface scatter size estimates to infer the existence during the Mississippian period of a three-level settlement hierarchy, consisting of large centers, villages, and hamlets. Using similar data, Pearson (1978) examined Mississippian settlement on Ossabaw Island, located at the mouth of the Ogeechee River in coastal Georgia, to infer the existence of a four-level hierarchy. Pearson's hierarchy was essentially identical to Lee's, differing only by the addition of a fourth and smallest special activity site class.

The use of surface data has fallen somewhat out of favor in the South Appalachian area in recent years. Since Lee's (1977) original analysis, extensive excavations have been conducted at a number of Mississippian sites in the upper Oconee River valley, much of it in conjunction with the construction of the Wallace Reservoir (P. Fish and Hally 1983). This work and comparable work in the nearby Russell Reservoir showed not only that a range of small, previously unrecognized special activity site types was present, but also that surface data were often unreliable for determining site size and function (Anderson and Joseph 1988; Shapiro 1983). Besides the need for caution in the use of surface data and the importance of detailed analyses of site function, another lesson learned from these exercises was the critical importance of having accurate, fine-grained chronologies capable of precisely dating components and hence delimiting approximately contemporaneous assemblages.

Recent settlement analyses undertaken in the South Appalachian area have been directed to resolving clusters of 16th-century sites that can be equated with early contact-era chiefdoms and, when comparable clusters of prehistoric sites are found, inferring the existence of similar polities. The most detailed work of this kind has been conducted in northwestern Georgia, where Hally and his colleagues have documented sites associated with the province of Coosa and have presumed earlier polities centered on sites such as Etowah (Hally 1989; Hally and Langford 1988; Hally, Smith, and Langford 1990). Thanks to this research, the spatial extent of the Coosa polity and its precursors are among the best delimited in the Eastern Woodlands.

Archaeological analyses directed to the resolution of decision-making hierarchies employing settlement data, as noted, typically equate site size classes with administrative levels. In analyses of political structures in prehistoric southeastern chiefdoms, paramount elites (caciques grandes or micos) are assumed to reside at the largest centers, that is, sites with the largest or greatest number of mounds or the largest surface extent. Lesser elites (micos or oratas) are assumed to have occupied the smaller, outlying centers and communities (or the centers of smaller chiefdoms). Finally, each village is assumed to have had one or more representatives of the ruling elite present (oratas). Burial/mortuary analyses directed to resolving status differences among the population is one method of determining whether or not individuals from superordinate decision-making groups were present at a site (J. Brown 1971; Milner 1984a; O'Shea 1984; Saxe 1970). Yet another way of determining the existence and nature of decision-making levels is to examine the occurrence of prestige goods on sites, under the assumption that the occurrence and amount of these items were related to the rank and importance of the elites living there in the regional political hierarchy (e.g., Peebles 1987a; Steponaitis 1991). Prestige goods flowing from a primary center in a Mississippian settlement system would presumably devolve primarily if not exclusively upon lesser elites in outlying settlements, rather than upon commoners (Welch 1991).

Analyses of both domestic and ceremonial architecture can also shed light on the nature of a decision-making hierarchy. If elites occupied larger structures that were spatially somewhat isolated from the commoner population, this would be evident in an examination of house size and location within and between communities. One trend that has been noted at a number of sites in the South Appalachian area is the replacement of earth lodges (actually earth-embanked structures that appear to have been council houses of some kind) by structures on platform mounds early in the Mississippian period. The replacement of earth lodges by platform/ temple mound complexes has been interpreted by J. Rudolph (1984) as reflecting broad changes in sociopolitical organization, specifically in the composition of groups permitted access to ceremonial facilities and hence to involvement in the decision-making process itself. As social stratification developed during the period of Mississippian emergence, presumed communal decision-making activity, once conducted in quasi-public forums in the earth lodges/council houses, was replaced by decision making by a much smaller group of elites resident on or with restricted access to structures on mounds. Platform mounds, as physically and symbolically elevated administrative/ceremonial centers, served to separate the elites that made use of them from the rest of the population, while simultaneously reinforcing their superior, sacred status.

DePratter (1983:207, 209, 1991a:163–65) has suggested that the presence of council houses in late prehistoric and early historic southeastern societies reflects consensus-based decision making characteristic of tribal-level groups or simple chiefdoms, and that their absence on Mississippian sites may indicate highly centralized authority structures. His argument is that:

> . . . as centralization developed in each area, there was a shift from control by councils (such as one might expect during the early stages of unification of kin-linked autonomous villages) toward more powerful chiefs deserving of mound residence, temple burials, and greatly increased social status.
> . . . By the time the Soto expedition passed through the Southeast in the 1540's, there were few if any councils or council houses operating in the chiefdoms visited. Instead, descriptions of or even mention of councils are rare and description of council houses are almost totally lacking. . . . By the eighteenth century, all of the southeastern chiefdoms had suffered periods

of decline, and only tribal level groups, sometimes organized into loose confederacies, were present (Swanton 1928a, 1928b, Hudson 1976). Detailed descriptions of council houses are provided for this time period by numerous writers. . . . This pattern of council house presence, disappearance, and later reappearance in the Southeast corresponds to the pattern of the rise, existence, and decline of chiefdoms being proposed here.

This argument is persuasive in broad outline. Many elite mound complexes in the South Appalachian area arose over earth-embanked structures or earth lodges, presumed communal social/ceremonial facilities. The few 16th-century accounts that do contain descriptions of council houses, furthermore, come from relatively simple coastal groups, where elite power appears to have been fairly limited. Finally, use of council houses is undeniably widespread during the later historic period, following the collapse of chiefdom organization over much of the region, among the Cherokee, Creek, and other groups.

How commoners fit into the administrative and political life of southeastern Mississippian society has received little investigation. Typically assumed to be pawns of the elite, with little say or influence, the commoners may actually have had much greater power, particularly in local matters. Some form of communal decision making almost certainly had to characterize every Mississippian community, if for no other reason than to provide assent to the decisions of the elite. Village-level administration, even in complex Mississippian chiefdoms, may have had to incorporate the rank and file in decision making in some fashion, perhaps under an orata, to conduct everyday life in an orderly fashion. The presence of communal decision-making bodies may have helped alleviate tensions and jealousies arising from the marked patterns of social inequality that characterized the more stratified chiefdoms. Local autonomy was also probably greater in villages located at some distance away from major centers and hence out from under the immediate control of the elites at those sites. The communal buildings so well documented in the later historic era may thus have been an aspect of ordinary Mississippian village life all along, rather than evidence of degeneration from a more complex organizational form. The nature of South Appalachian Mississippian archaeological research, which has focused primarily on mound sites with only minimal excavation in village areas, means resolution of this problem will have to await the completion of a great deal more fieldwork in village contexts. As we shall see, work in the Savannah River basin, at the Rucker's Bottom village site (chapters 5 and 8), provides some information about the nature of decision making and political control in subsidiary support communities.

Tributary Networks

The analysis of political economy, and specifically tributary networks, has received a great deal of attention in the Southeast in recent years. The most extensive and innovative of this work has been conducted with data from the Moundville chiefdom of west-central Alabama and has focused on relationships among site size, location, and surrounding agricultural productivity to patterns of tribute flow (Bozeman 1982; Peebles 1978, 1986, 1987a, 1987b; Steponaitis 1978, 1991; Welch 1991). During the initial development of the Moundville chiefdom, settlement size was closely correlated with the agricultural productivity of the surrounding terrain, measured using the occurrence of prime agricultural soils in catchment increments around each site in the settlement hierarchy (Bozeman 1982; Peebles 1978:400–410). As the chiefdom expanded, the population at Moundville rapidly exceeded its local catchment productivity, necessitating provisioning from surrounding, subsidiary communities. The extent of this provisioning, or subsistence goods produced by an outlying site that were submitted as tribute, could be calculated by comparing the size of the Moundville center's population with the size that could be supported by its local catchment. All personnel beyond the figure that could be provisioned locally had to be supported through external tribute (Steponaitis 1978, 1981). Because the agricultural production of outlying communities had to go to maintaining the Moundville center, surplus generation and mobilization were absolutely essential to the continued operation of this society.

How the tributary/political economy shaped settlement size and distribution has also been examined at Moundville. Steponaitis (1978:440–49) demonstrated that secondary centers in the chiefdom were strategically located to maximize the collection and flow of tribute. As Moundville grew in power, in fact, other centers in the Black Warrior River valley may have been relocated to increase the efficiency of this operation. The Moundville case suggests that the size of outlying centers in complex chiefdoms may be directly related to the proximity of the paramount center. Mounds at secondary centers closest to Moundville, for example, were appreciably smaller than mounds in centers at greater distances. This pattern was interpreted in terms of the logistics of operating a tributary economy. Centers closest to the paramount center were under more direct control and had the greatest tributary demands placed upon them, reducing the amount of surplus available to maintain local ceremonial facilities and elites. Populations at centers at a greater distance had greater control over their surplus and, exercising greater autonomy, were able to devote more effort to the construction of ceremonial or other site facilities. The number of elites and the size of facilities at outlying centers were also unquestionably related to the extent to which the primary center co-opted these ceremonial and administrative functions.

Not only was the regular production of agricultural surplus essential to the maintenance of an elite, who had to be supported, along with their families and retinues, but also means had to have been available for the efficient use of this surplus. Elite control of storage was thus as important as control of production. The kinds of crops or other subsistence goods that are available for storage, their periodicity of availability, and storage preservation technology itself will place constraints on how surplus is defined (Burns 1983). The number, size, and efficiency of storage facilities may thus have placed constraints on decision-making hierarchies. Comparing the size and locations of storage and living areas are means archaeologists have used to delimit how surplus was controlled (D'Altroy and Earle 1985; Lightfoot 1987:50).

Patterns of tribute flow can also be measured through the analysis of paleosubsistence evidence. A number of studies have shown that the health status of individuals in chiefdoms is directly related to food consumption patterns, specifically the amounts and kinds of food commoners had or the elite appropriated for their own use (e.g., Blakely and Beck 1981; Hatch 1987; Milner 1990; Powell 1988, 1992). The study of human skeletal remains can provide evidence about past diet, although in some cases this evidence may be ambiguous or open to multiple interpretations, requiring care in its use (Armelagos and Hill 1990; Huss-Ashmore, Goodman, and Armelagos 1982; Klepinger 1984; Wing and Brown 1979). Trace element and stable carbon and nitrogen isotope analyses, for example, offer the potential for identifying fairly specific dietary constituents. Stable carbon isotope analysis has been used in a number of areas of eastern North America and has shown that maize did not become an important source of food until the Early Mississippian period (Bender, Baerreis, and Steventon 1981; Buikstra 1991; Larsen et al. 1992; Lynott et al. 1986; Rose, Marks, and Tieszen 1991; Van der Merwe and Vogel 1978).

Stable isotope analysis proceeds by examining how differing plant and animal types incorporate differing isotopes of carbon into their system (Huss-Ashmore, Goodman, and Armelagos 1982:452–55; Larsen et al. 1992; Schwarcz and Schoeninger 1991). Two photosynthetic pathways are important with regard to the archaeological evaluation of maize in prehistoric diet, called C3 and C4. Most of the plant species in temperate North America are C3 plants, while maize, a tropical cultigen, is a C4 plant. Skeletal series showing a heavy utilization of C4 sources may thus indicate regular maize or other tropical plant consumption. Distinctive stable carbon and nitrogen isotope ratios also occur in marine and terrestrial resources and can indicate a reliance on one or the other, although, again, caution must be used (Larsen et al. 1992; Schoeninger et al. 1990; Seally and van der Merwe 1985).

Trace element analyses provide a more general indicator of diet, albeit one highly susceptible to the confounding effects of diagenesis. Zinc and copper values tend to be higher in skeletal remains of populations where meat intake was high in life, while strontium, manganese, and magnesium are higher in populations where vegetable foods were important (Huss-Ashmore, Goodman, and Armelagos 1982:450–52). Strontium values are higher in marine mollusks, crustaceans, and vertebrates (and in human populations that eat them) than in terrestrial animals, so like stable carbon isotope analysis, trace element analyses can also indicate extent of marine/terrestrial resource utilization. Trace element analyses have been used in a number of areas within the Eastern Woodlands to investigate sex- and status-related differences in diet, as well as changes in dietary patterns (Ambrose 1987; Cohen and Armelagos 1984; Gilbert 1985; Lambert, Szpunar, and Buikstra 1979; Larsen 1987; Larsen et al. 1992; Rose, Marks, and Tieszen 1991; Schoeninger et al. 1990).

Trace element analyses suggested, for example, that high-status individuals in the Moundville II/III chiefdom had more meat in their diet than did commoners (Peebles and Schoeninger 1981; Powell 1988), although little evidence for dietary stress was observed in any social segment (Peebles 1987a:29–31). The general health of the succeeding largely egalitarian Alabama River–phase populations, following the collapse of the Moundville chiefdom, was in marked contrast, with approximately half the individuals evincing evidence for severe dietary stress (Hill 1979, 1981; Peebles 1987a:31; Powell 1991). Effective regional political integration appears to have increased local populations' ability to dampen resource fluctuations through the allocation of resources from over a large area (although whether redistribution encompassed all members of society is unknown). The collapse of a complex chiefdom could thus have led to a much poorer standard of living for all members of society, and not just elites.

More indirect indicators of diet and the relative effectiveness of prehistoric provisioning strategies may also be obtained from skeletal remains. The incidence and severity of dietary stress during an individual's life can be approximated through examination of Harris lines, enamel hypoplasia, Wilson bands, evidence for porotic hyperostosis, dental attrition or decay, infectious lesions, osteoporosis, evidence for delayed growth or maturation, dental asymmetry, dental malocclusion and crowding, and metacarpal notching (Huss-Ashmore, Goodman, and Armelagos 1982). Measures of skeletal robusticity and trauma can indicate the workload and insults an individual was exposed to in life. Mortality patterns within skeletal population samples, such as life expectancy curves, can also provide a general indicator of subsistence or other stress. Goodman et al. (1984) used many of these measures, as well as indicators of the severity of infection at age of death and mortality information, for example, to examine changing patterns of stress in Late Woodland, Early Mississippian, and Late Mississippian populations at Dickson Mounds, Illinois. Increased stress loads, which were attributed to the subservient position of the site in a tributary hierarchy, were documented in the latter occupations. Similar results were obtained from analyses of skeletal remains along the upper Savannah River, from the Beaverdam Creek mound and Rucker's Bottom sites, a small Mississippian ceremonial center and a nearby tributary village, respectively (chapter 8).

Chiefdoms may be viewed as centralized risk-management organizations, which Hatch (1987:10) has described as "complex, problem-solving cultural systems that, in evolutionary terms, have a selective advantage [over less rigidly structured societies] through their ability to dampen internal and external stress" (see also Peebles 1987a:31; Peebles and Kus 1977). How successful they were may be reflected in the skeletal health of their constituent populations. A classic example of this type of analysis was conducted by Hatch (1974, 1976, 1987) using data from 1,284 burials at 19 sites of the Late Mississippian Dallas culture of eastern Tennessee. The Dallas societies were small, simple chiefdoms for the most part, located on the margins of the Mississippian area. Dallas mound interments were characterized by nonutilitarian prestige goods, described as "copper earspools and headdresses, ceremonial axes, painted and modeled pottery forms, and imported shell ornaments" (Hatch 1987:11). Adult males were the most common interments in the mounds, although individuals of all ages and both sexes were present, suggesting an ascribed social class. Burials with utilitarian grave goods, in contrast, tended to occur in village areas. Adult females and subadults were found in or near houses, commonly buried with simple shell jewelry and utilitarian ceramics, while adult males in village areas were interred with personal or utilitarian items, typically pipes, woodworking tools, and flint-knapping tools (10–11).

On the average, Dallas mound populations tended to be taller than villagers, suggesting a better diet (Hatch and Willey 1974). Analyses of tibia and femur cortical thickness, which are thought to reflect the amount of work-related stress an individual underwent in life, indicated that villagers were more physically active than individuals interred in mounds (Hatch, Willey, and Hunt 1983). This suggested that the elite stratum of Dallas society was exempted from arduous activity, such as farming or corvee labor, that is, communal construction projects such as erecting mounds, fortification lines, or community buildings. An analysis of childhood (defined as individuals from infancy to eight years in age) growth arrest, or Harris lines, in Dallas populations indicated greater prevalence among village children than in comparable mound populations, further evidence that higher-status individuals probably enjoyed a better or more regular diet. Surprisingly, however, high-status males interred in the mound had a higher incidence of growth arrest lines incurred during adolescence (defined as individuals from 8 to 16 years in age) than their village counterparts, a finding equated with participation in an arduous, probably ritually based training regimen (Hatch 1987:13). Dietary differences between elites and commoners in Dallas society, specifically in patterns of meat and vegetable consumption, were also documented through trace element analyses. Hatch and Geidel (1985:13) observed "statistically significant concentrations of those trace elements associated with a vegetable-rich diet in the village burial population, especially among subadults. Mound associated burials showed evidence of a more well-rounded diet." Even within the Dallas elite subsample, dietary differences may have been occurring, since the tallest burials tended to occur in the center of mounds (Hatch 1987:12). All of these findings suggest that diet improved with status in the simple chiefdoms that made up Dallas society.

Population health in Mississippian chiefdoms, as suggested previously, also appears to have been related to the degree of regional political centralization (Hatch 1987; Powell 1991:50). At both Etowah (Blakely and Beck 1981) and Moundville (Powell 1988), only minimal health differences were observed between higher- and lower-status groups. Hatch (1987:14), in a comparative analysis of Etowah, Moundville, and Dallas skeletal populations, has concluded that the Moundville and Etowah chiefdoms "provisioned their populations with a uniformly more adequate diet than did Dallas communities. One of the virtues of greater organizational complexity in Mississippian times appears to have been the ability to satisfy the basic needs of its members—be they related to diet, external resources, or protection from competing neighbors. Dallas villages, being smaller and organizationally less sophisticated, were likely to have been more susceptible to the predations of outsiders and interruptions in external supplies, as well as more frequently faced with the problem of how to allocate scarce but nutritionally significant food supplies. The answer here was predictable—let the lower ranks suffer first." These observations are important to the study of political change in Mississippian chiefdoms, since they indicate that the relative health of an archaeological skeletal population may provide clues about regional political organization.

Analyses of paleobotanical and zooarchaeological remains from archaeological sites can also indicate probable provisioning patterns and, from these, the position of sites and individuals in tributary networks and administrative hierarchies. The incidence of specific animal body parts within and between sites, measured using skeletal elements, can indicate how meat was distributed and consumed by various segments of the population. In some southeastern Mississippian societies, evidence has been found to suggest that elites were requisitioning prime cuts of meat, or specific species, for their own use (L. Kelly 1979:16; Scott 1982, 1983). At the late prehistoric/early historic Toqua site in eastern Tennessee, for example, faunal analyses by Bogan (1980) demonstrated that higher-status residential precincts received better cuts and a greater variety of meat. At the same site, Parham and Scott (1980) found that village (i.e., commoner) subadults suffered from porotic hyperostosis, a condition probably resulting from a meat-poor diet. Such a diet might also explain the greater frequency of Harris lines noted in Toqua village as opposed to mound populations (Hatch 1987:13). However, the presence of zooarchaeological remains in the archaeological record does not unequivocally indicate human consumption (barring coprolite evidence), since some species may have been used for purposes other than subsistence. Care must always be taken in the analysis of paleosubsistence data to eliminate possible sources of analytical error, by accounting for formation processes, including taphonomic factors, and resolving through independent means whether and how recovered species were utilized.

A most recent and innovative examination of Mississippian political economy has focused on ceramic vessel form and function, something quite different from more traditional uses of these artifacts for cultural identification and dating. In a series of papers, Hally (1983a, 1983b, 1984, 1986b) and Shapiro (1983, 1985a, 1985b, 1990) have explored the uses to which Mississippian vessels were put at mound, village, hamlet, and special activity sites in the central and northern Georgia area. Vessel form and use-wear analyses have been valuable in the resolution of intrasite activity areas and in determining the range of activities that occurred on particular sites. In an important illustration of the utility of this approach, Shapiro (1985a) demonstrated that large jars—possible communal or tribute storage vessels—were disproportionately represented in mound as opposed to village contexts at the Dyar site on the upper Oconee River in the central Georgia Piedmont. Elite control of surplus production, through the bulk storage of goods in mound temple complexes, may be indicated by this pattern (see also Blitz 1989, 1993a, 1993b).

Succession and Postmarital Residence

How chiefly succession occurred in prehistoric southeastern Mississippian societies is poorly understood, although it is possible to draw inferences from both the ethnohistoric and the archaeological record. Perhaps the most widely utilized method of exploring chiefly succession archaeologically, in the Southeast and elsewhere around the world, has been to examine the kind of public activities (i.e., episodes of monumental construction, ceremonial behavior, or mortuary presentations) associated with the interment of particular individuals (e.g., J. Brown 1971; Renfrew 1973, 1984). These analyses proceed under the assumption that a primary purpose of this kind of public behavior was the recognition and sanctification of the new leader—the linking of the successor with the power and sanctity of his or her predecessor—through the rebuilding, rededication, or interment of the old leader's symbols of power. In southeastern Mississippian society, as documented in chapter 3, mound stage construction, including the replacement and renewal of the leader's ancestral temple and/or place of residence, was sometimes associated with successional events.

A traditional method of examining succession in southeastern Mississippian society, accordingly, has been to examine the nature and frequency of construction stages and burials in temple mounds. These kinds of studies usually proceed by assuming that each new mound stage reflects a successional event, most probably the death of a chief and the literal elevation of his replacement to a place above society. Such an interpretation is supported by ethnohistoric accounts and from the archaeological record itself (DePratter 1983:179; Hally 1987, 1992; Schnell, Knight, and Schnell 1981:126–45; Waring 1968a:58–62, 66). If one divides the number of mound stages by the length of time the mound is assumed to have been in use, stage construction every 30 years or so is indicated at a number of sites in the South Appalachian area (table 2). This, probably not coincidentally, is about the duration of a generation and may indicate the average tenure of local chiefs or paramounts. Mound stage incidence (i.e., measured in terms of number of stages per century or, if available, more precise intervals) might indicate how often successional events occurred, while mound stage volume might provide clues about the size of the society, or at least of the power of the leader to mobilize labor, at each period of transition.

Knight (1986:678), alternatively, has argued that mound building was a product of communal/fertility cults, reflecting "a purely expressive act . . . a mortuary rite for the mound itself rather than for any individual . . . the symbolism of the earthen platform is that of an icon representative of earth, manipulated by periodic burial as a temporary means of achieving purification in the context of a communal rite of intensification." The comparatively infrequent occurrence of mound stage construction, however, on the order of once a generation or so at most examined sites, indicates that this activity was uncommon. While mound construction may have indeed been an intensification rite, I believe it most typically occurred in conjunction with the replacement of chiefly elites. Mound stage construction unquestionably had a profound ideological component, engendering communal participation in an activity directed to effacing evidence of the former chief, while simultaneously demonstrating and legitimizing the power of his successor. If the strength or necessity for legitimizing ideologies declined over the course of the Mississippian, as suggested in chapter 2, this would explain the diminished mound building observed in later Mississippian times.

The nature of chiefly succession can also be determined from other material remains, such as the quantity of prestige goods in circulation or the location of chiefly residences in relation to other symbols of elite power. The apparent relationship between prestige goods circulation and chiefly stability has been noted previously. Basically, according to this perspective, when the flow of these kind of goods declines or is inter-

Table 2. Number of Mound Stages and Estimated Occupation Spans at Selected Mississippian Sites in the South Appalachian Area

Site Number	Mound Group	Number of Stages	Period in Use	Years/ Stage	Phases of Occupation	Duration of Phase	References
9Mu102	Little Egypt, mound A	4	150	37.5	Little Egypt	1350–1500	Hally 1987: Figure 5; Hally and Langford 1988:68
40Mg31	Hiwassee Island	4	200	50	Dallas	1250–1450	T. Lewis and Kneberg 1946: Table 19
9Br1	Etowah, mound C	5	150	30	Late Etowah-Wilbanks	1200–1350	Hally and Langford 1988; King 1991a, 1991b
9Mu100	Sixtoe	2	100?	50?	Early Etowah (I/II)	1000–1100	A. Kelly et al. 1965; Hally 1987: Figure 5; Hally and Langford 1988:51
9Mu101	Bell Field	5–6?	150	25–30	(unnamed)	1300–1450?	A. Kelly 1970, 1972; Hally 1987: Figure 5; Hally and Langford 1988:62–63
9Fl13	Plant Hammond	3	100	33.3	Wilbanks	1200–1350	Wauchope 1966; Hally 1987: Figure 5; Hally and Langford 1988:63
9Br3	Two Run Creek	10	200?	20	Wilbanks	1200–1350	Wauchope 1966; Hally and Langford 1988:63
9Cl62	Cemochechobee, mound B	10	450	45	Rood	900–1350	Schnell, Knight, and Schnell 1981:145
9Cl62	Cemochechobee, mound A	5	450	90	Rood	900–1350	Schnell, Knight, and Schnell 1981:145
9Ch1	Irene, primary mound	7	150	22.5	Savannah I/II, III	1150–1300	C. Moore 1898:168; Caldwell and McCann 1941
9Ri1	Hollywood	2	100	50	Hollywood	1250–1350	C. Thomas 1894:317–326; DeBaillou 1965
9Eb85	Beaverdam Creek	6	100	16.7	Beaverdam	1200–1300	J. Rudolph and Hally 1985
9St1	Tugalo	4–5	100	22.5	Jarrett	1100–1200	C. Thomas 1894:314–15; Caldwell 1956
9St1	Tugalo	4	100	25	Tugalo	1450–1550	C. Thomas 1894:314–35; Caldwell 1956
9St3	Estatoe	5	100	20	Tugalo	1450–1550	A. Kelly and DeBaillou 1960
38Oc47	Chauga	6	100	16.7	Jarrett	1100–1200	A. Kelly and Neitzel 1959, 1961
38Oc47	Chauga	4	100	25	Tugalo	1450–1550	A. Kelly and Neitzel 1959, 1961

rupted, the position of the elite may grow precarious. As Peebles (1987a:34) has noted, in prestige goods economies, "the 'value' of goods is created in [terms of] both geographic and social distance. The exchanges link elites in different societies, and the act of exchange validates their relationship as equals and at the same time reinforces their superior status within their respective societies." The collapse of a number of southeastern chiefdoms, including Moundville and Spiro, has been attributed, in part, to interruptions in prestige goods exchange networks (e.g., Peebles 1987a:30; Rogers 1987). Prestige goods are not the only artifacts that can be used to explore matters of succession, however. Blake (n.d.), for example, has argued that where succession is poorly defined or the subject of intense competition (i.e., Goldman's open societies), chiefly residences will be in close proximity to other major symbols validating the chief's position, such as mortuary temples, storage facilities, or meeting houses. Where chiefly succession is more secure or where the position of the chief is not the subject of intense rivalry (as in Goldman's stratified and traditional societies, respectively), greater spatial separation of these facilities may occur, since validation of authority through proximity to legitimizing symbols is less critical. Brumfiel (1987) approached the same topic using the occurrence and characteristics of more mundane artifacts, notably serving vessels, to measure the extent of elite feasting and display-based public competition. Where public competition was extensive, leadership positions were probably widely coveted, and hence organizational structures were likely to be unstable and succession frequent.

Analyses of postmarital residence patterns have seen little exploration archaeologically in the Southeast. Matrilineal succession coupled with matrilocal residence, something documented in the ethnohistoric accounts, appears to be assumed rather than viewed as an inference to be tested. Limited support for the validity of this assumption may be forthcoming from physical anthropological analyses, if for example greater variability on male as opposed to female skeletal samples from sites or neighborhood cemeteries can be demonstrated, suggesting males married into the community (e.g., Hulse 1941). Artifact analyses directed to the resolution of postmarital residence patterns have not seen much consideration in the Southeast, something that may be due to the harsh criticism such work encountered in the Southwest (e.g., Plog 1976, 1980).

Environmental Constraints

Analyses of Mississippian settlement patterning and political organization in the South Appalachian area that have focused on the environmental associations of sites include Ward's (1965:45) correlation of major Mississippian settlement with "soils with a high degree of fertility and a highly friable texture" and L. Larson's (1971a, 1986) observation that major centers such as Etowah tended to occur at the boundaries of two or more major physiographic zones (see also Hally 1989). Ferguson (1971:245–47; see also Ferguson and Green 1984) noted that the locations of Mississippian ceremonial centers throughout the South Appalachian area were along major drainages and at macroecotones, at or near the junction of major physiographic provinces, and hence in areas suited to the exploitation of several different environmental zones. Centers were almost invariably found in areas of hardwood vegetation and on or near highly fertile soils, potentially rich agricultural and game/nut mast zones. More recently, M. Williams and Shapiro (1990a:165–73) have argued that some Mississippian populations in the region moved back and forth between closely spaced or "paired" communities, to counter factors of soil or firewood depletion. All of these models emphasize a linkage of Mississippian sites with easily tilled, highly fertile floodplain soils and with physiographic features influencing the spacing of centers and subsidiary sites across the region.

Environmental factors are unquestionably linked to territorial behavior, specifically the active defense of certain areas or resources. The difficulty of clearing southeastern river terrace vegetational communities, which were typically occupied by massive hardwood stands, for example, would have prompted some concern for their defense and maintenance. Fields in early stages of succession, which were far easier to clear than virgin forests, would have likewise been viewed as facilities to be controlled, regardless of their location in floodplains or uplands (Gilman 1981; Vayda 1961). Mississippian societies across the region, the contact-period accounts as well as the regional archaeological record demonstrate, were separated from their neighbors by empty, uninhabited areas. The sizes of these buffer zones are thought by some to have been related to the hide and protein requirements of individual societies and the need to ensure adequate supplies of these resources (e.g., Gramly 1977; Hickerson 1965; E. Turner and Santley 1979). If this view is correct, group population levels and territorial extent were directly linked in the prehistoric Southeast, with hunting territory/buffer zone size and permeability determined, in part, by resource needs of the population.

The emergence of complex societies is widely thought to have been facilitated in ecologically rich areas, an argument that has been explicitly linked with the emergence and spread of the Mississippian adaptation (Bruce Smith 1978). A range of ecological arguments has been proposed over the years, linking the demise of particular Mississippian chiefdoms to the overexploitation of local resources, such as soil, firewood, or game, or to changing environmental conditions, such as drought or a reduction in the growing season, bringing about a failure of the agricultural support system (e.g., Fowler 1975:100–101; Griffin 1961; M. Williams and Shapiro 1990a). The collapse of a number of Mississippian societies has even been attributed to global patterns of climate change, such as the onset of the

Little Ice Age (Baerreis and Bryson 1965; Griffin 1961:710–11; Peebles 1987b:31; Penman 1988).

Other environmental explanations for chiefdom collapse in the Southeast address themselves to the highly focused nature of the Mississippian adaptation itself, that is, to its great reliance on intensive agriculture and, in some cases, on a few key wild plant and animal species (*sensu* Speth and Scott 1985). Societies exploiting intentionally simplified ecosystems, such as those characteristic of intensive agriculturalists (i.e., with an economy directed to one or a few crop and game species), are particularly sensitive to environmental perturbations, particularly fluctuations in rainfall, hail, or growing season duration, or to population crashes in game animal species (e.g., Anderson, Stahle, and Cleaveland 1991, n.d.; J. Brown, Bell, and Wyckoff 1978; Chmurny 1973; Ford 1974, 1977). Catastrophic failure of the sociopolitical system can follow continued subsistence production failures, although it must be stressed that a primary purpose of chiefdom organization appears to be to dampen and hence overcome the worst effects of such failures. Localized and comparatively short-duration subsistence failures, therefore, are unlikely to affect greatly the stability of these systems and the ability of their ruling elites to maintain power. Widespread, long-term resource failures, in contrast, undoubtedly severely challenged these systems (chapter 7).

The Identification of Territories and Boundaries

Earle (1987:289) has described a number of methods used to infer the territorial extent of chiefdom societies. Perhaps the most simple and traditional method involves the examination of site or artifact distributions. Areas with large numbers of sites or artifacts dating to a particular period are interpreted as territorial cores, while areas of low density are interpreted as peripheries or buffers. In the Savannah River valley, for example, the distribution of Mississippian ceramics and projectile points appears to successfully differentiate areas used for settlement from those used for hunting (chapter 7). To give another example, some kind of barrier to direct contact and exchange appears to have separated the chiefdoms of western Alabama and northwestern Georgia during the Mississippian period, since both mundane and elite artifacts from the two areas were distinctive and nonoverlapping (Welch 1986:178–84, 1991:183–90). Prestige goods and raw material exchange "extended several hundred miles to the north, west, and south of Moundville, but it never extended to the northeast, east, or southeast" (Peebles 1987a:33). The minimal evidence for contact between these areas suggests that a major buffer zone, perhaps comparable to the "desert" separating Ocute and Cofitachequi in the 16th century, lay between the Wilbanks-phase Etowah and Moundville II/III chiefdoms.

The relative placement of settlements with respect to each other can also be used to infer the territorial extent of prehistoric chiefdoms, as the nearest-neighbor analyses noted previously suggest. One related method involves drawing Thiessen polygons around major sites or centers (Renfrew 1973, 1976). This type of analysis assumes each center controlled the terrain around it out to some distance between it and surrounding centers; calculation of this distance entails weighting each site according to its size and location in the overall regional hierarchy. In northwestern Georgia, the size and spacing of sites have been used to great effect to delimit the territorial extent of the constituent chiefdoms of the paramount chiefdom of Coosa (Hally, Smith, and Langford 1990), as discussed in a subsequent section. When an even spacing of settlement clusters is observed, it is commonly attributed to competition for the land in the intervening areas. Upham (1982:73–105), although working with southwestern data, has argued that the spacing of centers may be tied to regionwide alliance patterns.

Warfare

Military might and prowess appear to have played an important role in the maintenance of elite authority in many southeastern chiefdoms, and extensive archaeological and ethnohistoric evidence for warfare exists (e.g., Cohen and Armelagos 1984; DePratter 1983:44–67, 1991a:26–56; Dye 1990; Lafferty 1973; Lahren and Berryman 1984; L. Larson 1972:384–90; Milner 1993; Milner and Smith 1989; Milner, Smith, and Anderson 1991; Powell 1988:196, 1992:87). Architectural and skeletal data make up the bulk of the archaeological evidence for warfare from the region (i.e., fortifications such as palisades, bastions, and ditches at many sites; burning of communities; and evidence of trauma, such as trophy skulls, or bodies with embedded arrows, parry fractures, or signs of scalping or other inflicted wounds). Perhaps the most widely accepted explanation for Mississippian warfare is that it was a result of competition between societies for arable land or some other scarce resource and was ultimately brought about by population pressure (e.g., L. Larson 1972). The land best suited for intensive Mississippian agriculture, sandy and silt loams in close proximity to rivers, was so restricted in distribution that its control was of critical importance: "perhaps the primary cultural objective of warfare was the seizure of a town and, hence, the territory it controlled. This territory was of critical economic importance because of its rich, but restricted, agricultural land and its environmental diversity. . . . [W]arfare seems to have been essentially an adaptive mechanism whereby the pressure generated by an increasing population was relieved either by predatory expansion or a relatively large number of deaths" (389). Southeastern warfare, in this view, also served as a mechanism by which population growth was both fostered (for victorious societies) and checked (for losing societies). A strong correlation between Mississippian site location and floodplain terrace settings has, in fact, been noted by a number of scholars working in the South Appalachian area (e.g., Anderson 1975; Ferguson 1971; Murphy and Hudson 1968; Ward 1965).

While such an argument might be applicable in severely circumscribed settings such as Polynesia, where land of any kind was limited, little evidence suggests that pressure on agricultural land was a particularly critical factor constraining settlement or population growth in chiefdoms on continental land masses (Fallers 1973; Goody 1971; D. Taylor 1975:41, 81). Motives for warfare in the ethnohistoric accounts from the Southeast, for example, make no mention of agricultural *land* (Gibson 1974). Instead, warfare appears to have been about power—to gain control over people and the agricultural *surplus* they could produce—and, related to this, increasing personal prestige. Furthermore, a primary assumption in Larson's model, that floodplain soils were the only soils that could be intensively utilized by Mississippian populations, is no longer considered tenable. Mississippian populations are now known to have made use of a range of microenvironmental settings and soil types, and the argument that farming was restricted to floodplain areas is directly controverted by the evidence for numerous upland farmsteads observed in some areas (Kowalewski and Hatch 1991; Rudolph and Blanton 1980; Shapiro 1983:68–74, 1986). A better argument can be made that it was not the soils themselves that might be defended but the fields cleared on these soils, which represented a considerable labor investment (Gilman 1981). An alternative "resource control" argument that has appeared in recent years has focused on the control of animal protein and hide resources rather than of arable floodplain soils (Gramly 1977; Bruce Smith 1975; E. Turner and Santley 1979). Territorial extent, in these frameworks, was determined by game animal population density and distribution (i.e., most likely white-tailed deer) and the need to have access to an area sufficient to ensure a regular supply of hides and protein.

Unfortunately, these arguments about the causes of southeastern warfare, while seemingly plausible, are not well supported by the regional archaeological record. The most telling evidence against the primacy of any of the ecologically based "resource control" arguments that have been advanced is the fact that while large areas of the Southeast underwent depopulation and abandonment at one time or another over the course of the Mississippian, these areas were not immediately or in some cases ever occupied again, even though chiefdoms continued in neighboring areas (Anderson 1991; Milner, Anderson, and Smith 1982). Much of the central Mississippi River valley, for example, was abandoned around 1400, when it became the "vacant quarter" (S. Williams 1982, 1990). Complex chiefdoms such as the Nodena phase of northeastern Arkansas continued to the south, however, as did the Caborn-Wellborn and Madisonville societies along the Ohio River. The abandonment of the central Tennessee River valley after circa 1300 is another example of a large area that was precipitously abandoned without reoccupation, even though complex chiefdoms continued to exist in the nearby Black Warrior River valley to the south and the Coosa River valley to the northeast. Finally, as we shall see, the entire lower course of the Savannah River was abandoned after 1400 or so and remained unoccupied for over two centuries during both favorable and unfavorable climatic conditions. While environmental degradation may be responsible for population decline in some parts of the Southeast, it cannot explain patterns of abandonment on this scale.

Given the rivalry between elites in many southeastern chiefdoms, as observed at the time of contact, I believe that sociopolitical rather than ecological factors played a major role in at least some of these depopulations. That is, some patterns of territorial abandonment within the region appear to have been politically motivated or instigated, reflecting the relocation of populations to or away from more successful elites, either by choice or through the threat or use of force. Furthermore, given the absence of evidence for large-scale population reduction resulting from conflict in either the ethnohistoric literature or the archaeological record, it is debatable whether warfare had much of an effect on population levels within the Mississippian culture area. Chronic hostilities could, of course, result in considerable population movement and relocation, as alliance networks and political entities (i.e., complex chiefdoms) formed and collapsed. Sustained aggression between the polities occupying a region could support elite control, since it would reduce the likelihood that dissatisfied populations could relocate. The need for mutual defense might also tend to strengthen alliance ties.

As an alternative to ecological arguments about the causes and consequences of Mississippian warfare, Gibson (1974) has suggested that it served as a psychological safety valve. In this view, Mississippian warfare helped to bleed off tensions created by the inegalitarian status hierarchy by allowing commoners demonstrating prowess in warfare to achieve honored status and enhanced social position. This appears to have carried over to subsistence pursuits, notably the hunting of large game. A linkage among hunting, masculinity, and warfare is evident in many southeastern Mississippian societies. This appears to be because, to be a hunter, one was also forced to be a warrior, because of the possibility of hostile encounters with members of rival polities the farther one traveled from the central communities of a polity. Accordingly, higher social status accrued to those who ranged far from settlements in the hunt (i.e., into areas where game would have presumably been more plentiful) than to those who remained near fields and communities. Dickson (1981), in a reasoned synthesis, argued that Mississippian warfare was caused by both ecological and sociological factors, notably the need to defend highly circumscribed floodplain resource zones as well as the mediation of social tensions. I would suggest that warfare also was critical to the definition of territorial buffers and boundaries, the maintenance of the tributary economy, and the elimination or co-opting of rival elites.

Factional Competition

Resolving correlates of factional competition is a major challenge facing southeastern archaeologists, one directly relevant to the study of chiefly cycling (see Anderson 1993 for an extended discussion of this topic). Competition between rival factions among elites is widely recognized as a primary factor contributing to the instability of chiefdom political structures, and shifts in centers of power indicate changing power relationships, as differing factions obtained control of society. As competition between factions increased, prestige goods design complexity and quality also sometimes increased, since these goods were used in competitive display (Brumfiel 1987; Feinman 1980). Measuring levels of competition through analyses of elite goods occurrence and quality, however, is difficult in the Southeast. Contact-period ceramic assemblages in many areas known to have been dynamic chiefdoms often seem fairly drab, such as the Barnett- and Mulberry-phase ceramics from the 16th-century polities of Coosa and Cofitachequi, respectively, suggesting prestige-based elite display and exchange were either reduced compared with earlier periods or were in other, more perishable commodities (DePratter 1987b; Hally 1984, 1986b; Hally, Smith, and Langford 1990; Judge 1987). The latter interpretation is suggested by the ethnohistoric accounts, which repeatedly describe the gifts given to Spanish explorers as consisting of perishables such as food, bark and deerskin blankets, and furred and feathered capes. Ceramics, while occasionally illustrated or described, go unmentioned as a valued commodity.

Elaborate incised, engraved, or painted wares were present in some areas of the Southeast at various times during the Mississippian period, and when these wares are geographically widespread, they send a strong signal that elite exchange was occurring (Pauketat and Emerson 1991). The contrast these wares provide when compared with most Mississippian ceramics from the region has prompted discussion about the existence of "sacred" as opposed to "secular" ceramic assemblages in these societies (Sears 1961, 1973). The differences between elaborate and simple ceramics are usually expressed in terms of use in mortuary or ceremonial as opposed to domestic contexts or use by elites as opposed to commoners. Elaborate Mississippian ceramics may have seen considerable use in elite consumption rituals, a form of factional competition centered on feasting and the public display of wealth, as expressed through food-serving behavior (Brumfiel 1987).

Factional competition in the Southeast can also be examined using settlement data. The emergence of complex chiefly centers in some areas of the Southeast occurred at the expense of other nearby villages or centers, which frequently underwent a reduction in size and importance or were even abandoned. Major episodes of mound building and population increase at a primary center, coupled with the reduction in importance or abandonment of nearby secondary villages and centers, have been documented in the Moundville chiefdom during the Middle Mississippian period, in the American Bottom around Cahokia during the Early Mississippian Lohmann phase (Milner 1987a, 1990; Peebles 1987a; Steponaitis 1978, 1983), and, as we shall see, in the Savannah River valley (chapter 6).

The intensity of factional competition in various parts of the Southeast also appears to be related to physiographic factors. Paramounts should be able to exercise greater control over elites in subsidiary communities or polities when they are situated in fairly uniform or homogeneous landscapes. Few natural barriers would exist to interaction between centers, and social systems could develop optimal distributions (i.e., hexagonal matrices; Wright and Johnson 1975). Such a situation appears to characterize developments within the Apalachee province in northern Florida and, possibly, within the American Bottom (Porter 1974; J. Scarry 1990a, 1990b; J. Scarry and Payne 1986; Shapiro 1986). Less control over outlying populations, resulting in a greater likelihood of factional competition, would be likely in more irregular or patchy environments. Throughout most of the Southeast, Mississippian populations occur along widely separated linear river systems, an environmental structure that fosters considerable local autonomy and hence a greater likelihood of factional competition in any complex chiefdoms that may arise.

Ideological and Secular Authority Structures

In the Southeast, elite goods production and interregional exchange seem to peak about 1150 to 1300, at the height of the occurrence and distribution of the elaborate iconography and mortuary ceremonialism of the Southeastern Ceremonial Complex (SCC) (Galloway 1989; Muller 1989:15; Prentice 1990). Religious symbolism pervades the region at this time and is expressed on a wide range of materials, including marine shell, copper, and pottery. This period and that immediately before saw the greatest monumental construction in the region, with extensive mound building and elaborate mortuary ritual documented at centers such as Cahokia, Etowah, Lake Jackson, Moundville, and Spiro. Far-flung alliance, exchange, and ritual/ceremonial networks were apparently operating throughout the region. Warfare, while undoubtedly common if not endemic (i.e, witness the elaborate fortifications at Moundville and Etowah), does not appear to have constrained interpolity elite interaction and intrapolity monumental construction.

This pattern of elite goods exchange, monumental construction, and warfare changes dramatically in the Southeast after circa 1350 to 1400. Mound building diminishes in many areas, while evidence for settlement nucleation and large-scale warfare increases markedly, the former apparently in response to the latter. Interregional elite goods exchange falls off, as the widespread exchange of icons and other artifacts between elites characteristic of the SCC is increasingly replaced by localized, intrapolity exchange (e.g., J. Brown 1984; Milner 1987b, 1990; D. Morse and Morse 1983:247–50, 255, 281–84; Muller 1989:16; Schambach 1991). Elite exchange in this latter period appears directed more toward developing and maintaining alliances between the elites of local and proximate communities than with the elites in comparable positions at widely scattered centers throughout the region. This may be attributed, in part, to a rise in warfare throughout the region and the need to devote greater energy to defense than to ceremonialism. While ritual and mound building continued to occur, the energy invested in these efforts is markedly diminished. Monumental construction efforts comparable to those producing the mound complexes at Cahokia, Etowah, or Moundville are nonexistent, and the kind of elaborate mortuary behavior seen at mound 72 at Cahokia, at mound C at Etowah, or in the Craig mound at Spiro, centers that were in marked decline or gone by 1400, is certainly not evident.

Over the course of the Mississippian, I believe, the strategy by which elites legitimized their privileged position and authority apparently changed dramatically, with appeals to ideology giving way, over time, to more secular measures, including the overt use of force. The sacred position of the elite during the Middle Mississippian was indicated by their participation in regionwide ceremonial and exchange networks, which emphasized their control over events and materials at great distances, what Helms (1979) has called "esoteric knowledge." In the Late Mississippian, as regional populations grew, competition and warfare rather than cooperation and exchange came to dominate interpolity relationships. The arena of elite competition changed in both scale and scope, as the cooperation of local rather than more distant allies increasingly came to be required to maintain social prerogatives. The complex chiefdoms encountered by the mid-16th-century Spanish explorers were densely populated, complex, and geographically extensive and, with the exception of 11th- and 12th-century Cahokia, were probably equal in scale to anything that came before. Where they differed was in emphasis, specifically in the means of maintaining and exercising power and in the areas where surplus labor and societal energy were channeled.

Case Studies of Chiefly Cycling

In the pages that follow, cycling is illustrated using three southeastern archaeological examples, the complex Mississippian chiefdoms centered at Cahokia, Moundville, and Coosa. Two of these polities, Cahokia and

Moundville, were complex chiefdoms that had collapsed before European contact, while the Coosa polity was apparently at or near its height at the time of initial contact. These societies, perhaps the best-documented complex chiefdoms in the region, have dramatic developmental histories, information that can help illustrate how and why chiefly cycling occurs.

The Cahokia Polity

The American Bottom of the central Mississippi River valley was occupied by one of the densest concentrations of chiefly centers in the Eastern Woodlands, including what was unquestionably the most complex chiefdom-level society to emerge during the Mississippian period, the Cahokia polity. A series of single and multiple mound centers arose throughout this circa 3,000-square-kilometer area after A.D. 800, the largest of which, the site of Cahokia, covered more than 10 square kilometers in extent at its height around 1250 (figure 13). Over 100 earthen mounds were built at Cahokia, the largest of which, Monks mound, measured 300 meters by 212 meters at the base and stood 30 meters high. This mound was the largest earthen structure erected in the New World and was exceeded in size only by the Pyramid of the Sun and the great pyramid at Cholula in Mexico. By 1400, however, a few centuries after its peak, Cahokia and many of the other centers in the American Bottom had been largely abandoned. The decline of Cahokia is perhaps the most dramatic example of chiefdom collapse that exists anywhere in the world.

Milner (1987a, 1987b, 1990) has recently summarized developments over the course of the Mississippian period in the American Bottom, using four descriptive stages (coalescence, florescence, maintenance, and social fissioning), corresponding to developments during the Emergent Mississippian period and the Mississippian period Lohmann/Stirling, Moorehead, and Sand Prairie phases; his synthesis forms the basis for much of the discussion presented here (but see also Emerson 1991; Fowler 1975, 1978; Pauketat 1991). During the Emergent Mississippian period (circa 800 to 1000; see also J. Kelly 1987, 1990a, 1990b, J. Kelly et al. 1984), intensive maize agriculture was first adopted, and numerous small, nucleated communities oriented around central plazas appear on the bottomland ridges. Many of the area's mound centers, especially Cahokia, Lohmann, and Lunsford-Pulcher, have extensive Emergent Mississippian components, although the extent of mound construction activity and the details of the political landscape (i.e., whether a hierarchy existed among these settlements) remain unknown (Milner 1990). Local ceramic traditions occur in several areas, suggesting societies characterized by a fair degree of autonomy (J. Kelly et al. 1984). While simple chiefdoms probably emerged in a number of areas within the American Bottom at this time, how this process occurred is not fully understood (e.g., Emerson 1991; J. Kelly 1990b; Pauketat 1991).

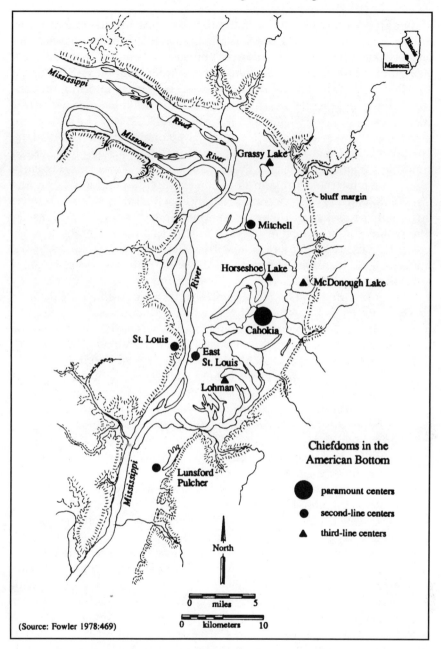

Figure 13 Cahokia in Archaeological Perspective: Major and Minor Centers in the American Bottom during the Stirling Phase.

Dramatic events are evident in the archaeological record after A.D. 1000, during the Lohmann (1000 to 1050) and Stirling (1050 to 1150) phases, what one researcher has called a pattern of "punctuated change in the political economy and the social organization of the American Bottom" (Pauketat 1991:309). Population grew rapidly within the region, and mound construction is documented at many centers, some of which increase markedly in size (Fowler 1974; Gregg 1975; Milner 1986, 1990). The emergence of a superordinate elite social stratum is evident from mortuary data, notably the occurrence of segregated burial areas and facilities for elite and commoner elements of society (Milner 1984a). This is most spectacularly represented by the Lohmann-phase burials within mound 72 at the Cahokia site, which were accompanied by lavish grave goods and numerous retainer sacrifices (Fowler 1974). The larger centers were internally differentiated, with mortuary, residential, and temple/ceremonial areas present. Evidence for interaction with societies over large areas of the midcontinent increases throughout the Emergent Mississippian and Lohmann phases and peaks during the Stirling phase. A wide range of extralocal raw materials is documented at Cahokia (Milner 1990:23–25; Pauketat 1991:113–24), while distinctive Ramey Incised and Powell Plain Stirling-phase vessels (or imitations thereof) are found at sites from the Yazoo River basin of northeastern Mississippi to Aztalan in Wisconsin (J. Kelly 1980; Milner 1987a, 1990; Pauketat and Emerson 1991:924).

The small outlying nucleated villages characteristic of the Emergent Mississippian were replaced by a larger number of dispersed farmsteads during the Lohmann phase, a settlement pattern that continued throughout the remainder of the Mississippian occupation of the area. Public structures such as sweat lodges and possible men's houses, probably accompanied by a few domestic buildings, have been identified at some of these outlying sites, suggesting some form of communal integration among these presumed commoner populations (J. Kelly et al. 1987:421–30; J. Kelly 1990a; Mehrer 1982; Milner 1984b:44, 1990:15). Larger-scale integration, however, was coordinated through ceremonial centers, replacing the village-level integration present previously.

The adoption of a dispersed settlement pattern has been attributed to the emergence of greater regional integration and a concomitant reduction in intergroup conflict, reducing the need for populations to aggregate for defensive purposes. Additionally, it has been suggested that dispersing the farming population would have greatly increased agricultural production, by ensuring that most tillable areas within the patchy bottomland habitat could be efficiently brought under cultivation, and at the same time would have minimized the risk of crop failure brought about by varied rainfall and flooding patterns (Chmurny 1973:95; Milner 1987a, 1990). Finally, as Pauketat (1991:319–20) has elegantly argued, the dissolution of smaller communities and the scattering of their inhabitants would have been a particularly effective way by which dominant elites at centers could separate possible competitors in outlying villages from their supporters. This would also have the effect of alienating or suppressing traditional forms of cooperation and interaction among the populace, facilitating the implementation of the elites' own agendas, including increased demands for tribute. Given the rapid population growth and political centralization that occurred during and immediately following the Emergent Mississippian period, such innovations are not altogether unexpected.

Complex chiefdoms are assumed to have been present in the American Bottom during the Lohmann and Stirling phases, with one unquestionably centered on Cahokia. The relationship of outlying centers to Cahokia at this time, specifically their degree of autonomy, is the subject of some debate. Some authorities (e.g., Fowler 1974, 1975; O'Brien 1989) see Cahokia as the paramount center in the region, at the apex of an inferred three-level decision-making hierarchy (over a four-level settlement hierarchy) and exercising direct control over all the other centers in the American Bottom, approaching or actually at a state level of organizational complexity. Milner (1987a, 1990:21–23), in contrast (and taking into account the complete absence of evidence for formal, differentiated administrative structures), finds it unlikely that any chiefdom society, given their fragile kin-based administrative structures, could be so highly organized, rigidly hierarchical, and internally differentiated. Instead, Milner (1990:29) views Cahokia as something of a *primes inter pares*, the dominant political entity among a number of organizationally similar if less complex quasi-autonomous chiefdoms exercising considerable control over events in their own territories. While Cahokia dominated these other societies and got them to operate in its interest, this control was probably indirect. That is, as long as the position of Cahokia was acknowledged and its interests maintained, perhaps through the periodic submission of tribute or corvee labor or through support in warfare, these other societies were allowed more or less to go their own ways.

Cahokia's dominance has been variously attributed to its near-central location within and immediately proximate to the extensive floodplain habitats of the American Bottom, as well as its central and potentially strategic location in the midcontinent riverine network (Fowler 1974, 1978; Milner 1990; Peregrine 1991). Cahokia is geographically admirably situated to control the flow of information and goods throughout the American Bottom, and its rise in importance was undoubtedly related to its position at the center of this flow, regardless of the degree of actual control it exercised over outlying centers. Whether the relationships between the elite at Cahokia at its height and the elite in other centers were based on force, ideology, or kinship is something that is currently unknown. As Milner (1990:28–29) has observed:

> It is not known how formerly separate and initially more-or-less equiva-

lent sociopolitical groups were integrated as part of a single Cahokia-dominated regional system. Previously unrelated elite lineages may have been incorporated into an expanding Cahokia superordinate social stratum. Alternatively, individuals from Cahokia may have replaced previously important personages in affiliated town-and-mound centers. . . . Linkages among members of the superordinate strata at major sites presumably facilitated the movement of exotic raw materials and artifacts used by elite groups in rituals to reinforce the aura of authority and to emphasize their close association with a regional social order dominated by Cahokia. . . . Once the political centralization process was initiated, it may have progressed at an ever-escalating rate as once roughly equivalent polities became dwarfed by the manpower mobilization potential of a Cahokia dominated system. Expansion must have been played out against an existing background of antagonistic and alliance relationships among the social groups of the region. The Cahokia regional system would not have been able to expand infinitely without a major structural reorganization of society. Eventually it would have been limited by the capacity of members of the principal lineage(s) to project their authority and to control effectively a number of geographically dispersed subsidiary sociopolitical units featuring locally influential leaders who were busy pursuing their own potentially divisive interests.

Thus there were very real limits to the growth of Cahokia, limits placed there by the nature of chiefdom political organization.

Cahokia reached its height during the Stirling phase, when what Pauketat (1991:323) has called a "divine chiefship" appears to have been present. During the subsequent Moorehead phase (1150 to 1250), however, Mississippian occupations in the American Bottom began to go into a state of decline or, at best, an attempt at system maintenance. The number of outlying communities that were occupied decreased, something attributed in part to environmental degradation, specifically a reduction in the amount of bottomland consistently available for cultivation as well as the possible overexploitation of firewood, game, and agricultural soils (Fowler 1975:100–101; Milner 1987b, 1990:30). Occupation of progressively higher portions of the floodplain is observed, a pattern that may well reflect increases in erosion, runoff, and flooding brought on by overcutting. Increasing factionalization of the elite, perhaps resulting from the stresses associated with maintaining a polity of this size and complexity (which would have required placing large numbers of subsidiary elites in positions where they could compete for more power or even supreme authority), is a plausible alternative to these ecologically based explanations (Pauketat 1991:325–26). Furthermore, given a cessation in the expansion of the political economy, which appears to have reached the limits possible for a chiefdom form of organization, this elite competition would have played out against decreasing (or at best stable) patterns of tribute flow (326). The out-migration of dissatisfied or less successful elites and their retinues would have been a logical response to these increasingly difficult political conditions.

Mound construction at Cahokia continued during the Moorehead phase, however. The pattern of continued or expanded monumental construction activity has been interpreted as an attempt on the part of the elites to maintain their positions, through legitimizing enterprises, in the face of increasing problems (Milner 1987a, 1990:31). A bastioned palisade was erected around the central portion of the site, suggesting intrasocietal or intersocietal conflict was on the increase. Long-distance exchange continued, although apparently on a diminished scale. Cahokia Cordmarked and Wells Incised vessels occur over a wide but more restricted area than Stirling-phase ceramics. Interestingly, during both the Moorehead and Sand Prairie phases, analyses of skeletal samples indicate that the general population remained in good health, indicating that the decline of the political system did not immediately "translate into measurable health-related problems" (Milner 1990:30, 1991); this evidence renders questionable ecologically based explanations for the decline of the polity, since patterns of overexploitation leading to resource stress would have likely translated into a visible decline in population health.

During the ensuing Sand Prairie phase (1250 to 1400), complex chiefdom organization collapsed throughout the American Bottom. Population decline continued in outlying areas, but now many of the large centers were themselves abandoned or were minimally occupied. At Cahokia, residential structures were erected in former ceremonial precincts, intrusive burials were placed in a range of mound types, and the bluff-crest cemeteries characteristic of the preceding Lohmann through Moorehead phases were replaced by scattered graves near residential areas in the floodplain (Milner 1984a, 1987a, 1991). As the traditional centers of the American Bottom declined, however, at least two polities on the periphery of the region, thought to have been simple chiefdoms, appear to have expanded in size and influence, one in the vicinity of the Emerald mound some 25 kilometers to the east, and another centered on the Common Field site approximately 100 kilometers to the south (Milner 1990:32). While these societies were small when compared to Cahokia at its height, their presence indicates that power and organization may have been in the process of shifting rather than disappearing entirely from the general region. Whether these or other centers in the central Mississippi River valley or elsewhere in the Southeast would have eventually come to rival Cahokia will remain forever unknown, since European contact precluded this possibility (see chapter 9).

Although Mississippian chiefdoms were present in the American Bottom for several hundred years, the period of florescence was comparatively brief, on the order of a century or so, during the Lohmann and Stirling phases. The decline of Cahokia was extended, however, lasting as long as its period of florescence, if not longer. Milner (1986, 1990), based on counts of structures in extensive excavations in outlying areas, has noted that, given the population peak in the Stirling phase, population decline during the ensuing Moorehead phase could have been quite gradual, on the order of 1% or less per year, and still yield the dramatic cumulative effects observed archaeologically by the end of this phase. Organizational collapse in the case of Cahokia appears to have been gradual rather than precipitous.

The extent of Cahokia's influence on chiefdoms elsewhere in the Eastern Woodlands has been the subject of extensive investigation. Traditionally, the American Bottom was viewed as something of a font from which all Mississippian arose, even the source of invading waves of population (e.g., Willey et al. 1956). In recent years, the extent to which migration played a role in the spread of this culture has been seriously questioned, to the point that Mississippian emergence is now believed to have occurred from local Woodland traditions in most parts of the Southeast, and any recourse to population movement is suspect (Bruce Smith 1984, 1990). Cahokia's impact on Mississippian societies throughout the surrounding region is viewed as substantial but largely indirect (e.g., Emerson 1991; Griffin 1993; Milner 1990:23–26; Peregrine 1992a), although a few investigators envision its elites dictating tribute and production from societies over large parts of the Eastern Woodlands, including as far away as the New York Iroquois (e.g., Dincauze and Hasenstab 1989; O'Brien 1989; Porter 1969, 1974). Other investigators see its role as more passive, attracting goods and people and rising to regional prominence by virtue of a favorable location and environment, but, as appears to be the case with all chiefdoms, organizationally incapable of coordinating economic activities in societies hundreds of kilometers away (Griffin 1993; Harn 1978:260; Milner 1990:21–23). While prestige goods exchange and even tribute extraction may have occurred among many of the societies contemporary with Cahokia, the volume probably declined rapidly with distance.

Within the American Bottom itself, over and above the long-term trend of emergence and decline, clear evidence exists for shifts in power indicative of cycling behavior over the course of the Mississippian. Fowler (1978:462), for example, has noted that the intensity of occupation at the secondary centers in the American Bottom was linked, to some degree, to the direction of Cahokia's external relations. During the Lohmann phase, when appreciable evidence for contact with societies in the lower Mississippi River valley and Caddoan area was evident, the Lunsford-Pulcher site in the southern part of the American Bottom appears to have been second only to Cahokia in importance. Later, during the Stirling and Moorehead phases, when contacts with the Plains are evident, the Mitchell site at the northern end of the bottom near the mouth of the Missouri River assumed a prominent role. The occupational histories of the other centers within the locality also varied appreciably. Both Lunsford-Pulcher and

Lohmann appear to have been abandoned or were only minimally occupied after the early part of the Mississippian period (Esarey and Good 1981; Griffin 1977:487; Milner 1990:19). At the Mitchell site, which was occupied for hundreds of years, there is evidence to suggest that much of the major construction occurred during a comparatively brief period (Porter 1974:151–54, 174–81, cited in Milner 1990). Finally, as noted previously, as Cahokia itself declined, there is some evidence to suggest that other centers were emerging. Thus the chiefdoms in the American Bottom illustrate, in microcosm, developmental processes occurring throughout the Mississippian area. Chiefdoms emerged and declined, and power shifted over the landscape.

The Moundville Polity

The evolution of the Moundville chiefdom in west-central Alabama, which at its height was one of the most powerful Mississippian chiefdoms in the Southeast, has been the focus of extended research in recent years, work that has been summarized by Peebles (1986, 1987a, 1987b), Steponaitis (1978, 1983, 1991), and Welch (1991), among others. The process by which this chiefdom emerged, expanded, and declined provides a classic illustration of cycling, not only by showing how organizational change occurred within the Moundville chiefdom itself, but also by showing how events at Moundville shaped the developmental trajectories of chiefdoms throughout the surrounding region.

The immediate precursors of the Moundville chiefdom were the Late Woodland West Jefferson–phase peoples (circa A.D. 850 to 1000), who lived in a series of scattered communities and practiced a hunting and gathering way of life supplemented by the cultivation of maize, with no evidence for hierarchical social organization. The Moundville community, the site of the later center, was a small village during this period, undistinguished from its neighbors. A series of simple Mississippian chiefdoms arose in the Black Warrior River valley between 1000 and 1250, during the Moundville I phase (figure 14). These were roughly equal in size and clustered around small single-mound centers, one of which was Moundville, which covered approximately 2 hectares and was otherwise apparently undistinguished from the other centers (Steponaitis 1983:151–61). The vast majority of the population during this and succeeding periods is assumed to have lived in outlying smaller hamlets and villages, whose production was controlled, to some degree, by elites living at one of the centers. Intensive agriculture provided an important contribution to subsistence, and a hierarchical form of social organization is assumed to have emerged, although evidence in support of this remains minimal (C. Scarry 1986; Welch 1991).

By circa 1200, the Moundville paramount chiefdom was beginning to emerge, a polity that expanded markedly in extent and influence during the Moundville II phase (1250 to 1400), until by the Moundville III phase

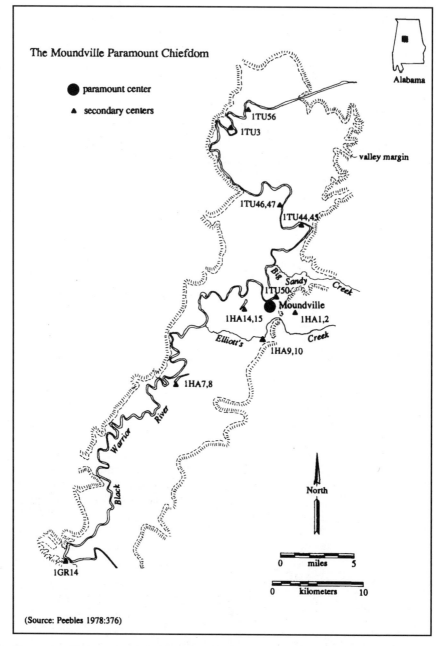

The Moundville Paramount Chiefdom

● paramount center

▲ secondary centers

Alabama

valley margin

1TU56
1TU3

1TU46,47 ▲

1TU44,45

Big Sandy Creek

1TU50
Moundville

1HA14,15   1HA1,2

Elliott's   Creek

1HA9,10

▲ 1HA7,8

Black Warrior River

North

1GR14

0   miles   5

0   kilometers   10

(Source: Peebles 1978:376)

Figure 14   Moundville in Archaeological Perspective: Major and Minor Centers in
the Black Warrior River Valley during the Moundville III Period.

(1400 to 1500), it was one of the major centers in the region. During the Moundville II phase, the center at Moundville assumed dominance within the valley, growing in size from 2 to 50 hectares, and from one mound to at least five (Peebles 1987b:9; Steponaitis 1983:157). Population throughout an approximate 50-kilometer section of the Black Warrior River valley around Moundville was brought under the control of the paramount center. Other centers in this part of the valley continued to be occupied but were clearly subsidiary. Centers closest to Moundville were small and their locations were displaced toward Moundville, presumably to reduce transportation costs and facilitate administrative control (Bozeman 1982; Steponaitis 1978). Mound centers located farther away, in contrast, were larger and appear to have had greater autonomy. Settlements were positioned within the landscape in such a way as to "facilitate the flow of labor, goods, and information from the provinces to Moundville" (Peebles 1987a:27).

The emergence of the Moundville II paramount center was apparently coupled with a period of militaristic expansion. Chiefdoms in nearby drainages disappeared during this time, notably in portions of the upper Black Warrior, the central Cahaba, and the central Tennessee river valleys, and their defeat and incorporation into or relocation or movement away from the Moundville chiefdom is inferred. This rearrangement of regional population may have been the result of an intentional policy on the part of the Moundville elite to strengthen their position by eliminating potential threats from neighboring polities. Eliminating these societies' roles as middlemen would also ensure Moundville a more prominent place in regional prestige goods and alliance networks. At the same time that Moundville was expanding and nearby areas were being abandoned, the occurrence of extralocal prestige goods in mortuary contexts at Moundville, presumably brought in under the auspices of long-distance exchange, declined markedly. Peebles (1987a:36) has summarized the overall process: "As Moundville achieved both local and regional dominance nearby polities were eliminated as exchange partners and potential rivals. In effect, Moundville insulated itself by eliminating proximate societies at a similar level of development and then instituted direct exchange relationships with polities to the north and northwest." Warfare may have taken resources formerly used for long-distance exchange, but the rewards obtained from military action, Welch (1991:195–96) has suggested, probably more than offset the temporary decline in extralocal prestige goods.

The emergence of the Moundville paramount chiefdom thus brought about changes in the Mississippian societies throughout the surrounding region, changes that appear directly linked to events taking place in the Black Warrior River valley. If neighboring societies were not eliminated altogether, it appears they were brought under some form of control. Fortifications, which were present in the Summerville I–phase (1000 to

1200) community at Lubbub Creek, a small Mississippian center on the Tombigbee River some 40 kilometers west of Moundville, for example, disappeared during Summerville II/III times (1200 to 1500) (Blitz 1993a). Only after 1500, when Moundville had collapsed, did they reappear. Fortifications were present at Lubbub Creek during periods of minimal regional integration, when the landscape was dominated by numerous small societies presumably in competition with one another for power, prestige, subsistence products, or other commodities. The disappearance of fortifications at Lubbub Creek, furthermore, occurred precisely when Moundville began to dominate the region and in all probability reflects the emergence of fairly stable political landscape, under what Peebles (1987b:23) has called a *Pax Moundvilliana*. A subordination of elites in outlying centers and polities appears to have occurred in conjunction with this inferred military domination. The burials in the Summerville II/III and Summerville IV occupations at Lubbub Creek, unlike those in the earlier Summerville I phase, had only domestic ceramics in association. A disenfranchisement of local elites is indicated, although it should be noted that the samples are small (Peebles 1987b:14; Powell 1983).

The chiefdom reached its peak in power and influence during the Moundville III phase. The central town at Moundville grew in size from 50 to 120 hectares and from 5 to 20 mounds surrounding a 40-hectare plaza (Peebles 1987b:9; Steponaitis 1983:159–60). Burial and midden data from the site have been used to infer resident population levels, with differing results. Examining burial data by phase, Peebles (1987b:9–10) estimated that population grew approximately 400% between Moundville I and II and another 50% between Moundville II and III, when it peaked at approximately 3,000 people. Over the same interval, population within the overall chiefdom was estimated to have grown from 10,000 to 30,000, although these figures are, in the absence of reliable settlement data, largely speculative. Steponaitis (1991:200), in an analysis of midden debris from Moundville, noted that identifiable potsherds declined fourfold between the Moundville I and the Moundville II and III phases. A decline in residential population was inferred, even as the site itself was seeing increased use as a ceremonial and burial center for people from across a large area, probably encompassing the entire chiefdom. If population growth actually occurred at the center or at least within the chiefdom itself between the Moundville I and the Moundville II and III phases, some of it may reflect the relocation of people from the northern and eastern chiefdoms that collapsed about this time, an inference that could be tested through comparative skeletal analyses. The emergence of a complex chiefdom organization, capable of accommodating fluctuations in subsistence productivity that are likely to have occurred, may have permitted considerable internal population growth.

The burial data from Moundville suggest that elite population may have increased in proportion to total population over time. Elites, defined as individuals characterized by sumptuary mortuary ritual, represented approximately 1% of the Moundville I population but rose to approximately 5% of the Moundville II– and III–phase populations. Reasons why this elite population growth occurred (if it is indeed correctly documented) remain to be determined, although the increase in complexity of the chiefdom itself, in terms of size and constituent population, may have necessitated an increase in the number of elite decision-making personnel. Additionally, some of this growth may reflect the incorporation of defeated or co-opted elites and their retinues from the northern and eastern societies that declined at this time. Alternatively, these figures may reflect changing use of the center itself, from a settlement with both elite and nonelite resident populations, to one increasingly occupied by elites. Whether elite population levels remained stable in relation to the rest of the population throughout the Moundville II and III phases is unknown. It would be interesting to see how elite population levels changed as the chiefdom declined toward the end of the Moundville III phase.

During the Moundville III phase, the chiefdom was once again deeply involved in long-distance exchange, with goods circulating to and from societies at considerable distances to the north, south, and west (Welch 1991:183–90). Interaction with contemporaneous societies in the central Mississippi River valley is indicated, although, interestingly, no ceramic artifacts made in the South Appalachian area have been found in the Moundville chiefdom: "Of the 153 imported ceramic vessels found thus far at Moundville, not one can be traced to a source due east of the Black Warrior River. There are vessels from the Nashville Basin and from southeast Missouri; there are vessels from Arkansas and from the Gulf Coast; but there is not a single example from the upper portions of the Coosa, Tallapoosa, and Chattahoochee Rivers" (Peebles 1986:32). The absence of interaction among these areas suggests that the enmity between the paramount elites of Coosa and Tastaluca observed by the Spanish during the 16th century (chapter 3) may have had considerable time depth and may have markedly affected regional exchange patterns.

Sometime around or shortly after 1500 and prior to the time of European contact, the Moundville chiefdom collapsed. The succeeding Alabama River phase (1500 to 1700) was characterized by small, egalitarian settlements evenly dispersed along the drainage. Population skeletal health in the western Alabama area declined markedly, as the organization that had previously buffered subsistence crises disappeared; Alabama River–phase burials in the general region exhibit a much higher incidence of iron deficiency anemia than burials dating to the Moundville III period or its equivalent (Hill 1981; Powell 1988:189–91, 1991).

Peebles (1986:30, 1987a, 1987b) has argued that the collapse of the Moundville III chiefdom was brought on by population pressure. Growing population levels within the chiefdom led to a reduction in the agricultural surpluses necessary to maintain the elite prestige goods economy (i.e, by feeding specialists and by providing wealth that could be used to purchase exotic materials). A decline in the occurrence of imported prestige goods in mortuary context, notably worked copper and marine shell, and of extralocal ceramics has been documented at Moundville over the course of the Moundville III phase (Peebles 1987b:14–15). With the collapse of the prestige goods economy, the organizational system that was legitimized by and predicated upon it also collapsed. Once effective organizational controls over the subsistence economy went, a marked reduction occurred in the population levels that could be maintained.

The collapse of the Moundville III chiefdom thus is inferred to have occurred because increasing population pressure siphoned off resources that could otherwise have been directed toward maintaining the prestige goods network. As the flow of prestige goods diminished, the position of the elites was undermined; with the collapse of chiefly authority, the subsistence and settlement system based upon it likewise collapsed. Peebles (1987a:34) has noted that prestige goods economies can also be disrupted by competition for control of exchange relationships by competing groups within a society; by the cutting off or redirecting of exchange routes by outside groups, effectively isolating the original node; and through the decline of surpluses necessary to maintain elite participation in the network through the support of craft specialists, procurement expeditions, and other essential labor.

Elite population growth over the course of the Moundville chiefdom may have affected the stability of the tributary economy, by placing increasing demands on the system for prestige goods and other services. Localized participation in the prestige goods exchange network diminished not only when the Moundville chiefdom was in decline, however, but also when the center was consolidating its hold over the immediate region during the Moundville II phase. During the period of consolidation, it appears that local affairs took precedence over the maintenance of external connections and, as Welch has suggested, because successes in warfare were an accepted substitute for prestige goods. The Moundville case thus indicates that a decline in prestige goods in circulation cannot be invariably equated with a decline in organizational stability and complexity. Instead, the circumstances within which organizational change occur must be carefully evaluated.

The Coosa Polity

The 16th-century paramount chiefdom of Coosa, one of the largest and most complex Mississippian societies in the southeastern United States at the time of European contact, has been the subject of extended archaeological and ethnohistoric investigation in recent years by a research team led by David J. Hally and Charles M. Hudson (Hally and Langford 1988;

Hally, Smith, and Langford 1990; Hudson et al. 1985, 1987). Visited by the De Soto, De Luna, and Pardo expeditions in the middle third of the 16th century, the province of Coosa was a complex chiefdom, a series of linked polities stretching for approximately 400 kilometers along the Coosa and Tennessee river valleys from northeastern Alabama through northwestern Georgia and into eastern Tennessee. A series of seven 16th-century Mississippian site clusters has been identified in this area, which Hally, Smith, and Langford (1990:122) argue were "largely independent chiefdoms that were unified, perhaps only briefly, by Coosa, the chiefdom represented by the largest and geographically most central site cluster." The location of these site clusters, their archaeological phase designation, and the Spanish province each probably represents are illustrated in figure 15. Procedures by which these clusters were recognized archaeologically, including information on survey methods and biases, site location and size, the number and size of associated mounds, each site or center's nearest neighbor, and estimated population for each site within individual clusters, have been published by Hally and his colleagues (Hally and Langford 1988; Hally, Smith, and Langford 1990). Much of the discussion that follows is drawn from these works.

The seven site clusters forming the Coosa paramount chiefdom each had between 4 and 7 sites larger than 1 hectare, with an average of 5.3 large sites per cluster (Hally, Smith, and Langford 1990:127–128; these sites are presumed to have been contemporaneous, since they are identifiable at the phase level). In five of the site clusters for which adequate survey data existed, site size ranged between 1 and 5.6 hectares and averaged approximately 2.8 hectares. Using data from excavated sites, Hally and his colleagues calculated the number of possible domestic structures at each site and used these data in turn to develop population estimates. Individual towns within the clusters were found to have an average of 59 households (range = 21 to 119) and average populations of either 350 (range = 124 to 702) or 652 (range = 253 to 1,309), depending on whether Naroll (1962) or S. Cook's (1972) formula for estimating population from dwelling size was used (Hally, Smith, and Langford 1990:128). The total population of the Carter's cluster, the presumed political center of the Coosa paramount chiefdom, was calculated to be either approximately 2,850 or 5,400 people, while the total population in all seven clusters was either approximately 12,000 or 22,400.

Platform mounds in use in the 16th century, with archaeologically documented construction episodes, are present on sites in four of the seven site clusters and may have been present in the other three, although the periods of occupation at the mound sites in these clusters remain to be documented (Hally, Smith, and Langford 1990:128). However, only in the Carter's cluster is there evidence for more than one mound group occupied simultaneously, at the Little Egypt site, which had two or three mounds, and at the Thompson site, which had one mound. The internal

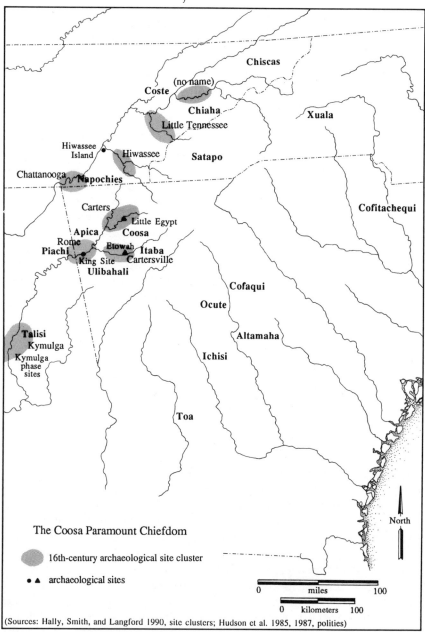

Figure 15   Coosa in Archaeological Perspective: Individual Sites and Centers in the 16th-century Complex Chiefdom.

political organization of six of the seven site clusters thus appears to have been that of a simple chiefdom, with one central town coordinating activities in a number of outlying communities. The internal political organization of the seventh site cluster, the Carter's cluster, may have been that of a complex chiefdom, with a primary center at Little Egypt and a secondary center at Thompson. Not surprisingly, the Little Egypt site has been identified as the probable central town of Coosa (Hudson et al. 1985:726–27).

The size of the seven site clusters, which Hally and his colleagues determined using "the linear distance between the two most widely separated large sites" in each cluster, ranged between 10.8 and 23.5 kilometers and averaged 19.5 kilometers (Hally, Smith, and Langford 1990:129–30). Large sites within these clusters ranged from 0.1 to 13.8 kilometers apart and averaged 5.5 kilometers apart. The lowest average distance between large sites, 3.3 kilometers, was observed in the Carter's cluster, something that may reflect the high degree of political organization of this polity and its role in the regional political landscape. The clusters themselves were widely separated from one another, with mound centers an average 49 kilometers apart (range = 29 to 69 kilometers) and the cluster edges, defined in terms of the distance between nonmound sites in neighboring clusters, an average of 33 kilometers apart (range = 16 to 50 kilometers) (130). Areas between the clusters were unoccupied and presumably served as buffer zones/hunting territories.

Hally and his colleagues (129–33) have interpreted the site clusters as politically more or less autonomous chiefdoms, with subsidiary communities under the direct control of an elite administrative hierarchy centered at the mound sites. The size of each cluster was small enough in terms of travel time to permit effective direct control of each community within it from the center, while the number of communities within each cluster, averaging under six, was low enough to preclude elite administrative overload, following scalar stress arguments advanced by Johnson (1978, 1982). The unoccupied buffer zones between these polities, they further argued, may have formed through processes of military competition between the leaders of each polity. Finally, the distance between each cluster was considered too great to permit leaders in one cluster to control activities directly in other nearby or more distant clusters.

How these site clusters were bound together to form the Coosa paramount chiefdom and the political organization of this entity are less clear. The early accounts indicate that subsidiary polities were drawn under the control of a cacique grande at a paramount center through military conquest or threat or through a series of presumably defensive alliances. Elites at subsidiary polities acknowledged the paramount's position through the periodic submission of tribute and in all probability received, in return, prestige and other goods from the paramount center, as well as support in times of crisis. The De Luna expedition account of the raid on the

Napochies by a combined force of Spaniards and Indians from Coosa, to rein in a subsidiary polity seeking autonomy, indicates competition between elites, ultimately leading to the exercise of military force, which sometimes played an important role in the formation and maintenance of these chiefdoms (chapter 3).

Knowledge about the size and importance of Coosa comes almost exclusively from early Spanish sources. Archaeological evidence for the existence of the Coosa paramount chiefdom is minimal, to the point that Hally and his colleagues (1990:133) describe the polity as "essentially invisible." The Little Egypt site, assumed to be the central town of the complex chiefdom, is not particularly distinctive. While three mounds were present and apparently in use, more than at any other site in the chiefdom, these mounds were much smaller than those present at Citico, Etowah, and Toqua in the Chattanooga, Cartersville, and Little Tennessee site clusters, respectively. The impressive mounds at these other sites, however, had been built much earlier and were no longer in use when Coosa was at its height.

Ceramics, an artifact category widely used to define the existence and extent of phases in the late prehistoric Southeast (e.g., Phillips 1970; S. Williams and Brain 1983), provide no clue to the extent of Coosa. The province boundaries not only crosscut two major ceramic traditions, the Dallas tradition of eastern Tennessee and the Lamar tradition of Georgia, but the pottery within each site cluster "for which ceramic counts are available can be distinguished at the phase level" (Hally, Smith, and Langford 1990:133). These phase assemblages would almost certainly be equated with distinct societies if ceramic analysis formed the primary method used to infer political relationships or ethnicity.

The only distinctive artifact found to be coextensive and contemporaneous with the historical province of Coosa to date, in fact, is the Citico-style gorget (133). Found almost exclusively with adult female and adolescent interments, these gorgets have been interpreted as some kind of badge of office or affiliation "symbolically associated with some institutional order or status group within the chiefdom of Coosa" (Hudson et al. 1985:732–33). The association with females may point to the existence of a female leadership category within the chiefdom. The artifact style may additionally or alternatively document the geographic extent of marital alliance networks binding the chiefdom together.

Hally and his colleagues concluded by arguing that, since there was little archaeological evidence for strong political ties binding polities into the paramount chiefdom of Coosa, southeastern paramount chiefdoms in general were probably fragile and short-lived. Relationships between paramount and subordinate elites are thought to have been primarily personal and symbolic in nature and characterized by few overt demands for tribute or services. The rapid decline in the power of Coosa in the 20 years between the De Soto and De Luna expeditions and the apparent resurgence in power within the chiefdom in the half-dozen years between the De Luna and Pardo expeditions indicate how quickly dramatic organizational change may occur in these societies. In the case of Coosa, however, there is little doubt that European contact precipitated some of these changes.

While the recent work with Coosa indicates that Mississippian paramount chiefdoms may be very difficult to recognize archaeologically, it also illustrates a number of methods by which this may be accomplished. Extensive regional survey followed by locational analyses, for example, may permit the resolution of site clusters that represent individual chiefdoms. The analysis of settlement and administrative structures within site clusters may indicate which of them, if any, may have been the center of a larger, paramount chiefdom. The Carter's site cluster had the only two-level administrative hierarchy evident in the seven clusters forming the Coosa paramount chiefdom and had the largest and most closely spaced settlements, further evidence of a high degree of internal political organization. Analysis of the material assemblage within and between site clusters over a region may reveal distinctive categories of artifacts shared between large numbers of sites, something that in turn may indicate the existence and extent of alliance relationships. Comparative mortuary analyses may indicate status differences and hence political relationships between elites at differing centers. Finally, paleopathological analyses may yield similar results, if secure relationships do indeed exist between level of political organization and subsistence stress.

Conclusions

In these first four chapters, I have attempted to show how ethnography, ethnohistory, and archaeology can aid in the archaeological examination of political and organizational change in chiefdom societies, specifically the emergence and decline of complex chiefdoms against a regional backdrop of simple chiefdoms. The focus on ethnographic examples of chiefdoms from around the world and the ethnohistoric documentation of the chiefdoms in the archaeological study area follows from the belief that understanding how living cultural systems operated is critical to effectively designing research directed to understanding past cultural systems. The archaeological analysis of political and organizational change in chiefdom society, it has been seen, can be addressed using a number of different but complementary kinds of evidence, including data about settlement patterning, mortuary behavior, individual health, regional exchange patterns, and local and regional resource structure.

In the next five chapters, these approaches are used to examine in considerable detail archaeological evidence for cycling in one part of the late prehistoric Southeast. Attention is directed to a series of Mississippian chiefdoms that were present in the Savannah River valley during the period from circa 1000 to 1600. A goal of this research is the linking of observations about the dynamics of living cultural systems—in this case, processes of organizational change in chiefdoms—to the evidence in the archaeological record. This activity, a major challenge before archaeologists, has been called middle-range theory (Binford 1981:25–30). The extent to which the archaeological record can tell us about past cultural systems is directly tied to how well we advance logical, well-grounded, and carefully constructed arguments showing how certain kinds of human behavior can be expected to leave behind certain kinds of archaeological signatures. If our arguments are plausible and our conclusions supported by multiple lines of evidence, we can have reason to believe them.

5

Evidence for Mississippian Occupation in the Savannah River Valley

In this chapter, archaeological evidence documenting the Mississippian occupation of the Savannah River valley is summarized, with an emphasis on the major survey and excavation projects conducted to date. Following more than a century of archaeological research, a considerable body of information exists about Mississippian occupations in the Savannah River basin. To date, approximately one-tenth of the basin has seen at least reconnaissance-level survey, and over 500 Mississippian components have been identified, most typically by the presence of diagnostic complicated stamped pottery or small triangular arrow points. Fourteen Mississippian mound sites are currently known, and most have seen at least some level of professional archaeological excavation. Much of this work took place 30 or more years ago, however, and it has only been in the past two decades that appreciable fieldwork directed to nonmound sites or much survey activity of any kind has occurred. This change in emphasis has been largely the result of federal historic preservation legislation exacted since the mid-1960s, which has mandated consideration of the research potential of all sites encountered, rather than only those characterized by large size, extensive debris scatters, or monumental architecture, the criteria that influenced previous excavation decisions. As a result, a large number of Mississippian village, hamlet, and special activity sites have been examined in recent years, and it is fair to state that, given modern research and recovery considerations, our knowledge of the archaeological assemblages at most of these sites is far better than it is at all but the most recently examined mound centers.

To facilitate a better understanding of the mound centers in the basin, some of which were badly damaged or destroyed during the 18th and 19th centuries, annotated historic accounts of these sites are provided in appendix A. For some sites, unfortunately, these early descriptions are virtually the *only* information that has survived. At the two largest mound groups in the basin, Mason's Plantation and Rembert, for example, most architectural features had been plowed, looted, or washed away by the time professional archaeological investigation began locally in the late 19th century. Late prehistoric cultural sequences have been developed in three parts of the basin, and most component assemblages with 50 or more sherds with identifiable surface finishes can be placed within approximately 100- to 150-year intervals (figure 16). This degree of chronological control, when combined with the extensive survey and excavation data that is available, permits the fine-grained diachronic examination of evidence for Mississippian settlement and household and political change in the basin. Details about these sequences, specifically information on each of the designated phases and how they are recognized, are provided in appendix B. The information in this chapter and the appendixes, accordingly, provides the necessary background for the basinwide analysis of chiefly cycling, presented in chapters 6 and 7, and the more focused examination of the subject, employing the results of research at specific sites, presented in chapter 8.

A vivid, if still incompletely understood, picture is emerging of the kinds of changes that occurred over the approximate seven-century period of Native American settlement from circa 1100 to 1750, from the first appearance of seemingly stratified societies in the 11th century, through the rise and fall of a number of simple and complex chiefdoms throughout the basin until a nearly valleywide organizational collapse occurred in the 15th century, to the ultimate decline and abandonment of the remnant populations remaining in the headwaters before the encroachment of European soldiers and settlers in the mid-18th century. It should be noted that the brief history of the work producing this picture, which follows in the next section, complements more detailed overviews that have appeared elsewhere (Anderson 1989; Anderson, Hally, and Rudolph 1986; Hally and Rudolph 1986).

Mississippian Archaeological Investigations in the Savannah River Valley

The earliest records of Mississippian sites in the Savannah River valley date from the colonial period. During the late 17th century through much of the 18th century, a number of Lower Cherokee towns were present in the upper reaches of the drainage. These towns were visited by traders, travelers, and military parties operating primarily out of Charleston and Savannah, and some descriptions from these visits included references to ancient monuments. The most detailed accounts from this period are by the naturalist William Bartram (1791:313–15, 324–26, 332; see appendix A in this text), who traveled along the Savannah River in the spring of 1776 and described Indian mounds and other earthworks at Silver Bluff, Rembert, and Keowee (figure 17). While a number of other Indian groups were in residence along the lower course of the Savannah during the 17th and 18th centuries, many of which had been relocated to this area by the colonial authorities to provide a buffer for the Carolina colony, archaeological and ethnohistoric research on these groups has been limited until quite recently (but see DePratter 1988, 1990; Green 1991; Green and DePratter 1990; McKivergan 1991).

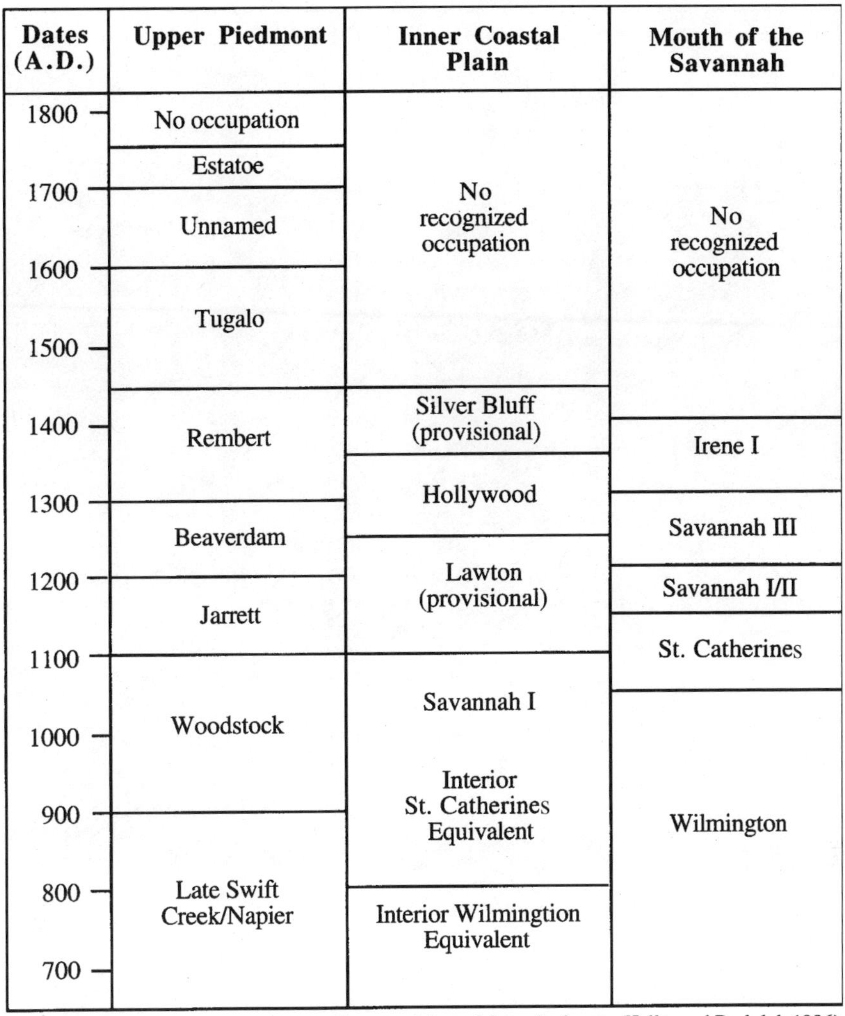

Dates (A.D.)	Upper Piedmont	Inner Coastal Plain	Mouth of the Savannah
1800 —	No occupation		
	Estatoe		
1700 —		No recognized occupation	No recognized occupation
	Unnamed		
1600 —			
	Tugalo		
1500 —			
1400 —	Rembert	Silver Bluff (provisional)	Irene I
1300 —		Hollywood	Savannah III
	Beaverdam		
1200 —		Lawton (provisional)	Savannah I/II
	Jarrett		
1100 —			St. Catherines
1000 —	Woodstock	Savannah I	
900 —		Interior St. Catherines Equivalent	Wilmington
800 —	Late Swift Creek/Napier		
		Interior Wilmingtion Equivalent	
700 —			

(Source: Adapted from Anderson, Hally, and Rudolph 1986)

Figure 16   The Later Prehistoric Cultural Sequence in the Savannah River Valley.

Antiquarian interest in the prehistoric monuments of the Savannah River valley dates to the mid-19th century. George White's (1849:230) *Statistics of the State of Georgia* contains a brief description of the Rembert mound group, a site that was later visited and described in detail by Charles C. Jones (1878:283–86; appendix A in this text). Jones, a resident of Augusta, maintained a lifelong interest in the native antiquities of the Georgia area, contributing descriptions of his findings to the Smithsonian and publishing two major books on the subject, *Monumental Remains of Georgia* and *Antiquities of the Southern Indians, Particularly of the Georgia*

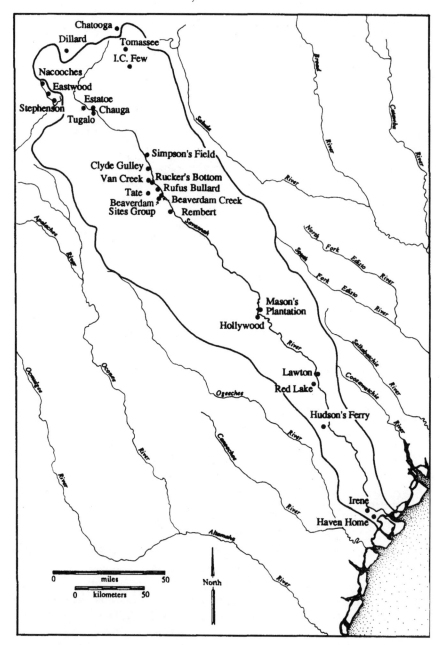

Figure 17   Major Mississippian Sites in the Savannah River Basin.

Tribes (Jones 1861, 1873, 1878, 1880). His detailed description of the mounds on Mason's Plantation near Silver Bluff (Jones 1873:148–57; appendix A in this text) provides the only data we have about this important site, which had washed away by the end of the 19th century. His romantic discussion of "the memorable meeting between the Spanish Adventurer and the Cacica of the Savannah" at this site helped to entrench the belief that dense Indian populations were present in the central Savannah River valley during the 16th century, and that the town of Cofitachequi, which was visited by De Soto in 1540, was located near Silver Bluff. As we shall see, basis for this belief no longer exists.

Excavations along the Savannah were conducted at several sites during the late 19th century, under the direction of archaeologists from the Smithsonian Institution and by Clarence B. Moore, a wealthy industrialist. From 1881 to 1891, the Mound Division of the Bureau of Ethnology explored over 2,000 mounds in the eastern United States (J. Powell 1894: xlv). Of this total, only three mound groups were examined along the Savannah River, at Hollywood, Rembert, and Tugalo. The work at these sites was described in the classic summary *Report of the Mound Explorations of the Bureau of Ethnology,* by Cyrus Thomas (1894:314–26; see appendix A in this text). The work at Hollywood produced a rich Southeastern Ceremonial Complex artifact assemblage, while the investigations at Rembert and Tugalo, although less successful in terms of artifact recovery, provided valuable descriptive information about these sites. The only other formal excavations conducted along the Savannah River during the 19th century were by Clarence B. Moore, who conducted limited testing at a number of sites.

During the winter of 1897–98, Moore (1898:167), "in a rapid steamer of light draught," examined 13 mound sites at six locations along the Savannah. Aside from limited testing at the Lawton mound group in Allendale County, South Carolina, Moore confined his work to the Georgia side of the river, working at the Irene mound near Savannah and at several low sand burial mounds in Screven and Burke counties. His explorations extended from the coast to the Fall Line and focused on what are now known to be late prehistoric habitation and burial sites. The results of this work were published, extensively illustrated, in the *Journal of the Philadelphia Academy of Natural Sciences* (1898). Although his descriptions were brief, they set a high standard for the period and are valuable references today, since many of these sites no longer exist.

The mounds that were examined by Moore were found to be either natural clay rises in the swamp with thin layers of habitation debris or low sand burial mounds. Moore had little luck at Lawton and at the other Savannah River sites he examined, however, something that prompted him to note: "The few mounds found back from the river were small . . . therefore, we did not pursue usual custom, totally to demolish each mound discovered, as we had done, as a rule, in Florida and on the Georgia coast" (167). Given this excavation strategy, it is probably fortunate that Moore's investigations were by his standards unsuccessful. Moore also visited the Stony Bluff quarry (9Bk5), one of several major chert outcrops that occur in the central Coastal Plain portion of the drainage. His observation that the site had been heavily scavenged by local residents documents a long history of artifact collecting in the basin (172). Moore found few rich sites, by his standards, and, commenting that "the Savannah River . . . did not offer a promising field," soon abandoned his effort (167).

Limited archaeological investigations were undertaken in the vicinity of the upper Savannah River during the early part of the 20th century. The most extensive work at a Mississippian site was that conducted at the Nacoochee mound near the headwaters of the Chattahoochee River in White County, Georgia (Heye, Hodge, and Pepper 1918). Etowah- and Middle/Late Lamar–period occupations were documented, and the report that was produced was of exceptional detail for the time, containing numerous artifact illustrations. In 1917, local citizens opened a shaft into the top of the Lindsey mound near Greenville, South Carolina, in the upper Saluda River basin, documenting superimposed occupation floors or construction episodes (Bragg 1918). The site has since been tentatively identified as belonging to the late prehistoric Pisgah culture (Dickens 1976:92), although its precise age and nature remain unknown. No further extensive archaeological investigations were conducted in the upper Savannah River basin until the middle of the 20th century, when reservoir construction was initiated.

In 1928 and 1929, Waring (1968b) conducted excavations at the Savannah I/II–period Haven Home burial mound near Savannah. Waring, a local physician, was a lifelong avocational archaeologist whose writings, posthumously collected and edited in the late 1960s by Stephen Williams (1968), provide the best overview produced to date about prehistoric occupations along the lower Savannah River. In 1929, the Cosgroves, now well known for their work in the Southwest, conducted excavations at the Late Archaic Stallings Island shell midden site near Augusta for the Peabody Museum of Harvard University (Claflin 1931). In addition to the well-known Late Archaic fiber-tempered ceramic complex (see Sassaman 1993), minor Mississippian components were also found at Stallings Island, including two Savannah culture urn burials.

During the late 1930s and early 1940s, extensive archaeological investigations were conducted in North Carolina and Georgia, mostly as a part of federally funded WPA relief activity. This work has had a profound and continuing effect on our understanding of the late prehistoric sequence and occupation of the Savannah River valley (see appendix B). Cultural sequences were established in three areas, in northern Georgia, at the mouth of the Savannah, and in central North Carolina, sequences that to this day guide the dating and interpretation of prehistoric archaeological sites in these areas. Of particular importance for the establishment of a local Mississippian cultural sequence was the WPA-sponsored survey activity in northern Georgia and a major program of survey and excavation undertaken at the mouth of the Savannah, in Chatham County, Georgia. Although the northern Georgia work was not synthesized until the 1960s, when Wauchope's (1966) classic volume *Archaeological Survey in Northern Georgia* appeared, descriptions of the Mississippian sequence for the area were published in a series of articles in the late 1940s and early 1950s (Fairbanks 1950, 1952; Wauchope 1948, 1950). Investigations at the mouth of the Savannah have never been fully reported, although an overview of the major findings are recounted in *The Collected Works of Antonio J. Waring, Jr.* (S. Williams 1968) and, most recently, in an overview by DePratter (1991b). The fieldwork in central North Carolina at Town Creek and surrounding sites was first summarized by Coe (1952) and has been the subject of extensive research by his students (e.g., Ferguson 1971; Oliver 1987; Reid 1965, 1967).

In 1948, the area of the Clark Hill (now Strom Thurmond) Reservoir above Augusta on the Savannah River was surveyed by Caldwell and Miller (Miller 1974). A total of 128 sites were located during preliminary survey work, and limited testing occurred at four of them, at Rembert mounds, Lake Spring, Fort Charlotte, and 38Mc6 (Caldwell 1953, 1974b; Miller 1949, 1950, 1974). The only excavations undertaken at a Mississippian site were a series of test pits excavated at the Rembert mound group on the west side of the river in Georgia (Caldwell 1953). The ceramic collections from the testing at Rembert were used by Hally (in Anderson, Hally, and Rudolph 1986:41–42; J. Rudolph and Hally 1985:456–59) to help define the Rembert phase, a late prehistoric (circa 1350 to 1450) Mississippian occupation along the upper Savannah and immediately adjacent portions of South Carolina and Georgia. To the north of Clark Hill Lake, the area of the Hartwell Reservoir was surveyed by Caldwell in 1953 (Caldwell 1974c), and three mound sites were examined over the next decade, at Chauga, Tugalo, and Estatoe (Caldwell 1956; A. Kelly and De Baillou 1960; A. Kelly and Neitzel 1959, 1961).

From 1966 to 1968, a program of survey and excavation was undertaken in the proposed flood pool of the Keowee-Toxaway Reservoir in Oconee and Pickens counties, South Carolina, in the extreme upper reaches of the Savannah River watershed. Excavations were conducted at a number of prehistoric and historic sites, including I. C. Few, Wild Cherry, Rock Turtle, Toxaway, and Fort Prince George, although to date only a general summary of the investigations has appeared (Beuschel 1976). Middle/Late Woodland through protohistoric Connestee, Pisgah, and Qualla components were found, a late prehistoric cultural sequence comparable to that noted in the Appalachian summit to the north. In fact, aside from detailed efforts at the late prehistoric Chauga, Estatoe, I. C. Few, and Rembert mound sites (Caldwell 1953; Grange 1972; A. Kelly and De Baillou 1960; A. Kelly and Neitzel 1961), Mississippian-period archaeological work conducted during the construction of the Clark Hill, Hartwell, and Keowee-Toxaway reservoirs was minimal in both scope and reporting.

Mississippian components were identified in Allendale County, South Carolina, along the lower Savannah River in the early 1960s by Stoltman (1974), during work on Groton Plantation. Stoltman (1974:30–31, 91) noted a general contemporaneity of Etowah-like and Savannah Complicated Stamped ceramic design motifs at a number of sites, something subsequently recognized as a primary characteristic of Early Mississippian components throughout the basin. Stoltman (241–43) also noted that while Woodland sites were found in a wide array of settings, Mississippian components were concentrated near the main channel. This was interpreted as the result of a switch from upland horticulture, presumably practiced by local Woodland populations, to intensive floodplain agriculture. This observation marked the first serious attempt to explore Mississippian settlement and subsistence systems in the Savannah River area, although it should be noted that evidence for Woodland horticulture is minimal at this time.

Very little work has been done on early historic Indian occupations along the Savannah. Historical summaries have appeared, however, and the general locations of a number of towns occupied after 1670 have been delimited (DePratter 1988; Milling 1940). A number of 18th-century Lower Cherokee sites have been examined in the upper reaches of the basin, including work conducted in the 1950s at the Chauga, Tugalo, and Estatoe mound complexes (described below) and at recent excavations in village areas at Tomassee (M. Smith et al. 1988) and Chattooga (Schroedl and Riggs 1989). The only report on a postcontact Indian site in the lower part of the basin appeared in 1948, when Caldwell described a number of artifacts found in association with burials at the early Creek town of Palachacolas, located on the Savannah River in Hampton County, South Carolina. The site, which had been abandoned during the Yamassee War of 1715, produced glass trade beads, kaolin pipe fragments, European ceramics, and other historic artifacts. These were intermingled with Indian shell beads and Ocmulgee- and Kasita-like pottery, which Caldwell (1948, 1952:321) equated with late protohistoric assemblages in central Georgia.

Since the late 1960s, considerable archaeological survey and excavation have occurred in all parts of the basin, for the most part as the result of cultural resource management projects. These projects have complemented research programs conducted in the drainage over the same interval, such as Ferguson's 1971 (n.d.) survey for Mississippian sites, Goodyear and Charles's (1984) survey of the Allendale chert quarries, and Brooks and colleagues' (1986) geoarchaeological analyses documenting changing channel morphology. Two major programs of archaeological research conducted in the basin in recent years are the mitigation program for the Richard B. Russell Reservoir and the ongoing cultural resources program on the Department of Energy's Savannah River Site. The Russell Reservoir project in the central Piedmont brought together researchers from throughout the region for a comparatively brief but intense period in the late 1970s and early 1980s, producing a massive body of research, the results of which have only recently been synthesized (Anderson and Joseph 1988). On the Savannah River Site in the inner Coastal Plain, in contrast, a small team of investigators has been conducting an intensive program of archaeological survey, excavation, and analysis for almost 15 years, yielding a reasonably detailed picture of prehistoric occupations in this part of the drainage (Sassaman et al. 1990).

Mississippian Survey Coverage in the Savannah River Valley

As of January 1990, almost 100 major archaeological survey projects had been conducted in the Savannah River basin (figure 18). Information about archaeological investigations in the Savannah River valley was obtained from the manuscript and site files maintained at the Laboratory of Archaeology at the University of Georgia and at the South Carolina Institute of Archaeology and Anthropology, the primary repositories for report and site data in Georgia and South Carolina (Anderson 1990a:262–79). Table 3, which is cross-referenced with figure 18, lists these projects and provides data about the intensity of survey coverage, area examined, number of prehistoric sites recorded, number of Mississippian components on these sites, and primary bibliographic references. In localities where numerous survey and excavation projects have occurred, such as in the Russell Reservoir and the Sumter National Forest and on the Savannah River Site, summary data from syntheses of work on these localities were employed (Anderson and Joseph 1988; Anderson et al. n.d.; Sassaman et al. 1990).

To date, just under one-tenth (2,058.4 square kilometers, or 7.5%) of the 27,450-square-kilometer Savannah River basin has been surveyed at some level of coverage (table 3). Much of this total comes from opportunistic reconnaissance-level survey projects, where typically only the largest or most obvious sites were recorded. Approximately 2.6% of the basin has been intensively surveyed using field procedures (theoretically) designed to locate and record all possible sites. These intensive survey projects have occurred throughout the basin, providing at least some intensive coverage in each of the major physiographic zones, including the Sea Island, Coastal Plain, Fall Line, Piedmont, and Blue Ridge provinces. While sites are reported from most areas of the basin, intensive survey of large contiguous areas is restricted to a few localities where coverage, designed to meet historic preservation inventory requirements, has been mandated by federal environmental legislation and executive order. These localities include the Wassaw and Savannah national wildlife refuges, the Savannah

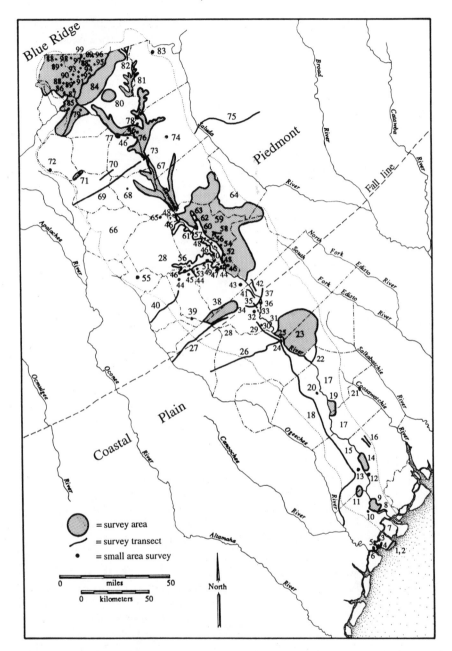

Figure 18   Major Survey Projects in the Savannah River Basin.

Table 3. Archaeological Survey in the Savannah River Valley: Major Survey Localities

Project Number	Locality (proceeding from mouth to interior, south to north)	Type of Survey/Project	Area Examined (ha)	No. of Prehistoric Sites	Total Sites	Mississippian Sites	Unknown	Mississippian Components E	M	L	References
1	Wassaw National Wildlife Refuge	reconnaissance	29.4	4	9	1		1			Pearson and Pearson 1978
2	Wassaw National Wildlife Refuge	intensive	n/a	38	69	7		5	2		DePratter 1977
3	Skidaway Island State Park	reconnaissance	n/a	3	7	0					Weinland 1981a
4	Skidaway Island	reconnaissance	613	84	101	13		7	11		Caldwell · 970: DePratter 1975
5	Landings Development, Skidaway Island	intensive	40.9	6	8	3			3		Elliott 1986a
6	Green Island	intensive	n/a	55	72	2		1	1		Crook 1975
7	Chatham County WPA archaeological survey	reconnaissance	n/a		/						DePratter 1991b; S. Williams 1968
8	Savannah Harbor sediment basin-widening project	reconnaissance	n/a	3	5	0					Ferguson 1973; Scurry and Brooks 1978
9	Savannah National Wildlife Refuge	reconnaissance	n/a	20	36	3	2				Marrinan 1979
10	Chatham County development tract	intensive	81	1	1	0					Haecker and Williams 1978
11	Eli Whitney watershed	reconnaissance	655.1	5	5	0					W. Mitchell and Hally 1975
12	Purrysburg tract	intensive	123.1	15	19	4	4				Elliott 1985
13	Fort Howard Paper Company tract	intensive	809.7	31	54	2	2		2	1	Elliott and Smith 1985; M. Smith 1986:239, 296
14	Jasper County geoarchaeological project	reconnaissance	n/a	58	58	21	12	6	4		Brooks and Sassaman n.d.
15	Ebenezer Creek watershed	reconnaissance	522.1	99	108	11	3	5	2	2	P. Fish 1976
16	New River watershed swamp	reconnaissance	61.3	0	0	0					Bianchi · 975
17	Coastal Plain Mississippian survey	reconnaissance	n/a	78	78	17	8	7	2		Ferguson n.d.
18	Vogtle-Thalmann transmission line	intensive	2,252.5	76	90	6	6				Garrow 1984
19	Groton Plantation	reconnaissance	9,097.60	21	21	13		13	3	1	Stoltmar 1974
20	Lower Brier Creek	reconnaissance	n/a	5	5	2		1	1		Elliott 1987
21	Brunson wastewater treatment facility	intensive	10	2	2	0					Judge 1988a
22	Allendale/Burke County chert quarry survey	reconnaissance	n/a	27	27	3	2	1			Goodyear and Charles 1984:42, 72, 83
23	Department of Energy Savannah River Site	intensive	48,664	755	853	101	89	31	19		Sassaman et al. 1990, Anderson 1990a:700–702
24	Vogtle Nuclear Power Plant Site	reconnaissance	n/a	8	8	1	1	1			Honerkamp 1973
25	Talatha Unit, Sumter National Forest	reconnaissance	2,437.70	34	34	0					Hanson and Most 1978
26	Vogtle-Wadley transmission line	intensive	331.2	43	60	2	2				Wheaton et al. 1982:92, 127, 130
27	Fall Line Freeway (southern alternate)	intensive, 10%	55.2	13	16	0					Gresham et al. 1986
28	Central Savannah basin archaic survey, Georgia	reconnaissance	n/a	39	39	8	5	1		3	Bruce Smith 1974:57–59, 216–17
29	Vogtle-Goshen transmission line	intensive	125.4	27	31	1	1	1			Garrow and Bauer 1984
30	Kimberly-Clark Plant tract	reconnaissance	182.2	9	21	1	1	1			Garrow, Herbert, and Savage 1980
31	Silver Bluff	intensive	81	1	1	1		1	1		Scurry, Joseph, and Hamer 1980
32	Cedar Ridge Farms development	intensive	96.8	0	0	0					Betty Smith 1979a
33	Butler Creek sewage pipeline	intensive	11.8	9	10	3	3				Ledbetter, Doyon, and Wood 1980
34	Bobby Jones Expressway, Richmond County, Georgia	reconnaissance	153.1	20	24	3	2	1	2	1	Ferguson and Widmer 1976:107

Table 3. (Continued)

Project Number	Locality (proceeding from mouth to interior, south to north)	Type of Survey/Project	Area Examined (ha)	No. of Prehistoric Sites	Total Sites	Mississippian Sites	Unknown	Mississippian Components E	M	L	References
35	Augusta 201 facilities	intensive	2.8	1	1	0					Garrow et al. 1978
36	Augusta railroad relocation project	intensive	n/a	38	42	5	5				Bowen 1979; Elliott and Doyon 1981
37	Bobby Jones Expressway, Aiken County, S.C.	reconnaissance	103.1	5	5	0					Cable et al. 1978
38	Fort Gordon Military Reservation	intensive	1,600	81	89	16	4	5	10	3	Campbell, Weed, and Thomas 1981
39	Mill Branch impoundment	intensive	48	14	14	2	1		1		Ledbetter and Gresham 1988:39, 65–67
40	Fall Line freeway (northern alternate)	intensive, 10%	40.5	6	6	0					Gresham et al. 1986
41	Murrey Road extension project	intensive	103.1	8	8	1				1	Bowen 1984; Ledbetter 1988:84–85
42	Pole Branch and southwest interceptors	intensive	40.5	2	6	0					Martin and Drucker 1987
43	Columbia County Industrial Park	intensive	130	5	10	0					Drucker and Anthony 1983
44	Clarks Hill Lake recreation areas	intensive	24	1	1	0					Jameson 1986
45	McDuffie County Water Treatment Facility	intensive	30	3	8	1	1				Judge 1988b
46	Fifteen tracts, Clark Hill and Hartwell reservoirs	intensive	20.4	3	5	1	1				Rudolph et al. 1979
47	Wildwood Park wastewater treatment plant	intensive	0.62	3	4	0					R. Webb 1987
48	Eighteen private club lease tracts, Clark Hill Lake	intensive	61.9	8	13	0					Anuskiewicz 1982
49	Lake Springs recreation area, Clarks Hill Lake	intensive	72.9	1	2	0					J. Wood 1980
50	Clarks Hill Lake land exchange/recreation areas	intensive	23.6	12	12	0					Anuskiewicz 1984
51	Cherokee recreation area, Clarks Hill Lake	intensive	51.6	4	7	1	1				Cridlebaugh 1985a, 1985b
52	Catfish recreation area, Clarks Hill Lake	intensive	208.4	19	47	1					Cridlebaugh 1985a, 1985b
53	Mistletoe State Park	intensive	2	4	4	0					Ledbetter 1983; Ledbetter, Wood, and Miller 1985
54	Brunswick Pulp and Paper, Augusta Archaeological Society	reconnaissance	2,024	44	44	0					George S. Lewis, personal communication, 1989
55	Alexander H. Stephens State Park	reconnaissance	n/a	5	7	0					Weinland 1981b
56	Clarks Hill recreational club lease tracts	intensive	146.1	15	19	0					Drucker 1983
57	Clark Hill Reservoir	reconnaissance	31,781.4	128	128	29	29				Miller 1974
58	Baker Creek State Park connector	intensive	4	0	1	0					Espenshade 1988
59	Long Cane Division, Sumter National Forest	reconnaissance	45,838.1	391	698	24	18	5	1		Anderson, Amer, and Elliott 1992; Bates, personal communication, 1989
60	McCormick County Law Enforcement	intensive	3.2	1	1	0					Charles and Smith 1988
61	Little River development	intensive	404.9	19	49	0					Holschlag and Rodeffer 1976
62	Little River–Buffalo Creek land disposal tract	intensive	931.2	63	108	1	1				Drucker et al. 1984:3–20
63	John De La Howe School	intensive	76.1	12	16	0					Martin, Drucker, and Jackson 1987
64	Greenwood County archaeological survey	reconnaissance	1,905.6	295	560	24	21	1	2	1	Rodeffer, Holschlag, and Cann 1979:53
65	Anthony Shoals Site (9WS51) evaluation	intensive	3.44	1	1	1					W. Wood and Smith 1988:43–47
66	Oglethorpe County clear-cuts	intensive	478	173	173	29	13	3	2	16	Freer 1989

No.	Project	Survey type	Area (sq km)	Sites						Reference
67	Richard B. Russell Reservoir	intensive	5,394.70	600 / 732	153	74	27	46	6	Anderson and Joseph 1988
68	Georgia Kraft Mill, Elbert County	intensive	185	14 / 18	0					R. Webb and Garrow 1981
69	Powder Springs pipeline corridor	intensive	36.8	5 / 6	0					Garrow 1978
70	Transco pipeline	intensive	29.5	18 / 19	0					Meyer 1988
71	Hudson River watershed	reconnaissance	n/a	18 / 20	1	1				Barber, Rudolph, and Hally 1979
72	Grove River watershed	reconnaissance	371.6	9 / 10	3	1			2	Jefferies and Hally 1975
73	Colonial Pipeline Company	intensive	0.7	0 / 0	0					Foss and Warner 1977
74	Broadway Lake dredging project	reconnaissance	n/a	3 / 3	0					Brooks 1977
75	Laurens-Anderson Highway corridor	intensive	772.9	125 / 165	8	8				Goodyear 1978; Goodyear, House, and Ackerly 1979
76	Hartwell Reservoir	reconnaissance	n/a	70 / 70	8					Caldwell 1974
77	Lake Hartwell State Park	intensive	242.9	29 / 33	0					Drucker, Anthony, and Harmon 1979; Anthony and Drucker 1980, 1984
78	Pioneer utility line	intensive	1.4	0 / 0	0					Judge 1939
79	Thrift exchange tract, Chattahoochee National Forest	intensive	194.3	1 / 5	0					Wynn 1982b
80	Oconee County wastewater project	intensive	126.6	5 / 13	1	1				Rodeffer and Holschlag 1976
81	Keowee-Toxaway Reservoir	reconnaissance	7,489.90	38 / 39	10		1	3	9	Beuschel 1976
82	Oconee-Jocassee-Bad Creek transmission lines	intensive	31.9	5 / 5	0					Brockington 1978
83	Oolenoy watershed	intensive	20.2	0 / 0	0					Brockington 1978
84	Andrew Pickens District, Sumter National Forest	reconnaissance	31,439.30	53 / 71	10	6	2	1	7	Anderson, Amer, and Elliott 1992; Bates, personal communication, 1989
85	Littleton Land Exchange, Chattahoochee National Forest	intensive	152.3	1 / 3	0					Gaffney and Wynn 1981
86	Stamp Creek Road, Chattahoochee National Forest	intensive	14.5	1 / 1	0					Wynn 1980a, 1981a
87	Georgia Power Co. land exchange, Chattahoochee National Forest	intensive	26.3	0 / 0	0					Wynn 1980b
88	Tallulah District, Chattahoochee National Forest	intensive	1,088.20	3 / 11	1	1				Wynn 1983
89	Seven compartments, Chattahoochee National Forest	reconnaissance	1,619.40	38 / 38	4	1			4	Seckinger and Graybill 1976
90	Six timber sale areas, Chattahoochee National Forest	intensive	501.6	3 / 4	0					Willingham and Wynn 1984
91	Worley Ridge tracts, Chattahoochee National Forest	reconnaissance	2,773.30	11 / 13	0					Willingham 1984b
92	Rabun County landfill	intensive	24.3	2 / 2	0					J. Rudolph et al. 1979
93	Warwoman Wildlife Openings, Chattahoochee National Forest	intensive	2.4	2 / 2	1	1				Willingham 1984b
94	Walnut Fork Road, Chattahoochee National Forest	intensive	9.8	2 / 2	0					Wynn 1981b
95	Pounding Mill Creek timber sale, Chattahoochee National Forest	intensive	234.8	2 / 9	0					Willingham 1983a
96	Three site testings, Chattahoochee National Forest	intensive	n/a	3 / 3	0					K. Schneider 1977
97	Ramey Creek timber sale, Chattahoochee National Forest	intensive	649.8	12 / 20	1				1	Willingham 1983b
98	Hoojah Branch, Chattahoochee National Forest	intensive	573.7	11 / 12	2	1				Willingham 1983c:17, 1984c
99	Darnell Creek Road, Chattahoochee National Forest	intensive	11.5	4 / 4	0				1	Wynn 1980c
	GRAND TOTALS		205,840	3,917 / 5,129	551	323	125	121	58	

Note: totals exclude data from project no. 75 outside of basin

27,450 square kilometers = size of Savannah River basin

2,058.4 square kilometers, or 7.5%, of basin surveyed at any level of intensity

702.22 square kilometers, or 2.6%, of the basin intensively surveyed

River Site, Fort Gordon, the Clark Hill, Russell, and Hartwell reservoirs, and portions of the Oconee, Chattahoochee, and Sumter national forests. Fortunately, these localities are dispersed along the river and encompass portions of all of the major physiographic zones.

As of January 1990, a total of 6,871 archaeological sites had been recorded in the 35 counties in Georgia and South Carolina encompassing the Savannah River basin. Of these, 5,129, or 74.6%, were found during the survey projects documented in table 3. The remaining 1,742 sites either lie in portions of these counties outside the basin proper or are isolated sites reported by amateurs or professionals and not derived from systematic survey coverage. As best as I have been able to determine, the data in table 3 represent over 90% of the sites recorded in the basin and almost all of the sites found through intensive survey activity. If projects or sites have been overlooked in the basin, it is because information from them was not on file in the Georgia and South Carolina state repositories when the analyses were conducted. It should be noted that no sites or records from North Carolina are included in the totals, even though a tiny fraction (less than 1%) of the basin, consisting of rugged terrain at the extreme headwaters, extended into this state.

In spite of the large numbers of sites recorded in the basin, gaps in survey coverage are evident. Comparatively few sites have been recorded in the extreme western part of the basin in Georgia, for example, where several counties have fewer than 50 recorded sites. A particularly crucial gap in intensive coverage occurs immediately below the Fall Line on both sides of the river. A number of Indian groups were reported in this area during the early historic era, and two major mound groups, Hollywood and Mason's Plantation, were built here during the late prehistoric era. The surveys that have been conducted to date along the river in this area have been comparatively minimal in extent, along narrow highway or railroad corridors. Only one project explicitly directed to locating Mississippian sites has been conducted in the basin, an opportunistic survey undertaken in 1971 by Ferguson, who followed up on leads provided by local informants. A total of 78 sites were found during this project, which was restricted to the Coastal Plain. Accordingly, while it is likely that most or all of the major mound centers in the basin have been found, information about other Mississippian site types must be viewed as incomplete. Furthermore, since many reported sites have small and probably nonrepresentative artifact collections, great care must be taken in interpreting this data.

Excavation Assemblages: The Mound Centers

Fourteen Mississippian mound centers, presumably the ceremonial and political focus for life during this period, are known from the Savannah River basin (table 4). These sites, proceeding inland from the mouth of the drainage, are Haven Home, Irene, Hudson's Ferry, Red Lake, Lawton, Hollywood, Mason's Plantation, Rembert, Beaverdam Creek, Tate, Tugalo, Estatoe, Chauga, and I. C. Few; they include both platform and burial mounds, with the former typically much larger than the latter. Given the century or more of effort directed to finding and excavating these sites, it is probable that most of the surviving platform mounds in the basin have been found. The sample of burial mounds, in contrast, is probably incomplete, because of their small size, particularly those dating to the initial Mississippian period, which are little more than low rises of earth. Archaeological investigations at the basin's mound sites are summarized in the pages that follow, proceeding from the mouth of the river into the interior.

Haven Home

In 1928 and 1929, Antonio J. Waring conducted excavations at the St. Catherines– or Savannah I/II–period Haven Home burial mound (9Ch15) near Savannah, Georgia, a site shown on an early map of the city as the "Indian King's Tomb" (Waring 1968b). At the time of excavation, the mound was circular and slightly conical in shape and was between 1.8 and 2.4 meters high and 22.9 meters in diameter (figure 19). Two construction episodes were recognized. The initial mound was built over a large concentration of burned human bone approximately 3 meters in diameter and several centimeters thick. The presence of a communal ossuary was inferred since "the bone showed the typical checking and cracking seen when dry bone is burned, and we may therefore deduce that the bones of a series of individuals had their flesh removed and were saved either in a special mortuary house or in houses of individuals until the mound was ready to be started" (Waring 1968b:212). The burned-bone lens was covered with a thin layer of sand and a 30-centimeter-thick layer of oyster shell, which was in turn covered with earth, into which were subsequently placed a number of individual flexed burials. The thin soil horizon observed in the profile suggested that this initial mound was in place for a number of years before the second episode of construction was begun, a layer of earth more than 1 meter thick into which, again, a number of individual flexed burials were placed.

Forty-four burials were recorded in the mound, including the central cremation (which was counted as a single interment, even though the remains of numerous individuals were represented). The subsequent burials were almost invariably flexed and covered with hematite, although two extended burials, both with vessels, were found. The bones were in very poor condition and were not saved, but most appear to have been from adults. Approximately one-third of the burials had grave goods

Table 4. Mississippian Excavation Assemblages and Mound Sites from the Savannah River Basin

Site Number	Site Name	Year Excavated	Site Type	Phases of Primary Occupation	References
	Mason's Plantation	-	platform mounds? (n = 6)	Savannah III/Hollywood?	C. Jones 1873:148–57; C. Moore 1898:167–68
9Eb86	Tate		platform mound (n = 1)	Beaverdam	Hutto 1970:23–25
9Eb1	Rembert	1883, 1948	platform mounds? (n = 5)	Beaverdam, Rembert	C. Thomas 1894:315–17; Caldwell 1953; J. Rudolph and Hally 1985:453–59; Anderson, Amer, and Elliott 1992
9Ri1	Hollywood	1891, 1965	platform mound (n = 2)	Hollywood	C. Thomas 1894:317–26; DeBaillou 1965
9Ch15	Haven Home	1897–98	burial mound (n = 1)	Savannah I/II	Waring 1968b
9Sn3	Hudson's Ferry	1897–98	burial mound (n = 1)	Lawton/Hollywood	C. Moore 1898:169–71
38Al11	Lawton	1897–98	platform mound (n = 2)	Lawton	C. Moore 1898:171–72; Anderson 1990a:662–68
9Ch1	Irene	1939–41	platform and burial mound (n = 2)	Savannah I/II, III, Irene I	C. Moore 1898:168; Caldwell and McCann 1941
9St1	Tugalo	1956–57	platform mound (n = 1)	Jarrett, Rembert, Tugalo	C. Thomas 1894:314–15; Caldwell 1956
38Oc47	Chauga	1958	platform mound (n = 1)	Jarrett, Tugalo, Estatoe	A. Kelly and Neitzel 1959, 1961
9St3	Estatoe	1959–60	platform mound (n = 1)	Tugalo, Estatoe	A. Kelly and DeBaillou 1960
38Pn2	I. C. Few	1967	burial mound? (n = 3)	Beaverdam, Rembert, Estatoe	Grange 1972
9Eb92	Beaverdam site group	1980	hamlet?	Beaverdam, Rembert	Campbell and Weed 1984
9Eb207	Beaverdam site group	1980	hamlet?	Beaverdam	Campbell and Weed 1984
9Eb208	Beaverdam site group	1980	hamlet?	Beaverdam	Campbell and Weed 1984
9Eb219	Beaverdam site group	1980	hamlet?	Jarrett, Beaverdam	Campbell and Weed 1984
38An126	Big Generostee Creek	1980	hunting camp?	Rembert	W. Wood et al. 1986
9Eb382	Van Creek	1980–81	village	Rembert	W. Wood et al. 1986
9Eb357	Clyde Gulley	1980–81	hamlet?	Jarrett	Tippitt and Marquardt 1984
38An8	Simpson's Field	1980–81	village?	Beaverdam/Rembert	Wood et al. 1986
9Eb76	Rufus Bullard	1980–81	platform mound (n = 1)	Beaverdam, Rembert	Anderson and Schuldenrein 1985
9Eb85	Beaverdam Creek	1980–81	village	Beaverdam	J. Rudolph and Hally 1985
9Eb91	Rucker's Bottom	1980–82	village	Beaverdam, Rembert	Anderson and Schuldenrein 1985
38Oc186	Tomassee	1986	village	Estatoe	M. Smith et al. 1988
9Sn4	Red Lake	1988	platform mound (n = 1)	Lawton	J. Mark Williams, personal communications, 1989
38Oc18	Chattooga	1989–92	village	Estatoe	Schroedl and Riggs 1989

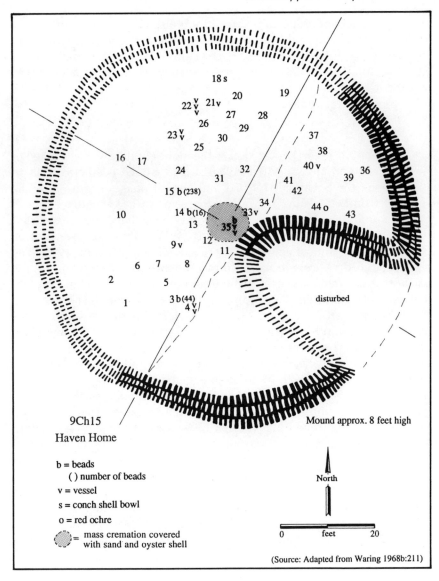

Figure 19 The Haven Home Burial Mound (9Ch15).

present: three burials had shell beads (16, 44, and 238 beads); eight burials had between one and three associated vessels (including two "boat-shaped" containers in the central cremation); and one burial had a conch shell bowl. Of 16 vessels described from the mound, 8 were Savannah Burnished Plain (2 apparently painted red or coated with ochre), 5 were Savannah Fine Cord-Marked, 2 were "boat-shaped" and presumably plain, and 1 was described as a red-and-black dog effigy pot, which may point to contact with Mississippian cultures elsewhere in the region. Few artifacts were found in the initial mass cremation, suggesting egalitarian communal treatment reminiscent of the Huron Feast of the Dead (Tooker 1964:134–40), if indeed all members of society were represented in the interment.

Irene

The Irene site (9Ch1), located near the mouth of the river, consisted of two mounds and an associated village area occupied from circa 1200 to 1450 during the Savannah I/II, III and Irene I phases (figure 20). The subject of limited testing by C. B. Moore in 1897 (appendix A), both mounds and almost 6 acres of the surrounding village were excavated from September 1937 to January 1940 by WPA crews of upward of 50 people working almost continuously (Caldwell and McCann 1941). The work produced a Mississippian cultural sequence for the lower part of the valley that has remained essentially unmodified to this day, and the site remains the most intensively examined mound center in the basin.

Eight construction stages with associated temple structures were found in the large mound at Irene, which was approximately 48.8 meters in diameter and 4.7 meters high in 1937. The first seven construction epi-sodes—the first three earth-embanked structures and the next four trun-cated pyramidal platform mounds—belonged to the Savannah I/II, III phases (circa 1150–1300), while mound stage 8, a circular earthen mound with a rounded summit (with no evidence for associated structures) dated to the succeeding Irene I phase (circa 1300–1400). A low circular mound with 106 burials was located west of the large mound that saw use during both the Savannah and Irene occupations. A large mortuary structure and a rotunda or council house were built during the Irene occupation. Finally, a series of fence lines or enclosures was found, and different segments were dated to one major occupation or the other. No evidence for Euro-pean contact was found (Caldwell and McCann 1941:72), and the site appears to have been abandoned some time around or shortly after circa 1450.

Primary Mound Construction Episodes.   Based on ceramic evidence, spe-cifically the presence of Savannah Check and Complicated Stamped pot-tery, the earliest mound construction at Irene apparently began sometime around 1150 to 1200 (Caldwell and McCann 1941:78). While evidence for earlier occupations was found, in the form of small numbers of Wilmington, Deptford, and Stallings sherds and a range of Archaic and Woodland point types, the first major use of the site appears to be during the Mississippian period. Mound stages 1 and 2 were earth-embanked structures with central fire basins built on the original ground surface. The structures were fairly small and squared, measuring approximately 7.6

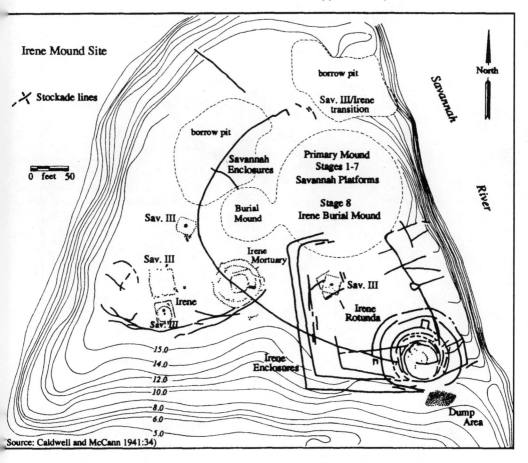

Figure 20 Major Architectural Features at the Irene Site (9Ch1). (Courtesy The University of Georgia Press)

meters on a side, with an entrance and a ramp on the southeastern side, while the area covered by the surrounding embankments measured approximately 18 meters by 12 meters. The embankment for mound stage 1 was 38 centimeters high, while that for mound stage 2 was 51 centimeters high. Mound stage 2 had a somewhat more complex central structure than the first stage, with a low modeled ledge of clay around its interior wall and a number of internal posts, suggesting the presence of partitioned seating areas (figure 21). The floor of the second stage was only approximately 5 centimeters higher than that of the first stage and was built right over it.

Mound stage 3 was very poorly defined and only slightly larger than the preceding mound, at 21.3 meters by 19.5 meters. Its summit had been removed, presumably during leveling/construction operations associated with the construction of stage 4. An earth-embanked structure is

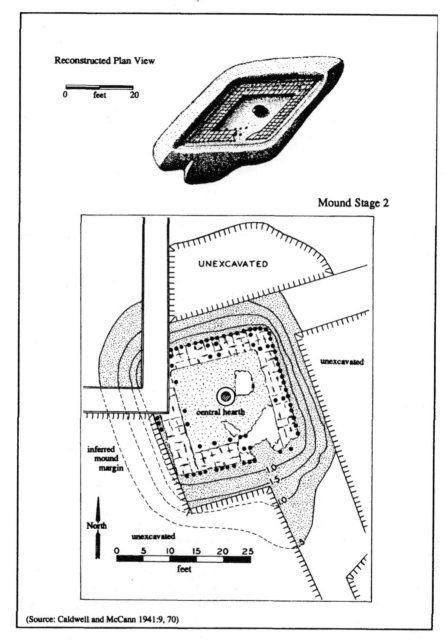

Figure 21   Mound Stage 2 in the Primary Mound at the Irene Site (9Ch1). (Courtesy The University of Georgia Press)

assumed to have been present, although its elevation above the preceding stage could not be determined. A human skull was found just under the western margin of this mound, under a Savannah Fine Cord-Marked vessel, but whether it was associated with the mound construction or something left from an earlier occupation could not be determined. A series of palisade or screening wall lines, suggesting multiple rebuilding episodes, was found around the periphery of the mound and extending out from it approximately 21 meters from the entranceway on the south-eastern side, enclosing a roughly rectangular-shaped area. Mound stage 4 was approximately 1.07 meters high, 21.3 meters on a side at the base, and 13.1 meters on a side at the summit, with a central depression approximately 15 centimeters lower where a building had apparently stood. Scattered post molds and linear alignments were observed, and the presence of fired daub and charred cane suggests one or more structures had been present and had burned.

Stage 5 was flat topped, a true platform mound measuring approximately 1.37 meters high, 29.3 meters by 18.3 meters at the base, and 15.5 meters by 14.9 meters at the summit (figure 22). Shell was placed in a layer on the sides of the mound away from the entrance area, possibly to "strengthen and drain the mound slopes" (Caldwell and McCann 1941:21) or as a special capping. As with the preceding stages, a ramp was located on the southeastern side, although for this stage a series of logs had been placed on the slope, creating steps. A central structure measuring 6.1 meters by 4.9 meters was present, with a fire basin surrounded by a shallow teardrop-shaped gutter extending to the edge of the mound, possibly to drain fluids. Palisades were erected at the base and on the summit of the mound, although openings at the ramp and mound corners suggest their use for screening rather than defensive purposes. A clay layer with cane matting impressions in its upper surface was observed by the southwestern wall, which may have been an open seating area.

Mound stage 6 was built directly over stage 5 and was somewhat larger, measuring 1.5 meters in height, 32.6 meters by 25.9 meters at the base, and 18.9 meters by 14.9 meters at the summit (figure 23). Once again shell was placed on the sides away from the entrance. The entrance ramp, while larger than that for stage 5 and built directly over it, lacked log steps. The summit had two central structures, one behind the other, and was almost completely enclosed by a palisade, with the only opening by the ramp. The first, southernmost building was 6.7 meters by 5.8 meters and had a central fire basin and an elaborate surrounding gutter running to the entrance; in some ways, this gutter resembles the forked-eye motif common on engraved shell masks from the South Appalachian area (M. Smith and Smith 1989:13). While this may be a fortuitous association, three fragments of copper sheeting with repoussé decorations were also found nearby, suggesting that ceremonial activities associated with the use of prestige goods occurred on the summit.

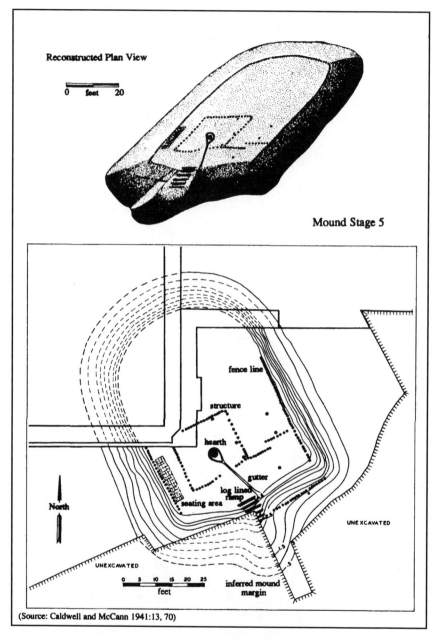

(Source: Caldwell and McCann 1941:13, 70)

Figure 22   Mound Stage 5 in the Primary Mound at the Irene Site (9Ch1). (Courtesy The University of Georgia Press)

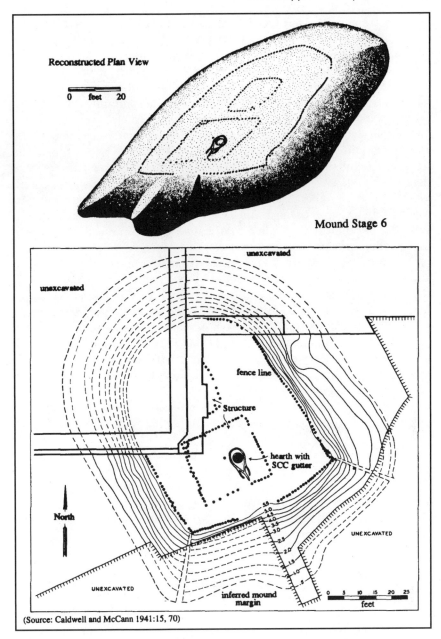

Figure 23   Mound Stage 6 in the Primary Mound at the Irene Site (9Ch1). (Courtesy The University of Georgia Press)

Mound stage 7 was appreciably larger than stage 6, standing 2.9 meters in height and measuring 25.9 meters across at the base and 19.8 meters wide at the summit. Its length could not be determined, since portions of the northern side had been removed for fill. Two ramps were present, on the southeastern and southwestern sides, neither with log steps. Evidence for two structures and a palisade was found on the summit, although the defining post lines were eroded and fragmentary. The first structure, near the southeastern ramp, was particularly poorly defined, consisting of little more than a line of posts 10 meters long with a hint of two corners. The second structure, located in the northeastern corner, was much more clearly defined, was approximately 4 meters on a side, was squared with rounded corners, and had a projecting entranceway. The summit and particularly the sides of the mound were extensively eroded, indicating it and possibly the site had fallen into disuse some time well prior to the construction of mound stage 8.

Mound stage 8 differed appreciably from the preceding stages in a number of respects. At approximately 48.8 meters in diameter, it was much larger than the previous mounds, was circular instead of rectangular in shape, and had a rounded instead of a flat summit. Stage 8 partially covered the burial mound to the east, which appears to have been used primarily during the Savannah occupations. In the construction of stage 8, shell was first placed over stage 7, including two layers on the flanks, with sand used as fill around and over the shell. Except where it overlapped the burial mound, stage 8 was capped with clay. The construction of stage 8, which was 1.8 meters higher, on the average, than stage 7, required as much fill as in all the preceding stages combined.

The Burial Mound.   The low burial mound to the west of the primary mound at Irene saw use during both the Savannah and Irene periods. In a pattern almost identical to that observed at the nearby Haven Home site, initial activity involved the placement of cremated secondary burials in a central shell deposit (approximately 5.5 meters in diameter and 61 centimeters thick). Five cremated burials were found below the shell, four with associated grave goods, including three unusually shaped Savannah Plain–like vessels, a clay elbow pipe, and a conch shell bowl. Two cremations were found in the shell lens itself, one in a Savannah Burnished Plain vessel. Only one other cremation was found at the site, in the Irene rotunda. A low sand-and-shell mound approximately 76 centimeters high and 16.8 meters in diameter was built over the central shell lens in a number of discrete construction episodes, each with a seemingly associated cluster of burials located either in the fill or placed in the underlying subsoil prior to construction. The 99 burials that came from this accretional mound were predominantly primary or secondary interments, the great majority of which were flexed, with a lesser number disturbed or fragmentary (Caldwell and McCann 1941:24). While grave goods were found with

5 of the 7 cremated individuals in the central shell deposit, only 8 of the 99 burials in the overlying mound had associated grave goods. One of these was an infant buried in an Irene Complicated Stamped urn, five were adults with varying but typically low numbers of shell beads, and one had a bone awl and a conch shell bowl (22–24). Except for the infant, it was not possible to determine precisely the date of the remaining burials, although most are assumed to date to the Savannah occupation.

The Mortuary. An apparent mortuary dating to the Irene period was located on a low rise 25 meters south of the primary mound (figure 24). A semisubterranean structure inset approximately 30 to 40 centimeters into the ground was in the central part of this complex, surrounded by two circular palisade lines. Approximately 7.3 meters on a side, square with rounded corners, and with a pronounced wall-trench entranceway, this building resembles domestic structures found at Rucker's Bottom in the Piedmont portion of the drainage (see below) and elsewhere in northern Georgia (Hally 1979, 1980; M. Smith 1981). No central hearth was found, however, arguing for a special function for the structure. The building had been destroyed by fire, as evidenced by burned roof debris over much of the floor and fired clay walls standing to a height of approximately 36 centimeters in several areas. Four burials, three flexed and the fourth an isolated skull, were found on the floor. One of the flexed burials showed signs of burning and may have been undergoing defleshing when the structure burned. Five Irene pottery vessels were also found on the floor, including two complicated stamped urns, one plain and one incised bowl, and one plain bottle. The presence of these vessels, the condition of the burials, and the presence of a small cluster of food refuse on the floor suggest the structure was in use when it burned.

The mortuary structure was covered over with a low sand mound soon after it burned. How far this mound extended beyond the structure could not be determined, since it had been greatly reduced by plowing. Thirty-four burials were placed in the fill of this mound, 21 infants or children in urns and the remainder flexed or fragmentary adult interments. In all, 25 Irene vessels were found in the mound, 21 Irene Complicated Stamped urns (filfot motif), two small incised (toy?) pots, and two plain bowls, one the cover of an urn burial. Excluding the urns themselves, only two of the burials had other associated grave goods. One infant had two small Irene Incised vessels inside its burial urn, while an adult located near the center of the mound was buried with five celts, four stone disks, two polished pebbles, and a incised schist plate. The death of this latter individual may have prompted the burning of the structure and the subsequent construction of the mound.

The immediate area around the mortuary structure was used as a cemetery, demarcated by two circular enclosures approximately 13.7 meters and 18.3 meters in diameter, respectively. The presence of a post

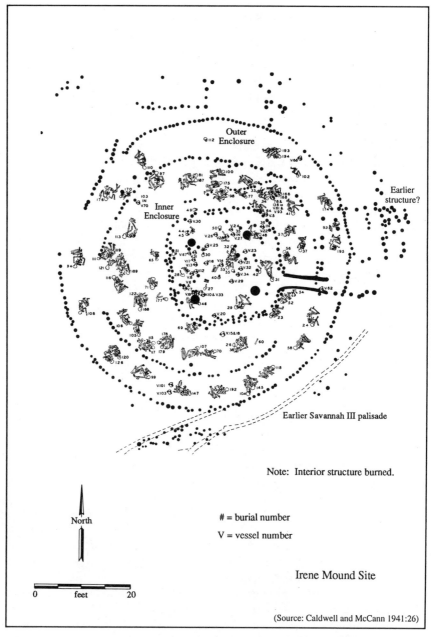

Figure 24   The Mortuary at the Irene Mound Site (9Ch1). (Courtesy The University of Georgia Press)

from the inner enclosure inside the entranceway of the mortuary indicates these enclosures were built after the mortuary had been destroyed. Forty-one burials were found inside the inner enclosure, many near and oriented parallel to the wall, and most flexed or fragmentary. Six double burials were present, three adult females with a child, two double burials of children, and one adult double burial. Only two urn burials were found, a double burial in two separate Irene Complicated Stamped urns. Nineteen of the 41 individuals were buried with grave goods, mostly isolated or small numbers of shell pins, gorgets, beads, or bone awls. Twenty-three burials were found in the outer enclosure, two of which were double burials (both adult females with children) and one an isolated skull. Two possible infant/child burial urns were also found, both Irene Complicated Stamped vessels and one covered with an Irene Plain bowl, although no bone was noted. Five of these burials had associated grave goods, again simple inclusions of one or a few artifacts such as ear pins, points, awls, pipe bowls, or fragments of red ochre. Seven burials in the inner and ten burials in the outer enclosure were placed in clay-sealed pits.

The Rotunda.   The remains of a probable council house or rotunda dating to the Irene period were found south of the primary mound, connected to it and enclosed by a large rectangular enclosure that had been rebuilt and expanded at least once (figure 20). The structure was defined by six concentric rings of wall trenches and post molds, the outermost 36.6 meters across. Short breaks in the northern side of the two outer circles probably served as entranceways, which faced the primary mound. The inner circles of posts represent either interior supports or, possibly, earlier building episodes. This latter interpretation is supported by the fact that the smaller and presumably earlier enclosure surrounded only the inner three post rings, while the outer enclosure passed outside of all six. The council house was thus apparently originally much smaller, on the order of 18.3 meters across, and was later expanded in one or more construction episodes to its final 36.6 meter diameter. A trash dump consisting mostly of large ceramic fragments was found to the south of the building, all of it Irene material. These vessels are assumed to have been used in the rotunda; the absence of other midden debris suggested to Caldwell and McCann (1941:31) use in ceremonial activity, such as black drink consumption. The floor of the Irene rotunda had been badly eroded, precluding determination of the presence of a central hearth.

Fifteen Irene Complicated Stamped urns were found buried upright near the center of the rotunda, ten with inverted Irene Plain or Irene Incised bowls over the top. All but two were empty; the exceptions included one with an infant skeleton and another with a plain water bottle. Whether the vessels were buried when the building was in use, or later, could not be determined. Their function is uncertain, although use in the preparation and storage of items such as the black drink is possible.

Caldwell and McCann's (1941:31) interpretation that these vessels originally held infants whose bones had since deteriorated is discounted, given
the fact that ten of the urns were covered. Seven burials were also found
near the center of the building, five flexed, one cremated, and one of
indeterminate arrangement. One of the burials was partially charred, and
another was missing its head. The charred individual was the only one
with associated grave goods, having been buried with nine small triangular points and three objects of worked stone. When these burials were
placed here is uncertain but is assumed to have been when the rotunda
was in use.

Other Site Features.   Numerous wall lines and enclosures were found at
the Irene site (figure 20). A series of small palisades surrounded the
primary Savannah-period mound, beginning at least as early as mound
stage 3, and after stage 4, the summit itself was palisaded. At some point
during the Savannah period, a large semicircular palisade approximately
150 meters long was built, beginning near the river and encircling the
platform and low burial mound. The dating of this palisade can be inferred
from the fact that it passed through the Irene mortuary and rotunda, which
had obviously not yet been built. Whether the palisade extended all the
way to the bluff overlooking the river could not be determined. A large
borrow pit, possibly created during the construction of stage 8 in the
primary mound, was present where the northern end would have been,
and the later Irene rotunda was located at the southern end.

During the Irene occupation, sometime after the completion of stage 8,
three squared enclosures were built to the southwest of the large mound,
enclosing the area from it to and including the rotunda (Caldwell and
McCann 1941:20). This enclosure was expanded twice, with the third and
final fence line built to accommodate the enlargement of the rotunda,
which doubled in size. One or more fragmentary palisade lines, which
may have formed enclosures or screening walls, were also found in the
western part of the site. The fact that one of these palisades ran near the
outer fence line of the Irene mortuary suggested to Caldwell and McCann
(34) that it dated to this period.

In spite of the large area examined at Irene, few permanent domestic
structures were found, supporting an interpretation that this site was a
largely "vacant" ceremonial center. Three Savannah, one apparent transitional Savannah/Irene, one Irene, and one structure of undetermined
period were the only buildings other than the mortuary and the rotunda
identified at the site (figure 20). Of these, the five that could be assigned to
a particular occupation had central fire basins and midden debris on the
floor and appear to have been domestic structures, perhaps occupied by
chiefly elites and, perhaps later, priests or caretakers maintaining the
mortuary and council house. The first Savannah structure, approximately
6.1 meters on a side, was located south of the large mound; the second, a

semisubterranean squared structure approximately 4.6 meters by 5.2 meters in size with rounded corners and a wall-trench entranceway, was located just west of the later Irene mortuary; the third, a rectangular semisubterranean structure of indeterminate size, with two projecting wall-trench entranceways, possibly reflecting an episode of rebuilding, was located just outside the semicircular enclosure to the west of the burial mound. The transitional Savannah/Irene structure, identified by the presence of Savannah and Irene pottery with riveted nodes and other rim decorations known to appear at the end of the Savannah period, was approximately 3.3 meters on a side and was located about 25 meters north of the primary mound. The Irene structure was square and approximately 6.1 meters on a side and was located just west of the mortuary, having been built over the Savannah structure found in this area. The final structure, a rectangular arrangement of post molds approximately 10.1 meters by 9.1 meters in size, was located just north of the Irene structure in the western part of the site. No floor features were identified, and the function of this structure or possible small enclosure is unknown. Both the transitional Savannah/Irene and the Irene structures had burned.

Large numbers of isolated post molds were found in the area away from the mounds, perhaps the remains of temporary structures erected by visitors congregating for ceremonial purposes (Caldwell and McCann 1941:69). The fact that extensive midden debris was found over the site area indicates it saw considerable use, even if it was not permanently occupied by a large number of people. Forty isolated burials were scattered over the village area, most in shallow pits. Five contained simple grave goods, which included a shell gorget, a bone fish hook, a stone disk, a point, and a clay elbow pipe. The 40 burials included 31 that were single and flexed, a double burial of an adult female and a child, one bundle burial, one partial burial (the upper body and skull of an adult male), and one that was fragmentary. Two adults were found flexed in deep clay-sealed pits. Finally, two burials of adult males, each extended with crushed skulls, were found near the southern margin of the large mound. Forty-two Irene vessels were also found scattered over the site, including 15 complicated stamped urns with plain or incised covering bowls. Burials were found in seven of the urns, six children and one adult. As with the burials, the urns were placed just below the surface.

The Human Skeletal Assemblage.   While a detailed analysis and description of the human skeletal remains from Irene have yet to be published, a wealth of information on the diet, disease load, and mechanical stress/ work loads of the site's inhabitants has been obtained from the assemblage (e.g., Hulse 1941; Larsen 1982, 1990; Larsen et al. 1992; M. Powell 1990; Ruff and Larsen 1990). In all, 280 individuals from 265 discrete burials were found at the site, representing 74 adult males, 75 adult females, 16 adolescents, 38 children and infants, and 62 skeletons of indeterminate age and sex (Hulse 1941). The low occurrence of children and adolescents at Irene, much lower than the expected incidence for a Mississippian agricultural community (Powell 1988:94–95; 1990:26–27; Weiss 1973), reinforces interpretations of the site's ceremonial (i.e., nondomestic) nature and indicates interment was typically reserved for important or full members of society. The even sex ratio, which persisted over all contexts, suggests a fair degree of equality in adult mortuary treatment, at least for those interred. In an innovative attempt to resolve aspects of social structure, Hulse (1941:59–62) suggested that an apparent pattern of greater skeletal variability in males as opposed to females in the burial mound sample could be attributed to exogamous marriage and matrilocal residence, that is, the in-marriage of males from outside the local community. Additionally, the presence of an unusual dental anomaly in two individuals, one buried in the mortuary and the other in the burial mound, was used to suggest genetic continuity between the occupations. The comprehensive examination of the assemblage, of course, will be needed to evaluate these inferences.

Stable carbon and nitrogen isotope analyses of skeletal remains from Irene indicate that a decrease in the use of marine resources and an increase in the use of maize characterized the initial Mississippian Savannah sample, at least when compared with earlier Woodland populations from the Georgia coastal area (Larsen et al. 1992). Interestingly, a pronounced decrease in the use of maize was indicated in the later Irene sample, with some evidence for an increase in the use of wild (C3) terrestrial resources, a dietary shift markedly unlike that observed in most other late Mississippian populations from the region, but one that may be linked with change in political organization at the site and in the Savannah River basin (chapter 8). A decrease in postcranial skeletal robusticity and an increase in incidence of dental caries between preagricultural and agricultural populations locally suggests that, while the transition to agriculture might have resulted in a reduced work load, it was not without its attendant problems (Larsen 1982; Larsen and Ruff 1991; M. Powell 1990; Ruff and Larsen 1990). On the whole, the Irene population appears to have been in good health, although it did exhibit a low incidence of porotic hyperostosis and cribia orbitalia and a much higher incidence of treponemal bone lesions, suggesting chronic low-level skeletal infection (Larsen 1982; M. Powell 1990:26).

Hudson's Ferry Mounds

Two low sand burial mounds of probable Lawton or Hollywood phase age were excavated by Clarence B. Moore (1898:169–71) near Hudson's Ferry in Screven County, Georgia, some 110 kilometers upriver from the mouth (see appendix A). The first mound (9Sc3), which was completely excavated, was 22.6 meters in diameter and 75 centimeters high, with four burials found near the center. Three of the four burials had grave goods, including, respectively, two stone discoidals; a knobbed clay pipe and a mussel shell fragment; and a clay owl effigy pipe. The knobbed pipe is identical to pipes found at other Mississippian sites in the drainage, including at Rucker's Bottom (Anderson and Schuldenrein 1985: figure 10:68,d) and Irene (Caldwell and McCann 1941: plate 18:f), and a similar bird effigy pipe was reported from the Hollywood mound (C. Thomas 1894: figure 205)(see appendix A in this text). The smaller mound, located approximately 1 kilometer to the southeast, was 18.6 meters across and 1.4 meters high. Moore cut a trench 30 feet wide through the center but found only calcined fragments from what was apparently a single cremation. No other artifacts were reported, and its age remains unknown. Both mounds resemble the burial mounds at Irene and Haven Home in size and shape, indicating that late prehistoric use of low sand mounds for burial, a common feature on the coast, occurs some distance into the interior along the Savannah.

Red Lake

The Red Lake site (9Sn4) is a small double mound complex located on an old oxbow meander scar of the Savannah River (figure 25). The site consists of two mounds, one 3 meters and the other approximately 0.75 meters high, located side by side near a bluff overlooking the river swamp. The site was examined in 1988 by Fred Cook and Mark Williams, who mapped the area around the mounds and opened two small test units on the northeastern side of the large mound (Cook n.d.). No record of earlier archaeological work at the site exists, although a narrow trench had been opened at some time in the past on the eastern side of the mound. The assemblage that was recovered was dominated by Savannah Plain, Check Stamped, and Burnished Plain finishes, together with small quantities of Etowah and Savannah Complicated Stamped (nested diamond and concentric circle motifs), indicating the site was occupied during the Lawton phase. The presence of two openings or inlets in the bluff below the mounds suggests the presence of paths down to the water or, alternatively, ditches like those at the nearby Lawton mound group. The area around the mounds was shovel tested in the summer of 1993 with little evidence for village deposits found (Espanshade et al. 1993); how the site was used in the past remains unknown.

The Lawton Mound Group

The Lawton mound group (38Al11) is located in western Allendale County, South Carolina, on a terrace overlooking the river swamp. The site covers approximately 3.5 acres, includes two flat-topped platform mounds and an associated village area surrounded by a fortification ditch and

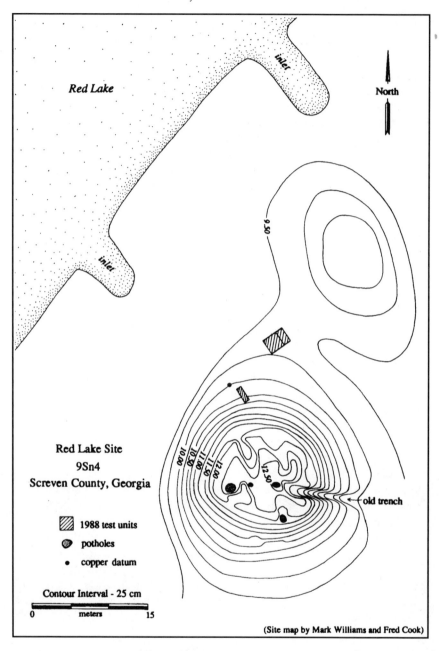

Figure 25 The Red Lake Mounds (9Sn4).

embankment, and was apparently occupied for about two centuries from circa 1150 to 1350, during the Lawton and Hollywood phases (figure 26). The site has seen limited archaeological examination, first in 1898 by Clarence B. Moore (1898; see appendix A in this text) and again in 1970 and 1989 by archaeologists from the South Carolina Institute of Archaeology and Anthropology (SCIAA)(Anderson 1990a:662–68). Moore directed his efforts to the northern mound and, finding no burials, elaborate artifacts, or evidence for construction stages in the fill, soon abandoned work. In 1970, SCIAA archaeologists prepared a map of the site, cleaned up and profiled several potholes, and made a small artifact collection. Except for a brief reconnaissance in 1989, the site has seen no other professional investigation. The 1970 and 1989 investigations indicate the mounds were built in stages, and evidence for a wattle-and-daub structure was noted in the upper part of the southern mound. Extensive midden debris was observed in the area around the mounds, indicating that the area saw considerable use and that domestic structures might be present.

The ceramics from Lawton consist of Savannah Check Stamped, Plain, Burnished Plain, Fine Cord-Marked, and Complicated Stamped (bulls-eye concentric circles motif), with corncob impressed and rectilinear Etowah-like complicated stamped finishes also noted. Assuming a sufficient excavation sample can be collected, recognition of a Lawton phase (now provisionally designated) may prove appropriate. The Lawton ceramic assemblage appears identical to that collected from the Red Lake site located across the river. The two sites may represent the ceremonial foci of a small chiefdom occupying this part of the basin.

Hollywood

The Hollywood site (9Ri1) consists of two mounds and an associated village area located just below the Fall Line in Georgia. In 1891, Henry L. Reynolds of the Mound Division of the Bureau of Ethnology conducted extensive excavations in the smaller of the two mounds (C. Thomas 1894:317–26; see appendix A in this text), and three-quarters of a century later, DeBaillou (1965) conducted test excavations in both mounds and in the adjacent nonmound area. Reynolds's work was described at length in the 12th Annual Report of the Bureau of Ethnology, while a summary of DeBaillou's work appeared in 1965. The assemblage appears to be transitional between the late Savannah III and Irene I phases, leading Hally to propose a Hollywood phase (circa 1250–1350) to accommodate these occupations along the central Savannah (Anderson, Hally, and Rudolph 1986:40–41; Hally and Rudolph 1986:62–63).

The 1891 excavations are described as of unrivaled competence for the period (Waring 1968c:293). At the time of excavation, the small mound,

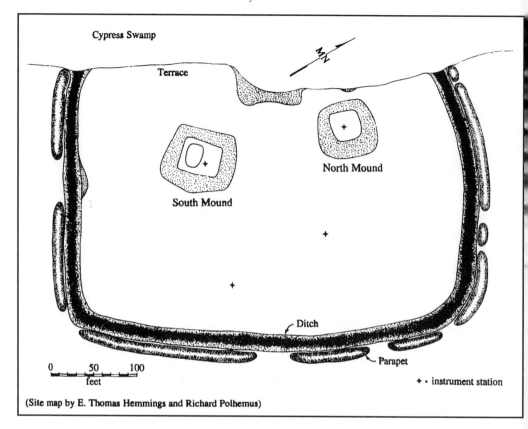

Figure 26   The Lawton Mound Group (38Alll).

mound B, was 3 meters in height, 21.3 meters in diameter, and conical in form and was located 85 meters north of the large mound, mound A. A small barn had protected it from looting. Two major construction stages were documented, the earliest of which contained two groups of burials. The lower stage of mound B was 2.1 meters thick and rested upon a rich premound midden deposit approximately 23 centimeters thick. The stratigraphically early burial group was found resting either on or just above a well-defined premound midden surface, near a large hearth approximately 3 meters in diameter located just southwest of the center of the mound. Seven adult extended burials were found, six to the west of the hearth and one to the east. Elaborate grave goods with classic Southeastern Ceremonial Complex iconography were found with several of these burials.

The most elaborate burial in the lower stage was located due west of the hearth and had a number of highly unusual nonlocal grave goods, including a tripodal bottle with human effigy heads for feet, a bottle painted with a cross and sunburst motif, a seated human effigy pipe of soapstone, and five clay elbow pipes. Three other pots and a copper ax head wrapped in cloth and bark were found to the northeast. A second burial with unusual grave goods was found to the northwest of the first. Near the head of this individual were two vessels, one engraved with a plumed serpent motif. The design on this engraved vessel resembles materials from Moundville as well as from Spiro, with some specific design motifs exactly duplicated on artifacts found at the latter site (Phillips and Brown 1978:194–95). Under the engraved vessel were fragments of copper plates of falcon warriors and some mica and shell fragments, while under the other vessel was a biconcave quartz discoidal, underlain by two copper cloth-and-bark-wrapped celts and several large pieces of mica.

The remaining five burials had less elaborate but still unusual grave goods. One had two groups of shell beads, a possible copper-plated wooden earplug, and a lump of galenite. A second had a string of shell beads, a copper celt encased in wood, a *Busycon* columella, and a piece of glauconite. The columella may have functioned as a special status marker, since it is found with elite burials throughout the Southeast at this time level. A pipe was found with the third burial, which was beside the individual with the elaborate painted vessels. An owl effigy pipe, three stone celts, five stone discoidals, a weathered shell ornament of some kind, an amorphous pebble, and a piece of glauconite were found near the fourth burial, while the final burial had a stone celt. The burial of these seven individuals at or near the base of the mound suggests a cohort, perhaps the founding elites at this center. Construction of the first major mound stage over these burials may have been deferred, in fact, until all the members of this group died. It is also possible that one or more of the interments may have been retainers sacrificed upon the death of a chief. The burials with only single grave goods may be of this type. Contemporaneity of interment cannot be assumed, however, even though all the burials were found in or no more than 45 centimeters above the premound midden.

The later burial group was placed from 30 to 60 centimeters below the upper surface of the first mound stage, approximately 1.5 meters above the earlier burials and about 1.2 to 1.5 meters below the modern ground surface. Four extended adult burials were found, together with 13 vessels and a piece of copper plating with a repoussé figure on it. Because no burial pit outlines were recognized, the relationship of the artifacts to the burials is uncertain. The copper plate and two vessels, one inside the other, were apparently associated with two of the burials. Four sets of two vessels each were found together, which appear to represent urn burials. Each apparently consisted of a large jar with a smaller pot or bowl inside. The four larger pots had been "killed" by breaking a small hole in the base, a practice observed at the contemporaneous Pee Dee–phase Town Creek site in North Carolina (Reid 1965:23). The presence of small bone fragments in two of the Hollywood vessels suggests they were urn burials, like those reported from the Irene site. As with the lower stage, the contemporaneity of these burials cannot be assumed. While all appear to date to the transitional Savannah/early Irene Hollywood phase, the interments may have taken place over several generations.

A hearth approximately 1.5 meters in diameter by 60 centimeters deep was found in the center of the upper burial cluster. Three posts were found in a line near the edge of this hearth, and traces of fire were seen about one of the burials. The hearth and posts, along with the occurrence of the burials and other artifacts at this level, point to the existence of an upper mound stage, probably surmounted by a temple or mortuary structure of some kind. The traces of fire further suggest that this structure may have burned. The site, which dates to between circa 1250 and 1350 on the basis of associated ceramics, was abandoned shortly after these burials were placed in the mound, given the absence of later Mississippian or protohistoric Indian ceramics (Anderson, Hally, and Rudolph 1986:40–41; Hally and Rudolph 1986:62–63). The scattered Irene urn burials in this upper level may be somewhat later than the extended burials, which otherwise resemble the earlier interments.

The upper "stage" or strata in mound B at Hollywood was just over 1 meter thick. The presence of European pottery and wrought-iron nails mixed in with Indian midden debris in the fill, which was of a distinctly different character from that in the lower stage, indicates that it is of historic origin and probably associated with the construction of the historic barn on the summit. This conclusion is also reinforced by the presence of a drawing knife and a wrought-iron nail at the juncture of the two stages and the presence of glass and porcelain as apparent intrusions into the upper level of the lower stage (Anderson 1990c).

The 1965 test excavations at Hollywood were largely directed to opening a trench, 70 feet by 10 feet, from the adjoining field to the southwest side of mound A, which appears to have originally been at least 30 meters on a side and over 1 meter high. This mound had been described by Reynolds as "of the pyramidal type" but even in 1891 was reported "almost entirely lost" as a result of flooding and the penning of cattle on its summit (C. Thomas 1894:318). Approximately 1.5 meters of historic alluvium were found to cover the field around the mound. While possible post stains were noted, the presence of a village area has been inferred primarily from the large numbers of surface artifacts found to date. Two construction stages were identified in mound A; charcoal on the slope of the upper mound stage suggested that there may have been structures atop it that had been consumed by fire (DeBaillou 1965:7). The lower stage was only about half the diameter of the upper stage and was resting on a premound humus with associated prehistoric midden debris. Two burials were found at the base of the mound, one associated with "a broken mortar and some unworked stones" (DeBaillou 1965:9–10); the absence of elaborate grave goods suggests these may have been commoners from the village.

Two squares, 10 feet by 10 feet, were also opened in the area of mound B in 1965, which had been recently bulldozed by the landowner and was assumed to have been completely destroyed. Undisturbed mound fill, however, was found at a depth of about 1.5 meters, about 30 centimeters above the premound midden. DeBaillou (1965:11) concluded that the edges of the mound were intact, that future excavations might uncover additional burials, and that the use of heavy equipment to remove overburden might expose features in the surrounding village area. Although no further work has been conducted at Hollywood, the dating of its assemblages has been the subject of heated debate, with the point of controversy being whether or not the site was an outlier of a Savannah River–based province of Cofitachequi, the capital of which has been placed across the river at Silver Bluff or Mason's Plantation (cf. Anderson 1990c, Eubanks 1989, 1990a, 1990b, 1991). As we have seen, however, no credible evidence currently exists for Indian occupation at Hollywood after circa 1450.

Mason's Plantation

The Mason's Plantation mound group may have been the largest Mississippian center in the Savannah River valley, although, unfortunately, the site washed away late in the last century, and our only descriptions of it are all over a century old. As best as can be determined, six mounds were originally present. The naturalist William Bartram (1791:315) visited the area in the mid-1770s, noting that "various monuments and vestiges of the residence of the ancients, as Indian conical mounts, terraces, areas &c" were located on the South Carolina side of the river near the Silver Bluff trading post. Charles C. Jones (1873:148–57) apparently visited the site on several occasions in the 1860s and early 1870s and prepared a lengthy description as well as a map showing the location and size of the two largest mounds. When Clarence B. Moore was working in the valley in the winter of 1897–98, he explicitly noted that, of the six mounds observed by Jones, "all have totally disappeared" and that, for this reason, "the archaeological examination of the Savannah river has been too long deferred" (1898:167–68). Bartram's, Jones's, and Moore's accounts are given in appendix A.

The Mason's Plantation site was thought by Swanton (1939:180–83, 1946:45) to have been the location of Cofitachequi, which was visited by De Soto in May of 1540. Swanton's opinion was no doubt influenced by Jones, whose account included a romantic discussion of De Soto's visit and an impassioned plea as to the importance of the site. Because Bartram reported mounds near Silver Bluff, the Mason's Plantation mound group became all but synonymous with Silver Bluff and was assumed to lie nearby. Efforts to locate major Mississippian sites, mounds, or assemblages in the vicinity of Silver Bluff, however, have proved singularly unsuccessful through the years, to the point that one team concluded that the "archeological data does not support the traditional designation of Silver Bluff as the location of the village of Cofitachique" (Scurry, Joseph, and Hamer 1980:77).

Historic land plats from the area around Silver Bluff at the South Carolina Department of Archives and History revealed no evidence for mounds or other Indian features (Richard D. Brooks, personnel communication, 1990). The Mason's Plantation land records themselves were quickly found, although the tract proved to be several kilometers north of Silver Bluff, just across and upriver from the Hollywood site. Gilmer's 1853 navigation map of the Savannah River, furthermore, shows the location of three mounds on Mason's Plantation, with the two largest in approximately the same location with regard to one another, as described by Jones (see appendix A). A reconnaissance of this same area by the author in 1990 failed to locate any traces of these mounds, suggesting they had indeed been washed away, although over 1 meter of modern flood deposits were noted in riverbank profiles, which may mask surviving portions of the site. Artifacts found on sandbars in the river at and below the presumed area of the site are dominated by Savannah III and early Irene motifs, suggesting a Hollywood-phase occupation, if the ceramics indeed come from the former mound center (Anderson 1990a:709–10). Given the extent of historic alluvium in the area, a deep testing program will be needed to determine whether portions of Mason's Plantation have survived.

Rembert

The Rembert mound group was a cluster of five mounds located in the central Piedmont along the Savannah River, just above the confluence of the Broad River. Occupied from circa 1100 to 1450, Rembert was one of the largest Mississippian mound groups in the Savannah River valley, with only the Mason's Plantation group below Augusta comparable in size. Limited archaeological investigations were conducted at Rembert in the 1880s and again in the 1940s before the site was inundated by the waters of Clark Hill Lake in 1952. Rembert was first described by the naturalist William Bartram in May of 1776 and was revisited and described on three separate occasions in the 19th century, by George White (1849:229–30), Charles C. Jones (1878:284–85), and John Rogan, who also conducted limited stratigraphic testing in the two largest mounds under the auspices of the Mound Division of the Bureau of Ethnology (C. Thomas 1894:315–

17; appendix A in this text). These early accounts provide important information about the number and size of the mounds that were present at the site, which had been largely destroyed by flooding and agricultural practices by the start of the 20th century.

In 1948, limited test excavations were undertaken at Rembert by Caldwell and Miller as part of River Basin Survey salvage investigations associated with the construction of Clark Hill Lake (Caldwell 1953). Unfortunately, by this time the large mound had been almost completely reduced, and no trace of the smaller mounds could be found. Eleven test pits were opened during a three-week field program, two pits in and three near the surviving remnant of the large mound and six others scattered over the surrounding area in presumed village deposits. Much of the primary mound base was found to be intact, resting on an artifact-rich premound midden. The mound fill sloped downward toward the center of the mound, suggesting that the earliest construction stages may have been earth-embanked structures. Artifacts were also found in four of the six test pits opened to the south of the mound, suggesting a large village area was present. Fired-clay wall plaster was found in some units, indicating wattle-and-daub structures were present. Unfortunately, in spite of the preservation encountered in both the mound and village area and the fact that additional excavations were recommended, no further work was conducted.

The materials collected during the 1948 testing were reexamined by Hally in the early 1980s to form the basis for a late prehistoric Mississippian archaeological culture in the upper Savannah, the Rembert phase, dated to circa 1350–1450 (Anderson, Hally, and Rudolph 1986:41–42; J. Rudolph and Hally 1985:453–59). Mississippian occupation at Rembert appears to have begun sometime in the 11th or early 12th century and continued until sometime in the 15th century. Present in the 1948 excavation sample were sherds with ladder-based diamond motifs, which are either Woodstock or early Etowah Complicated Stamped (Caldwell 1953:317, plate 56p; J. Rudolph and Hally 1985:453). More traditional Etowah two-bar nested diamond motifs were also present, and Hally has suggested that the initial occupation assemblage is equivalent to the Etowah II phase in the Allatoona Reservoir, which has been dated to circa 1050–1150 (Caldwell 1957; J. Rudolph and Hally 1985:456). A succeeding Beaverdam-phase occupation is indicated by the presence of several Savannah Complicated Stamped, Check Stamped, and corncob-impressed sherds. Unfortunately, as is the case with Mason's Plantation, the other large multimound group in the valley, our knowledge of Rembert is extremely limited. However, limited underwater archaeological investigations were conducted in the summer of 1990 at the suspected location of the site in Clark Hill Lake, and an extensive prehistoric artifact scatter was found that included Woodstock-, Beaverdam-, and Rembert-phase ceramics, as well as earlier Middle Archaic through Late Woodland materials, suggesting it may be possible to obtain more information about Rembert in the future (Anderson, Amer, and Elliott 1994).

Beaverdam Creek Mound and Village

The Beaverdam Creek site (9Eb85), located in the central Piedmont approximately 0.8 kilometer from the confluence of Beaverdam Creek with the Savannah, consisted of a small mound and an approximate 1.5-hectare adjacent village area. The type site for the Beaverdam phase (circa 1200 to 1300), the center was occupied during the 12th and 13th centuries, when two superimposed earth lodges followed by four platform stages were erected on the mound. Extensive excavations undertaken in 1980 and 1981, during the Richard B. Russell Reservoir investigations, documented the mound's construction and use, while wide-area stripping at several locations away from the mound exposed numerous features, including one structure (J. Rudolph and Hally 1985). Although evidence for permanent structures away from the mound was minimal, lithic, ceramic, and subsistence-related artifacts were found throughout the midden, indicating a range of domestic activities took place at the site, much like the use of the "vacant" ceremonial center at Irene.

Primary Mound Construction Episodes.   Two superimposed earth lodges and four successive mound stages were documented during the excavations (J. Rudolph and Hally 1985:69–197). The premound midden was from 15 to 20 centimeters thick and was contiguous with the village midden surrounding the mound. Several burial pits, portions of three structures, and a large number of miscellaneous post molds were found on this surface, representing occupations at the time of and immediately prior to the construction of the mound. The first two mound structures were surrounded by earth embankments. The first, structure A1 (figure 27), was square, 7.5 meters on a side, and oriented 24° west of magnetic north; covered an area of 56 square meters; and had a wall-trench entranceway on the southern side. It was built of individually set posts 10 to 15 centimeters in diameter and spaced 10 to 30 centimeters apart, with appreciably larger corner posts approximately 30 to 60 centimeters in diameter. The embankment itself was approximately 1.7 to 1.8 meters wide and was constructed of midden fill to a height of from 40 to 70 centimeters above the ground surface. It was erected flush with the wall line, after the posts had been set in place. The structure had not been burned or abandoned but appeared to have been quickly replaced. A male aged 30 to 35 years, designated burial 2, was found in a basin-shaped pit above the structure A1 embankment and under the embankment for structure A2 (figure 27). The presence of approximately 7,000 shell beads, a whelk columella, several *Olivella* shells, two copper-covered ear spools, a crescent-shaped copper head ornament,

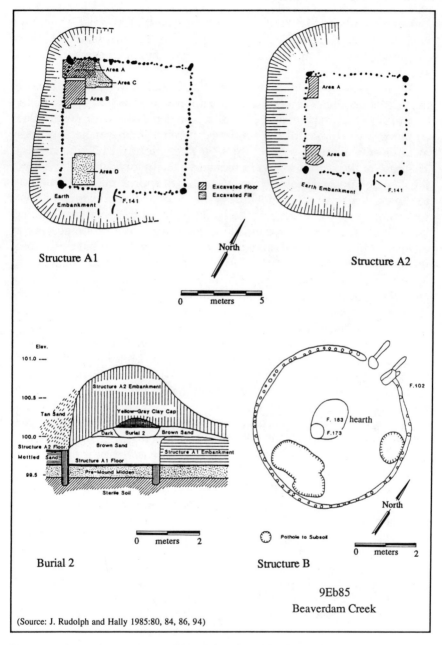

Figure 27   Structures A1, A2, and B and Burial 2 at the Beaverdam Creek Mound Site (9Eb85).

and a shell gorget and button indicate this individual occupied a very high position in the local society, and it is possible that his death may have triggered the abandonment and rebuilding of the initial earth-embanked structure.

Structure A2 resembled structure A1, although it was smaller, measuring 6.2 meters on a side and covering approximately 38.4 square meters (figure 27). Oriented the same direction as structure A1, with a wall-trench entranceway to the south, the building differed primarily in having a more massive embankment, from 2.2 to 2.7 meters wide and 1.25 meters high. The floor of the structure was raised above the fill over structure A1 by a thin layer of mottled grayish brown sand up to approximately 15 centimeters thick. Structure A2 did not burn but appeared to have been abandoned for a short period of time prior to being replaced by a platform mound. Water-laid sands around the northern side of structure A2 suggest it may have been inundated and damaged, something that may have prompted the rebuilding. Structure B, a small circular wall-trench building that may have been in use at the same time, was found to the north of structures A1 and A2 (figure 27). The inside of the structure had water-laid sand over the floor, suggesting that it too had been abandoned because of flooding. A prepared clay hearth with a pronounced rim was found just west of the center of the structure, while the floor had a moderate amount of occupational debris on it, suggesting it was a domestic building, perhaps for a caretaker elite or priest. Structure B appears to have been dismantled prior to the construction of the nearby earth-embanked structures or one of the early mound stages overlying it.

Structure A2 was replaced with a platform mound, termed stage 1, which was raised approximately 20 centimeters higher than the embankment. The stage was very badly disturbed, with only traces of the northwestern corner found intact. Measuring an estimated 17 meters east-west by 14 meters north-south, the platform was oriented the same direction as the two earth lodges, suggesting continuity of site use. Traces of two possible structures were found, a hard-packed floorlike surface and two lines of posts. Water-laid sand mixed with clay and ash found around the base of stage 1 was thought to represent burned material washed down from the summit. Whether this meant the summit structure for stage 1 was abandoned or burned prior to rebuilding is unknown. Above the water-laid sands was a gray ashy layer, approximately 1 to 28 centimeters thick, that was rich in pottery, bone, and other debris, including a number of pine log fragments. Given its excellent preservation, stage 1 is thought to have been quickly covered by stage 2 (J. Rudolph and Hally 1985:119, 126). The logs were interpreted as debris from the mound summit, rather than steps or a facing like that found covering stage 1 at Tugalo (see below).

Stage 2 measured approximately 18 meters by 18 meters and was oriented 13° west of magnetic north, a shift in orientation of about 11° from the earlier stage and structures. A ramp 2.25 meters wide with step remnants cut into the clay was built on the northwestern corner of the mound facing the creek, and the shift in mound orientation may have been to improve access to the waterway (J. Rudolph and Hally 1985:125). The mound was composed of dark red clay and rose approximately 13 centimeters higher than stage 1. The sides were steep, and furrows were evident in the red clay face, suggesting intentional roughening. The summit of stage 2, like that of stage 1, had been largely destroyed by pot hunting, and no evidence for structures was found (122–29).

Later mound stages were progressively more heavily disturbed. Stage 3 measured approximately 21 meters on a side and appears to have been at least 12 centimeters higher than stage 2. The orientation of the mound itself could not be determined, but a fragmentary wall line from a possible summit structure was oriented almost exactly the same direction as that of stage 2. The summit structure was represented by two wall line fragments and a small patch of floor surface. Some of the posts were charred, indicating the structure had burned. Water-laid sands were found on the northern side of the mound, suggesting sheet wash from the summit, while on the southeastern side a dark midden layer was found, with lenses indicating at least two or more episodes of deposition. Whether this reflected normal trash discard from the summit or debris from the destruction of a structure could not be determined.

Stage 4 was very poorly preserved, was apparently no more than a few centimeters in height above stage 3, and was about the same overall size. Fragments of a wall-trench structure found on the summit were oriented 3° west of magnetic north; if this was the same as that of the mound, some realignment appears to have occurred. A dense concentration of small boulders was found on the northwestern side of stage 4, over an approximate 90-square-meter area. Most had been moved about by pot hunters but appeared to have originally been on the side of the mound. Not enough boulders were present to provide a mantle like those found at Estatoe (see below) or Garden Creek (Dickens 1976:79–83), nor do they seem to have been used to control erosion, cover a smaller structure, or serve as post supports (J. Rudolph and Hally 1985:141–42). Their purpose remains unknown, although they may have been placed to flank and accentuate an entrance ramp.

Village Area Results. A number of excavation units dispersed across the floodplain indicated that Mississippian settlement was restricted to the area immediately around the mound (J. Rudolph and Hally 1985:199–259). One possible structure, a dense square cluster of post molds approximately 9 meters on a side, suggesting one or more episodes of rebuilding, was found about 50 meters southeast of the mound (figure 28). No evidence for a central hearth or a wall-trench entranceway was found, although any shallow features would have been destroyed by plowing in this area. While somewhat larger than the premound structures A1 and A2

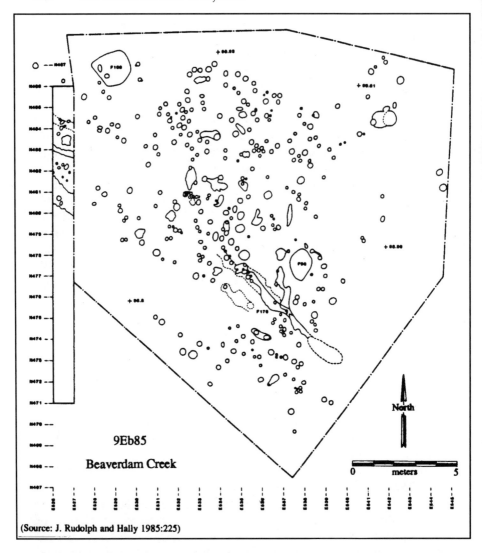

9Eb85

Beaverdam Creek

North

0   meters   5

(Source: J. Rudolph and Hally 1985:225)

Figure 28   Probable Domestic Structure in the Village Area at the Beaverdam Creek Mound Site (9Eb85).

or the residential structures at Rucker's Bottom, the size and shape were within the range for domestic structures at other sites in northern Georgia (J. Rudolph and Hally 1985:226). Midden in most areas was characterized by occupational debris, including lithic, ceramic, and subsistence-related artifacts, indicating a range of domestic activities. A possible plaza was found immediately south of the mound, characterized by a low feature density and no evidence for structures. Pecked and polished discoidals or chunky stones were common on the site, further supporting the inference that some kind of a plaza/gaming area had probably been present.

Artifact Analyses. The Beaverdam-phase ceramic assemblage was defined by Hally using a stratigraphic sample of 25,002 sherds from the premound midden, the midden strata in the village, and the gray ashy layer associated with stage 1 (J. Rudolph and Hally 1985:261–80; see appendix B in this text). Five principal types dominate the assemblage: Etowah Complicated Stamped, Savannah Complicated Stamped, Savannah Check Stamped, Savannah Plain, and Savannah Burnished Plain. Corncob impressions, typically below the lip on the neck and shoulder area of jars, were common. A minority of the rims were collared, formed by the addition of a strip of clay below the lip, and featured such decorations as cane punctations, fine incised lines, notching, and vertical ridges; these are common forms in Pisgah assemblages to the north (Dickens 1976:178; D. Moore 1981). Folded rims, more common in the ensuing Early Lamar Rembert phase, were present but rare, with those found either plain or notched.

The presence of quartz crystals, lumps of pigment, and sheet mica fragments in various midden proveniences (J. Rudolph and Hally 1985:305–11), as well as artifacts of shell and copper in a number of the mound burials, clearly indicates the site elite participated in long-distance prestige goods exchange. Their own contribution may have been worked soapstone goods, such as discoidals and pipes. An outcrop of soapstone was located approximately 1 kilometer away along the Savannah, and small soapstone fragments were found scattered over the site, indicating local manufacturing activity. Moderate numbers of small Mississippian triangular points were found at Beaverdam Creek (n = 139) and at the nearby Rucker's Bottom village site (n = 308). While a number of varieties could be differentiated, separable primarily by basal morphology (i.e., straight, concave, convex), no temporally or behaviorally significant categories were evident within these assemblages (Anderson n.d.; J. Rudolph and Hally 1985:287–89). Other flaked tools found at Beaverdam Creek included a small number of drills and perforators, other bifaces, and utilized flakes that may have been used to work shell, bone, or soapstone, although only evidence for soapstone manufacture was found.

The Burial Assemblage. Fifty-two burials were excavated at Beaverdam Creek, ten in the village area and the remainder in the mound or premound areas (Anderson 1990a: 569–70; Blakely et al. 1985; J. Rudolph and Hally 1985:317–51). Preservation was highly variable, ranging from excellent to extremely poor. Burials were typically extended to semiflexed, and approximately two-thirds were oriented along a northwest-to-southeast axis, with about an equal preference for southwest- and northeast-facing positions. Age determinations were possible for 43 individuals, and the resulting mortality curve (figure 29), with a high infant and childhood peak followed by decreased mortality in adolescence and increasing mortality thereafter, is fairly typical of prehistoric agricultural populations

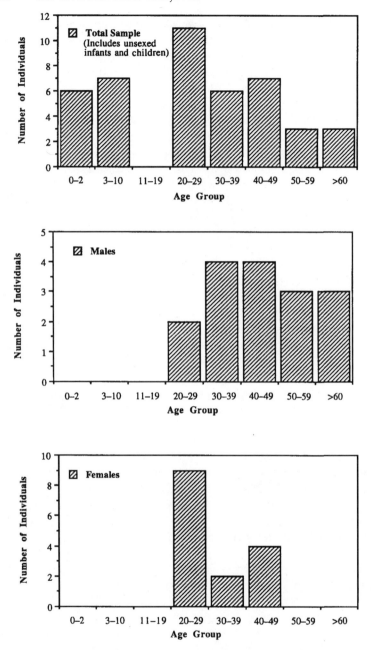

Figure 29   Mortality Distribution for the Beaverdam Creek Mound Site (9Eb85).

(Weiss 1973). Nine of the 11 burials, aged between 20 and 30 years at time of death, were female, perhaps reflecting deaths associated with the stresses of childbirth and lactation. Stature estimates could be calculated for seven males and five females, with males ranging from 166 to 178 centimeters and females from 156 to 163 centimeters (Blakely et al. 1985:343). Fronto-occipital cranial deformation was common among females at Beaverdam Creek and appeared to have been caused by binding a board to the back of the head. Nine of 16 identifiable adult females and 1 of 15 adult males had this trait; the adult male was elderly (more than 65 years of age), and the observed cranial deformation may have been due to age-thinning and postdepositional warping. General skeletal pathologies such as arthritis, localized periostitis, chronic osteomyelitis, blastomycosis, and possibly tuberculosis were present but were uncommon, as was evidence for dental decay.

Burial in the mound apparently demarcated high status at Beaverdam Creek, and this status was age and sex linked. Approximately one-third of the interments in the mound were characterized by grave goods or unusually elaborate burial treatment. Only one of the burials found in the village, in contrast, had associated grave goods. All of the identifiable burials found in the village area were either female or subadolescents; no identifiable adult males were found in this area. Within the mound the average age of death for males receiving special mortuary treatment (46.7 years; n = 6) was virtually identical to that for males buried with no special treatment (46.2 years; n = 8) (J. Rudolph and Hally 1985:345). In contrast, the average age of death of adult females receiving special mortuary treatment (40.2 years; n = 5) was considerably higher than that for adult females buried without special treatment (27.7 years; n = 11). Female status seems to have depended, in part, on surviving peak child-bearing years. Adults of both high and low status tended to be buried considerably deeper than subadults, with burial pit depth averaging 79 centimeters as opposed to 39 centimeters (J. Rudolph and Hally 1985:348).

Paleosubsistence Analyses.   Beaverdam Creek is currently the only Mississippian mound center in the basin where detailed paleosubsistence analyses have been conducted. A wide range of carbonized plant remains was identified at the site, including maize, squash, gourd, sunflower, sumpweed, hickory, acorn, walnut, hazelnut, maypops, persimmon, grape, bramble (raspberry), strawberry, plum, maygrass, panic grass, chenopodium, purslane, carpetweed, amaranth, and eyebane (P. Gardner 1985:400–411). Wood charcoal was not identified to species, but both hardwoods and softwoods were noted in the collection. Both acorn and hickory nuts were common, occurring in over 80% of the samples; hazelnut and walnuts were much less common and may not have played a major role in subsistence. Maize was the most frequently occurring plant food, present in 93% of the samples and accounting for 53% of the food remains by weight. Cobs were common, with the majority being 8-rowed Northern Flint but with lesser quantities of 10- and 12-rowed corn also present (405). Squash and gourd were represented by one rind and one seed fragment, and one rind fragment, respectively, while the sunflower and sumpweed were present in incidental quantity. Fruits appear to have been extensively utilized. Maypop seeds were present in almost 75% of the samples and grape in almost 40% of the samples, while the other fruits occurred in much lower incidence. The fairly wide range of plant foods exploited indicated something of a generalist strategy, with clear dietary preferences for certain plants, particularly maize, nuts, and fruits (409–11).

A sample of 7,573 bones representing a minimum of 161 animals was collected and examined from Beaverdam Creek, from both 1/4-inch (0.63-centimeter) mesh and flotation samples (Reitz 1985:416–28). A wide range of species from a number of habitats was exploited, most occurring in close proximity to the site. Both aquatic and terrestrial resources were exploited in some quantity, although terrestrial mammals, particularly deer, contributed the bulk of the food. Assemblage diversity and equability were high, indicating a diffuse or generalist subsistence strategy was practiced (427). An analysis of deer elements indicated that kills were returned intact to the site. The approximately equal occurrence of both hindquarters and forequarters indicated that meat probably did not leave the site as tribute, something that was suggested at the nearby Rucker's Bottom village. Many of the bones were burned, suggesting that roasting over an open fire was a common cooking practice. Carnivore gnawing was also observed, but no dog remains, one of the probable scavengers, were found.

Community Organization.   Beaverdam Creek undoubtedly served as a ceremonial focus for populations dispersed into subsidiary hamlet and village communities in this part of the upper Savannah River basin. The extent of its influence is unknown, however, since only minimal investigations have occurred at the two other centers located in this part of the drainage, Tate and Rembert. Whether use of the Beaverdam Creek site overlapped with or was temporally separate from the use of these other two centers will remain unknown until we can more precisely determine their periods of occupation. The number of people actually living at the Beaverdam Creek site on a year-round or permanent basis is unknown but is thought to have been small. Examination of approximately 2,640 square meters of the "village" area revealed large numbers of post features but only one definite house pattern, a squared structure approximately 9 meters on a side. One other structure, a circular wall-trench building approximately 5 meters in diameter in the premound midden area near the earth lodges, may have been a habitation or possibly a specialized structure associated with the communal building (i.e., a storage facility or caretaker/priest's residence). The presence of only two probable domestic structures, given the area examined, points to low resident populations, a pattern like that noted at Irene. However, the extensive midden deposits around the mound and the large numbers of post molds found in the village area argue for fairly intensive use, even if only for short periods. Rudolph and Hally (1985:356) have suggested that the post molds in the village lacking obvious patterning may have supported "racks, screens, platforms, arbors, and other short-lived constructions" such as those inferred at Irene. If Beaverdam Creek was indeed the ceremonial center for populations dispersed over a large area, evidence for these kinds of structures would be expected, to provide temporary shelter for groups visiting the site for ritual or other public activities.

Tate

Tate (9Eb86), a single-mound site overlooking the floodplain of Beaverdam Creek about 8 kilometers upstream from its confluence with the Savannah, was found during Hutto's reconnaissance survey in the Georgia portion of the then-proposed Russell Reservoir in 1969 (Hutto 1970:23–25). The mound was described as approximately 30 meters in diameter and 4.6 meters high, although because of erosion and looting, its original shape could not be determined. Approximately one-sixth of the mound had been destroyed by looters at the time of the survey, with most of the damage occurring on the northeastern side and the rest from isolated potholes scattered over the summit. Hutto (24) thought that at least five successive mound stages were present, although how he arrived at this cannot be determined. A village area to the north and west of the mound was inferred from the distribution of surface debris. In 1977, R. Taylor and Smith (1978:193, 388, 427) revisited the site and made a general surface collection; at that time, the mound was estimated to cover approximately 400 square meters, and its preservation was urged. Because it lay just outside of the reservoir flood pool, no further work occurred. The two collections argue for assignment to the Beaverdam phase (Hally and Rudolph 1986:54); Tate is the only surviving mound site in the basin where no formal excavation has occurred.

Tugalo

The Tugalo mound and village site (9St1), located near the headwaters of the Savannah in Georgia, was a major Lower Cherokee town in the 18th century (W. Williams and Branch 1978). In the 1880s, the single mound, which at that time was approximately 4.3 meters high and 30 meters in diameter, was explored with a vertical shaft with little result (C. Thomas 1894:314–15; see appendix A in this text). In 1952, an approximate 2,540-

square-meter area was examined in village deposits southeast of the mound by Edwards; aside from brief descriptions of the historic artifacts (Harmon 1986; M. Smith and Williams 1978), this work remains unpublished. A possible ditch line was found, suggesting the site may have been fortified at some point in its history, but the loss of all fieldnotes precludes our ever knowing for certain what features were present. Because Tugalo was in the flood pool of the then-proposed Hartwell Reservoir, federally funded excavations were conducted at the site between October 1956 and March 1957 under the direction of J. R. Caldwell (1956). The mound was extensively examined, and a small block was opened immediately to the north, in the presumed village area. Although no final report was ever produced, fairly detailed fieldnotes, maps, and photographs are on file at the University of Georgia, and brief summaries of the investigations have been prepared by W. Williams and Branch (1978) and Duncan (1985:17–25). Caldwell had prepared a series of detailed illustrations of the mound profile and structures prior to his death, and some are reproduced here for the first time.

Tugalo appears to have been continuously occupied from late Swift Creek/Woodstock to historic Cherokee times, with an apparent break only during the Savannah period. Nine construction episodes were recognized in the mound. The first four stages, each consisting of a rectangular mound surmounted by a well-defined earth-embanked structure, were found to be largely intact, while evidence for the remaining stages, which had been truncated by plowing and erosion, was found on the edge of the mound. Stages 1 through 4 were erected during the Jarrett phase (circa 1100 to 1200), and the upper flanks of stages 2 through 4 were covered by mantles of logs arranged parallel with the summit margin. Square earth-embanked structures approximately 7 meters on a side with well-defined corner posts, a series of lesser posts suggesting inner partitions, and a large central fire basin were atop stages 2 through 4 and appear to have been elite residences.

Because of the comparatively small amount of excavation that occurred in the lower portion of the mound, very little was determined about mound stage 1. From the profile, it appears an earth-embanked structure approximately 8 to 9 meters across was built immediately above the premound surface, possibly on a layer of fill approximately 10 to 20 centimeters thick. A cremation, burial 11, was found in a deep pit below the western margin of the structure and may have been roughly contemporaneous. Stage 2 (Caldwell's Mound III) stood about 1.5 meters high and was surmounted by a squared structure approximately 7 meters on a side with well-defined corner and wall posts, a central hearth, and a number of smaller interior posts suggesting the presence of partitions (figure 30). The summit structure was in a shallow depression approximately 50 centimeters deep formed by the surrounding embankment. The sides of the mound were covered with logs arranged parallel to the

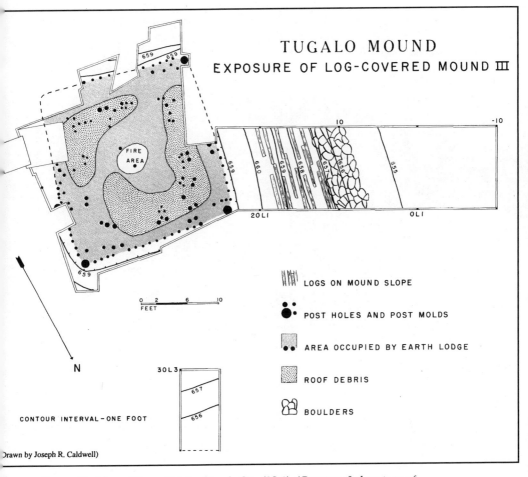

Figure 30   Mound Stage 2 at the Tugalo Site (9St1). (Courtesy Laboratory of
Archaeology, University of Georgia)

summit, and a layer of boulders had been placed around the base, presumably to hold the slope and logs in place.

Stage 3 (Caldwell's Mound II) was approximately 2.1 meters high and
20 meters across at the base, with a squared structure approximately 7
meters on a side on the summit (figure 31). This structure lay within a
shallow depression bounded by a low embankment and had well-defined
corner posts, a central hearth, and evidence for internal partitions. The fill
over the floor had an appreciable quantity of roof debris on it, indicating
the structure had collapsed or been pulled down prior to the construction
of the next stage. The flanks of mound stage 3 had been covered with logs
arranged parallel to the summit. As with stage 2, whether this mound
covering and the summit structure had burned could not be determined,

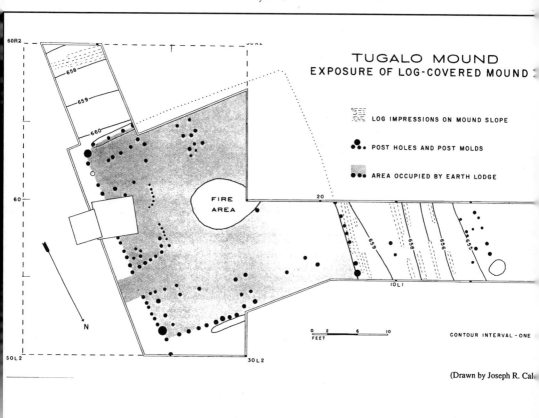

Figure 31   Mound Stage 3 at the Tugalo Site (9St1). (Courtesy Laboratory of Archaeology, University of Georgia)

although Caldwell's profile refers to "burnt mound stages," suggesting this may have happened. Observed at the base of the mound on the eastern side were scattered posts that appear to be from a structure, although a fence line may have been present (see below).

Mound stage 4 (Caldwell's Mound I) was approximately 23.8 meters on a side, with rounded corners and elevated about 2.4 meters (figure 32). The summit was surmounted by a square earth-embanked structure approximately 7 meters on a side with four well-defined corner posts, a series of lesser posts suggesting inner partitions, and a large central fire basin. The summit and upper sides of the mound were covered with an orange sand, while the lower portion was covered with a bluish clay, like the capping noted over the Jarrett-phase stages at Chauga (see below). A

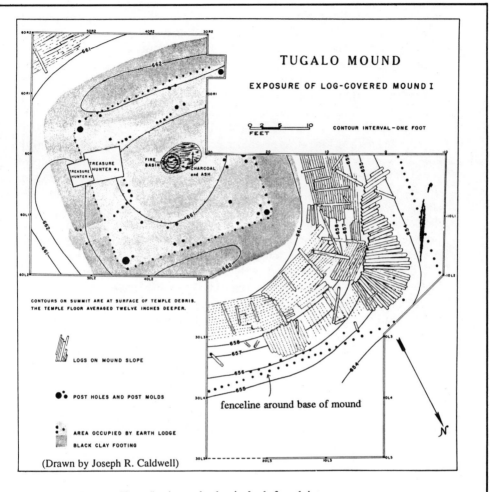

TUGALO MOUND

EXPOSURE OF LOG-COVERED MOUND I

CONTOUR INTERVAL – ONE FOOT

CONTOURS ON SUMMIT ARE AT SURFACE OF TEMPLE DEBRIS.
THE TEMPLE FLOOR AVERAGED TWELVE INCHES DEEPER.

LOGS ON MOUND SLOPE

POST HOLES AND POST MOLDS

AREA OCCUPIED BY EARTH LODGE

BLACK CLAY FOOTING

fenceline around base of mound

(Drawn by Joseph R. Caldwell)

Note: The "Treasure Hunter" unit may be the single shaft sunk into
this mound by BAE Mound Division archaeologists in the mid 1880s.

Figure 32   Mound Stage 4 at the Tugalo Site (9St1). (Courtesy Laboratory of
Archaeology, University of Georgia)

mantle of logs covered the sides; those higher on the slopes were arranged
parallel with the summit margin and had possible covering logs every 1 to
2 meters or so, while the logs near the base of the mound were perpendicular to the summit margin. This mantle had burned, accounting for its
unusual preservation. Orange clay from probable wall debris was found in
the fill above the mantle, which may have come from the summit. Two
rows of posts approximately 18 centimeters in diameter and 30 centimeters apart from a screening fence or palisade were found around the base

of stage 4, suggesting either one episode of rebuilding during the period when stage 4 was in use or an inner fence line belonging to the previous mound, stage 3. The presence of blue clay in the fill of the post molds in the inner row and the fact that burned posts from this wall extended through the clay cap, which covered the earlier wall line, indicate the wall was burned prior to the construction of stage 4 and may indeed be associated with stage 3. Both fence lines had burned, and the absence of fired clay indicates they were not wattle-and-daub walls.

Above stage 4, the summit area had been destroyed by plowing and erosion, and construction episodes were recognizable only on the periphery of the mound. Five strata from later occupations, spanning late Etowah through historic Cherokee periods, were recognized. These strata included two ash layers, the first probably terminal Jarrett phase in age and the second dating to the Early Lamar Rembert phase. Above this was a brown earthen layer that dated to the Rembert phase. A dense concentration of later, Tugalo-phase debris on the northeastern side of the mound was found above this, a deposit that was in turn overlain by a layer of historic Estatoe-phase Cherokce material (W. Williams and Branch 1978). How many true mound stages were present above the four Jarrett-phase levels is unknown, although one possible Jarrett-phase stage, one or two Rembert stages, and one Tugalo stage may have been present.

Immediately outside the fence lines around stage 4, a small block was opened on the northern side of the mound. Eleven semiflexed burials were found, all apparently lacking grave goods, which caused Caldwell (1956:4) to suggest they were of "less distinguished members of the community." These were in poor condition and were apparently not saved. A large ash bed (might be debris from summit occupations) was also found in this area. Perhaps the most important finding was a thick stratified deposit containing thousands of large sherds from vessels presumably used and discarded in the mound area. This finding has prompted the discovery of debris dumps at several other mounds in the general region (Shapiro 1985a; M. Williams 1990a:61–70; M. Williams and Shapiro 1986). Duncan's (1985) functional analysis of the Tugalo-phase vessel forms found in the dump suggests that the summit structures were probably elite residences.

Ceramics from the northeast dump at Tugalo were examined by Hally to define the Late Lamar Tugalo phase in the upper Savannah River valley, dated from circa 1450 to 1600 (Anderson, Hally, and Rudolph 1986:42–43). Tugalo ceramics also occur at Estatoe and Chauga, and the phase appears restricted to the upper part of the basin. Hally (1986a) has argued that the Tugalo phase developed directly out of the preceding Rembert phase with no break in continuity and in turn developed into the historic Cherokee Estatoe phase. Williams and Branch (1978:36), while noting that the change in the ceramic assemblage at Tugalo between the Jarrett and Rembert occupations was dramatic, suggested that "the lower Cherokee whose discards formed the historic stratum in the mound had occupied Tugalo at least since the third quarter of the 15th century A.D." and additionally suggested that they may have been intruders, taking over the site from earlier groups. While continuity in ceramic tradition throughout the Mississippian period is indicated in the upper Savannah River valley (Hally 1986a), evidence also suggests that fairly dramatic population realignments were occurring in the 15th century (see chapters 6–8).

Estatoe

The site of Estatoe was located about 10 kilometers north of Tugalo on the southern side of the Tugaloo River in extreme northeastern Georgia. Components from the late prehistoric Tugalo phase through historic Cherokee Estatoe phase (circa 1700 to 1750; see Hally 1986a:98–111) were documented in the single mound, which was excavated in 1959 and 1960 as part of the investigations in the Hartwell Reservoir (A. Kelly and De-Baillou 1960). Six construction episodes were identified, the lower five of which were surmounted by a series of superimposed structures approximately 12 meters on a side, separated from one another by thin earthen platforms approximately 5 to 10 centimeters thick. A layer of large cobbles and small boulders up to 1 meter thick was placed over the fifth stage, evenly covering the underlying structure (figure 33). At least one mound stage was erected above this, surmounted by a structure, although this and any possible later stages that may have been present had been truncated by plowing. As at Tugalo, a dump was found on the northeastern side of the mound. Two tests were opened in the village area southeast of the main mound, disclosing evidence for both burials and structures. Limited earlier occupation in the general site area is also indicated by the presence of some Woodland- and Etowah-like materials, but the nature of these occupations is unknown.

Continuous occupation of the site during the period the six mound stages were in use is indicated by the reuse of the same corner support post holes in each succeeding summit structure. These holes even extended through the rock layer separating stages 5 and 6 and were used in the construction of the structure on stage 6 (A. Kelly and DeBaillou 1960:9). The placement of the rock layer over stage 5, however, marked a major change in construction procedures and suggests that a major transition of some kind had occurred in the society (19). Based on ceramic evidence, use of the Estatoe mound began during the Late Lamar Tugalo phase (and possibly as early as the end of the preceding Rembert phase), coeval with the use of stages 8 to 10 at Chauga and with the deposition of the northeastern mound dump at Tugalo (29). The stone layer was laid down during the Tugalo phase, probably sometime around or shortly after 1500. As at Tugalo, during the late 15th and early 16th centuries, major changes seem to have occurred in the ceremonial centers of the upper Savannah

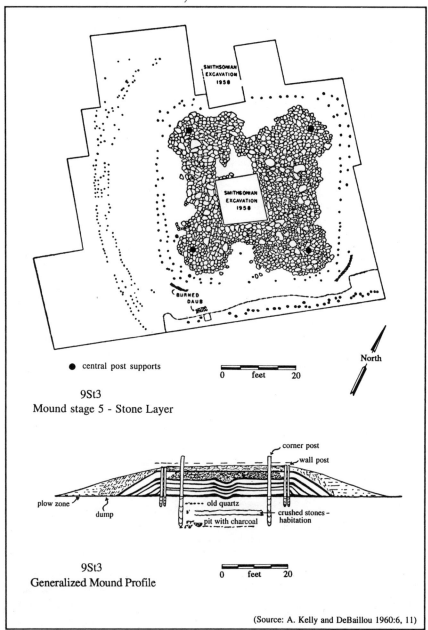

central post supports

0   feet   20

North

9St3
Mound stage 5 - Stone Layer

corner post

wall post

plow zone

dump

old quartz

pit with charcoal

crushed stones –
habitation

9St3
Generalized Mound Profile

0   feet   20

(Source: A. Kelly and DeBaillou 1960:6, 11)

Figure 33   Mound Stage 6 and Generalized Mound Profile at the Estatoe Site (9St3).
(Courtesy North Carolina Archaeological Society)

River basin. Site use continued into the succeeding Estatoe phase, which was defined in large measure on the basis of materials from this site (Hally 1986a; Hally, Hudson, and DePratter 1985). Occupation continued through the historic Cherokee period until the site was destroyed and abandoned near the end of the American Revolution.

Chauga

The Chauga mound and village site, located in Oconee County, South Carolina, was examined from August through December 1958 as part of salvage investigations undertaken in the Hartwell Reservoir (A. Kelly and Neitzel 1959, 1961). The site was a Lower Cherokee town that had been intermittently documented by colonial travelers during the first half of the 18th century. A single mound was present at the site, which, upon excavation, was found to have ten construction stages, most with associated structures. Site occupation appears to have taken place during two major periods, the Early Mississippian Woodstock and Jarrett phases and the late prehistoric/early historic Tugalo and Estatoe phases (Hally 1986a:97, 1987). Although a substantial terminal Woodland/initial Mississippian Woodstock component is present in the premound and early mound levels at Chauga, the first six mound stages are assigned to the Etowah culture Jarrett phase and the last four stages to the Late Lamar Tugalo phase. Historic 18th-century Cherokee Estatoe-phase ceramics were found in the associated village area and in slope wash near the mound, which led Hally (1986a:97; see also A. Kelly and Neitzel 1961:6–7) to conclude that these occupants used but did not add to the mound.

The mound had been badly damaged by cultivation and looting, and evidence for structures was minimal. No evidence for submound earth-embanked structures was evident. The first six stages were built in a consistent fashion, with "a zone of [basket] loaded fill surmounted by a clay cap," and had a truncated pyramidal shape (A. Kelly and Neitzel 1961:9). The clay capping was of a distinctive blue-gray clay ranging in thickness from a few centimeters on the summit to 30 centimeters or more on the margins and extending up to 3 meters away from the mound base in places. The upper four mound stages (7 to 10), in contrast, were not capped, although these were very badly disturbed and could only be reconstructed from remaining portions of the sides.

No evidence for structures was found atop stages 1 or 2, which, occurring in the central part of the mound, had been largely cored out by looters. Evidence for a palisade or screening fence was found around stage 1, suggesting a concern for defense or elite segregation among the first chiefly inhabitants of the site. A number of small boulders were found in the northeastern side of the mound, in the same manner as the boulders noted on the northwestern side of stage 4 at the slightly later Beaverdam

Creek site; the function of these stones could not be determined, although they may have flanked an entrance. Water-worn boulders were also found in low numbers in the clay cap on the southwestern, northwestern, and northeastern margins of the mound, and scatters of boulders and an occasional log proved to be characteristic features of the clay lining on the slopes of each of the six Jarrett-phase stages.

Stage 2 was similar in size to stage 1, although appreciably more boulders were observed on the slopes. Again, no evidence for structures was observed. Fragments of what may have been an extensive log covering were observed on mound stage 3, on the northwestern and northeastern sides of the mound (figure 34). This log mantle is like that noted over mound stages 2 through 4 at Tugalo, which also dated to the Jarrett phase. Traces of a large wall-trench structure were found atop stage 3; this structure had burned, and the debris had been cleared off prior to the construction of stage 4.

Stage 4 was poorly preserved, although large numbers of boulders occurred on the northwestern and northeastern margins of the mound. Both stages 2 and 4 at Chauga had unusually large numbers of boulders on their margins, although no evidence exists for a cap of boulders over either summit, in the same manner as that observed over stage 5 at Estatoe, which dated appreciably later in time. Linear arrangements of post molds were also noted atop stage 4, indicating a structure had been present. The presence of ash on the side of the mound suggested an episode of burning, but since the summit surface had been damaged by plowing, this could not be ascertained. Whether these summit structures were temples or elite residences could not be determined.

Evidence for the remaining stages survived only on the mound flanks. Stage 6 was the last capped, and a palisade or retaining wall was built around at least part of its base (A. Kelly and Neitzel 1961:19). While an association of this palisade with burials placed around the mound perimeter was inferred, its appearance just prior to site abandonment may suggest an increased concern for security at this time. The site was apparently unoccupied for about 200 years, after which the final four stages were added to the mound. Only traces of these latter stages remained. Stages 7 and 8 apparently represented fairly appreciable additions, raising the height of the mound 30 centimeters or more. The final two construction episodes, stages 9 and 10, in contrast, were minor and may have been little more than "apron-like appendages" or ramps added to the mound (57).

A large block unit encompassing 2,450 square feet (248.8 square meters) was opened in the village area about 25 meters southeast of the mound (figure 35). Numerous post molds were found, including a number of lines and arcs, suggesting the presence and rebuilding of a number of structures, but none were conclusively identified. Two faint narrow parallel linear stains, possibly from a palisade or plank wall line, were found at the edge of the block in two areas, but their age and function could not be

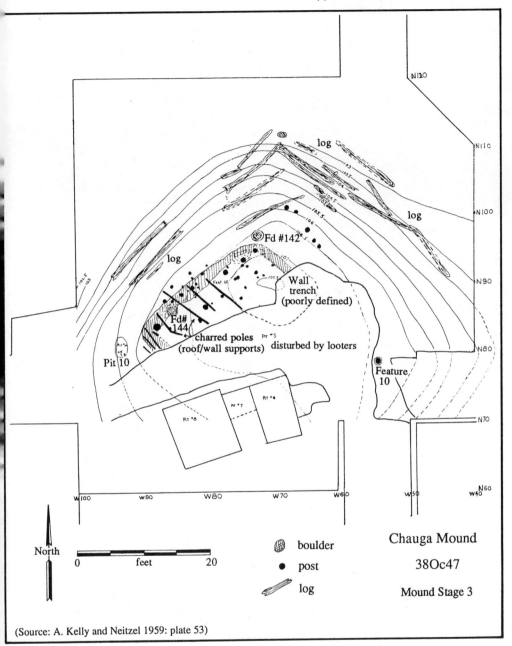

Figure 34 Mound Stage 3 at the Chauga Site (38Oc47). (Courtesy Laboratory of Archaeology, University of Georgia)

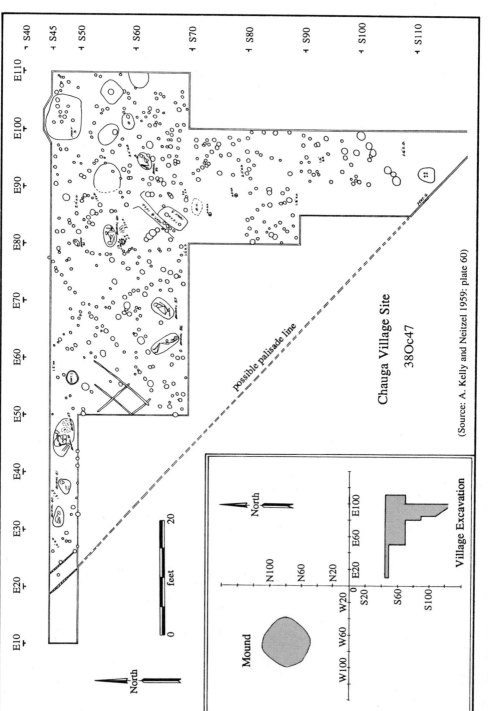

Figure 35 The Village Excavations at the Chauga Site (38Oc47). (Courtesy Laboratory of Archaeology, University of Georgia)

(Source: A. Kelly and Neitzel 1959: plate 60)

Chauga Village Site
38Oc47

possible palisade line

Village Excavation

Mound

North

determined. The features in the village included both prehistoric and historic Cherokee materials. In all, 53 burials were found in the mound and 9 in the associated village area (Anderson 1990a:580–82; A. Kelly and Neitzel 1961:33–34); this assemblage is discussed in greater detail in chapter 8.

I. C. Few

At the I. C. Few site (38Pi2) near the headwaters of the basin in South Carolina, evidence for Late Woodland through Mississippian Napier, Etowah, Savannah, Early Lamar/Pisgah, and historic Cherokee components was found during excavations conducted in 1967 as part of the Keowee Reservoir project (Grange 1972). Fieldwork at the site included the excavation of one of three small low circular mounds present, and a number of transects in what was interpreted as an associated village area. Located near Fort Prince George, which was established in the mid-18th century, the area was visited in the 1770s by Bartram (1791:332; see appendix A in this text), who reported the presence of "several Indian mounts or tumuli, and terraces, monuments of the ancients, at the old site of Keowe." Because of the documented Cherokee occupations near the fort, prior to the fieldwork the site was assumed to date to the historic era.

Historic artifacts were rare at I. C. Few, and none were found in features, indicating most occupation dated to the prehistoric era. The mound examined appears to have been built in a single construction episode over a burned, poorly defined structure (Grange 1972:52). The presence of numerous hearth, pit, and post features, including evidence for two or more small circular structures, indicated a village area was located around the mound. Ceramic evidence suggests the primary period of use of the site was during the Rembert phase, from circa 1300 to 1450, with construction of the mound possibly beginning somewhat earlier, during the Beaverdam phase (Grange 1972:110–75; Anderson, Hally, and Rudolph 1986:35).

The mound, which was approximately 20 meters in diameter, was elevated approximately 0.5 to 0.7 meter above the surrounding floodplain. Unfortunately, it had been very badly damaged by looting and plow reduction, so its original shape is unknown. Two bundle and eight flexed burials were found in the mound, and four other flexed burials were found in the village area to the north of the mound (Anderson 1990a:376). Eight of the burials in the mound had associated grave goods, compared to only one in the village area. All but one of the burials that could be identified as to sex were male, while two of the three identifiable burials in the village were female. Children and infant remains were underrepresented in both areas. One of the bundle burials, of an adult male, had 1,373 shell beads around the skull. The long bones of this burial, which was fragmentary, had rodent gnawing marks on them, indicating the body may have been exposed for some time prior to burial. Burials with shell beads were found only in the southern part of the mound, suggesting this area was reserved for higher-status individuals.

The I. C. Few site appears in most respects to have been a fairly ordinary village, although the presence of low (burial?) mounds suggests it also served as a ceremonial center of some kind. The lack of evidence for platform mound architecture suggests that social differentiation at this site, and possibly in the society occupying the immediate area, may have been minimal, or that the center was a minor one. Why mound construction never proceeded further than it did is unknown, although it is possible that the site's ceremonial functions were subsumed by the elites at the nearby Chauga, Estatoe, and Tugalo centers, which all had major occupations following the end of the Rembert phase.

Excavation Assemblages: Nonmound Sites

While most of the mound sites in the Savannah River valley have seen at least some level of professional archaeological examination, until it was mandated by federal cultural resource management legislation, little attention was directed to nonmound sites. However, a number of Mississippian village, hamlet, and special activity sites were examined in the Savannah River basin from 1980 to 1982, during investigations conducted prior to the flooding of the Richard B. Russell Reservoir (Anderson 1988b)(table 4). Our knowledge of these types of sites, aside from what we can infer from survey data (see chapter 6), thus comes from only a small part of the basin. The evidence that has been found from these sites, however, clearly demonstrates their importance for exploring sociopolitical change.

While the discussion and examples presented here focus on the prehistoric nonmound sites examined and reported to date in the basin, within the past five years, fieldwork has also occurred at two 18th-century Lower Cherokee town sites near the headwaters, Tomassee and Chattooga (M. Smith et al. 1988; Schroedl and Riggs 1989). The work at Tomassee was a fairly limited, largely voluntary testing program designed to assess the condition of the site deposits, which were found to be extensive and well preserved. Little information about the nature and organization of the community could be inferred, given the small area examined, although the fieldwork demonstrated this kind of data could be gathered, given sufficient time and resources. At Chattooga, such a large-scale investigation program was initiated in the late 1980s by archaeologists from the University of Tennessee, with funding and other assistance provided by the university and by the U.S. Forest Service. Four field seasons have been conducted to date, and large areas of the site have been exposed. As the data from this community are reported, they will offer a valuable baseline for comparison with village assemblages gathered elsewhere in the basin.

Rucker's Bottom (9Eb91)

Appreciable portions of two Mississippian villages dated to between circa 1200 and 1450, during the Beaverdam and Rembert phases, and were documented at the Rucker's Bottom site (9Eb91) from 1980 to 1982 in conjunction with the work in the Richard B. Russell Reservoir (Anderson and Schuldenrein 1985:251–590). The site extended for almost 1 kilometer along the Savannah and was located on a well-drained terrace elevated 4 to 6 meters above the river channel, immediately to the north of the confluence of Van Creek, a small tributary. A low-lying swale was situated behind the terrace, and the site, in one of the largest tracts of bottomland along this stretch of the Savannah, had access to extensive arable land and a range of riverine and backswamp resources. Mississippian artifacts were found in a dark, well-defined midden extending over almost 2 hectares, and approximately 10,000 square meters in the center of the scatter were examined, revealing several thousand features, including two ditch and stockade lines, upward of 20 structures, and well over 100 large pits (figure 36). A thin stratum of Mississippian pottery was also found at a depth of almost 1 meter in the swale, indicating use of this area.

Community Organization. Settlement was found to have shifted from an open, roughly circular arrangement of houses about a central plaza in the south-central part of the terrace during the Beaverdam phase, to a similar arrangement of structures around a plaza in the north-central part of the terrace during the Rembert phase. This later community was fortified, however, occurring first within a semicircular and later a rectangular ditched and stockaded enclosure.

The initial, Beaverdam-phase community was centered about a comparatively open area, which may have been a plaza. Besides having a markedly lower feature density, several large rock-filled pits that were present may have functioned as trophy or gaming post supports. Comparable major post supports, it should be noted, have been found in the plazas at many southeastern sites, including Cemochechobee, King, Ledford Island, Mitchell, and Zebree (Hally, Garrow, and Trotti 1975:60; D. Morse and Morse 1980:21–23; Porter 1969; Schnell, Knight, and Schnell 1981:34–35; Sullivan 1987:20). Around the plaza area were the remains of numerous structures, although resolving patterns in the dense feature scatter proved difficult. When they could be identified, buildings were typically circular in shape and from 4 to 8 meters in diameter, although evidence for a few squared structures was also noted. A large building approximately 14 meters in diameter appears to have been present in the

Rucker's Bottom
(9Eb91)
Wide-area Stripping 1981-82

North

0 meters 10

Mississippian Analytical Strata

1. Circular house (?) in the western part of the Rembert-phase village.

2. Squared house (?) in the western part of the Rembert-phase village.

3. Circular house (?) in the southern part of the Rembert-phase village.

4. Circular house (?) in the southern part of the Rembert-phase village.

5. Squared house (?) in the eastern part of the Rembert-phase village.

6. Circular house (?) in the eastern part of the Rembert-phase village.

7. Large public (?) building in the southern part of the Rembert-phase village.

8. Large semicircular enclosure in the area between the two villages.

9. Circular house (?) in the northwestern part of the Beaverdam-phase village.

10. Circular house (?) in the northwestern part of the Beaverdam-phase village.

11. Rectangular house (?) in the southern part of the Beaverdam-phase village.

12. Northeastern part of the Beaverdam-phase village (incompletely stripped).

13. Southeastern part of the Beaverdam-phase village (high feature density area).

14. Large public (?) building in the southern part of the Beaverdam-phase village.

15. Southwestern part of the Beaverdam-phase village (high feature density area).

16. Northwestern part of the Beaverdam-phase village (high feature density area).

17. Central part of the Beaverdam-phase village (low feature density area). Plaza (?)

18. Area between the two villages (low feature density area).

19. Southern side of the Rembert-phase semicircular ditch.

20. Northern side of the Rembert-phase semicircular ditch.

21. Southern side of the Rembert-phase rectangular ditch.

22. Northwestern side of the Rembert-phase rectangular ditch.

23. Southern part of the Rembert-phase village (high feature density area).

24. Western part of the Rembert-phase village, area between the two enclosures.

25. Central part of the of the Rembert-phase village (low feature density area). Plaza (?)

26. Eastern part of the Rembert-phase village (high feature density area).

27. Northern part of the Rembert-phase village (high feature density area).

(Source: Anderson and Schuldenrein 1985:475)

south-central part of the village, facing the plaza. This building is roughly similar in plan to descriptions of 18th-century Cherokee and Creek town houses or rotundas (e.g., Bartram 1791:448–49; Hawkins 1848:71–72; Swanton 1928:170–88) and may have served a similar function. Burials were found scattered over the village, some below house floors. Several tight clusters of burial pits were also found, suggesting family interments. One burial from the plaza had a large number of shell beads with it, suggesting higher-status individuals (i.e., possible village headmen or their kin?) may have been interred in this area. No ditches or well-defined stockade lines were found associated with this early village, which appears to have been unfortified.

Sometime during the transition period between the Beaverdam and Rembert phases, the community relocated 100 or so meters to the north along the terrace. This later, Rembert-phase village was initially characterized by a semicircular and then later a rectangular ditch-and-stockade network. Like that of the earlier village, a pattern of houses or areas of high feature density about a plaza or an area of comparatively low feature density characterized this community. Also as in the earlier village, several large rock filled pits, which are interpreted as major post supports, were found in the presumed plaza area inside the enclosures. Although containing up to several hundred kilograms of large rocks, these pits typically had only low to moderate amounts of sherds, bone, or other midden debris in their fill. Low artifact density, in fact, characterized many of the features found in the plazas on the site, suggesting somewhat less surface debris or intentional refuse disposal elsewhere. Such a pattern is in keeping with historic accounts of Cherokee and Creek village maintenance, which describe the sweeping of plaza areas (e.g., Bartram 1789:34–36; Swanton 1928:170–90).

A large circular structure approximately 13 to 14 meters in diameter, a possible town house or rotunda, was found in the southern part of the enclosed village, in roughly the same position with respect to the plaza as the large structure observed in the earlier village. A quotation from Bartram (1971:448–49) illustrates how Creek rotundas functioned: "The great council house or rotunda is appropriated to much the same purpose as the public square, but more private, and seems particularly dedicated to political affairs. It is a vast conical building or circular dome. . . . [T]here are people appointed to take care of it, to have it daily swept clean, and to provide canes for fuel, or to give light." The use of cane for light and fuel was supported by the ethnobotanical analysis at Rucker's Bottom; charred cane was found in appreciable numbers of Mississippian features, includ-

Figure 36 (facing page) The Mississippian Feature Assemblage at Rucker's Bottom (9Eb91).

ing in several possible hearths (J. Moore 1985). As at Irene, extensive debris was found behind the Rembert-phase council house at Rucker's Bottom, in this case in the fortification ditch, although unlike at Irene, where only vessel fragments were found, in this case both pottery and food remains were present. The presence of an entrance gap and the fact that the council house was in an occupied village may explain the more generalized trash disposal. Unlike with the Irene rotunda, which doubled in size over its period of use, no clear evidence for rebuilding or enlargement of these structures was observed at Rucker's Bottom.

Smaller circular and square, presumably domestic structures were also found, as well as evidence for smaller, possibly more temporary buildings. Summer and winter houses have been reported from throughout the Southeast on prehistoric Mississippian sites (Faulkner 1977), and comparable structures were undoubtedly present in both villages at Rucker's Bottom. A 1540 account from the De Soto entrada of a Mississippian village in south-central Georgia illustrates this nicely: The houses of this town "were covered with canes in the manner of tile. Those houses are very clean and some have their walls plastered and appear to be made of mud. Throughout the cold lands each of the Indians has his house for the winter plastered inside and out. They shut the very small door at night and build a fire inside the house so it gets as hot as an oven, and stays so all night long so there is no need of clothing. Besides these houses they have others for summer with kitchens nearby where they build their fires and bake their bread" (Elvas in Robertson 1993:75; see also Bourne 1904, 1:53). Considerable variability in size and construction was evident at Rucker's Bottom; some structures had well-defined wall lines with closely set posts, while others were more open or ambiguous in size and shape. The larger well-defined buildings may have been winter houses, while the less-well-defined post clusters as well as many of the seemingly isolated or unconnected posts may have been summer houses, lean-tos, storage buildings or barbacoas, or other, currently unrecognized structure types. Evidence from the site suggests that, over time, squared buildings with rounded corners became more prevalent.

The two enclosures fronted on the river; the rectangular enclosure clearly intruded the semicircular one and, given its larger extent (approximately 50% greater), indicates the Rembert village expanded somewhat over its history. Traces of stockade lines were found inside both ditches, suggesting a probable ditch-and-bank arrangement, with the ditch fill used to elevate and support the stockade posts. The ditches at Rucker's Bottom were from 1 to 2.5 meters across and from 0.5 to 1.2 meters deep. The shallow depth and narrow width of these features suggest they were not serious defensive works but were, instead, minor obstacles and may have been little more than borrow areas for fill used to tamp around the palisade, which was a more substantial barrier. Distinct gaps were found in both ditch lines, three in the earlier and one in the later, which may delimit entranceways, something that reinforces the inference that these features had little military significance. Ditch fill near the gaps contained large quantities of artifactual debris, suggesting a pattern of intentional refuse disposal near village entranceways.

Rows of posts from probable banked stockade lines were found in several areas from 3 to 6 meters inside these ditch lines, and at least one of the entrance areas had what appears to be an interior screening wall, suggesting these were indeed defensive lines. Furthermore, the largest surviving sections of the semicircular post line were typically noted just inside these openings, suggesting that portions of the palisades near entrance areas were better constructed than other sections. Ditches like those found at Rucker's Bottom are noted at a number of sites in the South Appalachian area in early historic and early archaeological accounts (Blanding 1848; Hawkins 1848:33), and they have been found and excavated at a number of Mississippian sites in the Southeast (e.g., Cole and Albright 1983; Lafferty 1973; Morgan 1984; D. Morse and Morse 1980, 1983). Gaps, furthermore, have been noted in the ditch lines at well-fortified sites, including at Etowah (Cornelius 1818; Morgan 1984:42), indicating these were normal features designed to facilitate normal access to the community.

The nature of the stockade/defensive system along the river could not be determined. A description of what Rucker's Bottom might have looked like from the river was provided by Henry Woodward (in Salley 1911:132–33), who in 1674 visited an Indian village on the Savannah somewhere just north of Augusta: "we came in sight of the Westo town . . . which stands upon a point of the river . . . upon the western side. . . . [T]he next day I viewed the Town, which is built in a confused manner, consisting of many houses whose sides and tops are both artificially done with bark, upon the tops of most wherof fastened to the ends of long poles hang the locks of hair of Indians that they have slain. The inland side of the town being doubly palisaded, and that part which fronts on the river having only a single one. Under whose steep banks seldom lie less than one hundred fair canoes ready upon all occasions." The approximately 4-meter-high riverbank would have afforded some protection, but it is probable that a stockade of some kind was also present. A large depression approximately 20 meters across and cutting 5 to 10 meters into the bank was present in the bank margin below the center of the semicircular enclosure and may have been an eroded entrance area. Canoes could have been kept tied up in this area for use in both fishing and travel, and access to the river margin by the village inhabitants for water, bathing, subsistence pursuits, and other activities would have been facilitated by a path of some kind.

The Burial Assemblage. A total of 41 human burials were identified during the fieldwork at Rucker's Bottom, and 24 of these were removed and examined in detail; isolated human bones were also found in another 8 features (Weaver et al. 1985). Large pits, excluding those filled with rocks in the plaza areas, commonly contained burials (41 of 69 examined, or 59.4%). The burial pits occurred in isolation or in small clusters, which may be fortuitous associations or may reflect kin or sodality groupings. No mortuary buildings like those reported from Irene or Town Creek (Caldwell and McCann 1941:25–26; Graham 1973) were found, and burial appears to have been far less formal an affair than at the larger centers.

The 24 burials included 9 from inside and 15 from outside the enclosures. Diagnostic artifacts were recovered in the fill of a number of the burial pits, and this, along with general locational data, that is, whether they occurred inside or outside the Rembert-phase enclosure, permitted the rough dating of 23 of the 24 burials. Thirteen burials were assigned to the Beaverdam and ten to the Rembert phase. Most adults were found semiflexed lying on their side. Two infants, however, were found in vessels, and three individuals (two adults and a child) were found lying side by side in extended positions on their backs near the Rembert-phase plaza. Grave goods were simple and were found with about half (n = 7, or 53.8%) of the individuals in the earlier Beaverdam-phase sample, and with one of the ten burials in the later Rembert-phase sample. Other than the possible elite burial found in the plaza of the Beaverdam-phase village, no spectacular grave associations indicative of marked status differentiation were noted at the site, nor was an appreciable age or sex bias evident in the occurrence of grave goods. Adult males, however, did tend to have slightly more elaborate grave goods than adult females, that is, more pots or beads instead of bone pins, rattles, or cobble tools.

Stature estimates were calculated for eight of the adults and yielded a range from 156 to 175 centimeters. Based on this very small sample, the mean stature for males was 170.6 centimeters, while the mean stature for females was 163.9 centimeters. Each individual was examined for the presence of gross skeletal pathology, radiographic anomaly and pathology, microscopic anomaly and pathology, and dental enamel hypoplasia and, using atomic absorbtion spectrometry, for concentrations of zinc, calcium, magnesium, and strontium (Butler 1986; Weaver et al. 1985; see chapter 8). Individual trace element values exhibited no discernible patterns between age- or sex-defined groups, although a significant difference in zinc values was observed between the earlier and later skeletal samples, suggesting possibly greater meat consumption during the Beaverdam phase. This was also suggested by the mean strontium values, although the difference was not statistically significant.

The primary epidemiological problems in the sample were dental diseases and their attendant consequences. The skeletal remains exhibited no evidence for violence or trauma but instead showed gradual, progressive dental problems, as well as a range of general systemic and skeletal pathologies, including the accumulation of osteophytes and osteomyelitic bone infections. Osteomyelitis was surprisingly frequent in the skeletal sample, occurring in 8 of the 24 individuals. Although occurring on six of the Beaverdam-phase individuals, as opposed to on only two individuals dated to the Rembert phase, this difference was not found to be statistically significant (Fischer's Exact Test, p = 0.343; Butler 1986:173). Enamel hypoplasia was observed on about half of the burials in each phase (Beaverdam = 6; Rembert = 5), again with no statistically significant difference observed (Fischer's Exact Test, p = 0.272; Butler 1986:172). Combined with the somewhat surprising rarity of Harris lines in the radiographs of the long bones, the incidence of dental enamel hypoplasia implied that childhood stresses, while moderate, were not extraordinarily severe. In general, the sample presented a picture of a population of rather short stature, gracile physique, and subject to considerable disease stress.

Paleosubsistence Analyses. Standardized 4-liter flotation samples were collected from 119 Mississippian features at Rucker's Bottom and from 54 1-meter squares from the floor of one of the Rembert-phase structures. The heavy and light fractions were examined for ethnobotanical remains by Josselyn Moore (1985), and three standardized measures were employed in the analyses: species density, diversity, and ubiquity. Species density is the count or weight of a species in a standardized sample, with count per liter and weight per liter used at Rucker's Bottom. Species diversity is a measure of the number of different species of a given analytical category (i.e., cultigens, seeds, nuts, wood types) in a given sample. Species ubiquity refers to the percentage of all samples or features in which a specific species is present.

Corn was common at Rucker's Bottom, occurring in over half of the Mississippian features, with a ubiquity of 57% (figure 37). Corncob fragments represented the bulk of the sample, with only a few kernels and one small complete cob recovered. Although corn was found in a greater number of Beaverdam-phase features (ubiquity of 65%, as opposed to 48% in the Rembert-phase features), considerably more corn was found in the later occupation. Carbonized nutshells were recovered from just under half of the Mississippian features at Rucker's Bottom. Hickory and acorn were the only species identified. While hickory nut showed a fairly constant pattern of utilization between the earlier and later Mississippian occupations, use of acorns increased dramatically, measured over both ubiquity and density (figure 37). Four identifiable species of seeds were found in the Mississippian features: maypops, grape, lambs-quarter, and doveweed. Maypops and grape were found in both the early and later occupations, while lambs-quarter was identified only in Beaverdam-phase features and doveweed in later Rembert features. Seeds were more common in the later occupation (ubiquity of 33%, as opposed to 21% in the Beaverdam phase), suggesting some subsistence intensification was occurring.

Examining the ubiquity of the wood versus nut charcoal for hickory

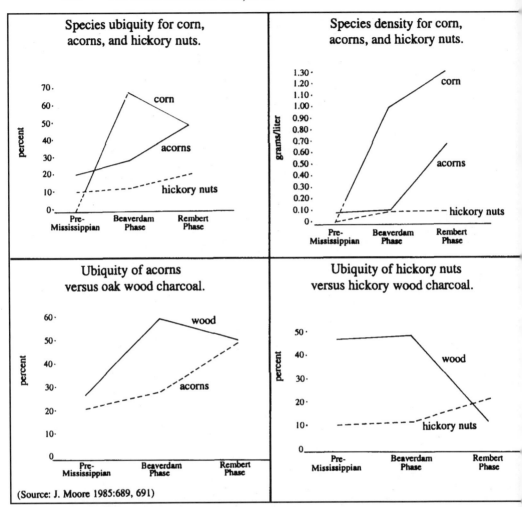

Species ubiquity for corn, acorns, and hickory nuts.

Species density for corn, acorns, and hickory nuts.

Ubiquity of acorns versus oak wood charcoal.

Ubiquity of hickory nuts versus hickory wood charcoal.

(Source: J. Moore 1985:689, 691)

Figure 37   Species Ubiquity and Density among Paleoethnobotanical Samples at Rucker's Bottom (9Eb91).

and oak between the earlier and later Mississippian occupations, a slight decline in oak occurred, together with a sharp drop for hickory (figure 37). If wood charcoal ubiquity can be considered an indicator of species availability and nutshell a measure of species utilization, then a decline in both tree species, but particularly hickory, appears to have occurred in the Rucker's Bottom area. The utilization of hickory nuts, in contrast, increased slightly, while acorn use increased dramatically. Margaret Scarry (1981:95) has suggested that changes such as these in wood and nut utilization may have been the result of intensive land clearance associated with agricultural intensification. As larger areas were cleared, the availability of wild resources would have declined. Plant succession would have been affected by this farming activity, with subclimax plant communities (which include pine and oak) becoming dominant. The high incidence of pine observed in the wood charcoal from the site, a pattern also noted in the pollen samples collected at the Beaverdam Creek mound (S. Fish 1985), was probably due in part to this clearing.

A total of 13,094 identifiable bone fragments were found at Rucker's Bottom and were examined by Scott (1985). All bone was weighed, with counts and minimum-number-of-individuals (MNI) data recorded for identified taxa. The bone sample from Rucker's Bottom was typically poorly preserved, exhibiting extensive predepositional and postdepositional modification, although in some contexts preservation was quite good. Besides natural weathering, carnivore scavenging had removed some portion of the assemblage. Gnawed bones were found in several features, although, surprisingly, no dog remains were found on the site. In general, many of the bones that survived did so because they were relatively dense and hence more resistant to normal weathering processes.

Three species dominated the assemblage: white-tailed deer, wild turkey, and box turtle. In terms of economic importance, white-tailed deer was the most important species, followed by wild turkey. The apparent abundance of box turtles was probably related more to factors of preservation and the use of carapaces for vessels and rattles than to subsistence importance. Elements associated with the forequarters and hindquarters of large mammals, mostly deer, were more common in the assemblage than expected, based on bone density, indicating these relatively meaty sections were probably brought onto the site in greater quantities than other, economically less valuable parts. A very high frequency of burned deer phalanges was also observed in the assemblage, which suggests the roasting of whole limbs over open fires. Limb elements from Rucker's Bottom also exhibited a high degree of intentional fragmentation, suggesting a concern for subsistence maximization, possibly to facilitate boiling and marrow extraction. Given the evidence for subsistence stress observed in the skeletal sample, this procedure may have helped reduce famine. The degree of fragmentation may have been influenced by the size of the cooking vessel used to boil the bones, which may have in turn been related to the size of the consumer group. The degree of fragmentation was similar to that observed at the Yarborough site (Scott 1981, 1982), where family unit cooking practices were documented. Comparable family- or household-sized groups were probably present at Rucker's Bottom. Once the flesh had been removed from these limbs and stored or eaten, the bones may have then been smashed and boiled, something that would explain the high degree of fragmentation observed. Shellfish remains were found in varying but typically low quantity and were more common in the earlier Beaverdam-phase occupation than in the later Rembert-phase occupation (Blanchard and Claassen 1985).

Clyde Gulley

What appear to be the remains of an Early Mississippian Jarrett-phase village were found at the Clyde Gulley site (9Eb387) in 1981 during the investigations in the Richard B. Russell Reservoir (Tippitt and Marquardt 1984: 8-9 to 8-14, 8-20 to 8-37). The site was located on a low rise on the first terrace just below the confluence of Pickens Creek with the Savannah River. A dark midden stain was found extending over a roughly 0.5-hectare area, measured using a split-spoon sampling auger (figure 38). The midden was thickest on a low rise on the levee crest and thinned rapidly away from this area. Slightly thicker deposits were observed in three places, which may represent the locations of structures (i.e., house clusters?) or refuse disposal areas. A number of pits, post molds, and artifact concentrations, including the outline of a small circular structure 3 meters in diameter were found in a block, 10 meters by 10 meters, which opened into the midden in the largest of these concentrations. Two pits within this structure contained burned earth and bone, while a ground-stone tool fragment, several large sherds, and a number of small triangular points were found on the floor, suggesting a domestic residence (Tippitt and Marquardt 1984: 8-23). Given the low artifact density, the structure, which had not burned, appeared to have been cleaned prior to abandonment. No other evidence for structures was found.

The ceramic assemblage was dominated by plain, burnished plain, and complicated stamped finishes; the complicated stamped designs were predominantly two-bar and two-bar cross diamonds, supporting a Jarrett-phase assignment. A similar ceramic assemblage was found at 9Eb388, a small surface scatter on a ridge overlooking the site, which may have been an outlying hamlet or some other activity area, such as a seasonally occupied agricultural camp (9-5). Burnished bowls were common, and one had a duck-head effigy lug. Other artifacts recovered included plain and incised pipe fragments, pottery disks, small isosceles triangular points, and a number of small bipolar cores and small blades with lateral wear retouch. Use of the small blades in composite tools for a range of tasks, including cleaning fish, drilling, scarification, or working shell or bone was suggested (8-37). Almost all of the flaked-stone artifacts were made from very finely veined or clear crystal quartz.

Flotation samples were taken from all of the unit levels and features, but comparatively few identifiable charred plant remains were recovered, something attributed to the minimal evidence for burning found at the site (8-37). Seeds from maypops, passion flower, and grass were found, together with hickory nutshell and pinecone fragments (Aulbach-Smith 1984). Only one corn fragment was found, from the area of the structure. The fruit seeds suggested late summer to fall occupation, something also indicated by the nutshells. The low incidence of corn, with a ubiquity far below that observed at Rucker's Bottom and Beaverdam Creek, may be

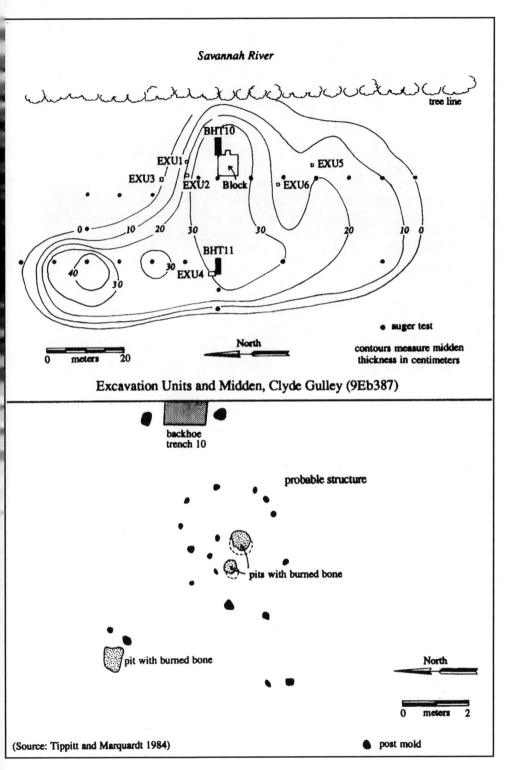

Savannah River

tree line

BHT10

EXU1

EXU3   EXU2   Block

EXU5

EXU6

0   10   20   30   30   20   10   0

BHT11

40   EXU4

30

30

• auger test

North

0   meters   20

contours measure midden
thickness in centimeters

Excavation Units and Midden, Clyde Gulley (9Eb387)

backhoe
trench 10

probable structure

pits with burned bone

pit with burned bone

North

0   meters   2

(Source: Tippitt and Marquardt 1984)   ● post mold

Figure 38 The Mississippian Component at the Clyde Gulley Site (9Eb387).

due to the poor preservation observed or may indicate that local use of this food source was comparatively minimal during the early part of the Mississippian period. Faunal remains recovered included bones from white-tailed deer, mud or musk turtles, softshell turtles, bullhead catfish, one unidentifiable bird, and one or more nonpoisonous snakes (Ruff 1984). Mammal and turtle bone accounted for over 98% of the assemblage. Given the proximity of the river, the presence of catfish and aquatic turtles was not surprising, although the incidence of fish remains was thought to be low (Ruff 1984: B-3). Deer elements from both the front and hind legs were recovered, suggesting that complete skeletons were returned to the site. Unlike at the Beaverdam-phase village at Rucker's Bottom, the populations occupying the Clyde Gulley site may not have had extensive tribute demands placed upon them.

Simpson's Field (38An8)

A single structure, possibly the remains of a hamlet, was found during investigations in the Richard B. Russell Reservoir in 1980 and 1981 at the Simpson's Field site (38An8), located on a Pleistocene terrace adjacent and parallel to the Savannah (W. Wood et al. 1986:49–119). The structure, located in the northeastern corner of the primary excavation block, was an oval-to-rectangular cluster of post molds approximately 10 to 12 meters in length by 7.5 meters wide (figure 39). This structure slightly overlapped a transitional Swift Creek/Napier Late Woodland house with several associated earth ovens located just to the south. Two burials lay within the Mississippian structure, while a small pit was found just outside of it to the north. Present were a number of internal posts that may represent benches or dividers, but no other features beyond these posts and the two burials were found inside the structure. The burials consisted of a child with five accompanying miniature vessels and a middle-aged female with a single bowl. Subfloor burials were also observed at Rucker's Bottom and may have been common during this period in this portion of the drainage (Weaver et al. 1985; W. Wood et al. 1986:119). Site use during the late Beaverdam phase and continuing into the transitional period between the Beaverdam and Rembert phases was indicated. Skeletal pathologies on the adult female, specifically antemortem tooth loss and bone resorption and the presence of excessive wear, caries, and abscesses in the remaining teeth, suggest a fairly stressful existence (Tyzzer 1986), similar to that seen in many of the burials recovered at Rucker's Bottom, particularly in the Beaverdam-phase village assemblage (Weaver et al. 1985:593–94). If a hamlet or small village was present at Simpson's Field, occupation by commoners rather than high-status individuals appears likely.

Faunal remains were rare and were dominated by deer, with rabbit, opossum, raccoon, turkey, and box turtle also identified (W. Wood

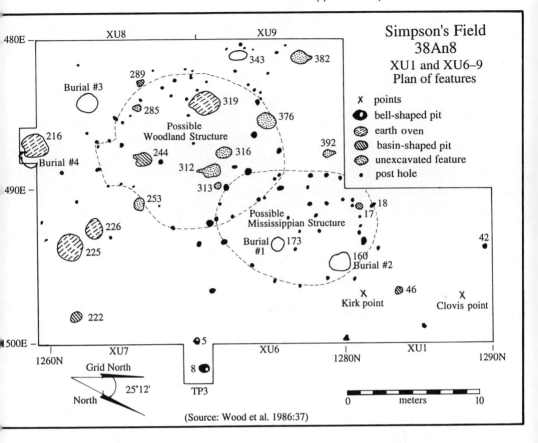

Figure 39   The Late Woodland and Mississippian Components at the Simpson's Field Site (38An8).

1986:374). The lack of identifiable riverine species was somewhat surprising, given the close proximity of the channel. Domesticated plants recovered included corn and a gourd rind fragment (P. Gardner 1986a:377–86). Wild plant foods included acorn and hickory nut fragments, grape, persimmon, strawberry, raspberry, and maypops. The presence of these open-habitat species suggested possible localized field clearing and abandonment and the exploitation of early successional communities (P. Gardner 1986b:378). An analysis of the ethnobotanical remains by fill zone within burial 2 was conducted by Dickens (1985:55–56), who documented seasonal differences between the two lower zones around and above the burial and an upper zone that accumulated sometime later:

> This pit, which appears to be of the shaft-and-side chamber variety (Dickens 1976:103), contained three garbage-laden soil zones: (1) a zone of fill in the lower part of the pit around the skeletal remains, (2) a zone of fill

in the central part of the pit, and (3) a zone of postburial slump in the upper part of the pit.

. . . Plant remains from the lower fill zone produced a seasonal profile indicating Late Spring–Early Summer deposition (i.e., interment). The middle zone (probably fill) also produced a Late Spring–Early Summer profile. The upper zone, undoubtedly representing post-burial slump, produced a Late Fall–Early Winter profile. It is important to note that the ratio of corn to nuts shifts from the lower to the upper zones. This feature provides an excellent example of the importance of separating, in recovery and analysis, fill from slump material in any feature.

This example illustrates the importance of careful field recovery and suggests how paleosubsistence remains may help delimit periods of feature use, abandonment, and filling.

Beaverdam Site Group

In the only explicit attempt conducted to date to determine whether hamlets were present in the upper Savannah River basin, four Mississippian sites within 2 kilometers of the Beaverdam Creek mound were examined in 1980 during the work in the Russell Reservoir (Campbell and Weed 1984; W. Gardner, Rappleye, and Barse 1983). Systematically dispersed surface collection or shovel-test units were dispersed over each site to locate artifact concentrations, which were then examined by small machine-stripped block units or hand-excavated test pits. The Mississippian artifact and feature concentrations at each of these sites were found to be spatially limited, indicating the presence of household- or hamlet-sized occupations. Post stains were found at all four sites, suggesting structures were once present, although at only one of them, 9Eb208, was a fairly well-defined circular post mold pattern from a probable domestic structure found (Campbell and Weed 1984:98–110). At this site, which was located on an upland ridge nose some 450 meters south of the mound, a semicircular outline of posts approximately 7 meters across was found, together with a nearby hearth and several isolated posts, suggesting a residential complex. A Beaverdam-phase occupation was indicated, contemporaneous with the occupation of the mound. The hearth may have been an exterior or summer hearth used by the occupants of the structure. At Rucker's Bottom, comparable features were observed near at least two structures, and they were interpreted as cooking pits (Anderson and Schuldenrein 1985:559).

Big Generostee Creek

A single disturbed burial of an adult female was found in one of five 2-meter test units opened at the Big Generostee Creek site (38An126) in 1980 during work in the Richard B. Russell Reservoir (W. Wood et al. 1986:197). The presence of Mississippian small triangular points and a ceramic assemblage characterized by notched appliquéd rim strips, finger-pinched appliquéd rim strips, bold incising, corncob impressions, and two-bar nested diamonds in the upper levels of the test units argue for a Beaverdam- or Rembert-phase age for the interment (203–5). Although Rembert-phase ceramics and two triangular points were present in the pit fill, its dating must be considered provisional. The burial had been badly disturbed by a historic excavation, and earlier Woodland materials as well as two historic square nails were also present in the fill (178, 185–86). The burial was apparently an adult female of comparatively short stature (150 to 155 centimeters) and indeterminate age, although probably somewhere between 20 and 40 years (Tyzzer 1986:367–69). In the absence of pelvic remains, the sex determination was tentative, having been based on the presence of a gracile cranial and facial morphology. Antemortem molar and premolar loss with significant resorbtion, caries, and wear to the secondary dentine on many of the surviving teeth implied a stressful existence. The pathologies were comparable to those noted on presumed commoner burials from the Rucker's Bottom and Simpson's Field sites. A hamlet or a small village appears to have been present.

Rufus Bullard

A series of posts from a possible structure were observed immediately below the plow zone in a block, 10 meters by 10 meters, opened on the levee crest at the Rufus Bullard site (9Eb76) in the Richard B. Russell Reservoir (Anderson, Cantley, and Schuldenrein 1985). Twelve posts, four rock clusters from probable hearths, and two large diffuse stains were found, defining an oval approximately 7 meters by 4 meters in extent, and a probable Late Woodland or Mississippian age was inferred (Flint and Suggs 1980:8, 67). The site occupies a large bottom adjacent to the Savannah River, and Mississippian artifacts were observed over an appreciable area, occurring in all of the units excavated. The principal occupation during the Mississippian period appears to be during the Rembert phase, given the high incidence of decorated rim strips (Anderson, Cantley, and Schuldenrein 1985:164). A number of hamlets or possibly a small village may have been present.

Van Creek

A probable special purpose butchering/processing area was examined at the Van Creek site (9Eb382) during the investigations in the Richard B. Russell Reservoir in 1980 (Anderson and Schuldenrein 1985:115–47). The site was a predominantly surface and plow zone artifact scatter extending over approximately 0.5 hectare on an old Pleistocene terrace overlooking Van Creek and about 1 kilometer upstream from the confluence of the creek with the Savannah River. The diagnostic assemblage was dominated by lithic artifacts, specifically small triangular arrow points, which was somewhat unusual given that the site was just 400 meters west of the dense village occupation at Rucker's Bottom, across a swampy swale. A controlled surface collection was conducted, and ten 2-meter test pits were opened at the site, which was found to lie entirely in the plow zone, with no evidence for sub-plow-zone features.

The most extensive use of the Van Creek site was during the Mississippian period. Diagnostics included 29 small triangular points and 10 complicated stamped sherds, and the fragmentary design elements on the pottery suggest a Beaverdam- or Rembert-phase age for the assemblage. The artifacts tended to occur adjacent to and overlooking either the swale or a swampy tributary of Van Creek. Many of the triangulars were broken, although roughly equivalent numbers of tips and bases were found, suggesting extensive hafted biface use and breakage, and probably discard, in the immediate site area. Other probable Mississippian tools present included expedient unifaces and crude bifaces. The high incidence of projectile points and the low incidence of ceramics was the opposite of the pattern observed at the Rucker's Bottom village across the swale, where ceramics far outnumbered points. Contemporaneous use of the Van Creek site is indicated, apparently for short-term tasks or otherwise exploiting the swale margin. The site is interpreted as an animal butchering and processing station that may have been intentionally located a discrete distance from the main village.

6

The Record of Political Change in the Savannah River Chiefdoms

Evidence from the Mound Centers

Over 500 Mississippian sites, including 14 Mississippian mound centers, have been documented in the Savannah River valley. Occupational histories at most of the centers are at least generally known, since excavation or surface data are available from all but Mason's Plantation. As recounted in chapter 5, excavation activity has occurred at 11 of the 14 centers, including at Haven Home, Irene, Hudson's Ferry, Red Lake, Hollywood, Rembert, Beaverdam, Tugalo, Chauga, Estatoe, and I. C. Few. Furthermore, at several of these sites where extensive excavations have been conducted, periods of occupation and construction are known within fairly tight intervals. The archaeological record from the basin thus offers a strong empirical foundation from which to examine political change over time. In this chapter, this changing record is examined, to the limits of our current chronology, and is used to advance inferences about political conditions in the basin.

No ceremonial centers are known from within the Savannah River valley at the end of the Late Woodland period, circa A.D. 1000. Low sand burial mounds, the focus of collective, largely egalitarian mortuary behavior, were probably in use in the lower part of the drainage, as were those documented during the preceding Deptford and Wilmington phases (Brooks et al. 1982; Caldwell 1952; D. Thomas and Larsen 1979); however, none are currently documented. Circa 1100, however, collective cremation ossuaries covered by low mounds appear at both Haven Home and Irene (figure 40). In the upper part of the drainage, the presence of Woodstock ceramics at both Chauga and Rembert suggests that these centers began about this time, although only at Chauga, where Woodstock barred oval motifs were common in the premound and initial mound stage deposits, is there an indication of mound construction (A. Kelly and Neitzel 1961:37). The founding of these centers appears to date to between 1000 and 1100 and probably toward the end of this span, coeval with Early Mississippian developments in northwestern Georgia at Etowah and Wilbanks.

Between 1100 to 1150, at least four Mississippian centers emerged in the basin, two in the upper reaches and two near the mouth. Platform mound construction began at Tugalo and either began or continued at Chauga, small single-mound centers located within a few kilometers of each other

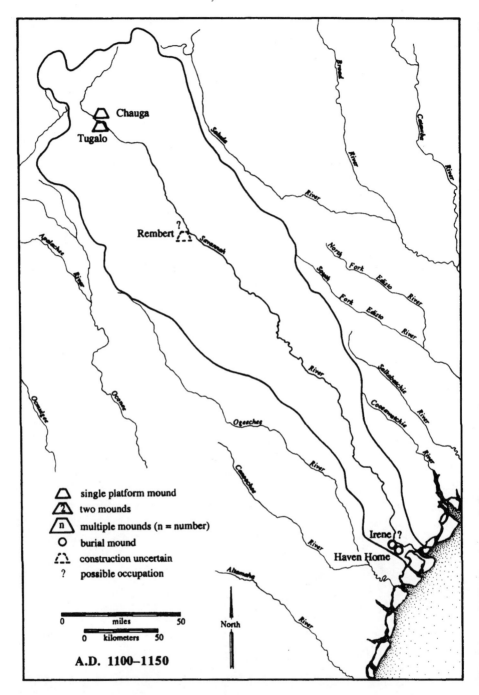

Figure 40   Mississippian Centers in the Savannah River Valley, A.D. 1100–1150.

in the extreme northern part of the valley. The Jarrett-phase assemblages at these sites are dominated by Etowah motifs, and some form of interaction with groups to the west along the Chattahoochee and beyond is indicated. These are the only platform mound centers known in the valley from this early period, although the presence of Etowah (Jarrett-phase) ceramics in collections obtained from the Rembert mounds prior to their destruction suggests construction may have begun there during this period as well. At the opposite end of the basin, near the river mouth, the Haven Home burial mound was constructed at this time, and perhaps only slightly later, the low sand burial mound was begun at Irene. A change from largely egalitarian and collective to individual burial treatment, with some individuals clearly receiving preferential treatment, is evident at these sites, particularly at Haven Home, suggesting the emergence of social ranking.

After 1150, Mississippian centers emerged throughout the basin. By 1200, at least seven and possibly as many as nine centers were in use, in three and possibly four clusters located about 50 kilometers apart in the central Piedmont, upper Coastal Plain, lower Coastal Plain, and near the river mouth (figure 41). Curiously, the centers in the northern part of the basin, at Chauga and Tugalo, were abandoned and remained unoccupied for over a century. This abandonment may reflect the southward movement of the populations of these centers down the basin into its broader and presumably more fertile lower reaches. Three centers appeared in the central Piedmont circa 1200, at Beaverdam Creek, Tate, and Rembert, the first two of which were single-mound centers. Whether Rembert was a single-mound center at this time as well or was already on the way to becoming the dominant multimound center it would become a century or so later is unknown. At least four simple chiefdoms, or possibly one complex chiefdom, were thus present in the central Piedmont by 1200.

In the inner Coastal Plain, occupation of the Hollywood and Mason's Plantation centers may have begun at this time, although this is uncertain. Farther south, the Lawton and Red Lake centers appear, and the nearby Hudson's Ferry burial mound was built either at this time or slightly later. Finally, at the mouth of the river, a major period of construction was initiated at Irene. Irene, Lawton, and Red Lake all apparently had two mounds (although at Red Lake the second mound, if actually present, was quite small), suggesting that these chiefdoms may have been somewhat more complex than those farther upriver. Three and possibly four groups of chiefdoms thus appear to have been present in the basin by 1200, with complex chiefdoms (possibly) emerging in one or more areas.

The situation was essentially the same 50 years later, in 1250, although by this time four clusters of mounds were undoubtedly present in the valley (figure 42). In the central Piedmont, Beaverdam Creek and Tate remained occupied (or at least no evidence indicates their abandonment at this time), as did the Rembert site, which may have begun to emerge as a paramount center. In the inner Coastal Plain, the Hollywood site was

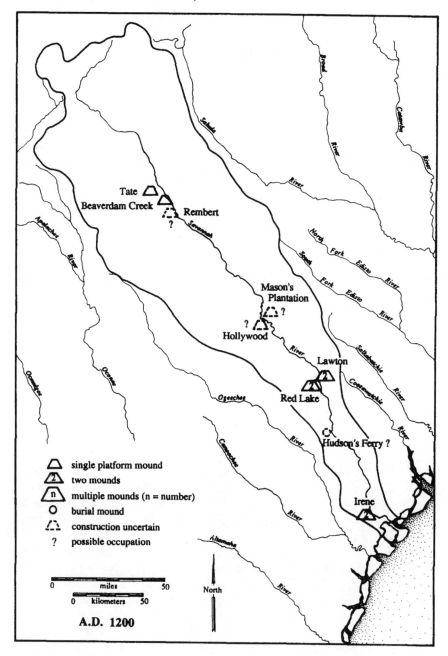

Figure 41   Mississippian Centers in the Savannah River Valley, A.D. 1200.

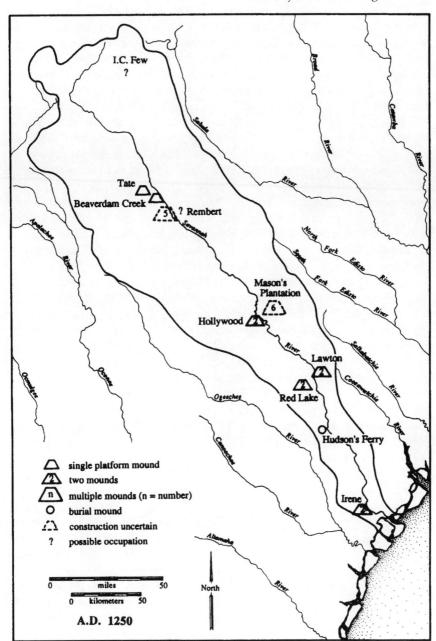

Figure 42 Mississippian Centers in the Savannah River Valley, A.D. 1250.

occupied, and elaborate Southeastern Ceremonial Complex interments were placed in the mound, suggesting the elites at that center were well connected. The Mason's Plantation site across the river was also probably occupied by this time as well, given the materials observed in collections from the river below the site. Like Rembert, Mason's Plantation may have also been emerging as a paramount center. Lower in the drainage, the Lawton and Red Lake sites continued to be occupied, and this is the probable period when the Hudson's Ferry mound was in use. Whether Red Lake and Lawton were paired sites within a larger chiefdom or were discrete chiefdoms is unknown. At the mouth of the river, the upper stages on the platform mound at Irene were under construction, and some Southeastern Ceremonial Complex iconography is evident at this site as well. While a pattern of simple chiefdoms is indicated throughout the valley, more complex political entities appear to have been forming.

Between 1250 and 1350, the political situation changed dramatically in the Savannah River valley, although, unfortunately, our chronological controls are not sufficiently refined to delimit precisely when and in what order events occurred. At the beginning of this period, small centers were scattered throughout the basin, while by the end of it, circa 1350, most of these were gone, and two major multimound centers had emerged, at Rembert and apparently at Mason's Plantation (figure 43). In the central Piedmont, occupation apparently ceased at Beaverdam Creek and Tate, and the Rembert site had emerged as a major center, with at least five mounds present. The abandonment of the smaller single-mound centers appears to have taken place by or shortly after 1300, about the same time that Rembert rose to preeminence. Evidence for elite impoverishment was observed at Beaverdam Creek, suggesting power and prestige were being subsumed by elites at the larger center (see chapter 8).

In the inner Coastal Plain, a second multimound center apparently emerged at this time, at Mason's Plantation. The nearby Hollywood site was abandoned sometime between circa 1300 and 1350, also with evidence for an impoverishment of the local elites, although the site saw some use later during the early Irene period as a burial mound. In the lower Coastal Plain, both the Lawton and Red Lake mound centers were abandoned during this same period, and at the mouth of the river, a century or more of continuous mound construction came to an end at Irene. The Irene site apparently fell into disuse for a time, prior to undergoing a dramatic if comparatively brief renewal in the ensuing Irene I period. For the first time in a century and a half, a Mississippian center reappeared in the upper part of the basin, at the Tugalo site, and the use of the I. C. Few burial mound may have begun at this time as well. While Mississippian populations in the extreme reaches of the basin thus may have had some degree of local autonomy, most of the upper and lower portions appear to have been dominated by polities based at Rembert and Mason's Plantation, respectively. The replacement of small localized centers and probable simple

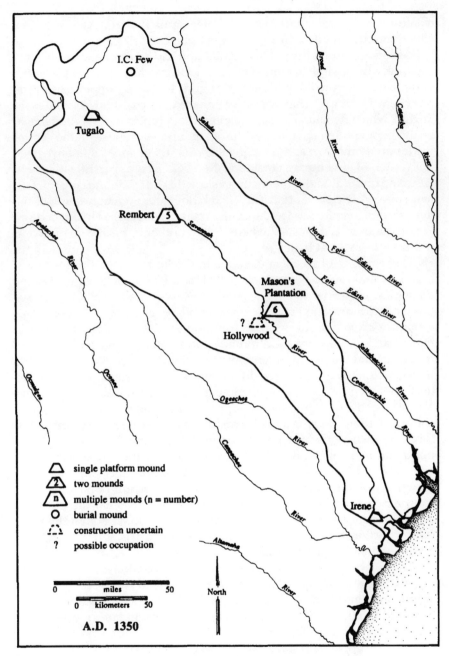

Figure 43   Mississippian Centers in the Savannah River Valley, A.D. 1350.

chiefdoms by large multimound centers and two probable complex chiefdoms apparently took place in the basin circa 1300.

Within a century, the political landscape had again changed. By circa 1400, only two platform mound centers appear to have been in use in the entire basin, at Tugalo and Rembert (figure 44). In the upper part of the basin, fairly simple chiefdoms are inferred. Occupation continued at Tugalo, which remained a small single-mound center, and this appears to be the period when the I. C. Few burial mound was in use. In the central Piedmont, Rembert reached its greatest extent and appears to have been the center of a complex chiefdom. Rembert was apparently the only occupied multimound center in the basin at this time. Mound construction had apparently ceased at Mason's Plantation, although our dating of the demise of this center is uncertain. Only sporadic use of the Hollywood site across the river is indicated, where urn and other burials were placed in the mounds by local Irene groups.

At the mouth of the Savannah, the Irene site was revitalized between circa 1350 and 1400, possibly the result of the abandonment of the Mason's Plantation center farther upriver and the reestablishment of local autonomy. Within a comparatively brief period, probably on the order of half a century or so, the former platform mound was converted to a burial mound and doubled in size, a rotunda and mortuary were built and then modified, and an extensive series of fence lines was erected. By 1400, the Irene site thus may have been dominating events in the lower basin and may have been a focus for ceremonial life, while the Rembert mound center played a similar role in the upper basin. While a traditional hierarchical chiefdom organizational structure may have been present in the Piedmont, where the use of platform mounds continued, less well-organized and more egalitarian decision-making structures are indicated below the Fall Line. This dichotomy is epitomized by the continuation of platform mound use at Rembert and the construction of a rotunda, or council house, and then its enlargement at Irene. Whether these centers were antagonistic to one another remains unknown, although the presence of fortifications and occasional trauma on burials at Irene suggest a period of increased militarism.

By 1450, both Rembert and Irene had been abandoned, and all of the centers in the basin from the central Piedmont to the river mouth lay empty and unoccupied (figure 45). None of these sites apparently saw subsequent reuse, even though a number of historic Indian groups moved into the area during the late 17th century. Only the area around the headwaters appears to have escaped and may have even benefited by whatever brought about the abandonment of the centers in the middle and lower portions of the valley. The Tugalo site in the extreme upper reaches of the basin continued to be occupied, however, and two new centers emerged nearby, at Chauga, which was reoccupied following a hiatus of about two centuries, and at Estatoe, where mound construction began for

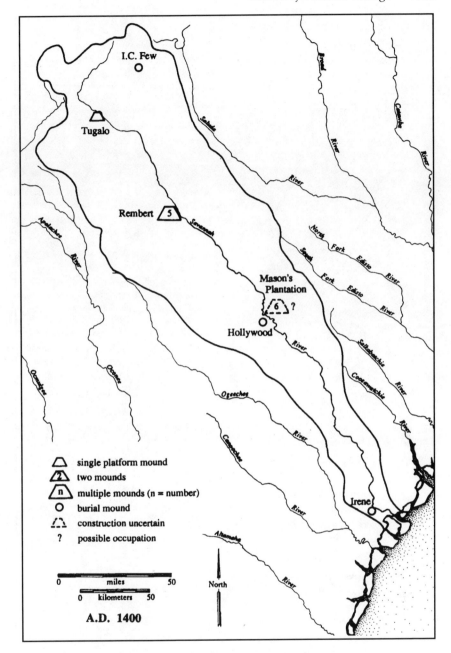

Figure 44   Mississippian Centers in the Savannah River Valley, A.D. 1400.

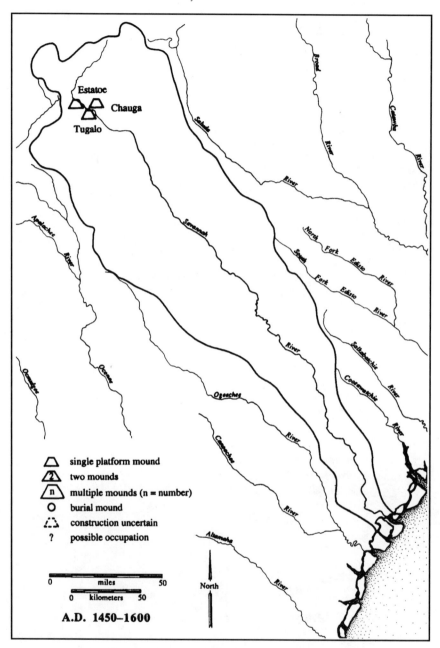

Figure 45   Mississippian Centers in the Savannah River Valley, A.D. 1450–1600.

the first time. All three of these sites, which were small single-mound centers, continued to be occupied into the 18th century, although mound construction apparently stopped at all of them sometime toward the end of the Tugalo phase, circa 1600, a pattern observed throughout the region (M. Smith 1987).

Evidence from General Survey Data

The Mississippian political history writ large at the mound centers is supported by the more prosaic general survey data available from the Savannah River basin. As documented in chapter 5, a total of 3,917 sites with prehistoric components have been found so far during survey projects in the basin, 551 or 14.1% of which had Mississippian components (table 3). Surface collections exist from many of these sites, and given the detailed cultural sequence and chronology available for the later prehistoric and protohistoric period, it has been possible to date many of these assemblages fairly precisely, using ceramic design motifs, rim treatments, and other sorting criteria. As part of the present research, artifact collections from 2,081 of these sites were examined in an effort to resolve periods of occupation. Artifactual data from Mississippian components identified during this analysis have been described elsewhere (Anderson 1990a:685–717). Where surface collections were not available for analysis, published descriptions were used to resolve periods of occupation, where these were detailed enough to make a precise temporal assignment.

Identifiable components were placed into one of three major subperiods, corresponding to the Early, Middle, and Late Mississippian locally, and by location within the drainage (table 5; figure 46). Subperiods rather than specific phase assignments were used to facilitate the comparison of contemporaneous assemblages in various parts of the basin. In all, 304 Early, Middle, and Late Mississippian components were identified on the 551 sites. Another 323 components, classified as Unknown Mississippian, had assemblages that could not be accurately placed within a specific subperiod or else were from sites where the collections were not available for analysis and where the published descriptions were ambiguous. Unidentifiable components were most common on sites with small ceramic assemblages or where artifacts such as Mississippian triangular points or otherwise nondiagnostic sherds were all that were present in the collections. The total number of identifiable and unidentifiable Mississippian components (n = 627) is larger than the number of Mississippian sites, it should be noted, because some sites had more than one component present.

Early Mississippian (circa 1000 to 1250) components, which encompassed assemblages attributable to the Savannah I/II, Savannah I, Woodstock, Jarrett, and Beaverdam phases, proceeding from the mouth to the headwaters, were fairly common (n = 125, or 41.1% of all identifiable

Table 5. Mississippian Components in the Savannah River Valley by Period and Major Physiographic Zone

Project Number	Locality (Proceeding from south to north)	Area Examined (ha)	No. of Prehistoric Sites	Total Sites	Total Mississippian Sites	Mississippian Components			
						Unknown	E	M	L
1–11	Mouth of the drainage	1,419.4 (0.69%)	219 / (5.59%)	313 (6.10%)	29 (5.26%)	2 (0.62%)	14 (11.2%)	17 (14.05%)	0 (0%)
12–22	Lower Coastal Plain	12,876.3 (6.26%)	412 / (10.52%)	462 (9.01%)	79 (14.34%)	37 (11.46%)	33 (26.4%)	14 (11.57%)	4 (6.9%)
23–43	Inner Coastal Plain/Fall Line	54,206.4 (26.33%)	1,118 / (28.54%)	1,278 (24.92%)	145 (26.32%)	114 (35.29%)	39 (31.2%)	34 (28.1%)	8 (13.79%)
44–71	Lower Piedmont	89,737.5 (43.6%)	1,860 / (47.49%)	2,703 (52.7%)	265 (48.09%)	160 (49.54%)	36 (28.8%)	51 (42.15%)	23 (39.66%)
72–99	Upper Piedmont/Blue Ridge	47,600.7 (23.13%)	308 / (7.86%)	373 (7.27%)	33 (5.99%)	10 (3.1%)	3 (2.4%)	5 (4.13%)	23 (39.66%)
	GRAND TOTALS	205,840 (100%)	3,917 / (100%)	5,129 (100%)	551 (100%)	323 (100%)	125 (100%)	121 (100%)	58 (100%)

27,450 square kilometers = size of Savannah River basin
2,058.4 square kilometers, or 7.5%, of basin surveyed at any level of intensity
702.22 square kilometers, or 2.6%, of the basin intensively surveyed

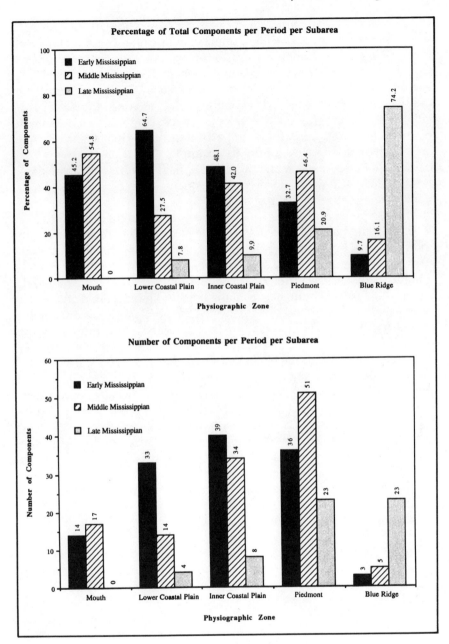

Figure 46   Mississippian Components by Period and Subarea in the Savannah River Valley: Summary Data.

components). The greatest number of Early Mississippian sites was observed in the central part of the drainage, in the inner Coastal Plain/Fall Line and lower Piedmont subareas. However, the greatest proportional occurrence of Early Mississippian components, compared with Middle and Late Mississippian components, occurred in the lower part of the drainage. The observed site distributions, while assumed to reflect population distributions, may also be linked in part to cropping practices and to general soil conditions in different parts of the basin. In areas where soils are poorly suited to agriculture, for example, as may be the case in the Coastal Plain (see chapter 7), movement of fields and possibly associated habitation sites may have been more frequent, leaving behind a proportionally larger number of sites.

Mississippian assemblages are rare everywhere in the basin until after 1100, it should be emphasized. Woodstock Complicated Stamped ceramics were noted on less than a dozen sites, and only at Chauga were more than a few sherds present. The first Mississippian assemblages in any quantity belong to the Jarrett phase and resemble Etowah II/III materials, suggesting possible influence from the northwestern Georgia area. Characteristic Etowah one- and two-bar nested diamond motifs occur throughout the basin. Surprisingly, only one Early Mississippian component was observed in the survey collections from the extreme upper reaches of the drainage, even though the Chauga and Tugalo centers were occupied at this time. Comparatively few prehistoric sites have been recorded in this part of the basin (n = 308), however, and the sample may be nonrepresentative. If this low density of Early Mississippian sites holds up, it may indicate that settlement was minimal away from these centers. Elsewhere in the drainage, where sample sizes are greater, Early Mississippian sites are found in some numbers. Details about site size and function remain elusive for most of these components, although the existence of both hamlets and small villages has been documented in the Russell Reservoir area.

Middle Mississippian (circa 1250 to 1450) components, encompassing assemblages from the Irene I, Hollywood, Silver Bluff, and Rembert phases, were also common in the basin (n = 121, or 39.8% of all identifiable components). They were fairly common everywhere, with the exception of in the headwaters, continuing the pattern noted during the Early Mississippian period and suggesting that occupation in this part of the drainage remained minimal. Only one center, Tugalo, was occupied throughout most of the Middle Mississippian in the upper part of the basin, and it was not until the very end of the period or early in the succeeding period that Chauga and Estatoe were occupied. Middle Mississippian components occur with greatest frequency in the area around the Rembert site, one of the two major mound centers that emerged in the valley during this period. The excavations in the Russell Reservoir have shown that at least some of these sites were small villages or hamlets.

Very little is known about settlement around Mason's Plantation, the other major mound group in the valley at this time, which lies in an approximate 20-kilometer section of the upper Coastal Plain that has seen little survey activity (figure 18). A slightly lower number of Middle Mississippian, as opposed to Early Mississippian, components are evident, suggesting some population decline or consolidation may have been occurring. This is clearly indicated in the lower Coastal Plain, where Middle Mississippian components (n = 14) occur with less than half the frequency of Early Mississippian components (n = 33). The decline in the number of sites in the lower Coastal Plain is probably related to the abandonment of the Lawton and Red Lake centers. No comparable decline was observed at the mouth of the river, however, where a slight increase in the number of sites is noted, although it was during this period that the occupation at Irene was revitalized.

Late Mississippian (circa 1450 to 1750) components, which include assemblages from the Irene II, Yamassee, Tugalo, and Estatoe phases, were appreciably less common in the basin than components dating to the earlier subperiods (n = 58, or 19.1% of all identifiable components). Late Mississippian components were infrequent everywhere except in the upper reaches of the valley above the Fall Line, where most of the components dating to this period were found (n = 46, or 79.3%). An increase in the frequency and proportional occurrence of Late Mississippian components is evident proceeding from the mouth to the headwaters, although the actual numbers of these components are still quite low everywhere but in the extreme northern part of the basin (figure 46). That is, while Late Mississippian components become progressively more common upriver, they remained infrequent and accounted for no more than approximately 20% of the identifiable components in any area below the headwaters. Furthermore, many of the components assigned to the Late Mississippian period in these areas were identified on the basis of sherds exhibiting one or a few bold incised lines, artifacts that could very well date to the Middle Mississippian Irene I or Rembert phases. With a very few exceptions, almost all the unambiguous Late Mississippian assemblages found in the basin with moderate or large numbers of diagnostic artifacts occurred in the headwaters area.

No Late Mississippian components were observed at the mouth of the basin, suggesting the area was abandoned after Irene I times. The unoccupied buffer present in this area in the 16th century, between the Guale of the central Georgia coast and the Orista and related groups along the lower and central South Carolina coast, may well have formed as early as 1450 or so. Light use of the lower and inner Coastal Plain is also indicated during the Late Mississippian period, with only four and eight components found in these areas, respectively. Appreciably more Late Mississippian components were identified in the lower Piedmont. While 23 Late Mississippian components were identified in this area, most of them (n = 18) were from the extreme western part of the basin in Oglethorpe and Banks counties near the Oconee River (Freer 1989; Jefferies and Hally 1975) and appear to reflect early historic movement into the area (see discussion of the Oglethorpe County data below). Nowhere below the upper Piedmont/ Blue Ridge area, in fact, does evidence exist for intensive occupation during the Late Mississippian period near the main channel. The low incidence of artifacts representing most of these components suggests the presence of isolated hamlets or villages or temporary camps used by populations based elsewhere.

Only in the headwaters area are Late Mississippian components fairly common, accounting for 23 of the 31 identifiable components found in this locality. Most of these components are historic Cherokee in age and probably come from hamlet or town sites such as those recently documented at Chattooga and Tomassee (Schroedl and Riggs 1989; M. Smith et al. 1988). The survey data for the Late Mississippian period thus complement the record from the mound centers, since only Chauga, Tugalo, and Estatoe, of all the centers in the basin, were occupied during this period.

Evidence from Specific Localities

Archaeological assemblages from three intensively surveyed localities offer additional detail on events taking place during the Mississippian period in the Savannah River valley. These localities include the Savannah River Site in the inner Coastal Plain and the Richard B. Russell Reservoir and the Oglethorpe County clear-cut project tracts in the central Piedmont (Anderson and Joseph 1988; Freer 1989; Sassaman et al. 1990). Several hundred prehistoric sites have been recorded in each area, and well-documented (and frequently extensive) collections are available from all of these sites. Encompassing as they do some of the most intensively examined terrain in the valley, the archaeological record from these localities is particularly well suited to fine-grained analyses of prehistoric settlement.

The Savannah River Site

The Savannah River Site (SRS) is a U.S. Department of Energy facility located in the inner Coastal Plain of South Carolina, encompassing approximately 777 square kilometers and extending for about 50 kilometers along and up to 40 kilometers away from the Savannah River, through upland sandhills dissected by several tributary streams (figures 18 and 47). Over the past 15 years, approximately 40% of the facility has been intensively surveyed, and 755 prehistoric sites have been recorded, 91 of which have Mississippian components (Anderson 1990a:700–702; Sassaman et al. 1990:276). Just prior to the Mississippian period, Late Woodland sites

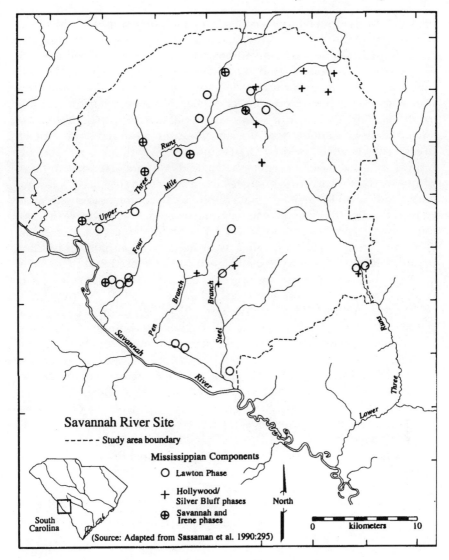

Figure 47   Distribution of Early and Middle Mississippian Sites on the Savannah River Site.

are widespread (more than 250 components), occurring in large number both near the Savannah River floodplain and throughout the interriverine uplands. A dispersed settlement strategy has been inferred, with the landscape occupied by numerous small, household-family groups, each intensively exploiting a wide range of microenvironmental settings (Brooks and Hanson 1987; Sassaman et al. 1990:300, 315–17). Political integration among these groups is assumed to have been minimal, as no evidence for ceremonial centers, burial areas, or even major settlements has been found.

A dramatic reduction in the number of sites is evident in the succeeding Early Mississippian period, when components are found for the most part near riverine or major tributary floodplain areas, with comparatively minor use of the interriverine uplands. Because these sites are typically small, most are assumed to represent special activity areas, hamlets, or small villages, although none have been examined in the kind of detail necessary to resolve function. Mississippian sites with ceramics, possibly representing habitation loci (i.e., households or hamlets), tend to occur primarily on terrace settings, suggesting a settlement orientation toward arable soils and a diversity of game resources. In contrast, sites with small triangular Mississippian projectile points, presumably indicative of hunting activity, tend to occur more widely over the landscape, suggesting game procurement in a wide range of settings. An appreciable proportion of the Mississippian survey assemblage (n = 29 sites, or 31.9%) consisted of sites with projectile points only, suggesting hunting was fairly extensive in the locality (Anderson 1990a:491, 700–702).

The distribution of Mississippian sites on the SRS seems to be linked to political conditions in this part of the basin, specifically the location of major political centers in the basin. The greatest number of these sites, for example, occur on the parts of the SRS that are closest to the Mason's Plantation and Hollywood mound groups, which are less than 20 kilometers upstream. The comparatively low incidence of Mississippian ceramics elsewhere on the SRS may reflect a fall-off in settlement away from these centers, although it must also be emphasized that the streams to the south are either much smaller (i.e., Four Mile, Pen Branch, and Steel Creek) or have been only partially surveyed (i.e., Lower Three Runs). The Lawton and Red Lake mound centers to the south of the SRS are smaller than those to the north and are considerably farther away, approximately 60 kilometers below the mouth of Upper Three Runs Creek and 15 kilometers below the mouth of Lower Three Runs Creek. They are thus unlikely to have exerted as much sway over populations on the SRS as the centers to the north, although once Mississippian settlement along the lower course of Lower Three Runs Creek is resolved, it will probably prove to be more closely tied to these southern centers.

Examining the number of Mississippian components by subperiod on the SRS, it appears that settlement was most extensive during the Early Mississippian Lawton phase (n = 28 identifiable components) and declined somewhat during the subsequent Middle Mississippian Hollywood and Silver Bluff phases (n = 19 identifiable components). In fact, no Late Mississippian or historic Indian components have been identified anywhere in the SRS to date, supporting the inference that population declined markedly in the lower part of the basin after the Middle Mississippian period. Interestingly, a marked change in settlement occurs between the Early and the Middle Mississippian periods (figure 47). Early Mississippian sites were found both along the river and in the interior, while Middle Mississippian sites are found almost exclusively in the interior, well away from the Savannah. During approximately this same period, as we have seen, political conditions apparently became unstable, as highlighted by the appearance or expansion of fortifications at both Rucker's Bottom and Irene, suggesting that an increase in warfare was occurring within the valley. The relocation of their settlements away from the river by the populations on the SRS may have been a defensive measure, an attempt literally to hide from raiding groups, who may have favored the major transportation arteries.

The Middle Mississippian marked the period when the center at Mason's Plantation reached and then passed its peak and when the abandonment of the Hollywood, Red Lake, and Lawton mound centers occurred. The settlement shift observed on the SRS may, therefore, also reflect a reaction of some kind to the absorption or consolidation of the valley's simple chiefdoms into complex chiefdoms, perhaps because the intensity of warfare or tribute demands may have increased. Some evidence suggests that conflicts between paramount chiefdoms were more intense than those between simple chiefdoms, primarily because of the greater numbers of warriors involved and the larger scale of the conflict (DePratter 1983:44ff; Dye 1989; Steponaitis 1991). If warfare or tribute burdens increased as a result of these changes in the political landscape, the dispersal of outlying settlements away from major transportation arteries may have been a practical evasive strategy.

The Richard B. Russell Reservoir

From 1969 to 1985, an extensive program of cultural resource investigations took place in the Richard B. Russell Reservoir, a 45-kilometer section of the main channel and its associated tributaries in the central Piedmont (figures 18 and 48). Approximately 5,400 hectares were intensively surveyed, locating 609 prehistoric sites; large scale excavations were conducted at more than 30 locations; and a detailed program of paleoenvironmental and geoarchaeological investigations was undertaken (Anderson and Joseph 1988; Foss, Wagner, and Miller 1985; Segovia 1985; Sheehan, Whitehead, and Jackson 1985; Schuldenrein and Anderson 1988). Late Woodland sites were found to be extremely rare, with only 13 Swift Creek and 7 Napier components recorded (Anderson, Cobb, and Joseph 1988:25). Because identification of components dating to this period remains controversial (see appendix B), discussion of Late Woodland settlement and comparison with subsequent Mississippian occupations are premature.

Mississippian assemblages, in contrast, were common and readily identifiable, occurring on 125 sites, and many could be dated to compara-

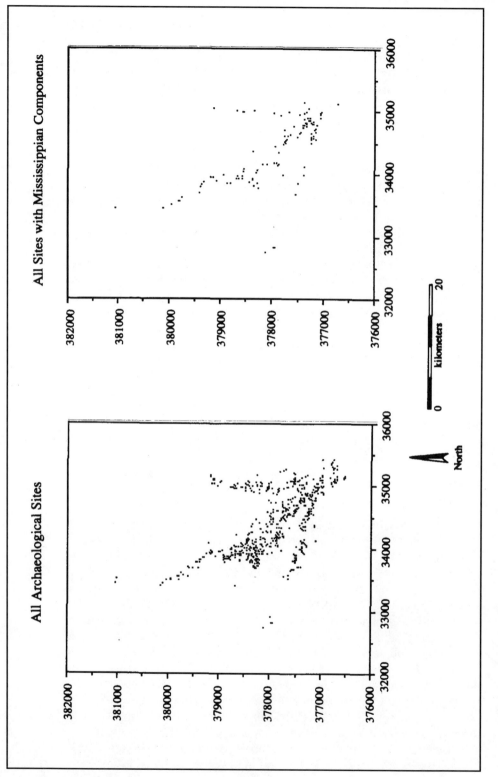

Figure 48 Distribution of All Sites and All Mississippian Sites in the Richard B. Russell Reservoir Area.

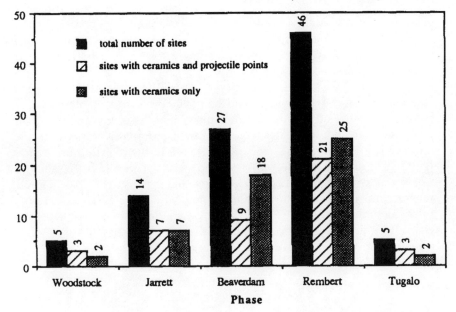

Figure 49   Mississippian Sites per Phase in the Richard B. Russell Reservoir Area.

tively narrow time intervals. The number of components increased from the Early to the Middle Mississippian, followed by a precipitous decline in the Late Mississippian (figure 49). The peak in settlement during the Rembert phase corresponds to the emergence of the Rembert site, which is located just to the south of the reservoir, as a major political entity in this part of the valley. Only five post-Early Lamar components were identified, characterized by one or a few sherds of bold incised pottery amid larger Rembert-phase or earlier Mississippian assemblages. Since bold incising also occurs in low incidence in the Rembert phase, it is possible some or all of these components may date to this time.

Nearly one out of every five prehistoric sites found in the reservoir had an identifiable Mississippian component, indicating that terrain near the Savannah was intensively utilized during the Mississippian period in the central Piedmont. As we have seen, the excavation activity that took place in the reservoir documented the presence of mound centers, small villages, hamlets, and special activity sites. Mississippian components occurred both along the Savannah and up the major tributaries in the Russell area, although by far the greatest number were observed along the main river channel (figure 48). How interior interriverine areas were utilized is unknown, since survey activity was restricted to in and near the flood pool. The limited survey work conducted in the adjacent uplands, however, found no evidence to indicate that settlement in this area was as extensive as that noted in the Late Mississippian period in the upper Oconee River valley to the west (Kowalewski and Hatch 1991; Rudolph and Blanton 1980; see below).

Most of the Mississippian assemblages (n = 110 of 125 sites, or 88%) had ceramics present and are assumed to have come from habitation loci. While 28 of the sites with ceramics also had Mississippian triangular projectile points, only 15 sites were found with projectile points alone; no appreciable difference was evident, however, in the distribution of sites with points and sites with ceramics. This incidence (n = 15 of 125 sites, or 12%) is far lower than that observed on the SRS in the upper Coastal Plain, where almost one-third of the identifiable Mississippian sites had only projectile points present. The SRS survey area, however, included appreciable terrain in the interriverine area, while the Russell survey was directed almost exclusively to floodplain areas.

Oglethorpe County Clear-cut Tracts

The final intensive survey data set examined encompassed eight clear-cut tracts totaling 1,198 hectares in the central Piedmont of eastern Georgia, which were surveyed in their entirety following timber harvesting in 1988 by archaeologists from the University of Georgia under the direction of Jennifer Freer (1989). The tracts were distributed in a near-linear fashion from the Oconee River to the Broad River, a tributary of the Savannah (figure 50). As such, they effectively straddled the divide between these two major watersheds and offered the opportunity to examine sites and assemblages in the interriverine zone at increasing distances from the major drainages in the area. A total of 313 prehistoric sites were located in the eight tracts, and Mississippian components were identified at 71 of them.

From an examination of the distribution of Mississippian components by period over the survey tracts, it is evident that settlement was greatest near the Oconee River and was most intense during the Late Mississippian period (figure 51). Early Mississippian components, identified by the presence of Woodstock and Etowah ceramics, were uncommon, occurring on one site each in four of the tracts. Three of these four sites were in the Savannah River basin, perhaps indicating population density was higher in this drainage during the Early Mississippian. Small triangular projectile points were found on three of the four sites, suggesting both domestic and resource procurement (i.e., hunting-related) activities may have been occurring. Middle Mississippian components, identified by the presence of Savannah materials, were only slightly more common, occurring on five sites. Interestingly, three of these sites were located in the Oconee River basin, suggesting a shift in settlement away from the Savannah River basin

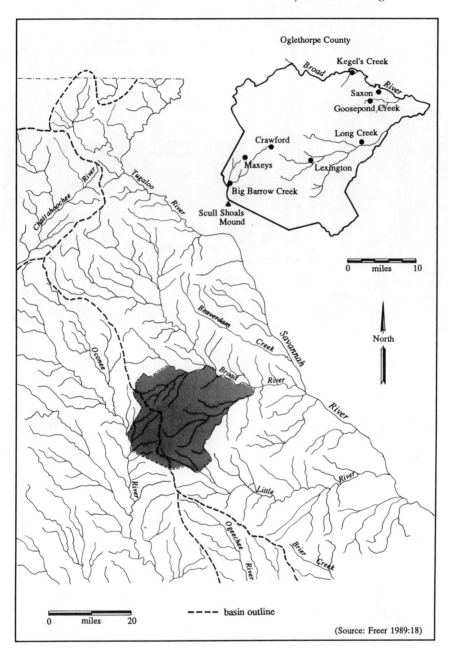

Figure 50   Oglethorpe County Clear-cut Tract Locations.

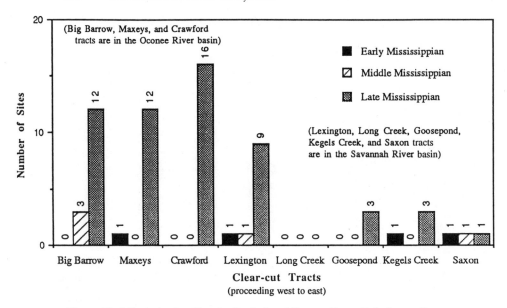

Figure 51   Mississippian Sites by Period and Survey Tract, Oglethorpe County
Clear-cut Survey.

or, more likely (given the growth of the Rembert chiefdom at this time), a
population increase in the Oconee River basin (Freer 1989:130–31). Only
one of the five sites yielded Mississippian triangular projectile points,
possibly indicating that hunting-related activity was becoming separated
in some fashion from habitation sites. The emergence of complex
chiefdoms in the Savannah and possibly the Oconee river basins during
the Middle Mississippian period may have resulted in a relocation of
population to areas closer to these centers. Intervening areas, in this view,
served as a combination boundary zone and hunting territory for these
groups and possibly as an area where warfare occurred (131).

Late Mississippian period components—identified by the presence of
assemblages from the Iron Horse (1450 to 1530), Dyar (1530 to 1590), and
Bell (1590 to 1650) phases in the Oconee River basin (Freer 1989:132–33; M.
Smith 1981:186–89, 245; M. Williams 1983:433–39, 1988:123–24)—were
extremely common, occurring on 56 sites. Major population increase and
a dramatic expansion of settlement into upland environments are indicated by the numbers of sites found and an examination of their environmental associations (Freer 1989:152). An appreciable majority of the sites
(n = 40, or 71.4%) were in tracts in the Oconee River basin, indicating a
continuation of the settlement trends observed during the preceding

Middle Mississippian period, that is, an increase in settlement in this part of the Oconee River basin and a comparative decrease in use of this part of the Savannah River basin.

Mississippian triangular projectile points were observed only infrequently on Late Mississippian sites (n = 10, or 17.9%), like the pattern observed during the preceding Middle Mississippian period, again suggesting separation of hunting activity or possibly warfare away from habitation sites. Interestingly, 6 of the 16 Late Mississippian sites found in tracts in the Savannah River basin had small triangular projectile points, while points were found on only 4 of 40 Late Mississippian sites in the Oconee River basin. Greater hunting-related activity associated with habitation sites or an increase in warfare may be indicated by this distribution, at least for populations in the Savannah River basin. The increased incidence of projectile points on sites does suggest that the western Savannah River basin was some kind of a boundary area.

The settlement changes documented in the Oglethorpe County survey tracts appear to reflect events occurring over a much larger area. Major population increase during the Late Mississippian period is well documented in the upper Oconee River valley, while, in contrast, by the start of the same period in the Savannah River basin in the vicinity of the Russell Reservoir, population had declined markedly. The Oglethorpe County survey data, however, indicate settlement continued in the Savannah River basin in areas near the Oconee River basin, although the number of sites declined rapidly with increasing distance from that basin. These patterns, particularly the comparatively large number of Late Mississippian sites (n = 9) observed in the Lexington tract in the extreme western reaches of the Savannah River basin, indicate that major watershed divides did not serve as strict territorial boundaries during the Late Mississippian period in this area. The depopulation that occurred farther to the east, however, may have facilitated population expansion from the Oconee River basin into the Savannah River basin.

7

Political Change in the
Savannah River Chiefdoms

Environmental Factors

The Effects of Local and Regional Physiographic Structure

If our reconstruction of Mississippian settlement history is correct, chiefdoms in the lower part of the Savannah River basin, encompassing the Coastal Plain below the Fall Line, declined sometime between circa 1300 and 1400. Only somewhat later, between circa 1400 and 1450, did the same fate befall the chiefdoms in the central Piedmont, while the area around the headwaters, in the Blue Ridge physiographic province, was occupied until well into the historic period. It is possible that the lower part of the basin was abandoned first, because the kinds of resources attractive to Mississippian populations were never very great in this area. The Coastal Plain lies within E. Braun's (1950:280) Southern Evergreen Forest. Low-lying floodplain, swamp, and Carolina Bay areas are dominated by water-tolerant hardwoods, while other vegetational communities, most typically in the interriverine zone, are characterized by xeric mixed scrub oak–turkey oak–pine barrens at higher elevations and mixed hardwood-pine forests at lower elevations (see also Barry 1980:95–190). Analyses of resource potential have indicated that the tributary/ floodplain bottomland forests would have offered the greatest food resources to native populations (Brooks et al. 1990:44–55; L. Larson 1980b:51–56), and large numbers of prehistoric sites have been found on the terraces adjacent to this zone throughout the Coastal Plain (Anderson 1975; Brooks and Scurry 1978; Sassaman et al. 1990).

Few major Mississippian sites, however, have been found in the lower Coastal Plain of either Georgia or South Carolina away from the Sea Island area (Anderson 1975; Ferguson 1971; Schnell and Wright 1990). This patterning has been attributed to the extensive pine forests or "barrens" in the area and to the decreased exploitable biomass away from major riverine swamps (L. Larson 1980b:56). The possibility that Mississippian agricultural technology, which may have first appeared locally in the Piedmont, may have been unable to adapt effectively to conditions in the Coastal Plain has also been advanced (Ferguson 1971:246). In the Savannah River valley, both of these factors may have constrained settlement somewhat. Below the Fall Line, the basin is quite narrow, with few large tributary streams (figure 52). Well-defined first terraces are comparatively rare along the lower part of the channel because of the great expanse of swamps. The broad, shallow valleys of the central and lower Coastal Plain are characterized by low sedimentation rates and channel switching rather than lateral migration (Brooks, Sassaman, and Hanson 1990:28), indicating areas where Mississippian floodplain agriculture might have been practiced were comparatively rare. Only in the upper Coastal Plain, and particularly in the Piedmont, where relief is more pronounced and channels more stable, are well-defined, periodically flooded terraces presumably better suited to Mississippian agriculture present.

The presence of only a few large tributaries in the Coastal Plain portion of the Savannah River basin, furthermore, meant that only a comparatively minor zone separated the floodplain forests of the main channel and its larger tributaries from the pine forests of the interriverine zone (Brooks et al. 1990). As a result, population levels probably remained fairly low in the lower basin. The large number of Mississippian sites noted along Upper Three Runs Creek, a major tributary passing through the Savannah River Site, however, indicates that where major streams were present, their margins were favored settlement areas. If this argument is correct, and the Coastal Plain portion of the Savannah River basin was indeed not particularly well suited to Mississippian settlement, it is possible that chiefdoms established in this area may have been unusually vulnerable to resource or political stress, helping to explain why they were abandoned before societies farther to the north in the basin.

Vegetation in the Piedmont falls within Braun's (1950:259) Eastern Oak-Hickory Formation and consists of a mixed mesophytic forest with a considerable range of hardwoods (Barry 1980:75–76). In the South Carolina Blue Ridge province, a wide range of species is found, from mixed hardwoods in the narrow floodplain forests, to oak-hickory forests in the uplands, to xeric pine–scrub oak associations on rocky ridge crests. The mixed, predominantly hardwood forests occupying both riverine and interriverine areas in the upper part of the basin meant that mast, and hence game, occurred throughout the region, unlike the situation in the Coastal Plain, where food resources of interest to human populations were largely concentrated in riverine habitats (Barry 1980; Ward 1983:68–69). Prehistoric sites of all periods have been found in large numbers in both the riverine and interriverine areas of the Georgia–South Carolina Piedmont (Anderson and Joseph 1988; P. Fish and Hally 1983; Freer 1989; Goodyear, House, and Ackerly 1979; House and Ballenger 1976; J. Kelly 1972; Sassaman 1983; Ward 1983; J. White 1982). While there is a tendency for larger sites to occur along the major rivers of the region, potential food resource distributions in the Piedmont and Blue Ridge areas do not appear to have constrained prehistoric land use to the extent noted in the Coastal Plain.

The organizational collapse and presumed associated abandonment of

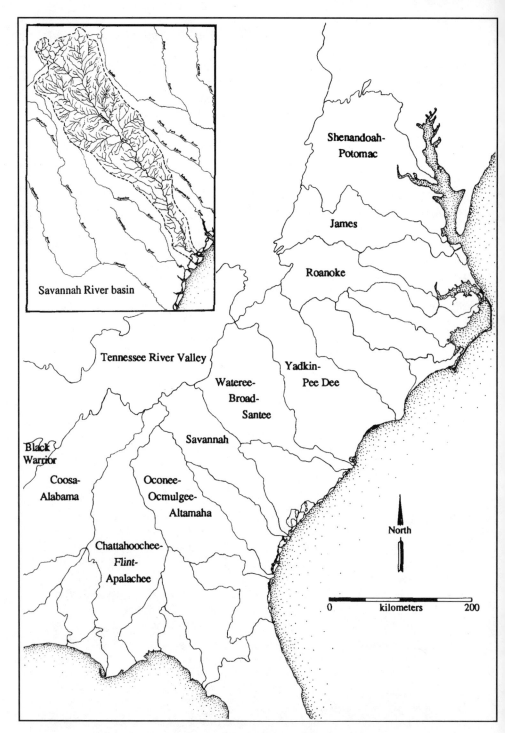

Figure 52 Tributary Drainage Patterns in the Savannah River Basin and the Size of the Basin in Comparison to Surrounding Drainages.

the central and lower Savannah River valley that took place in the late 15th century may also be tied, at least in part, to regional physiographic structure, specifically drainage patterns. The Savannah is a somewhat smaller basin (27,450 square kilometers) than the basins on either side, the Santee-Wateree-Congaree (41,500 square kilometers) to the east and the Ocmulgee-Oconee (35,200 square kilometers) to the west (Carver 1959; U.S.G.S. 1974) (figure 52). As documented in chapter 3, a number of major Mississippian polities were present in these drainages during the 16th century, while the Savannah itself lay largely abandoned. It is possible that societies in smaller basins could well have been at a disadvantage in any competition or conflict with societies in adjacent larger basins. Minimally, if land use was restricted largely to one's immediate basin, societies in smaller basins such as the Savannah would have had a smaller resource base to draw upon and, probably as a direct result, lower population levels. One method by which competition between societies occupying differing drainages can be explored archaeologically is offered below.

The Formation and Maintenance of Mississippian Buffer Zones

Theoretical Considerations

How local Mississippian populations interacted with societies in adjoining basins requires an examination of assemblages from large areas. Mississippian exploitation of wild plant and animal resources, as noted in chapter 3, was not restricted solely to the floodplain and immediately adjoining microenvironments but included forays into the interriverine areas, an activity that appears to have led to low-intensity warfare and the creation of buffer zones between groups. Buffer zones, or unoccupied areas, are well documented in the early 16th-century accounts, which indicate that skirmishes tended to occur when groups from differing polities met when hunting or fishing. Terrain near permanent settlements thus served as a fairly safe procurement territory for a range of resources, while hunting and gathering in areas at a greater distance was increasingly dangerous. The examination of archaeological assemblages over large areas, it is suggested, can shed light not only on the extent of buffer zones but can provide clues about the nature of relationships between the societies maintaining them.

Although studies of the patterns of human behavior leading to the formation and maintenance of buffer zones have been variously explored (DeBoer 1981; Durham 1976; Gage 1979; Gramly 1977; Gross 1975; Hickerson 1965; Bruce Smith 1974b), the detailed measurement of individual patterns of movement has only rarely occurred. This kind of information has, however, been collected for other animal species, notably social carnivores such as lions and wolves, and offers valuable lessons for the examination of human patterns of interaction. Territorial boundary avoidance behavior, measured in a sharp decline in the occurrence of kills near group boundaries, for example, has been observed among wolf populations, social carnivores that do not tolerate intruders into their territory (Fritts and Mech 1981:62–63; Mech 1977; Nelson and Mech 1981:40). Areas midway between groups were thus typically avoided, to reduce the possibility of conflict. It is probable that Mississippian populations in the Southeast acted the same way. The low incidence of contact across the buffers in place in the 16th-century Southeast was highlighted by the fact that De Soto repeatedly surprised native groups when he emerged from buffer zones, even though his party numbered 600 soldiers and was accompanied by hundreds of Indian bearers, close to 200 horses, and even a herd of pigs (DePratter 1983:39–42, 1991a:34–35). This example suggests that contacts between groups separated by buffers were few and far between and, given the pattern of skirmishing between hunting parties, that the central portions of buffers were avoided whenever possible. An ecological consequence of this behavior was that buffer zones served as game sanctuaries or refuges, from which species depleted closer to settlements might replenish themselves (Hickerson 1965; Mech 1977; see chapter 2). The maintenance of buffer zones thus likely prevented overhunting and potentially serious food shortages. The necessity of maintaining viable hunting territories, particularly if population levels were fairly high, is likely to have been an important reason for the occurrence of skirmish-type warfare in the Southeast during the Mississippian period.

Evidence for the existence and operation of buffer zones between southeastern chiefdoms should be recognizable archaeologically. In the discussion of Mississippian settlement in the Savannah River basin, the distribution of diagnostic projectile points and ceramics in three study localities was examined to infer land use strategies and political conditions, specifically where habitation, hunting, and warfare may have occurred and with what intensity. These same data should be able to help us understand how buffer zones were formed and maintained. In the Oglethorpe County clear-cut tracts discussed previously, for example, a decrease in presumed habitation sites and an increase in the incidence of projectile points on these presumed habitation sites were documented with increasing distance from the Oconee River. Over this same sample, the number of sites yielding only small triangular projectile points also increased with distance from the presumed core settlement area near the Oconee River (figure 53). Such patterns support the inference that areas away from major drainages served as hunting territories.

Given this, if the incidence of Mississippian habitation and hunting debris could be mapped over a large area, sufficient to encompass two or more polities, the resulting distributions might reveal the existence and extent of buffer zones and the intensity with which these areas were used.

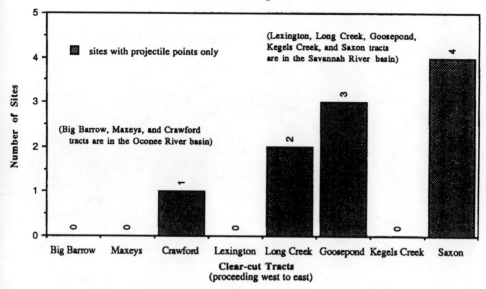

Figure 53   Sites with Mississippian Projectile Points Only, Oglethorpe County Clear-cut Tracts.

Two major patterns are predicted, depending on the nature of political relations between these societies. If individuals from differing polities were making a deliberate effort to avoid each other, then the area midway between these polities would probably be devoid or nearly devoid of artifacts. However, if conflict was occurring between two polities that were essentially equivalent in strength and if foraging parties were being actively challenged, an increased incidence of projectile points might be expected in intermediate areas, where the likelihood of conflict was great-est. Hypothetical artifact distributions are illustrated in figure 54, using the presence of ceramics to indicate habitation areas and small triangular projectile points for areas where hunting or warfare occurred. The location of artifact-free zones (assuming comparatively peaceful conditions, with groups avoiding each other) or areas where increased numbers of projec-tile points occurred (assuming a higher level of conflict or competition) would, of course, depend upon the size and military capability of the polities in question, with the distributional centroids likely displaced toward the weaker polity.

Projectile Point Distributions

In an attempt to evaluate these ideas, the occurrence of Mississippian triangular projectile points across South Carolina was examined, using

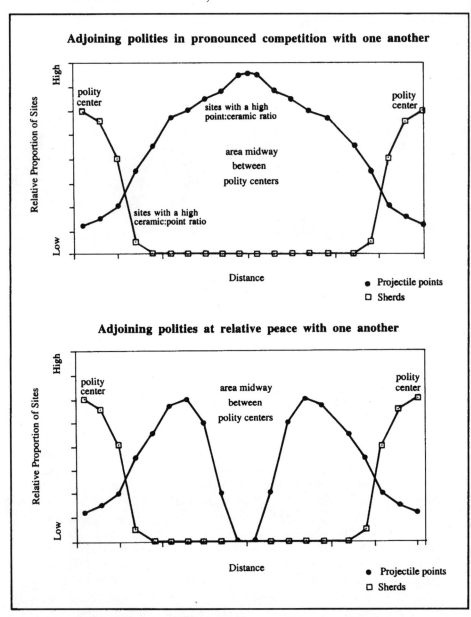

Figure 54 Hypothetical Artifact Distributions Created by the Operation of Buffer Zones between Societies at Relative Peace with One Another and in Intense Competition with One Another.

data from a statewide survey of amateur collections (Charles 1981, 1983, 1986). The number of Mississippian projectile points in each collection was recorded by raw material, along with the total number of points in the collection (Anderson 1990a:522–23). A total of 4,469 Mississippian triangular projectile points were present in the statewide sample of 85,102 points. The incidence of Mississippian projectile points, as a percentage of the total number of projectile points in each county and as a percent of the total number of Mississippian triangular points in the statewide sample, was examined employing a series of west-to-east transects across the state (figures 55 and 56). Because county-level proveniences are used and the data are derived from amateur collections, the resulting distributions are coarse grained and to some extent nonrepresentative. The uses of percentage values, that is, comparing the number of Mississippian points in a county to the total number of points collected in that county and to the total number of Mississippian points collected statewide, were attempts to standardize the differing artifact totals in each county. While ideally the distribution of projectile points should be compared with ceramics, so few Mississippian sites with ceramics have been recorded away from major drainages in South Carolina (in part because of collector bias toward projectile points) as to preclude this option. This dearth of ceramic Mississippian components is, however, what would be expected if the interriverine area served as a hunting territory.

Comparatively large numbers of Mississippian triangular projectile points were observed in the interriverine area in the upper part of the state, in Laurens and Greenville counties, which encompass the headwaters of the Saluda River (figure 55: middle, top). A much lower incidence of points occurred in the counties to either side, which lie along the Savannah and Broad rivers. This suggests that the upper Saluda may have been a hunting territory used by the Mississippian populations along the Savannah River as well as those around the Blair and McDowell centers along the Broad River in Fairfield and Chester counties, respectively (Ryan 1971a, 1971b; Teague 1979). The centers along the Broad River are thought to have been abandoned fairly early, by circa 1400 (DePratter 1989; Hudson, Worth, and DePratter 1990), and an appreciable buffer may have separated the major chiefdoms of the Savannah and Wateree/Catawba rivers during the later prehistoric era. While hunting appears most intense in the Saluda basin in the upper Piedmont, in the lower Piedmont the greatest incidence of projectile points away from the Savannah occurs in the vicinity of the Broad River, in Newberry and Fairfield counties (figure 55: bottom). These concentrations are near the Blair and McDowell centers, and some of the points undoubtedly derive from these occupations. The area also lies roughly midway between the Savannah and the upper Wateree/Catawba and may have been a zone of increased hunting or conflict for populations from these areas. During the late 17th and early 18th centuries, the western South Carolina Piedmont was a well-documented hunting territory and

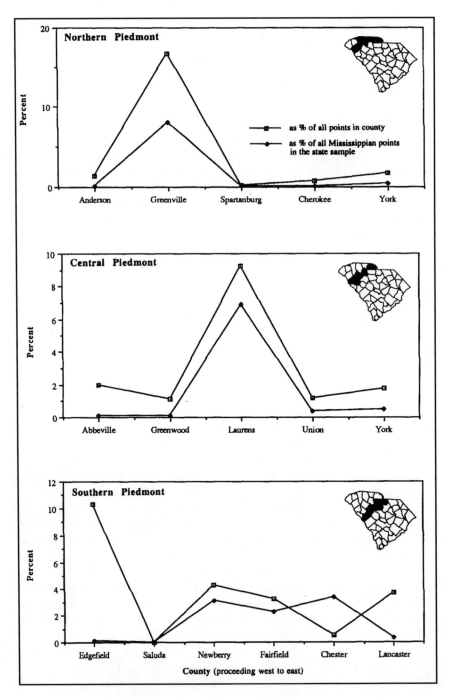

Figure 55 Incidence of Mississippian Triangular Projectile Points by County across the South Carolina Piedmont.

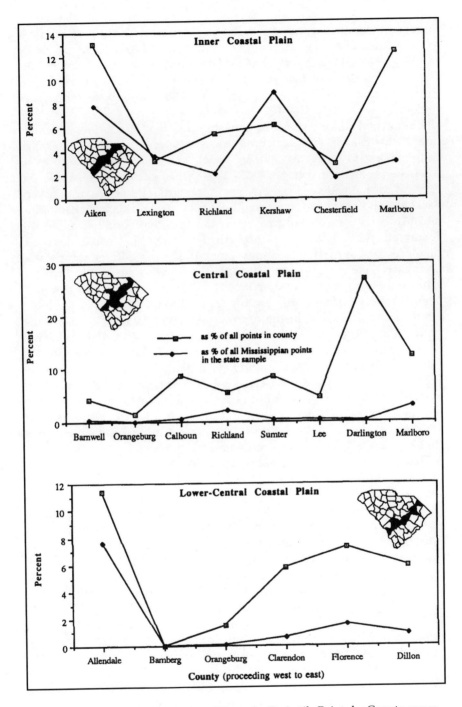

Figure 56 Incidence of Mississippian Triangular Projectile Points by County across the South Carolina Coastal Plain.

buffer zone separating the Lower Cherokee towns on the upper Savannah and the Catawba peoples along the upper Broad and Catawba rivers (Milling 1940:231–32, 266ff). The Catawba word for the Broad River, *Eswa Huppeday*, in fact, means "(boundary) line river." Use of the western Piedmont as a buffer appears to extend well back into the Mississippian period.

From the Fall Line south, appreciably different distributions are evident (figure 56). Mississippian projectile points occur primarily in counties near major river systems and are much less common in counties in interriverine areas. In counties located along the Fall Line, for example, the greatest concentrations of Mississippian triangular points occur in Aiken, Kershaw, and Marlboro counties (figure 56: top). The Mason's Plantation and Mulberry centers are present in the first two counties, along the Savannah and Wateree rivers, respectively, while an extensive Mississippian presence in Marlboro County, along the Pee Dee River, is indicated from early Spanish accounts that place the province of Ilapi in this area (Hudson, Smith, and DePratter 1984:73). The intervening counties have comparatively far fewer artifacts, suggesting hunting took place predominantly around centers. In the central and lower Coastal Plain, similar patterns are observed (figure 56: middle, bottom). Traveling eastward, projectile point incidence is low in predominantly interriverine counties such as Bamberg, Orangeburg, and Lee, until it picks up in the vicinity of the Santee/Wateree and Pee Dee rivers. The ethnohistoric evidence suggests that the Savannah River buffer, or the "desert of Ocute," was widest between the central Coastal Plain and the central Piedmont in the early 16th century, since chiefly polities were present in the headwaters along the Tugalo and in the central and lower Coastal Plain along the Salkehatchie and nearby drainages (Hudson 1990). This may be indicated by the projectile point data. While the interriverine area of the upper Coastal Plain includes such lesser drainages as the Edisto and the Lynches rivers, the upper reaches of these streams do not appear to have been utilized as heavily as the major drainages in hunting/warfare activity. Interestingly, along the Savannah, Mississippian projectile point incidence is fairly low in Barnwell County, which lies between the counties containing the Mason's Plantation and Lawton centers (i.e., Aiken and Allendale), suggesting that, even along the river systems of the Coastal Plain, the use of projectile points was greatest in areas near centers.

While the available projectile point data are not, unfortunately, sufficiently fine grained to permit full evaluation of the specific models of buffer zone use advanced previously (figure 54), they do reveal general patterns of Mississippian land use that can be refined as our assemblage information increases. The triangular projectile point distributions from South Carolina indicate that the Piedmont and Coastal Plain portions of the state were utilized quite differently during the Mississippian period. In the lower part of the state, as we have seen, triangular projectile points occur primarily in counties near major river systems, while in the upper part of the state, in the central and upper Piedmont, they occur in counties in predominantly interriverine areas. These distributions appear to be closely tied to physiographic conditions and particularly to plant and animal resource distributions in the two areas. As noted previously, in the discussion of basin physiographic characteristics, hardwoods and wild game resources are widely distributed in the interriverine Piedmont, while in the Coastal Plain these resources tend to be more concentrated along the riverine terraces and swamps. While for some time it has been known that Mississippian sites are infrequent along the minor drainages of the Coastal Plain, this pattern has been traditionally attributed to a preference for the rich floodplain areas of major drainages (Anderson 1975:189; Murphy and Hudson 1968). Instead, or in addition, these distributions may reflect the distribution of game resources, hunting patterns, and the operation of buffer zones.

Extralocal Lithic Raw Material Distributions

Raw material occurrence was also examined over the statewide Mississippian triangular projectile point sample, on the assumption that the incidence of extralocal lithic raw materials in assemblages might be a way of measuring interaction (i.e., trade or exchange) between peoples in different areas (figure 57). Perhaps not surprisingly, triangular points in most parts of the state were made of locally available raw materials. In counties in the southwestern Coastal Plain, for example, the vast majority of the Mississippian triangular points were made from Coastal Plain chert, which crops out in Allendale County (Goodyear and Charles 1984), while in the eastern Piedmont and northeastern Coastal Plain, metavolcanics, which occur in the Carolina Slate Belt of the lower Piedmont (Novick 1978), dominate assemblages. Quartz, which occurs widely in the upper part of the state (Novick 1978), dominates assemblages over much of the western Piedmont, while Ridge-and-Valley chert, from areas to the north and west of South Carolina (Goad 1979), is most common in the extreme northwestern part of the state and, to a lesser extent, along the Fall Line and in the lower Coastal Plain around Charleston.

The incidence of extralocal lithic raw material in each county over the Mississippian triangular assemblage was also examined (figure 57). Extralocal lithic raw materials were defined as those occurring outside of their physiographic province of origin. Thus Coastal Plain chert is considered an extralocal raw material when it is observed in Piedmont or Blue Ridge assemblages, while quartz and metavolcanics, which originate in the upper part of the state, are considered extralocal raw materials when they occur in Coastal Plain assemblages. Ridge-and-Valley chert, which originates in northwestern Georgia and eastern Tennessee (Goad 1979), is

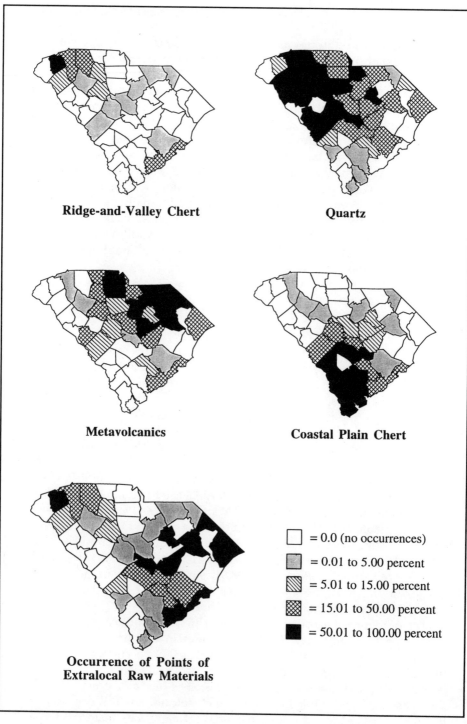

Figure 57   Specific Lithic Raw Materials and Extralocal Raw Material Incidence on Mississippian Triangular Projectile Points in South Carolina.

considered an extralocal material everywhere in South Carolina. Extralocal materials of Piedmont origin dominate Mississippian assemblages in the eastern Coastal Plain, along the Pee Dee River; the reason for this is that there are no major stone sources in this area. The only major Coastal Plain source, in Allendale County, is farther away than Piedmont sources and lies across several drainages.

Mississippian triangular points of extralocal lithic raw materials are common in the western Piedmont, an area previously interpreted as a buffer zone/hunting territory used by groups from along the Savannah, Broad, and Wateree rivers. The somewhat higher-than-usual incidence of projectile points made of extralocal raw materials in this area may, accordingly, reflect use by populations based at some distance. When specific raw material distributions are examined, this inference is even more strongly supported. A strip of three counties with points of Coastal Plain chert, for example, occurs in the area corresponding to the headwaters of the Saluda River. Points of Ridge-and-Valley chert and of metavolcanics, which seem to derive from the eastern Piedmont, are also found in these same counties. Both Ridge-and-Valley chert and Coastal Plain chert points are much less common in the counties to the west and east, along the Savannah and Broad rivers, while metavolcanic points are uncommon in the counties to the west, along the Savannah. These same counties along the upper Saluda also yielded large numbers projectile points (figure 55), so the raw material evidence complements the interpretation from the distributional data that the western South Carolina Piedmont saw use as a hunting territory.

The occurrence of a moderate incidence of points of extralocal lithic raw materials in the counties of the central Coastal Plain along and to the south and west of the Santee/Wateree River may reflect a use of Piedmont materials, since major high-quality lithic raw material sources do not occur along the lower reaches of the Santee. This explanation for the occurrence of extralocal raw materials would appear more likely than that the area saw extensive use as a hunting territory, something that is not indicated by the projectile point distributions (figure 56). Given the arguments noted previously about interriverine resource structure in the Coastal Plain, comparatively minimal interaction likely occurred between the populations in differing dainages in this area.

Ridge-and-Valley chert is most common in the extreme northwestern part of the state, the area in closest proximity to its sources in Georgia and Tennessee, and falls off away from this area across the western Piedmont. The raw material has been noted on Lower Cherokee sites, and when small triangular points of black or gray chert are found in surface context in South Carolina, they are sometimes referred to as Cherokee points (see also Goodyear, House, and Ackerly 1979:184–87, 228–29). As noted previously, the western Piedmont of South Carolina was a hunting territory of the Lower Cherokee towns in the early historic era (Milling 1940:266), so this distribution is not altogether surprising. However, Ridge-and-Valley chert also occurs in low incidence in Fall Line counties across the state and in the two counties around Charleston, well away from the probable source area and well away from the settlements of the people who appear to have used it. This distribution may illustrate the position of the Fall Line as a major transportation artery, along which unusual materials are likely to have flowed during both the historic period and the preceding late prehistoric era. It also likely reflects historic-period exchange between the Lower Cherokee towns and the European settlements and trading posts. Groups of Lower Cherokee are known to have visited or attacked European settlements along the Fall Line on the Savannah and Congaree rivers and around Charleston (Milling 1940:144, 266–306). Trade with the Cherokee was intensive during the century prior to the destruction of the Lower Cherokee towns during the American Revolution, so the occurrence of triangular projectile points of Ridge-and-Valley chert well outside the western Piedmont is not an improbable occurrence.

The distributional patterns observed in the statewide collections sample, while subject to a number of limitations, tend to be supported by data from areas where intensive survey work has been conducted (e.g., Anderson, Cobb, and Joseph 1988:25; Sassaman and Anderson 1990:164–68). Until larger and more representative artifact samples can be obtained and examined, the patterns presented here and the inferences based on them should be viewed as tentative. What this analysis does indicate, however, is that buffers were not merely empty areas occurring between groups but were zones characterized by their own varying dynamics.

The Effects of Climatic Change as Measured by Dendrochronology

Theoretical Considerations

In an important study from the southwestern United States, Burns (1983) examined long-term relationships among climate, agricultural production, storage technology, and political organization, the latter measured in terms of extent of public construction. He first determined that a relationship existed between tree-ring-width measurements and crop yields during the early historic period, prior to the adoption of modern farming techniques and fertilizers. From this base, he extrapolated crop yields into the past employing dendrochronological cores from a series of sites (Burns 1983:106–14). Examining the paleoclimatic and crop data over the period from A.D. 652 to the historic period, Burns (257–89) found that major public construction in the pueblos of the Four Corners area of the Southwest occurred during periods of extended or superabundant crop surpluses and that little or no construction occurred during periods of scarcity.

Through formal modeling and using reconstructed crop yields derived from the dendrochronological data, Burns examined the amounts of agricultural food products that would have been available each year, given differing storage strategies. Estimates of average annual production, consumption, and storage were made in terms of crop yield, that is, in bushels of corn or other crops (158, 167). Years with above-average rainfall were assumed to represent periods of food production above the needs of the population, or surplus, while years with below-average rainfall were assumed to represent periods of production shortfall, or food shortage. Production or crop-yield-per-acre figures were calculated over the study period (A.D. 652–1968) and were then used to calculate the total amount of food reserves on hand for each given year. The effects of storage technology to accommodate production surpluses or shortfalls were then considered, in a series of analyses assuming storage capability equivalent to 1.5, 2.0, 2.5, 3.0, 3.5, 4.0, and 5.0 years of consumption. For each model year, the amount of food already in storage (starting with zero) was added to the amount produced that year, calculated using the calibration of crop yield per tree ring. The amount of food was compared to need (for food and seed), figured as equivalent to a normal year's production, and any surplus or shortfall was calculated. Production surplus was put in storage, up to the given capacity, while production shortfalls were subtracted from the total food in storage. Once the upper storage limit had been reached, any additional production was considered "excess surplus" that had to be used immediately and was removed from the model. Deficits below zero, that is, when harvested and stored food reserves were exhausted, were also removed from consideration.

The results of the model were surprising. Famines, defined as "when the amount of food necessary to sustain a population at its normal level of consumption is lacking" (186, 220ff), occurred, as expected, when production shortfalls exhausted stored food reserves. This happened not only during periods of severe drought, however, but could also come about through a series of slightly below-average production shortfalls that combined gradually to exhaust reserves. Two of the most serious famines documented in the Southwest, in fact, occurred when average production shortfalls were no more than about 25% below normal for an extended series of years, with only a few years of severe production shortfall (202–7). This happened during the so-called Great Drought from 1276 to 1299, when many sites in the Four Corners area were abandoned, and during the period from 1772 to 1795, when the Spanish reported severe famines among the pueblos, particularly during the years from 1778 to 1780. Burns (147) cautioned, however, that not all historic crop failures and subsequent famines in the Southwest could be attributed to drought. Warfare, frosts, mismanagement, or insect pests might also lead to crop failure, yet this would not be detectable using dendrochronological data.

Burns's analyses document how the storage capabilities of a society determine its ability to buffer production shortfalls. Accordingly, political organization and storage technology "intervene between crop failure and famines. A crop failure's impact is only immediate and severe when few or no food resources are left in storage to cushion the effect of that failure. The importance of the years immediately preceding a particular crop failure thus become obvious. It is during these preceding years that the amount of food reserves is determined" (149). Obviously, a society that can store three years' supply of food (i.e., enough to meet the current year's demands, plus two extra years') would be able to weather shortfalls better than societies with only two years' storage capacity (i.e., enough to meet the current year's demands, plus one extra year's). Storage history is thus a critical aspect of this equation, particularly the amount of stored food available at the start of a period of stress (223). The order in which years of average, above-average, and below-average harvests occurs is also critical, since different sequences of the same production figures can yield widely varying cumulative effects (226, 239). Thus if in a ten-year period, five years had below-average harvests, the long-term effect would be much more severe if they occurred in succession than if poor years alternated with good ones. Famine can thus occur following periods where annual production shortfalls were comparatively minor but cumulatively great. A series of slightly below-average years, given inadequate or insufficient long-term storage, could be cumulatively as devastating as more severe droughts (141).

Burns's approach also permits the identification of favorable periods, when production was average to above average and food stress was minimal. A few years of above-average harvests, for example, would fill storage facilities to capacity. If favorable conditions persisted and production consistently exceeded storage capacity, the excess surplus (surplus over and above the storage capacity of the society) could be used to finance public ceremonial and construction activity. Periods of public construction in the Four Corners area, which are known very precisely from dendrochronological analyses delimiting years when wooden construction members were cut, were most extensive during periods of extended surplus and were rare to nonexistent during periods of production shortfall (215, 256, 264–89).

In chapter 2, it was argued that the historical trajectories of chiefdoms such as those in the southeastern United States were shaped, at least in part, by climatic fluctuations. The regular production of crop surpluses and their mobilization as tribute were regarded as critical to the stability of agriculturally based chiefdoms. Social unrest leading to organizational change or collapse is a common response to harvest failure and not merely in chiefdoms, as any reading of history will testify. If agricultural chiefdoms are indeed sensitive to climatic extremes and climatic change, as hypothesized, this sensitivity should be manifest in the archaeological record of settlement distribution and sociopolitical organization. These questions are explored with data from the Savannah River basin and immediately surrounding areas, in an effort to delimit long-term relationships among climate, agricultural production, storage technology, and political organization, following the example set by Burns in the Southwest.

Paleoclimatic Analyses in the Savannah River Area

Over the past decade, investigators at the Tree Ring Laboratory, Department of Geography, University of Arkansas, led by David Stahle and Malcolm K. Cleaveland, have been exploring paleoclimatic conditions in the Southeast using tree-ring data (Stahle, Cleaveland, and Hehr 1985a, 1985b,1988; Stahle et al. 1985). While several species have been investigated, including loblolly pine (*Pinus taeda*), shortleaf pine (*P. echinata*), longleaf pine (*P. palustris*), white oak (*Quercus alba*), post oak (*Q. stellata*), eastern red cedar (*Juniperus virginiana*), eastern hemlock (*Tsuga canadensis*), and red spruce (*Picea rubens*), most recent work has focused on bald cypress (*Taxodium distichum* L. Rich) annual growth-ring data (Stahle in Stockton, Boggess, and Meko 1985:91). By cross-dating and merging the tree-ring records from living trees with those from subfossil logs, five bald cypress chronologies greater than 800 years long have been produced to date in Georgia and the Carolinas (figure 58).

These long cypress chronologies exhibit a very strong warm-season climate signal and can provide a quantitative measurement of paleoclimate over long intervals. Bald cypress radial growth is positively correlated with rainfall and inversely correlated with temperature during the spring and summer, and cypress chronologies have been successfully used to reconstruct indices of drought severity (Stahle, Cleaveland, and Hehr 1985a, 1988), percent possible sunshine (Stahle, Cleaveland, and Cerveny 1991), and growing-season rainfall quantity (Stahle and Cleaveland 1992). Using ring-width data, warm-season precipitation reconstructions have been calculated for the past millennium for North Carolina, South Carolina, and Georgia (Stahle and Cleaveland 1992). The reconstructions are based on linear or multiple regression models that account for 54% to 68% of the variance in average rainfall, and all are strongly verified when compared with precipitation records available since circa 1890. The three reconstructions are highly intercorrelated in a spatial fashion consistent with their relative locations; specifically, they exhibit a southward increase in warm-season rainfall mean and variance from North Carolina to Georgia.

The warm-season precipitation reconstruction from 1005 to 1600 for South Carolina is plotted in figure 59. This reconstruction was based on two 1,000-year-long bald cypress chronologies, one from Four Hole Swamp, South Carolina (33°20' N, 80°25' W) and the other from Ebenezer Creek, Georgia (32°22' N, 81°15' W), a tributary of the Savannah River. The

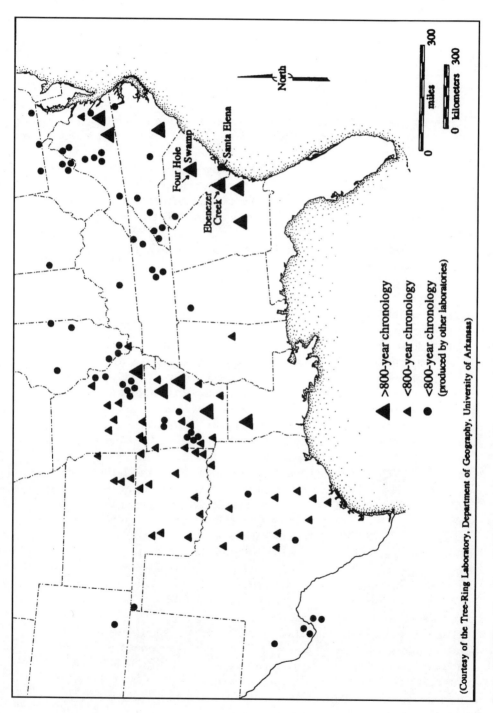

North

| 0 | miles | 300 |
| 0 | kilometers | 300 |

Four Hole Swamp
Santa Elena
Ebenezer Creek

▲ >800-year chronology

▲ <800-year chronology

● <800-year chronology
(produced by other laboratories)

(Courtesy of the Tree-Ring Laboratory, Department of Geography, University of Arkansas)

Figure 58   Millennium-long Bald Cypress Tree-ring Chronologies, North Carolina, South Carolina, and Georgia.

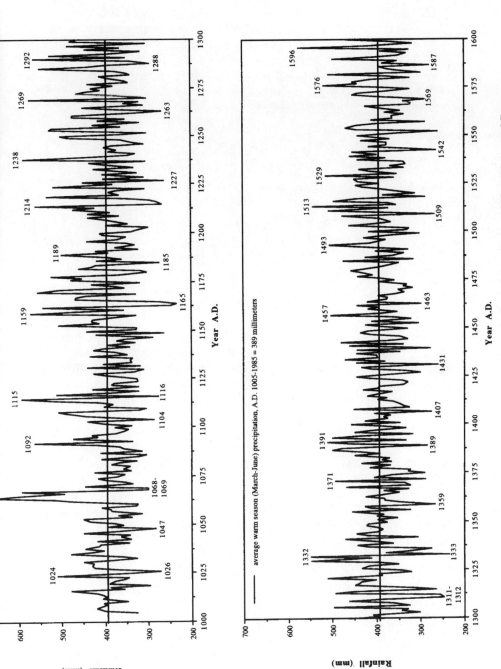

Figure 59 South Carolina Reconstructed Spring Precipitation (March through June): A.D. 1005–1600 Annual Data.

regression model used accounts for 58% of the variance in South Carolina rainfall from March to June between 1887 to 1936. Periods of significant drought are inferred based on the presence of three or more successive years of below-average rainfall values in the primary data (after Burns 1983:259–60). While a number of minor fluctuations are evident, there are several extended periods of appreciably higher- or lower-than-average precipitation that are assumed to have been either periods of unusual drought, when agriculture would have likely been stressed and harvests below normal levels, or periods of average to above-average moisture conditions, when favorable harvests may have occurred.

Modeling Stored Food Supplies in the Savannah River Chiefdoms

To examine more directly the relationship between climate and events in the local Mississippian archaeological record, analyses were conducted to determine the amount of agricultural food that could have been available each year over the interval from 1005 to 1600, given differing storage strategies and using reconstructed crop yields derived from the dendrochronological data (see also Anderson, Stahle, and Cleaveland 1991, n.d. for a more extended discussion of this research). The analysis reported here was conducted assuming a native storage capacity equivalent to two normal harvests, equating with a year's normal consumption, plus one year of reserves. While it is possible that local Mississippian societies could have maintained more than two years' reserve; given the Southeast's moist climate, preserving corn or other foodstuffs for longer than one or two years would have likely been difficult. Ethnohistoric accounts quantifying crop reserves are rare in the Southeast, but enough references exist, particularly from the 1539–43 DeSoto expedition, to indicate at least the possibility that up to a year or more of reserves were maintained in the complex chiefdoms observed during the 16th century (DePratter 1983:165).

Reconstructed rainfall values were assumed to reflect directly crop yields for the years in question. That is, all years with above-average rainfall were assumed to have yielded above-average harvests, or surplus, while all years of below-average rainfall were assumed to have yielded below-average harvests, or shortfalls. Critical to such an analysis, of course, is the assumption that periods with above- or below-average rainfall actually reflect periods of increased or decreased crop yields. Attempts to model the relationship between rainfall and crop yields locally, using historic data, indicate a relationship exists, although it is not always impressive. A number of factors, such as modern use of fertilizers, pesticides, and hybrid varieties, complicate such an analysis.

Beginning in 1005, and assuming no crops were in storage, the harvest and cumulative stored food resources were calculated for each successive year using the reconstructed warm-season rainfall values (figure 60). The average precipitation value for the period from 1005 to 1985, which was 388.85 millimeters, was assumed to represent the amount of rainfall needed to produce an average harvest. Departures above and below this figure were equated directly with crop yield. Years in which rainfall was 2 standard deviations or more below normal, or periods of severe to extreme drought, were assumed to reflect years of total crop failure. Rainfall values between 0 and 2 standard deviations below average, with mild to intensive drought conditions, were assumed to reflect years when crop production was below average. The extent to which rainfall was below average was considered to be directly proportional to the amount of crop shortfall. The negative standard deviation rainfall values were thus divided by 2 to ensure a range between 0 and -1, with values below -1 assigned a lower limit of -1. The rainfall values and shortfall ranges only go to -1 because numbers lower than this would imply more crops failed than were planted, an obvious impossibility (although years with rainfall greater than 2 standard deviations below average did sometimes occur). The same relationship was assumed on the positive side, with precipitation values above average assumed to represent years where crop production was above average. The amount of harvest surplus was allowed to range up to +1, corresponding to a maximum of two years' supplies (normal annual consumption plus one year's reserves).

Years with average harvests were assigned a crop value of 0, which was also assumed to represent normal annual consumption. Below average harvest values were subtracted from the running total (when the total was 0 or positive; it is not possible to accumulate successive negative shortfalls), while above average harvest values were added to it. The totals were never allowed to drop below -1 or above +1 for any given year, since, as noted previously, harvest values below -1 were an impossibility, while values greater than +1 exceeded storage capacity. When the surplus was greater than storage capacity (i.e., greater than +1), it was declared excess surplus (shown on figure 60 by a "+" indicating a year where this occurred). This excess surplus would need to have been consumed immediately and could have been used to sponsor trade, feasting, monumental construction, or other public activities. The negative values in figure 60 indicate the amount of shortfall that would have to be made up from other food sources. These are included to indicate the severity of the shortfall, which could range up to an entire year's consumption (-1), if a total crop failure occurred when no reserves were in storage.

Potential famines would have occurred when poor harvests led to an exhaustion of stored food reserves. Surprisingly, this could occur not only during severe droughts but could also come about through a series of comparatively minor production deficits that combined gradually to exhaust reserves. That is, an extended series of below-average harvests could

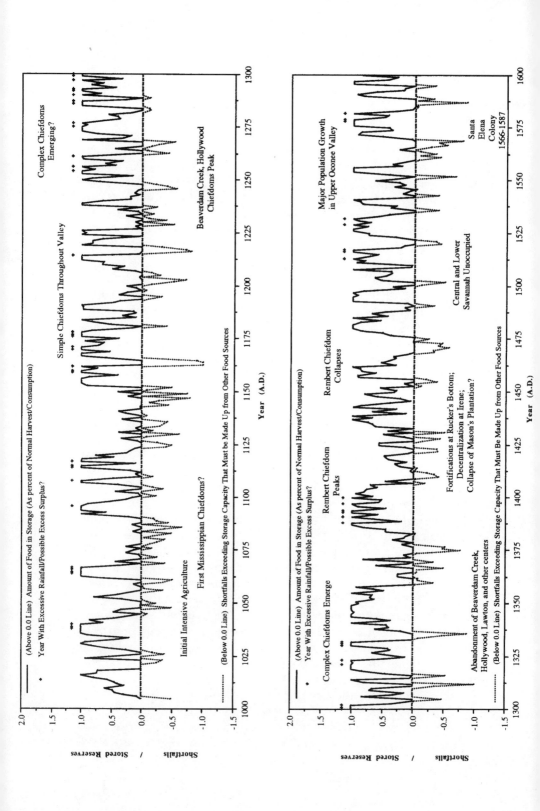

be cumulatively as devastating as shorter but more severe droughts. A storage strategy equivalent to one year's reserves (two normal harvests) would have enabled local populations to buffer most year-to-year shortfall in production, however, enabling them to overcome both isolated crop failures as well as a number of consecutive years of slightly below-average harvests. This was sufficient to ensure adequate or better food supplies just over three-fourths of the years (n = 449, or 75.5%) between 1005 and 1600. When extended periods of drought did happen, furthermore, maintaining a year's food reserves would have ensured that the effects of declining harvest yields were spread out, giving local populations more time to switch to other resources. No reasonable storage strategy, however, would have enabled local Mississippian populations to avoid stress during major periods of extended drought. Food shortfalls occurred during 12 of the years from 1359 and 1377, for example, while the period between 1407 and 1476 saw food shortfalls occurring 21 times, including during 7 of the last 8 years of this interval. These agricultural shortfalls would have had to have been made up from other sources (i.e., wild foods, or foods obtained through trade or conquest). It may not be altogether surprising, therefore, that several small chiefdoms are thought to have collapsed during the later 14th century and that the lower valley was apparently depopulated during the later 15th century. While the archaeological associations are admittedly coarse-grained, much better evidence for the importance of growing-season rainfall on Mississippian agricultural production and social conditions comes from the archival records of the 16th-century Spanish colony at Santa Elena.

The Effect of Climate on the Santa Elena Colony

The rainfall reconstruction indicates that below-normal rainfall occurred during every year from 1559 to 1569, except for 1565. The next year, the Spanish established the colony of Santa Elena on the lower South Carolina coast. This colony was placed on Paris Island, roughly midway between the two localities used to generate the South Carolina rainfall reconstruction (South 1980). Our best account of climatic conditions comes from April 1566, shortly after the Spanish attempted to settle. At this time, the land was undergoing a severe drought that had greatly reduced native food supplies. Descriptions of the native Orista, who appear to have been

Figure 60 (facing page) Crops in Storage and Food Shortfalls Exceeding Stored Reserves from A.D. 1005 to 1600, Calculated Using the South Carolina Warm Season Precipitation Reconstruction, and Assuming Storage Capacity Equivalent to Two Normal Harvests.

a simple agricultural chiefdom, included the observations that "there was little food in the land, as there had been no rain for 8 months" and that "their cornfields and farming lands were dry, whereat they were all sad, on account of the little food they had" (Merás in Quin 1979:492–93; see also Connor 1928:177, 210). Although Menéndez de Avilés stationed one of his officers and some 20 men with the Orista, they were in "great fear of lack of food," since "even if the Indians had been willing to give their food to Estébano de las Alas and his men, they had none, for it had not rained for many months" (Merás in Waddell 1980:147). These records lend credence to the paleoclimatic reconstruction, which indicates the period from 1566 to 1569 was particularly dry, and that the year 1566 was one of the driest of the decade, with only the years 1567 and 1569 drier.

The colony at Santa Elena had a precarious existence in its early years, something that was unquestionably due at least in part to the poor climatic conditions. The establishment of the colony, in fact, occurred toward the end of the driest period of the entire 16th century (figure 59), although the Spanish could have had no idea how atypical these conditions were. Food was scarce during the first years of settlement, and its acquisition preoccupied the local authorities (Connor 1928). The Pardo expeditions were sent into the interior at this time, not only to explore further but also to relieve the colony of the necessity of feeding his men. During Pardo's second expedition from 1567 to 1568, conditions were so desperate at Santa Elena that Pardo was ordered to bring food from the interior, and food shortages in the colony were at least part of the reason why he dispersed his forces into a series of small forts along his route (Hudson 1990:45, 152ff). These forts were all destroyed and their companies massacred within a few months of their establishment. The climatic reconstruction offers independent confirmation of these conditions and suggests reasons why the colony and its settlements in the interior ultimately failed.

Native rebellions during this period, the records indicate, were brought about by demands the Spanish placed on local populations for food and services. A minor rebellion occurred in 1570, for example, when the authorities at Santa Elena, short on food, "ordered three or four caciques, among them Escamacu, Orista, and Hoya, to bring some canoe loads of maize to Santa Elena" (Rogel in Waddell 1980:149). Rogel, a Jesuit living with the Indians, abandoned his mission at this time, knowing the Indians would not react well to these demands. When the Indians failed to provide the corn, the Spanish sent soldiers to their village, and rebellion ensued until the caciques were appeased with gifts. Although no mention of climatic conditions or amount of food on hand is given in Rogel's account, the reaction of the natives suggests they had little to spare, which would have likely been the case if, as indicated by the paleoclimatic reconstruction, the previous four years (1566–69) had been particularly dry. The attacks on the colony and its outposts, particularly the destruction of the forts in the interior, may well have been prompted, if not hastened, by the demands the Spanish placed on a native agricultural system that was likely already under considerable stress.

Above-average rainfall is indicated for most of the 1570s, but drought conditions returned in the 1580s, and the Santa Elena colony was abandoned in late 1587. The year 1587, the paleoclimatic reconstruction indicates, was the driest year during the entire approximate 20-year period of Spanish settlement (as well as the third driest year of the entire 16th century), and three of the four years before this (1583–85) were characterized by below-average rainfall. Consolidation of Spanish settlement in La Florida at St. Augustine rather than Santa Elena at this time was facilitated, in part, by perceptions that the former area was more fit for settlement (Lyon 1984:15). The role climate played in this decision is unknown but may be suggested by the precipitation reconstruction.

The Effect of Climatic Factors on Mississippian Occupations in the Savannah River Basin

Significant changes are observed in the Mississippian archaeological record from the Savannah River basin and immediately adjoining areas during the interval from 1000 to 1500 (chapter 6). As the Santa Elena example suggests, some of these changes may be linked to climatic factors. Before discussing associations between the paleoclimatic and archaeological records, however, it must be emphasized that the absolute time scale for the archaeological sites, occupations, and assemblages from the Savannah River valley is far coarser than the year-to-year time scale available from the dendrochronological record. Accordingly, the following inferences, linking together specific aspects of the archaeological and paleoclimatic record, should be viewed as tentative and as observations that will be refined or rejected through future investigation.

The initial appearance of intensive agricultural food production in the Savannah River basin likely occurred between circa 1000 and 1100, when the first evidence for Mississippian occupation is found, identified by Woodstock and Etowah ceramics at the Chauga and Rembert sites, later major centers, in the northern part of the basin. Climatic conditions conducive to agriculture were comparatively benign over the period from circa 1000 to 1125, with only two periods in our hypothetical reconstruction when food supplies would have been severely stressed, from 1056 to 1061 and from 1076 to 1090.

The second quarter of the 12th century witnessed a number of successive years of below-average rainfall, and food shortfalls are indicated 17 of the 28 years from 1124 to 1152. Only in the headwaters, where rainfall is extensive—almost twice that in the lower portions of the drainage (Kronberg and Purvis 1959:7)—would conditions suitable to agricultural food production likely have been present (and, as noted above, it was here that the first chiefdoms apparently originated). By 1150 or shortly thereafter, however, Mississippian centers emerged in several parts of the basin. During the second half of the 12th century, from 1153 to 1200, in fact, climatic conditions were quite good, with shortfalls indicated during only seven years (although those from 1162 to 1164 were quite severe). By the end of this interval, by about 1200, at least six and possibly as many as nine centers were in use, in three and possibly four clusters located approximately 50 to 75 kilometers apart. Interestingly, by this time the centers in the upper part of the basin were abandoned, suggesting a southward movement of population down the basin into its broader and presumably more fertile lower reaches. This relocation of settlement may have been facilitated by the favorable climatic conditions.

The first half of the 13th century was again apparently one of modest climatic deterioration, with food shortfalls occurring in 16 of the years between 1201 and 1250. The clusters of single chiefdoms remain, although there are suggestions that complex chiefdoms may have begun to emerge, at Rembert and Mason's Plantation, events that might have been stimulated by the increased subsistence uncertainty. Between circa 1250 and 1350, the political situation changed dramatically in the basin, although, unfortunately, our chronological controls are not sufficiently refined to delimit precisely when and in what order events occurred. At the beginning of this period, small centers were scattered throughout the basin, while by the end of it, circa 1350, most of these were gone, and two major multi-mound centers had emerged, at Rembert and Mason's Plantation. Climatic conditions were generally quite favorable throughout this interval, however, with only 16 years of shortfall predicted between 1251 and 1358.

Sometime after circa 1300, a number of small mound centers are inferred to have been abandoned throughout the drainage, including Hollywood, Lawton, and Red Lake in the Coastal Plain, and Beaverdam Creek and Tate in the central Piedmont, while at the mouth of the river, more than a century of continuous mound construction apparently came to an end at Irene. The 14th century is thought to have been the heyday of the presumed complex chiefdom centered at Mason's Plantation, and if so, the elites at this center may have stifled political ambitions among populations at Irene and elsewhere in the lower drainage. The reconstructed climatic data suggest that the growth of complex chiefdoms locally may have occurred at the expense of simple chiefdoms and was brought about, at least in part, by an extended period of favorable climatic conditions. The extensive regular agricultural surpluses that resulted were likely used by particularly competent elites to further their political agendas, with less successful elites at outlying centers absorbed into or eliminated by the elites in the larger chiefdoms.

A severe downturn in climate occurred after this interval, however, and food shortages are indicated 12 of the 19 years from 1359 to 1377. The abandonment of some of the basin's smaller centers, something inferred to have occurred during the previous period, may have actually taken place or been completed at this time. Occupation may have ceased at Mason's Plantation during this same period, which may also be the time when major fortifications appeared at Irene and Rucker's Bottom.

After 1377, crop surpluses would have been present in storage almost every year until 1407 (only in 1383 was there a slight shortfall). The Irene site, which apparently fell into disuse during the previous period, appears to have undergone something of a renewal about this time, although no evidence indicates that a chiefdom level of organization reappeared. This is also the time when the Rembert chiefdom, presumably encompassing the Mississippian populations of the central Piedmont, also apparently reached its peak. Evidence for the reoccupation or reemergence of centers occurred during this same general interval in the upper part of the basin at the single-mound Tugalo site, while in the lower part of the basin, the populations using the Irene site appear to have dominated the landscape, with evidence for their interments, in the form of urn burials, noted as far inland as Hollywood and Stallings Island.

A moderate deterioration in climate lasting almost three-quarters of a century occurred shortly after the start of the 15th century, and it is about this time that the most dramatic change in the regional political landscape occurred. Between 1407 and 1476 shortfalls occurred 21 of 69 years, and it is during this interval that the lower valley was apparently depopulated. By shortly after 1400, Tugalo and Rembert were the only platform mound centers known to have been in use in the basin and, with the fragmentation of the complex chiefdom at Mason's Plantation, the chiefdom centered at Rembert was apparently the only major polity. Fortifications are thought to have appeared at the Rucker's Bottom village site about this time, and this may have also been the period when major fortifications were erected around the rotunda and mound at Irene, events that suggest warfare or raiding, possibly as local groups sought to obtain food. By the late 15th century, however, Mississippian chiefdoms had disappeared throughout the central and lower Savannah River valley, and possibly in the nearby Broad River drainage as well, where the Blair and McDowell sites were abandoned (DePratter 1989).

The depopulation of the central and lower Savannah basin, which is thought to have occurred about this time, may thus have been brought about in part by climatic conditions. A long interval of decreased rainfall would have had a marked effect on crop yields and hence surplus production, affecting in turn the ability of local chiefly elites to finance their political systems. The changes in Mississippian settlement observed locally in the 15th century may reflect, in part, a drought-induced migration from the lower to the upper portion of the basin to exploit greater seasonal rainfall amounts or may reflect the movement of peoples to other, more favored polities in adjoining drainages. If true, population relocation analogous to the abandonment of the Colorado Plateau (Dean et al. 1985) and the Virgin Branch Anasazi (D. Larson and Michaelson 1990) may have occurred, if not entirely for the same reasons.

After 1476, an extended period of favorable moisture conditions returned, lasting over three-quarters of a century, until 1559, with food
shortfalls occurring only 10 years. Unfortunately, there do not appear to
have been any Mississippian populations in the central and lower Savannah River basin to take advantage of these conditions, suggesting that
factors other than environment were constraining settlement. Mississippian populations are reported from the nearby Coosawatchie and the
Salkehatchie rivers during the mid-16th century (Hudson 1990:78–80),
close to where the Four Hole Swamp cores used to develop the reconstruction employed here were taken, and it is possible that these groups were
taking advantage of favorable local conditions. During this same period, a
marked expansion in population, particularly into upland areas, occurred
in the upper Oconee River basin immediately to the west in Georgia
(Kowalewski and Hatch 1991), and it is also probably at this time that the
chiefdom of Cofitachequi, approximately 150 kilometers to the east along
the Wateree River, achieved regional prominence (DePratter 1989; Hudson
1990). In fact, in 1540, the year De Soto visited Cofitachequi on the nearby
Wateree River, the analysis indicates storage facilities would have been
close to capacity. The generosity that De Soto received from this society
(Vega in Varner and Varner 1951:300–301) may well have been genuine
rather than forced, since the chiefdom could have had plenty of food
reserves (assuming our reconstruction is accurate). All of these events
would have likely been facilitated by an extended period of favorable
climatic conditions.

A pronounced period of decreased rainfall occurred between 1559 and
1569, and food shortfalls would have occurred every year (save only 1565)
during this interval, including between 1566 to 1569, the first four years of
Spanish settlement at Santa Elena. The establishment of this colony apparently could not have taken place at a worse time, both from the perspective
of the Spanish, who were reduced literally to praying for relief, and from
the perspective of the Indians, upon whom the Spanish were placing
demands for food. The observation of the missionary Rogel (in Waddell
1980:147–53) that the native Orista, who lived near Santa Elena, had spent
much of the year wandering since "time immemorial" may have instead
been a reflection of the period of his mission, which encompassed the
worst part of this decade of drought and occurred at a time when the
natives had probably experienced greatly reduced harvests, if not total
crop failure, for several years running.

Political Change and Climate:
Lessons from the Savannah River Valley

Based on an examination of localized paleoclimatic data for the period
of Mississippian and early historic settlement, a direct relationship between growing-season climate and political conditions appears evident.

.Several extended periods of above- or below-average warm-season rainfall, from 1100 to 1600, occurred close enough in time to approximate periods of social change to suggest a connection. The suspected relationship between climate and political change, however, was not found to be invariable. The Savannah River valley remained unoccupied throughout the 16th century, even though climatic conditions ameliorated at the end of the 15th century and were unusually favorable for the first half of the next century.

Research linking paleoclimatic data to the archaeological record is currently in its infancy in the southeastern United States, and a great deal of research will be required to test the hypotheses advanced here. Refinement of the archaeological time scale is a particularly critical area, since at present our placement of assemblages is, at best, to within no more than approximate half-century intervals. Many more absolute dates will be needed than are available at present if we are to equate the archaeological and paleoclimatic records with any degree of precision (see also McGhee 1981:163). In addition to employing radiocarbon determinations in the refinement of cultural chronology, archaeologists locally must take advantage of other procedures (i.e., archaeomagnetic dating; hydration/patination-based dating procedures; correlation with palynological and geoarchaeological/geomorphological signatures, etc.).

While the paleoclimatic reconstructions are far more precise than the archaeological cultural sequence, additional bald cypress chronologies will need to be developed to refine our knowledge of past climatic conditions. Another topic that needs to be explored is how extensively the areas are covered by the dendroclimatological reconstructions. Are extended periods of above- and below-average precipitation synchronous over large areas, and if so how does this affect cultural and political developments, specifically warfare, alliance formation, habitation and field dispersal, and hunting and storage strategies? Finally, basic information about Mississippian storage technology and capacity will need to be developed, to see whether the assumptions in the models of crop yield and storage strategy presented here are warranted. Attempts to link archaeological and dendrochronological analyses have a long history in the Southeast, dating back to Gordon R. Willey's (1937) efforts to derive a central Georgia chronology while working at Macon Plateau in the 1930s (see also Bell 1951 and Hawley 1941). Only now, however, is the full potential of this type of information beginning to be realized. This study indicates that analyses linking paleoclimatic and archaeological data are likely to prove quite valuable in this part of the Southeast.

8

Political Change in the
Savannah River Chiefdoms

Events at Particular Sites and General Trends

Evidence from Particular Sites

In this chapter, evidence from individual sites in the Savannah River basin is examined in a further effort to determine the causes of the political and organizational changes observed in the archaeological record, specifically the formation and fragmentation of complex chiefdoms in the valley. Although information is available from over 500 Mississippian sites in the basin, the archaeological record from seven of them—the Irene, Hollywood, Beaverdam Creek, Chauga, Tugalo, and Estatoe mound centers and the Rucker's Bottom village site—is particularly extensive. The record from these sites, taken individually and then combined with data from the rest of the basin, indicates that organizational change in chiefdoms can leave pronounced archaeological signatures, which can be identified and examined using a wide range of evidence.

Irene (9Ch1)

The Irene site was occupied during the Savannah I/II, Savannah III, and Irene I phases in the mouth of the Savannah sequence, from circa 1150 to 1400. The site record details the emergence and subsequent collapse of what is assumed to have been a simple chiefdom occupying the area of the river mouth. Successive construction stages in the primary mound suggest local elites were able to increase their power and status for several generations, as evidenced by the growth in mound volume or the enlargement of structures and by the construction of multiple structures atop the mound. The elaborate hearth and gutter arrangements atop stages 5 and 6, furthermore, suggest ceremonial life was becoming more complex. The appearance of fortifications, if these are what the fences at the site are and not merely screening walls around a sacred precinct, suggests social tension or warfare also increased over time. The ceremonial complex atop the platform mound was abandoned during stage 7, and when construction resumed sometime later, it was channeled in new directions. The primary mound now served as a burial mound, and this, and the construction of a public building to the south of the main mound, suggests a more egalitarian society now occupied the site.

Major periods of organizational change that are well documented in the archaeological record occur two times at Irene, first during the transition from the Savannah III to the Irene I occupation, circa 1300, when the main platform mound fell into disuse for a number of years, and then again about a century later, circa 1400 to 1450, when the site was abandoned. The site record changed dramatically following the period when mound stage 7, the last Savannah III occupation prior to the Irene I phase, was in use. The mound and its associated ceremonial structures fell into disuse, indicating a collapse of the political hierarchy had occurred. The two structures identified atop mound stage 7 had been clearly abandoned for some time, as evidenced by the presence of considerable erosion on the mound slopes, to the point where portions of the southeastern structure and the palisade line around the summit had washed away. While a thin layer of ash and charcoal were found on the floor of the southeastern structure, there was no conclusive evidence that it, or the northeastern structure, where very little ash was found, had burned. The ceremonial complex appears to have been abandoned rather than destroyed.

While the chiefdom was operating, changes were occurring that hint at the conditions leading to chiefly collapse and abandonment. The seven Savannah stages each had an associated summit structure, and palisades had surrounded the base of stage 3 and the summits of stages 5, 6, and 7. The placement of palisades around first the base and then the summit of the Savannah mound may point to either the increasing isolation of the local elite or increasing warfare in the general region. A large semicircular palisade was built around the mounds at some point during the Savannah occupation as well, a further indication of hostilities. If the presence of palisades reflects the increasing physical isolation of the elite or an increase in regional patterns of warfare, either could have resulted in organizational destabilization, leading to the abandonment of stage 7. Increasing pomp and ceremony are implied in the successive Savannah mound stages, which, as noted, proceed from simple to more elaborate earth-embanked structures, to ever larger platform mounds with seemingly specialized central structures with unusual fire basin/gutter features. Whether this pattern continued in stage 7 could not be determined because of the erosion on the summit.

The artifactual evidence from the summit suggests that this was unlikely and that elite authority was in decline. Savannah Complicated Stamped pottery, which was present in each of the preceding mound stages (Caldwell and McCann 1941:2, 78), is absent in the occupation zone associated with mound stage 7 at Irene. Other Savannah finishes, specifically check stamping and burnished plain, are found, but no complicated stamped sherds were recovered from the mound. It is possible that this disappearance of complicated stamped wares may reflect an impoverishment of local elites, that is, a decline in the incidence of status-marking goods at the center or a decline in the manufacture of a ware minimally signaling affiliation with and continuity in a local Mississippian tradition. Savannah Complicated Stamping is most typically found on large jar forms, at least in the upper part of the basin, where detailed vessel functional analyses have been conducted (Rudolph and Hally 1985:373), and the same appears to be true of the sample recovered from Irene (Caldwell and McCann 1941:45). These large complicated stamped jars are thought to have had storage functions, and their absence in the last Savannah mound stage may point to a decline in the ability of local elites to mobilize tribute, some of which may have been stored in the structures atop the mound, following arguments developed by Shapiro (1985a) and Blitz (1989, 1993a, 1993b). All of this assumes, of course, that Savannah Complicated Stamped wares signaled elite status or group affiliation in some way, and that the comparatively small pottery sample from the summit of stage 7 (n = 111 sherds) is representative of site conditions.

The replacement or reinvigoration of local political structures is marked by the appearance of Irene I–phase materials across the site and the extensive construction activities associated with this occupation. How long an interval separated the two occupations is unknown, although stage 8 was built after the summit of stage 7 had been abandoned long enough for extensive erosion to occur, possibly for as long as one or two generations. The final episode of construction in the primary mound was much different than the preceding stages. The mound created by the construction of stage 8 was circular with a rounded summit, measured approximately 48.8 meters in diameter, and stood 4.7 meters high. Appreciably larger than the stage 7 mound, the stage 8 mound required a volume of fill that was larger than that of all of the previous stages combined, indicating considerable communal effort was involved in its construction. No evidence for structures was found on its summit, a major break with the earlier tradition.

The construction of stage 8 included a number of features that appear intended, in fact, to demarcate and separate, physically and symbolically, the new stage from its predecessors. These included the placement of shell layers over the old stage and the deliberate effacing of the ramps on the sides of the earlier mound. The new mound also functioned differently, over and above the absence of structures. Save for a skull associated with a Savannah Fine Cord-Marked pot found just under the western margin of mound stage 3, possibly representing a dedicatory offering, no formal burials were found in the first seven mound stages. A number of burials were present in the fill of stage 8; three apparently were interred during construction and several more some time later (Caldwell and McCann 1941:18, 20). The function of the mound had clearly changed, from an elite residence or temple to a burial mound, similar to the smaller mound at the site and the mounds at Haven Home and Hudson's Ferry. A return to earlier, more egalitarian burial practices is indicated.

Perhaps the most convincing evidence that dramatic organizational change was occurring at Irene, beyond the abandonment of platform mound architecture and the conversion of the primary mound into a rounded burial mound, was the construction of a probable rotunda or council house to the south of the main mound. This rotunda underwent one or more episodes of rebuilding and expansion, indicating it was in use for some time. This strongly suggests a change from decision making by elites to decision making by some form of public consensus. Council houses, which were observed in a number of southeastern Atlantic coastal groups during the early contact era, appear to have served as public forums in these societies (Hilton in Cheves 1897:21–22; Crook 1978:39–40; Waddell 1980:45–46). DePratter (1991a) has suggested that council houses were present only in Mississippian societies that were weakly integrated, specifically chiefdoms that were just getting started or that were falling apart, that is, becoming more egalitarian (chapter 4 and below). The latter appears to have been occurring at Irene. The expansion in size of the Irene council house over time may indicate either population growth or the inclusion of a larger percentage of adults in the decision-making process, or both. If the latter explanation is correct, it may indicate the society was growing more egalitarian over time. The construction and enlargement of the council house and the creation of the stage 8 mound indicate, however, that labor could still be mobilized for large-scale projects, albeit perhaps under the direction of leaders who, if no longer holding elite status, had considerable public authority or persuasive ability.

Subsistence practices appear to have changed markedly between the Savannah and Irene occupations, as evidenced by stable carbon and nitrogen isotope analyses (Larsen et al. 1992; Schoeninger et al. 1990). Decreased use of maize and a possible increased use of wild terrestrial resources is indicated between the earlier and later populations, suggesting the organizational shift had led to a decreased reliance on agriculture. That agricultural food production decreased appreciably in the period following the collapse of chiefly organizational structures suggests intensive cultivation strategies may have been dictated by the elite, both to maintain the political economy and to further their own personal agendas.

Some evidence indicates an increase in warfare during the Irene occupation, and this may have played a major role in the abandonment of the site at the end of the Irene I phase. One burial from the center of the rotunda was missing its head, another was charred, and five isolated skulls that may have represented war trophies were found around the site in Irene contexts (compared to one in Savannah context). Two adult males with crushed skulls, found buried near the edge of the stage 8 Irene mound, may have been victims of warfare or possibly were sentinels executed for failing in their duty, something explicitly depicted by LeMoyne (1875).

Another possible war casualty, an adult female buried in the Irene mortuary, had been killed by an arrow to the head. The appearance and elaboration of fortifications at the site, first around the Savannah mound and then around the Irene rotunda, also point to increasing hostilities, as noted previously. Of the six domestic structures at the site, furthermore, the two latest ones dating to the transitional Savannah/Irene and Irene I occupations had burned, as had the Irene mortuary.

Within the Irene mortuary complex itself, evidence suggests an increase in raiding and warfare and, if our reconstruction of its use life is correct, possibly the impoverishment of the site occupants during the period prior to abandonment. This complex was apparently built in three stages (as was the rotunda), first a mortuary structure and then two successively larger enclosures, the fence line for the first of which intruded the burned mortuary. A number of double (n = 6) and fragmentary (n = 4) burials were placed in these areas, suggesting multiple deaths were occurring and, possibly, that people were killed and their bodies recovered considerably later in a fragmentary condition (e.g., Hudson, Smith, and DePratter 1988). Almost half the burials in the inner, presumably earlier circular enclosure (19 of 41 individuals) had grave goods, compared to less than one-quarter (5 of 23 individuals) of those in the outer, presumably later circular enclosure (Caldwell and McCann 1941:28). A similar decline in the occurrence of grave goods in burials, as we shall see, has been noted at other sites in the Savannah River valley just prior to their abandonment.

Hollywood (9Ri1)

Striking evidence for an impoverishment of local elites during the period leading up to site abandonment was found at the Hollywood site. In mound B, which was excavated by Reynolds in 1891, a marked difference was evident in the kinds and amounts of grave goods found with the burials in the upper and lower divisions (possibly representing two stages?) of the lower mound fill (table 6). Elaborate materials were found associated with the burials in the lower division, including copper celts and engraved plates, painted and engraved ceramic vessels, shell beads, stone celts, pipes, lumps of galena and glauconite, and discoidals. In the upper division, in contrast, one or two pottery vessels and a repoussé copper plate fragment were all that were found with the burials. After these upper division burials had been interred (apparently toward the end of the Hollywood phase), mound construction ceased, although the mound was used for some time after by early Irene groups, who placed several urn burials in the fill just below the surface. In some ways, the use of mound B at Hollywood parallels events at Irene itself, where the Savannah-phase platform mound was subsequently used as a burial mound by (more egalitarian?) Irene populations.

Table 6. Mississippian Burials from the Hollywood Site: Summary Data by
Provenience

Upper Division	Grave Goods
Burial 11	1 repoussée figured copper plate, 1 small vessel
Burial (unnumbered)	2 vessels
Burial 10	1 vessel
Burial (unnumbered)	no grave goods

Lower Division	
Burial 2	1 long-necked jar (negative painted with sunburst, 1 tripodal bottle (tripod made of human heads), 5 clay and 1 soapstone pipes, 5 other pottery vessels, 1 copper ax head wrapped in cloth and bark, copper falcon warrior plates, 1 biconcave disk of quartz, 2 copper celts wrapped in cloth and encased in bark, several large pieces of mica
Burial 3	2 lots of shell beads, perforated shell disks, 1 copper-sheathed wooden earspool, 1 lump galenite
Burial 5	1 owl effigy pipe, 1 decayed shell ornament, 3 stone celts, 5 discoidal stones, 1 unusual stone implement, 1 lump of glauconite
Burial 6	1 stone celt
Burial 7	no grave goods (it is possible that 2 of the vessels, the falcon warrior plates, the biconcave disk, the mica, and 2 copper celts from burial 2 were actually associated with this burial)
Burial 8	1 lot of shell beads, 1 copper ax encased in wood, 1 whelk columella, 1 lump of glauconite
Burial 9	1 pipe

The individuals buried in the lower division of mound B at Hollywood unquestionably occupied positions of high status in their society. Given the unusual nature of the associated grave goods, which included pottery styles from potentially as far afield as Spiro (see chapter 5 and appendix A), they were also clearly in some kind of contact with other chiefly elites at considerable distances. The placement of the lower-division burials immediately above the premound midden suggests these individuals were interred soon after the site had been founded and a chiefdom level of organization had arisen locally. Because the associated grave goods are so unusual and elaborate, it is difficult to believe that they were acquired by an indigenous emerging elite, particularly since there appears to be little of value locally that such an elite could offer in exchange, at least as far as we have been able to determine to date. How and why elites at various centers acquired the kinds and quantities of prestige goods they did is, of course, the subject of appreciable research and speculation. The inhabitants of Hollywood, which is just below the Fall Line, may have been in a strategic position to control trade in one or more commodities (i.e., shell, soapstone); there may have been valued local products that are currently unrecognized, or, possibly, Hollywood was the center where elites from the Mason's Plantation center across the river were interred (much as Talimeco was for Cofitachequi). It is even possible, if one can accept the idea of elite population movement during the Mississippian, that these grave goods were brought to the site by a founding elite originating elsewhere, possibly from a society such as the contemporaneous and unquestionably lavishly equipped late Etowah/Wilbanks-phase chiefdom of northwestern Georgia.

Beaverdam Creek (9Eb85)

Evidence for increasing social complexity followed by elite impoverishment and then site abandonment, something noted at Irene, is also indicated at Beaverdam Creek. The small mound at this site went through six separate construction episodes during the Beaverdam phase, from circa 1200 to 1300. Two earth-embanked structures, or earth lodges, were built initially, one on top of the other, followed by four platform mound stages. The transition from earth lodges to platform mound stages at the site suggests society was becoming increasingly hierarchical. The site also provides important clues as to why episodes of mound stage construction occurred. The presence of a high-status burial between the two earth lodges, for example, indicates rebuilding may mark the death of one chief and the succession of his or her replacement, as argued in chapters 3 and 4. The evidence that some rebuilding took place following flooding, however, indicates that more prosaic reasons than the death of an elite may have also prompted this activity and that it may have been a necessary renewal ceremony (Knight 1986).

An analysis of the relative age of the burials in the Beaverdam Creek mound, based on the provenience where the burial was *found*, documented an apparent decline in the incidence of interments with grave goods over time (figure 61: top). Most of the burials with grave goods occurred in the earliest phases of site use, presumably when the chiefdom was just emerging. Unfortunately, given the extent to which the site had been looted prior to excavation, most of the burials upon which this analysis is based came from the lowest stages. While an impoverishment of the center well prior to abandonment is suggested, the extensive destruction of the upper stages renders this interpretation open to question.

Rudolph and Hally (1985:348–51) made an attempt to arrive at a more precise relative placement of the burials at Beaverdam Creek, that is, to determine where the burials likely *originated*, by examining their position within the premound midden in relation to the location and extent of the overlying stages. Burials found at some depth in the premound midden were assumed to be contemporaneous with the mound just prior to the mound stage that covered them; that is, these burials are assumed to have been placed around the edge of the mound. Burials in the premound midden that were extremely shallow, however, were assumed to have been placed in (and hence intruded from) the immediately overlying stage. Rudolph and Hally's arrangement of the burials, while less conservative than the preceding analysis, may more closely represent the interment history of the site (figure 61: bottom). Burials with grave goods occur much more evenly over time, making claims of site impoverishment more difficult to justify. However, based on the incidence of elaborate burials, defined as those with shell or copper grave goods, it is evident that a majority (five of eight) of these burials occur in the group assigned to pre–mound stage 1. Five of the 11 burials in this earliest group (45.5%), in fact, have elaborate grave goods, as opposed to only 3 of the 24 burials (12.5%) in the stages above them (although 2 of these 3 burials may have occurred during the last construction stage). Thus while both analyses suggest an impoverishment of local elites was occurring, this cannot be conclusively demonstrated.

A detailed analysis of vessel form and function was conducted using all of the intact or reconstructible vessels from the site and those rim sherds (n = 198) large enough to permit accurate vessel shape determinations and orifice diameter measurement (J. Rudolph and Hally 1985:367–98; see also Hally 1983a, 1983b, 1984, 1986b). Eight distinct vessel forms were identified, each exhibiting a fair degree of size variability, and this absence of size standardization has been interpreted as reflecting household rather than community or specialist patterns of manufacture and use (J. Rudolph and Hally 1985:384). Most of the ceramic vessels from Beaverdam Creek indicated domestic or secular use, with little evidence for a class of "sacred" vessels (*sensu* Sears 1973). The scarcity of elaborate vessels such as those found with the lower burials at Hollywood suggests elite prestige-based

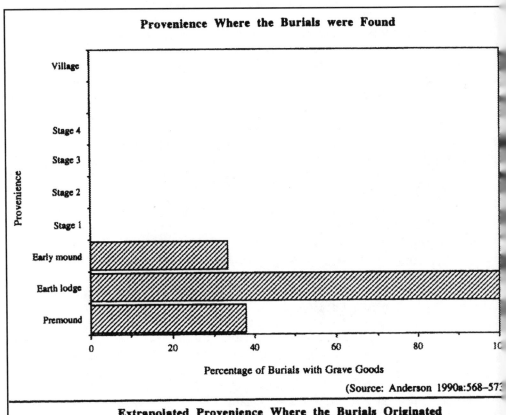

Provenience Where the Burials were Found

Percentage of Burials with Grave Goods

(Source: Anderson 1990a:568–573)

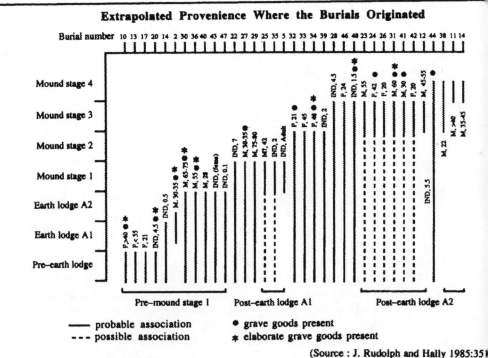

Extrapolated Provenience Where the Burials Originated

(Source : J. Rudolph and Hally 1985:35)

display and competition were not well developed in the Beaverdam Creek society or at least was not conducted using this medium. On the basis of arguments developed by Brumfiel (1987) and recounted in chapter 4, this suggests that factional competition may have been fairly minimal in the simple chiefdom assumed to have been centered on the site. If so, then, the abandonment of the site may well have resulted from external causes, such as extended periods of inclement weather or the emergence of a complex chiefdom nearby (i.e., Rembert), as suspected, rather than from internal dissension and conflict.

Rucker's Bottom (9Eb91)

The Rucker's Bottom site was a small agricultural community occupied during the Beaverdam and Rembert phases, from circa 1200 to 1450. Throughout its occupation, the village remained fairly small, never exceeding 1 hectare in size, although it did relocate 100 or so meters along the terrace between the Beaverdam and Rembert phases. Both the earlier and later villages at the site were characterized by structures about plazas, a typical southeastern Mississippian arrangement. Large circular structures, which have been interpreted as council houses, were found in both villages to the south of the plazas, and their presence may indicate considerable local decision making occurred. The portions of the community plans that were recovered indicate that between 15 and 30 houses were present at any one time. Total village population was probably somewhere between 90 and 330, depending on whether Naroll's (1962; 5.9 people per house) or S. Cook's (1972; 11 people per house) estimate is used. Given the small size of the site's presumed domestic structures, which ranged between approximately 25 and 50 square meters, a community size toward the lower end of this range is suggested, on the order of 90 to 150 people.

The earlier, Beaverdam-phase village at Rucker's Bottom was probably a tributary community to the Beaverdam Creek mound center, which was located approximately 12 kilometers downstream. Comparative mortuary and paleosubsistence analyses indicate that the inhabitants of this village did not live as well as those at the center (see below). On the average, they were in much poorer health and shorter in stature, and when they died, they were interred with less elaborate grave goods, if any at all. While both of these Beaverdam-phase components, at the mound center and at Rucker's Bottom, made use of a fairly wide range of wild plant and animal foods as well as cultigens, some evidence suggests that food, specifically deer hindquarters, was leaving the village as tribute. If food was being

Figure 61 (facing page) Frequency of Burials with Grave Goods by Provenience at the Beaverdam Creek Site (9Eb85).

removed from one site to the other, it might explain the differences in health and stature observed between the two populations.

Shortly after 1300, the Beaverdam Creek mound site was abandoned, with the Rembert mounds to the south becoming the principal ceremonial center in this part of the drainage. About this time, the village at Rucker's Bottom was relocated to the northern part of the terrace, and simple ditch and stockade fortifications appeared. No evidence has been found that food left the site as tribute during this later occupation, and the villagers appear to have been in better health, suggesting the community exercised greater autonomy than previously. Subsistence became increasingly focused, with a narrower range of species exploited and a particular emphasis made on deer and acorns.

The size of the village increased between the earlier and later enclosures, from 5,600 to 7,200 square meters. The rectangular enclosure, surrounding the final occupation at the site, surrounded an area about a quarter again as large as that within the semicircular enclosures. These figures suggest at least some increase in local population. With the apparent eclipse of the Beaverdam Creek mound by Rembert, a site over twice as far away, the Rucker's Bottom community may have attained greater prominence in the local settlement system, possibly becoming somewhat more autonomous.

The size of the fortifications in the Rembert-phase village increased over time, from a fence line composed of posts 15 centimeters in diameter in the semicircular enclosure, to one of posts up to 30 centimeters wide in the later rectangular enclosure. This may reflect increasing hostilities in the general region, although, if so, it was an unsuccessful response, since the site was abandoned toward the end of the Rembert phase. Some evidence for conflict, in the form of a multiple burial of three individuals lying extended on their backs, was found inside the Rembert enclosure. This may have been a family group, since it consisted of two adults (one female and the other unidentifiable as to sex) and a young child of about six or seven years (Weaver et al. 1985:631–34). No evidence for trauma was observed on the remains, which were, however, in a shallow pit in very poor condition. The fact that three apparently contemporaneous deaths occurred may reflect an increase in low-intensity conflict at this time (no multiple burials were found in the Beaverdam-phase village), if these individuals were indeed killed rather than having died of other causes.

The greater emphasis on fortifications may also reflect the somewhat greater isolation of the community, which probably had to serve as a center or defended area for surrounding populations. Sites with Mississippian components, most of these appreciably smaller than the Rucker's Bottom site, have been found throughout the floodplain along this stretch of the Savannah and appear to represent isolated hamlets or smaller communities. The inhabitants of these nearby sites may have gravitated to Rucker's Bottom in times of stress and possibly at other times for communal activities or ceremonies. The fact that the fortifications are not particularly elaborate, however, suggests that while defense was a consideration, it was not a preeminent concern.

Some evidence indicates a greater concern with food storage and with preventing the theft or otherwise unsanctioned use of food during the Rembert-phase occupation, something that may be linked both to the extended period of drought that occurred toward the end of this phase and to the evidence for increasing hostilities. During the Beaverdam phase and presumably during the initial Rembert occupation, storage is assumed to have been in above-ground facilities or in barbacoas such as those reported by the early Spanish explorers. A number of small circular and rectangular post arrangements were found at Rucker's Bottom, which were interpreted as possible storage sheds or corncribs. Three of these structures (figure 36: nos. 3, 4, and 6) were located in prominent positions in the Rembert village, two adjacent to the probable rotunda and the third to the east near the rectangular palisade wall (Anderson and Schuldenrein 1985:538–39, 551–52). Anyone accessing these facilities would have been clearly visible throughout the village, something that may have deterred theft, and at the same time, their exposed position would have facilitated rallying to their defense or the targeting of raiders stealing from them.

What appear to be massive subterranean storage features also occurred for the first time at the site during the Rembert-phase occupation. Two of these were excavated, one (feature M1143) having been found behind a house against the inner wall of the semicircular palisade, the other (feature M1193) in the center of the plaza area (Anderson and Schuldenrein 1985:536, 554). These features had little in their fill besides small amounts of pottery fragments and other midden debris, something that distinguished them from the other large pits found on the site, which either invariably contained burials or extensive debris or, if found in plaza areas, were filled with boulders and appear to have served as massive post supports. Each had a capacity of about 1 cubic meter and would have thus been able to hold approximately 28.4 bushels of shelled corn (see D. Morse 1980: 21-8 to 21-11, and DeBoer 1988 for further discussion of how these features functioned in southeastern Mississippian societies). Their locations suggest a desire to hide food supplies, to restrict them to use by a single family (as in the case of M1143), or to maintain them in public view and hence ensure their access was known to the community (as in the case of M1193). Two other large pits were found near M1193 in the center of the plaza in the Rembert village. These pits, features M1183 and M1184, were interpreted as major post supports, although, unlike similar pits in the Beaverdam-phase village, they did not have well-defined rock-lined post molds in them (Anderson and Schuldenrein 1985:488–90, 552–54). These features had volumes approaching 2 cubic meters and may have been used for storage at some point, although they were ultimately filled with more than 500 kilograms of rock.

The Rucker's Bottom site and indeed the entire lower Savannah River basin below the headwaters were abandoned by the end of the Rembert phase, indicating that the various measures taken by the site's inhabitants to maintain their position were not sufficient. The fact that there is no evidence that the community burned suggests it was abandoned by its inhabitants rather than destroyed by outsiders. At least one of the Rembert-phase houses, structure 2, was, in fact, abandoned and was later used as a butchering area, although this could have occurred during normal village occupation (Anderson and Schuldenrein 1985:561–78).

Chauga (38Oc47)

The Chauga site was occupied during the Early Mississippian Jarrett phase, when the first six mound stages were built. After a hiatus of about two centuries, the site was reoccupied during the Late Mississippian Tugalo phase, when four additional stages were built over the first six. The six Jarrett-phase mound stages each had a well-defined clay cap. This clay capping, while potentially functioning to reduce erosion of the underlying basket-loaded fill, also would have symbolically sealed and separated the earlier stages from the most recent stage. A palisade was built around the mound at the time stage 6 was erected. While an earlier palisade had been erected around stage 1 and was assumed to demarcate a burial area or serve a screening function for elites using the mound, these fences may have also had a defensive purpose. The fact that palisades were present during both the initial and the final periods of the Early Mississippian occupation points to a greater concern with defense at the times when the chiefdom was just getting established and when it was falling apart.

The absence of clay caps on the summits of stages 7 through 10 indicates a different approach to mound building had emerged in the two centuries since the Jarrett occupation. Stages 7 and 8 were large, indicating extensive construction was occurring and suggesting the founding society was vibrant. However, a second decline of mound building occurred during stages 9 and 10, which were much smaller than stages 7 and 8. The timing of this decline, late in the Tugalo phase, suggests it is linked with the decline in mound building observed throughout the interior Southeast during the late 16th century, a pattern equated with a European contact–induced collapse of chiefly political organization (M. Smith 1987).

In all, 62 burials were excavated at Chauga, 53 in or near the mound and 9 in the village area (figure 62). Although several were found buried in the mound itself within particular stages, most came from the premound midden in a small area on the southeastern side of the mound. There was some indication that the burials in this cluster were placed at the edge of each successive mound stage, and this, along with the presence of a number of recognizable pit outlines, permitted the approximate dating of

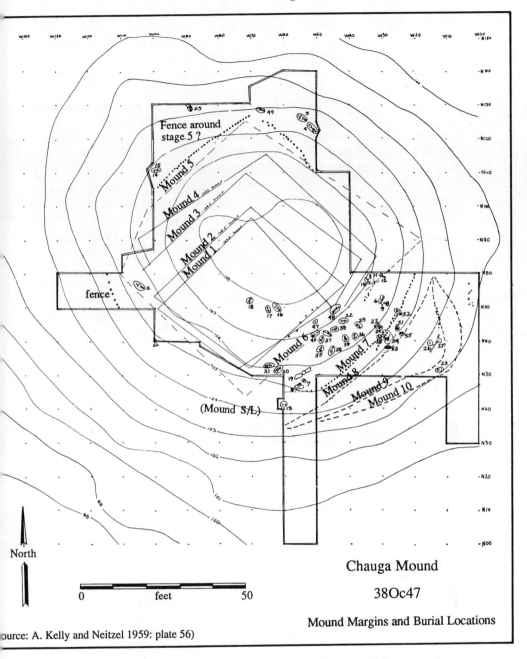

Figure 62   Burial Locations at the Chauga Site (38Oc47). (Courtesy Laboratory of
Archaeology, University of Georgia)

many of the interments by the excavators (A. Kelly and Neitzel 1961: table 1; Anderson 1990a:578–85). Most of the burials were intact enough to place in coarse age groups, and 26 were identified as to sex. Almost all of the burials were either flexed or partially flexed, a few were bundle burials, and one was a cremation. Twenty-four of the burials had accompanying grave goods, mostly in the form of shell beads or pins, with an occasional gorget, celt, discoidal, projectile point, or a piece of unusual rock or mineral. No truly elaborate interments such as the ones noted at Hollywood and Beaverdam Creek were found, however, suggesting elite-commoner distinctions may not have been pronounced.

Evidence for a progressive impoverishment of the site occupants is evident over the course of the Jarrett occupation and is suggested for the Tugalo occupation (figure 63). The number of burials with grave goods of any kind during the Early Mississippian Jarrett-phase occupation declined markedly after the initial stages of mound construction, and no grave goods are found with burials in the last four stages leading up to the abandonment of the center. When the site was later reoccupied, a similar pattern is indicated. While grave goods are found with an appreciable number of the interments associated with stage 7, the initial Tugalo-phase mound addition, this incidence declined appreciably in subsequent stages. Although the sample sizes are small, this patterning suggests that these two chiefdoms were each initially quite successful, with the elites in control of more wealth than in later times.

Organizational change in the Mississippian populations occupying the headwaters of the Savannah River basin at the beginning of the Tugalo phase is indicated by the new mound construction at Chauga, at Estatoe, and possibly at Tugalo (see chapter 5 and below). All of these events took place around or shortly after 1450, when the lower portion of the basin was abandoned. An influx of people from the collapsing chiefdoms to the south may have occurred, resulting in social reorganization. This is suggested in part by symbolic termination and rebuilding episodes in the mound at Estatoe and by the reoccupation of other previously abandoned centers such as Chauga and Tugalo. While the occupations that emerged in the late 15th century appear to have continued into the historic period and hence represent the formation of the Lower Cherokee towns, this is a subject of some debate. Appreciable stylistic and technological continuity is evident between the ceramic assemblages of the Tugalo and Estatoe phases (Hally 1986a:112), although assemblages from the interval between these phases, from circa 1600 to 1700, remain to be documented.

Some evidence from the early historic period supports the idea that Cherokees may not have been living in the upper Savannah area in the mid-16th century but may have only later moved into this area. A number of the mountain Cherokee leaders Pardo met in western North Carolina, at the towns of Tocae near Asheville and Cauchi near Marshall, had names suggesting possible affiliation with the Cherokee towns located along the

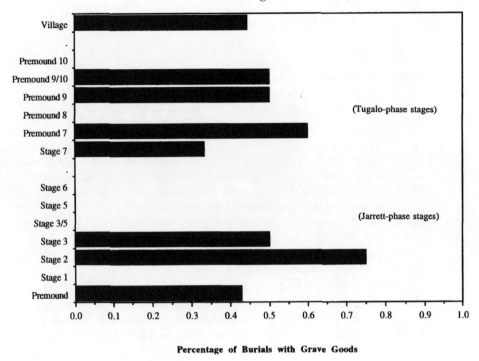

Figure 63   Incidence of Burials with Grave Goods by Provenience at the Chauga Site (38Oc47).

upper Savannah River during the early 18th century, such as Estate Orata (after Estatoe?) and Tacoru Orata (after Tugalo?) (Hudson 1990:94–99). Given current reconstructions of Pardo's route, these communities were either farther into the mountains at this time or the chiefs had traveled appreciable distances to see Pardo (something that is distinctly possible, given the numbers of elites he met at various towns). Hudson is uncertain which interpretation is correct and notes that the possibility must at least be considered that the Lower Cherokee moved into the Savannah River valley from towns farther into the mountains sometime after the 1560s, perhaps replacing or combining with the inhabitants of the chiefdoms already present in the area (96). While the archaeological evidence on hand indicates continuity of occupation, refinement of our knowledge of sites and assemblages in the headwaters should permit a resolution of this problem.

Tugalo (9St1)

The Tugalo mound and village site was apparently occupied through-out the Mississippian period, with a possible break only during the Beaverdam phase. As at Irene and Beaverdam Creek, a change from earth-embanked structures to substructure mounds apparently occurred during the Early Mississippian period. The four lowest stages or construction episodes, dating to the Jarrett phase, were characterized by square earth-embanked structures with central fire basins. The stages above this, unfortunately, had been plowed down and were very poorly defined. At least one of these dated to the Jarrett phase, however, and may have been a first formal mound stage. As at the other sites, a transition from more to less egalitarian decision making and the emergence of a social elite are indicated by these architectural changes.

The presence of well-defined log mantles over mound stages 2 through 4 at Tugalo (figures 30–32) is different from the clay capping noted over the Jarrett-phase mound stages at the nearby Chauga site, although the blue clay layer present around the base of stage 4 at Tugalo was similar to the capping noted at Chauga. At both occupations, the inhabitants appear to have gone to considerable trouble to separate earlier from later construction stages. This effort also served to emphasize the importance of the mound itself and presumably of the elites who made use of it. Unfortunately, no burial data are available from the mound, and the burials from the adjoining off-mound block remain unanalyzed, precluding the kind of diachronic mortuary analyses conducted at Hollywood, Beaverdam Creek, and Chauga. As at Chauga, a fence line appears around the later Jarrett mounds at Tugalo, specifically around stage 4 (and possibly stage 3) prior to the abandonment of the center following stage 5. The log mantle and fence line associated with stage 4 had burned, as had the fence line that may have been associated with stage 3. This pattern of burning supports either increasing hostilities or the use of fire in mound renewal/rebuilding activity.

While the later Mississippian occupations at Tugalo are currently poorly understood, they appear to have begun in the Rembert phase, following a hiatus in occupation of a century or more. This reoccupation of the site in the late 14th or early 15th century may reflect a population relocation, perhaps from the Rembert-phase chiefdom lower in the basin. As noted in chapter 5, ceramics from a refuse area on the northeastern side of the mound were used by Hally (1986a) to define the Late Lamar Tugalo phase, which he argued developed directly out of the preceding Rembert phase. Continuity in ceramic manufacture from the Rembert through the historic Cherokee Estatoe phases is indicated at sites such as Tugalo in the upper Savannah River basin, although, as noted previously, assemblages dating from circa 1600 to 1700 are currently undocumented and the events of this period remain uncertain.

Estatoe (9St3)

The occupation of the Estatoe site appears to have begun about the same time that the construction of stages 8 through 10 occurred at Chauga and the northeastern dump deposit was formed at Tugalo. Six construction episodes were identified in the primary mound at Estatoe, all apparently dating to the Tugalo phase. The first five were each only a few centimeters thick and were surmounted by large squared structures approximately 12 meters on a side. These buildings resemble the presumed public structures erected during the Early Mississippian occupations at Irene, Beaverdam Creek, and Tugalo, although they are appreciably larger and the earth embankments are missing. It is possible that the inhabitants were initially under the control of elites at another center, such as Tugalo or Chauga, where formal platform mounds were apparently in use at this time. If so, the presence of possible public structures suggests some decision-making responsibility remained in the hands of the local community, something also indicated at Rucker's Bottom. If Estatoe was founded to accommodate an influx of people from lower in the basin, as is suspected, it is reasonable to assume that the older centers would have exercised some kind of control over these people, at least initially. Of these older centers, Chauga may have been preeminent, since evidence for mound construction is present, while at Tugalo it is equivocal.

The emergence of elites at Estatoe proper may be indicated by the placement of a thick layer of stone over stage 5, evenly covering the underlying structure, and the erection of a fairly appreciable mound stage above this. The rock layer clearly differentiates the upper from the lower stages and suggests some kind of change had occurred in the local society. Whether subsequent stages were built above stage 6 could not be determined, since the upper part of the mound had been reduced by plowing, although no traces of such stages were found around the mound margin. Interestingly, even though stage 6 is differentiated from the preceding stages, continuity is indicated by the reuse of major corner support post holes for the structure built atop the mound. These holes extended through the rock layer separating stages 5 and 6, suggesting, if the emergence of an elite is indeed indicated, they may have come from within the community and the tradition that used the earlier structures. Alternatively, since the post supports were rock lined and durable, their reuse may have been from purely practical considerations. Given the absence of evidence for later stages, however, if an elite group had emerged locally, it was apparently not in power for long. As at Chauga and possibly also at Tugalo, mound construction ceased in the drainage and across much of the region at this time.

General Trends Associated with Organizational Change at Mississippian Sites in the Savannah River Basin

Council Houses and Political Change

At present, the occurrence and function of council houses on prehistoric Mississippian sites in the region are uncertain. By analogy, they are assumed to have functioned in the same manner as the council houses in historic Creek and Cherokee towns, serving as combination men's houses and the loci of community decision making. Archaeological and ethnohistorical summaries of evidence pertaining to Dallas and Cherokee town houses have been prepared by investigators working in eastern Tennessee (e.g., Baden 1983; Lewis and Kneberg 1946:70–72; Polhemus 1987:247–59; Schroedl 1978, 1986:228–34). Evidence for the occurrence of large circular structures that are interpreted as council houses has been reported from a number of locations across the region, including Cemochechobee in southwestern Georgia (Schnell, Knight, and Schnell 1981:63–66), at Macon Plateau in central Georgia (Fairbanks 1956), at Bessemer in central Alabama (DeJarnette and Wimberly 1941:53), at Rucker's Bottom and Irene in the Savannah River valley, and, most recently, at historic Chattooga town (Schroedl and Riggs 1989). A public structure was recognized at the Julien site in the American Bottom (Milner 1984b:43–44, 195), and other presumed public (but noncircular) council houses have been reported from the region. An occurrence of council houses throughout the Mississippian era and on sites of widely varying sizes is thus indicated from the regional archaeological record. The actual temporal and spatial distribution of these structures, however, will remain incompletely known until much larger portions of communities can be excavated than typically occurs at present.

Evidence from several sites in the region suggests that the appearance or disappearance of public structures signaled changes in political organization, specifically from decision making by consensus to decision making in the hands of elites, or vice versa. At the Bessemer site in central Alabama, for example, large public buildings were replaced by mounds (Welch 1990). A replacement of earth-embanked structures, possible council houses, by mound stage construction is documented at a number of sites in the South Appalachian area, including at Irene and Beaverdam Creek and possibly at Tugalo in the Savannah River valley. James Rudolph (1984) has suggested that this replacement of earth lodge by platform/temple mound architecture reflected a replacement of communal meeting places by the residences and temples of a much smaller group of elite decision makers. DePratter (1983:209, 1991a:163–65), as noted previously, believed council houses occurred in weakly centralized societies and that, as chiefly authority increased, councils would have grown weaker and their architectural correlates would have disappeared.

The Savannah River data support the idea that the appearance or disappearance of council houses at centers is linked to the emergence or replacement of egalitarian decision-making structures, but the data also suggest that council houses were present in outlying communities even at the height of chiefly power. The appearance of a rotunda at Irene occurred shortly after the temple mound (a visible architectural symbol of chiefly organizational structure) disappeared and at about the same time that the complex chiefdom centered at Mason's Plantation farther upriver apparently collapsed. A general replacement of chiefdom-level organization by more egalitarian social forms appears to have been occurring throughout the lower part of the valley at this time. The probable council house in the Beaverdam-phase village at Rucker's Bottom, however, occurred when chiefly elites were in place at the nearby Beaverdam Creek mound. The Rucker's Bottom site record, in fact, indicates that probable council houses or public buildings were present throughout the period of Mississippian occupation, during the periods when first the Beaverdam Creek and then the Rembert mound centers were in ascendancy. The existence and use of council houses, it is suggested, probably occurred throughout the Mississippian period in this part of the Southeast. Their role as decision-making centers, however, may have been diminished in more complex chiefdoms, particularly at ceremonial centers.

Fortifications and Political Change

Two types of fortifications were documented in the Savannah River valley: stockade or ditch and stockade lines around entire communities; and stockade lines around the base or summit of platform mounds or rotundas. Whether these enclosures served as true fortifications or merely as screening walls demarcating public or ceremonial precincts in each case is unknown. What is evident, however, is that their appearance signaled either the establishment of a chiefly center at a site, as indicated at Chauga, or the onset of a period of (presumably) increasing tension that in most cases resulted in organizational collapse or site abandonment, as documented at Irene (both occupations), Rucker's Bottom, Chauga, Tugalo, and possibly Lawton.

Fortifications surrounding entire communities or centers are documented at the Irene, Lawton, and Rucker's Bottom sites and possibly at Chauga and Tugalo. At Irene, the Savannah III–phase semicircular enclosure surrounds both mounds, while smaller enclosures were built around and atop the platform mound itself beginning with stage 3. In size, shape, and orientation with respect to the river, the large Savannah III enclosure at Irene is nearly identical to the early Rembert-phase semicircular enclosure at Rucker's Bottom, which dates to just after circa 1375, somewhat later than the one at Irene. Sixty kilometers southwest of Rucker's Bottom, a circular enclosure is also inferred to have been present from circa 1350 to 1400 at the Shoulderbone site along the Oconee River (M. Williams and Shapiro 1986, 1990a:152). At all three sites, the semicircular to circular enclosures were replaced by rectangular enclosures somewhat later, after circa 1350 to 1400. Both Irene and Rucker's Bottom were abandoned sometime fairly soon after the rectangular fortifications were built, although occupation at Shoulderbone may have continued. When the rectangular ditch line surrounding the mounds at Lawton was built is unknown, although the site itself was apparently abandoned at the end of the Lawton phase or very early in the ensuing Hollywood phase, around or shortly after circa 1300. Stockade lines may have also surrounded the villages at Chauga and Tugalo, although our information about these features is limited (chapter 5).

Fortifications are documented around the margin or summit of the primary mounds at the Irene, Chauga, and Tugalo sites. At Chauga, a stockade was built around the first mound stage, during the Jarrett phase. The presence of fortifications at this site, which appears to have been (with Tugalo) one of the first chiefly centers in the valley, suggests that the Mississippian emergence locally may not have been an entirely peaceful process. That is, the new chiefly elites may have had to maintain fortified centers until they consolidated their position. If these chiefdoms were established by people from outside the valley (one possible scenario, given the strong Etowah-like appearance of the ceramic assemblage), some protection from local populations may have been necessary. No fortifications were built around the next several stages at Chauga, however, suggesting this inferred period of tension passed fairly quickly. While the initial mound stage at the nearby Tugalo site may have been surrounded by a fence (as stages 3 and 4 were), the excavations were not extensive enough to determine this one way or the other.

At Irene, palisades appeared around the Savannah III platform mound for the first time in stage 3 and continued through stage 7, when the mound was abandoned. At Chauga, a palisade reappeared around the platform mound during stage 6, just prior to the end of the Jarrett-phase occupation and the abandonment of the site for some two centuries. At Tugalo, fence lines were found around both stages 3 and 4, the final (?) Jarrett-phase occupations of the site, and both had burned. The presence of these fences, coupled with evidence for burning and abandonment, suggests increased hostilities were occurring. It is not known, however, whether the presence of fortifications signaled conflict with other polities or increased factional competition locally. That is, fortifying mounds, if a result of increased hostilities, may have been to make them defensive retreats for entire populations or, if indicative of increased factional competition, to make access to elites more difficult. It is also possible that these fortifications may reflect the increasing (physical and hierarchical) separation of elite and commoner members of these societies, a gap that became too great to continue. In this view, the fortifications were first to demarcate and later to protect and maintain the position of the elite. Whatever the explanation, the appearance of fortifications locally was almost invariably soon followed by organizational change or collapse.

The similarity in the fortifications at Irene, Rucker's Bottom, and Shoulderbone, including how they changed over time, suggests a common tradition about what constituted proper defensive works in this part of the South Appalachian area. The absence of obvious bastions or multiple stockade lines, however, suggests that community defense may not have been an overwhelming preoccupation. The De Soto chroniclers, for example, did not report substantial aboriginal fortifications in their travels through the Southeast until they reached Chiaha in eastern Tennessee. The apparent absence of substantial fortifications in the central Georgia and South Carolina areas in 1540 is interesting, since a pronounced rivalry was reported between the provinces occupying these areas, Ocute and Cofitachequi (Hudson et al. 1985, 1987). However, direct contact between these complex chiefdoms, including warfare, appears to have been infrequent, as De Soto's army, assisted by recruits from Ocute, got thoroughly lost attempting to reach Cofitachequi (see Elvas in Robertson 1993:80–81; see also Bourne 1904, 1:59–64). While skirmishes between smaller groups may have occurred from time to time, massive attacks on settlements do not appear to have occurred or to have been expected.

Although fortifications do appear at Irene and Rucker's Bottom prior to abandonment, these do not appear to have been substantial defensive works and may have only been intended to defer small raiding parties rather than large armed groups. The absence of major fortifications at the sites along the Savannah in the years immediately prior to the abandonment of much of the basin, in fact, suggests that something other than large-scale warfare brought about the observed depopulation. A pattern of continuing low-intensity conflict, something hinted in the burials at Irene and Rucker's Bottom, may have achieved the same result, albeit more gradually. Interestingly, the appearance of fortifications in the Savannah River valley, after the initial period when chiefdoms were first becoming established, appears to have occurred first at Irene and Lawton in the lower part of the basin and only somewhat later at upriver sites such as Rucker's Bottom and possibly Chauga and Tugalo. This pattern is in agreement with the survey data from the basin, which suggest the lower portion was abandoned first. A gradual retreat of populations upriver and possibly into adjoining drainages may be indicated.

Mortuary Behavior and Political Change

Mortuary data from five sites in the Savannah River valley indicate chiefdom organizational collapse was preceded by the relative impoverishment of local populations, as measured by the incidence of grave goods in burials. At Irene, Hollywood, Beaverdam Creek, Rucker's Bottom, and Chauga, burials from the period immediately prior to site abandonment all exhibit a lower incidence of grave goods and typically much less elaborate grave goods than burials from earlier periods of occupation. This decline in grave goods incidence appears to reflect the diminishing involvement of local elites in prestige goods exchange networks. How this affected their ability to legitimize their status and position, however, appears less certain.

At the Hollywood, Beaverdam Creek, and Chauga sites, elaborate prestige goods were most common during the earliest occupations, when these chiefdoms were presumably just getting started. At Chauga and possibly Beaverdam Creek, comparatively few burials in the final three mound stages had grave goods, suggesting that the impoverishment of these sites occurred over a period of several generations. If this is indeed the case (the burial data from the upper stages at both sites are very limited), it indicates that possession of prestige goods was not critical to the maintenance of power in these societies, at least in the short run (see also Welch 1986:189). Even after access to these symbols of power diminished or disappeared, elites were apparently able to maintain control for two or three more generations. While the Savannah River data thus support the argument that a decline in the occurrence of prestige goods likely signals a chiefdom in trouble, the fact that these societies were able to continue for some time anyway suggests organizational collapse probably occurred for a number of reasons. The incidence of prestige/grave goods at a center may thus indicate the relative stability of that society, but it does not tell us the reasons for this condition.

The decline in the incidence of grave goods observed in the burials from the inner and outer enclosures at the mortuary at Irene and from the Beaverdam- to the Rembert-phase villages at Rucker's Bottom occurs in contexts where chiefly organizational structures either were not present or were centered elsewhere. At Irene, during the period when the mortuary was in use, the presence of a council house suggests a fairly egalitarian form of social organization was present, while at Rucker's Bottom, which also had a council house at this time, chiefly authority appears to have been based at Rembert. In both cases, however, a decline in the incidence of grave goods characterizes the period prior to site abandonment. The fact that commoner populations were affected indicates patterns of impoverishment were society-wide and not just centered on elites.

The mortuary data from the lower Savannah indicate the emergence of chiefdoms in this area was accompanied by not only a change from collective to individual interment but also an increasing concern with distinguishing individual status differences. In the initial Mississippian or immediate pre-Mississippian components at Haven Home and Irene, burials were placed in low sand burial mounds. The first burials in these mounds were mass cremations, suggesting collective interment with little concern for individual status distinctions. Soon after, a pattern of individual interment began, with burials placed in low mounds (as at Irene and Hudson's Ferry) or buried individually in village areas.

A pattern of individual interment of commoners in village or low burial mounds and elites in or near more elaborate earth lodge/temple mound complexes becomes common throughout the valley once chiefdoms have been established. Elite status was marked not only by placement in or at the margin of mounds, but also by the quantity and quality of grave goods. Some individuals were placed in vessels during the Middle Mississippian period, with this pattern most common among peoples using Savannah and early Irene ceramics. The pattern of individual interment continues through the Cherokee occupations in the upper part of the drainage. The only exception, occasional multiple burials, apparently reflects unusual circumstances (i.e., conflict-related deaths). After the disintegration of the chiefdom centered at Irene, however, a mortuary complex and enclosed cemetery area were built during the Irene I–phase occupation, suggesting something of a reversion to earlier Woodland burial practices in this part of the drainage.

Limited evidence to indicate when and how chiefly succession may have occurred at chiefdoms in the valley was found at Hollywood and Beaverdam Creek. At Hollywood, a series of burials with elaborate grave goods occurred seemingly together in the base of mound B, suggesting the interment of a founding and certainly dominant elite. Mound construction may have proceeded upon the interment of the final individual, although, given the period when this site was examined, the early 1890s, evidence about the existence of burial pits and mound stages and structures was not carefully recorded, at least by modern standards. At Beaverdam Creek, as noted previously, a burial with unusual grave goods was found between the two earth-embanked structures, A1 and A2. The Beaverdam Creek burial, which was unquestionably interred during the period between the construction of these two structures, offers the best evidence locally for an association between the death of an elite and mound stage construction (although at this same site evidence also suggests some mound construction may have been necessary to repair flood damage). If an association between mound stage construction and chiefly succession is (usually) valid, most of the centers in the Savannah River valley that have been examined appear to have been occupied by chiefdoms having lifespans on the order of a few generations (tables 2 and 4). Hally (1987, 1992, 1993), in analyses of occupation span at a number of mound centers from northern Georgia, noted that continuous occupation rarely exceeded 100 to 150 years, which he inferred was about the maximum time a Mississippian chiefdom could remain intact. This evidence illustrates the fragility of chiefdom political structures and suggests even the most successful polities were unlikely to remain in place for more than five or six generations.

Paleobiological Evidence for Political Change

Throughout the Savannah River valley exists evidence that commoners lived differently in life and were treated differently in death than elites
during the Mississippian period, and that the same patterns hold to a
somewhat lesser extent to females as opposed to males. Summary data on
the total burial sample recovered to date from the valley, by site, are
presented in table 7. At the Beaverdam Creek, Chauga, and I. C. Few sites,
burials were recovered from both mound and village contexts. In each
case, the burials in the village areas included a much higher incidence of
females than did burials from the mounds. In addition, mound burials
tended to have a much higher incidence of grave goods. The only exception to this pattern was at Chauga, where a slightly higher proportion of
the burials in the village area had grave goods than those in the mound.
Interment of higher-status individuals, a higher proportion of which was
male, in mound as opposed to village contexts is indicated at these sites. At
Irene, where data on individual interments are difficult to reconstruct from
the report in some cases, Caldwell and McCann (1941:38) note that 40
burials were found scattered over the site in shallow pits, suggesting little
care was taken in their interment. Furthermore, only five of these burials
had grave goods, supporting the implication that they were lower-status
individuals.

These status differences appear to have translated into differences in
health and diet, something most clearly documented in the skeletal
samples from Beaverdam Creek and Rucker's Bottom, where elite and
commoner segments of the same society were examined. Mortality data
from Beaverdam Creek, where a detailed analysis of the skeletal materials
was conducted (Blakely et al. 1985), indicate mound interment was reserved either for children or adults, with adolescents excluded (figure 29).
This pattern is also indicated at the Chauga and I. C. Few sites, although
the physical anthropological analyses conducted on the burials from these
sites were far more limited, consisting of little more than approximate
aging and sexing. The data from these three sites do suggest that, once past
early childhood, elite status accrued, in part, by surviving adolescence.
Hatch (1987), noting an unusually high incidence of stress markers on
Dallas skeletons, has argued that adolescence was a period of intense
stress for the children of elites (chapter 4); survival of this period of
training and testing appears to have been necessary to warrant burial in
mound contexts in the Savannah River chiefdoms. The relative health of
the individuals from Beaverdam Creek was found to be quite good, with
little evidence for disease or pathology (Blakely et al. 1985:343–45).

Burials recovered from village contexts at Rucker's Bottom, presumed
commoners, were also subjected to a detailed series of analyses (Butler
1986; Weaver et al. 1985; see also chapter 5 in this text). Although the
evidence is inconclusive, the individuals dating to the Rembert phase

Table 7. Mississippian Mortuary Data from the Savannah River Basin: Summary Data by Site

Site	Provenience	Total Burials	Male	Female	Child	Indeterminate	Incidence of Grave Goods	Dominant Burial Type	Relative Health
Haven Home (Early Mississippian)	central feature	n/a	n/a	n/a	n/a	n/a	(100.0%)	cremation	n/a
	outer mound	43	n/a	n/a	n/a	43	(28.6%)	flexed	fair
Irene burial mound (Early Mississippian)	central feature	7	n/a	n/a	n/a	n/a	(71.4%)	cremation	n/a
	outer mound	99	22	19	n/a	n/a	(7.1%)	flexed	n/a
Chauga (Early Mississippian)	stages 1–6	32	14	9	4	5	(34.3%)	semiflexed	n/a
	village	9	1	4	2	2	(44.4%)	semiflexed	n/a
Beaverdam Creek (Middle Mississippian)	mound	37	15	11	10	1	(35.1%)	flexed	good
	village	9	n/a	5	3	1	(0.0%)	semiflexed	good
Hollywood (Middle Mississippian)	lower division	7	n/a	n/a	n/a	7	(85.7%)	n/a	n/a
	upper division	4	n/a	n/a	n/a	4	(75.0%)	n/a	n/a
Rucker's Bottom (Middle Mississippian)	Beaverdam-phase village	14	4	6	2	2	(50.0%)	semiflexed	fair
	Rembert-phase village	10	1	3	0	6	(10.0%)	semiflexed	good
I. C. Few (Middle Mississippian)	mound	10	4	1	2	3	(80.0%)	flexed	n/a
	village	4	1	2	0	1	(25.0%)	flexed	n/a
Irene* (Middle/ Late Mississippian)	stage 8	12	n/a	n/a	n/a	n/a	n/a	flexed	n/a
	mortuary structure	25	n/a	n/a	n/a	n/a	(100.0%)	flexed; urn burials	n/a
	inner enclosure	41	n/a	n/a	n/a	n/a	(34.1%)	flexed	n/a
	outer enclosure	23	n/a	n/a	n/a	n/a	(21.7%)	flexed	n/a
Chauga (Late Mississippian)	stages 7–10	21	7	2	5	7	(42.9%)	semiflexed	n/a
Totals**		407	69	62	28	82			
Irene	entire site	265	74	75	54	62			
	mortuary	89	23	24					

* Partial figures obtained from report. The total figures from the site at the bottom are from Hulse (1941:57).

** Based on total figures from Irene as provided by Hulse (1941).

appeared to be in somewhat better skeletal health than those dating to the Beaverdam phase. Six of the 13 Beaverdam-phase burials exhibited osteomyelitis, as opposed to only 2 of the 10 Rembert individuals, although this incidence was not found to be statistically significant. The seemingly poorer health of the earlier population may be due to the inferred position of the village as a tributary community of the Beaverdam Creek center, which may have requisitioned food resources. Evidence for a fairly stressful existence was also noted on the presumed commoner burials found at the Simpson's Field and Big Generostee Creek sites (Tyzzer 1986; see also chapter 5 here).

If the Rembert-phase villagers were indeed in better health than those in the Beaverdam-phase community at Rucker's Bottom, then the abandonment of the Beaverdam center and the emergence of a complex chiefdom centered at Rembert, considerably farther away, may have resulted in a better diet for the inhabitants of Rucker's Bottom. This may have been brought about by the greater ability of the complex chiefdom to buffer periods of uncertainty, or it may be simply because Rembert was much farther away and hence the village enjoyed greater autonomy. Finally, the climatic data indicate that the early (but not the final) part of the Rembert phase was a period of unusually favorable conditions, which would have meant favorable harvests and probably some reduction in dietary stress.

Detailed paleobiological analyses have also been conducted with skeletal samples from the Irene site, indicating the populations were in fairly good health, although the demands of agricultural food production brought about a decline in skeletal robusticity and an increase in health problems, at least when compared with preceding Woodland populations (Larsen 1982; Larsen et al. 1992; M. Powell 1990; Ruff and Larsen 1990). The skeletal sample from the site, with few children or adolescents present, is most unusual for agricultural populations such as these and supports an interpretation that the site saw use in periodic ceremonial functions rather than served as a residential community. These findings and the evidence for pronounced subsistence change between the Savannah and Irene occupations (see below) indicate the potential of paleobiological data for delimiting site function and the role dietary evidence can play in recognizing and interpreting patterns of organizational change. The analyses conducted to date in the basin also indicate that political conditions and status relations can be explored and documented using human skeletal remains.

Paleosubsistence Evidence for Political Change

Detailed paleoethnobotanical and zooarchaeological analyses of subsistence remains have been conducted at only four Mississippian sites in the Savannah River valley, at Beaverdam Creek (S. Fish 1985; P. Gardner 1985; Reitz 1985), Clyde Gulley (Aulbach-Smith 1984; Ruff 1984), Rucker's Bottom (J. Moore 1985; Scott 1985), and Simpson's Field (P. Gardner 1986a, 1986b; K. Wood 1986), all in the central Piedmont. These are the only assemblages for which published and quantifiable information is available, although floral and faunal remains are sometimes mentioned in other reports (Caldwell and McCann 1941:78–79; see also Campbell and Weed 1984:134; Grange 1972:205–9; Reitz 1988:149–51). Comparatively few remains were found at two of the four Piedmont sites, Clyde Gulley and Simpson's Field, which dated to the Early Mississippian Jarrett phase and the later Middle Mississippian Rembert phase, respectively. At Beaverdam Creek and Rucker's Bottom, in contrast, much larger sets of paleosubsistence data were collected and analyzed. Comparison of the Beaverdam-phase assemblages at these sites, a small mound center and a nearby village, indicates political relationships can be inferred from paleo-subsistence data, specifically tributary demands and their effects on subsistence. Furthermore, at Rucker's Bottom, comparison of subsistence data from the earlier and later communities indicates that the emergence of a complex chiefdom in this part of the drainage, coupled with a presumed pattern of greater subsistence autonomy, may have led to more focused hunting strategies and apparently an increase in the use of wild plant foods, specifically acorns, as a source of carbohydrates beyond what was provided by maize.

Dependence upon intensive agriculture has been defined as a hallmark of Mississippian culture (Griffin 1967:189), and given the frequency with which domesticated plant remains, most typically corn, have been found on late prehistoric sites in the Georgia–South Carolina area, there is little doubt that intensive, agriculturally based food production characterized the local Mississippian adaptation, particularly after the Early Mississippian period (Anderson 1989; Hally and Rudolph 1986:46, 69). The dates of the initial appearance and subsequent large-scale adoption of agriculture in the area away from the river mouth (see below), however, remain unknown. Evidence for the use of cultigens prior to the Mississippian period in the Savannah drainage is minimal, and later Woodland-period subsistence locally appears to have been directed primarily to wild plant and animal resources. The only evidence for the cultivation of domesticates found to date in the basin in Woodland context consists of a single squash rind fragment found in a late Swift Creek context at Simpson's Field (Gardner 1986a:390–91). No reliable evidence for the cultivation of corn has been found in Late Woodland features from anywhere in the drainage to date. As flotation processing comes to be increasingly utilized, however, our knowledge of later prehistoric plant use will improve.

By 1100 or shortly thereafter, Mississippian settlement in the upper Savannah River area was characterized by a range of site types, including ceremonial centers, smaller villages, and isolated farmsteads. Maize agriculture was presumably established by this time, although the only paleo-botanical evidence for this is a single fragment from the Jarrett-phase structure at Clyde Gulley (Tippitt and Marquardt 1984:8-37). It is not until the subsequent Beaverdam phase, in fact, that corn remains are found in any quantity, at Beaverdam Creek and Rucker's Bottom (Gardner 1985; J. Moore 1985) and in lesser incidence at 9Eb92 (Campbell and Weed 1984:134). While agriculture may have only become important to subsis-tence after circa 1200 locally, the samples upon which this inference is based are extremely limited. The actual contribution of maize to subsis-tence at various periods in the valley's prehistory will remain unknown until stable carbon isotope and related analyses can be conducted on securely dated local Late Woodland and Mississippian skeletal series.

To date, such analyses have been conducted with skeletal samples from Irene and other pre-Mississippian as well as postcontact sites in the Georgia coastal zone. The stable carbon/nitrogen isotope analyses from the mouth of the basin indicate maize agriculture was not adopted in this area until after the St. Catherines phase, circa 1150 or later (Larsen et al. 1992; Schoeninger et al. 1990; see also Reitz 1988:150). As noted previously, these same analyses provide indirect evidence for dietary change between the Savannah and Irene occupations, notably a decreased emphasis on maize and an apparent increased use of wild terrestrial plant and animal resources. A decreased emphasis on intensive agriculture appears to be associated with the collapse of the Savannah-phase chiefdom at Irene, perhaps as populations were no longer required to grow maize to further elite political agendas.

Indirect evidence for agricultural intensification has also been found through analyses of paleoethnobotanical remains in the Savannah River valley. A shift from mature to immature successional communities was indicated in the floral remains found at both Rucker's Bottom and Beaverdam Creek, something probably the result of increased land clear-ance associated with agricultural food production. At Rucker's Bottom, a marked increase in the number of floodplain tree species that were ex-ploited (i.e., found carbonized in site features) occurred between the Beaverdam and Rembert phases, suggesting the vegetation around the site was becoming increasingly disturbed as a result of clearance (J. Moore 1985:690–92). The increase in species diversity, coupled with a high inci-dence of pine (a pioneer species) and a decline in oak and hickory, suggests an increasingly immature floodplain forest community. Similar findings were also noted in palynological investigations conducted at the Beaverdam Creek site, which documented a mixed pine and oak commu-nity during the premound era (S. Fish 1985). Both pine and nonarboreal pollen were heavily represented, indicating that the area around the site was in an early stage of succession, something possibly related to field clearing. When the platform mound stages were under construction, the incidence of pine was even higher, and traces of maize pollen were found, almost certainly indicating increased field clearing associated with intensive agriculture (S. Fish 1985:411–16; Rudolph and Hally 1985:27–28).

The Beaverdam-phase village at Rucker's Bottom, as noted in chapter 5, was characterized by a highly diversified subsistence economy, making use of a wide range of plant and animal resources in addition to agricultural domesticates. This may have been a reaction to tribute demands, since at this time the village was apparently subservient to the center at Beaverdam Creek. The use of a wide range of species might result from a need to replace the kinds of foodstuffs presumably leaving the site, such as corn and deer or other large mammal meat, with wild plant foods and meat from a range of smaller animals. The skeletal analyses described previously indicated the Beaverdam-phase inhabitants of Rucker's Bottom were in rather poor health, supporting such an inference.

The early Beaverdam-phase population at Rucker's Bottom and at Beaverdam Creek apparently made greater use of corn than nuts and greater use of hickory nuts than acorns. In the later Rembert-phase village at Rucker's Bottom, in contrast, a relative decline in the use of corn and an increase in the use of nuts occurred, with a particular emphasis on acorns (J. Moore 1985:686–92). A high incidence of nut remains, particularly acorns, was also observed in the Rembert-phase component at Simpson's Field (Gardner 1986b:377–86). The increased use of wild plant resources in the later Mississippian occupation at Rucker's Bottom and Simpson's Field, notably the increased use of acorns, may reflect an attempt to augment carbohydrate yields, which may indicate the population was under some stress. Alternatively, if local Rembert-phase populations had become relatively free of tributary obligations, given the abandonment of the Beaverdam Creek mound center, less emphasis may have been placed on corn production (something also indicated at Irene).

In this case, subsistence stress may be the more plausible alternative, given the fact that the entire central and lower Savannah drainage was apparently abandoned at the end of the Rembert phase and the fact that climatic conditions deteriorated in the period just prior to this abandonment. During the probable period of repeated harvest shortfalls that ensued, use of acorns may have been necessary to overcome the loss of agriculturally produced carbohydrates. The highly focused hunting practices observed at the site at this time also appear tied to greater labor investment in other activities, which could include the gathering of wild plant foods as well as attempting to maintain the agricultural system. Interestingly, greater possible use of wild foods does not appear to have translated into poorer health for the Rembert-phase inhabitants; if anything, the opposite appears to have occurred.

Beaverdam-phase occupations at both Rucker's Bottom and Beaverdam Creek were characterized by fairly high species diversity, something that was interpreted as reflecting either procurement during warm weather or a diversified subsistence strategy (Reitz, Marrinan, and

Scott 1987:217; Scott 1985:661–63). A greater abundance of fish at the Beaverdam Creek mound and a greater abundance of small mammals at Rucker's Bottom were the principal differences between these assemblages. The difference in fish probably reflects proximity to suitable fishing grounds, since major shoals occur both to the north and south of Beaverdam Creek on the Savannah but were not present for several kilometers above or below Rucker's Bottom (Rudolph and Hally 1985:444). The greater use of small mammals at Rucker's Bottom probably, as noted above, reflects a higher level of dietary stress among village or commoner populations than among the elites at the center, who apparently had their diet supplemented by tributary foodstuffs from outlying areas (see below).

The Rembert-phase faunal assemblage at Rucker's Bottom, in contrast, had a much lower species diversity and consisted almost entirely of large mammal remains, suggesting either fall/winter procurement or a shift toward an increasingly focused subsistence economy. Fall/winter hunting is not implausible, since this is the period when deer were presumably in the best condition, with the greatest amounts of protein and fat (Bruce Smith 1975:33). Considerable evidence indicates that human hunting strategies are linked to fat quantity in the target prey population (Binford 1978:157–63, 465–66; Jochim 1976, 1981:82–90; Speth and Spielmann 1983:18–21). Since both villages at Rucker's Bottom and the center at Beaverdam Creek are assumed to have been occupied year-round, a change from a diversified to a more focused hunting strategy, with perhaps more fall/winter hunting, is considered the more plausible explanation for the observed patterning at the two sites (Rudolph and Hally 1985:444). The faunal assemblage from Rembert-phase components at Simpson's Field, assumed to be a hamlet, also indicates focused game procurement, with white-tailed deer (*Odocoileus virginianus*) accounting for much of the assemblage (K. Wood 1986:372).

The apparent intensification in large mammal procurement between the Beaverdam phase and Rembert phase may have been brought about by a need to maximize hunting return and to reduce the amount of labor such procurement entailed, labor that might have been needed elsewhere, possibly for farming or defense. Given the evidence that Rucker's Bottom was occupied for an extended period, it might also reflect the depletion of game in the locality. Speth and Scott (1985:257) have documented reasons why increasingly focused game procurement may occur in agricultural populations: "Greater horticultural commitment increases the need for efficient sources of high-quality protein, at least seasonally. It also introduces time and labor constraints that necessitate the rescheduling of hunting activities to more restricted periods of the year. Larger and more stable communities also degrade their immediate environs and deplete locally available game, forcing hunters to travel greater distances to productive hunting areas. Together, these factors favor the taking of selectively greater proportions of larger, higher-yield prey. . . ." Hunting directed to a few large species is clearly indicated during the Rembert phase at Rucker's Bottom and (although the sample is small) at Simpson's Field. Early in the Rembert phase, when favorable climatic conditions apparently occurred over an extended period, agricultural intensification may have taken place, since harvest returns would have been consistently favorable. An increasingly focused hunting strategy may have been one consequence of this. Moreover, given the decline in agricultural food production later in the Rembert phase, wild food resources would have become even more important, as local populations attempted to find alternative food resources. Hunters may have had to go even farther to find game. In light of the evidence for increased conflict, specifically the appearance of fortifications at Rucker's Bottom, Mississippian populations from the upper Savannah may have been forced to spend increasing amounts of time in the interriverine buffer zones precisely when it was increasingly precarious to do so. This may have in turn led to increased casualties and hastened the organizational collapse that ensued.

The trace element analyses conducted at Rucker's Bottom provide additional indirect evidence for dietary change that may be linked to the political fortunes of that site (Butler 1986:103–18; Weaver et al. 1985:602–3). Levels of calcium, magnesium, zinc, and strontium were determined and compared over the individuals dating to the two phases. No statistically significant differences were noted in the levels of calcium, magnesium, and strontium, although the Rembert-phase burials were found to have lower zinc levels, suggesting decreased meat consumption or possibly a more diverse diet (Butler 1986:180–81; Underwood 1977). The Rembert-phase sample also exhibited much greater variability in the incidence of zinc and magnesium and in the ratio of strontium to calcium than did the Beaverdam-phase sample, something also suggesting greater variability in dietary patterns. This may reflect the conditions that are assumed to have existed toward the end of the phase, when poor climatic conditions presumably resulted in repeated harvest shortfalls, maize consumption was reduced or varied, and other food sources were exploited. It must be emphasized, however, that the samples on which these inferences are based are quite small and that effects of diagenesis were not controlled.

The faunal remains from Rucker's Bottom also provide clues as to the apparent position of the community in the local political hierarchy. Scott (1981, 1982), in a faunal analysis employing materials from a small hamlet (Yarborough) and a ceremonial center (Lubbub Creek) located along the Tombigbee River, has shown that the occurrence of skeletal elements may indicate whether and in what direction subsistence resources were being transferred between communities. Some evidence was found to suggest that the Beaverdam-phase village at Rucker's Bottom was submitting tribute elsewhere, probably to the Beaverdam Creek center some 12 kilometers downstream, and that this pattern ceased in the Rembert occupation (Scott 1985:662–64). A reduced incidence of limb bones indicated these meaty elements (i.e., hindquarters or forequarters) may have been leaving the site, possibly as tribute. An analysis of deer element incidence at Beaverdam Creek, interestingly, found almost twice as many hindquarter elements, probably the most preferred meaty cut on the animal, than forequarters (n = 75 forequarter and n = 132 hindquarter elements; Reitz 1985:424), supporting the inference that the occupants at this site were the recipients. In contrast, in the later Mississippian Rembert-phase community at Rucker's Bottom, this pattern was not evident, and the sample was more similar to that expected at a ceremonial center. Scott (1985:664) has noted: "The differences between the early and later Mississippian components at Rucker's Bottom suggest a change in settlement function through time, from a more subservient role during the earlier period (with greater quantities of meat being transported from the village) to a higher position in the socio-political hierarchy in the later period (perhaps with meat coming in, but certainly with less meat going out)." This patterning is consistent with changing political relationships along the Savannah, notably the decline of the Beaverdam Creek site and an apparent relocation of power to Rembert after the Beaverdam phase. These changing political fortunes may have resulted in increased autonomy for the Rucker's Bottom community and may have reduced tribute demands on the local population.

9

Exploring Political Change in Chiefdom Society

Investigating Cycling

This study has explored how and why political change occurs in chiefdoms. The emergence and collapse of complex chiefdoms amid a regional landscape of simple chiefdoms, a process I have called cycling behavior, is an ingrained aspect of chiefdom life. The changes in decision-making levels that are characteristic of the cycling process may be triggered, we have seen, by the operation of one or more of a wide array of factors promoting organizational instability. These factors encompass areas as diverse as the characteristics of primary and secondary chiefdoms; the strength and importance attached to legitimizing ideological structures, such as ties with ancestral elites, the occupation of centers of power, and the role of chiefly iconography; scale/time-depth dependent relationships between sacred and secular mechanisms for maintaining authority structures; rules of succession, inheritance, marriage formation, and postmarital residence; and ecological parameters, including both coarse-grained and fine-grained environmental structure, climatic perturbations, and the structure and stability of resource procurement/buffer zones. This study has attempted to show, through example, how cycling can be explored using archaeological data, as well as information from a number of other disciplines, including history and ethnohistory, paleobiology, and paleoclimatology. The use of multiple lines of argument and evidence, I believe, is the best way to achieve new insights about how complex societies emerge and evolve.

In the examination of cycling, the Mississippian chiefdoms of the southeastern United States and specifically within the Savannah River basin have been examined at some length. We have seen that political change was common in the late prehistoric Southeast and that an extensive archaeological record exists documenting these patterns and processes of change. Chiefdoms varied appreciably in size and organizational complexity across the regional landscape and over time, and hundreds of these societies emerged, expanded, and then fragmented during the period from circa 800 to 1600. In the absence of written records for most of them, archaeological analyses are critical to understanding their history. For the most recent chiefdoms, though, accounts from the early contact era can complement the archaeological record and can offer guidance in its interpretation. The chiefdoms of the Southeast existed just a moment ago in time, when compared to those in many other parts of the world, but nonetheless have a great deal to contribute to the study of political change and to the understanding of cultural evolution in general.

Lessons from the Savannah River Chiefdoms

In the Savannah River basin, we have seen how aspects of cycling brought on by changes in climate and within the regional political landscape resulted in identifiable changes in health, subsistence, demography, mortuary behavior, and architecture. The emergence of major multimound centers in the basin (presumably complex chiefdoms), for example, was coupled with the abandonment of smaller centers. That is, the development of increasing social complexity was coupled with increasing centralization of authority at the expense of smaller centers and, presumably, their chiefly elites. At the same time, however, commoner populations in outlying villages may have exercised greater autonomy than previously, perhaps to fill the localized leadership vacuum.

Physiography and resource structure also shaped the different historical trajectories observed. The post-1450 abandonment of much of the basin, with the lower reaches depopulated earlier than those upriver, indicates that societies in areas most prone to circumscription and most vulnerable to subsistence stress succumbed more readily to destabilizing processes than societies in more favored areas. How buffer zones between polities formed and operated was measured and was shown apparently to depend on conditions in both the natural and the political landscape.

A direct relationship between climate, agricultural surplus generation, and political conditions is also apparent. Social and political changes were observed in the basin chiefdoms about the same time that extended periods of increased or decreased rainfall occurred. The relationship between climate and political change was not found to be invariant, however. The basin was largely unoccupied throughout the 16th century, even though climatic conditions were unusually favorable much of the time. Storage would have enabled local populations to buffer most temporary shortfalls, although the effects of extended periods of climatic deterioration would have probably been quite serious. Such periods occurred, in fact, circa 1450, about the time the lower basin was abandoned, and in the 1560s through 1580s, when the Spanish tried to colonize the nearby South Carolina coast.

A number of archaeological correlates of political change were observed in the basin. The emergence of stratified chiefdoms was characterized by a replacement of communal structures by buildings atop platform mounds at several sites, and on at least one site, a council house reappeared following the abandonment of the platform mound. These architectural changes are linked to changes in organizational structure, between decision making by consensus and decision making in the hands of an elite. The presence of council houses on a site does not invariably document an egalitarian social system, since these structures were observed in tributary communities when chiefdoms were present. Their presence under such circumstances indicates at least some autonomy or control over local affairs, though, and also suggests that public decision-making forums were probably in use throughout the Mississippian period, although their role was probably diminished at chiefly centers.

The appearance of fortifications indicates that the position of the elite and the sociopolitical environment were becoming less secure, but it may also signal the emergence or collapse of chiefly organizational structures. Collapse does not appear to have inevitably or at least immediately followed once fortifications appeared, however, nor does it signal the occurrence of extensive warfare, since little evidence exists for large-scale conflict in the period leading up to the abandonment of the central and lower basin. Low-intensity conflict, which was suggested, may have played a large role in the decision to abandon areas.

Evidence for an impoverishment of chiefly centers prior to their abandonment was documented through mortuary analyses at several mound sites, where a decline in the proportional occurrence of burials with elaborate grave goods occurred in the later periods of occupation. A similar decline in the occurrence of grave goods was observed in village commoner burials, indicating these trends may have reached all levels of society. Elite impoverishment did not lead immediately to organizational collapse, however. Instead, at several centers, one or more later stages of mound construction occurred during periods characterized by a significant decline in the occurrence of prestige goods in burials. Evidence indicating impoverishment of burials may signal trouble in more egalitarian societies as well (i.e., at Irene).

The collapse of chiefdom organization or a reduction in tributary demands can lead to decreased reliance on intensive agriculture or at least on maize, something indicated by paleobiological (stable isotope) and ethnobotanical analyses. These changes may also translate into better overall population health. The status of a site in a tributary economy, specifically whether it was a donor or a recipient of foodstuffs, can be indicated by zooarchaeological analyses. The extent to which diet was diversified may have been prompted by subsistence stress, notably the imposition of tributary demands or the increased labor requirements of intensive agriculture. The emergence of intensive agriculture was recognizable not only by the presence of corn and other domesticates in the archaeological record and through stable isotope analyses, but also from evidence for land clearing and successional change in forest composition.

Why Was the Savannah River Basin Abandoned?

The archaeological record from the basin indicates that something dramatic happened in the 15th century. That a large-scale abandonment took place can no longer be seriously challenged. After circa 1450, no evidence indicates any mound centers were occupied below the headwaters of the river. Only a few Late Mississippian components, most of them near the Oconee River, in fact, have been found among the thousands of prehistoric sites that exist from the central and lower valley. Artifacts dating from the interval circa 1450 to 1600 are virtually nonexistent in this part of the valley, and Mississippian components, which showed a pattern of increase over the centuries from circa 900 to 1450, exhibited a pronounced drop after this time.

Most of the post-1450 occupation of the central and lower valley, at least until the late 17th century, when evidence for native occupation reappears, is minimal and probably derives from ephemeral occupations, possibly representing little more than hunting camps or temporary settlements by groups based elsewhere. The only area where later sites occur with fairly extensive assemblages, indicative of more permanent hamlet or village occupations, is in the extreme western part of the basin along the upper Little and Broad rivers near the Oconee River. These occupations have been interpreted as representing an eastern boundary of the dense 16th-century Oconee province and are possibly indicative of populations' moving into the political and settlement vacuum left by the abandonment of the Savannah River.

The abandonment of the central and lower Savannah thus was caused by a combination of factors, of which changes in environmental conditions and in the regional political landscape were perhaps the most important. The rise of the rival provinces of Ocute and Cofitachequi, which were separated by an extensive buffer zone at the time of the De Soto entrada in 1540, appears to be an important part of this story. The populations of Cofitachequi and Ocute observed in the early contact era were extensive and, at least in the case of Ocute, were apparently also increasing dramatically (Elvas in Robertson 1993:77–87; Ranjel in Worth 1993a:272–281; see also Bourne 1904, 1:55–69, 2:89–102, respectively; Rudolph and Blanton 1980). It is suggested that the successful growth of these chiefdoms was, at least in part, at the expense of the polities along the Savannah River. Fortifications, appearing at several sites along the Savannah in the last century prior to the abandonment, offer possible evidence for political circumscription and increasing tension and, perhaps, overt hostilities among the chiefly polities along the Savannah, the Oconee, and the Santee/Wateree rivers. The populations of Cofitachequi and possibly Ocute as well may have encroached on the Savannah River polities' traditional hunting preserves or may have even been actively raiding settlements.

The mid-15th century was, at least locally, a period of environmental deterioration, specifically decreased rainfall, which would have put additional stress on Mississippian political systems throughout the immediate region. Groups may have attempted to overcome food shortages by obtaining the stored resources of their neighbors. The abandonment of villages that were weakened by drought and famine conditions and thus increasingly subject to raiding is a probable consequence. Furthermore, faced with repeated harvest shortfalls, the inhabitants of the Savannah River basin would have been forced to make increasing use of alternative resources, including game from the interriverine buffer zones. Given a moderate level of storage, food shortages resulting from deceased rainfall would have been deferred long enough for local populations to switch over to these food resources. Unfortunately, the populations of the Savannah River basin would have been seeking alternative resources at precisely the period when the expansion of their neighbors would have made their use (i.e., game and other foodstuffs from the buffer zones) increasingly precarious.

Repeated years of poor harvests would have put a great deal of strain on the agriculturally based political structures, particularly the ability of the elites to mobilize tribute. It is unlikely that climatic deterioration by itself could have brought about the collapse of chiefly authority observed in the basin after circa 1450, since the valley's chiefdoms survived earlier periods of prolonged drought. The Savannah River chiefdoms do not appear to have been threatened by rivals in the regional political landscape during these earlier periods, however. A continued pattern of crop failure or harvest shortfall, coupled with small but steady (if not increasing) losses in warfare or hunting activity, would pose increasingly insurmountable challenges to the authority of the Savannah River elites, by deflating their aura of sanctity, ability, and invincibility. It would also affect their abilities to mobilize tribute and hence maintain their positions and that of their followers. Thus the elites in the Savannah River chiefdoms of the mid-15th century were facing difficulties both locally, in the form of crop failures, and externally, in the political arena, where their neighbors were gaining the upper hand both in power and prestige.

While the circumscription of the Savannah River chiefdoms may have developed gradually, over the course of several generations, the effects were quite severe. That circumscription could operate over great distances is indicated a century later, when one of the leaders of Ocute told De Soto that, because of the power of Cofitachequi, the local populations were "intimidated and submissive, not daring to go any distance or leave their own boundaries" (Vega in Shelby 1993:274; see also Varner and Varner 1951:284). Given this testimony of the effect Cofitachequi had on its neighbors in central Georgia in 1540, it is possible that province may have had an equally or more marked impact on the Savannah River chiefdoms of a century earlier.

The relocation of much of the valley's population to other areas, and specifically to more successful leaders, is interpreted as the ultimate result of the gradual circumscription and demoralization of the Savannah River chiefdoms. Since little clear evidence for intensive warfare has been found anywhere along the middle and lower Savannah (although only a few sites have been extensively examined), an immediate question that arises is what happened to the people when these centers collapsed and the whole lower portion of the drainage was abandoned? It has been suggested that only the organizational structures collapsed, with local populations remaining but reverting to more typically "Woodland" settlement patterns and social organization, including ceramic finishes popular during that period, such as cordmarking (K. Stephenson and King 1992). To date, however, no direct evidence for these kinds of occupations has been found in the central and lower Savannah drainage.

At least some of the people appear to have retreated to the north, into the headwaters area. Late Mississippian sites are common in this area, much more so than earlier Mississippian sites, suggesting considerable localized population increase occurred. The Estatoe center appears, Chauga was reoccupied after lying deserted for two centuries, and occupations continued at Tugalo, which had itself been reoccupied only about a century earlier. At Estatoe, the replacement of earth-lodge-like structures by a true platform mound after stage 5 suggests this center acquired greater prominence within a few generations of its founding. Although mound construction ceased in the headwaters by or shortly after circa 1600, as it did throughout most of the region, the upper part of the valley continued to be occupied until well into the colonial period, when it was the location of many of the Lower Cherokee towns. The formation of these towns and thus of the historic Lower Cherokee may be partially a response to political developments between the 15th-century Mississippian chiefdoms of central Georgia and South Carolina.

A major increase in population has also been documented in the central Oconee drainage during later Mississippian times, after circa 1500 (Kowalewski and Hatch 1991; Rudolph and Blanton 1980). Some of this increase, it is argued, is the result of a direct relocation of people from the Savannah River valley. Tenuous evidence for this has been suggested by the appearance of ceramic assemblages resembling Rembert-phase materials at one site along the upper Oconee (Ledbetter and Wynn 1988), although a massive influx of such materials on a range of sites would be much more convincing. A relocation of Savannah River valley populations into the Oconee River basin and the province of Ocute, rather than eastward into the Santee/Wateree River basin, which was controlled by Cofitachequi, seems more probable for two reasons.

First, in the central Piedmont, the Oconee and Savannah river basins lie adjacent to one another, making travel and communication between these two areas straightforward. The Little and Broad rivers, major tributaries of the Savannah, in fact, extend almost to the main channel of the Oconee. The center of the province of Ocute was thus only approximately 75 kilometers from the upper Savannah, and its margins were accessible by major waterways. The center of Cofitachequi along the Wateree River, in contrast, lay approximately 150 kilometers to the east, across both the Saluda and Broad rivers, a much longer journey. Second, little evidence exists for interaction between the populations of the Savannah and Santee/Wateree basins. The major pathway De Soto followed for seven days after leaving Ocute, for example, apparently ran eastward from the Oconee River to the general vicinity of the Savannah River, after which the trail deteriorated and disappeared (Hudson, Smith, and DePratter 1984:72). The fact that this pathway was present in 1540 suggests the inhabitants of east-central Georgia regularly visited areas to the east as far as the Savannah. That they went little farther was dramatically illustrated by the fact that De Soto's party, accompanied by hundreds of natives from Ocute, got lost trying to find Cofitachequi, with near-disastrous results for the expedition.

If the chiefdoms in the Savannah and Oconee drainages had a long history of contact and interaction, it would have facilitated the westward relocation of population out of the Savannah River valley, assuming the events of the latter half of the 15th century made relocation their most attractive option. There is ample ethnographic precedent for this. Patterns of expansion tend to be toward those individuals, groups, or polities that are genealogically the most remote and hence the least likely to draw in on their side any neighboring or related kin into any struggles that may ensue (Bohannon and Bohannon 1954:5; Vayda 1961). Patterns of population relocation or retreat, in contrast, tend to be toward groups that are closest genealogically.

One thing is clear: the patterns of chiefly competition that apparently led to the abandonment of the Savannah River valley do not appear to have been over prime agricultural land or to have been brought about solely by climatic deterioration. The entire central and lower Savannah River valley contains extensive rich farmland and yet remained abandoned for almost two centuries after 1450. It was not reoccupied, in fact, in spite of the marked improvement in climatic conditions that occurred after circa 1500. For this reason, resorting to environmental determinism to explain the events observed in the archaeological record of the Savannah River basin is untenable. Environment had its role, but so too did politics.

Cycling and the Evolution of Organizational Complexity in the Eastern Woodlands

The emergence and collapse of complex chiefdoms, or cycling, typifies the later prehistoric archaeological record of the Eastern Woodlands, rather than the emergence of primary states. To understand why cycling is so common, we must look to the basic structure of chiefdom social organization. We have seen that an internal contradiction in the kin-based structure of chiefdom societies sows the seeds of repeated organizational collapse. In these societies, the chief's assistants are his closest relatives, who are also his potential rivals and successors. While it is in a chief's best interest to suppress potential rivals, he is forced to place them in positions of power if he is to maintain himself. These positions of power are often used to mount challenges to chiefly authority and succession. Only when this pattern is broken, something that occurs rarely, are chiefdoms replaced by states or simpler sociopolitical entities (Yoffee 1993).

Why one or more Mississippian societies in the Eastern Woodlands never developed into state-level polities is a question of some interest, since chiefdoms elsewhere in the New World made this transition. In some areas of the Eastern Woodlands, notably in the American Bottom, societies approaching primary states in size (if not in information-processing capability) were unquestionably present. The extent of the monumental construction at the Cahokia site during the period from circa 1000 to 1250 and the level of mortuary ritual accompanying some of its leaders, where retainer sacrifice reminiscent of Ur's royal tombs occurred, suggest something quite close to a state was present. However, environmental deterioration coupled with administrative failures apparently led to the decline of Cahokia after circa 1200, and the region had not rebounded by the time European contact truncated the native developmental sequence.

There appear to be a number of reasons why cycling, and not steplike evolution to ever greater social complexity, if indeed this is even the route to state formation, characterizes the Mississippian archaeological record. First, the existence of chiefdoms was actually comparatively brief in the region. European contact destroyed the region's agricultural chiefdoms within a millennium after their initial emergence, and in many areas within no more than a few hundred years after their first appearance. Research in four areas where primary states did emerge indicates that a minimum of approximately 1,000 years (Oaxaca) and in some cases almost 2,000 years (Peru, Mesopotamia, India) elapsed between the emergence of chiefdoms and states (Wright 1986). The process of primary state formation, it is suggested, may require evolutionary changes at the chiefdom level, which typically take a considerable amount of time to work through, time the Mississippian societies of the Eastern Woodlands did not have.

This process appears to involve changes in authority structures. Chiefly cycling, I believe, tends to select for increasingly secular or power-based authority structures and, to some extent, for the emergence of ever more complex chiefdoms. This selection process requires many generations and, given the presence of cycling, is not unilineal but is instead punctuated by periods where societies of greater or lesser complexity dominated portions of the landscape. The cumulative effect of repeated successional events within individual complex chiefdoms and competition between these chiefdoms, however, can be viewed as a process of selection for secular-based power structures that could ultimately lead to state formation. The selection events necessary for this development, such as the development of a writing system or the emergence of nonkin-based administrative structures (i.e., bureaucratic apparatus), however, did not happen in the Eastern Woodlands.

The societies of the Eastern Woodlands also apparently developed in isolation, with little or no direct contact with other New World states, precluding the likelihood of secondary state formation. The nearest state-level societies were located in central Mexico, at a considerable distance across major geographic barriers. Currently no conclusive evidence has been found for direct or regular contact between the Middle American states and the Mississippian or pre-Mississippian societies of the Eastern Woodlands. The only Latin American artifacts reaching the Eastern Woodlands were domesticates such as corn and beans, and they apparently spread fairly gradually from group to group.

The physiographic and biotic resource structure of the Eastern Woodlands also appears to have hindered the easy development of complex societies in many areas. Carneiro (1981:67) has suggested that "the smaller an area in which [chiefdoms arise], the easier it will be to unify." The area occupied by Mississippian chiefdoms in the Eastern Woodlands was appreciably larger than nuclear Mesoamerica, but areas of densely packed chiefdoms favorable for state formation were patchily distributed. Given the area involved and the comparatively limited area suitable for the emergence and development of agricultural/game-based chiefdoms, for the most part along narrow, widely spaced riverine floodplains, the distances between individual chiefly societies appear to have hindered the formation of stable multipolity aggregates. While chiefdom-level societies in the region appear to have exerted influence over considerable areas, as the Coosa case illustrates, direct administrative control appears to have been within fairly small areas. If primary states had developed in the Eastern Woodlands, it is unlikely that they would have first appeared in the narrow, widely spaced river valleys characteristic of much of the region. Instead, it is likely such societies would have emerged first, if anywhere, in the ecologically rich central and lower Mississippi River valley, where large numbers of chiefdoms occurred in comparatively small areas.

Given the prevalence of warfare at the time of early state formation and the apparent association of early state formation with the unification of a number of chiefdom-level societies, predominantly through conquest and subsequent administrative reorganization, it is probable that state-level societies would have eventually emerged in the Eastern Woodlands. Low-intensity warfare was a way of life among the Mississippian chiefdoms of the region, occasionally giving way to major episodes of apparent conquest or extermination. The unification of widely spaced chiefdoms would have been difficult in most areas, however, so conquest-based states would probably have emerged in such areas as the central and lower Mississippi River valley, where complex chiefdoms were closely packed together in the landscape. Whether and when this outcome would have occurred, however, will remain forever unknown.

Final Remarks

The Savannah River case indicates the importance of a regional perspective in the investigation of cycling. The changes that were observed in the individual centers and societies in the valley, we have seen, could only be understood when the larger picture of change along the basin, in adjoining basins, and, indeed, throughout the region was examined. Within the Savannah River valley, chiefdoms rose and fell, and centers of power rotated over the landscape. These changes occurred for a variety of reasons, indicating the futility of searching for single causes and the need to consider multiple lines of evidence in the explanation of long-term political change.

Much remains to be done in the study of the Mississippian chiefdoms of the Savannah River valley. In particular, the Lawton, Mason's Plantation, and Tate mound centers, which are largely unknown, need to be mapped and tested. This is particularly critical in the case of Mason's Plantation, which was one of the largest centers in the basin; finding any remains from this site would be important. Village, hamlet, and special activity site types, about which we know less than we do about the centers, also need to be recognized and examined. Survey data need to continue to be collected from across the region, so that our understanding of settlement patterns and land use strategies can continue to advance. Finally, we need to strive continually to bring new ways of thinking to our data.

Early Historic Descriptions of
Mississippian Centers in the Savannah River Basin
[Bracketed annotations by David G. Anderson]

Mounds near Pipemaker's Creek,
Chatham County, Georgia
[The Irene Site, 9Ch1]

[Taken from "Certain Aboriginal Mounds of the Savannah River," by Clarence B. Moore, p. 168, first published in 1898]

At the union of Pipemaker's creek and the Savannah river, about four miles [6.4 kilometers] above Savannah, in view from the river, on property belonging to Henry Taylor, Esq., of Savannah, who kindly gave us permission to investigate, are two aboriginal mounds.

The larger, a truncated cone in shape, has a base irregularly circular in outline with a diameter of about 130 feet [39.6 meters]. [Note that the diameter was 160 feet or 48.8 meters in 1937, when the WPA excavations began, suggesting considerable plow reduction had occurred in the intervening years.] The diameter of the summit plateau, which is also circular, is about 60 feet [18.3 meters]. The mound, which has a height of 19 feet [5.8 meters], presents a picturesque appearance. [In 1937, the top was described as rounded and 15.5 feet, or 4.7 meters, high, suggesting an upper, Irene stage may have been present and subsequently lost.] The sides are steep and on them grow cedars and liveoaks, the oaks covered with trailing moss. A large excavation had been made previous to our visit, by treasure seekers, we were told. The exposed portions were carefully examined by use and a certain amount of digging done without showing traces of burials. [Use of the large mound for burial purposes does not appear common, a finding reinforced by the WPA work.] The mound seemed to be composed of clayey sand with oyster shells in places.

Contiguous to the southwest margin of the large mound was a rise in the ground, circular in a general way, with a diameter of about 60 feet [18.3 meters] and a height of 3 feet [91 centimeters] at the center. The mound, which was more than half dug through by us, seemed to have been a refuse heap formed by long-continued occupation. It had also been used as a place of burial. Human remains were met with at eighteen places—the usual flexed burials, the head as a rule, though not always, pointing to the east. [In the fill of Moore's excavation, ten disturbed burials were found during the WPA excavations, one, partially undisturbed, with several hundred disk-shaped shell beads (Caldwell and McCann 1941:24).] With the burials were small shell beads on two occasions and with one was a pebble-hammer roughly pecked to leave a central encircling ridge. In the midden debris were: many pebbles, some broken; bits of chert; two earthenware discs; one-half of a discoidal stone; numerous sherds bearing the check, the diamond-shaped, and the complicated, stamp.

Mounds near Hudson's Ferry, Screven County, Georgia

[Taken from "Certain Aboriginal Mounds of the Savannah River," by Clarence B. Moore, pp. 169–71, first published in 1898]

Hudson's Ferry, about 68 miles [109 kilometers] by water above Savannah, is the steamboat landing for Enecks, a settlement and post-office about two miles [3.2 kilometers] inland. A man named Golden stated he had found two vessels of earthenware, one above the other, by the roadside at the landing, which contained cremated human bones [probably a Savannah or Irene urn burial]. We visited Mr. T. J. Enecks, of Enecks, who showed us the vessels, which are of a type [unfortunately not described here] found on the Georgia coast.

In a field about 1 mile [1.6 kilometers] west of Hudson's ferry, on the property of Mr. William Prior, of Enecks, to whom we are indebted for permission to investigate, was a mound, much spread out by plowing, in a cultivated field [now recorded as 9Sn4 in the Georgia archaeological site files]. Its diameter was 74 feet [22.5 meters]; its height, 2 feet 5 inches [76 centimeters, almost identical in size to the burial mound at Irene]. The mound had been dug into previously to a certain extent. The holes remained unfilled. We were informed by the son of Mr. Prior that the digging was done by him and that he had found nothing except two skeletons. The mound was thoroughly investigated by us. It was of dark yellow sand without stratification or pits. A dark band ran through it at the level of the surrounding field [an old A-horizon or midden?].

Burial No. 1 was 4 feet [1.2 meters] S.E. by E. from the point taken by us as the center of the mound. The skeleton, of a male, heading S., was partly flexed, with trunk and face to the right. The legs were drawn up, the knees turned to the right, the upper arms lay along the body with the forearms bent across it. Near the skull was a chip of chert and a quantity of charcoal, though neither skull nor sand showed trace of fire. On either side of the right arm were two handsome discoidal stones each flat on one side and convex on the other, 2.3 inches [5.8 centimeters] and 2.7 inches [6.9 centimeters] in diameter, respectively. This skeleton had doubtless been buried, after exposure, with most of the parts held in place by the ligaments [a probable secondary burial]. The right foot, however, except the astragalus, was missing. The heel bone lay by the skull. The skeleton, which was 3 feet [91 centimeters] from the surface, had been let into the dark band at the base of the mound.

Burial No. 2 was 8 feet [2.4 meters] S. of the center and 2 feet 9 inches [84 centimeters] down, just through the black basal band. It was of a male, was flexed on the right and headed S.S.W. Back of the skull was a broken mussel shell and a tobacco pipe of earthenware covered as to the bowl with projecting knobs. [The pipe (figure 64 in this text) is a common Mississippian form observed at other sites in the Savannah basin, as noted in chapter 5.]

Burial No. 3, 6 feet [1.8 meters] W.N.W., 2.5 feet [76 centimeters] down, head S., included the upper portion of a skeleton, the rest having been dug away during one of the excavations to which we have referred. In the sand, which had been thrown back and left, was an interesting tobacco pipe of light-colored clay consisting of an effigy of a bird, probably an owl. The wings, tail, and "horns" are distinctly shown, as are the legs and eyes. Part of the bill is missing [figure 64 here]. An interesting feature of this pipe is that the bird faces the smoker, the pipe evidently having been made more for the satisfaction of the owner than to attract the attention of others. [This seems unlikely, given the dramatic profile the pipe would have presented.] We have before noticed this tendency in aboriginal pipes,

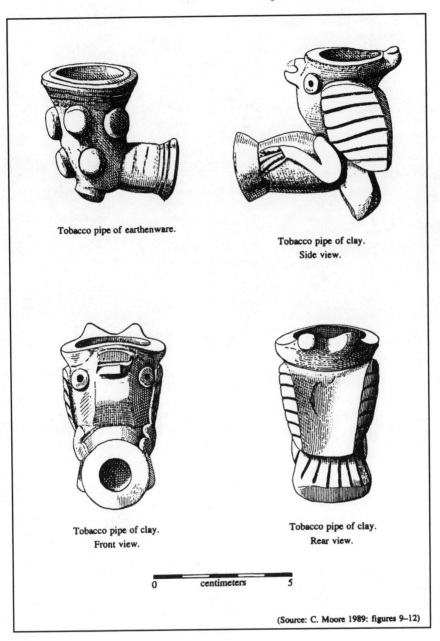

Tobacco pipe of earthenware.

Tobacco pipe of clay.
Side view.

Tobacco pipe of clay.
Front view.

Tobacco pipe of clay.
Rear view.

0   centimeters   5

(Source: C. Moore 1989: figures 9–12)

Figure 64   Pipes from Hudson's Ferry Mound.

notably in one found by us in the great Grant mound, Florida, where a small piece of copper had been fastened to the near side of the bowl.

Mr. J. D. McGuire, who has made an especial study of aboriginal tobacco pipes and whose memoir on the subject will shortly be brought out by the National Museum, says of this pipe that the specimen is the most interesting one of the pipes of this type, which belongs to Georgia and South Carolina, that has come under his observation and by far the most elaborate one he knows of, though the pipe is related to other interesting pipes from the same locality [i.e., Hollywood, as noted in chapter 5; see below] and also from North Carolina and possibly from Tennessee.

Mr. Andrew E. Douglass, whose superb collection of pipes may be seen at the Museum of Natural History, New York, writes of the bird-pipe as follows: "The pipe represented in the cuts is, so far as I know, entirely unique. It represents what I take to be a conventional owl, and, as you observe, the face is turned to the smoker, which would be considered a legitimate Indian conception. It is not likely to have any duplicate, as it is hand-work and the artist is not likely to have adhered to the same design in modeling another. I regard it as a fine specimen of original Cherokee work." [The Cherokee identification is, of course, incorrect and must be viewed in the context of the time when this work was undertaken.]

Burial No. 4, 8 feet [2.4 meters] W.S.W., 10 inches [25 centimeters] from the surface had been disturbed in part by the second pit of the previous digging. Charcoal lay near the skull.

Together, and unassociated with human remains, were three fossil shark's teeth, each somewhat over one inch in length, with bases and points considerably worn, showing use in handles as pointed tools. With them was a mussel-shell containing two bones with cores of spurs, doubtless belonging to a wild turkey. A pitted smoothing stone lay loose in the sand, as did two arrow-points of chert.

In a field formerly under cultivation, about half a mile [0.8 kilometers] south-east from the mound just described, was a mound of sand 4 feet 5 inches [1.4 meters] high and 61 feet [18.6 meters] across the base. It had been somewhat spread out by cultivation. Previous to our visit a small hole had been dug into the top. A trench 30 feet [9.1 meters] wide was dug, in from the margin through the center. About the middle of the mound were calcined fragments of bones probably belonging to one individual. Similar fragments were seen in the sand thrown out by the former digger.

Mounds near Brooks Landing, Barnwell County, S.C.
(The Lawton Mound Group, Allendale County, S.C.)

[Taken from "Certain Aboriginal Mounds of the Savannah River," by Clarence B. Moore, pp. 171–72, first published in 1898]

Brooks' Landing [Lawton Mounds, 38Al11], not given on the government chart, is about 121 miles [195 kilometers] from Savannah by the river. About half a mile [0.8 kilometers] in an easterly direction from the landing, in the cypress swamp, are two mounds on the property of Mr. S. G. Lawton, of Allendale, S.C., who courteously placed them at our disposition. The mounds, about the same size and almost contiguous, stand close to the edge of the terrace, which borders the river in high water and is itself submerged in times of freshet. The northernmost mound was chosen for investigation. It was the usual shape, a greatly truncated cone with markedly level summit plateau. The diameter of base was 68 feet [20.7 meters]; of the summit plateau 36 feet [11 meters]. Measured from the terrace on which it stands, its average height is 5 feet 4 inches [1.62 meters], though, to an observer looking from the north and including the height of the terrace, its altitude would seem much greater. [These measurements are slightly larger than those recorded in 1970 when the site was revisited.] Trenches, aggregating 45 feet [13.7 meters] in length from 3 to 4 feet [0.91 to 1.22 meters] wide and from 5 to 6 feet [1.52 to 1.83 meters] deep, were dug into the summit plateau. About five feet down there seemed to be a black basal line indicating the original surface [premound midden?]. The mound was of unstratified clay with occasional fire-places, perhaps in use during its construction. Three or four sherds were met with, and 5 feet [1.52 meters] from the surface was a deposit of small fragments of calcined bones, some of which were undoubtedly human. Probably this mound was domiciliary and the burial incidental. [The absence of burials or much debris suggests few stages were present. Each stage would have probably been characterized by an occupation surface and possibly associated burials.]

The Silver Bluff Area

[Taken from *Travels through North and South Carolina, Georgia, East and West Florida, the Cherokee Country . . .* , by William Bartram, pp. 313–15, first published in 1791]

Next morning [late April 1776] I set forward prosecuting my tour. I pursued the high road leading from Savanna to Augusta for the distance of one hundred miles [160 kilometers] or more, and then recrossed the river at Silver Bluff, a pleasant villa, the property and seat of G. Golphin, Esquire, a gentleman of very distinguished talents and great liberality, who possessed the most extensive trade, connections, and influence, amongst the South and South-West Indian tribes, particularly with the Creeks and Chactaws, of whom I fortunately obtained letters of recommendation and credit to the principal traders residing in the Indian towns.

Silver-Bluff is a very celebrated place; it is a considerable height upon the Carolina shore of the Savanna River, perhaps thirty feet [9.1 meters] higher than the low lands on the opposite shore, which are subject to be overflowed in the spring and fall; this steep bank rises perpendicular out of the river, discovering various strata of earth . . . [a lengthy discussion of local geology and fossils follows]. The surface of the ground upon this bluff, which extends a mile and a half or two miles [2.4 or 3.2 kilometers] on the river, and is from an half mile [0.8 kilometers] in breadth, nearly level, and a good fertile soil, as is evident from the vast Oaks, Hickory, Mulberry, Black walnut and other trees and shrubs, which are left standing in the old fields which are spread abroad to a great distance, and discover various monuments and vestiges of the residence of the ancients, as Indian conical mounts, terraces, areas &c. as well as remains or traces of fortresses of regular formation, as if constructed after the modes of European military architects, and are supposed to be ancient camps of the Spaniards who formerly fixed themselves at this place in hopes of finding silver. [This statement provides virtually the sole documentary evidence for major Indian and Spanish earthen constructions in the vicinity of Silver Bluff. In a very real sense, the later 19th-century and early 20th-century equation of the town of Cofitachequi with Silver Bluff originates with this description. Bartram's statement is puzzling from a late 20th-century perspective, since no archaeological evidence has been found from the Silver Bluff area to support the presence of either Spanish or late prehistoric Mississippian earthworks or even extensive occupation.]

Tumuli on Mason's Plantation

[Taken from *Antiquities of the Southern Indians, Particularly of the Georgia Tribes*, by Charles C. Jones, pp. 148–57, first published in 1873]

Tradition designates "Silver Bluff," or its vicinity, as the site of the ancient village of Cutifachiqui. There, if we rightly interpret the geography of the Fidalgo of Elvas, dwelt an Indian queen, young and attractive, who with royal hospitality welcomed to her capital and the freedom of her nation the adventurous De Soto and his daring companions, lone wandering and not yet lost amid the unbroken forests and howling wildernesses of a vast region hitherto untrodden by the white man.

No storied urn or monumental bust, no epitaph deeply graven on enduring marble, no sepulchral column, perpetrates her memory or her greatness; and yet certain tumuli, sternly wrestling with all-subduing time, lonely and voiceless in this generation, even now repeat the story of the Indian queen, whose cordial welcome of and generous hospitality to the adventurous, travel worn stranger, were requited by unkindness, ingratitude, and dishonor.

In 1776, Mr. Bartram [excerpt presented previously] states that there were in this vicinity what he is pleased to denominate Indian conical mounts, terraces, and areas, and also the remains or traces of fortresses which were supposed to be ancient camps of the Spaniards, who formerly fixed themselves at this place in the hope of finding silver.

It is not our purpose to pursue the track of the Spanish expedition, or to recount the traditions of the locality. Our object is simply to chronicle the existence and perpetuate the recollection of the prominent physical peculiarities of a marked group of ancient tumuli resting upon the left bank of the Savannah River, some twelve or fifteen miles [19.3 or 24.1 kilometers] by water below the city of Augusta. Thirty-five years ago [circa 1835] this group numbered six mounds, but the restless river, with recurring freshets, encroaching steadily upon the Carolina shore, has already rolled its turbid waters over two of them, while [an]other two have so far yielded to the leveling influence of the plowshare as to be almost entirely obliterated. [The 1853 Gilmer map of the Savannah River channel, the portion of which illustrates these mounds, is presented in figure 65. This map shows three mounds in this area, suggesting two had been plowed down in the 15 to 20 years from circa 1835 to the early 1850s.] Consequently but two remain, and they only in major part, one-third of each having been washed away by the current; and the day is probably not far distant when tradition only will designate the spot once memorable in the annals of a former race as the site of monuments of unusual size and interest. [Six mounds is the most recorded at any site along the Savannah, the next largest being Rembert with five. The reference to two mounds plowed flat suggests they were to the south of the two surviving mounds fronting on the river, between the mounds and the oxbow lake. The bases of these mounds may still be present under the alluvial deposits now blanketing this field. Likewise, traces of the apparent moat or ditch may also be present.]

These tumuli are located on Mason's Plantation, upon the very edge of the Savannah River, and in the midst of the wide, deep swamp, which here on either bank stretches away for miles, exhibiting one uniform, level, alluvial surface. What was once a mighty forest, grand and impenetrable in its majestic trees and tangled brakes, is now a rich cornfield whose harvests have for many years with a yield of a hundred-fold rewarded the toil of the intelligent husbandman. The

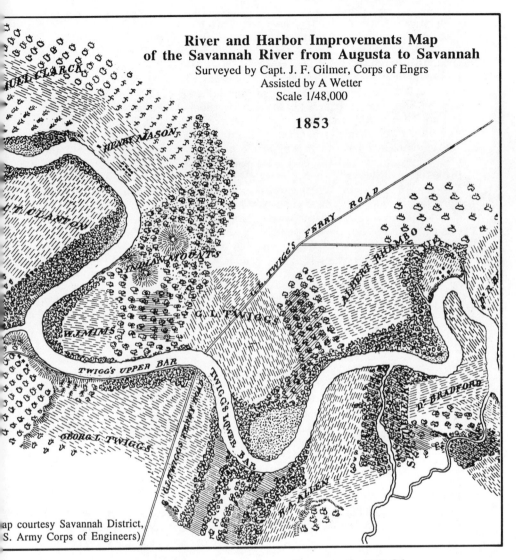

River and Harbor Improvements Map
of the Savannah River from Augusta to Savannah
Surveyed by Capt. J. F. Gilmer, Corps of Engrs
Assisted by A Wetter
Scale 1/48,000

1853

ap courtesy Savannah District,
S. Army Corps of Engineers)

Figure 65   The Mounds at Mason's Plantation, as Shown on the 1853 Gilmer
Navigation Map of the Savannah.

surrounding space being thus denuded of its original growth, the tumuli loom up
in uninterrupted proportions, while from the river, which has wellnigh cut them
in twain, the observer enjoys a most favorable opportunity, as presented by their
perpendicular fronts, for closely examining their physical composition. Freshets
have performed what it would have required long days of toil to have accomplished, and even then the work would not have been done half so well. It is sad
to realize, however, that these encroachments which at present bring hidden
things to view, and enable the examiner to pursue his investigations with facility,
are dooming the objects themselves to early and absolute annihilation. Some

forest-trees, chiefly beech and locust, still crown the summits and flanks of these fragmentary mounds trembling upon the brink of the remorseless river.

The largest tumulus, designated in the accompanying sketch by the letter A (Plate III) [figure 66 in this text], rises thirty-seven feet [11.3 meters] above the plain, and forty-seven [14.3 meters] above the water-line as it existed at the date of this visit. Measured east and west, its summit diameter was fifty-eight feet [17.7 meters], while, in consequence of the encroachment of the river, when measured in a northerly and southerly direction, it fell a little short of thirty-eight feet [11.6 meters]. Its base diameter, ascertained in an easterly and westwardly direction, was one hundred and eighty-five feet [56.4 meters]. Although its outlines have been somewhat marred by the whirling eddies of the river, as its swelling waters, in the spring of the year gathering marvelous volume and impetus, have again and again swept by, inundating the entire swamp-region, this tumulus may be truth-fully described as a truncated cone—its sides sloping gently and evenly, and its apex surface level [i.e., a flat-topped pyramidal temple mound]. If terraces ever existed, they are no longer apparent. The western flank of this mound was extended for a distance of some twenty yards [18.3 meters] or more beyond the point where it would otherwise have terminated, respect being had to the configu-ration of the eastern and southern slopes. About two feet [61 centimeters] below the present surface of this extension is a continuous layer of charcoal, baked earth, ashes, broken pottery, shells, and bones. This layer is about twelve inches [30 centimeters] thick. So far as our examination extended—and it was but partial—the admixture of human bones was very slight—the bones, of which there are vast numbers, consisting of those of animals and birds native to this region. One is at a loss to explain the existence of this stratum of charcoal, ashes, shells, fragmentary pottery and bones, unless upon the hypothesis that it comprises the debris of a long-seated encampment or permanent abode of the aborigines upon this little bluff. This stratum can be traced along the water-front of the mound, as though it existed prior to its construction. The superincumbent mass of earth seems to have been heaped above it. Where it penetrates the tumulus, it is wellnigh coincident with a prolongation of what was at the time the surface of the surrounding swamp. [This is an excellent early case of stratigraphic recording, including as it does the clear recognition of a premound midden layer extending under the main mound. Traces of this village midden may well remain in the surviving field.]

The mound itself is composed of the alluvium of the adjacent field, which is a micaceous clay, richly impregnated with vegetable mould. No traces of in-humation could be perceived, and the composition of the tumulus was homoge-neous as far as ascertained. [No obvious evidence for stages or use as a burial mound is indicated, suggesting fairly rapid construction.]

It is earnestly hoped that some one will carefully note from time to time the encroachments of the river, as in all likelihood the central portions of this mound will soon be laid bare, and then, its contents, if any, will be fully disclosed. Thus will an opportunity be afforded for a most satisfactory examination.

One hundred and twenty-five feet [38.1 meters] due east of this large tumulus, is the smaller mound designated by the letter B [figure 66 in this text]. Its appearance, general outline, and composition, are so nearly analogous to those of the larger mound, that a specific description is scarcely necessary. It may be remarked, however, that, possessing a base-diameter of one hundred and fourteen feet [34.7 meters], it rises fifteen feet [4.6 meters] above the surface of the ground and twenty-five feet [7.6 meters] above the level of the river.

It will be perceived by a reference to the accompanying sketch (Plate III) [figure

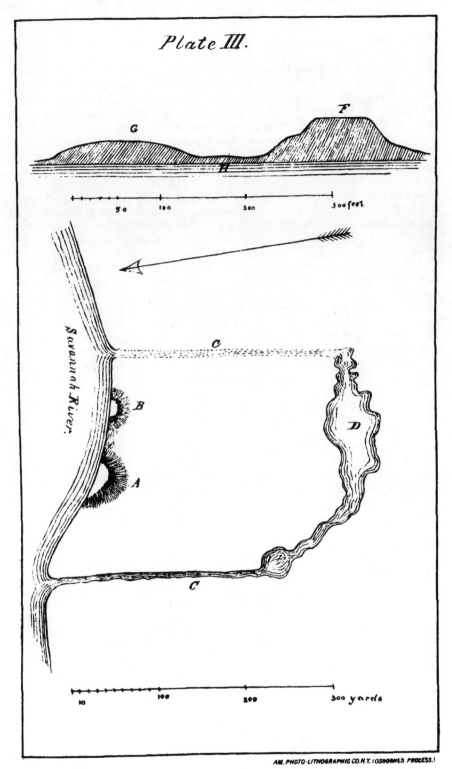

Figure 66 The Mounds at Mason's Plantation, as Reported by C. C. Jones in 1873.

66 in this text] that these tumuli were, in days long since numbered with an unrecorded past, isolated by a moat (C C), whose traces are still quite observable. The enclosed space—the river forming the northern boundary—contains a conjectured area of about eight acres [3.2 hectares; this is much smaller than the area between the oxbow and the river at present, which encompasses approximately 50 acres]. Commencing at the river, eastwardly of the smaller mound and distant from its flank some thirty yards [27.4 meters], this ditch extends in a southerly direction until it merges into what now seems to be a natural lagoon (D). Following this in a westwardly course, it finally leaves it, and thence runs almost due north to the river into which it empties at a remove of about eighty yards [24.4 meters] from the western flank of the larger tumulus. Here the communication with the river is still perfect, but the upper mouth of this moat is now dry. It varies in width from twenty to forty feet [6.1 to 12.2 meters], and is in some parts wider still.

In all probability the earth removed in the construction of this canal was devoted to the erection of these tumuli; and there are here and there in their vicinity physical evidences of the fact that the surrounding soil contributed to their further elevation. Terra-cotta vases, pots and pans, arrow and spear heads, stone articles of use and ornament, mortars, pipes, and bone and shell beads, are found in the adjacent fields, but there lives not a tradition of the time when, and of the tribes by whom, these tumuli were built. [The absence of a folk tradition of native habitation at the Mason Plantation mound group indicates it was abandoned prior to extensive European contact and exploration along the Savannah. Such extended contact postdates the 1670 English settlement of Charles Towne and suggests the site was abandoned prior to this time. No Savannah polity other than the intrusive Westo, visited by Woodward in 1673, is noted in the Charles Towne colonial records. Parenthetically, Cofitachequi, a comparable center located near Camden, South Carolina, was occupied in the 1670s and is repeatedly mentioned in the Charles Towne colony records. No such center is noted along the Savannah.] Lonely, storm-beaten, freshet-torn, they stand nameless and without a history in this generation—silent, yet convincing illustrations of the ephemeral character of the nomadic races which for centuries peopled this entire region, and, departing, left behind them neither rude letters nor monuments of art—nothing save these rude earth-mounds and occasional relics to give assurance of their former existence.

In the twilight of what by-gone and unrecorded century were these tumuli built? Whence came, and who the peoples that lifted them from out the bosom of our common mother? Served they as friendly refuge in seasons of freshet and of storm? [Probably, particularly for the elite.] Were sacred fires ever kindled upon your summits and within this consecrated area? [Almost certainly.] Within your hidden depths do the brave and honored of your generation sleep that sleep which knows no waking until the final trump shall summon alike the civilized and the savage to the last award? [Again, almost certainly so.] Or are ye simple watch-towers, deserted of your sentinels—forts, abandoned of your defenders? We question, but there are no voices of the past in the ambient air. We search among these tombs, but they bear no epitaphs. The sacred fires, if ever kindled, were turned into ashes long ago, and naught but darkness is here. [This perspective enables us to appreciate the accomplishments of modern archaeology, which have truly helped us to hear the voices of the past inhabitants of the basin.] We gaze upon these monuments, but they are inscriptionless, and the Savannah rolling its swollen waters about them will soon sweep even these mute earth-mounds out of existence. For a few short moments this tawny-hued river will grow more turbid with the dissolving mass of native clay, and then, borne away upon its bosom, and settling darkly in the depths of this swiftly moving stream, nothing will evermore be seen of these august witnesses of the memorable meeting between the Spanish Adventurer and the Cacica of the Savannah. [One can see from this passage how the episode of De Soto at Cofitachequi was romanticized in the 19th century by writers such as C. C. Jones, and how the equation of the Silver Bluff area with the location of Cofitachequi became entrenched in local folklore and ultimately scholarship.]

Silver Bluff and Mason's Plantation

[Taken from "Certain Aboriginal Mounds of the Savannah River," by Clarence B. Moore, pp. 167–68, first published in 1898]

In 1776, William Bartram saw a number of mounds at Silver bluff, about 27 miles by water below Augusta, of which no trace is now apparent. Colonel Jones describes large mounds on Mason's Plantation, below Augusta on the Carolina side, and examined a section of one which had been exposed by the river, finding no burials [C. Jones 1873:155]. He earnestly hopes that the mounds may be carefully watched during the process of destruction. All have totally disappeared. The archaeological examination of the Savannah river has been too long deferred.

The Hollywood Mounds

[Taken from Henry L. Reynolds's description of the fieldwork, summarized in *Report of the Mound Explorations of the Bureau of Ethnology*, by Cyrus Thomas, pp. 317–26, first published in 1894]

While this report was being prepared Mr. Henry L. Reynolds, one of my assistants, was sent to certain points in Georgia and South Carolina to make examination of some works to which my attention had been called. The result of this examination is given in the following report, made by him. This includes the Hollywood mound of Richmond County, Georgia, which proved to be of unusual interest, and the McDowell [Mulberry, 38Ke1] mound, Kershaw County, South Carolina.

The Hollywood Mound

There are two mounds situated in a bend of the Savannah river, in Richmond County, Georgia, 3 miles [4.8 kilometers] east from Hollywood, a small flag station on the Georgia Central railroad about 10 miles [16 kilometers] below Augusta and 5 miles [8 kilometers] above Silver bluff. This latter, which is on the South Carolina side, seems to me, after a special investigation of this question, to be the most probable site of the ancient town of Cutifachiqui, where De Soto and his army were so generously entertained. [No evidence for this investigation, which may have included fieldwork or interviews with local citizens, has been found. From the expressive wording, Reynolds may have been relying on C. C. Jones's 1873 account for this conclusion.]

The mounds are situated on the lowest river land, which is annually subject to inundation. The overflows of the Savannah are very destructive, particularly at this point. Cattle are drowned, the rich riparian crops are destroyed, and the farmers impoverished. At such times these mounds are the only land visible above a broad expanse of water, and it is this fact which has given rise to the tradition among people of the vicinity that they were thrown up by some former owner of the property to serve as places of refuge for his cattle during their inundations. [Extensive historic flooding and deposition in this area are indicated by the approximate 4 to 5 feet of sediments found by DeBaillou's excavations at Hollywood in the 1960s.] A quarter of a mile [0.4 kilometers] to the north of the mounds near the river bank is an extensive shell heap, composed chiefly of the shells of Unio. Upon the larger of the two mounds [mound A, which DeBaillou examined in the 1960s] a simple barn has been erected. This mound appears to have been originally of the pyramidal type, but since its surface has suffered so greatly from the cattle that have been penned in upon it and the washing occasioned by floods, its original character, as well as whatever smaller physical features it may have presented, is now almost entirely lost. [It appears that the upper portion of the mound has seen considerable damage, possibly removing most of the evidence for one or more of the final stages.]

Mound No. 2, the one excavated [mound B], is in an adjoining field, the property of a gentleman of Augusta, Georgia. It is 280 feet [85.3 meters] due north of No. 1, is conical in form, 10 feet [3 meters] high, and 70 feet [21.3 meters] in diameter. Though originally surmounted by a small log barn, which a former flood removed to a point at its base, the mound has evidently remained unmolested since that time, for several small cottonwood trees, as well as considerable underbrush, were growing upon it. [From this description, it is evident that both mounds had historic structures on them at one time. Mound A appears to have been a pyramidal platform mound, possibly a substructure mound, while mound B, from its conical shape, may have been a burial mound. Given the conversion of the platform mound at Irene to a conical burial mound during the Irene I occupation, the same thing may have happened to mound B, since the upper surface was intruded by a number of Irene burials.]

The excavation was conducted as follows: First two trenches, each 10 feet [3 meters] wide, were cut crosswise through the center, one north and south, the other east and west. These were carried down to the bottom, and in some places to the original pure micaceous soil that underlies the mixed loam of the surrounding field. The segments that remained were then cut down several feet beyond the radius that covered the interments found in the trenches. In this manner the mound was thoroughly excavated and all its buried contents exposed. [From this description, it is probable, as DeBaillou noted in his 1965 report, that portions of the mound margin were left intact, and any burials placed around the margin would have been missed.]

The mound is stratified, or, in other words, constituted of two different kinds of soil, the upper being strictly sandy micaceous loam, 3 feet [91 centimeters] thick; the lower a hard, compact vegetable earth, taken from what is commonly called in the south "crawfish land." This rested at the bottom upon 9 inches [23 centimeters] of a very black and rich vegetable mould, permeated throughout with innumerable small pieces of burnt pottery, charcoal, shell, mica, chipped flint, and charred and decayed bones too small for identification. The surface of this black mold appeared to be the original surface upon which the mound was built. [A rich premound midden, apparently with well-preserved paleosubsistence remains, underlay mound B.]

All the interments lay within the lower division of the mound [initial stage or stages built during the Savannah occupation]. The absence of burial in the upper division, the different character of the earth, and the presence of fragmentary pottery (N.M. 135278–84) unlike that found in the subsoil, seems to indicate a subsequent addition. It also seems to indicate that the original builders or others who succeeded them were disposed to utilize these their old tombs for some purpose in connection with floods, for this additional earth seems to have been cast upon the mound to increase its elevation. [Given the different character of the soil in the upper mound division and the presence of historic artifacts in its fill, as described below, it appears that the upper part of the mound dates to the postcontact period and probably after circa 1750, when the area was settled; see also Anderson 1990c for a detailed discussion of this interpretation.]

It will also be seen from the sectional diagram that there were two general series of interments which comprise the find, or rather the important contents of the mound. The lowermost of these contained specimens either resting on the black mold at the bottom or within a foot and a half [46 centimeters] above it, and the upper from a foot to 2 feet [30 to 61 centimeters] below the line separating the two strata, or from 4 to 5 feet [1.22 to 1.52 meters] below the surface of the mound. [Given that the mound was approximately 10 feet, or 3 meters, high, the two burial episodes in the lower division were thus separated by approximately 2 to 3 feet, or 61 to 91 centimeters, and probably come from stages missed in the fieldwork.] Fire played some part in the ceremony of burial, for hearth remains of burnt earth and ashes were seen with each series of burials. [This suggests that the two groups of burials may have been placed inside structures that were covered over, with only the central (?) hearth and a few posts detected in the fieldwork.] These burials were made before the subdivision was finally completed; in other words, they were not intrusive, for there was no disturbance of the soil above them. [This statement, if correct, may indicate that the Irene I peoples using the site, who placed the series of urn and other burials that make up the interments in the upper part of the lower division, built this part of the mound. An alternative interpretation would be that some or all of these burials were intrusive.]

Scattered indiscriminately throughout the soil composing the upper division of the mound were the following articles: One stone chisel (N.M. 135271), one stone celt, eight small pieces of white and blue glazed European crockery (N.M. 135279), many small fragments of Indian ware, and five pieces of old-fashioned rudely wrought iron nails much oxidized (N.M. 135280). These appeared to have been thrown up with the earth in the construction of this part of the mound. [From this statement, the upper division of the mound would appear to have been built during the historic period and to have made use of soil containing both European and Indian midden debris. The European artifacts, particularly the crockery, which may be delft or pearlware, will need to be examined to determine its precise age. This evidence and the absence of native American burials in the upper division reinforce the interpretation that it is of historic age.]

In the subsoil the hearth A (Figure 196)[figure 67, top, in this text] was first discovered almost touching the line of division [i.e., it was found just below the surface in the upper part of the lower construction division]. It was of reddish burnt earth, covered with pure wood ashes and a small quantity of charcoal. It was 5 feet [1.52 meters] in diameter, 2 feet [61 centimeters] thick, and rested at the bottom on fine sand. [The size and thickness suggest it saw extensive use; comparably sized hearths were found on the summits of several of the stages in the primary mound at Irene.] Adjoining it on the southeast lay a large culinary pot (N.M. 135205), indicated on the diagram (Fig. 196) [figure 67] as No. 1, the rim being 10 inches [25 centimeters] below the line dividing the lower from the upper strata and 3 feet 10 inches [1.17 meters] below the surface of the mound. Decomposed animal matter was found in the bottom mingled with scattered particles of

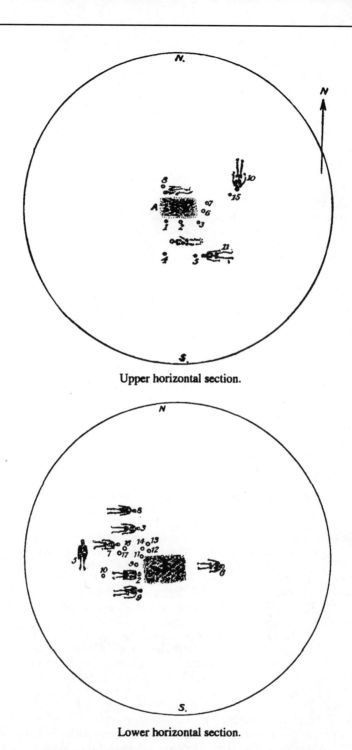

Upper horizontal section.

Lower horizontal section.

Note: Numbers refer to artifacts discussed in the text.

(Source: C. Thomas 1894:320–321)

Figure 67 Mississippian Burials at the Hollywood Site (9Ri1). (Courtesy Smithsonian Institution Press)

black and white ashes. [The presence of bone suggests the vessel was interred with food inside or may have been a human burial.] One foot and a half [46 centimeters] east from pot No. 1, on the same level, lay another pot, 2 (N.M. 135209), having inside of it another pot (N.M. 135208). In consequence of their inferior composition, badly decayed condition, and the pressure of the hard superincumbent earth, these vessels were so badly injured that they fell apart when taken out. Almost alongside of the last, on the same level, lay another, 3 (N.M. 135211), inside of which was an inverted pot (N.M. 135210). Decayed animal matter, a few bone beads, a fragment of the tooth of some animal, and some scattered charcoal cinders were found in the bottom. [This suggests that the vessel contained a food offering or, given the beads, a human burial, possibly that of a child, in light of the poor condition of the bone.] In the earth alongside of these pots was found a piece of iron (N.M. 135275). Directly south of pot No. 1, on the same level, 6 feet [1.8 meters] distant, lay another pot (N.M. 135212). In the earth surrounding it were found pieces of white European porcelain (N.M. 135279, Fig. 197 [figure 68, upper left, in this text]). [The presence of European artifacts with the burials and vessels in the upper part of the lower construction division suggests either that intrusion and disturbance from the historic construction division occurred immediately above this level or that the native burials and associated artifacts date to the historic period. Given the fact that the associated vessels apparently date to the early Irene period, this latter explanation is considered implausible. The fact that more historic artifacts, described below, were found at and just below the boundary between the upper and lower construction divisions further supports the dating of the upper stage to the historic period and the probability that the highest deposits in the lower stage were disturbed somewhat during the historic period.] East of this last, 6 feet [1.8 meters] distant, lay a small pot, 5 (N.M. 135198). The rims of these two pots appeared to be about on the same level. Not far from pot No. 5 were the decayed remains of a repoussé figured copper plate (N.M. 135226) so thin and brittle that it was with difficulty that it could be handled without breaking. Alongside were the faint indications of human burial, as seen in small pieces of decayed bone and human teeth. Between these last and those indicated by the figures 1, 2, 3 was a scant line of decayed bone, so scant and decayed that it was impossible to tell whether or not it was human. Traces of fire were seen about these bones. North of these traces of bone, and immediately under the line of pots Nos. 1, 2, 3, were three small upright timber molds, varying from 1 to 1 1/2 feet long [30 to 46 centimeters; these posts are presumably from a structure atop this mound stage]. No traces of the timbers remained. Apparently lying on the dividing line between the two strata, 14 feet [4.3 meters] northwest of the center, was the fragment of an old drawing knife (N.M 135261). A rude old iron nail, very much oxidized, was found on the surface of the subsoil, 3 feet [91 centimeters] deep and 12 feet [3.7 meters] southwest of the center. Another rude though sharp-pointed ancient iron nail was found not far from the last, but eight inches [20 centimeters] below the surface of the subsoil. A small piece of green glass was found three inches [7.6 centimeters] below the surface of the subsoil, in the southwest segment and east of the hearth. [The presence of these historic artifacts, clearly located at the base of the upper construction division and up to several inches below the surface of the lower division, permits the dating of the upper deposit to the historic period and indicates that the materials in the lower deposit were disturbed somewhat, as noted previously.] Resting on the sand that seemed to stretch over the entire area beneath these pots and the fire bed between them were the pots indicated by Nos. 6 (Pl. XIX, N.M. 135192) [figure 69 in this text; this vessel is an Irene filfot stamped jar with reed punctated nodes and dates to the

348   *Appendix A*

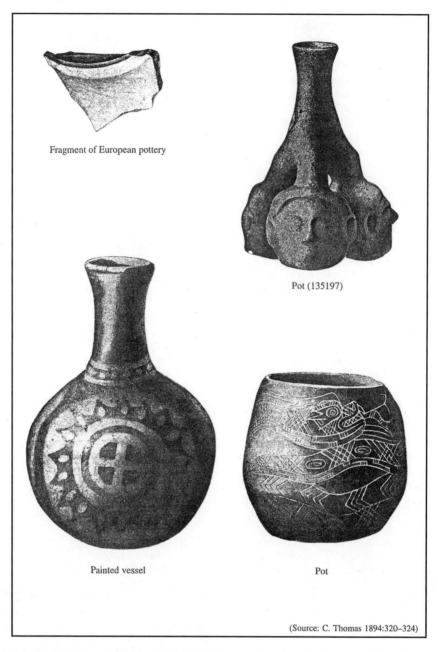

Fragment of European pottery

Pot (135197)

Painted vessel

Pot

(Source: C. Thomas 1894:320–324)

Figure 68   Artifacts from the Hollywood Mound. (Courtesy Smithsonian Institution Press)

(Source: C. Thomas 1894: plate 19)

Figure 69   Pee Dee/Irene Filfot Stamped Vessel from the Hollywood Mound.
(Courtesy Smithsonian Institution Press)

Irene I/Hollywood phase from circa 1300 to 1400] and 7 (N.M. 135200). A large
bowl (N.M. 135199) was found inside of pot No. 6, and by the side of the two
vessels, at the bottom, were the scanty remains of some fabric [this description
suggests a covered urn]. Two feet 8 inches [81 centimeters] from the surface of the
mound were the remains of decayed timber, which ran down about 1 1/2 feet [46
centimeters] to the east of the pot at 6, almost touching its eastern rim. It is not
unlikely that this was the remnant of some post planted on the surface of the
mound by some of its white owners [more evidence for historic period intrusion
into the upper part of the lower construction division and for historic construction
atop the final mound].

Alongside of the northwestern edge of the hearth A was a line of decayed
bones, which, from the small pieces of skull and two or three teeth that remained,
were found to be human. Though in the very last stages of decay, the remains were

so remarkably meager as to give the impression that all the bones of the body could not have been buried. The soil about all of the bones found in this upper layer was absolutely free from any trace of animal or vegetable matter, which leads to the opinion that the bones were buried after having been denuded of flesh. [This level of detail indicates the care with which Reynolds conducted his excavation. Whether his interpretation is correct or not remains unknown, but the example is a testimony to his powers of observation and reasoning.] A pot, No. 8 (N.M. 135193), lay close to the skull remains thus found. Like pots 1, 6, and 8, it had a small hole in the bottom, but had another sturdier pot (N.M. 135200) placed within it. [This indicates the occupants of the site occasionally "killed" their pots, something also noted in Pee Dee vessels from the Town Creek site, as documented by Reid (1965, 1967).] Seven and a half feet [2.3 meters] to the northeast of the fire bed, on a level apparently 5 inches [12.7 centimeters] lower than that of the pots heretofore described, lay pot No. 15 (N.M. 135213). Near it to the northeast were the remains of human bones (No. 10).

In the lower division, as in that last described, all the articles seemed to be clustered about a hearth B [figure 67, bottom, in this text] and on the same general level [i.e., suggesting most of the burials were all placed about the same time]. Here most of the human remains were found, but, like those in the upper burial, only the merest traces were observed. The conditions of this locality are very conducive to decay. Decayed and meager as they were, sufficient evidence was had in the case of each skeleton to show that it was human, such as the presence of teeth and certain identifiable bones.

The hearth B, which in some places was 10 feet [3 meters] in diameter, was situated wholly southwest of the center. [The large size of the hearth and the layering within it (see below) again suggests intensive use, possibly within a structure missed in the fieldwork. Its off-center location suggests the size and orientation of the mound shifted somewhat during later construction, most probably during the historic addition that gave the mound its final shape.] Its composition was peculiar. It consisted of four layers of pure white ashes each one-half inch [1.27 centimeters] thick, separated by red burnt earth averaging an inch [2.54 centimeters] in thickness. Ashes formed the bottom as well as the topmost layer. The hearth rested on the curious black mold at the bottom [i.e., a premound midden?]. This black mold did not penetrate to the north and east border of the mound, but lay only over an area of which this hearth was the center. [This suggests the black staining may have been associated with a structure of some kind, possibly a public building later covered over by mound fill.]

Southwest of the hearth B and in connection with the remains of skeleton No. 2 was pot 9 (N.M. 135197), a bottle standing on a tripod of human heads, shown in Fig. 199 [figure 68, upper right, in this text; this vessel resembles forms from the central Mississippi Valley and may come from there]. As traces of fire were noticed above this pot and skeleton, there seems to have been more than one ceremony attendant upon the burial of these articles. The pot 10 (N.M. 135194), which was found at the foot of this skeleton, seemed to have had originally a wooden cover, for in the earth taken from the top some small traces of decayed wood were noticed, and in the earth about it lay a clay pipe (N.M. 135223). Northeast of pot No. 9, and also near the fire bed, was a long-neck jar, 11 (N.M. 135295). (See Fig. 200) [figure 68, lower left, in this text; this vessel also resembles forms from the central Mississippi River valley, specifically Sikeston Negative Engraved from southeastern Missouri]. At its western base lay the pipes (N.M. 135216, 135218, 135219, 135220, 135222), five typical forms of which are shown in Pl. XXIV [figure 70 in this text]. Pipe 3a and 3b (135216) was carved from soapstone; the remainder

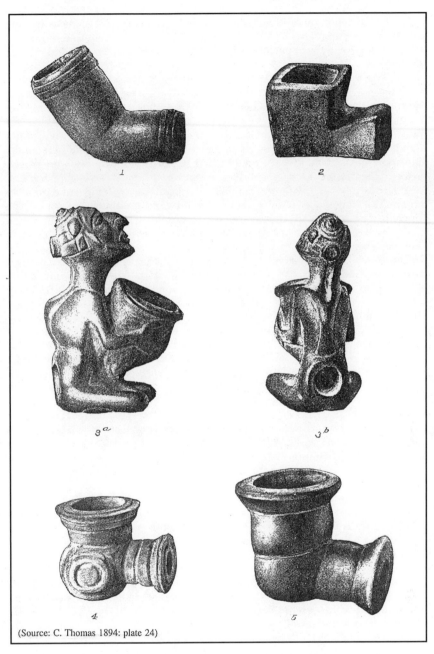

(Source: C. Thomas 1894: plate 24)

Figure 70 Pipes from the Hollywood Mound. (Courtesy Smithsonian Institution Press)

are of clay. Adjoining these articles on the northeast and on the same level were pots 12, 13, and 14 (N.M. 135196, 135204, 137215), and 6 inches [15 centimeters] below the former lay a copper ax head (N.M. 135228) wrapped in cloth and incased in bark.

Three or 4 feet [0.91 or 1.22 meters] west of these, lying against each other, were two other pots, 16 and 17 (N.M. 135202, 135203). No. 16 (Fig. 201) [figure 68, lower right, in this text; this vessel is engraved with a plumed serpent motif, whose design and execution has affinities with Moundville vessels as well as vessels found at Spiro, with some specific design motifs exactly duplicated on artifacts found at the latter site (Phillips and Brown 1978:194–95)] was found lying on its side upon the black mold at the bottom, and beneath it, as if the pot were placed on top of them, were the fragments of thin and very brittle plates of copper (N.M. 135227), bearing Mexican figures in relief [i.e., falcon warrior images and possibly a cat mask], some flakes of mica, and decayed pieces of unidentified shells. The copper had been originally first wrapped in some kind of leather, then in fine, rush matting, and whole incased in bark. Beneath No. 17, which was also lying on its side, was a beautiful biconcave disk of quartz (N.M. 135260). Beneath this last, 3 or 4 inches [7.6 or 10 centimeters] deeper, and lying on the black mold at the bottom, were two copper celts (N.M. 135229) wrapped in cloth together and incased on both sides in bark. Accompanying this were several large pieces of mica. There were scarcely more than a handful of decayed bones in connection with these objects, identifiable only by the help of a few human teeth.

About the neck bones of skeleton 3, which lay 13 feet [4 meters] northwest of the center, were found a lot of shell beads (N.M. 135247, Fig. 202) [figure 71 in this text], and below these, a foot [30 centimeters] to the south, another lot of shell beads (N.M. 135242), a lot of perforated shell disks (N.M. 135248), the copper-sheathed ornament of wood (N.M. 135256) shown in Fig. 203 [figure 71 in this text; this appears to be an ear ornament], and a lump of galenite.

Immediately north of the remains last described, on the same level and about 15 feet [4.6 meters] northwest of center, lay the bones and teeth of what seemed to be another skeleton (No. 8). With it were found the lot of shell beads (N.M. 135233) shown in Fig. 204 [figure 71 here], a copper ax or celt incased in wood (N.M. 135232), the decayed remains of the columella of the Busycon perversum, and a lump of soggy glauconite.

Nothing was found with skeleton No. 9, which lay southwest of the fire bed and near to skeleton 2 on the south, except a pipe (N.M. 135224). [This suggests the individual was of lower status than the four previous interments.]

Skeleton No. 5 lay about 23 feet [7 meters] west of the center, almost on the black mold at the bottom, and near its head were found a pipe (N.M. 135217), representing the head of an owl (Fig. 205) [figure 71, lower left, in this text]; one decayed shell ornament, three stone celts, five discoidal stones, an anomalous stone implement, and a lump of glauconite. The apparent remains of another human burial were seen to the east of the hearth (skeleton No. 6), and near the teeth was discovered a well-shaped stone celt.

A pipe (N.M. 135225) was found in the earth two feet [61 centimeters] to the south of hearth B.

The piece of blue porcelain (N.M. 135279) shown in Fig. 206 [figure 71, lower right, in this text] was found 4 feet [1.22 meters] southwest of the center and six feet [1.8 meters] beneath the surface of the mound. [This would suggest the blue porcelain sherd came from about 1 foot, or 30 centimeters, below the boundary between the upper and lower divisions of the mound, within the zone of historic disturbance. All of the artifacts from the excavation, both historic and prehistoric,

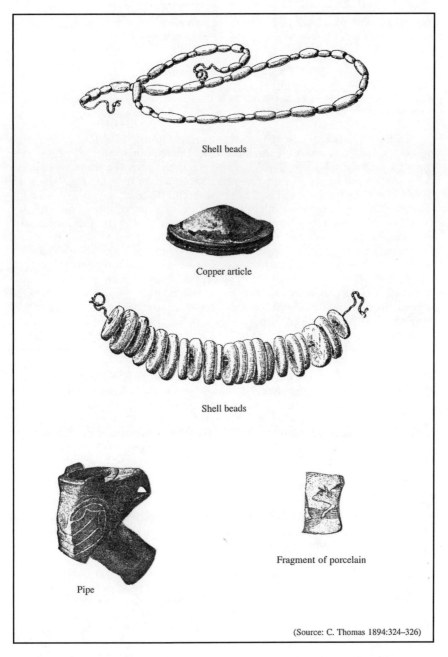

Shell beads

Copper article

Shell beads

Pipe

Fragment of porcelain

(Source: C. Thomas 1894:324–326)

Figure 71   Artifacts from the Hollywood Mound. (Courtesy Smithsonian Institution Press)

need to be reexamined to date precisely the activities documented archaeologically and the nature of these activities themselves (Anderson 1990c).]

The Rembert Mound Group

[Taken from *Travels through North and South Carolina, Georgia, East and West Florida, the Cherokee Country . . .* , by William Bartram, pp. 324–26, first published in 1791]

I made a little excursion up the Savanna river [spring 1776], four or five miles [6.4 or 8 kilometers] above the fort [Fort James Dartmouth, at the confluence of the Broad and Savannah rivers], with the surgeon of the garrison, who was so polite as to attend me to shew me some remarkable Indian monuments, which are worthy of every travelers notice. These wonderful labors of the ancients stand in a level plain, very near the bank of the river, now twenty or thirty yards [18.3 or 27.4 meters] from it; they consist of conical mounts of earth and four square terraces, &c. [what is meant by this reference to "four square terraces" is unclear, unless the presumed plaza area in front of the mound was bounded or elevated in some way]. The great mount is in the form of a cone, about forty or fifty feet [12.2 or 15.2 meters] high, and the circumference of its base two or three hundred yards [183 or 274 meters; it is obvious from these statements that no effort was made to obtain precise measurements, or even close approximations using pacing or similar procedures], entirely composed of the loamy rich earth of the low grounds; the top or apex is flat; a spiral path or track leading from the ground up to the top is still visible, where now grows a large, beautiful spreading Red Cedar (*Juniperus Americana*) there appear four niches, excavated out of the sides of this hill, at different heights from the base, fronting the four cardinal points; these niches or sentry boxes are entered into from the winding path, and seem to have been meant for resting places or lookouts. [The mound appears to be a pyramidal substructure mound. The spiral path leading to the summit is a feature also seen on the primary mound at the Lamar site near Macon. Whether this is a historic feature, perhaps to facilitate access to the summit, is unknown. The niches are a curious feature seemingly without parallel; if not historic potholes, they may have indeed served as sentry posts. The idea that they served as resting places seems improbable.] The circumjacent level grounds are cleared and planted with Indian Corn at the present, and I think the proprietor of these lands, who accompanied us to this place, said that the mount itself yielded above one hundred bushels [3,523.8 liters] in one season [this seems improbable but at least suggests the summit and perhaps even the slopes were in cultivation]: the land hereabouts is indeed exceeding fertile and productive.

It is altogether unknown to us, what could have induced the Indians to raise such a heap of earth in this place, the ground for a great space around being subject to inundations, at least once a year, from which circumstance we may conclude they had no town or settled habitations here [probably wrong]: some imagine these tumuli were constructed for lookout towers. It is reasonable to suppose, however, that they were to serve some important purpose in those days, as they were public works, and would have required the united labor and attention of a whole nation, circumstanced as they were, to have constructed one of them almost in an age. There are several less ones round about the great one, with some very large tetragon terraces on each side, near one hundred yards [91 meters] in length, and their surface four, six, eight, and ten feet [1.22, 1.8, 2.4, and 3 meters] above the ground on which they stand.

We may however hazard a conjecture, that as there is generally a narrow space or ride in these low lands, immediately bordering on the rivers bank, which is eight or ten feet [2.4 or 3 meters] higher than the adjoining low grounds, that lie betwixt the stream and the heights of the adjacent main land, which, when the river overflows its banks, are many feet under water, when, at the same time, this ridge on the river bank is above water and dry, and at such inundations appears as an island in the river. Now these people might have had a town on this ridge, and this mount raised for a retreat and refuge in case of inundations, which are unforeseen and surprise them very suddenly, spring and autumn. [Bartram appears to be suggesting native settlement may have focused on the levee crest, to avoid flooding. The levee would have been the driest area within the floodplain. Bartram's explanation, however, does not help us understand why people lived here, since it would have presumably been easier to live in the adjoining uplands than build elaborate refugia in the floodplain.]

Ancient Tumuli on the Savannah River,
Visited by William Bartram, in 1776
(The Rembert Mounds)

[Taken from *Annual Report of the Board of Regents of the Smithsonian Institution . . . for the Year 1877*, by Charles C. Jones, pp. 283–86, first published in 1878]

Near the close of a spring day in 1776, Mr. William Bartram, who, at the request of Dr. Fothergill, of London, had been for some time studying the flora of Carolina, Georgia, and Florida, forded Broad River just above its confluence with the Savannah, and became the guest of the commanding officer at Fort James. This fort was situated on an eminence in the forks of the Savannah and Broad, equidistant from those rivers, and from the extreme point of land formed by their union [figure 72 in this text; the mounds are shown in relation to 1870s settlements]. Fort Charlotta [later excavated by Caldwell (1974)] was located about a mile [1.6 kilometers] below, on the left bank of the Savannah. The stockade of Fort James was an acre [0.4 hectare] in extent.

Attended by the polite surgeon of the garrison, Bartram made an excursion up the Savannah River, "to inspect some remarkable Indian monuments" four or five miles [6.4 or 8 kilometers] above the fort. Of them he writes as follows: [see the first paragraph from Bartram reprinted above] . . . .

Unable satisfactorily to determine the precise object the aborigines had in contemplation in the erection of this striking monument, he hazards the conjecture that the Indians formerly possessed a town on the river bank, and raised this mound "as a retreat and refuge in case of inundations, which are unforeseen, and surprise them very suddenly, spring and autumn." What were the uses of the smaller elevations he does not suggest.

Wishing to note the changes which might have occurred during the past hundred years, we visited these tumuli a few weeks since [circa 1876]. The attendant mounds, which are mainly grave-mounds, had been materially wasted by the plowshare and the influences of the varying seasons. The tetragon terraces had lost their distinctive outlines, and were little more than gentle elevations; their surfaces littered with sherds of pottery and flint chips, and occasionally with fragments of human bones. Freshets had sadly marred the level of the adjacent space. Overleaping the river bank, the turbid waters had carved deep pathways in the surface of the valley on both sides of the "great mount." There it remained,

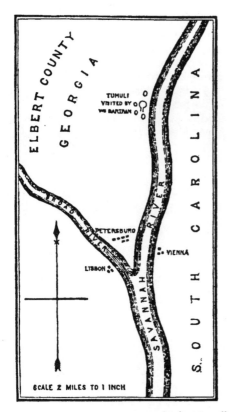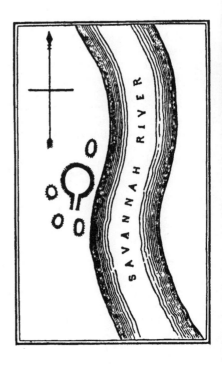

Ancient tumuli on the Savannah River.

(Source: C. Jones 1878:283–84)

Figure 72   The Rembert Mound Group in the 1870s. (Courtesy Smithsonian Institution Press)

however, wholly unaffected by these unusual currents. It had evidently suffered no perceptible diminution in its recorded dimensions. The Savannah River still pursued its long-established channel, but "the four niches or sentry-boxes," if they formerly existed, were entirely gone, and of "the spiral path or track leading from the ground up to the top" we could discover no trace. [Given the reference to cultivation of the mound below, this is not a surprising observation if plowing had occurred.] On the south a roadway, about 15 feet [4.6 meters] wide and commencing at a point some distance from the base of the mound, leads with a regular grade to the top. This manifestly furnished the customary means of ascent, as the sides are too precipitous for convenient climbing. This feature seems to have escaped Mr. Bartram's observation. [This may refer to a ramp, something indicated in figure 72 here, or it may be a recent construction.]

Not having been cultivated for many years, the apex and sides of this truncated cone are now clothed in a luxuriant growth of trees and swamp cane. Attired in such attractive garb, this tumulus forms a marked object in the profile of the valley from which it springs. Proofs of long-continued occupancy, by the aborigines, of the adjacent territory are abundant. Ancient burial-places, the sites of old villages, traces of open-air workshops for the manufacture of implements of jasper, quartz, chert, greenstone, and soapstone, refuse piles, and abandoned fishing resorts [presumably this refers to weirs in the river], are by no means infrequent along both banks of the Savannah River. Upon the advent of the European the circumjacent valley was found cleared and in cultivation by the red men, who here had fixed abodes and were associated in considerable numbers. [Here Jones seems, given the following references to the 16th century and De Soto, to be referring to the De Soto expedition and to his erroneous belief that the well-populated province of Cofitachequi was along the Savannah. There is no evidence for appreciable 16th-century native occupation of this portion of the Savannah River valley.] The Southern tribes, in the sixteenth century, subsisted largely upon maize, beans, pumpkins, and melons. These they planted, tended, and harvested regularly. Of their agricultural labors at the dawn of the historic period we have full accounts.

So vast are the proportions of this largest mound that we are persuaded it rises beyond the dignity of an artificial place of retreat, elevation for chieftain-lodge, or mound of observation.

It appears entirely probable that it was a temple-mound, built for sun-worship, and that it forms one of a well-ascertained series of similar structures still extant within the limits of the Southern States. These Florida tribes, as they were called in the days of De Soto, worshipped sun and were frequently engaged in the labor of mound-building [a fact not widely acknowledged in the 19th century]. Over them ruled kings who exercised powers well-nigh despotic. Often were the concentrated labors of the nation directed to the accomplishment of allotted tasks. Hence, within the territory occupied by these people, we find many traces of early constructive skill of unusual magnitude.

The material employed in erecting this large tumulus differs from the soil of the surrounding bottom. It is a dark-colored, tenacious clay, while the surface of the valley is covered with a micaceous loam readily dissolving into an almost impalpable powder. Near by are no traces of pits or excavations [but see Thomas's 1894 comment below]. Nor are there indications that any earth was scraped up around the base. These facts afforded confirmation of the statement made by the present owner of the plantation upon which these tumuli are located, that the big mound had been built with clay brought from the Carolina side of the Savannah River. There clay abounds; and we were informed that in the side of the hill immediately opposite, the excavations may still be seen whence the tough material was obtained for heaping up this mound. This tumulus is one of the finest within the limits of Georgia, and should be classed with the truncated pyramids on Tumlin's plantation in the Etowah Valley, with the largest of the East Macon mounds, and with that frustum of a four-sided pyramid on Messier's place, in Early County.

The Rembert Mounds

[Taken from John P. Rogan's description of the fieldwork, summarized in *Report of the Mound Explorations of the Bureau of Ethnology*, by Cyrus Thomas, pp. 315–17, first published in 1894]

These mounds were visited by Bartram in 1773 [the correct date is 1776], who describes them: [see the first paragraph from Bartram reprinted above] . . . .

In 1848 George White (author of White's *Statistics of Georgia*) visited this group, in regards to which he remarks as follows:

> The large mound corresponds exactly with Bartram's description of it, with this exception, that the sides and summit are covered with a growth of cane and several large trees. The smaller mounds have been almost destroyed. Capt. Rembert has excavated the smaller mounds and found human skeletons, jars, pipes, beads, breastplates [of copper?], stone hammers, hatchets, arrowheads, etc. Some of these are now in our possession and are really objects of curiosity.

If these descriptions were correct at the time they were made, very decided changes have taken place in the appearance of the works since then. The group, consisting of 2 mounds, is situated on the farm of Mr. Z. A. Tate, near the bank of the Savannah river, 4 miles [6.4 kilometers] above the mouth of Broad river. They stand on the level bottom, one 130 and the other 390 feet [39.6 and 118.9 meters] from the bank of the river. This bottom extends several miles north and south, and three-fourths of a mile [1.2 kilometers] back from the river to the hills. As will be seen by reference to Fig. 193 [figure 73, top, in this text], which shows a section, north and south, of the area, there are 2 "washouts" flanking these mounds. The one on the north (a), commencing at the river, extends a fourth of a mile [0.4 kilometers] back in a southwest direction, covering an area of 7 or 8 acres [2.8 or 3.2 hectares]. This approaches within about 200 feet [61 meters] of the large mound (b). The one on the south (c) also commences at the river and extends back southeastward only a few hundred feet beyond the mounds and runs within a few feet of them. These excavations are denominated "washouts" because the present owner of the land, Mr. Tate, remembers when they were made by high water. Nevertheless, judging from present appearances, there are reasons for believing that at least a portion of the earth used in the construction of the mounds was obtained here, leaving depressions, and that, during high water, when the land was overflowed, as is frequently the case, channels were washed out from them to the river. The south margin of the southern "washout" is fully 4 feet [1.22 meters] higher than the land on which the mounds stand.

Mound No. 1.—This, which is much the larger of the two, stands 130 feet [39.6 meters] from the river bank, and is, exclusive of the ramp or projection, an exact circle 151 feet [46 meters] in diameter, nearly flat on top, and 30 feet [9.1 meters] high at the highest point (north side), but only 27 feet [8.2 meters] near the south side. The diameter of the top is about 70 feet [21.3 meters]. The plan of the ramp or rather extension, as it seems to be, is shown in Figure 194 [figure 73, middle, in this text]. The vertical outline of the mound, with a section of the shaft, is presented in Fig. 195 [figure 73, bottom]. The right or southern end of this shows the slope of the extension. This has an average width on top of 20 feet [6.1 meters].

The mound is covered with trees such as sugarberry, walnut, hickory, and oak. One sugarberry is 6 feet [1.8 meters] in circumference (at stump height); a walnut, 5 feet [1.5 meters]; a hickory, 3 1/2 feet [1.06 meters]; and an oak, 10 feet [3 meters]. [This strongly suggests the mound summit was not cultivated, contrary to the implication in the Jones account, circa 1877.] The shaft was carried down to the bottom. The first foot [30 centimeters] was of soil (a), then 7 feet [2.1 meters] of dark sandy loam (b), next 1 1/2 feet [15 centimeters] of thoroughly burned yellowish clay and sand (c), with a large percentage of ashes. This layer had the appearance of having been put down and packed while wet and then burned; it was so hard that it was difficult to break it. Next 3 feet [91 centimeters] of black earth also

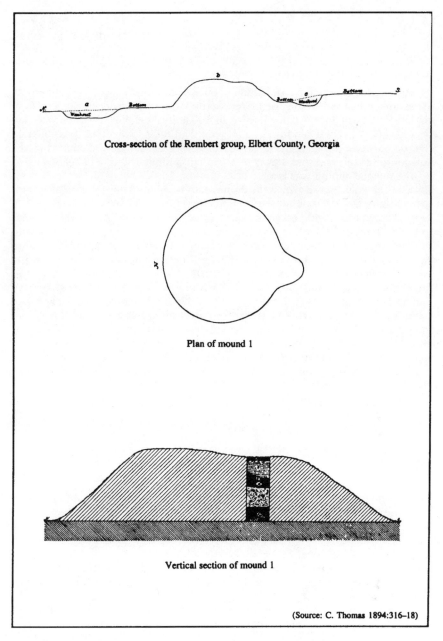

Cross-section of the Rembert group, Elbert County, Georgia

Plan of mound 1

Vertical section of mound 1

(Source: C. Thomas 1894:316–18)

Figure 73   The Rembert Mound Group in the 1880s. (Courtesy Smithsonian Institution Press)

packed (d); then 8 1/2 feet [2.6 meters] of pure sand (e); and last, resting on the original surface, 6 feet [1.8 meters] of hard bluish muck (f). All of these layers, except the bottom one, had charcoal, mica, fragments of pottery, and animal bones scattered through them, but the last were so far decomposed that none of them could be saved.

As fragments of pottery and animal bones were found in spots, together with ashes and other indications of fire, it is probable these were fire beds where cooking had been done. All that portion of the shaft below the layer of burned clay was so very dry that when turned up it would crumble to dust. It is possible that the bottom layer of blue "muck" is partly the original soil, as it is much like the surrounding soil, and that a part of the surrounding surface has been washed away since the mound was built.

Mound No. 2 (not shown in the figure) stands about 40 feet [12.1 meters] west of the base of No. 1. It is oblong in form, 58 feet [17.7 meters] long north and south, 41 feet [12.5 meters] wide, and 6 feet [1.8 meters] high. A large shaft had been sunk in the middle by some previous explorer, hence investigations were confined to the eastern and western sides, which presented one or two peculiarities. With the exception of the top layer of soil, 1 foot [30 centimeters] thick, the remainder on the east side consisted of river sand, with particles of charcoal and vegetable matter mixed through it, while on the west it was composed of small masses of red clay and dark earth. In this, at a depth of 2 1/2 feet [76 centimeters], were the bones of a single adult skeleton. These were packed together in a space 2 feet [61 centimeters] square and 18 inches [46 centimeters] deep; the skull was placed face down and all the other bones piled about it. Immediately over the bones was a layer of red 2 inches [5.1 centimeters] thick, burned hard. Resting on this layer were remains of a pretty thoroughly burned fire. A few fragments of pottery and a small clay pipe were found.

Tugalo

[Taken from John P. Rogan's description of the fieldwork, summarized in *Report of the Mound Explorations of the Bureau of Ethnology*, by Cyrus Thomas, pp. 314–15, first published in 1894]

But one mound in this county was examined. This is situated on the farm of Mr. Patton Jarrett, in the western part of the county, on the south bank of Tugalo River, one-fourth of a mile [0.4 kilometer] above the mouth of Toccoa Creek. It is conical in form, the base almost exactly circular, precisely 100 feet [30.5 meters] in diameter, and a little over 14 feet [4.3 meters] high. The owner would permit no further examination than could be made by sinking one shaft. [This shaft may be one of the units marked "Treasure hunter #1" and "Treasure hunter #2" on Caldwell's 1956 plan of mound stage 1, illustrated in figure 32 in this text.] Nothing further than the stratification was ascertained, which is as follows: (1) top layer, 2 1/2 feet [76 centimeters] of soil similar to that of the surrounding surface, but with a quantity of charcoal scattered through it; (2) a layer 1 inch [2.54 centimeters] thick of charcoal; (3) 6 inches [15 centimeters] of dark red clay or muck; (4) 2 feet [61 centimeters] of sandy loam; (5) 6 inches [15 centimeters] of bright red, very hard, clay, apparently sun-dried; (6) 4 feet [1.22 meters] of dark, rich loam, with a little charcoal scattered through it; (7) 6 inches [15 centimeters] of dark clay or muck; (8) 6 inches [15 centimeters] of sandy loam; (9) 2 feet [61 centimeters] of dark, rich loam; and, lastly, resting on the original surface, 2 feet [61 centimeters] of river sand. In the sixth and ninth layers were a few fragments of pottery.

Keowee

[Taken from *Travels through North and South Carolina, Georgia, East and West Florida, the Cherokee Country* . . . , by William Bartram, pp. 332, 372, first published in 1791]

There are several Indian mounts or tumuli, and terraces, monuments of the ancients, at the old site of Keowe, near the Fort Prince George, but no Indian habitations at the present . . . . [Bartram appears to be referring to the low circular burial mounds at the I. C. Few site, one of which was examined by Grange (1972) in 1967, during investigations in the Keowee Reservoir. If other earthworks or mound were present, they appear to have been reduced in the intervening years.]

I observed in the environs of Keowe, on the bases of the rocky hills, immediately ascending from the low grounds near the river bank, a great number of very singular antiquities, the work of the ancients; they seem to me to have been altars for sacrifice or sepulchres; they were constructed of four flat stones, two set on an edge for the sides, one closed one end, a very large flat one lay horizontally at top, so that the other end was open; this fabric was four or five feet [1.22 or 1.52 meters] in length, two feet [61 centimeters] high, and three [91 centimeters] in width. I enquired of the trader what they were, who could not tell me certainly, but supposed them to be ancient Indian ovens; the Indians can give no account of them; they are on the surface of the ground and are of different dimensions [features possibly related to stone mound burials along the upper Oconee in Georgia, or stone box graves in Tennessee?].

Mississippian Cultural Sequences in the Savannah River Valley

Fine-grained late prehistoric cultural sequences have been developed in three parts of the basin (figure 18). Because these sequence differ appreciably in the lower, central, and upper portions of the valley, these areas are discussed separately. At present, thanks to an extensive history of research, temporal resolution on the order of 100- to 150-year intervals is currently possible in most areas. While these intervals will need to be and in fact are continually being narrowed, they are sufficiently fine grained enough to permit the detailed examination of local Mississippian political change. Absolute chronological control for these sequences has been provided by a number of radiocarbon dates (Hally and Rudolph 1986:21–26; these dates are, however, in need of updated calibration) and by the cross-dating of materials from sequences developed in nearby areas of South Carolina, Georgia, and North Carolina.

In the South Appalachian area, the complicated stamped pottery tradition established in the Woodland period continued into the Mississippian, and variations in design motif, rim treatment, and other incidental decoration have proved to be highly sensitive chronological markers. Rim modification has proved particularly important. A sequence of unmodified to collared rims, to rims with rosettes or punctations, and then to applied and pinched rim strips is evident over much of the region (Hally and Rudolph 1986:63; Reid 1967; J. Rudolph 1983; M. Smith 1983). While plain (unmodified) rims continue to occur, the incidence of folded and punctated, pinched, or notched rim strips increases over time in the region, with the later treatments typically larger and more poorly executed. This phenomenon was originally noted by A. Kelly (1938:48) at Macon Plateau and by Caldwell and McCann (1941:41) in the Irene mound report, where "transitional" rim forms belonging to the period between the Savannah and Irene occupations were illustrated. It has recently been documented in Mississippian assemblages from central South Carolina (DePratter and Judge 1990; South 1973; Stuart 1975). Finally, in central Georgia, J. Rudolph and Blanton (1980:16) have documented an increase in rim strip width over time, and both M. Smith (1981:185–88) and J. Rudolph (1983:90–93) have documented an increase in finger pinching and a decrease in punctation over time.

Design motifs are also useful for identifying assemblages to specific periods (figure 74). Some complicated stamped motifs, such as Irene filfot crosses or line blocks, have fairly tight temporal occurrences. A decrease in check stamping, to give another example, is well documented over the course of the Mississippian along the Savannah, both at the mouth and well into the interior (DePratter 1979:111; J. Rudolph and Hally 1985). Some caution is essential, however. Recent work along the upper Savannah and Oconee rivers indicates that some supposedly "diagnostic" design motifs—such as nested diamonds, which are traditionally linked with Etowah/Early Mississippian components—actually occur somewhat later in time as well (Anderson, Hally, and Rudolph 1986:38; Hally and Rudolph 1986:37–51; M. Smith 1981:182–86, 1983:75–81). Care must thus be used when dating local assemblages, and large sherd samples are essential for fairly precise age determinations. In spite of these limitations, well-documented ceramic sequences have been produced for the Savannah, upper Oconee, and upper Wateree river valleys in recent years (Anderson 1987b; Anderson, Hally, and Rudolph 1986; DePratter 1979, 1991b; DePratter and Judge 1990; Hally and Rudolph 1986; J. Rudolph and Hally 1985; Sassaman and Anderson 1990; M. Smith 1981, 1983; M. Williams and Shapiro 1987).

The discussion that follows focuses on ceramics, since these artifact types have been found to be chronologically sensitive. Traditional taxonomic categories and temporal assignments have been noted for each period as appropriate. Specific types and varieties employed here follow criteria reported in previous ceramic analyses conducted within the Savannah River basin and immediately adjoining areas. The emphasis on ceramics, it should be noted, is the result of necessity, not choice. Attempts to use other artifact categories to date components, such as pipes and projectile points, have had little success so far (Anderson n.d.; J. Rudolph and Hally 1985:287–95), although temporal trends may be present within these artifact categories that may ultimately prove of chronological value. A decrease in the size of triangular arrow points has been documented between the Late Woodland and Mississippian period, for example, in the Coastal Plain portion of the drainage (Sassaman et al. 1990), although, unfortunately, no such changes have been observed in the small triangular points that characterize Mississippian occupa-

---

Key for Figure 74 (pages 364–365)
Late Woodland/Mississippian Complicated Stamped Design Motifs Found in Savannah River Basin

Swift Creek series
1   snoeshoes
2   concentric circles with cross-in-circle
3   concentric circles with rectilinear design
4   spirals
5   concentric loops or "owl eye"

Napier series
6   zigzag multiline strands with block filler
7   multiline strands crossing over each other, with block filler
8   combination curvilinear/rectilinear multiline strands

Woodstock series
9   barred oval (curvilinear designs)
10 barred rectangle/diamond (rectilinear designs)

Etowah series
11 nested diamonds -1 bisecting line
12 nested diamonds - 2 bisecting lines
13 nested diamonds - 2-bar
14 nested diamonds - 3-bar
15 nested diamonds - 1 horizontal, 1 vertical bisector
16 nested diamonds - 2-bar cross
17 nested diamonds - 3-bar horizontal, 2-bar vertical bisector

Savannah series
18 concentric circles - bulls eye
19 concentric circles - hollow center
20 concentric circles - 1 bisecting line
21 concentric circles -1 horizontal, I vertical bisector
22 concentric circles - 2-bar cross
23 figure 8
24 keyhole
25 figure 9/nested P's
26 interlocking circles

Irene series
27 filfot cross
28 filfot scroll
29 line block
30 line block/nested squares

Lamar series
31 nested rectangles/frets with cross
32 herring bone
33 herring bone, bisected
34 nested T
35 arc-angle
36 nested squares

Pisgah series
37 ladder

Irene/Lamar series
38 brackets and circles
39 scrolls
40 brackets and ovals
41 line-filled triangles
42 nested triangles

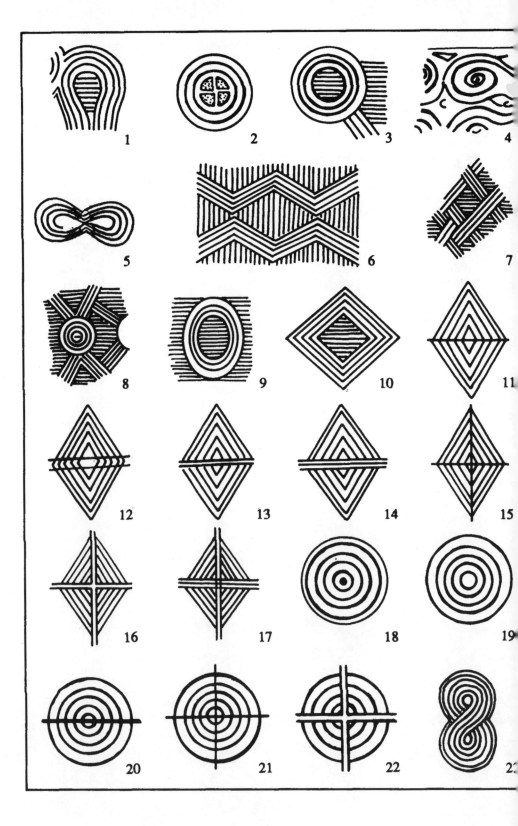

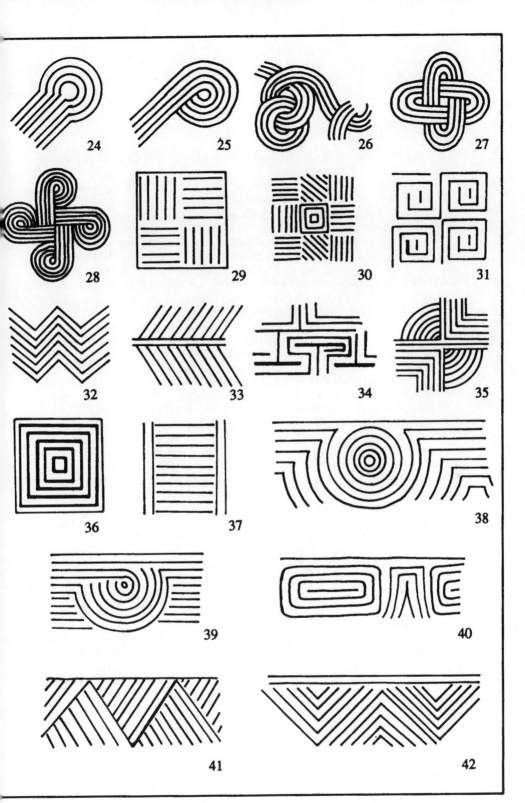

tions in the drainage. Pipe forms are also thought to have temporal significance, but to date little attention has been directed to these artifact types.

The Mississippian Ceramic Sequence
in the Lower Savannah River Area

Background

Arthur Kelly (1941:vi), in the foreword to the Irene mound report, noted that "the importance of the Lower Savannah Basin in southeastern archaeology can hardly be overemphasized." During the WPA era, extensive excavations were conducted at a number of Late Archaic through Mississippian period sites near the mouth of the Savannah River in Chatham County, Georgia. This work, at Bilbo, Deptford, Oemler, Irene, and other sites in the area, enabled Caldwell and Waring (1939a, 1939b; Waring 1968d) to devise a prehistoric ceramic sequence for the lower Savannah drainage. The basic outline of this sequence, encompassing the Stallings, Deptford, Wilmington, Savannah, and Irene series in chronological order from earliest to latest, was established at this time.

Described as "one of the finest local sequences based on stratigraphic evidence that exists in southeastern archaeology" (S. Williams 1968:101), the mouth-of-the-Savannah sequence has seen only minor revision in the intervening half-century since its formulation, including the addition in the late 1940s of the Refuge series, intermediate between Stallings and Deptford (Waring 1968e), and the addition in the early 1970s of the St. Catherines series, intermediate between the Wilmington and Savannah series (Caldwell 1971:91; DePratter 1979:119, 131–32). In 1979, DePratter presented a detailed overview of the sequence, with a description of many of the types used to define periods. Since then, only minor revisions to the Mississippian portion of the sequence have been proposed, specifically that the Savannah Check Stamped and Complicated Stamped types appear to have had a longer duration (Anderson, Hally, and Rudolph 1986:42–44; but see DePratter 1991b:157–93). For the later prehistoric and protohistoric era, the sequence in its present form provides chronological control on the order of 150- to 200-year intervals for the period from roughly A.D. 800 to 1700. Until quite recently, the mouth-of-the-Savannah sequence was used, with varying degrees of success, throughout lower South Carolina and Georgia. As work has progressed in the region, however, the development of more applicable local sequences has occurred, eliminating the need for its application far afield.

The Lower Savannah Sequence

Late Woodland components in the extreme lower portions of the Savannah River basin are characterized by the lumpy, poorly finished clay/grog-tempered wares of the Wilmington and St. Catherines series and by intermediate-sized triangular projectile points (DePratter 1979). Clay/grog-tempered paste has rounded, subrounded, and irregular lumps of sherd, clay, or fired clay ranging in size from approximately 2 to 10 millimeters mixed into it. These inclusions typically differ appreciably in color and texture from the surrounding body of the sherd. Two Wilmington phases have been established in the mouth-of-the-Savannah sequence. The first, Wilmington I, dates from A.D. 500 to 600 and is characterized by clay/grog-tempered Wilmington Check Stamped, Heavy Cordmarked, and Plain and Walthour Complicated Stamped ceramics, the latter an apparent late Swift Creek variant. No interior equivalent for this phase has been observed, although there was undoubtedly a period when the manufacture of Deptford and interior Wilmington wares overlapped. Wilmington II–phase components, which date from circa 600 to 1050, are identified by the presence of Wilmington Plain, Brushed, Fabric-Marked, and Heavy Cordmarked pottery. The bold parallel cord-marked assemblages are particularly diagnostic of the period.

St. Catherines–phase assemblages, which date from circa 1050 to 1150 (DePratter 1991b:11), continue to be dominated by grog tempering, although the size of the temper inclusions decreases compared with the previous period. St. Catherines Plain, Burnished Plain, Fine Cordmarked, and Netmarked all occur, with the grog-tempered fine cross cord-marked the key diagnostic. Cord impressions are much narrower and more carefully executed than on the preceding Wilmington period vessels, and St. Catherines vessels are much better made than their Wilmington predecessors, with well-smoothed to burnished interiors. The only appreciable difference between St. Catherines and the succeeding Savannah I/II phase, which dates from circa 1150 to 1200, is a change from grog to sand tempering. While the Savannah I phase has been dated from 1200 to 1300 in DePratter's (1991b:11) most recent revision of this sequence, I believe the earlier range is more likely. Plain, burnished plain, fine cross cord-marked, and net-marked exterior finishes continue to be present, although they are now typed within the Savannah series, with Savannah Fine Cordmarked the key diagnostic. Net marking, a rare type during the St. Catherines phase, drops out in the Savannah I phase.

The Savannah II (1200 to 1250) and Savannah III (1250 to 1300) phases at the mouth of the river are distinguished by the appearance of check stamping and complicated stamping, respectively (DePratter 1979:111; his most recent revision of this sequence combines these phases and has them falling within a 25-year span from 1300 to 1325, an interval I find to be far too short). Savannah III Complicated Stamped pottery, which is dominated by curvilinear, concentric circle, or oval motifs, occurs in the first seven mound stages at Irene. It is highly unlikely that all of this construction occurred within a 50-year (much less a 25-year) period, that is, from 1250 to 1300, much less from 1300 to 1325. Likewise, it seems unlikely that the widespread occurrence of both Savannah Check Stamped and Savannah Complicated Stamped pottery in the lower basin reflects no more than a 100-year (much less a 25-year) period. A somewhat broader span for these phases, from circa 1150 to 1200 for Savannah I/II and from 1200 to 1300 for Savannah III, is proposed here.

The Irene I phase (1300 to 1400) at the mouth of the river is identified by the appearance of Irene Complicated Stamped pottery, characterized by filfot cross and line block motifs and a variety of rim decorative treatments (DePratter 1979:111; his recent revision has this phase dating from 1325 to 1425, which seems plausible, although slightly later than the range advanced here). Bold incising, a hallmark of later periods, appears for the first time, but in low incidence and with relatively simple one- to three-line designs placed just below the rim, primarily on bowls. Rim treatment has proved a particularly sensitive temporal indicator during this period. Plain folded rims occur in small numbers late in Savannah III, followed by hollow cane punctations and riveted nodes during the transition from Savannah III to Irene I, with rosettes and narrow folded rims with cane punctations and, rarely, finger-pinched appliquéd rim strips characteristic of Irene I assemblages. The mouth of the Savannah River was apparently abandoned by the end of the Irene I phase, since succeeding Irene II–phase (1400 to 1550) components, characterized by a marked increase in bold incising, are almost unknown.

Discussion

Although the broad outline of the late prehistoric cultural sequence in the lower Savannah River basin has been known for over half a century, room exists for considerable refinement, particularly determining precise periods of occurrence of specific surface finishes, design motifs, and rim treatments. While evidence indicates that folded and stamped or incised rims become more common on cord-marked vessels in later St. Catherines/Savannah I times, for example, this remains to be conclusively demonstrated. Likewise the temporal range of design motifs now used somewhat uncritically to identify phases, such as concentric circles, line blocks, and filfot crosses/scrolls or certain types of rim treatment, remains to be determined. Finally, the nature of occupation at the river mouth after 1450 needs to be resolved. While the area is thought to have been abandoned (Anderson, Hally, and Rudolph 1986), this remains to be fully documented.

Exactly how late Late Woodland assemblages, specifically those dominated by cord marking, persist in the lower and middle Savannah River valley is currently the subject of some debate. Along the southern coast, in Beaufort County, excavations at three sites on Pinckney Island tested and demonstrated the general utility of the mouth-of-the-Savannah sequence in that area (Trinkley 1981). The fieldwork did suggest that St. Catherines pottery, dated from 1050 to 1150 in the mouth-of-the-Savannah sequence, might occur as late as the 16th century in that area (Trinkley 1981:82; see also Braley 1983; Brooks 1983). Excavations at the St. Catherines/Savannah I period Callawassie Island burial mound (Brooks et al. 1982) have also suggested that an essentially "Woodland" burial tradition may have continued into the Early Mississippian period in the southern coastal area. Similar phenomena may have occurred in the middle Savannah River area, where it has been suggested that Woodland ceramics continued in use during and even after the period Mississippian chiefdoms occupied the area, from circa 1200 to 1600 (Mark J. Brooks, personal communication, 1990; see also K. Stephenson and King 1992). This inference, although unlikely, given the low incidence of cord marking in later Mississippian assemblages from the Middle Savannah, cannot be dismissed out of hand and will require testing. The relationships between Woodland and Mississippian occupations in the lower and middle Savannah drainage, particularly the mechanisms bringing about the transition between these seemingly markedly dissimilar forms of social organization and subsistence adaptation, will undoubtedly serve as a focus for much future research.

The Mississippian Ceramic Sequence in the Middle Savannah River Area

Background

Unlike the situation at the river mouth, where a lengthy and dynamic history of research has occurred, sequence development in the middle and upper part of the Savannah River basin was practically nonexistent prior to the 1980s. The only major attempt at sequence definition in the central portion of the drainage was conducted in the 1960s on Groton Plantation in Allendale and Hampton counties, South Carolina, by Stoltman (1974) and Peterson (1971a, 1971b). These investigations, which consisted of intensive excavations at two sites, Clear Mount and Rabbit Mount, and also survey and limited testing at approximately 20 other sites, provided a wealth of descriptive information on the kinds of ceramics present in the lower middle portion of the drainage. A major contribution of this research was the dating of Stallings and Refuge materials to between circa 2500 and 600 B.C. in this area and the description of the surface finishes and design elements in these early series. Unfortunately, comparatively little effort was directed to refining the later Woodland and Mississippian sequence, and materials of this period were interpreted using the sequence at the river mouth.

The ceramic sequence devised for the middle Savannah River encompasses late prehistoric occupations in the basin from the area just above the mouth to the Fall Line (figure 16). The distinctiveness of the area during the late prehistoric era is highlighted by a near-complete absence of grog-tempered Wilmington and St. Catherines ceramics and by the presence of upper valley attributes and assemblages mixed in among classic lower valley assemblages. The middle Savannah River sequence was developed in the mid-1980s (Anderson 1987b; Anderson, Hally, and Rudolph 1986, 1990), as part of an analysis of ceramics from the L-Lake project area on the Savannah River Site (excavations described in Brooks and Hanson 1987) and building on earlier observations about late prehistoric assemblages in this portion of the drainage (Caldwell 1952; Hally and Rudolph 1986; Reid 1965; Stoltman 1974). Subsequent analyses of additional assemblages from the Savannah River Site and elsewhere in the middle Savannah River valley have permitted some refinement of this initial formulation (Anderson 1990a; Sassaman and Anderson 1990).

The Middle Savannah Sequence

The early Late Woodland period (circa 500 to 800) in the middle Savannah River ceramic sequence is characterized by sand-tempered plain, cord-marked, and fabric-impressed pottery. The principal difference between the Late Woodland assemblages at the mouth of the river and those in the middle portion of the drainage lies in the type of temper employed in each area. Wilmington and St. Catherines series ceramics along the lower Savannah are characterized by clay/grog tempering, while assemblages in the interior are sand tempered. Clay/grog-tempered paste is extremely rare in the middle and upper Savannah River valley. No unambiguous diagnostic indicators exist dating assemblages exclusively to the early Late Woodland period, although sand-tempered cord-marked pottery characterized by closely spaced, carefully applied wide (greater than 2 millimeters) parallel impressions is common. The cord-marked material appears to be an inland equivalent of Wilmington Heavy Cordmarked, *var. Wilmington* observed at the river mouth. The cord width may be up to approximately 10 millimeters wide in extreme cases on this finish. Finer cord-marked pottery (less than 2 millimeters in width) characterized by cross and parallel stamped impressions may also occur as minority finishes. Stamping varies considerably in care and execution over these latter finishes. Rims tend to be unmodified, although narrow folds are sometimes observed. Sand-tempered fabric-impressed pottery occurs in some assemblages as a minority ware. No phase names have been assigned to the early Late Woodland period, which is provisionally described as an interior Wilmington equivalent.

The later Late Woodland in the middle Savannah falls within what is locally described as the Savannah I phase (circa 800 to 1100), an inland equivalent of the St. Catherines and Savannah I phases from the mouth of the drainage. Fine cross cord-marked sand-tempered pottery is common, characterized by closely spaced and carefully applied narrow (approximately 0.5 to 2 millimeters) impressions;

folded, incised, and stamped rims are sometimes observed and appear to become more common later in the period. Separation of St. Catherines equivalents
from Savannah Fine Cord-Marked, *var. Savannah* material is currently impossible
in the middle Savannah. Cord-Marked vessels found with Mississippian assemblages typically have highly smoothed or burnished interiors, but these are an
unreliable criteria to use with small samples. Other, minority finishes that may
occur include Santee Simple Stamped, *var. Santee,* fabric-impressed, and, possibly
late in the period, Savannah Check Stamped, although this finish is currently
placed in the subsequent Early Mississippian Lawton phase. Napier Complicated
Stamped and Woodstock Complicated Stamped ceramics also occur but are
extremely rare; these series are more common in the Piedmont portion of the
drainage (see below).

Early Mississippian (circa 1100 to 1250) occupations in the middle Savannah
River valley are roughly equivalent to the Savannah I–III phases at the mouth of
the river and the Jarrett/Beaverdam phases in the central Piedmont, differing only
in the incidence of certain finishes within assemblages. No formal phase names
have been assigned, although the occupations at the Lawton Mound group
suggest a provisional Lawton-phase designation for components of this period.
Diagnostic indicators include Savannah Complicated Stamped, Plain, Burnished
Plain, Fine Cordmarked, and Check Stamped. The Savannah series materials
typically have plain, unmodified rims lacking punctations, rosettes, or nodes.
Other finishes that may occur include plain (nonburnished) and, as a minority,
cross V-shaped simple stamping (Santee Simple Stamped, *var. Santee).* The Savannah Check Stamped, Cordmarked, and Burnished Plain types may occur earlier
than Savannah Complicated Stamped. Concentric circle motifs dominate the
complicated stamped assemblages, with one- and two-bar diamond (Etowah
motifs) less common.

The Middle Mississippian period in the middle Savannah River valley dates
from 1250 to 1450, during the Hollywood and (provisional) Silver Bluff phases.
Transitional Savannah/Irene or Early/Middle Mississippian assemblages in the
middle Savannah River valley are assigned to the Hollywood phase (1250 to 1350).
Savannah Check Stamped is common, followed by Mississippian Plain, Burnished Plain, and both Savannah and Irene Complicated Stamped, the latter
dominated by variations on the filfot cross motif. As at Irene during Caldwell and
McCann's (1941:41–42) contemporaneous "transitional" period, cane punctations
and riveted nodes with cane punctations are present. Corncob impressing occurs
in low incidence.

Assemblages reflecting a mixture of attributes from the Irene I phase at the
mouth of the basin and the Rembert phase in the central Piedmont appear
following the Hollywood phase, during what is here provisionally described as
the Silver Bluff phase (circa 1350 to 1450). Diagnostic indicators include Pee Dee/
Irene and Lamar Complicated Stamped pottery, characterized by modified rims
with punctations, rosettes, nodes, and, less commonly, folded rims or applied rim
strips. Rectilinear line blocks and filfot crosses and scrolls dominate complicated
stamped assemblages; less common motifs include the herringbone and arc-angle.
Other finishes present include burnished plain and check stamping, the latter in
low incidence. As at the mouth of the river, incising of any kind is rare, occurring
as simple one- to three-line designs below the rim of bowls and sometimes, in
conjunction with rim modification, on folds. The Silver Bluff–phase designation
for assemblages of this period is provisional. If ceramic collections can be obtained
from the area of the Mason's Plantation mound group, they may provide the basis

for establishing a local equivalent of the Irene I/Rembert phases that could be called either Silver Bluff or Mason's Plantation.

No assemblages that date to the Late Mississippian period (circa 1450 to 1600) are currently reported from the middle Savannah River. The middle and lower valley is assumed to have been unoccupied during this period, following the collapse of local chiefdoms. If occupations dating to this period are eventually documented, phase designation will be appropriate. Native settlement in the middle Savannah River valley resumed sometime after 1600, possibly as late as circa 1670, and continued until 1715, when these groups were destroyed in the Yamassee War (DePratter 1979). A number of Indian groups from widely scattered areas in the Southeast and the East lived along the drainage during this period, and the ceramic assemblages from these occupations are undoubtedly diverse, although to date they have been reported from only one site, Palachacolas Town (Caldwell 1948). Kasita Red Filmed, Walnut Roughened, and Ocmulgee Fields Incised pottery were found at Palachacolas Town (Caldwell 1948:322–24), and shell-tempered plain, brushed, and cord-marked pottery, presumably dating to this period, has been observed on a number of other local sites. The ceramic assemblages dating to this period are provisionally assigned to a Yamassee phase, although finer subdivision will undoubtedly occur as the sites of specific groups are examined.

Discussion

As with the mouth-of-the-Savannah sequence, while the broad outlines of the late prehistoric sequence in the middle Savannah are known, many details remain to be filled in. Late Woodland assemblages dominated by sand-tempered cord-marked pottery are widespread in the interior Coastal Plain along the Savannah River, both along the floodplain and in the interriverine uplands. Chronological control within local cord-marked assemblages is poor, however, with only a rough separation between earlier and later Late Woodland currently possible, made on the basis of cord size and the occurrence of cross stamping. There is some suggestion that rim and lip treatment has chronological significance, particularly in the Ocmulgee basin (Snow 1977; K. Stephenson 1990), but this remains to be explored locally. Late Woodland diagnostics prevalent in nearby areas, such as Swift Creek and Napier Complicated Stamped pottery, found primarily to the north of the Fall Line, and Santee Simple Stamped ceramics, which are common in central South Carolina, occur in low incidence along the middle Savannah and provide some basis for cross-dating occupations between these regions. These regional correlations are examined in the discussion of the upper Savannah River sequence.

The Mississippian cultural sequence in the middle Savannah River valley, as currently developed, provides chronological resolution on the order of approximate 150-year intervals. However, of the three mound groups present in this part of the drainage—Lawton, Mason's Plantation, and Hollywood—only the last has been examined in any detail. While Hollywood provides a baseline for identifying mid-13th- through mid-14th-century Middle Mississippian components, recognition of earlier and later components relies on the sequences developed at the mouth of the river and in the Piedmont and hence incorporate the strengths and weaknesses noted with these sequences. Considerable refinement of this sequence should be possible once sites dating to these periods are examined locally, particularly when and if assemblages can be obtained from Lawton and Mason's Plantation.

Late Mississippian and historic-period Native American occupation of the middle Savannah River is currently very poorly documented archaeologically. The area was apparently unoccupied until late in the 17th century, when the Westo and other groups, some intentionally relocated along the river to provide a buffer for the expanding South Carolina colony, are reported (DePratter 1988). Although the locations of a number of towns occupied after 1670 have been delimited, archaeological evidence for these historic Indian settlements is minimal. As noted, the only report on a postcontact Indian site in the middle part of the basin appeared in 1948, when Caldwell described a number of artifacts found in association with burials at the early Creek town of Palachacolas, located on the Savannah River in Hampton County, South Carolina (Caldwell 1948). This site was occupied by a group of Appalachicola Indians sometime between 1680 and 1716, when it was abandoned following the Yamassee War. Kasita Red Filmed, Walnut Roughened, and Ocmulgee Fields Incised pottery was found at Palachacolas Town, together with six shell-tempered sherds, four of them "decorated with a carelessly applied cord-wrapped stick or paddle" (Caldwell 1948:322–24). Glass trade beads, kaolin pipe fragments, European ceramics, and other historic artifacts were also found, intermingled with Indian shell beads and pottery. Shell-tempered pottery has been found in several other surface collections from the middle Savannah River valley, where it is assumed to reflect comparable early historic occupations. The documentation of these late occupations, however, remains a major research challenge.

The Mississippian Ceramic Sequence in the Upper Savannah River Area

Background

In the late 1970s and early 1980s, a detailed cultural sequence was developed in the upper Savannah River basin, as a direct result of the extensive archaeological investigations undertaken in the Richard B. Russell Reservoir (Anderson and Joseph 1988; Hally 1990). Prior to this time, no work directed to sequence definition had been done in this portion of the basin. The large-scale surveys that took place in the Clarks Hill, Hartwell, and Keowee-Toxaway reservoirs from the late 1940s through the late 1960s, unfortunately, were characterized by only minimal analysis and reporting. While intensive excavations were conducted in conjunction with these reservoir projects at the Chauga, Estatoe, I. C. Few, Lake Spring, Rembert, and Tugalo sites (Caldwell 1953, 1956; A. Kelly and DeBaillou 1960; A. Kelly and Neitzel 1961; Miller 1949), the reports that did appear were largely descriptive, with little emphasis directed to sequence definition or refinement. The sequence that has emerged in the upper Savannah River valley, while resting upon a considerable body of primary evidence, also owes a great deal to work conducted in three adjoining areas, in northern Georgia, south-central North Carolina, and western North Carolina.

Extensive archaeological survey and testing activity took place in northern Georgia during the WPA era and in the Allatoona Reservoir shortly after the Second World War, work that yielded the classic northwestern Georgia Kellogg-Cartersville-Etowah-Savannah/Wilbanks-Lamar ceramic and cultural sequence (Fairbanks 1950; Wauchope 1948, 1950, 1966). The northern Georgia sequence, as modified through the years by the inclusion of later Woodland/initial Mississippian series such as Swift Creek, Napier, and Woodstock and by better dating of the initial Woodland Kellogg series, continues to be a basic framework for identifying and dating ceramic prehistoric assemblages in northern Georgia and South Carolina (Bowen 1982; Caldwell 1957; Hally and Langford 1988; Hally and Rudolph 1986; Sears 1958; Wauchope 1966; W. Wood and Ledbetter 1988).

Under the direction of Joffre Coe and his colleagues at the Research Laboratories of Anthropology at the University of North Carolina, Chapel Hill, archaeological investigations have been carried out since 1937 at the Town Creek site, located on a tributary of the Pee Dee River in south-central North Carolina. The mound and associated stockaded village area, an enclosure encompassing approximately 2 hectares, have been almost completely excavated. The site assemblage was used to define the Pee Dee focus by Coe (1952:308–9), and the associated ceramics, formally described by Reid (1967) as the Pee Dee series, have since been recognized at sites across South Carolina, including within the Savannah River valley (Anderson 1975, 1982; Ferguson 1971; Reid 1965). Pee Dee series material, which has been dated to the 13th to 14th centuries (Dickens 1976:198), thus serves as a temporal benchmark for local Middle Mississippian remains. Recent descriptive and comparative analyses of Pee Dee materials from the Wateree Valley of central South Carolina, furthermore, are clarifying the placement of this series, and its associated decorative attributes, in the overall Mississippian sequence (DePratter and Judge 1986; DePratter 1987b).

Work in the Appalachian Summit area of western North Carolina, conducted in the 1960s and early 1970s, produced the third extralocal sequence that has been used with fair effect in the upper Savannah River basin (Dickens 1976; Egloff 1967; Keel 1976; D. Moore 1981; Purrington 1983). The ceramic prehistoric and protohistoric portions of this sequence encompass the Swannanoa, Pigeon, Connestee, Pisgah, and Qualla phases and accommodate at least some of the materials found on sites in northern and northwestern South Carolina. Swannanoa series ceramics are Early Woodland in age, appearing around 700 B.C. Pigeon series materials date to the initial Middle Woodland, while Connestee materials are of later Middle Woodland and possibly Late Woodland age. The Pisgah phase, which spans the prehistoric Mississippian period, remains to be subdivided but encompasses the immediate precursors of the historic Cherokee peoples, represented by the Qualla phase. The utility of this sequence in northern South Carolina remains to be determined, although it appears to work fairly well along the upper Savannah River (Anderson and Joseph 1988; Beuschel 1976).

In the early 1980s, the ceramic collections from the Rembert, Chauga, Tugalo, and Estatoe mound sites were reanalyzed by Hally, in conjunction with analyses of the collections obtained during the Russell Reservoir investigations, to develop a Mississippian sequence for the upper Savannah River (Anderson, Hally, and Rudolph 1986:38–42; Hally and Rudolph 1986; J. Rudolph and Hally 1985:261–80, 447–70). The massive, well-controlled excavation assemblage from the Beaverdam Creek mound, coupled with the collections from sites such as at Rucker's Bottom and Clyde Gulley and comparisons with assemblages from farther afield, provide the basis for this sequence. Documented Mississippian phases include Jarrett (circa 1100 to 1200), Beaverdam (circa 1200 to 1300), Hollywood (circa 1250 to 1350), Rembert (circa 1350 to 1450), and Tugalo (circa 1450 to 1600), followed in the colonial era by the Estatoe phase (circa 1700 to 1750). This absolute chronology is supported by a lengthy series of calibrated radiocarbon dates from the Savannah and, through cross-dating, from other nearby drainages (J. Rudolph and Hally 1985:462–70)(figure 16). The calibration used to delimit these phase ranges has recently been revised (cf., Ralph, Michael, and Han 1973; Stuiver and Pearson 1986), although inspection of these recalibrated dates indicates no major shifts. The Late Woodland portion of the sequence was developed by a number of investigators, again largely using materials from the Russell Reservoir (Anderson 1988a; Anderson and Schuldenrein 1985; T. Rudolph 1991; W. Wood et al. 1986).

The Upper Savannah Sequence

Late Woodland occupations in the upper Savannah River are currently unequivocally recognized by the presence of late Swift Creek and Napier ceramics. While Swift Creek ceramics have been documented from circa A.D. 100 to 750 in the Georgia area, enough work has been done to differentiate earlier from later assemblages within this series (A. Kelly and Smith 1975; T. Rudolph 1985, 1986; W. Wood et al. 1986:339). Late Swift Creek components in the upper Savannah River date from circa 500 to 750 and may occur slightly earlier. Some overlap of these Swift Creek (as well as later Napier and Woodstock) materials with Cartersville-like and Connestee Simple Stamped assemblages is indicated in the upper Savannah River basin, although the relationships between these series is not well understood at the present, either here or elsewhere in Georgia (Anderson 1990a:459–64; Elliott and Wynn 1991; Worth and Duke 1991).

Swift Creek ceramics, originally reported from the type site near Macon (A. Kelly and Smith 1975), are characterized by a wide range of complicated stamped design motifs and are common in southwestern Georgia and on the Florida Gulf coast, where they have been dated to between A.D. 100 and 450 at such sites as Mandeville (Betty Smith 1979b). Early Swift Creek ceramics are characterized by complicated stamped designs with concentric circles, ovals, and, usually, simple curvilinear design motifs. Rims are typically notched or scalloped, and tetrapods are common. The ware continues into the Late Woodland in central and northern Georgia, well after its replacement in the Gulf coastal region by Weeden Island types (Milanich and Fairbanks 1980; Willey 1949). Along the upper Savannah River, Swift Creek and later Napier finishes are present but not widespread, and they are extremely rare along the middle and lower Savannah (DePratter 1979; Hanson and DePratter 1985; Stoltman 1974).

Late Swift Creek ceramic assemblages, which date from circa A.D. 500 to 750, were defined in large part through work with materials from the Swift Creek and Kolomoki sites (A. Kelly and Smith 1975; Sears 1956). These assemblages are characterized by an increase in the incidence of plain pottery and folded rims, a decline in the incidence of notched and scalloped rims, and more complex complicated stamped designs with some zoned stamping. A fine-lined variant of Swift Creek, called B-Complex to differentiate it from classic southern and central Georgia materials, was defined by Caldwell in the Buford Reservoir on the upper Chattahoochee River (T. Rudolph 1991; W. Wood et al. 1986:340–41). This material, which seems transitional between Swift Creek and Napier, appears to be a regional variant and is most commonly found in the northern and eastern Georgia Piedmont, including within the Russell Reservoir (T. Rudolph 1986; W. Wood et al. 1986:340–41). Similar Swift Creek/Napier materials were found at the Anneewakee Creek site in northwestern Georgia, where uncorrected dates of 1345±85 B.P. (GX-2825, calibrated circa A.D. 664; Stuiver and Pearson 1986:812, 832) and 1195±110 B.P. (GX-2826, calibrated circa A.D. 820, 845, or 855; Stuiver and Pearson 1986:812, 831) were reported (Dickens 1975:36, 38). Late Swift Creek components in the upper Savannah River date from circa A.D. 500 to 750 (calibrated) and may occur slightly earlier. The Late Swift Creek materials were infrequently found in the Russell Reservoir and, based on excavations at Simpson's Field (38An8), were provisionally given an Anderson-phase designation (W. Wood et al. 1986:342), although this appears premature, given how little is actually known about these occupations (Anderson 1988a:247).

Later Late Woodland components (circa 750 to 900) in the upper Savannah River are identified by the presence of Napier ceramics, originally recognized during the excavations at Macon Plateau in the 1930s. These ceramics are characterized by narrow, well-executed rectilinear complicated stamping and a typically dark gray to black color, suggesting firing in a reducing atmosphere (Caldwell 1957:313–14, 1958:44; Fairbanks 1952:288; A. Kelly 1938; Wauchope 1948:204, 1966:57–60). Overlap with both earlier Swift Creek and later initial Mississippian Woodstock series ceramics has been documented at a number of sites (Wauchope 1966:60–63, 437–38), suggesting the series represents terminal Woodland occupations in the area. Napier ceramics are uncommon in the vicinity of the upper Savannah River basin (Ferguson 1971:67; Garrow 1975:24; Keel 1976:221; T. Rudolph 1986). No formal phases have been assigned to this period in the upper Savannah River valley.

In the upper Savannah River, initial Mississippian Woodstock components (circa 900 to 1100) are identified by the presence of Woodstock Complicated Stamped ceramics, which have been shown to be ancestral to Etowah in northwestern Georgia (Sears 1958). Like the preceding Napier and Swift Creek series, Woodstock assemblages are infrequent in the upper Savannah River, and no major components have been excavated (Anderson 1988b). Sites of the succeeding Jarrett phase (1100 to 1200), which has been documented at the Chauga, Clyde Gulley, and Tugalo sites, are characterized by Etowah Complicated Stamped (primarily variations on the nested diamond motif), check-stamped, and red-filmed ceramics. Complicated stamped designs are dominated by rectilinear motifs; corncob impressions around vessel necks and shoulders and collared rims forms occur in low numbers. While corncob impressing is observed on some sites in the Coastal Plain, collared rims appear restricted to above the Fall Line.

The ensuing Beaverdam phase (1200 to 1300) is comparable in many ways to the Lawton phase in the middle part of the drainage (Anderson, Hally, and Rudolph 1986:38–40; Hally and Rudolph 1986:61–62; J. Rudolph and Hally 1985). Beaverdam-phase components have been examined in some detail at the Beaverdam Creek and Rucker's Bottom sites. The incidence of Etowah Complicated Stamped declines appreciably and red filming disappears. Check stamping increases and Savannah Complicated Stamped appears, with concentric circles the most common motif. The incidence of curvilinear design motifs increases markedly, while the incidence of collared rims (with notched, fine incised, or punctated designs) and corncob impressing increases slightly. The Hollywood phase (circa 1250 to 1350), which overlaps with the Beaverdam phase, is sometimes used to characterize transitional Beaverdam/Rembert-phase assemblages in the upper part of the drainage (Anderson, Hally, and Rudolph 1986:40–41; Hally and Rudolph 1986:62–63). Transitional assemblages were noted at Rucker's Bottom, although the incidence of check stamping was far below that noted at Hollywood.

During the Rembert phase (1350 to 1450) in the upper Savannah River, assemblages were characterized by Lamar Complicated Stamped pottery, with both curvilinear and rectilinear motifs present (Anderson, Hally, and Rudolph 1986:41–42; J. Rudolph and Hally 1985:456–59). Design motifs included concentric circles, figure nines, filfot crosses, line blocks, and herringbones. Check stamping nearly disappears, while Lamar Bold Incised makes its first appearance, albeit in low incidence. Incised vessels dating to this period are characterized by simple designs formed using typically two or three broad lines. Cane punctations, rosettes, and nodes continue on vessel rims, and finger pinching appears. Rims included both folded and unfolded forms, and narrow appliquéd strips appear. Rembert components have been identified at Rembert, Rucker's Bottom, and Tugalo.

Late prehistoric/protohistoric Tugalo-phase (1450 to 1600) components in the upper Savannah are characterized by Lamar Complicated Stamped and Lamar Incised pottery (Anderson, Hally, and Rudolph 1986:38–42; Duncan 1985). The complicated stamped design motifs are similar to those from the preceding Rembert phase, although the stamping is larger and more carelessly applied. The incised ware, in contrast, has more complex designs than during the preceding period, made from a larger number of narrower lines. Folded and pinched rims dominate jar assemblages, and rim fold and appliquéd strip width increases over earlier periods (J. Rudolph 1983:90–93). Red filming again appears as a minority ware. Tugalo-phase components are restricted to the extreme upper reaches of the Savannah River, where they have been identified at Chauga, Estatoe, and Tugalo. Mississippian groups present in the upper Savannah River valley during this period may have been the ancestors of the groups of the Lower Cherokee towns found in this area at the end of the 17th century by European explorers and traders.

No phase designation has as of yet been assigned to materials dating from 1600 to 1700 in the upper Savannah River. Materials from the Dillard Mound on the Little Tennessee River in Rabon County, Georgia, appear to date to this period, however, and may provide the basis for eventual phase definition (David J. Hally, personal communication, 1990). Using materials from the Chauga, Estatoe, and Tugalo sites in the extreme upper reaches of the Savannah River, Hally (1986a) defined the historic Cherokee Estatoe phase (1700 to 1750). Estatoe-phase assemblages are dominated by Lamar Complicated Stamped and Lamar Incised and simple stamped, check-stamped, plain, and burnished plain ceramics (Hally 1986a:98–111). Hally's detailed summary of Estatoe phase ceramics represents a refinement and improvement over Egloff's (1967) Qualla phase, which was formulated using ceramics from these same sites but was based on ceramics now known to span the 15th through 18th centuries.

Discussion

Even after the Russell Reservoir investigations, knowledge about the Late Woodland in the upper Savannah River remains the subject of considerable ambiguity, in large measure because components of this period appear to encompass presumably earlier simple stamped as well as the more readily identifiable Swift Creek and Napier Complicated Stamped finishes (Anderson 1988a:245–47; 1990a:459–64; Anderson and Schuldenrein 1985:338–65; W. Gardner 1984:48–61; W. Wood et al. 1986:339–43). The cultural sequence for the period after circa 1000 in the upper Savannah River, as developed by Hally, fortunately, is much better grounded and permits the dating of most assemblages to within approximate 100-year intervals, the finest-grained temporal resolution currently available in the basin. As in other portions of the basin, however, considerable work remains to be done tying down design motifs and decorative treatments in space and time. In some cases, this necessitates revising cherished assumptions. As an example, nested or cross diamond motifs, traditionally associated with Etowah components in the South Appalachian area, have recently been found to encompass a much broader temporal range. They are common during both the Jarrett and subsequent Beaverdam phases in the upper Savannah, although a decrease in incidence is evident. The nested diamond motif also continues to occur in post-Etowah-period assemblages in the middle Oconee drainage (M. Smith 1981:183–84, 1983). At the Dyar Mound, nested diamonds were reported as the most common motif throughout both the Early and Middle Mississippian Stillhouse and Duvall phases, which roughly correspond to the Etowah/Early Savannah Beaverdam and Late Savannah/Early Lamar Rembert phases in the Russell Reservoir area.

The position of cord-marked pottery within the upper Savannah River sequence also remains largely unknown. This finish is widespread during both the Late Woodland and Early Mississippian periods throughout the middle and lower portions of the drainage but is rarely reported in the Piedmont. While Savannah Fine Cord-Marked has been dated from circa 1150 to 1300 at the mouth of the river and from circa 800 to 1300 in the interior (DePratter 1979:111; Anderson, Hally, and Rudolph 1986:42–43), no cord-marked pottery was reported among the more than 25,000 sherds recovered at the Beaverdam mound, which was occupied from circa 1200 to 1300. The finish did occur in low incidence at Rucker's Bottom, where it was found in clear Rembert-phase context on the floor of structure 2. Characterized by carefully applied, closely spaced parallel cord impressions and well-smoothed interior surfaces, many of the sherds resembled Savannah Fine Cord-Marked. The position of this and other finishes such as check stamping, fabric marking, and simple stamping, however, needs to be better resolved.

Conclusions

The ceramic sequences presented in the preceding pages have received empirical support from a series of stratigraphic excavations undertaken in various parts of the Savannah River basin. These sequences were used to sort the late prehistoric site assemblages from the valley examined in the present study. Although the broad outline of the late prehistoric ceramic sequence in the Savannah basin may be said to be fairly well known, there is room for considerable refinement. Determining the precise periods of occurrence for specific surface finishes, design motifs, and rim treatments is particularly critical, given the temporal utility these attributes have demonstrated. Care should be taken to identify properly the design motifs or other attributes advanced here to date assemblages, and the sequences themselves should not be employed too far afield.

References Cited

Adams, Robert McCormick
1966   *The Uruk Countryside: The Natural Setting of Urban Societies.* Chicago: University of Chicago Press.
1974   Historic Patterns of Mesopotamian Irrigation Agriculture. In *Irrigation's Impact on Society,* edited by T. E. Downing and M. Gibson, pp. 1–6. Anthropological Papers, no. 25. Tucson: University of Arizona Press.
1981   *The Heartland of Cities.* Chicago: University of Chicago Press.

Ambrose, S. H.
1987   Chemical and Isotopic Techniques of Diet Reconstruction in Eastern North America. In *Emergent Horticultural Economies of the Eastern Woodlands,* edited by William F. Keegan, pp. 78–107. Occasional Papers, no. 7. Carbondale: Southern Illinois University, Center for Archaeological Investigations.

Anderson, David G.
1975   Inferences from Distributional Studies of Prehistoric Artifacts in the Coastal Plain of South Carolina. *Southeastern Archaeological Conference Bulletin* 18:180–94.
1982   The Mattassee Lake Ceramic Artifact Assemblage. In *Mattassee Lake: Archaeological Investigations along the Lower Santee River in the Coastal Plain of South Carolina,* by David G. Anderson, Charles E. Cantley, and A. Lee Novick, pp. 207–321. Special Publication. Atlanta: National Park Service, Interagency Archeological Services.
1985a The Internal Organization and Operation of Chiefdom Level Societies on the Southeastern Atlantic Slope: An Examination of Ethnohistoric Sources. *South Carolina Antiquities* 17:35–69.
1985b Middle Woodland Societies on the Lower South Atlantic Slope: A View from Georgia and South Carolina. *Early Georgia* 13:29–66.
1986   Comments. In *Mississippi Period Archaeology of the Georgia Piedmont,* by David J. Hally and James L. Rudolph, pp. 94–102. Report, no. 24. Athens: University of Georgia, Laboratory of Archaeology.
1987a Warfare and Mississippian Political Evolution in the Southeastern United States. Paper presented in the symposium Warfare and the Evolution of Chiefdoms, 20th annual Chacmool Conference, Calgary, Alberta, November 13.
1987b Prehistoric Ceramics from Four Sites along the Middle Savannah River: 38Br259, 38Br495, 38Br527, and 38Br528. In *Late Archaic–Late Woodland Adaptive Stability and Change in the Steel Creek Watershed, South Carolina,* edited by Mark J. Brooks and Glen T. Hanson. Savannah River Archaeological Papers, no. 2. Columbia: University of South Carolina, South Carolina Institute of Archaeology and Anthropology.
1988a Emergent Horticultural Economies: The Woodland Period. In *Prehistory and History along the Upper Savannah River: Technical Synthesis of Cultural Resource Investigations, Richard B. Russell Multiple Resource Area,* edited by David G. Anderson and J. W. Joseph, pp. 205–47. Russell Papers. Atlanta: National Park Service, Interagency Archeological Services.
1988b The Rise and Demise of Chiefdoms: Mississippian Occupations. In *Prehistory and History along the Upper Savannah River: Technical Synthesis of Cultural Resource Investigations, Richard B. Russell Multiple Resource Area,*

edited by David G. Anderson and J. W. Joseph, pp. 248–320. Russell Papers. Atlanta: National Park Service, Interagency Archeological Services.

1989   The Mississippian in South Carolina. In *The Archaeology of South Carolina: Papers in Honor of Robert L. Stephenson,* edited by Albert C. Goodyear III and Glen T. Hanson, pp. 101–32. Anthropological Studies, no. 9. Columbia: University of South Carolina, South Carolina Institute of Archaeology and Anthropology.

1990a   *Political Change in Chiefdom Societies: Cycling in the Late Prehistoric Southeastern United States.* Ph.D. dissertation, Department of Anthropology, University of Michigan. Ann Arbor: University Microfilms.

1990b   Stability and Change in Chiefdom Level Societies: An Examination of Mississippian Political Evolution on the South Atlantic Slope. In *Lamar Archaeology: Mississippian Chiefdoms in the Deep South,* edited by Mark Williams and Gary Shapiro, pp. 187–213. Tuscaloosa: University of Alabama Press.

1990c   The Mississippian Occupation and Abandonment of the Savannah River Valley. *The Florida Anthropologist* 43(1):13–35.

1991   Examining Prehistoric Settlement Distribution in Eastern North America. *Archaeology of Eastern North America* 19:1–22.

1992   Explaining Change: Evaluating Southeastern Evolutionary Models from the Multiscalar Perspective. Paper presented in the symposium Great Towns, Regional Polities, and Macro-Regional Interaction: Multiscalar Approaches to North American Cultural Evolution, 57th annual meeting of the Society for American Archaeology, Pittsburgh, Penn. April.

1994   Factional Competition and the Evolution of Mississippian Chiefdoms in the Southeastern United States. In *Factional Competition in the New World,* edited by Elizabeth M. Brumfiel and John W. Fox, pp. 45–59. Cambridge, England: Cambridge University Press.

n.d.   Variability in Mississippian Triangular Assemblages: An Example from Northeast Georgia. Manuscript on file at the South Carolina Institute of Archaeology and Anthropology, University of South Carolina.

Anderson, David G., and J. W. Joseph

1988   *Prehistory and History along the Upper Savannah River: Technical Synthesis of Cultural Resource Investigations, Richard B. Russell Multiple Resource Area.* Russell Papers. Atlanta: National Park Service, Interagency Archeological Services.

Anderson, David G., and Joseph Schuldenrein (editors)

1985   *Prehistoric Human Ecology along the Upper Savannah River: Excavations at the Rucker's Bottom, Abbeville, and Bullard Site Groups.* Russell Papers. Atlanta: National Park Service, Interagency Archeological Services.

Anderson, David G., Christopher Amer, and Rita F. Elliott

1994   *Archaeological Survey along the Upper Savannah River, 1990, Including Underwater Investigations at the Rembert Mound Group.* Atlanta: National Park Service, Interagency Archeological Services.

Anderson, David G., Charles E. Cantley, and A. Lee Novick

1982   *The Mattassee Lake Sites: Archaeological Investigations along the Lower Santee River in the Coastal Plain of South Carolina.* Special Publication. Atlanta: National Park Service, Interagency Archeological Services.

Anderson, David G., Charles E. Cantley, and Joseph Schuldenrein

1985   The Rufus Bullard Site (9Eb76) Archeological Record. In *Prehistoric Human Ecology along the Upper Savannah River: Excavations at the Rucker's Bottom,*

Abbeville, and Bullard Site Groups, edited by David G. Anderson and Joseph Schuldenrein, pp. 149–74. Russell Papers. Atlanta: National Park Service, Interagency Archeological Services.

Anderson, David G., James E. Cobb, and J. W. Joseph
1988   Research Framework. In *Prehistory and History along the Upper Savannah River: Technical Synthesis of Cultural Resource Investigations, Richard B. Russell Multiple Resource Area,* edited by David G. Anderson and J. W. Joseph, pp. 19–55. Russell Papers. Atlanta: National Park Service, Interagency Archeological Services.

Anderson, David G., David J. Hally, and James L. Rudolph
1986   The Mississippian Occupation of the Savannah River Valley. *Southeastern Archaeology* 5(1):32–51.
1990b   Central Savannah River. In *Lamar Archaeology: Mississippian Chiefdoms in the Deep South,* edited by Mark Williams and Gary Shapiro, pp. 55–56. Tuscaloosa: University of Alabama Press.

Anderson, David G., David W. Stahle, and Malcolm K. Cleaveland
1991   Paleoclimates and Prehistoric Mississippian Economic Systems: Linking Archaeological and Dendrochronological Data in the Southeastern Woodlands. Paper presented in the symposium Approaches to Mississippi Period Political Economy in the Southeastern United States, 56th annual meeting of the Society for American Archaeology, New Orleans, La., April.
n.d.   Paleoclimate and the Potential Food Reserves of Mississippian Societies in the Southeastern United States. *American Antiquity* (in press).

Anderson, David G., Trisha Logan, Robert Morgan, and James Bates
n.d.   *A Cultural Resources Overview of the Sumter National Forest.* U.S. Department of Agriculture Forest Service, Columbia, South Carolina (manuscript in preparation).

Anghiera, Pietro Martire d'
1912   *De Orbe Novo: The Eight Decades of Peter Martyr D'Anghera.* Translated by Francis Augustus MacNutt. New York: G. P. Putnam's Sons.

Anthony, David W.
1990   Migration in Archaeology: The Baby and the Bathwater. *American Anthropologist* 92:895–914.

Anthony, Ronald W., and Lesley M. Drucker
1980   *Hartwell Destination Park: An Archaeological Study of a Piedmont Locality, Oconee County, South Carolina.* Resource Study Series, no. 19. Columbia, S.C.: Carolina Archaeological Services.
1984   *Archaeological Testing and Data Recovery at Lake Hartwell Destination Park, Oconee County, South Carolina.* Resource Study Series, no. 74. Columbia, South Carolina: Carolina Archaeological Services.

Anuskiewicz, Richard J.
1982   *An Archaeological Reconnaissance of Eighteen Private Club Lease Tracts at Clarks Hill Lake, Georgia and South Carolina.* Manuscript on file at the University of Georgia, Laboratory of Archaeology.
1984   *Cultural Resource Investigations of Proposed Recreation Areas and Land Exchange Areas at Clarks Hill Lake Georgia and South Carolina.* Manuscript on file at the University of Georgia, Laboratory of Archaeology.

Armelagos, George J., and M. Cassandra Hill
1990   An Evaluation of the Biocultural Consequences of the Mississippian Transformation. In *Towns and Temples along the Mississippi,* edited by David H. Dye and Cheryl Anne Cox, pp. 16–37. Tuscaloosa: University of Alabama Press.

Asch, David L., and Nancy E. Asch
1985   Prehistoric Plant Cultivation in West-Central Illinois. In *Prehistoric Food Production in North America*, edited by Richard I. Ford, pp. 149–203. Anthropological Papers, no. 75. Ann Arbor: University of Michigan, Museum of Anthropology.

Aulbach-Smith, Cynthia A.
1984   Botanical Remains from 9Eb259 and 9Eb387, Richard B. Russell Reservoir Project, Elbert County, Georgia. In *Archaeological Investigations at Gregg Shoals, a Deeply Stratified Site on the Savannah River*, edited by V. Ann Tippitt and William H. Marquardt, pp. C-1 to C-3. Russell Papers. Atlanta: National Park Service, Interagency Archeological Services.

Baden, William W.
1983   *Tomotley: An Eighteenth Century Cherokee Village*. Report of Investigations, no. 36. Knoxville: University of Tennessee, Department of Anthropology.

Baerreis, David A., and Reid A. Bryson
1965   Climatic Episodes and the Dating of the Mississippian Cultures. *Wisconsin Archaeologist* 46:203–20.

Baker, Steven G.
1974   Cofitachique: Fair Province of Carolina. M.A. thesis, Department of History, University of South Carolina.
1975   The Historic Catawba Peoples: Exploratory Perspectives in Ethnohistory and Archaeology. Manuscript on file with the Department of History, University of South Carolina.

Bandera, Juan de la
1568   Account written by Juan de la Bandera of the villages and what kind of land is each one through which Captain Juan Pardo passed in the provinces of Florida; he set out at the order of Pedro Menéndez de Avilés to discover a road to New Spain, from the point of Santa Elena of the said provinces, in the years 1566 and 1567 (Bandera I manuscript). In *Explorations in Interior South Carolina by Hernando De Soto (1540) and Juan Pardo (1566–1568)*, edited by Chester B. DePratter, pp. 32–34. South Carolina Institute of Archaeology and Anthropology, University of South Carolina. *The Notebook* 19.
1569   The "Long" Bandera Relation AGI, Santa Domingo 224. Proceedings for the Account Which Captain Juan Pardo Gave of the Entrance Which He Made into the Land of the Floridas. In *The Juan Pardo Expeditions: Exploration of the Carolinas and Tennessee, 1566–1568*, by Charles M. Hudson (translation by Paul E. Hoffman), pp. 205–96. Washington, D.C.: Smithsonian Institution Press, 1990.

Barber, Gary, James L. Rudolph, and David J. Hally
1979   An Archaeological Survey in the Hudson River Watershed. Manuscript on file at the University of Georgia, Laboratory of Archaeology.

Barcia Carballido y Zuñiga, Andrés G.
1723   *Ensayo cronológico para la historia general de la Florida, 1522–1722, por Gabriel de Cardenas Z. Cano*. Madrid.

Barker, Alex W., and Timothy R. Pauketat (editors)
1992   *Lords of the Southeast: Social Inequality and the Native Elites of Southeastern North America*. Archaeological Papers of the American Anthropological Association, no. 3.

Barry, J. M.
1980   *Natural Vegetation of South Carolina*. Columbia: University of South Carolina Press.

Bartram, William
1789   *Observations on the Creek and Cherokee Indians*. London. Reprinted in *Trans-actions of the American Ethnological Society* 3(1): 2–81.
1791   *Travels through North and South Carolina, Georgia, East and West Florida, The Cherokee Country: The Extensive Territories of the Muscogulges or Creek Confederacy, and the Country of the Choctaws; Containing an Account of the Soil and Natural Production of these Regions, Together with Observations on the Manners of the Indians*. Philadelphia: James and Johnson.

Bell, R. E.
1951   Dendrochronology at the Kincaid Site. In *Kincaid: A Prehistoric Illinois Metropolis*, edited by Faye Cooper Cole. Chicago: University of Chicago Press.

Bender, Barbara
1985   Emergent Tribal Formulations in the American Midcontinent. *American Antiquity* 50:52–62.
1989   The Roots of Inequality. In *Domination and Resistance*, edited by D. Miller, M. Rowlands, and C. Tilley, pp. 83–95. London: Unwin Hyman.

Bender, Margaret M., David A. Baerreis, and Raymond L. Steventon.
1981   Further Light on Carbon Isotopes and Hopewell Agriculture. *American Antiquity* 46:346–53.

Bennett, Charles E.
1975   *Three Voyages [by] René Laudonnière*. Gainesville: University Presses of Florida.

Betzig, Laura L.
1982   Despotism and Differential Reproduction: A Cross Cultural Correlation of Conflict Asymmetry, Hierarchy, and Degree of Polygyny. *Ethology and Sociobiology* 3:209–21.
1986   *Despotism and Differential Reproduction: A Darwinian View of History*. Hawthorne, N.Y.: Aldine.
1988a   Redistribution: Equity or Exploitation? In *Human Reproductive Behavior: A Darwinian Perspective*, edited by Laura L. Betzig, Monique Borgerhoff Mulder, and Paul W. Turke, pp. 49–63. Cambridge, England: Cambridge University Press.
1988b   Mating and Parenting in Darwinian Perspective. In *Human Reproductive Behavior: A Darwinian Perspective*, edited by Laura L. Betzig, Monique Borgerhoff Mulder, and Paul W. Turke, pp. 3–20. Cambridge, England: Cambridge University Press.

Betzig, Laura L., Monique Borgerhoff Mulder, and Paul W. Turke (editors)
1988   *Human Reproductive Behavior: A Darwinian Perspective*. Cambridge, England: Cambridge University Press.

Beuschel, Leslie
1976   Keowee-Toxaway Reservoir Project: A Partial Report of the Archaeology, 1967–1968 and 1970. Manuscript on file at the South Carolina Institute of Archaeology and Anthropology, University of South Carolina.

Bianchi, Travis L.
1975   *An Archaeological Survey of a Portion of the Upper New River Watershed in Jasper County, South Carolina*. Research Manuscript Series, no. 70. Columbia: University of South Carolina, South Carolina Institute of Archaeology and Anthropology.

Biedma, Luys Hernandez de
1904   Relation of the Conquest of Florida, Presented by Luys Hernandez de Biedma in the Year 1544 to the King of Spain in Council. Translated by

Buckingham Smith. In *Narratives of the Career of Hernando De Soto in the Conquest of Florida as Told by a Knight of Elvas and in a Relation by Luys Hernandez de Biedma, Factor of the Expedition, Translated by Buckingham Smith, Together with an Account of De Soto's Expedition Based on the Diary of Rodrigo Ranjel, His Probate Secretary, Translated from Ovideo's Historia General y Natural de las Indias,* edited by Edward Gaylord Bourne, 2:3–40. New York: A. S. Barnes.

1993   Relation of the Island of Florida by Luys Hernández de Biedma. In *The De Soto Chronicles: The Expedition of Hernando De Soto to North America in 1539–1543,* vol. 1, edited by Lawrence A. Clayton, Vernon James Knight, Jr., and Edward C. Moore, pp. 221–246. Tuscaloosa: University of Alabama Press.

Binford, Lewis R.
1978   *Numamiut Ethnoarchaeology.* New York: Academic Press.
1981   *Bones: Ancient Men and Modern Myths.* New York: Academic Press.

Blake, Michael
n.d.   Status and Power Symbolism in Chief's Residence. Manuscript on file with the author.

Blake, Michael, and John E. Clark
n.d.   Environmental Restrictedness and the Evolution of Complex Societies. Manuscript on file with the authors.

Blakely, Robert L. (editor)
1988   *The King Site: Biocultural Adaptations in Sixteenth Century Georgia.* Athens: University of Georgia Press.

Blakely, Robert, and Lane A. Beck
1981   Trace Elements, Nutritional Status, and Social Stratification at Etowah, Georgia. *Annals of the New York Academy of Sciences* 376:417–31.

Blakely, Robert, D. Mathews, James L. Rudolph, R. Tyzzer, and Paul Webb
1985   Burial Descriptions. In *Archaeological Investigation of the Beaverdam Creek Site (9Eb85), Elbert County, Georgia,* edited by James L. Rudolph and David J. Hally, pp. 317–45. Russell Papers. Atlanta: National Park Service, Interagency Archeological Services.

Blanchard, Scott, and Cheryl Claassen
1985   Mollusc Remains from the Rucker's Bottom Site (9Eb91), Elbert County, Georgia: Identification and Seasonality Estimate. In *Prehistoric Human Ecology along the Upper Savannah River: Excavations at the Rucker's Bottom, Abbeville, and Bullard Site Groups,* edited by David G. Anderson and Joseph Schuldenrein, pp. 665–72. Russell Papers. Atlanta: National Park Service, Interagency Archeological Services.

Blanding, William
1848   Remains on the Wateree River, Kershaw District, South Carolina. In *Ancient Monuments of the Mississippi Valley,* edited by E. G. Squier and E. H. Davis, pp. 105–8. Smithsonian Contributions to Knowledge, no. 1. Washington, D.C.: Smithsonian Institution Press.

Blanton, Richard, Stephen Kowalewski, Gary Feinman, and Jill Appel
1981   *Ancient Mesoamerica.* Cambridge, England: Cambridge University Press.
1982   *Monte Alban's Hinterland.* Part 1: *The Prehispanic Settlement Patterns of the Central and Southern Parts of the Valley of Oaxaca, Mexico.* Memoirs, no. 7. Ann Arbor: University of Michigan, Museum of Anthropology.

Blitz, John
1989   Vessel Size as a Measure of Mississippian Mound Activities. Paper presented at the 46th annual Southeastern Archaeological Conference, Tampa, Fla., November 11.

1993a   *Ancient Chiefdoms of the Tombigbee.* Tuscaloosa: University of Alabama Press.
1993b   Big Pots for Big Shots: Feasting and Storage in a Mississippian Community. *American Antiquity* 58:80–96.

Bogan, Arthur E.
1980   *A Comparison of Late Prehistoric Dallas and Overhill Cherokee Subsistence Strategies in the Little Tennessee River Valley.* Ph.D. dissertation, Department of Anthropology, University of Tennessee. Ann Arbor: University Microfilms.

Bohannan, Paul, and Laura Bohannan
1954   The Migration and Expansion of the Tiv. *Africa* 24:2–16.

Boone, James L., III
1988   Parental Investment, Social Subordination, and Population Processes among the 15th and 16th Century Portuguese Nobility. In *Human Reproductive Behavior: A Darwinian Perspective,* edited by Laura L. Betzig, Monique Borgerhoff Mulder, and Paul Turke, pp. 201–20. Cambridge, England: Cambridge University Press.

Bourne, Edward Gaylord (editor)
1904   *Narratives of the Career of Hernando De Soto in the Conquest of Florida as Told by a Knight of Elvas and in a Relation by Luys Hernandez de Biedma, Factor of the Expedition, Translated by Buckingham Smith, Together with an Account of De Soto's Expedition Based on the Diary of Rodrigo Ranjel, His Probate Secretary, Translated from Ovideo's Historia General y Natural de las Indias.* 2 vols. New York: A. S. Barnes.

Bowen, William Rowe
1979   Augusta Railroad Relocation Demonstration Project: Intensive Archaeological Survey Identification of Resources and Assessment of Impacts. Manuscript on file at the Georgia Department of Transportation, Atlanta.
1982   *Archaeological Investigations at 9Ck(DOT)7, Cherokee County, Georgia.* Occasional Papers in Cultural Resource Management, no. 1. Atlanta: Georgia Department of Transportation.
1984   An Intensive Archaeological Survey of GDOT Project M-7050(1), Richmond County Murray Road Extension. Manuscript on file at the Georgia Department of Transportation, Atlanta.

Boyd, C. Clifford, Jr., and Gerald F. Schroedl
1987   In Search of Coosa. *American Antiquity* 52:840–44.

Bozeman, Tandy K.
1982   *Moundville Phase Communities in the Black Warrior River Valley, Alabama.* Ph.D. dissertation, Department of Anthropology, University of Michigan. Ann Arbor: University Microfilms.

Bragg, Laura M.
1918   Indian Mound Excavations in South Carolina. *Bulletin of the Charleston Museum* 14(4):17–20.

Braley, Chad O.
1983   The Pinckney Island Survey: Some Thoughts on the Cord Marked Pottery of the Lower South Carolina Coast. *South Carolina Antiquities* 15:5–9.

Braun, David, and Stephen Plog
1982   Evolution of "Tribal" Social Networks: Theory and Prehistoric North American Evidence. *American Antiquity* 47:504–25.

Braun, E. Lucy
1950   *Deciduous Forests of Eastern North America.* Philadelphia: Bleakston.

Brockington, Paul B.
1971   A Preliminary Investigation of an Early Knapping Site in Southeastern Georgia. South Carolina Institute of Archaeology and Anthropology, University of South Carolina. *The Notebook* 3:34–46.
1978a   *An Archaeological Survey of Duke Power's Oconee–Red Creek 500 kV and Jocassee–Bad Creek 100 kV Transmission Lines, Oconee County, South Carolina.* Research Manuscript Series, no. 130. Columbia: University of South Carolina, South Carolina Institute of Archaeology and Anthropology.
1978b   *An Archaeological Survey of Oolenoy Watershed Project 40, Pickens County, South Carolina.* Research Manuscript Series, no. 135. Columbia: University of South Carolina, South Carolina Institute of Archaeology and Anthropology.
Brooks, Mark J.
1977   *An Archeological Survey of Areas to Be Impacted by the Dredging of Broadway Lake, Anderson County, South Carolina.* Research Manuscript Series, no. 152. Columbia: University of South Carolina, South Carolina Institute of Archaeology and Anthropology.
1983   St. Catherines Pottery from the Callawassie Island Burial Mound, Beaufort County, South Carolina. *South Carolina Antiquities* 15:11–15.
Brooks, Mark J., and Glen T. Hanson (editors)
1987   *Late Archaic–Late Woodland Adaptive Stability and Change in the Steel Creek Watershed, South Carolina.* Savannah River Archaeological Papers, no. 2. Columbia: University of South Carolina, South Carolina Institute of Archaeology and Anthropology.
Brooks, Mark J., and Kenneth E. Sassaman
n.d.   Westvaco Archaeological Project. Notes and records on file at the Savannah River Archaeological Research Program, South Carolina Institute of Archaeology and Anthropology, University of South Carolina.
Brooks, Mark J., and James D. Scurry
1978   *An Intensive Survey of Amoco Realty Property in Berkeley County, South Carolina, with a Test of Two Subsistence-Settlement Hypotheses for the Prehistoric Period.* Research Manuscript Series, no. 147. Columbia: University of South Carolina, South Carolina Institute of Archaeology and Anthropology.
Brooks, Mark J., Kenneth E. Sassaman, and Glen T. Hanson
1990   Environmental Background and Models. In *Native American Prehistory of the Middle Savannah River Valley: A Synthesis of Archaeological Investigations on the Savannah River Site, Aiken and Barnwell Counties, South Carolina,* edited by Kenneth E. Sassaman, Mark J. Brooks, Glen T. Hanson, and David G. Anderson, pp. 19–66. Savannah River Archaeological Research Papers, no. 1. Columbia: University of South Carolina, South Carolina Institute of Archaeology and Anthropology.
Brooks, Mark J., Larry Lepionka, Ted A. Rathbun, and John Goldsborough
1982   *Preliminary Archaeological Investigations at the Callawassie Island Burial Mound(38Bu19), Beaufort County, South Carolina.* Research Manuscript Series, no. 185. Columbia: University of South Carolina, South Carolina Institute of Archaeology and Anthropology.
Brooks, Mark J., Peter A. Stone, Donald J. Colquhoun, Janice G. Brown, and Kathy B. Steele
1986   Geoarchaeological Research in the Coastal Plain Portion of the Savannah River Valley. *Geoarchaeology* 1:293–307.

Brose, David S.
1979   A Speculative Model of the Role of Exchange in the Prehistory of the Eastern Woodlands. In *Hopewell Archaeology: The Chillicothe Conference*, edited by David S. Brose and N'omi Greber, pp. 3–8. Kent, Ohio: Kent State University Press.
1989   From the Southeastern Ceremonial Complex to the Southern Cult: "You Can't Tell the Players without a Program." In *The Southeastern Ceremonial Complex: Artifacts and Analysis, the Cottonlandia Conference*, edited by Patricia Galloway, pp. 27–37. Lincoln: University of Nebraska Press.

Brose, David S., and N'omi Greber (editors)
1979   *Hopewell Archaeology: The Chillicothe Conference.* Kent, Ohio: Kent State University Press.

Brose, David S., and George W. Percy
1978   Fort Walton Settlement Patterns. In *Mississippian Settlement Patterns*, edited by Bruce D. Smith, pp. 81–114. New York: Academic Press.

Brown, Ian W.
1980   *Salt and the Eastern North American Indian: An Archaeological Study.* Bulletin 6. Cambridge, Mass.: Harvard University, Peabody Museum of Archaeology and Ethnology, Lower Mississippi Survey.

Brown, James A.
1976   The Southern Cult Reconsidered. *Midcontinental Journal of Archaeology* 1:115–35.
1984   Arkansas Valley Caddoan: The Spiro Phase. In *Prehistory of Oklahoma*, edited by Robert E. Bell, pp. 241–263. New York: Academic Press.
1985   The Mississippian Period. In *Ancient Art of the American Woodland Indians*, by David S. Brose, James A. Brown, and David W. Penny, pp. 92–145. New York: Harry N. Abrams.

Brown, James A. (editor)
1971   *Approaches to the Social Dimensions of Mortuary Practices.* Society for American Archaeology Memoir 25.

Brown, James A., Robert E. Bell, and Don G. Wyckoff
1978   Caddoan Settlement Patterns in the Arkansas River Drainage. In *Mississippian Settlement Patterns*, edited by Bruce D. Smith, pp. 169–200. New York: Academic Press.

Brown, James A., Richard A. Kerber, and Howard D. Winters
1990   Trade and the Evolution of Exchange Relations at the Beginning of the Mississippian Period. In *The Mississippian Emergence*, edited by Bruce D. Smith, pp. 251–80. New York: Academic Press.

Brumfiel, Elizabeth M.
1987   Consumption and Politics at Aztec Huexotla. *American Anthropologist* 89:676–86.

Brumfiel, Elizabeth M., and John W. Fox (editors)
1994   *Factional Competition in the New World.* Cambridge, England: Cambridge University Press.

Buikstra, Jane E.
1991   Out of the Appendix and into the Dirt: Comments on Thirteen Years of Bioarchaeological Research. In *What Mean These Bones? Studies in Southeastern Bioarchaeology*, edited by Mary Lucas Powell, Patricia S. Bridges, and Ann Marie Wagner Mires, pp. 172–188. Tuscaloosa: University of Alabama Press.

Bullen, Ripley P., and H. Bruce Green
1970   Stratigraphic Testing at Stalling's Island, Georgia. *Florida Anthropologist* 23:8–28.
Burling, Robbins
1974   *The Passage of Power*. New York: Academic Press.
Burns, Barney T.
1983   *Simulated Anasazi Storage Behavior Using Crop Yields Reconstructed from Tree Rings:* A.D. *652–1968*. Ph.D. dissertation, Department of Anthropology, University of Arizona. Ann Arbor: University Microfilms.
Butler, Carol Roetzel
1986   Diet, Disease, and Culture: Evidence from Rucker's Bottom (9Eb91), a Late Mississippian Site in Northeast Georgia. M.A. thesis, Department of Anthropology, Wake Forest University.
Butzer, Karl W.
1980   Civilizations: Organisms or Systems. *American Scientist* 68:517–23.
1982   *Archaeology as Human Ecology*. Cambridge, England: Cambridge University Press.
Byrd, Kathleen M. (editor)
1991   *The Poverty Point Culture: Local Manifestations, Subsistence Practices, and Trade Networks*. Geoscience and Man, no. 29. Baton Rouge: Louisiana State University, Department of Geography and Anthropology.
Cable, John S., and Charles E. Cantley
1979   An Intensive Archaeological Survey of the South Carolina 151 Highway Widening Project. Manuscript on file at the South Carolina Institute of Archaeology and Anthropology, University of South Carolina.
Cable, John S., Charles E. Cantley, and Jim Sexton
1978b   *A Study of Prehistoric Utilization of the Inter-riverine Piedmont: The U. S. 176 By-pass Survey from Union to Pacolet, South Carolina*. Research Manuscript Series, no. 131. Columbia: University of South Carolina, South Carolina Institute of Archaeology and Anthropology.
Cable, John S., Charles E. Cantley, James L. Michie, and Stephen M. Perlman
1978a   *An Archaeological Reconnaissance of the Bobby Jones Expressway Corridor, Aiken County, South Carolina*. Research Manuscript Series, no. 124. Columbia: University of South Carolina, South Carolina Institute of Archaeology and Anthropology.
Caldwell, Joseph R.
1948   Palachacolas Town, Hampton County, South Carolina. *Journal of the Washington Academy of Sciences* 38(10):321–324.
1952   The Archeology of Eastern Georgia and South Carolina. In *Archeology of the Eastern United States*, edited by James B. Griffin, pp. 312–21. Chicago: University of Chicago Press.
1953   The Rembert Mounds, Elbert County, Georgia. In Bulletin 154, pp. 303–20. Washington, D.C.: Bureau of American Ethnology.
1954   The Old Quartz Industry of Georgia and South Carolina. *Southern Indian Studies* 6:37–39.
1956   Progress Report on Excavation at Tugalo (9St1–Georgia). Manuscript on file at the Laboratory of Archaeology, University of Georgia.
1957   Survey and Excavations in the Allatoona Reservoir, Northern Georgia. Manuscript on file at the Laboratory of Archaeology, University of Georgia.
1958   *Trend and Tradition in the Prehistory of the Eastern United States*. American

Anthropological Association Memoir 88. Springfield: Illinois State Museum.

1964   Interaction Spheres in Prehistory. In *Hopewellian Studies*, edited by Joseph R. Caldwell and Robert L. Hall, pp. 133–43. Scientific Papers, no. 12. Springfield: Illinois State Museum.

1970   Proposal to the Branigar Organization Inc. for Archaeological Investigations on Skidaway Island, Chatham County, Georgia. Manuscript on file at the Laboratory of Archaeology, University of Georgia.

1971   Chronology of the Georgia Coast. *Southeastern Archaeological Conference Bulletin* 13:89–92.

1974a   Study of Mulberry Pottery. South Carolina Institute of Archaeology and Anthropology, University of South Carolina. *The Notebook* 6(3–4):88–98.

1974b   Preliminary Report: Archeological Investigation of Fort Charlotte, McCormick County, South Carolina. South Carolina Institute of Archaeology and Anthropology, University of South Carolina. *The Notebook* 6(2):45–56.

1974c   Appraisal of the Archaeological Resources of Hartwell Reservoir, South Carolina and Georgia. South Carolina Institute of Archaeology and Anthropology, University of South Carolina. *The Notebook* 6(2):35–44.

Caldwell, Joseph R., and Catherine McCann (editors)
1941   *Irene Mound Site, Chatham County, Georgia*. Athens: University of Georgia Press.

Caldwell, Joseph R., and Antonio J. Waring, Jr.
1939a   Some Chatham County Pottery Types and Their Sequence. *Southeastern Archaeological Conference Newsletter* 1:5–6.

1939b   The Use of Ceramic Sequence in the Classification of Aboriginal Sites in Chatham County, Georgia. *Southeastern Archaeological Conference Newsletter* 2:6–7.

Caldwell, Joseph R., C. E. Thompson, and S. K. Caldwell
1952   The Booger Bottom Mound: A Forsyth Period Site in Hall County, Georgia. *American Antiquity* 17:319–28.

Campbell, Janice L., and Carol S. Weed
1984   *The Beaverdam Group Archaeological Investigations at 9Eb92, 9Eb207, 9Eb208, and 9Eb219, Richard B. Russell Multiple Resource Area, Elbert County, Georgia.* Russell Papers. Atlanta: National Park Service, Interagency Archeological Services.

Campbell, Janice L., Carol S. Weed, and Prentice M. Thomas, Jr.
1981   *Archaeological Investigations at the Fort Gordon Military Reservation, Georgia.* Report of Investigations, no. 33. Final report prepared by New World Research. Atlanta: National Park Service, Interagency Archeological Services.

Capello, H., and R. Ivens
1882   *From Benguella to the Territory of Yacca*. Translated by A. Elwes. London: Sampson Low.

Carneiro, Robert L.
1962   Scale Analysis as an Instrument for the Study of Cultural Evolution. *Southwestern Journal of Anthropology* 18(2):149–69.

1967   On the Relationship between Size of Population and Complexity of Social Organization. *Southwestern Journal of Anthropology* 23(3):234–43.

1968   Ascertaining, Testing, and Interpreting Sequences of Cultural Development. *Southwestern Journal of Anthropology* 24(4):354–74.

1970   A Theory of the Origin of the State. *Science* 169:733–38.
1981   The Chiefdom: Precursor of the State. In *The Transition to Statehood in the New World*, edited by Grant D. Jones and Robert R. Kautz, pp. 37–79. Cambridge, England: Cambridge University Press.
1990   Chiefdom Level Warfare as Exemplified in Fiji and the Cauca Valley. In *The Anthropology of War*, edited by J. Haas, pp. 190–211. Cambridge, England: Cambridge University Press.
1991   The Nature of the Chiefdom as Revealed by Evidence from the Cauca Valley of Columbia. In *Profiles in Cultural Evolution Papers from a Conference in Honor of Elman R. Service*, edited by A. Terry Rambo and Kathleen Gillogly, pp. 167–90. Anthropological Papers, no. 85. Ann Arbor: University of Michigan, Museum of Anthropology.

Carneiro, Robert L., and Stephen Tobias
1963   The Application of Scale Analysis to the Study of Cultural Evolution. *Transactions of the New York Academy of Sciences* 26 (series 2):196–207.

Carver, R. F.
1959   *Drainage Area for Georgia Streams*. Atlanta: Georgia Department of Natural Resources.

Chagnon, Napoleon A., and William Irons (editors)
1979   *Evolutionary Biology and Human Social Behavior: An Anthropological Perspective*. North Scituate, Mass.: Duxbury Press.

Champion, Timothy, and Sara Champion
1986   Peer Polity Interaction in the European Iron Age. In *Peer Polity Interaction and Socio-political Change*, edited by Colin Renfrew and John F. Cherry, pp. 59–68. Cambridge, England: Cambridge University Press.

Champion, Timothy, Clive Gamble, Stephen J. Shennan, and A. Whittle
1984   *Prehistoric Europe*. New York: Academic Press.

Chapman, Jefferson, and Bennie C. Keel
1979   Candy Creek–Connestee Components in Eastern Tennessee and Western North Carolina and Their Relationship with Adena-Hopewell. In *Hopewell Archaeology: The Chillicothe Conference*, edited by David S. Brose and N'omi Greber, pp. 157–61. Kent, Ohio: Kent State University Press.

Chapman, J. Jefferson, and Andrea Shea
1981   The Archaeobotanical Record: Early Archaic to Contact in the Lower Little Tennessee River Valley. *Tennessee Anthropologist* 6:61–84.

Charles, Tommy
1981   Dwindling Resources: An Overture to the Future of South Carolina's Archaeological Resources. South Carolina Institute of Archaeology and Anthropology, University of South Carolina. *The Notebook* 13:1–85.
1983   Thoughts and Records from the Survey of Private Collections of Prehistoric Artifacts throughout South Carolina: A Second Report. South Carolina Institute of Archaeology and Anthropology, University of South Carolina. *The Notebook* 15:1–37.
1986   The Fifth Phase of the Collectors Survey. South Carolina Institute of Archaeology and Anthropology, University of South Carolina. *The Notebook* 18:1–27.

Charles, Tommy, and Steven D. Smith
1988   An Archaeological Survey of the Proposed Law Enforcement Complex, J. Strom Thurmond Reservoir, McCormick County, South Carolina. Manuscript on file at the South Carolina Institute of Archaeology and Anthropology, University of South Carolina.

Cheves, Langdon (editor)
1897   *The Shaftesbury Papers and Other Records Relating to Carolina and the First Settlement on Ashley River Prior to the Year 1676*. Vol. 5. Collections of the South Carolina Historical Society. Charleston: The Society.

Chicken, George
1916   Journal of Colonel George Chicken's Mission from Charleston, South Carolina, to the Cherokees, 1726. In *Travels in the American Colonies*, edited by Newton Mereness. New York: Antiquarian Press.

Childe, V. G.
1952   *New Light on the Most Ancient Near East*. London: Routledge and Kegan Paul.

Chmurny, William W.
1973   *The Ecology of the Middle Mississippian Occupation of the American Bottom*. Ph.D. dissertation, Department of Anthropology, University of Illinois at Urbana-Champaign. Ann Arbor: University Microfilms.

Claassen, Cheryl P.
1986   Shellfishing Seasons in the Prehistoric Southeastern United States. *American Antiquity* 51:21–37.

Claflin, William H., Jr.
1931   *The Stalling's Island Mound, Columbia County, Georgia*. Papers of the Peabody Museum of American Archaeology and Ethnology, no. 14(1). Cambridge, Mass.: Harvard University, The Museum.

Clark, John E.
1987   Politics, Prismatic Blades, and Mesoamerican Civilization. In *The Organization of Core Technology*, edited by Jay K. Johnson and Carol A. Morrow, pp. 259–84. Boulder, Colo.: Westview.
1988   *The Lithic Artifacts of La Libertad, Chiapas, Mexico: An Economic Perspective*. Papers of the New World Archaeological Foundation, no. 52. Provo, Utah: Brigham Young University.
1994   *The Development of Early Formative Rank Societies in the Soconusco, Chiapas, Mexico*. Ph.D. dissertation, Department of Anthropology, University of Michigan, Ann Arbor: University Microfilms.

Clark, John E., and Michael Blake
1989   The Emergence of Rank Societies on the Pacific Coast of Chiapas, Mexico. Paper presented at the Circum-Pacific Prehistory Conference, Seattle, Wash., August.
1994   The Power of Prestige: Competitive Generosity and the Emergence of Rank Societies in Lowland Mesoamerica. In *Factional Competition in the New World*, edited by Elizabeth M. Brumfiel and John W. Fox, pp. 17–30. Cambridge, England: Cambridge University Press.

Clayton, Lawrence A., Vernon James Knight, Jr., and Edward C. Moore (editors)
1993   *The De Soto Chronicles: The Expedition of Hernando De Soto to North America in 1539–1543*. Tuscaloosa: University of Alabama Press.

Clignet, R.
1970   *Many Wives, Many Powers: Authority and Power in Polygynous Families*. Evanston, Ill.: Northwestern University Press.

Coe, Joffre L.
1952   The Cultural Sequence of the Carolina Piedmont. In *Archeology of the Eastern United States*, edited by James B. Griffin, pp. 301–9. Chicago: University of Chicago Press.

Cohen, Mark N., and George J. Armelagos (editors)
1984   *Paleopathology at the Origins of Agriculture*. New York: Academic Press.

Cole, Gloria, and Caroline H. Albright
1983   Summerville I–II Fortifications. In *Prehistoric Agricultural Communities in West-central Alabama: Excavations in the Lubbub Creek Archaeological Locality*, edited by Christopher S. Peebles, pp. 140–96. Atlanta: National Park Service, Interagency Archeological Services.

Colquhoun, Donald J., and Mark J. Brooks
1986   New Evidence from the Southeastern U.S. for Eustatic Components in the Late Holocene Sea Levels. *Geoarchaeology* 1:275–91.

Colson, Elizabeth
1951   The Plateau Tonga of Northern Rhodesia. In *Seven Tribes of Central Africa*, edited by Elizabeth Colson and Max Gluckman, pp. 94–162. Manchester, England: Manchester University Press.

Colson, Elizabeth, and Max Gluckman (editors)
1951   *Seven Tribes of Central Africa*. Manchester, England: Manchester University Press.

Connor, Jeanette Thurber (editor)
1928   *Pedro Menéndez de Avilés: Adelantado, Governor and Captain-General of Florida; Memorial by Gonzalo Solís de Merás; First published in La Florida su Conquista y Colonizacion por Pedro Menéndez de Avilés by Eugenio Ruidíaz y Caravia*. Publications of the Florida State Historical Society, no. 3. Deland, Fla.: The Society.

Cook, Fred C.
n.d.   Investigations at the Red Lake Site, Screven County, Georgia (manuscript in preparation).

Cook, Fred C., and Charles E. Pearson
1989   The Southeastern Ceremonial Complex on the Georgia Coast. In *The Southeastern Ceremonial Complex: Artifacts and Analysis, the Cottonlandia Conference*, edited by Patricia Galloway, pp. 27–37. Lincoln: University of Nebraska Press.

Cook, S. F.
1972   *Prehistoric Demography*. McCaleb Module in Anthropology. Reading, Mass.: Addison-Wesley.

Cordy, Ross H.
1981   *A Study of Prehistoric Social Change: The Development of Complex Societies in the Hawaiian Islands*. New York: Academic Press.

Cornelius, Elias
1818   On the Geology, Mineralogy, Scenery, and Curiosities of Parts of Virginia, Tennessee, and of the Alabama and Mississippi Territories, etc. *Stillman's American Journal of Science* 1:322–24.

Cowan, C. Wesley
1985   Understanding the Evolution of Plant Husbandry in Eastern North America: Lessons from Botany, Ethnography, and Archaeology. In *Prehistoric Food Production in North America*, edited by Richard I. Ford, pp. 205–43. Anthropological Papers, no. 75. Ann Arbor: University of Michigan, Museum of Anthropology.

Creamer, Winifred, and Jonathan Haas
1985   Tribe versus Chiefdom in Lower Central America. *American Antiquity* 50:738–54.

Cridlebaugh, Patricia A.
1985a *A Cultural Resource Survey of the Clarks Hill Lake Cherokee Recreation Area, Lincoln County, Georgia and Catfish Recreation Area, McCormick County, South Carolina*. Savannah, Ga.: U.S. Army Corps of Engineers.

1985b *Intensive Archaeological Survey and Testing of Five Archaeological Sites in Catfish Recreation Area, Clarks Hill Lake, McCormick County, South Carolina.* Savannah, Ga.: U.S. Army Corps of Engineers.

Crook, Morgan R., Jr.
1975 An Archaeological Survey of Green Island, Chatham County, Georgia. Manuscript on file at the Laboratory of Archaeology, University of Georgia.
1978 *Mississippian Period Community Organizations on the Georgia Coast.* Ph.D. dissertation, Department of Anthropology, University of Florida. Ann Arbor: University Microfilms.

D'Altroy, Terence N., and Timothy K. Earle
1985 Staple Finance, Wealth Finance, and Storage in the Inka Political Economy. *Current Anthropology* 26:187–206.

Davis, R. P. Stephen, Jr., Larry R. Kimball, and William Baden (editors)
1982 *An Archaeological Survey and Assessment of Aboriginal Settlement within the Lower Little Tennessee River Valley.* Norris, Tenn.: Tennessee River Valley Authority.

Dean, J. S., R. C. Euler, G. J. Gummerman, F. Plog, R. H. Hevly, and T. N. V. Karlstrom
1985 Human Behavior, Demography, and Paleoenvironment on the Colorado Plateau. *American Antiquity* 50:537–54.

DeBaillou, Clemens
1965 A Test Excavation of the Hollywood Mound (9Ri1), Georgia. *Southern Indian Studies* 17:3–11.

DeBoer, W. R.
1981 Buffer Zones in the Cultural Ecology of Aboriginal Amazonia: An Ethnohistorical Approach. *American Antiquity* 46:364–77.
1988 Subterranean Storage and the Organization of Surplus: The View from Eastern North America. *Southeastern Archaeology* 7:1–20.

De Brÿ, Theodoro
1591 *Brevis narratio eorvm ovae in Florida Americae Provîncia Gallis acciderum, secunda in illam navigatione, du ce Renato de Laudóniere classis praefecto: anno MDLXIIII. Qvae est secunda pars Americae. Additae figurae & incolarum eicones ibidem ad vivú expressae brevis item declaratio religionis, rituum, vivendique ratione ipsorum. Auctore Iacobo le Moyne, cui cognomen de Morgues, Laudónierum in ea navigatione sequnto.* Francoforti ad Moenvm.

DeJarnette, David L., and Steven B. Wimberly
1941 *The Bessemer Site.* Geological Survey of Alabama Museum Paper 17. Tuscaloosa: University of Alabama.

DePratter, Chester B.
1975 An Archaeological Survey of P. H. Lewis Property, Skidaway Island, Chatham County, Georgia. Manuscript on file at the Laboratory of Archaeology, University of Georgia.
1977 Report on an Archaeological Survey of Portions of Wassaw National Wildlife Refuge, Chatham County, Georgia, and Blackbeard Island National Wildlife Refuge, McIntosh County, Georgia. Manuscript on file at the Laboratory of Archaeology, University of Georgia.
1979 Ceramics. In *The Anthropology of St. Catherine's Island.* Vol. 2: *The Refuge-Deptford Mortuary Complex,* edited by David H. Thomas and Clark S. Larsen., pp. 109–32. Anthropological Papers of the American Museum of Natural History, no. 56(1). New York: The Museum.
1983 *Late Prehistoric and Early Historic Chiefdoms in the Southeastern United States.*

Ph.D. dissertation, Department of Anthropology, University of Georgia. Ann Arbor: University Microfilms.

1987a   *Explorations in Interior South Carolina by Hernando De Soto (1540) and Juan Pardo (1566–1568).* South Carolina Institute of Archaeology and Anthropology, University of South Carolina. *The Notebook* 19.

1987b   The Pee Dee Pottery Tradition: From Town Creek to the Wateree. Paper presented at the Town Creek Indian Mound 50th anniversary celebration, Southern Pines, N.C., April 11.

1988   Indian Occupations of the Savannah River Valley during the Late Prehistoric and Early Historic Periods. Manuscript on file at the South Carolina Institute of Archaeology and Anthropology, University of South Carolina.

1989   Cofitachequi: Ethnohistorical and Archaeological Evidence. In *Studies in South Carolina Archaeology: Papers in Honor of Robert L. Stephenson,* edited by Albert C. Goodyear III and Glen T. Hanson, pp. 133–56. Anthropological Studies, no. 9. Columbia: University of South Carolina, South Carolina Institute of Archaeology and Anthropology.

1990   The Apalachee in South Carolina: The Documentary Record. Paper presented at the 47th annual meeting of the Southeastern Archaeological Conference, Mobile, Ala. November 8.

1991a   *Late Prehistoric and Early Historic Chiefdoms in the Southeastern United States.* New York: Garland.

1991b   *W.P.A. Archaeological Excavations in Chatham County, Georgia: 1937–1942.* Laboratory of Archaeology Series, no. 29. Athens: University of Georgia.

DePratter, Chester B., and Christopher Judge
1990   Wateree River. In *Lamar Archaeology: Mississippian Chiefdoms in the Deep South,* edited by Mark Williams and Gary Shapiro, pp. 56–58. Tuscaloosa: University of Alabama Press.

DePratter, Chester B., and Marvin T. Smith
1980   Sixteenth Century European Trade in the Southeastern United States: Evidence from the Juan Pardo Expeditions (1566–1568). In *Spanish Colonial Frontier Research,* edited by Henry F. Dobyns, pp. 67–77. Albuquerque, N.M.: Center for Anthropological Studies.

DePratter, Chester B., and Stanley A. South
1990   *Charlesfort: The 1989 Search Project.* Research Manuscript Series, no. 210. Columbia: University of South Carolina, South Carolina Institute of Archaeology and Anthropology.

1993   The Search for Charlesfort. Paper presented at the 19th annual meeting of the Archaeological Society of South Carolina, Columbia, April 3.

DePratter, Chester B., Charles M. Hudson, and Marvin T. Smith
1983   The Route of Juan Pardo's Explorations in the Interior Southeast, 1566–1568. *Florida Historical Quarterly* 62:125–58.

DeSchlippe, Pierre
1956   *Shifting Cultivation in Africa: The Zande System of Agriculture.* London: Routledge and Kegan Paul.

De Soto, Hernando
1539   Letter. In *Narratives of the Career of Hernando De Soto in the Conquest of Florida as Told by a Knight of Elvas and in a Relation by Luys Hernandez de Biedma, Factor of the Expedition, Translated by Buckingham Smith, Together with an Account of De Soto's Expedition Based on the Diary of Rodrigo Ranjel, His Probate Secretary, Translated from Ovideo's Historia General y Natural de las Indias,* edited by Edward Gaylord Bourne, 2:160–62. New York: A. S. Barnes.

Dickemann, M.
1979   Female Infanticide and the Reproductive Strategies of Stratified Human Societies: A Preliminary Model. In *Evolutionary Biology and Human Social Behavior: An Anthropological Perspective*, edited by Napoleon A. Chagnon and William Irons. North Scituate, Mass.: Duxbury Press.

Dickens, Roy S.
1975   A Processual Approach to Mississippian Origins on the Georgia Piedmont. *Southeastern Archaeological Conference Bulletin* 18:31–42.
1976   *Cherokee Prehistory: The Pisgah Phase in the Appalachian Summit Region.* Knoxville: University of Tennessee Press.
1985   The Form, Function, and Formation of Garbage Filled Pits on Southeastern Aboriginal Sites: An Archaeobotanical Analysis. In *Structure and Process in Southeastern Archaeology*, edited by Roy S. Dickens, Jr., and H. Trawick Ward, pp. 34–59. Tuscaloosa: University of Alabama Press.

Dickson, D. Bruce
1981   The Yanomamo of the Mississippi Valley? Some Reflections on Larson (1972), Gibson (1974) and Mississippian Warfare in the Southeastern United States. *American Antiquity* 46:909–16.

Dincauze, Dena F.
1987   Strategies for Paleoenvironmental Reconstruction in Archaeology. In *Advances in Archaeological Method and Theory*, edited by Michael B. Schiffer, 11:255–336. New York: Academic Press.

Dincauze, Dena F., and R. J. Hasenstab
1989   Explaining the Iroquois: Tribalization on a Prehistoric Periphery. In *Centre and Periphery: Comparative Studies in Archaeology*, edited by Timothy C. Champion, pp. 67–87. London: Unwin Hyman.

Dobyns, Henry F.
1983   *Their Number Become Thinned.* Knoxville: University of Tennessee Press.

Drennan, Robert D.
1985   *Regional Archaeology in the Valle de la Plata, Columbia: A Preliminary Report on the 1984 Season of the Proyecto Arqueólogico Valle de la Plata.* Museum of Anthropology Research Reports in Archaeology, no. 11. Ann Arbor: University of Michigan.
1987   Regional Demography in Chiefdoms. In *Chiefdoms in the Americas*, edited by Robert D. Drennan and Carlos A. Uribe, pp. 307–23. Lanham, Md.: University Press of America.
1988   Household Location and Compact versus Dispersed Settlement in Prehispanic Mesoamerica. In *Household and Community in the Mesoamerican Past: Case Studies in the Maya Area and Oaxaca*, edited by Richard Wilk and Wendy Ashmore, pp. 273–93. Albuquerque: University of New Mexico Press.
1991a   Cultural Evolution, Human Ecology, and Empirical Research. In *Profiles in Cultural Evolution: Papers from a Conference in Honor of Elman R. Service*, edited by A. Terry Rambo and Kathleen Gillogly, pp. 113–35. Anthropological Papers, no. 85. Ann Arbor: University of Michigan, Museum of Anthropology.
1991b   Prehispanic Chiefdom Trajectories in Mesoamerica, Central America, and Northern South America. In *Chiefdoms: Power, Economy, and Ideology*, edited by Timothy K. Earle, pp. 263–87. Cambridge, England: Cambridge University Press.

Drennan, Robert D., and Carlos A. Uribe (editors)
1987   *Chiefdoms in the Americas.* Lanham, Md.: University Press of America.

Drucker, Lesley M.
1983   *An Archaeological Survey of 30 Club Lease Tracts in Columbia, Lincoln, and McDuffie Counties, Georgia–Clarks Hill Lake.* Resource Study Series, no. 64. Columbia, S.C.: Carolina Archaeological Services.
1984   *A Cultural Resources Investigation for the Williston Interceptor Project, Barnwell County, South Carolina.* Resource Study Series, no. 72. Columbia, S.C.: Carolina Archaeological Services.
Drucker, Lesley M., and Ronald W. Anthony
1983   *An Archaeological Study of the Proposed Columbia County Industrial Park, Columbia County, Georgia.* Resource Study Series, no. 70. Columbia, South Carolina: Carolina Archaeological Services.
Drucker, Lesley M., Ronald W. Anthony, and Michael A. Harmon
1979   *A Cultural Resources Inventory Survey for the Proposed State Park on Lake Hartwell, Oconee County, South Carolina.* Resource Study Series, no. 11. Columbia, South Carolina: Carolina Archaeological Services.
Drucker, Lesley M., Ronald W. Anthony, Susan H. Jackson, Susan J. Krantz, and Carl R. Steen
1984   *An Archaeological Study of the Little River–Buffalo Creek Special Land Disposal Tract, Clarks Hill Lake, McCormick County, South Carolina.* Resource Study Series, no. 75. Columbia, S.C.: Carolina Archaeological Services.
Dumont de Montigny
1753   *Mémoires historiques sur la Louisiane*, edited by Le Mascrier. 2 vols. Paris.
Duncan, Gwyneth A.
1985   A Morphological Analysis of the Tugalo Phase Vessel Assemblage. M.A. thesis, Department of Anthropology, University of Georgia.
Du Pratz, Le Page
1758   *Histoire de la Louisiane.* 3 vols. Paris.
Durham, William H.
1976   Resource Competition and Human Aggression. Part 1: A Review of Primitive War. *The Quarterly Review of Biology* 51:385–415.
Dye, David H.
1990   Warfare in the Sixteenth Century Southeast: The De Soto Expedition in the Interior. In *Columbian Consequences*, vol 2: *Archaeological and Historical Perspectives on the Spanish Borderlands East*, edited by David H. Thomas, pp. 211–22. Washington, D.C.: Smithsonian Institution Press.
Dyson-Hudson, Rada, and Eric A. Smith
1978   Human Territoriality: An Ecological Reassessment. *American Anthropologist* 80:21–41.
Earle, Timothy K.
1977   A Reappraisal of Redistribution: Complex Hawaiian Chiefdoms. In *Exchange Systems in Prehistory*, edited by Timothy K. Earle and Jonathan E. Ericson, pp. 213–29. New York: Academic Press.
1978   *Economic and Social Organization of a Complex Chiefdom: The Halelea District, Kaua'i, Hawaii.* Anthropological Papers, no. 63. Ann Arbor: University of Michigan, Museum of Anthropology.
1987   Chiefdoms in Archaeological and Ethnohistorical Perspective. *Annual Review of Anthropology* 16:279–308.
1989   The Evolution of Chiefdoms. *Current Anthropology* 30:84–88.
1991   The Evolution of Chiefdoms. In *Chiefdoms: Power, Economy, and Ideology*, edited by Timothy K. Earle, pp. 1–15. Cambridge, England: Cambridge University Press.

Earle, Timothy K. (editor)
1991   *Chiefdoms: Power, Economy, and Ideology*. Cambridge, England: Cambridge University Press.

Earle, Timothy K., and Jonathan E. Ericson (editors)
1977   *Exchange Systems in Prehistory*. New York: Academic Press.

Ecija, Francisco Fernandez de
1605   Testimonio del viaje que hizo el Capitan Francisco Fernandez de Ecija a la visita de la coste de la Canda del Norte de este pressidio: anõ 1605. Translated by Day Wardlow. In *The Spanish Settlements within the Present Limits of the United States*, edited by Woodbury Lowery, vol. 5. Washington, D.C.: Library of Congress Manuscript Division, undated.
1609   Orden del Gobernador D. Pedro de Ibarra (de S. Augustin de la Florida) a el Capitan Francisco Fernandez de Ecija para reconocer las costas del norte de aquella provincia y relacion de este viaje llevado a cavo por el mismo capitan. In *The Spanish Settlements within the Present Limits of the United States*, edited by Woodbury Lowery, vol. 6. Washington, D.C.: Library of Congress Manuscript Division, undated.

Egloff, Brian J.
1967   An Analysis of Ceramics from Historic Cherokee Towns. M.A. thesis, Department of Anthropology, University of North Carolina.

Elliott, Daniel T.
1985   *Archaeological Reconnaissance of the Purrysburg Tract, Jasper County, South Carolina*. Atlanta, Ga.: Garrow and Associates.
1986a   *Archaeological Survey for the Landings Development, Chatham County, Georgia*. Atlanta, Ga.: Garrow and Associates.
1986b   *CRM: Vogtle-Effingham-Thalmann 500 kV Electric Transmission Line. GP-SN-08:Data Recovery*. Atlanta, Ga.: Garrow and Associates.
1987   Surface Collections from Five Sites near Brier Creek in Screven County, Georgia. Manuscript on file at the Laboratory of Archaeology, University of Georgia.

Elliott, Daniel T., and Dennis B. Blanton
1985   *Archaeological Survey of Elbert and Coldwater Creek Recreation Areas, Richard B. Russell Multiple Resource Area, Elbert County, Georgia*. Atlanta, Ga.: Garrow and Associates.

Elliott, Daniel T., and Roy Doyon
1981   *Archaeological and Historical Geography of the Savannah River Floodplain near Augusta, Georgia*. Report, no. 22. Athens: University of Georgia, Laboratory of Anthropology.

Elliott, Daniel T., and Stephen A. Kowalewski
1987   Fortson Mound, 9Ws2. *Lamar Briefs* 10:4.

Elliott, Daniel T., and Lisa D. O'Steen
1987   Anatomy of the Brier Creek Archaic. Paper presented at the 44th annual Southeastern Archaeological Conference, Charleston, S.C., November 12.

Elliott, Daniel T., and Marvin T. Smith
1985   *Final Report on Archaeological Survey of the Fort Howard Paper Company Tract, Effingham County Tract*. Atlanta, Ga.: Garrow and Associates.

Elliott, Daniel T., and Jack T. Wynn
1991   The Vinning Revival: A Late Simple Stamped Phase in the Central Georgia Piedmont. *Early Georgia* 19:1–18.

Elvas, Fidalgo de
1904   True Relation of the Vicissitudes That Attended the Governor Don

Hernando De Soto and Some Nobles of Portugal in the Discovery of the Province of Florida Now Just Given by a Fidalgo of Elvas. 1557. Evora, Portugal. Reprint. In *Narratives of the Career of Hernando De Soto in the Conquest of Florida as Told by a Knight of Elvas and in a Relation by Luys Hernandez de Biedma, Factor of the Expedition, Translated by Buckingham Smith, Together with an Account of De Soto's Expedition Based on the Diary of Rodrigo Ranjel, His Probate Secretary, Translated from Ovideo's Historia General y Natural de las Indias,* edited by Edward Gaylord Bourne, 2:1–223. New York: A. S. Barnes.

1993   True Relation of the Hardships Suffered Governor Hernando De Soto & Certain Portuguese Gentlemen During the Discovery of the Province of Florida. Now Newly Set Forth by a Gentleman of Elvas. In *The De Soto Chronicles: The Expedition of Hernando De Soto to North America in 1539–1543,* vol. 1, edited by Lawrence A. Clayton, Vernon James Knight, Jr., and Edward C. Moore, pp. 19–219. Tuscaloosa: University of Alabama Press.

Emerson, Thomas E.

1991   Some Perspectives on Cahokia and the Northern Mississippian Expansion. In *Cahokia and the Hinterlands: Observations from the American Midwest,* edited by Thomas E. Emerson and R. Barry Lewis, pp. 221–36. Urbana: University of Illinois Press.

Esarey, Duane, and Timothy W. Good

1981   *Final Report on FAI-270 and Illinois Route 460 Related Excavations at the Lohmann Site 11-S-49, St. Clair County, Illinois.* FAI-270 Archaeological Mitigation Project Report, no. 39. Macomb: Western Illinois University, Department of Sociology and Anthropology.

Espenshade, Christopher T.

1986   *CRM: Vogtle-Effingham-Thalmann 500 kV Electric Transmission Line. GP-SN-13: Data Recovery.* Atlanta, Ga.: Garrow and Associates.

1988   An Archaeological Survey of the Proposed 329/43 Connector, McCormick County, South Carolina. Report prepared by Brockington and Associates, on file at the South Carolina Institute of Archaeology and Anthropology, University of South Carolina.

Espenshade, Christopher T., Thomas Pluckhahn, Marian Roberts, David C. Jones, and Eric C. Poplin

1993   *Cultural Resources Survey and Testing of the Georgia Pacific (Thompson-Towns) Tract Screven County, Georgia.* Atlanta, Ga.: Brockington and Associates.

Eubanks, W. S., Jr.

1989   Studying De Soto's Route: A Georgian House of Cards. *Florida Anthropologist* 42(4):369–80.

1990a   Swanton: Four . . . Hudson: Zero. A Response to Hudson, Smith, Anderson, Chardon. *Soto States Anthropologist* 90(1):2–32.

1990b   The Lattimire Urn. *Soto States Anthropologist* 90(2):112–23.

1991   De Soto: Still Another Look. *Soto States Anthropologist* 91(2):149–90.

Fairbanks, Charles H.

1950   A Preliminary Segregation of Etowah, Savannah, and Lamar. *American Antiquity* 16:142–51.

1952   Creek and Pre-Creek. In *Archaeology of the Eastern United States,* edited by James B. Griffin, pp. 285–300. Chicago: University of Chicago Press.

1956   *Archaeology of the Funeral Mound, Ocmulgee National Monument, Georgia.* Archaeological Research Series, no. 3. Washington, D.C.: National Park Service.

Fallers, Lloyd A.
1973   *Inequality*. Chicago: University of Chicago Press.

Faulkner, Charles H.
1977   The Winter House: An Early Southeastern Tradition. *Midcontinental Journal of Archaeology* 2:141–59.

Feinman, Gary
1980   *The Relationship between Administrative Organization and Ceramic Production in the Valley of Oaxaca, Mexico*. Ph.D. dissertation, Department of Anthropology, City University of New York. Ann Arbor: University Microfilms.

Feinman, Gary, and Jill Neitzel
1984   Too Many Types: An Overview of Sedentary Prestate Societies in the Americas. In *Advances in Archaeological Method and Theory*, edited by Michael B. Schiffer, 7:39–102. New York: Academic Press.

Ferguson, Leland G.
1971   *South Appalachian Mississippian*. Ph.D. dissertation, Department of Anthropology, University of North Carolina. Ann Arbor: University Microfilms.
1973   *Sediment Basin Project, Savannah Harbor, Georgia*. Research Manuscript Series, no. 52. Columbia: University of South Carolina, South Carolina Institute of Archaeology and Anthropology.
1975   Mississippian Artifacts and Geography. Paper presented at the annual meeting of the Southern Anthropological Society, Clearwater Beach, Fla. April.
n.d.   Lower Savannah River Survey. Notes and records on file at the South Carolina Institute of Archaeology and Anthropology, University of South Carolina.

Ferguson, Leland G. (editor)
1974   Archaeological Investigations at the Mulberry Site. South Carolina Institute of Archaeology and Anthropology, University of South Carolina. *The Notebook* 6 (3–4).

Ferguson, Leland G., and Stanton W. Green
1984   South Appalachian Mississippian: Politics and Environment in the Old, Old South. *Southeastern Archaeology* 3:139–43.

Ferguson, Leland G., and Randolph J. Widmer
1976   *Archaeological Examination of a Transect through the Middle Savannah River Valley: The Bobby Jones Expressway*. Research Manuscript Series, no. 89. Columbia: University of South Carolina, South Carolina Institute of Archaeology and Anthropology.

Firth, Raymond W.
1936   *We, the Tikopia: A Sociological Study of Kinship in Primitive Polynesia*. London: George Allen and Unwin.
1961   *History and Traditions of Tikopia*. Wellington, New Zealand: Polynesian Society.

Fisch, Eva
1982   The Early and Middle Formative Periods. In *Monte Alban's Hinterland*, part 1: *The Prehispanic Settlement Patterns of the Central and Southern Parts of the Valley of Oaxaca, Mexico*, edited by Richard E. Blanton, Stephen Kowalewski, Gary Feinman, and Jill Appel, pp. 27–36. Memoirs of the Museum of Anthropology, no. 7. Ann Arbor: University of Michigan.

Fish, Paul R.
1976   *Patterns of Prehistoric Site Distribution in Effingham and Screven Counties, Georgia*. Report, no. 11. Athens: University of Georgia, Laboratory of Archaeology.

Fish, Paul R., and Suzanne K. Fish (editors)
1984   *Prehistoric Agricultural Strategies in the Southwest.* Anthropological Research Papers, no. 33. Tempe: Arizona State University.

Fish, Paul R., and David J. Hally
1983   The Wallace Reservoir Archaeological Project: An Overview. *Early Georgia* 11:1–18.

Fish, Suzanne K.
1985   Palynology. In *Archaeological Investigations at the Beaverdam Creek Site (9Eb85), Elbert County, Georgia,* by James L. Rudolph and David J. Hally, pp. 411–16. Russell Papers. Atlanta: National Park Service, Interagency Archeological Services.

Flannery, Kent V.
1972   The Cultural Evolution of Civilizations. *Annual Review of Ecology and Systematics* 3:399–426.

Flannery, Kent V. (editor)
1976   *The Early Mesoamerican Village.* New York: Academic Press.

Flannery, Kent V., and Joyce Marcus (editors)
1983   *The Cloud People: Divergent Evolution of the Zapotec and Mixtec Civilizations.* New York: Academic Press.

Flint, Lawrence L., and Robert C. Suggs
1980   An Archaeological Investigation of the Bullard Group Sites 9Eb76 and 9Eb348, Richard B. Russell Multiple Resource Area, Elbert County, Georgia. Report on file at the Interagency Archeological Services Division, National Park Service, Atlanta.

Ford, Richard I.
1974   Northeastern Archaeology: Past and Future Directions. *Annual Review of Anthropology* 3:385–413.
1977   Evolutionary Ecology and the Evolution of Human Ecosystems: A Case Study from the Midwestern United States of America. In *Explanation of Prehistoric Change,* edited by James N. Hill, pp. 153–84. Albuquerque: University of New Mexico Press.
1980   The Color of Survival. In *Discovery,* pp. 17–29. Santa Fe, N.M.: School of American Research.

Fortes, Meyer
1945   *The Dynamics of Clanship among the Tallensi.* Oxford, England: Oxford University Press.

Foss, John, D. P. Wagner, and F. P. Miller
1985   *Soils of the Savannah River Valley, Richard B. Russell Multiple Resource Area, Elbert County, Georgia.* Russell Papers. Atlanta: National Park Service, Interagency Archeological Services.

Foss, Robert W., and Richard A. Warner
1977   *A Cultural Resource Survey of Proposed Savannah River Pipeline Crossing, Hart County, Georgia, and Anderson County, South Carolina.* Report ES-906. Marietta, Ga.: Soil Systems.

Fowler, Melvin R.
1974   *Cahokia: Ancient Capital of the Midwest.* McCaleb Module in Anthropology. Reading, Mass.: Addison-Wesley.
1975   A Pre-Colombian Urban Center on the Mississippi. *Scientific American* 233:92–101.
1978   Cahokia and the American Bottoms: Settlement Archaeology. In *Mississippian Settlement Systems,* edited by Bruce D. Smith, pp. 455–78. New York: Academic Press.

Freer, Jennifer A.
1989   Archaeological Settlement Patterns in Oglethorpe County, Georgia. M.A. thesis, Department of Anthropology, University of Georgia.
1991   Prehistoric and Historic Settlement in Oglethorpe County, Georgia. *Early Georgia* 19:43–62.

Fried, Morton H.
1967   *The Evolution of Political Society*. New York: Random House.
1975   *The Notion of Tribe*. Menlo Park, Calif.: Cumings.
1983   Tribe to State or State to Tribe in Ancient China? In *The Origins of Chinese Civilization*, edited by David N. Keightley, pp. 467–93. Berkeley: University of California Press.

Friedman, Jonathan, and Michael J. Rowlands
1977   Notes toward an Epigenetic Model of the Evolution of "Civilization." In *The Evolution of Social Systems*, edited by J. Friedman and M. J. Rowlands, pp. 201–76. Pittsburgh: University of Pittsburgh Press.

Fritts, Steven H., and L. David Mech
1981   *Dynamics, Movements, and Feeding Ecology of a Newly Protected Wolf Population in Northwestern Minnesota*. Journal of Wildlife Management, Wildlife Monographs, no. 80, supplement. St. Paul: University of Minnesota Agriculture Experiment Station.

Gaffney, Lori A., and Jack T. Wynn
1981   *A Cultural Resources Survey of the Littleton Land Exchange, Habersham County, Georgia*. Report, no. 80-CA-230-E-1. Gainesville, Ga.: U.S.D.A. Forest Service.

Gage, Timothy B.
1979   The Competitive Interactions of Man and Deer in Prehistoric California. *Human Ecology* 7:253–68.

Galloway, Patricia
1990   Sources for the Soto Expedition: Intertextuality and the Elusivenesss of Truth. Paper presented at the annual meeting of the Society for Spanish and Portuguese Historical Studies, New Orleans, La.
1991   The Archaeology of Ethnohistorical Narrative. In *Columbian Consequences*, vol. 3: *The Spanish Borderlands in Pan-American Perspective*, edited by David H. Thomas, pp. 453–69. Washington, D.C.: Smithsonian Institution Press.
1992   The Unexamined Habitus: Direct Historic Analogy and the Archaeology of Text. In *Representations in Archaeology*, edited by Jean-Claude Gardin and Christopher S. Peebles, pp. 178–95. Bloomington: Indiana University Press.

Galloway, Patricia (editor)
1989   *The Southeastern Ceremonial Complex: Artifacts and Analysis, the Cottonlandia Conference*. Lincoln: University of Nebraska Press.
n.d.   The Historiography of the De Soto Expedition (manuscript in preparation).

Gardner, Paul S.
1985   Paleoethnobotany. In *Archaeological Investigation of the Beaverdam Creek Site (9Eb85), Elbert County, Georgia*, edited by James L. Rudolph and David J. Hally, pp. 400–11. Russell Papers. Atlanta: National Park Service, Interagency Archeological Services.
1986a   Carbonized Plant Remains from Parris Island South (9Eb21), Sara's Ridge (38An29), and Simpson's Field (38An8) Sites. In *Prehistory in the Richard B. Russell Reservoir: The Archaic and Woodland Periods of the Upper Savannah River: The Final Report of the Data Recovery at the Anderson and Elbert County Groups: 38An8, 38An29, 38An126, 9Eb17, 9Eb19 and 9Eb21*, edited by W.

Dean Wood, Dan T. Elliott, Teresa P. Rudolph, and Dennis B. Blanton, pp. 387–92. Russell Papers. Atlanta: National Park Service, Interagency Archeological Services.

1986b   Carbonized Plant Remains from Feature 160, Simpson's Field (38An8), Anderson County, South Carolina. In *Prehistory in the Richard B. Russell Reservoir: The Archaic and Woodland Periods of the Upper Savannah River: The Final Report of the Data Recovery at the Anderson and Elbert County Groups: 38An8, 38An29, 38An126, 9Eb17, 9Eb19 and 9Eb21*, edited by W. Dean Wood, Dan T. Elliott, Teresa P. Rudolph, and Dennis B. Blanton, pp. 377–86. Russell Papers. Atlanta: National Park Service, Interagency Archeological Services.

Gardner, William M.
1984   An Interpretive Overview of the Prehistory of Richard B. Russell Multiple Resource Area, Elbert and Hart Counties, Georgia, and Abbeville and Anderson Counties, South Carolina. Report prepared by Thunderbird Research Corporation, on file at the Interagency Archeological Services Division, National Park Service, Atlanta.

Gardner, William M., Lauralee Rappleye, and William Barse
1983   Results of Archaeological Reconnaissance and Testing of Previously Unsurveyed Floodplains and 35 Archaeological Sites in the Richard B. Russell Multiple Resource Area, Georgia and South Carolina. Report prepared by Thunderbird Research Corporation, on file at the Interagency Archeological Services Division, National Park Service, Atlanta.

Garrow, Patrick H.
1975   The Woodland Period North of the Fall Line. *Early Georgia* 3:17–26.
1978   *A Cultural Resource Survey of the Proposed 40 Inch O.D. Pipeline, Powder Springs, Georgia to the Savannah River: Phase II: The Sample Survey.* Report, no. ES-968, Marietta, Ga.: Soil Systems.
1980   *Cultural Resources Survey of Fifteen Proposed Shower and Restroom Facility Sites, Clarks Hill and Hartwell Lakes, Georgia and South Carolina.* Marietta, Ga.: Soil Systems.

Garrow, Patrick H. (editor)
1984   *Cultural Resource Management Vogtle-Effingham-Thalmann Transmission Line, Burke, Screven, Effingham, Chatham, Bryan, Liberty, Long, McIntosh, and Glynn Counties, Georgia. Resource Inventory II: Final Report.* Atlanta, Ga.: Garrow and Associates.

Garrow, Patrick H., and Bruce H. Bauer (editors)
1984   *Cultural Resource Management Vogtle to Goshen Transmission Line, Burke and Richmond Counties, Georgia. Resource Inventory II: Final Report.* Atlanta, Ga.: Garrow and Associates.

Garrow, Patrick H., Bertram S. A. Herbert, and Stephen H. Savage
1980   *Cultural Resource Reconnaissance: Kimberly-Clark Corporation Drinking and Sanitary Tissue Manufacturing Facility, Augusta, Georgia.* Marietta, Ga.: Soil Systems.

Garrow, Patrick H., Claudia Watson, Thomas R. Wheaton, and William H. Adams
1978   *A Cultural Resources Inventory and Archaeological Survey for the Augusta 201 Facilities Plan, Augusta, Georgia.* Report ES-1079. Marietta, Ga.: Soil Systems.

Gibson, Jon L.
1974   Aboriginal Warfare in the Protohistoric Southeast: An Alternative Perspective. *American Antiquity* 39:130–33.

Gilbert, Robert I., Jr.
1985   Stress, Paleonutrition, and Trace Elements. In *The Analysis of Prehistoric Diets*, edited by Robert I. Gilbert, Jr., and J. H. Mielke, pp. 339–58. New York: Academic Press.

Gilman, Antonio
1981   The Development of Social Stratification in Bronze Age Europe. *Current Anthropology* 22:1–8.

Gladfelter, B. G.
1981   Developments and Directions in Geoarchaeology. In *Advances in Archaeological Method and Theory*, edited by Michael B. Schiffer, 4:343–64. New York: Academic Press.

Gluckman, Max
1950   Kinship and Marriage among the Lozi of Northern Rhodesia and the Zulu of Natal. In *African Systems of Kinship and Marriage*, edited by A. R. Radcliffe-Brown and C. D. Forde. London: Oxford University Press.
1951   The Lozi of Barotseland in North-Western Rhodesia. In *Seven Tribes of Central Africa*, edited by Elizabeth Colson and Max Gluckman, pp. 1–93. Manchester, England: Manchester University Press.

Goad, Sharon I.
1979   *Chert Resources in Georgia: Archaeological and Geological Perspectives.* Report, no. 21. Athens: University of Georgia, Laboratory of Archaeology.

Godelier, Maurice
1986   *The Mental and the Material: Thought, Economy, and Society.* London: Verso Press.

Goldman, Irving
1955   Status Rivalry and Cultural Evolution in Polynesia. *American Anthropologist* 67:680–97.
1970   *Ancient Polynesian Society.* Chicago: University of Chicago Press.

Goodman, A. H., J. W. Lallo, G. J. Armelagos, and J. C. Rose
1984   Health Changes at Dickson Mounds, Illinois (A.D. 950–1300). In *Paleopathology at the Origins of Agriculture*, edited by M. N. Cohen and G. J. Armelagos, pp. 271–305. Orlando, Fla.: Academic Press.

Goody, Jack
1971   *Technology, Tradition, and the State in Africa.* London: Oxford University Press.

Goodyear, Albert C.
1978   *An Archeological Survey of the Primary Connector from Laurens to Anderson, South Carolina.* Research Manuscript Series, no. 152. Columbia: University of South Carolina, South Carolina Institute of Archaeology and Anthropology.

Goodyear, Albert C., and Tommy Charles
1984   *An Archaeological Survey of Chert Quarries in Western Allendale County, South Carolina.* Research Manuscript Series, no. 195. Columbia: University of South Carolina, South Carolina Institute of Archaeology and Anthropology.

Goodyear, Albert C., III, and Glen T. Hanson (editors)
1989   *Studies in South Carolina Archaeology: Papers in Honor of Robert L. Stephenson.* Anthropological Studies, no. 9. Columbia: University of South Carolina, South Carolina Institute of Archaeology and Anthropology.

Goodyear, Albert C., John H. House, and Neal W. Ackerly
1979   *Laurens-Anderson: An Archaeological Study of the Inter-riverine Piedmont.*

Anthropological Studies, no. 4. Columbia: University of South Carolina, South Carolina Institute of Archaeology and Anthropology.

Graham, Martha D.
1973   Dental Morphology, Attrition, and Pathology in Selected Skulls from Town Creek Indian Mound, Mount Gilead, North Carolina. M.A. thesis, Department of Anthropology, University of North Carolina.

Gramly, Richard Michael
1977   Deerskins and Hunting Territories: Competition for a Scarce Resource of the Northeastern Woodlands. *American Antiquity* 42:601–5.

Grange, Roger D.
1972   The I. C. Few Site (38Pn2). Manuscript on file at the South Carolina Institute of Archaeology and Anthropology, University of South Carolina.

Green, William
1991   The Search for Altamaha: The Archaeology and Ethnohistory of an Early 18th Century Yamasee Indian Town. M.A. thesis, Department of Anthropology, University of South Carolina.

Green, William, and Chester B. DePratter
1990   Origins of the Yamasee. Paper presented at the 47th annual meeting of the Southeastern Archaeological Conference, Mobile, Ala. November 8.

Gregg, Michael L.
1975   A Population Estimate for Cahokia. In *Perspectives in Cahokia Archaeology*, pp. 126–36. Illinois Archaeological Survey Bulletin. Urbana: University of Illinois.

Gresham, Thomas H.
1985a   *Archaeological Investigations at Two Ridge Top Lithic Scatter Sites, Lincoln County, Georgia.* Athens, Ga.: Southeastern Archaeological Services.
1985b   *Archaeological Investigations at 9Lc24, Lincoln County, Georgia.* Athens, Ga.: Southeastern Archaeological Services.

Gresham, Thomas H., and Karen G. Wood
1986   *Archaeological Data Recovery at 38Ab387 and 9Eb368, Richard B. Russell Lake, Abbeville County, South Carolina, and Elbert County, Georgia.* Athens, Ga.: Southeastern Archaeological Services.

Gresham, Thomas H., Teresa P. Rudolph, James L. Rudolph, and Karen G. Wood
1986   *Archaeological Survey of Alternative Routes for the Fall Line Freeway, Georgia.* Athens, Ga.: Southeastern Archaeological Services.

Griffin, James B. (editor)
1952   *Archeology of Eastern United States.* Chicago: University of Chicago Press.

Griffin, James B.
1952   Culture Periods in Eastern United States Archeology. In *Archeology of Eastern United States*, edited by James B. Griffin, pp. 325–64. Chicago: University of Chicago Press.
1961   Some Correlations of Climatic and Cultural Change in Eastern North American Prehistory. *Annals of the New York Academy of Sciences* 95:710–17.
1967   Eastern North American Archaeology: A Summary. *Science* 156:175–91.
1977   The University of Michigan Excavations at the Pulcher Site in 1950. *American Antiquity* 42:462–90.
1978   Foreword to *Mississippian Settlement Patterns*, edited by Bruce D. Smith, pp. xv–xxii. New York: Academic Press.
1985   Changing Concepts of the Prehistoric Mississippian Cultures of the Eastern United States. In *Alabama and the Borderlands: From Prehistory to Statehood*, edited by R. Reid Badger and Lawrence A. Clayton, pp. 40–63. Tuscaloosa: University of Alabama Press.

1991 Cahokia and Its Neighbors: Archaeological Myth-stakes. Paper presented in the symposium Exploring and Exploding Myths about Cahokia, 56th annual meeting of the Society for American Archaeology, New Orleans, La. April 26.

1993 Cahokia Interaction with Contemporary Southeastern and Eastern Societies. *Midcontinental Journal of Archaeology* 18:1–17.

Gross, Daniel R.

1975 Protein Capture and Cultural Development in the Amazon Basin. *American Anthropologist* 77:526–49.

Grove, Jean M.

1988 *The Little Ice Age*. London: Methuen.

Haas, Jonathan

1982 *The Evolution of the Prehistoric State*. New York: Columbia University Press.

1990 *The Anthropology of War*. Cambridge, England: Cambridge University Press.

Hack, J. T.

1942 *The Changing Physical Environment of the Hopi Indians of Arizona*. Papers of the Peabody Museum of American Archaeology and Ethnology, no. 35(1). Cambridge, Mass.: Harvard University, The Museum.

Haecker, Charles M., and George I. Williams

1978 *Archaeological Survey of the 200 Acre Development Tract, Chatham County, Georgia*. Report ES-965. Marietta, Ga.: Soil Systems.

Hally, David J.

1979 *Archaeological Investigation of the Little Egypt Site (9Mu102), Murrey County, Georgia, 1969 Season*. Report, no. 18. Athens: University of Georgia, Laboratory of Archaeology.

1980 Archaeological Investigation of the Little Egypt Site (9Mu102), Murrey County, Georgia, 1970–1972 Seasons. Manuscript on file at the Interagency Archaeological Services Division, National Park Service, Atlanta.

1983a Use Alterations of Pottery Vessel Surfaces: An Important Source of Evidence for the Identification of Vessel Function. *North American Archaeologist* 4:3–26.

1983b The Interpretive Potential of Pottery from Domestic Contexts. *Midcontinental Journal of Archaeology* 8:163–96.

1984 Vessel Assemblages and Food Habits: A Comparison of Two Aboriginal Southeastern Vessel Assemblages. *Southeastern Archaeology* 3:46–64.

1986a The Cherokee Archaeology of Georgia. In *The Conference on Cherokee Prehistory*, edited by David G. Moore, pp. 95–121. Swannanoa, N.C.: Warren Wilson College.

1986b The Identification of Vessel Function: A Case Study from Northwest Georgia. *American Antiquity* 51:267–95.

1987 Abandoned Centers and Change in Mississippian Societies: Platform Mounds and the Nature of Mississippian Chiefdoms. Paper presented at the 44th annual Southeastern Archaeological Conference, Charleston, S.C. November 13.

1989 The Ecological and Cultural Context of the Etowah Site. Paper presented at the 46th annual Southeastern Archaeological Conference, Tampa, Fla. November 10.

1990 Upper Savannah River. In *Lamar Archaeology: Mississippian Chiefdoms in the Deep South*, edited by Mark Williams and Gary Shapiro, pp. 52–55. Tuscaloosa: University of Alabama Press.

1992 Platform Mound Construction and the Instability of Mississippian

Chiefdoms. Paper presented at the 49th annual Southeastern Archaeological Conference, Little Rock, Ark. October 22.

1993   The Territorial Size of Mississippian Chiefdoms. In *Archaeology of Eastern North America: Papers in Honor of Stephen Williams*, edited by James B. Stoltman, pp. 143–168. Archaeological Report No. 25. Jackson: Mississippi Department of Archives and History.

Hally, David J., and James B. Langford, Jr.
1988   *Mississippi Period Archaeology of the Georgia Valley and Ridge Province.* Report, no. 25. Athens: University of Georgia, Laboratory of Archaeology.

Hally, David J., and James L. Rudolph
1986   *Mississippi Period Archaeology of the Georgia Piedmont.* Report, no. 24. Athens: University of Georgia, Laboratory of Archaeology.

Hally, David J., Patrick M. Garrow, and Wyman Trotti
1975   Preliminary Analysis of the King Site Settlement Plan. *Southeastern Archaeological Conference Bulletin* 18:55–62.

Hally, David J., Charles M. Hudson, and Chester B. DePratter
1985   The Proto-historic along the Savannah River. Paper presented at the 42nd annual Southeastern Archaeological Conference, Birmingham, Ala. November 7.

Hally, David J., Marvin T. Smith, and James B. Langford, Jr.
1990   The Archaeological Reality of DeSoto's Coosa. In *Columbian Consequences*, vol. 2: *Archaeological and Historical Perspectives on the Spanish Borderlands East*, edited by David H. Thomas, pp. 121–38. Washington, D.C.: Smithsonian Institution Press.

Halstead, Paul, and John O'Shea (editors)
1989a   *Bad Year Economics: Cultural Responses to Risk and Uncertainty.* Cambridge, England: Cambridge University Press.

1989b   Cultural Responses to Risk and Uncertainty. Introduction to *Bad Year Economics: Cultural Responses to Risk and Uncertainty*, edited by Paul Halstead and John O'Shea, pp. 57–67. Cambridge, England: Cambridge University Press.

Hames, Raymond B., and William T. Vickers (editors)
1983   *Adaptive Responses of Native Amazonians.* New York: Academic Press.

Hanson, Glen T., and Chester B. DePratter
1985   The Early and Middle Woodland in the Savannah River Valley. Paper presented at the 42nd annual Southeastern Archaeological Conference, Birmingham, Ala., November 7.

Hanson, Glen T., and Rachel Most
1978   *An Archaeological Reconnaissance of the Talatha Unit, Sumter National Forest, Aiken County, South Carolina.* Research Manuscript Series, no. 138. Columbia: University of South Carolina, South Carolina Institute of Archaeology and Anthropology.

Hanson, Glen T., Richard D. Brooks, and John W. White
1981   *The Human Occupation along the Steel Creek Floodplain: Results of an Intensive Archeological Survey for the L-Area Reactivation Project, Savannah River Plant, Barnwell County, South Carolina.* Research Manuscript Series, no. 173. Columbia: University of South Carolina, South Carolina Institute of Archaeology and Anthropology.

Hanson, Glen T., Rachel Most, and David G. Anderson
1978   *The Preliminary Archaeological Inventory of the Savannah River Plant, Aiken and Barnwell Counties, South Carolina.* Research Manuscript Series, no. 134.

Columbia: University of South Carolina, South Carolina Institute of Archaeology and Anthropology.

Harmon, Michael A.
1986   *Eighteenth Century Lower Cherokee Adaptation and Use of European Material Culture*. Volumes in Historical Archaeology, no. 2. Columbia: University of South Carolina, South Carolina Institute of Archaeology and Anthropology.

Harn, Alan D.
1978   Mississippian Settlement Patterns in the Central Illinois River Valley. In *Mississippian Settlement Patterns*, edited by Bruce D. Smith, pp. 233–68. New York: Academic Press.

Harner, M. A.
1972   *The Jivaro: People of the Sacred Waterfalls*. New York: Natural History Press.

Hassan, Fekri A.
1981   *Demographic Archaeology*. New York: Academic Press.

Hatch, James W.
1974   Social Dimensions of Dallas Mortuary Patterns. M.A. thesis, Department of Anthropology, Pennsylvania State University.
1975   Social Dimensions of Dallas Burials. *Southeastern Archaeological Conference Bulletin* 18:132–38.
1976   *Status in Death: Principles of Ranking in Dallas Culture Mortuary Remains*. Ph.D. dissertation, Department of Anthropology, Pennsylvania State University. Ann Arbor: University Microfilms.
1987   Mortuary Indicators of Organizational Variability among Late Prehistoric Chiefdoms in the Southeastern U.S. Interior. In *Chiefdoms in the Americas*, edited by Robert D. Drennan and Carlos A. Uribe, pp. 9–18. Lanham, Md.: University Press of America.

Hatch, James W., and Richard A. Geidel
1985   Status-specific Dietary Variation in Two New World Cultures. *Journal of Human Evolution* 14:469–76.

Hatch, James W., and Patrick Willey
1974   Stature and Status in Dallas Society. *Tennessee Archaeologist* 30:107–31.

Hatch, James W., Patrick Willey, and Edward E. Hunt, Jr.
1983   Indicators of Status-related Stress in Dallas Society: Transverse Lines and Cortical Thickness in Long Bones. *Midcontinental Journal of Archaeology* 8:49–71.

Hawkins, Benjamin
1848   A Sketch of the Creek Country in the Years 1798 and 1799. *Collections of the Georgia Historical Society* 3(1).

Hawley, Florence M.
1941   *Tree-Ring Analysis and Dating in the Mississippi Drainage*. University of Chicago Publications in Anthropology, Occasional Papers, no. 2. Chicago: University of Chicago Press.

Healan, Dan M.
1972   *Surface Delineation of Functional Areas at a Mississippian Ceremonial Center*. Missouri Archaeological Society Memoir 10. Columbia: University of Missouri.

Helms, Mary W.
1979   *Ancient Panama: Chiefs in Search of Power*. Austin: University of Texas Press.
1987   Art Styles and Interaction Spheres in Central America and the Caribbean: Polished Black Wood in the Greater Antilles. In *Chiefdoms in the Americas*,

edited by Robert D. Drennan and Carlos A. Uribe, pp. 67–83. Lanham, Md.: University Press of America.

1988   *Ulysses' Sail: An Ethnographic Odyssey of Power, Knowledge, and Geographical Distance.* Princeton, N. J.: Princeton University Press.

1992   Political Lords and Political Ideology in Southeastern Chiefdoms: Comments and Observations. In *Lords of the Southeast: Social Inequality and the Native Elites of Southeastern North America*, edited by Alex W. Barker and Timothy R. Pauketat, pp. 185–94. Archaeological Papers of the American Anthropological Association, no. 3.

Henige, David

1986   The Context, Content, and Credibility of *La Florida del Ynca. The Americas* 43:1–23.

Heye, George G., F. W. Hodge, and G. H. Pepper

1918   *The Nacoochee Mound in Georgia.* Contributions from the Heye Museum of the American Indian 2(1). New York: The Museum.

Hickerson, Harold

1965   The Virginia Deer and Intertribal Buffer Zones in the Upper Mississippi Valley. In *Man, Culture, and Animals*, edited by A. L. and A. P. Vayda, pp. 43–65. Washington, D.C.: American Association for the Advancement of Science.

Hill, Mary Cassandra

1979   The Alabama River Phase: A Biological Synthesis and Interpretation. M.A. thesis, Department of Anthropology, University of Alabama.

1981   The Mississippian Decline in Alabama: A Biological Analysis. *American Journal of Physical Anthropology* 54:233.

Hilton, William

1663   A True Relation of a Voyage upon Discovery of Part of the Coast of Florida, from the Lat. of 31 Deg. to 33 Deg. 45 m. North Lat. in the Ship Adventure, William Hilton Commander, and Commissioner with Captain Anthony Long and Peter Fabian Set Forth by Several Gentlemen and Merchants of the Island of Barbadoes; Sailed from Spikes Bay Aug. 10, 1663. In *The Shaftesbury Papers and Other Records Relating to Carolina and the First Settlement on Ashley River Prior to the Year 1676*, edited by Langdon Cheves, 5:18–28. Collections of the South Carolina Historical Society. Charleston: The Society, 1897.

Hodder, Ian

1978   Simple Correlations between Material Culture and Society: A Review. In *The Spatial Organization of Culture*, edited by Ian Hodder, pp. 3–24. Pittsburgh: University of Pittsburgh Press.

Hodder, Ian, and Clive Orton

1976   *Spatial Analysis in Archaeology.* Cambridge, England: Cambridge University Press.

Hoffman, Paul E.

1990a   *A New Andalucia and a Way to the Orient: A History of the Southeast during the Sixteenth Century.* Baton Rouge: Louisiana State University Press.

1990b   The Pardo Documents. In *The Juan Pardo Expeditions: Exploration of the Carolinas and Tennessee, 1566–1568*, by Charles M. Hudson, pp. 203–342. Washington, D.C.: Smithsonian Institution Press.

1993   Introduction: The De Soto Expedition, a Cultural Crossroads. In *The De Soto Chronicles: The Expedition of Hernando De Soto to North America in 1539–1543*, vol. 1, edited by Lawrence A. Clayton, Vernon James Knight, Jr., and Edward C. Moore, pp. 1–17. Tuscaloosa: University of Alabama Press.

Holmes, William H.

1903   Aboriginal Pottery of the Eastern United States. In Annual Report 20, pp. 1–201. Washington, D.C.: Bureau of American Ethnology.

Holschlag, Stephanie, and Michael J. Rodeffer

1976   A Preliminary Archaeological Reconnaissance of the Little River Development Project, Alternative A. Manuscript on file at the South Carolina Institute of Archaeology and Anthropology, University of South Carolina.

Honerkamp, Nicholas

1973   *Archaeological Field Survey of the Alvin W. Vogtle Nuclear Plant Property in Burke County, Georgia*. Report, no. 6. Athens: University of Georgia, Laboratory of Archaeology.

House, John H.

1982   Evolution of Complex Societies in East-central Arkansas: An Overview of Environments and Regional Data Bases. In *Arkansas Archaeology in Review*, edited by Neal L. Trubowitz and Marvin D. Jeter, pp. 37–47. Research Series, no. 15. Fayetteville: Arkansas Archaeological Survey.

House, John H., and David L. Ballenger

1976   *An Archeological Survey of the Interstate 77 Route in the South Carolina Piedmont*. Research Manuscript Series, no. 104. Columbia: University of South Carolina, South Carolina Institute of Archaeology and Anthropology.

Hudson, Charles M.

1976   *The Southeastern Indians*. Knoxville: University of Tennessee Press.

1986   Some Thoughts on the Early Social History of the Cherokees. In *The Conference on Cherokee Prehistory*, edited by David G. Moore, pp. 139–57. Swannanoa, N.C.: Warren Wilson College.

1987   Juan Pardo's Excursion beyond Chiaha. *Tennessee Anthropologist* 12:74–87.

1988   A Spanish-Coosa Alliance in Sixteenth-century North Georgia. *Georgia Historical Quarterly* 62:599–626.

1990   *The Juan Pardo Expeditions: Exploration of the Carolinas and Tennessee, 1566–1568*. Washington, D.C.: Smithsonian Institution Press.

Hudson, Charles M., Marvin T. Smith, and Chester B. DePratter

1984   The Hernando DeSoto Expedition: From Apalachee to Chiaha. *Southeastern Archaeology* 3:65–77.

1988   The King Site Massacre Victims: An Historical Detectives' Report. In *The King Site: Biocultural Adaptations in Sixteenth Century Georgia*, edited by Robert L. Blakely, pp. 117–34. Athens: University of Georgia Press.

Hudson, Charles M., John E. Worth, and Chester B. DePratter

1990   Refinements in Hernando DeSoto's Route through Georgia and South Carolina. In *Columbian Consequences*, vol. 2: *Archaeological and Historical Perspectives on the Spanish Borderlands East*, edited by David H. Thomas, pp. 107–19. Washington, D.C.: Smithsonian Institution Press.

Hudson, Charles M., Marvin T. Smith, Chester B. DePratter, and Emilia Kelley

1989   The Tristan de Luna Expedition, 1559–1561. *Southeastern Archaeology* 8:31–45.

Hudson, Charles M., Marvin T. Smith, David J. Hally, Richard Polhemus, and Chester B. DePratter

1985   Coosa: A Chiefdom in the Sixteenth Century United States. *American Antiquity* 50:723–37.

1987   In Search of Coosa: Reply to Schroedl and Boyd. *American Antiquity* 52:840–57.

Hulse, Frederick S.
1941   The People Who Lived at Irene. In *Irene Mound Site, Chatham County, Georgia*, edited by Joseph R. Caldwell and Catherine McCann, pp. 57–68. Athens: University of Georgia Press.

Huss-Ashmore, Rebecca, Alan H. Goodman, and George J. Armelagos
1982   Nutritional Inference from Paleopathology. In *Advances in Archaeological Method and Theory*, edited by Michael B. Schiffer, 5:395–474. New York: Academic Press.

Hutto, Brooks
1970   *Archaeological Survey of the Elbert County, Georgia, Portion of the Proposed Trotter's Shoals Reservoir, Savannah River.* Laboratory of Archaeology Series, no. 7. Athens: University of Georgia.

Ingram, M. J., G. Farmer, and T. M. L. Wigley
1981   Past Climates and Their Impact on Man: A Review. In *Climate and History: Studies in Past Climates and Their Impact on Man*, edited by T. M. L. Wigley, M. J. Ingram, and G. Farmer, pp. 3–50. Cambridge, England: Cambridge University Press.

Jameson, John H., Jr.
1986   *An Intensive Cultural Resource Survey of Proposed Expansions of the Raysville, Petersburg, and Winfield Recreation Areas, Clarks Hill Lake, Columbia and McDuffie Counties, Georgia.* Savannah, Ga.: U.S. Army Corps of Engineers.

Jefferies, Richard W., and David J. Hally
1975   An Archaeological Reconnaissance of Structures 1, 2, 3, 33, 51, 58 and 60, Grove River Watershed, Jackson and Banks Counties, Georgia. Manuscript on file at the Laboratory of Archaeology, University of Georgia.

Jochim, Michael A.
1976   *Hunter-Gatherer Subsistence and Settlement: A Predictive Model.* New York: Academic Press.
1981   *Strategies for Survival: Cultural Behavior in an Ecological Context.* New York: Academic Press.

John, Brian S.
1977   *The Ice Age Past and Present.* Glasgow, Scotland: William Collins Sons.

Johnson, Gregory A.
1973   *Local Exchange and Early State Development in Southwestern Iran.* Anthropological Papers, no. 51. Ann Arbor: University of Michigan, Museum of Anthropology.
1977   Aspects of Regional Analysis in Archaeology. *Annual Review of Anthropology* 6:479–508.
1978   Information Sources and the Development of Decision-making Organizations. In *Social Archaeology beyond Subsistence and Dating*, edited by C. L. Redman, M. J. Berman, E. V. Curtin, W. T. Langhorne, Jr., N. M. Versaggi, and J. C. Wanser, pp. 87–112. New York: Academic Press.
1980   Rank Size Convexity and System Integration. *Economic Geography* 56:234–47.
1982   Organizational Structure and Scalar Stress. In *Theory and Explanation in Archaeology: The Southampton Conference*, edited by Colin Renfrew, M. J. Rowlands, and Barbara A. Segraves, pp. 389–421. New York: Academic Press.
1987   The Changing Organization of Uruk Administration on the Susiana Plain. In *The Archaeology of Western Iran: Settlement and Society from Prehistory to the Islamic Conquest*, edited by Frank Hole, pp. 107–39. Washington, D.C.: Smithsonian Institution Press.

Jones, Charles C.
1861   *Monumental Remains of Georgia*. Savannah, Ga.: John M. Cooper and Co.
1873   *Antiquities of the Southern Indians, Particularly of the Georgia Tribes*. New York: D. Appleton and Co.
1878   Ancient Tumuli on the Savannah River, Visited by William Bartram, in 1776. *Annual Report of the Board of Regents of the Smithsonian Institution . . . for the Year 1877*, pp. 283–89. Washington, D.C.: Government Printing Office.
1880   Primitive Manufacture of Spear and Arrow Points along the Line of the Savannah River. *Annual Report of the Board of Regents of the Smithsonian Institution . . . for the Year 1879*, pp. 376–82. Washington, D.C.: Government Printing Office.

Jones, Grant D.
1978   The Ethnohistory of the Guale Coast through 1684. In *The Anthropology of St. Catherine's Island*, vol. 1: *Natural and Cultural History*, edited by David H. Thomas, pp. 178–210. American Museum of Natural History Anthropological Papers, no. 55(2). New York: The Museum.

Joseph, J. W.
1986   *CRM: Vogtle-Effingham-Thalmann 500 Kv Electric Transmission Line: GP-LI-01 Data Recovery*. Atlanta, Ga.: Garrow and Associates.

Judge, Christopher
1987   Aboriginal Vessel Function in Mississippian Society: A Case Study from the Mulberry Site (38Ke12). M.A. thesis, Department of Anthropology, University of South Carolina.
1988a   *Archaeological Inventory Survey of the Proposed Bruson Wastewater Treatment Plant Facilities, Hampton County, South Carolina*. Resource Study Series, no. 127. Columbia, S.C.: Carolina Archaeological Services.
1988b   *Archaeological Inventory of the Proposed Thomson-McDuffie County Water Treatment Plant Facilities, McDuffie County, Georgia*. Resource Study Series, no. 126. Columbia, S.C.: Carolina Archaeological Services.
1989   *Archaeological Inventory Survey of the Proposed Pioneer Rural Water District Utility Line at Hartwell Lake, Anderson County, South Carolina*. Resource Study Series, no. 134. Columbia, S.C.: Carolina Archaeological Services.

Karl, T. R., L. K. Metcalf, M. L. Nicodemus, and R. G. Quayle
1982   *Statewide Average Climatic History*. Historical Climatology Series, no. 6-1. Asheville, N.C.: National Climate Data Center.
1985   *Atlas of Monthly Palmer Moisture Anomaly Indices (1931–1983) for the Contiguous United States*. Historical Climatology Series, no. 3-9. Asheville, N.C.: National Climate Data Center.

Keel, Bennie C.
1976   *Cherokee Archaeology: A Study of the Appalachian Summit*. Knoxville: University of Tennessee Press.

Kellar, James H., Arthur R. Kelly, and Edward V. McMichael
1962   The Mandeville Site in Southwestern Georgia. *American Antiquity* 27:336–55.

Kelly, Arthur R.
1938   A Preliminary Report on Archaeological Explorations at Macon, Georgia. Bulletin 119. Washington, D.C.: Bureau of American Ethnology.
1941   Foreword to *Irene Mound Site, Chatham County, Georgia*, by Joseph R. Caldwell and Catherine McCann, pp. v–vii. Athens: University of Georgia Press.

1970 *Explorations at Bell Field Mound and Village: Seasons 1966, 1967, 1968.* Atlanta: National Park Service, Interagency Archeological Services.

1972 *The 1970–1971 Field Season at Bell Field Mound, Carters Dam.* Atlanta: National Park Service, Interagency Archeological Services.

1979 Hopewellian Studies in American Archaeology: Hopewell after Twenty Years. In *Hopewell Archaeology: The Chillicothe Conference*, edited by David S. Brose and N'omi Greber, pp. 1–2. Kent, Ohio: Kent State University Press.

Kelly, Arthur R., and Clemens DeBaillou

1960 Excavation of the Presumptive Site of Estatoe. *Southern Indian Studies* 12:3–30.

Kelly, Arthur R., and Betty A. Smith

1975 The Swift Creek Site, (9BI3), Macon, Georgia. Manuscript on file at the Laboratory of Archaeology, University of Georgia.

Kelly, Arthur R., and Robert S. Neitzel

1959 Chauga Mound and Village (38Oc1) and Other Sites in the Hartwell Basin. Manuscript on file at the Interagency Archaeological Services Division, National Park Service, Atlanta.

1961 *The Chauga Site in Oconee County, South Carolina.* Laboratory of Archaeology Series, no. 3. Athens: University of Georgia.

Kelly, Arthur R., Frank T. Schnell, Donald F. Smith, and Ann L. Schlosser

1965 Explorations in Sixtoe Field, Carter's Dam, Murray County, Georgia: Seasons of 1962, 1963, 1964. Manuscript on file at the Interagency Archaeological Services Division, National Park Service, Atlanta.

Kelly, John Edward

1972 An Archaeological Survey of the Piedmont Region in North Central South Carolina. M.A. thesis, Department of Anthropology, University of Wisconsin–Madison.

1980 *Formative Developments at Cahokia and the Adjacent American Bottom: A Merrell Tract Perspective.* Ph.D. dissertation, Department of Anthropology, University of Wisconsin–Madison. Ann Arbor: University Microfilms.

1987 Emergent Mississippian and the Transition from Late Woodland to Mississippian: The American Bottom Case for a New Concept. In *The Emergent Mississippian: Proceedings of the Sixth Mid-South Conference Archaeological Conference, June 6–9, 1985*, edited by R. A. Marshall, pp. 212–26. Occasional Papers, no. 87-01. Mississippi State: Mississippi State University, Cobb Institute of Archaeology.

1990a Range Site Community Patterns and the Mississippian Emergence. In *The Mississippian Emergence*, edited by Bruce D. Smith, pp. 67–112. New York: Academic Press.

1990b The Emergence of Mississippian Culture in the American Bottom. In *The Mississippian Emergence*, edited by Bruce D. Smith, pp. 113–52. New York: Academic Press.

Kelly, John E., Andrew C. Frontier, Steven J. Ozuk, and Joyce A. Williams

1987 *The Range Site (11-S-47): Archaic through Late Woodland Occupations.* American Bottom Archaeology FAI-270 Site Reports, no. 16. Urbana: University of Illinois Press.

Kelly, John E., Steven J. Ozuk, Douglas K. Jackson, Dale L. McElrath, Fred A. Finney, and Duane Esarey

1984 Emergent Mississippian. In *American Bottom Archaeology*, edited by Charles J. Bareis and James W. Porter, pp. 128–57. Urbana: University of Illinois Press.

Kelly, Lucretia S.
1979   *Animal Resource Exploitation by Early Cahokia Populations on the Merrell Tract.* Illinois Archaeological Survey Circular 4. Urbana: University of Illinois Press.

Kent, Susan (editor)
1989   *Farmers as Hunters: The Implications of Sedentism.* Cambridge, England: Cambridge University Press.

Ketcham, Herbert E.
1954   Three Sixteenth Century Spanish Chronicles Relating to Georgia. *Georgia Historical Quarterly* 38:66–82.

King, Adam
1991a Excavations at Mound B, Etowah: 1954–1958. M.A. thesis, Department of Anthropology, University of Georgia.
1991b A New Chronology for the Etowah Site. Paper presented at the annual meeting of the Society for American Archaeology, New Orleans, La. April.

King, Adam, and Jennifer A. Freer
1992   The Mississippian Southeast: A World Systems Perspective. Paper presented at the 49th annual Southeastern Archaeological Conference, Little Rock, Ark., October 23.

Kirch, Patrick V.
1984   *The Evolution of the Polynesian Chiefdoms.* Cambridge, England: Cambridge University Press.

Kirch, Patrick V. (editor)
1986   *Island Societies: Archaeological Approaches to Evolution and Transformation.* Cambridge, England: Cambridge University Press.

Kirchoff, Paul
1955   The Principles of Clanship in Human Society. *Davidson Journal of Anthropology* 1:1–10.

Klepinger, L. L.
1984   Nutritional Assessment from Bone. *Annual Review of Anthropology* 13:75–96.

Knight, Vernon James, Jr.
1981   *Mississippian Ritual.* Ph.D. dissertation, Department of Anthropology, University of Florida. Ann Arbor: University Microfilms.
1985   Symbolism of Mississippian Mounds. Paper presented at the 42nd annual Southeastern Archaeological Conference, Birmingham, Ala., November.
1986   The Institutional Organization of Mississippian Religion. *American Antiquity* 51:675–87.
1988   *A Summary of Alabama's De Soto Mapping Project and Project Bibliography.* Alabama De Soto Commission Working Papers, no. 9. Tuscaloosa: University of Alabama, State Museum of Natural History.
1990   Social Organization and the Evolution of Hierarchy in Southeastern Chiefdoms. *Journal of Anthropological Research* 46:1–23.

Kohl, Philip L.
1987   The Use and Abuse of World Systems Theory: The Case of the Pristine West Asian State. In *Advances in Archaeological Method and Theory,* edited by Michael B. Schiffer, 11:1–35. New York: Academic Press.

Kowalewski, Stephen A.
1990   The Evolution of Cultural Complexity in the Valley of Oaxaca. *Annual Review of Anthropology* 19:39–58.

Kowalewski, Stephen A., and James W. Hatch
1991 The 16th Century Expansion of Settlement in the Upper Oconee Watershed, Georgia. *Southeastern Archaeology* 10:1–17.

Kowalewski, Stephen A., and Mark Williams
1989 The Carroll Site (9Pm85): Analysis of 1936 Excavations at a Mississippian Farmstead in Georgia. *Southeastern Archaeology* 8:46–67.

Kowalewski, Stephen A., Gary M. Feinman, Laura Finstein, Richard E. Blanton, and Linda M. Nicholas
1989 *Monte Alban's Hinterland.* Part 2: *Prehispanic Settlement Patterns in Tlacolula, Etla, and Ocotlan, the Valley of Oaxaca, Mexico.* Memoir 23. Ann Arbor: University of Michigan, Museum of Anthropology.

Kroeber, A. L.
1939 *Cultural and Natural Areas of Native North America.* Berkeley: University of California Press.

Kronberg, Nathan, and John C. Purvis
1959 *Climate of the States: South Carolina.* Weather Bureau Climatograph of the United States, no. 60-38. Washington, D.C.: U.S. Department of Commerce.

Lafferty, Robert H., III
1973 An Analysis of Prehistoric Southeastern Fortifications. M.A. thesis, Department of Anthropology, Southern Illinois University.

Lahren, C. H., and H. E. Berryman
1984 Fracture Patterns and Status at Chucalissa: A Biocultural Approach. *Tennessee Anthropologist* 9:15–21.

Lamb, H. H.
1966 *The Changing Climate.* London: Methuen.
1977 *Climate: Present, Past, and Future.* 2 vols. London: Methuen.
1981 An Approach to the Study of the Development of Climate and Its Impact in Human Affairs. In *Climate and History: Studies in Past Climates and Their Impact on Man,* edited by T. M. L. Wigley, M. J. Ingram, and G. Farmer, pp. 291–309. Cambridge, England: Cambridge University Press.
1982 *Climate, History and the Modern World.* London: Methuen.

Lambert, J. B., C. B. Szpunar, and J. E. Buikstra
1979 Chemical Analysis of Excavated Human Bone from Middle and Late Woodland Sites. *Archaeometry* 21:115–29.

Larsen, Clark Spencer
1982 *The Anthropology of St. Catherines Island,* vol. 3: *Prehistoric Human Biological Adaptation,* pp. 155–270. Anthropological Papers of the American Museum of Natural History, no. 57. New York: The Museum.
1983 Behavioral Implications of Temporal Change in Cariogenesis. *Journal of Archaeological Science* 10:1–8.
1987 Bioarchaeological Interpretations of Subsistence Economy and Behavior from Human Skeletal Remains. In *Advances in Archaeological Method and Theory,* edited by Michael B. Schiffer, 10:339–445. New York: Academic Press.
1990 Biological Interpretation and the Context for Contact. In *The Archaeology of Mission Santa Catalina de Guale,* vol. 2: *Biocultural Interpretations of a Population in Transition,* edited by Clark S. Larsen, pp. 11–25. Anthropological Papers of the American Museum of Natural History, no. 68. New York: The Museum.

Larsen, Clark Spencer (editor)
1990 *The Archaeology of Mission Santa Catalina de Guale,* vol. 2: *Biocultural Interpre-*

tations of a Population in Transition. Anthropological Papers of the American Museum of Natural History, no. 68. New York: The Museum.

Larsen, Clark Spencer, and Christopher B. Ruff
1991 Biomechanical Adaptation and Behavior on the Prehistoric Georgia Coast. In *What Mean These Bones? Studies in Southeastern Bioarchaeology,* edited by Mary Lucas Powell, Patricia S. Bridges, and Ann Marie Wagner Mires, pp. 102–13. Tuscaloosa: University of Alabama Press.

Larsen, Clark Spencer, Margaret J. Schoeninger, Nikolaas J. van der Merwe, Katherine M. Moore, and Julia A. Lee-Thorp
1992 Carbon and Nitrogen Stable Isotope Signatures of Human Dietary Change in the Georgia Bight. *American Journal of Physical Anthropology* 89:197–214.

Larson, Daniel O., and Joel Michaelson
1990 Impacts of Climatic Variability and Population Growth on Virgin Branch Anasazi Cultural Developments. *American Antiquity* 55:227–49.

Larson, Lewis H., Jr.
1971a Settlement Distribution during the Mississippi Period. *Southeastern Archaeological Conference Bulletin* 13:19–25.
1971b Archaeological Implications of Social Stratification at the Etowah Site, Georgia. In *Approaches to the Social Dimensions of Mortuary Practices,* edited by James A. Brown, pp. 58–67. Society for American Archaeology Memoir 25.
1972 Functional Considerations of Warfare in the Southeast during the Mississippian Period. *American Antiquity* 37:383–92.
1978 Historic Guale Indians of the Georgia Coast and the Impact of the Spanish Mission Effort. In *Tacachale: Essays on the Indians of Florida and Southeastern Georgia during the Historic Period,* edited by Jerald T. Milanich and Samuel Proctor, pp. 120–40. Gainesville: University Presses of Florida.
1980a *Sapelo Papers: Researches in the History and Prehistory of Sapelo Island, Georgia.* Studies in the Social Sciences, no. 19. Carrollton: West Georgia College.
1980b *Aboriginal Subsistence Technology on the Southeastern Coastal Plain during the Late Prehistoric Period.* Ripley P. Bullen Monographs in Anthropology and History, no. 2. Gainesville: University Presses of Florida.
1986 Settlement Distribution during the Mississippi Period (revised). In *The Late Prehistoric Southeast: A Source Book,* edited by Chester B. DePratter. New York: Garland.
1989 The Etowah Site. In *The Southeastern Ceremonial Complex: Artifacts and Analysis, the Cottonlandia Conference,* edited by Patricia Galloway, pp. 133–41. Lincoln: University of Nebraska Press.

Lawson, John
1709 *A New Voyage to Carolina; Containing the Exact Description and Natural History of That Country Together with the Present State Thereof and a Journal of a Thousand Miles, Traveled thro' Several Nations of Indians, Giving a Particular Account of Their Customs, Manners, etc.* London.
1967 *A New Voyage to Carolina,* edited by Hugh T. Leffler. Chapel Hill: University of North Carolina Press.

Leach, E. R.
1954 *Political Systems of Highland Burma: A Study of Kachin Social Structure.* Monographs on Social Anthropology, no. 44. London: London School of Economics.

Ledbetter, R. Jerald
1983 *A Cultural Resources Survey on a Portion of Mistletoe State Park, Columbia County, Georgia.* Athens, Ga.: Southeastern Archaeological Services.

1988   *The Pig Pen Site: Archaeological Investigations at 9Ri158 Richmond County, Georgia.* Athens, Ga.: Southeastern Archaeological Services.

Ledbetter, R. Jerald, and Thomas H. Gresham
1988   *A Cultural Resources Survey of the Proposed Mill Branch Impoundment, Warren County, Georgia.* Athens, Ga.: Southeastern Archaeological Services.

Ledbetter, R. Jerald, and Jack Wynn
1988   *An Archaeological Assessment of Three Sites in the Oconee National Forest, Greene County, Georgia.* Athens, Ga.: Southeastern Archaeological Services.

Ledbetter, R. Jerald, Roy Doyon, and W. Dean Wood
1980   *A Cultural Resource Survey of a Proposed Butler Creek Sewage Pipeline Corridor.* Athens, Ga.: Southeastern Wildlife Services.

Ledbetter, R. Jerald, Karen G. Wood, and Cynthia Miller
1985   *Archaeological Investigations at Mistletoe State Park, Columbia County, Georgia.* Athens, Ga.: Southeastern Archaeological Services.

Lee, Chung H.
1976   The Beaverdam Creek Mound (9Eb85), Elbert County, Georgia. Manuscript on file at the Laboratory of Archaeology, University of Georgia.
1977   *Settlement Pattern Analysis of the Late Mississippian Period in Piedmont Georgia.* Ph.D. dissertation, Department of Anthropology, University of Georgia. Ann Arbor: University Microfilms.
1978   Locational Analysis of Late Mississippian Sites in the Southern Piedmont. *Early Georgia* 6:22–31.

Leeds, Anthony
1960   Ecological Determinants of Chieftainship among the Yaruro Indians of Venezuela. *Akten des 34. Internationalen Amerikanistenkongresses*, pp. 597–608. Reprinted in *Environment and Cultural Behavior: Ecological Studies in Cultural Anthropology*, edited by Andrew P. Vayda, pp. 377–94. Garden City, N.J.: Natural History Press.

Leffler, Hugh T. (editor)
1967   *A New Voyage to Carolina.* Chapel Hill: University of North Carolina Press.

LeMoyne, Jacques
1875   *Narrative of LeMoyne, an Artist Who Accompanied the French Expedition to Florida under Laudonnière 1564.* Translated from the Latin of De Brÿ. Boston.

Le Petit, Father
n.d.   Letter to d'Avaugour. In *Jesuit Relations and Allied Documents: In Travels and Explorations of the Jesuit Missionaries in New France, 1610–1791*, edited by Reuben Goldthwaites, 68:120–223. Cleveland, Ohio.

Lenski, Gerhard E.
1966   *Power and Privilege: A Theory of Social Stratification.* New York: McGraw-Hill.

Levy, Janet E., J. Alan May, and David G. Moore
1990   From Ysa to Joara: Cultural Diversity in the Catawba Valley from the Fourteenth to the Sixteenth Century. In *Columbian Consequences*, vol. 2: *Archaeological and Historical Perspectives on the Spanish Borderlands East*, edited by David H. Thomas, pp. 153–68. Washington, D.C.: Smithsonian Institution Press.

Lewis, Clifford M.
1978   The Calusa. In *Tacachale: Essays on the Indians of Florida and Southeastern Georgia during the Historic Period*, edited by Jerald T. Milanich and Samuel Proctor, pp. 19–49. Gainesville: University Presses of Florida.

Lewis, Thomas M. N., and Madeline Kneberg
1946   *Hiwassee Island: An Archaeological Account of Tennessee Indian Peoples.* Knox-
        ville: University of Tennessee Press.
Lightfoot, Kent G.
1984   *Prehistoric Political Dynamics: A Case Study from the American Southwest.*
        DeKalb: Northern Illinois University Press.
1987   A Consideration of Complex Prehistoric Societies in the U.S. Southwest. In
        Chiefdoms ,in the Americas, edited by Robert D. Drennan and Carlos A.
        Uribe, pp. 43–56. Lanham, Md.: University Press of America.
Lillios, Katina Tobias
1991   *Competition to Fission: The Copper to Bronze Age Transition in the Lowlands of
        West-central Portugal (3000–1000 B.C.).* Ph.D. dissertation, Department of
        Anthropology, Yale University. Ann Arbor: University Microfilms.
Lowery, Woodbury (editor)
n.d.   *The Spanish Settlements within the Present Limits of the United States.* 18 vols.
        Washington, D.C.: Library of Congress.
Lowie, Robert
1946   Social and Political Organization of the Tropical Forest and Marginal
        Tribes. In *Handbook of South American Indians,* edited by Julian Steward,
        5:313–67. Washington, D.C.: Bureau of American Ethnology.
Lundmark, Hans
1984   The Identification of Tribal Hierarchies. In *Settlement and Economy in Later
        Scandinavian Prehistory,* edited by Kristian Kristiansen, pp. 43–61. Interna-
        tional Series, no. 211. Oxford, England: British Archaeological Reports.
Lyon, Eugene
1984   *Santa Elena: A Brief History of the Colony, 1566–1587.* Research Manuscript
        Series, no. 193. Columbia: University of South Carolina, South Carolina
        Institute of Archaeology and Anthropology.
Lynott, Mark J., Thomas W. Boutton, James E. Price, and Dwight E. Nelson
1986   Stable Carbon Isotopic Evidence for Maize Agriculture in Southeast Mis-
        souri and Northeast Arkansas. *American Antiquity* 51:51–65.
Machiavelli, Niccolò
1950   *The Discourses.* London: Routledge and Kegan Paul.
Manning, Mary K.
1982   *Archaeological Investigations at 9Pm260.* Wallace Reservoir Project Contri-
        bution 16. Athens: University of Georgia, Department of Anthropology.
Marquardt, William H.
1986   The Development of Cultural Complexity in Southwest Florida: Elements
        of a Critique. *Southeastern Archaeology* 5:63–70.
1987   The Calusa Social Formation in Protohistoric South Florida. In *Power
        Relations and State Formation,* edited by Thomas C. Patterson and Christine
        W. Gailey, pp. 98–116. Washington, D.C.: American Anthropological Asso-
        ciation, Archeology Section.
1988   Politics and Production among the Calusa of South Florida. In *Hunters and
        Gatherers,* vol. 1, *History, Evolution, and Social Change,* edited by Tim Ingold,
        David Richs, and James Woodburn, pp 161–88. London: Berg Publishers.
1989   Agency, Structure, and Power: Operationalizing a Dialectical Anthropo-
        logical Archaeology. Paper presented at the Wenner-Gren Foundation for
        Anthropological Research Symposium 108, Critical Approaches in Arche-
        ology: Material Life, Meaning, and Power, Cascais, Portugal, March 17–25.

1992   Dialectical Archaeology. In *Archaeological Method and Theory*, edited by Michael B. Schiffer, 4:101–140. Tucson: University of Arizona Press.

Marrinan, Rochelle A.
1979   *The Cultural Resources of Savannah National Wildlife Refuge, South Carolina and Georgia*. Atlanta: National Park Service, Interagency Archeological Services.

Marrinan, Rochelle A., John F. Scarry, and Rhonda L. Majors
1990   Prelude to De Soto: The Expedition of Panfilo de Narváez. In *Columbian Consequences*, vol. 2: *Archaeological and Historical Perspectives on the Spanish Borderlands East*, edited by David H. Thomas, pp. 71–82. Washington, D.C.: Smithsonian Institution Press.

Martin, Debra K., and Lesley M. Drucker
1987   *Archaeological Inventory Survey of Pole Branch and Southwest Interceptors, Aiken County, South Carolina*. Resource Study Series, no. 113. Columbia, S.C.: Carolina Archaeological Services.

Martin, Debra K., Lesley M. Drucker, and Susan H. Jackson
1987   *A Cultural Resources Inventory Study of U.S. Forest Service Land Exchange Parcels, McCormick County, South Carolina*. Resource Study Series, no. 105. Columbia, S.C.: Carolina Archaeological Services.

Martínez, Francisco
1567   The Story of the Voyage and Reconnaissance into the Interior of Florida in 1566 by Captain Juan Pardo, by Order of Governor Pedro Menéndez de Avilés, written by the Soldier Francisco Martínez. In *Explorations in Interior South Carolina by Hernando De Soto (1540) and Juan Pardo (1566–1568)*, edited by Chester DePratter, pp. 31–32. South Carolina Institute of Archaeology and Anthropology, University of South Carolina. *The Notebook* 19.

McGhee, Robert
1981   Archaeological Evidence for Climatic Change during the Last 5000 Years. In *Climate and History: Studies in Past Climates and Their Impact on Man*, edited by T. M. L. Wigley, M. J. Ingram, and G. Farmer, pp. 162–79. Cambridge, England: Cambridge University Press.

McKivergan, David A., Jr.
1991   Migration and Settlement among the Yamasee of South Carolina. M.A. thesis, Department of Anthropology, University of South Carolina.
1992   Balanced Reciprocity and Peer Polity Interaction in the Late Prehistoric Southeastern United States. Paper presented at the 49th annual Southeastern Archaeological Conference, Little Rock, Ark., October 23.

MacNutt, Francis Augustus (translator and editor)
1912   *De Orbe Novo: The Eight Decades of Peter Martyr D'Anghiera*. New York: Burt Franklin.

Mech, L. David
1977   Wolf-Pack Buffer Zones as Prey Reservoirs. *Science* 198:320–21.

Mehrer, Mark W.
1982   *A Mississippian Community at the Range Site (11-S-47), St. Clair County, Illinois*. FAI-270 Archaeological Mitigation Project Report 52. Urbana: University of Illinois, Department of Anthropology.

Merás, Gonzalo Solís de
1567   Memorial que hizo el Doctor Gonzalo Solís de Merás de todas las jornadas y sucesos del Adelantado Pedro Menéndez de Avilés, su cuñado, y de la Conquista de la Florida y Justicia que hizo en Juan Ribao y otros Franceses.

Reprinted in *Pedro Menéndez de Avilés: Adelantado, Governor and Captain-General of Florida; Memorial by Gonzalo Solís de Merás; First Published in La Florida su Conquista y Colonizacion por Pedro Menéndez de Avilés by Eugenio Ruidíaz y Caravia,* edited by Jeanette Thurber Connor, pp. 39–245. Publications of the Florida State Historical Society, no. 3. Deland, Fla.: The Society, 1928.

Meyer, Joseph S.
1988   Cultural Resources Survey of a Proposed 12.05 Mile Pipeline Corridor, Elbert, Hart and Madison Counties, Georgia. FERC Docket no. CP88-760-000. Manuscript prepared by New World Research, on file at the Laboratory of Archaeology, University of Georgia.

Michie, James L.
1990   *An Initial Archeological Survey of the Wachesaw/Richmond Plantation Property, Georgetown County, South Carolina.* Research Manuscript Series, no. 191. Columbia: University of South Carolina, South Carolina Institute of Archaeology and Anthropology.
1992   The Search for San Miguel de Gualdape. Paper presented at the 18th annual conference on South Carolina Archaeology, Columbia, S.C., March 28.

Milanich, Jerald T., and Charles H. Fairbanks
1980   *Florida Archaeology.* New York: Academic Press.

Miller, Carl F.
1949   The Lake Spring Site, Columbia County, Georgia. *American Antiquity* 15:254–58.
1950   An Analysis and Interpretation of the Ceramic Remains from Site 38Mc6 near Clark's Hill, S.C. *Journal of the Washington Academy of Sciences* 40:350–54.
1974   Appraisal of the Archaeological Resources of the Clark Hill Reservoir Area, South Carolina and Georgia (1948). South Carolina Institute of Archaeology and Anthropology, University of South Carolina. *The Notebook* 6:27–34.

Milling, Chapman
1940   *Red Carolinians.* Columbia: University of South Carolina Press.

Milner, George R.
1980   Epidemic Disease in the Postcontact Southeast: A Reappraisal. *Midcontinental Journal of Archaeology* 5:39–56.
1984a   Social and Temporal Implications of Variation among American Bottom Mississippian Cemeteries. *American Antiquity* 49:468–88.
1984b   *The Julien Site.* American Bottom Archaeology FAI-270 Site Reports, no. 7. Urbana: University of Illinois Press.
1986   Mississippian Population Density in a Segment of the Central Mississippi River Valley. *American Antiquity* 51:227–38.
1987a   The Development and Dissolution of an Organizationally Complex Mississippian Period Culture in the American Bottom, Illinois. Paper presented at the symposium Between Emergence and Demise: Examining Political Change in Mississippian Societies, 44th annual Southeastern Archaeological Conference, Charleston, S.C., November 13.
1987b   Cultures in Transition: The Late Emergent Mississippian and Mississippian Periods in the American Bottom, Illinois. In *The Emergent Mississippian: Proceedings of the Sixth Mid-South Conference Archaeological Conference,*

June 6–9, 1985, edited by R. A. Marshall, pp. 194–211. Occasional Papers, no. 87-01. Mississippi State: Mississippi State University, Cobb Institute of Archaeology.

1990   The Late Prehistoric Cahokia Cultural System of the Mississippi River Valley: Foundations, Florescence, and Fragmentation. *Journal of World Prehistory* 4:1–43.

1991   Health and Culture Change in the Late Prehistoric American Bottom, Illinois. In *What Mean These Bones? Studies in Southeastern Bioarchaeology*, edited by Mary Lucas Powell, Patricia S. Bridges, and Ann Marie Wagner Mires, pp. 52–69. Tuscaloosa: University of Alabama Press.

1993   Osteological Evidence for Prehistoric Warfare. In *Regional Perspectives on Mortuary Analysis*, edited by Lane A. Beck (manuscript under review).

Milner, George R., and Virginia G. Smith

1989   Carnivore Alteration of Human Bone from a Late Prehistoric Site in Illinois. *American Journal of Physical Anthropology* 79:43–49.

Milner, George R., David G. Anderson, and Marvin T. Smith

1992   The Distribution of Eastern Woodlands Peoples at the Prehistoric and Historic Interface. Paper presented in the symposium Societies in Eclipse, annual meeting of the Society for American Archaeology, Pittsburgh. To appear in *Societies in Eclipse*, edited by C. Wesley Cowan, Washington, D.C.: Smithsonian Institution Press (in press).

Milner, George R., Virginia G. Smith, and Eve Anderson

1991   Warfare in Late Prehistoric West-central Illinois. *American Antiquity* 56:581–603.

Milner, George R., Dorothy A. Humpf, and Henry C. Harpending

1989   Pattern Matching of Age-at-Death Distributions in Paleodemographic Analysis. *American Journal of Physical Anthropology* 80:49–58.

Mitchell, J. C.

1951   The Yao of Southern Nyasaland. In *Seven Tribes of Central Africa*, edited by Elizabeth Colson and Max Gluckman, pp. 292–353. Manchester, England: Manchester University Press.

Mitchell, William W., and David J. Hally

1975   An Archaeological Field Study of the Eli Whitney Watershed, Effingham and Chatham Counties, Georgia. Manuscript on file at the Laboratory of Archaeology, University of Georgia.

Mooney, James

1975   *Historical Sketch of the Cherokee*. 1900. Reprint. Chicago: Aldine.

Moore, Clarence B.

1898   Certain Aboriginal Mounds of the Savannah River. *Journal of the Academy of Natural Sciences of Philadelphia*. 2, no. 2 (2nd series):162–172.

Moore, David G.

1981   A Comparison of Two Pisgah Ceramic Assemblages. M.A. thesis, Department of Anthropology, University of North Carolina.

Moore, Josselyn F.

1985   Archeobotanical Analyses at Five Sites in the Richard B. Russell Reservoir, Georgia and South Carolina. In *Prehistoric Human Ecology along the Upper Savannah River: Excavations at the Rucker's Bottom, Abbeville, and Bullard Site Groups*, edited by David G. Anderson and Joseph Schuldenrein, pp. 673–93. Russell Papers. Atlanta: National Park Service, Interagency Archeological Services.

Morgan, John R.
1984   An Archaeological Survey of an Area Proposed for Development at Etowah Mounds, Bartow County, Georgia. *Early Georgia* 9:33–55.

Morse, Dan F.
1977   The Penetration of Northeast Arkansas by Mississippian Culture. In *For the Director: Research Essays in Honor of James B. Griffin*, edited by Charles E. Cleland, pp. 186–211. Anthropological Papers, no. 61. Ann Arbor: University of Michigan, Museum of Anthropology.
1980   The Big Lake Household and the Community. In *Zebree Archaeological Project: Excavation, Data Interpretation, and Report on the Zebree Homestead Site, Mississippi County, Arkansas*, edited by Dan F. Morse and Phyllis A. Morse, pp. 21-1 to 21-35. Fayetteville: Arkansas Archeological Survey.
1982   Regional Overview of Northeast Arkansas. In *Arkansas Archaeology in Review*, edited by Neal L. Trubowitz and Marvin D. Jeter, pp. 20–36. Research Series, no. 15. Fayetteville: Arkansas Archeological Survey.
1990   The Nodena Phase. In *Towns and Temples along the Mississippi*, edited by David H. Dye and Cheryl Anne Cox, pp. 69–97. Tuscaloosa: University of Alabama Press.

Morse, Dan F., and Phyllis A. Morse (editors)
1980   *Zebree Archaeological Project: Excavation, Data Interpretation, and Report on the Zebree Homestead Site, Mississippi County, Arkansas*. Fayetteville: Arkansas Archeological Survey.
1983   *Archaeology of the Central Mississippi Valley*. New York: Academic Press.
1990   The Spanish Exploration of Arkansas. In *Columbian Consequences*, vol. 2: *Archaeological and Historical Perspectives on the Spanish Borderlands East*, edited by David H. Thomas, pp. 197–210. Washington, D.C.: Smithsonian Institution Press.

Morse, Phyllis A.
1981   *Parkin: The 1978–1979 Archeological Investigations of a Cross County, Arkansas Site*. Research Series, no. 13. Fayetteville: Arkansas Archeological Survey.
1990   The Parkin Site and the Parkin Phase. In *Towns and Temples along the Mississippi*, edited by David H. Dye and Cheryl Anne Cox, pp. 118–34. Tuscaloosa: University of Alabama Press.

Muller, Jon
1989   The Southern Cult. In *The Southeastern Ceremonial Complex: Artifacts and Analysis, the Cottonlandia Conference*, edited by Patricia Galloway, pp. 11–26. Lincoln: University of Nebraska Press.

Murdock, George P.
1967   *Ethnographic Atlas*. Pittsburgh: University of Pittsburgh Press.

Murphy, Christopher, and Charles M. Hudson
1968   On the Problem of Intensive Agriculture in the Aboriginal Southeastern United States. Working Papers 2(1):24–34. Athens: University of Georgia, Department of Sociology and Anthropology.

Nag, Moni
1962   *Factors Affecting Fertility in Non-industrial Societies: A Cross Cultural Study*. New Haven, Conn.: Human Relations Area Files Press.

Naroll, Raoul
1956   A Preliminary Index of Social Development. *American Anthropologist* 58:687–715.
1962   Floor Area and Settlement Population. *American Antiquity* 27:587–89.

Nassaney, Michael S.

1992a *Experiments in Social Ranking in Prehistoric Central Arkansas.* Ph.D. dissertation, Department of Anthropology, University of Massachusetts. Ann Arbor: University Microfilms.

1992b Communal Societies and the Emergence of Elites in the Prehistoric American Southeast. In *Lords of the Southeast: Social Inequality and the Native Elites of Southeastern North America,* edited by Alex W. Barker and Timothy R. Pauketat, pp. 111–43. Archaeological Papers of the American Anthropological Association, no. 3.

Nelson, Michael E., and L. David Mech

1981 *Deer Social Organization and Wolf Predation in Northwestern Minnesota.* The Journal of Wildlife Management, Wildlife Monographs, no. 77, supplement. Minneapolis: University of Minnesota, Department of Ecology and Behavioral Biology, Bell Musuem of Natural History, University of Minnesota.

Netting, Robert

1968 *Hill Farmers of Nigeria: Cultural Ecology of the Kofyar of the Jos Plateau.* Seattle: University of Washington Press.

Novick, Andrea Lee

1978 Prehistoric Lithic Material Sources and Types in South Carolina. *South Carolina Antiquities* 10:422–37.

O'Brien, Patricia

1989 Cahokia: The Political Capital of the "Ramey" State? *North American Archaeologist* 10:275–92.

Ogilvie, Robert Maxwell

1971 Introduction to *Livy: The Early History of Rome,* books 1–5 of *The History of Rome from Its Foundation,* translated by Aubrey de Sélincourt, pp. 7–29. Harmondsworth, Middlesex, England: Penguin Books.

Oliver, Billy L.

1987 Support Communities of the Pee Dee Phase in the Southern North Carolina Piedmont. Paper presented at the Town Creek Indian Mound 50th anniversary celebration, Southern Pines, N.C., April 11.

Orans, Martin

1966 Surplus. *Human Organization* 25:24–32.

O'Shea, John

1981 Coping with Scarcity: Exchange and Social Storage. *British Archaeological Reports International Series* 96:167–83.

1984 *Mortuary Variability: An Archaeological Investigation.* New York: Academic Press.

1989a The Role of Wild Resources in Small-scale Agricultural Systems: Tales from the Lakes and Plains. In *Bad Year Economics: Cultural Responses to Risk and Uncertainty,* edited by Paul Halstead and John O'Shea, pp. 57–67. Cambridge, England: Cambridge University Press.

1989b Conclusions: Bad Year Economics. In *Bad Year Economics: Cultural Responses to Risk and Uncertainty,* edited by Paul Halstead and John O'Shea, pp. 123–26. Cambridge, England: Cambridge University Press.

Oviedo y Valdéz, Gonzalo Fernández de (El Capitan)

1851–55 *Historia General y Natural de las Indias.* 4 vols. Madrid.

Padgett, Thomas

1980 Observations on Mossy Oak. *Southeastern Archaeological Conference Bulletin* 17:26–29.

Palmer, Edward
n.d.   McCollum Mound and House Site. Manuscript on file at the National Anthropological Archives, Smithsonian Institution.

Palmer, Wayne C.
1965   *Meteorological Drought Research*. Weather Bureau Research Paper 45. Washington, D.C.: U.S. Department of Commerce.

Pardo, Juan
1567   Report of the Entry and Conquest Made by Order of Pedro Menéndez de Avilés 1565 into the Interior of Florida by Captain Juan Pardo, Written by Himself. In *Explorations in Interior South Carolina by Hernando De Soto (1540) and Juan Pardo (1566–1568)*, edited by Chester DePratter, pp. 29–31. South Carolina Institute of Archaeology and Anthropology, University of South Carolina. *The Notebook* 19.

Parham, Kenneth R., and Gary T. Scott
1980   Porotic Hyperostosis: A Study of Disease and Culture at Toqua (40Mr6), A Late Mississippian Site in Eastern Tennessee. In *The Skeletal Biology of Aboriginal Populations in the Southeastern United States*, edited by P. Willey and Fred. H. Smith. Tennessee Anthropological Association Miscellaneous Papers, no. 5. Chattanooga, Tenn.: Tribute Press and Printing.

Parler, A. Robert, and Sammy T. Lee
1981   A Preliminary Report on the Allen Mack Site (38Or67). Paper presented at the 7th annual Conference on South Carolina Archaeology, Columbia, S.C., April 11.

Parsons, Jeffrey R., Elizabeth Brumfiel, Mary H. Parsons, and David J. Wilson
1982   *Prehispanic Settlement Patterns in the Southern Valley of Mexico: The Chalco Xochimilco Region*. Memoirs of the Museum of Anthropology, no. 14. Ann Arbor: University of Michigan.

Pauketat, Timothy R.
1991   *The Dynamics of Pre-state Political Centralization in the North American Midcontinent*. Ph.D. dissertation, Department of Anthropology, University of Michigan. Ann Arbor: University Microfilms.
1992   The Reign and Ruin of the Lords of Cahokia: A Dialectic of Dominance. In *Lords of the Southeast: Social Inequality and the Native Elites of Southeastern North America*, edited by Alex W. Barker and Timothy R. Pauketat, pp. 31–51. Archaeological Papers of the American Anthropological Association, no. 3.

Pauketat, Timothy R., and Thomas E. Emerson
1991   The Ideology of Authority and the Power of the Pot. *American Anthropologist* 93:919–41.

Paynter, Robert W.
1981   Social Complexity in Peripheries: Problems and Models. In *Archaeological Approaches to the Study of Complexity*, edited by Sander E. van der Leeuw, pp. 117–30. Amsterdam: Universeit van Amsterdam.

Pearson, Charles E.
1978   Analysis of Late Mississippian Settlements on Ossabaw Island, Georgia. In *Mississippian Settlement Patterns*, edited by Bruce D. Smith, pp. 53–80. New York: Academic Press.

Pearson, Charles E., and Sharon Goad Pearson
1978   *Cultural Resources Reconnaissance of Construction Project Areas of Wassaw National Wildlife Refuge, Georgia*. 2 vols. Report prepared for the U. S. Fish

and Wildlife Service. Atlanta: National Park Service, Interagency Archeological Services.

Peebles, Christopher S.

1978   Determinants of Settlement Size and Location in the Moundville Phase. In *Mississippian Settlement Patterns*, edited by Bruce D. Smith, pp. 369–416. New York: Academic Press.

1979   *Excavations at Moundville, 1905–1951*. Microfiche. Ann Arbor: University of Michigan Press.

1986   Paradise Lost, Strayed, and Stolen: Prehistoric Social Devolution in the Southeast. In *The Burden of Being Civilized: An Anthropological Perspective on the Discontents of Civilization*, edited by Miles Richardson and Malcolm C. Webb, pp. 24–40. Southern Anthropological Society Proceedings, no. 18. Athens: University of Georgia Press.

1987a   Moundville from 1000 to 1500 A.D. as Seen from 1840 to 1985 A.D. In *Chiefdoms in the Americas*, edited by Robert D. Drennen and Carlos A. Uribe, pp. 21–41. Lanham, Md.: University Press of America.

1987b   The Rise and Fall of the Mississippian in Western Alabama: The Moundville and Summerville Phases, A.D. 1000 to 1600. *Mississippi Archaeology* 22:1–31.

Peebles, Christopher, and Susan M. Kus

1977   Some Archaeological Correlates of Ranked Societies. *American Antiquity* 42:421–48.

Peebles, Christopher S., and Margaret J. Schoeninger

1981   Notes on the Relationship between Social Status and Diet at Moundville. *Southeastern Archaeological Conference Bulletin* 24:96–97.

Penman, John T.

1988   Neo-boreal Climatic Influences on the Late Prehistoric Agricultural Groups in the Upper Mississippi Valley. *Geoarchaeology* 3:139–45.

Peregrine, Peter N.

1991   A Graphic-Theoretic Approach to the Evolution of Cahokia. *American Antiquity* 56:66–75.

1992a   *Mississippian Evolution: A World-System Perspective*. Monographs in World Archaeology, no. 9. Madison, Wis.: Prehistory Press.

1992b   Networks of Power: The Mississippian World-System. Paper presented at the 49th annual Southeastern Archaeological Conference, Little Rock, Ark., October 23.

Petersen, Glenn

1982   *One Man Cannot Rule a Thousand: Fission in a Ponapean Chiefdom*. Ann Arbor: University of Michigan Press.

Peterson, Drexal A.

1971a   *Time and Settlement in the Archaeology of Groton Plantation, South Carolina*. Ph.D. dissertation, Department of Anthropology, Harvard University. Ann Arbor: University Microfilms.

1971b   The Refuge Phase in the Savannah River Region. *Southeastern Archaeological Conference Bulletin* 13:76–81.

Phillips, Philip

1970   *Archaeological Survey in the Lower Yazoo Basin, Mississippi, 1947–1955*. 2 vols. Papers of the Peabody Museum of Archaeology and Ethnology, no. 60. Cambridge, Mass.: Harvard University, The Museum.

Phillips, Philip, and James A. Brown
1978   *Pre-Colombian Shell Engravings from the Craig Mound at Spiro, Oklahoma.*
       Cambridge, Mass.: Harvard University, Peabody Museum of Archaeology
       and Ethnology.

Plog, Stephen
1976   The Inference of Prehistoric Social Organization from Ceramic Design
       Variability. *Michigan Discussions in Anthropology* 1:1–47.
1980   *Stylistic Variation in Prehistoric Ceramics: Design Analysis in the American
       Southwest.* Cambridge, England: Cambridge University Press.

Polhemus, Richard B.
1987   *The Toqua Site: A Late Mississippian Dallas Phase Town.* Report of Investiga-
       tions, no. 41. Prepared by the Tennessee Valley Authority. Knoxville:
       University of Tennessee, Department of Anthropology.

Pollock, Susan
1983   Style and Information: An Analysis of Susiana Ceramics. *Journal of Anthro-
       pological Archaeology* 2:354–90.

Porter, James W.
1969   The Mitchell Site and Prehistoric Exchange Systems at Cahokia: A.D. 1000
       ± 300. In *Explorations in Cahokia Archaeology*, edited by Melvin L. Fowler,
       pp. 137–64. Illinois Archaeological Survey Bulletin 7. Urbana: The Survey.
1974   *Cahokia Archaeology as Viewed from the Mitchell Site: A Satellite Community at
       A.D.1150–1200.* Ph.D. dissertation, Department of Anthropology, Univer-
       sity of Wisconsin. Ann Arbor: University Microfilms.

Powell, Mary Lucas
1983   Biocultural Analysis of Human Skeletal Remains from the Lubbub Creek
       Archaeological Locality. In *Prehistoric Agricultural Communities in West
       Central Alabama*, vol. 2, *Studies of Material Remains from the Lubbub Creek
       Archaeological Locality*, edited by Christopher S. Peebles, pp. 430–77. At-
       lanta: National Park Service, Interagency Archeological Services.
1988   *Status and Health in Prehistory: A Case Study of the Moundville Chiefdom.*
       Washington, D.C.: Smithsonian Institution Press.
1990   On the Eve of Conquest: Life and Death at Irene Mound, Georgia. In *The
       Archaeology of Mission Santa Catalina de Guale*, vol. 2: *Biocultural Interpreta-
       tions of a Population in Transition*, edited by Clark Spencer Larsen, pp. 26–35.
       Anthropological Papers of the American Museum of Natural History, no.
       68. New York: The Museum.
1991   Ranked Status and Health in the Mississippian Chiefdom at Moundville.
       In *What Mean These Bones? Studies in Southeastern Bioarchaeology*, edited by
       Mary Lucas Powell, Patricia S. Bridges, and Ann Marie Wagner Mires, pp.
       22–51. Tuscaloosa: University of Alabama Press.
1992   In the Best of Health? Disease and Trauma among the Mississippian Elite.
       In *Lords of the Southeast: Social Inequality and the Native Elites of Southeastern
       North America*, edited by Alex W. Barker and Timothy R. Pauketat, pp. 81–
       97. Archaeological Papers of the American Anthropological Association,
       no. 3.

Powell, John Wesley
1894   Report of the Director. *Annual Report* 12:xxi–xxviii. Washington, D.C.:
       Bureau of Ethnology.

Prentice, Guy
1990   Review of *The Southeastern Ceremonial Complex*, edited by Patrica Gallo-
        way. *Southeastern Archaeology* 9:69–75.
Price, T. Douglas, and James A. Brown
1985   Aspects of Hunter-Gatherer Complexity. In *Prehistoric Hunter-Gatherers:
        The Emergence of Cultural Complexity*, edited by T. Douglas Price and James
        A. Brown, pp. 3–20. New York: Academic Press.
Price, T. Douglas, and James A. Brown (editors)
1985   *Prehistoric Hunter-Gatherers: The Emergence of Cultural Complexity.* New
        York: Academic Press.
Priestley, Herbert I.
1928   *The Luna Papers: Documents Relating to the Expedition of Don Tristán de Luna
        y Arellano for the Conquest of La Florida in 1559–1561.* 2 vols. Deland: Florida
        State Historical Society.
Purrington, Burton L.
1983   Ancient Mountaineers: An Overview of Prehistoric Archaeology of North
        Carolina's Western Mountain Region. In *The Prehistory of North Carolina:
        An Archaeological Symposium*, edited by Mark A. Mathis and Jeffrey J. Crow,
        pp. 83–160. Raleigh, N.C.: Department of Cultural Resources, Division of
        Archives and History.
Quattlebaum, Paul
1956   *The Land Called Chicora.* Gainesville: University Presses of Florida.
Quinn, David B. (editor)
1979   *New American World: A Documentary History of North America to 1612*, vol. 5:
        The Extension of Settlement in Florida, Virginia, and the Spanish Southwest.
        New York: Arno.
Radcliffe-Brown, A. R.
1952   Patrilineal and Matrilineal Succession. 1935. Reprint. In *Structure and
        Function in Primitive Society*, by A. R. Radcliffe-Brown, pp. 32–48. Glencoe,
        Ill.: Free Press.
Rafferty, Jim, and Rich Norling
1986   *Cricket Graph: Presentation Graphics for Science and Business.* Malvern, Penn.:
        Cricket Software.
Ralph, E. K., H. N. Michael, and M. C. Han
1973   Radiocarbon Dates and Reality. *MASCA Newsletter* 9(1).
Ramenofsky, Ann F.
1987   *Vectors of Death: The Archaeology of European Contact.* Albuquerque: Univer-
        sity of New Mexico Press.
1990   Loss of Innocence: Explanations of Differential Persistence in the Sixteeeth-
        century Southeast. In *Columbian Consequences*, vol. 2. *Archaeological and
        Historical Perspectives on the Spanish Borderlands East*, edited by David H.
        Thomas, pp. 31–48. Washington, D.C.: Smithsonian Institution Press.
Ranjel, Rodrigo
1904   A Narrative of De Soto's Expedition Based on the Diary of Rodrigo Ranjel,
        His Private Secretary, by Gonzalo Fernandez de Oviedo y Valdes. 1539–41.
        In *Narratives of the Career of Hernando De Soto in the Conquest of Florida as Told
        by a Knight of Elvas and in a Relation by Luys Hernandez de Biedma, Factor of the
        Expedition, Translated by Buckingham Smith, Together with an Account of
        DeSoto's Expedition Based on the Diary of Rodrigo Ranjel, His Probate Secretary,
        Translated from Ovideo's Historia General y Natural de las Indias*, edited by
        Edward Gaylord Bourne, 2:41–149. New York: A. S. Barnes.
1993   Account of the Northern Conquest and Discovery of Hernando De Soto. In

The De Soto Chronicles: The Expedition of Hernando De Soto to North America in 1539–1543, vol. 1, edited by Lawrence A. Clayton, Vernon James Knight, Jr., and Edward C. Moore, pp. 247–306. Tuscaloosa: University of Alabama Press.

Rappaport, Roy A.
1971   The Sacred in Human Evolution. *Annual Review of Ecology and Systematics* 2:23–44.
1979a   The Obvious Aspects of Ritual. In *Ecology, Meaning, and Religion*, edited by Roy A. Rappaport, pp. 173–221. Richmond, Calif.: North Atlantic Books.
1979b   Sanctity and Lies in Evolution. In *Ecology, Meaning, and Religion*, edited by Roy A. Rappaport, pp. 223–246. Richmond, Calif.: North Atlantic Books.

Reay, Marie
1959   *The Kuma*. Melbourne, Australia: Melbourne University Press.

Reid, J. Jefferson
1965   A Comparative Statement of Ceramics from the Hollywood and Town Creek Sites. *Southern Indian Studies* 17:12–25.
1967   Pee Dee Pottery from the Mound at Town Creek. M.A. thesis, Department of Anthropology, University of North Carolina.

Reitz, Elizabeth J.
1985   Faunal Analysis. In *Archaeological Investigation of the Beaverdam Creek Site (9Eb85), Elbert County, Georgia*, edited by James L. Rudolph and David J. Hally, pp. 416–28. Russell Papers. Atlanta: National Park Service, Interagency Archeological Services.
1988   Evidence for Coastal Adaptations in Georgia and South Carolina. *Archaeology of Eastern North America* 16:137–58.

Reitz, Elizabeth J., Rochelle A. Marrinan, and Susan L. Scott
1987   Survey of Vertebrate Remains from Prehistoric Sites in the Savannah River Valley. *Journal of Ethnobiology* 7(2):195–221.

Renfrew, Colin
1973   Monuments, Mobilisation, and Social Organization in Neolithic Wessex. In *The Explanation of Culture Change: Models in Prehistory*, edited by Colin Renfrew, pp. 539–58. Pittsburgh: University of Pittsburgh Press.
1974   Beyond a Subsistence Economy: The Evolution of Prehistoric Social Organization in Prehistoric Europe. In *Reconstructing Complex Societies*, edited by C. B. Moore, pp. 69–95. Bulletin Supplement, no. 20. Cambridge, Mass.: American Schools of Oriental Research.
1975   Trade as Action at a Distance: Questions of Integration and Communication. In *Ancient Civilization and Trade*, edited by J. A. Sabloff and C. C. Lamborg-Karlovsky, pp. 1–60. Albuquerque: University of New Mexico Press.
1976   Megaliths, Territories and Populations. In *Acculturation and Continuity in Atlantic Europe*, edited by S. J. de Laet, pp. 198–220. Bruges, Belgium: De Tempel.
1984   *Approaches to Social Archaeology*. Cambridge, Mass.: Harvard University Press.
1986   Introduction: Peer Polity Interaction and Socio-Political Change. In *Peer Polity Interaction and Socio-Political Change.*, edited by Colin Renfrew and John F. Cherry, pp. 1–18. Cambridge, England: Cambridge University Press.

Renfrew, Colin, and John F. Cherry (editors)
1986   *Peer Polity Interaction and Socio-political Change*. Cambridge, England: Cambridge University Press.

Renfrew, Colin, and Stephen J. Shennan (editors)
1982 *Ranking, Resource and Exchange: Aspects of the Archaeology of Early European Society.* Cambridge, England: Cambridge University Press.

Robertson, James Alexander (translator)
1993 True Relation of the Hardships Suffered Governor Hernando De Soto & Certain Portuguese Gentlemen During the Discovery of the Province of Florida. Now Newly Set Forth by a Gentleman of Elvas. In *The De Soto Chronicles: The Expedition of Hernando De Soto to North America in 1539–1543,* vol. 1, edited by Lawrence A. Clayton, Vernon James Knight, Jr., and Edward C. Moore, pp. 19–219. Tuscaloosa: University of Alabama Press.

Rodeffer, Michael J., and Stephanie Holschlag
1976 *An Archaeological Reconnaissance of the Oconee County Wastewater Project.* Greenwood, S.C.: Lander College.

Rodeffer, Michael J., Stephanie Holschlag, and M. K. Cann
1979 *Greenwood County: An Archaeological Reconnaissance.* Greenwood, S.C.: Lander College.

Rogel, Juan
1570 Habana 9 de Diciembre de 1570.—Carta del Padre Juan Rogel á Pedro Menéndez de Avilés, residente en la Florida, lamentándose de las pocas ó ningunas esperanzas que tenía de la conversión de aquellos inconstantísimos habitantes. Translated by W. G. Brinton. In *The Historical Magazine, and Notes and Queries Concerning the Antiquities, History, and Biography of America,* edited by John Dawson Gilmary Shea, 5(11):327–30. New York: Charles B. Richardson.

Rogers, J. Daniel
1987 Markers of Social Integration: The Development of Centralized Authority in the Spiro Region. Paper presented in the symposium Between Emergence and Demise: Examining Political Change in Mississippian Societies, 44th annual Southeastern Archaeological Conference, Charleston, S.C., November 13.

Rose, Jerome C., Murray K. Marks, and Larry L. Tieszen
1991 Bioarchaeology and Subsistence in the Central and Lower Portions of the Mississippi Valley. In *What Mean These Bones? Studies in Southeastern Bioarchaeology,* edited by Mary Lucas Powell, Patricia S. Bridges, and Ann Marie Wagner Mires, pp. 7–21. Tuscaloosa: University of Alabama Press.

Rudolph, James L.
1983 Lamar Period Exploitation of Aquatic Resources in the Middle Oconee River Valley. *Early Georgia* 11:86–103.
1984 Earthlodges and Platform Mounds: Changing Public Architecture in the Southeastern U.S. *Southeastern Archaeology* 3:33–35.

Rudolph, James L., and Dennis B. Blanton
1980 A Discussion of Mississippian Settlement in the Georgia Piedmont. *Early Georgia* 8:14–36.

Rudolph, James L., and David J. Hally (editors)
1985 *Archaeological Investigation of the Beaverdam Creek Site (9Eb85), Elbert County, Georgia.* Russell Papers. Atlanta: National Park Service, Interagency Archeological Services.

Rudolph, James L., Jack Tyler, and Patricia Quillian
1979 An Archaeological Survey in the Clark Hill and Hartwell Reservoirs, Georgia and South Carolina. Manuscript on file at the Laboratory of Archaeology, University of Georgia.

Rudolph, James L., Marvin T. Smith, John W. Strand, and David J. Hally
1979   An Archaeological Survey of a Proposed Landfill Site, Rabun County, Georgia, for the Georgia Mountains Planning and Development Commission. Manuscript on file at the Laboratory of Archaeology, University of Georgia.

Rudolph, Teresa P.
1985   Late Swift Creek and Napier Settlement in Northern Georgia. Paper presented at the 42nd annual Southeastern Archaeological Conference, Birmingham, Ala., November 7.
1986   Regional and Temporal Variability in Swift Creek and Napier Ceramics from North Georgia. Paper presented at the Ocmulgee National Monument 50th anniversary conference, Macon, Ga., December 13.
1991   The Late Woodland "Problem" in North Georgia. In *Stability, Transformation, and Variation: The Late Woodland Southeast*, edited by Michael S. Nassaney and Charles R. Cobb, pp. 259–83. New York: Plenum Press.

Ruff, Barbara
1984   Vertebrate Faunal Remains from the Clyde Gulley Site, 9Eb387. In *Archaeological Investigations at Gregg Shoals, a Deeply Stratified Site on the Savannah River*, edited by V. Ann Tippitt and William H. Marquardt, pp. B-1 to B-5. Russell Papers. Atlanta: National Park Service, Interagency Archeological Services.

Ruff, Christopher B., and Clark Spencer Larsen
1990   Postcranial Biomechanical Adaptations to Subsistence Stress. In *The Archaeology of Mission Santa Catalina de Guale*, vol. 2: *Biocultural Interpretations of a Population in Transition*, edited by Clark S. Larsen, pp. 94–120. Anthropological Papers of the American Museum of Natural History, no. 68. New York: The Museum.

Ryan, Thomas M.
1971a   Some Brief Field Trips in South Carolina. South Carolina Institute of Archaeology and Anthropology, University of South Carolina. *The Notebook* 3(4):93–101.
1971b   Test Excavations at McCollum Site. South Carolina Institute of Archaeology and Anthropology, University of South Carolina. *The Notebook* 3(5): 104–10.

Sahlins, Marshall D.
1958   *Social Stratification in Polynesia*. Seattle: University of Washington Press.
1963   Poor Man, Rich Man, Big Man, Chief: Political Types in Melanesia and Polynesia. *Comparative Studies in Society and History* 5(3):285–303.
1968   *Tribesmen*. Englewood Cliffs, N.J.: Prentice-Hall.
1981   *Historical Metaphors and Mythical Realities: Structure in the Early History of the Sandwich Islands Kingdom*. Ann Arbor: University of Michigan Press.

Salley, Alexander S., Jr.
1911   *Narratives of Early Carolina, 1650–1708*. New York: Charles Scribner's Sons.

Sanders, William T., and Joseph Marino
1970   *New World Prehistory*. Englewood Cliffs, N.J.: Prentice-Hall.

Sanders, William T., and Barbara J. Price
1968   *Mesoamerica: The Evolution of a Civilization*. New York: Random House.

Sanders, William T., and David Webster
1978   Unilinealism, Multilinealism, and the Evolution of Complex Societies. In *Social Archaeology: Beyond Subsistence and Dating*, edited by Charles L. Redman, M. J. Berman, E. V. Curtin, W. T. Langhorne, Jr., N. M. Versaggi, and J. C. Warner, pp. 249–302. New York: Academic Press.

Sassaman, Kenneth E.
1983   Middle and Late Archaic Settlement in the South Carolina Piedmont. M.A. thesis, Department of Anthropology, University of South Carolina.
1989   Prehistoric Settlement in the Aiken Plateau: Archaeological Investigations at 38Ak158 and 38Ak159, Aiken County, South Carolina. *South Carolina Antiquities* 21:31–64.
1993   *Early Pottery in the Southeast: Tradition and Innovation in Cooking Technology.* Tuscaloosa: University of Alabama Press.
Sassaman, Kenneth E., and David G. Anderson
1990   Typology and Chronology. In *Native American Prehistory of the Middle Savannah River Valley: A Synthesis of Archaeological Investigations on the Savannah River Site, Aiken and Barnwell Counties, South Carolina*, by Kenneth E. Sassaman, Mark J. Brooks, Glen T. Hanson, and David G. Anderson, pp. 143–215. Savannah River Archaeological Research Papers, no. 1. Columbia: University of South Carolina, South Carolina Institute of Archaeology and Anthropology.
Sassaman, Kenneth E., Glen T. Hanson, and Tommy Charles
1988   Raw Material Procurement and the Reduction of Hunter-Gatherer Range in the Savannah River Valley. *Southeastern Archaeology* 7:79–94.
Sassaman, Kenneth E., Mark J. Brooks, Glen T. Hanson, and David G. Anderson
1990   *Native American Prehistory of the Middle Savannah River Valley: A Synthesis of Archaeological Investigations on the Savannah River Site, Aiken and Barnwell Counties, South Carolina.* Savannah River Archaeological Research Papers, no. 1. Columbia: University of South Carolina, South Carolina Institute of Archaeology and Anthropology.
Saxe, Arthur A.
1970   *Social Dimensions of Mortuary Practices.* Ph.D. dissertation, Department of Anthropology, University of Michigan. Ann Arbor: University Microfilms.
Scarry, C. Margaret
1981   Plant Procurement Strategies in the West Jefferson and Moundville I Phases. *Southeastern Archaeological Conference Bulletin* 24:94–96.
1986   *Changes in Plant Procurement and Production during the Emergence of the Moundville Chiefdom.* Ph.D. dissertation, Department of Anthropology, University of Michigan. Ann Arbor: University Microfilms.
Scarry, John F.
1987   Stability and Change in the Apalachee Chiefdom: Centralization, Decentralization, and Social Reproduction. Paper presented in the symposium Between Emergence and Demise: Examining Political Change in Mississippian Societies, 44th annual Southeastern Archaeological Conference, Charleston, S.C., November 13.
1990a Mississippian Emergence in the Fort Walton Area: The Evolution of the Cayson and Lake Jackson Phases. In *The Mississippian Emergence*, edited by Bruce D. Smith, pp. 227–50. Washington, D.C.: Smithsonian Institution Press.
1990b The Rise, Transformation, and Fall of Apalachee: A Case Study of Political Change in a Chiefly Society. In *Lamar Archaeology: Mississippian Chiefdoms in the Deep South*, edited by Mark Williams and Gary Shapiro, pp. 175–86. Tuscaloosa: University of Alabama Press.
Scarry, John F., and Claudine Payne
1986   Mississippian Polities in the Fort Walton Area: A Model Generated from the Renfrew-Level XTENT Algorithm. *Southeastern Archaeology* 5:79–90.

Schambach, Frank F.
1989 The End of the Trail: The Route of Hernando De Soto's Army through Southwest Arkansas and East Texas. *Arkansas Archeologist* 27/28:9–33.
1991 A Reinterpretation of the Place of the Spiro Site and the Northern Caddoan Area in Southeastern Prehistory. Paper presented at the 33rd annual Caddo Conference, Nacogdoches, Tex., March 23.

Schapera, I.
1956 *Government and Politics in Tribal Societies*. London: Watts Press.

Schneider, David, and K. Gough
1961 *Matrilineal Kinship*. Berkeley: University of California Press.

Schneider, Kent A.
1977 Archeological Investigations at Sites 9Ra52, 9Ra53, and 9Ra54, Rabun County, Georgia. Manuscript on file at the Laboratory of Archaeology, University of Georgia.

Schnell, Frank T., and Newell O. Wright, Jr.
1992 *Mississippian Period Archaeology of the Georgia Coastal Plain*. Report, no. 26. Athens: University of Georgia, Laboratory of Archaeology.

Schnell, Frank T., Vernon J. Knight, Jr., and Gail S. Schnell
1981 *Cemochechobee: Archaeology of a Mississippian Ceremonial Center on the Chattahoochee River*. Ripley P. Bullen Monographs in Anthropology and History, no. 3. Gainesville: University Presses of Florida.

Schoeninger, Margaret J., Nikolaas J. van der Merwe, Katherine Moore, Julia Lee-Thorp, and Clark Spencer Larsen
1990 Decrease in Diet Quality between the Prehistoric and Contact Periods. In *The Archaeology of Mission Santa Catalina de Guale*, vol. 2: *Biocultural Interpretations of a Population in Transition*, edited by Clark S. Larsen, pp. 78–93. Anthropological Papers of the American Museum of Natural History, no. 68. New York: The Museum.

Schoolcraft, Henry R.
1851–57 *Historical and Statistical Information Respecting History, Conditions, and Prospects of the Indian Tribes of the United States*. 6 vols. Collected and prepared under the direction of the Bureau of Indian Affairs. Philadelphia.

Schortman, Edward M., and Patricia A. Urban
1987 Modeling Interregional Interaction in Prehistory. *Advances in Archaeological Method and Theory*, edited by Michael B. Schiffer, 11:37–95. New York: Academic Press.

Schroedl, Gerald F.
1978 Louis-Philippe's Journal and Archaeological Investigations at the Overhill Town of Toqua. *Journal of Cherokee Studies* 3:206–20.
1986 *Overhill Cherokee Archaeology at Chota-Tanasee*. Report of Investigations, no. 38. Knoxville: University of Tennessee, Department of Anthropology.

Schroedl, Gerald F., and Brett Riggs
1989 Cherokee Lower Town Archaeology at the Chattooga Site (38Oc18). Paper presented at the 46th annual Southeastern Archaeological Conference, Tampa, Fla., November 10.

Schuldenrein, Joseph, and David G. Anderson
1988 Paleoenvironmental History and Archaeology in the Russell Lake Area. In *Prehistory and History along the Upper Savannah River: Technical Synthesis of Cultural Resource Investigations, Richard B. Russell Multiple Resource Area*, edited by David G. Anderson and J. W. Joseph, pp. 56–93. Russell Papers. Atlanta: National Park Service, Interagency Archeological Services.

Schwarcz, H. P., and Margaret J. Schoeninger
1991   Stable Isotope Analyses in Human Nutritional Ecology. *Annual Yearbook of Physical Anthropology* 34:283–321.

Scott, Susan L.
1981   Economic and Organizational Aspects of Deer Procurement during the Late Prehistoric Period. Paper presented at the 38th annual Southeastern Archaeological Conference, Asheville, N.C., November.
1982   Yarborough Site Faunal Remains. In *Archaeological Investigations at the Yarborough Site (22Ci814), Clay County, Mississippi,* edited by Carlos Solis and Richard Walling, pp. 140–52. Report of Investigations, no. 30. Tuscaloosa: The University of Alabama, Office of Archaeological Research.
1983   Analysis, Synthesis, and Interpretation of Faunal Remains from the Lubbub Creek Archaeological Locality. In *Prehistoric Agricultural Communities in West Central Alabama,* vol. 2: *Studies of Material Remains from the Lubbub Creek Archaeological Locality,* edited by Christopher S. Peebles, pp. 272–390. Atlanta: National Park Service, Interagency Archeological Services.
1985   Analysis of Faunal Remains Recovered at the Rucker's Bottom Site (9Eb91), Elbert County, Georgia. In *Prehistoric Human Ecology along the Upper Savannah River: Excavations at the Rucker's Bottom, Abbeville, and Bullard Site Groups,* edited by David G. Anderson and Joseph Schuldenrein, pp. 639–64. Russell Papers. Atlanta: National Park Service, Interagency Archeological Services.

Scurry, James D., and Mark J. Brooks
1978   *An Archeological Reconnaissance of Areas to Be Impacted by the Widening and Dredging of Savannah Harbor, Georgia.* Research Manuscript Series, no. 125. Columbia: University of South Carolina, South Carolina Institute of Archaeology and Anthropology.

Scurry, James D., J. Walter Joseph, and Fritz Hamer
1980   *Initial Archaeological Investigations at Silver Bluff Plantation, Aiken County, South Carolina.* Research Manuscript Series, no. 168. Columbia: University of South Carolina, South Carolina Institute of Archaeology and Anthropology.

Seally, Judith C., and Nikolaas J. van der Merwe
1985   Isotope Assessment of Holocene Human Diets in the Southwestern Cape, South Africa. *Nature* 315:138–40.

Sears, William H.
1956   *Excavations at Kolomoki: Final Report.* University of Georgia Series in Anthropology, no. 5. Athens: University of Georgia Press.
1958   The Wilbanks Site (9Ck5), Georgia. In Bulletin 169, pp. 129–94. Washington, D.C.: Bureau of American Ethnology.
1961   The Study of Social and Religious Systems in North American Archaeology. *Current Anthropology* 12:223–46.
1973   The Sacred and the Secular in Prehistoric Ceramics. In *Variation in Anthropology: Essays in Honor of J. C. McGregor,* edited by D. W. Lathrap, pp. 31–42. Urbana: Illinois Archaeological Survey Publications.

Seckinger, Ernest W., and Donald A. Graybill
1976   *Final Report on Archaeological Survey 1, Chattahoochee National Forest (Rabun County, Georgia).* Gainesville, Ga.: U.S.D.A. Forest Service.

Segovia, Antonio V.
1985   *Archeological Geology of the Savannah River Valley and Main Tributaries in the*

Richard B. Russell Multiple Resource Area. Russell Papers. Atlanta: National Park Service, Interagency Archeological Services.

Serrano y Sanz, Manual
1912   *Documentos Históricos de la Florida y la Luisiana, Siglos 16 al 18*. Madrid: Librería General de Victoriano Suárez.

Service, Elman R.
1971   *Primitive Social Organization*. 1962. Reprint. New York: Random House.

Shanks, Michael, and Christopher Tilley
1982   Ideology, Symbolic Power and Ritual Communication: A Reinterpretation of Neolithic Mortuary Practices. In *Symbolic and Structural Archaeology*, edited by Ian Hodder, pp. 129–54. Cambridge, England: Cambridge University Press.
1987   *Re-constructing Archaeology: Theory and Practice*. Cambridge, England: Cambridge University Press.

Shapiro, Gary
1983   *Site Variability in the Oconee Province: A Late Mississippian Society of the Georgia Piedmont*. Ph.D. dissertation, Department of Anthropology, University of Florida. Ann Arbor: University Microfilms.
1985a   Ceramic Vessels and Site Variability. Paper presented at the 50th annual meeting of the Society for American Archaeology, Denver, Colo., May.
1985b   Ceramic Vessels, Site Permanence, and Group Size: A Mississippian Example. *American Antiquity* 49:696–712.
1986   Rivers and Boundaries. Paper presented at the 43rd Meeting of the Southeastern Archaeological Conference, Nashville, Tenn., November.
1990   Bottomlands and Rapids: A Mississippian Adaptive Niche in the Georgia Piedmont. In *Lamar Archaeology: Mississippian Chiefdoms in the Deep South*, edited by Mark Williams and Gary Shapiro, pp. 147–62. Tuscaloosa: University of Alabama Press.

Sheehan, Mark C.
1986   Analyses of Fossil Pollen from 38An8 and 38An29. In *Prehistory in the Richard B. Russell Reservoir: The Archaic and Woodland Periods of the Upper Savannah River: The Final Report of the Data Recovery at the Anderson and Elbert County Groups: 38An8, 38An29, 38An126, 9Eb17, 9Eb19 and 9Eb21*, edited by W. Dean Wood, Dan T. Elliott, Teresa P. Rudolph, and Dennis B. Blanton, pp. 393–98. Russell Papers. Atlanta: National Park Service, Interagency Archeological Services.

Sheehan, Mark C., Donald R. Whitehead, and Stephen T. Jackson
1985   *Late Quaternary Environmental History of the Richard B. Russell Multiple Resource Area*. Russell Papers. Atlanta: National Park Service, Interagency Archeological Services.

Shelby, Charmion (translator)
1993   La Florida by the Inca. History of the Adelantado Hernando De Soto, Governor and Captain General of the Kingdom of La Florida, and of Other Heroic Gentlemen, Spaniards and Indians; Written by the Inca Garcilasso de la Vega, Captain of his Majesty, a Native of the Great City of El Cuzco, Capital of the Kingdoms and Provinces of El Peru. In *The De Soto Chronicles: The Expedition of Hernando De Soto to North America in 1539–1543*, vol. 2, edited by Lawrence A. Clayton, Vernon James Knight, Jr., and Edward C. Moore, pp. 25–559. Tuscaloosa: University of Alabama Press.

Shennan, Stephen
1982   Exchange and Ranking: The Role of Amber in the Earlier Bronze Age of

Europe. In *Ranking, Resource, and Exchange: Aspects of the Archaeology of Early European Society*, edited by Colin Renfrew and Stephen J. Shennan, pp. 33–45. Cambridge, England: Cambridge University Press.

1987 Trends in the Study of Later European Prehistory. *Annual Review of Anthropology* 16:365–82.

Shryock, Andrew J.
1987 The Wright Mound Reexamined: Generative Structures and the Political Economy of a Simple Chiefdom. *Midcontinental Journal of Archaeology* 12:243–68.

Silverberg, Robert
1968 *Mound Builders of Ancient America: The Archaeology of a Myth.* Greenwich, Conn.: New York Graphic Society.

Smith, Betty A.
1979a Archaeological Survey of the Cedar Ridge Farms Development, Richmond County, Georgia. Manuscript on file at the Laboratory of Archaeology, University of Georgia.

1979b The Hopewell Connection in Southwest Georgia. In *Hopewell Archaeology: The Chillicothe Conference*, edited by David S. Brose and N'omi Greber, pp. 181–87. Kent, Ohio: Kent State University Press.

Smith, Bruce D.
1974a Middle Mississippian Exploitation of Animal Populations: A Predictive Model. *American Antiquity* 39:274–91.

1974b Predator-Prey Relationships in the Southeastern Ozarks, A.D. 1300. *Human Ecology* 2:31–43.

1975 *Middle Mississippian Exploitation of Animal Populations.* Anthropological Papers, no. 57. Ann Arbor: University of Michigan, Museum of Anthropology.

1978 Variation in Mississippian Settlement Patterns. In *Mississippian Settlement Patterns*, edited by Bruce D. Smith, pp. 479–503. New York: Academic Press.

1984 Mississippian Expansion: Tracing the Historical Development of an Explanatory Model. *Southeastern Archaeology* 3:12–32.

1985 The Archaeology of the Southeastern United States: From Dalton to DeSoto, 10,500–500 B.P. *Advances in World Archaeology* 5:1–88.

1990 *The Mississippian Emergence.* Washington, D.C.: Smithsonian Institution Press.

Smith, Marvin T.
1981 *Archaeological Investigations at the Dyar Site, 9Ge5, Wallace Reservoir, Georgia.* Wallace Reservoir Project Contribution, no. 5. Athens: University of Georgia, Department of Anthropology.

1983 The Development of Lamar Ceramics in the Wallace Reservoir: The Evidence from the Dyar Site. *Early Georgia* 11:74–85.

1984 *Depopulation and Culture Change in the Early Historic Period Interior Southeast.* Ph.D. dissertation, Department of Anthropology, University of Florida. Ann Arbor: University Microfilms.

1986 *Archaeological Testing of Sixteen Sites on the Fort Howard Tract, Effingham County, Georgia.* Atlanta, Ga.: Garrow and Associates.

1987 *Archaeology of Aboriginal Culture Change in the Interior Southeast: Depopulation during the Early Historic Period.* Ripley P. Bullen Monographs in Archaeology and History, no. 6. Gainesville: University Presses of Florida.

Smith, Marvin T., and David J. Hally
1992 Chiefly Behavior: Evidence from Sixteenth Century Spanish Accounts. In

Lords of the Southeast: Social Inequality and the Native Elites of Southeastern North America, edited by Alex W. Barker and Timothy R. Pauketat, pp. 99–109. Archaeological Papers of the American Anthropological Association, no. 3.

Smith, Marvin T., and Stephen A. Kowalewski
1980   Tentative Identification of a Prehistoric Province in Piedmont Georgia. *Early Georgia* 8:1–13.

Smith, Marvin T., and Julie Barnes Smith
1989   Engraved Shell Masks in North America. *Southeastern Archaeology* 8:9–18.

Smith, Marvin T., and J. Mark Williams
1978   European Materials from the Tugalo Site, 9St1. *Early Georgia* 6:38–53.

Smith, Marvin T., J. Mark Williams, Chester B. DePratter, Marshall Williams, and Mike Harmon
1988   *Archaeological Investigations at Tomassee (38Oc186), a Lower Cherokee Town.* Research Manuscript Series, no. 206. Columbia: University of South Carolina, South Carolina Institute of Archaeology and Anthropology.

Smith, Richard L.
1974   The Archaic Period in the Central Savannah River Area: A Study of Cultural Continuity and Innovation. Manuscript on file at the Research Laboratories of Anthropology, University of North Carolina.

Snow, Frankie
1977   *An Archaeological Survey of the Ocmulgee Big Bend Region: A Preliminary Report.* Occasional Papers from South Georgia, no. 3. Douglas: South Georgia College.

South, Stanley A.
1970   A Ceremonial Center at the Charles Towne Site. South Carolina Institute of Archaeology and Anthropology, University of South Carolina. *The Notebook* 2(6–7):3–5.

1973   Indian Pottery Taxonomy for the South Carolina Coast. South Carolina Institute of Archaeology and Anthropology, University of South Carolina. *The Notebook* 5(2):54–55.

1979   *The Search for Santa Elena on Paris Island, South Carolina.* Research Manuscript Series, no. 150. Columbia: University of South Carolina, South Carolina Institute of Archaeology and Anthropology.

1980   *The Discovery of Santa Elena.* Research Manuscript Series, no. 150. Columbia: University of South Carolina, South Carolina Institute of Archaeology and Anthropology.

1982   *Exploring Santa Elena 1981.* Research Manuscript Series, no. 184. Columbia: University of South Carolina, South Carolina Institute of Archaeology and Anthropology.

1991   *Archaeology at Santa Elena: Doorway to the Past.* Popular Series, no. 2. Columbia: University of South Carolina, South Carolina Institute of Archaeology and Anthropology.

Southall, Aidan
1956   *Alur Society: A Study in Process and Types of Domination.* Cambridge, England: W. Heffer & Sons.

Spencer, Charles S.
1987   Rethinking the Chiefdom. In *Chiefdoms in the Americas,* edited by Robert D. Drennan and Carlos A. Uribe, pp. 369–89. Lanham, Md.: University Press of America.

1990   On the Tempo and Mode of State Formation: Neoevolutionism Reconsidered. *Journal of Anthropological Archaeology* 9:1–30.

1991   Coevolution and the Development of Venezuelan Chiefdoms. In *Profiles in Cultural Evolution: Papers from a Conference in Honor of Elman R. Service*, edited by A. Terry Rambo and Kathleen Gillogly, pp. 137–65. Anthropological Papers, no. 85. Ann Arbor: University of Michigan, Museum of Anthropology.

Speth, John D., and Susan L. Scott
1985   The Role of Large Mammals in Late Prehistoric Horticultural Adaptations: The View from Southeastern New Mexico. *Archaeological Survey of Alberta Occasional Paper* 26:233–66.

Speth, John D., and Katherine A. Spielmann
1983   Energy Source, Protein Metabolism and Hunter-Gatherer Subsistence Strategies. *Journal of Anthropological Archaeology* 2:1–31.

Squier, Ephraim G., and E. H. Davis (editors)
1848   *Ancient Monuments of the Mississippi Valley*. Smithsonian Contributions to Knowledge, no. 1. Washington, D.C.: Smithsonian Institution Press.

Stahle, David W., and Malcolm K. Cleaveland
1992   Reconstruction and Analysis of Spring Rainfall over the Southeastern U.S. for the Past 1000 Years. *Bulletin of the American Meteorological Society* 73:1947–61.

Stahle, David W., Malcolm K. Cleaveland, and R. S. Cerveny
1991   Tree-ring Reconstructed Sunshine Duration over the Central USA. *International Journal of Climatology* 11:285–95.

Stahle, David W., Malcolm K. Cleaveland, and John G. Hehr
1985a   A 450-Year Drought Reconstruction for Arkansas, United States. *Nature* 316:530–32.
1985b   Tree-ring Dating of Bald Cypress and the Potential for Millennia-long Chronologies in the Southeast. *American Antiquity* 50:796–802.
1988   North Carolina Climate Changes Reconstructed from Tree Rings: A.D. 372 to 1985. *Science* 240:1517–20.

Stahle, David W., John G. Hehr, Graham G. Hawks, Jr., Malcolm K. Cleaveland, and John R. Baldwin
1985   *Tree-ring Chronologies for the South-central United States*. Fayetteville: University of Arkansas, Department of Geography, Tree Ring Laboratory and Office of the State Climatologist.

Steinbock, R. T.
1976   *Paleopathological Diagnosis and Interpretation*. Springfield, Ill.: Charles C. Thomas.

Steinen, Karl T.
1992   Ambushes, Raids and Palisades: Mississippian Warfare in the Interior Southeast. *Southeastern Archaeology* 11:132–39.

Stephenson, Keith
1990   Investigation of Ocmulgee Cord-marked Pottery Sites in the Big Bend Region of Georgia. M.A. thesis, Department of Anthropology, University of Georgia.

Stephenson, Keith, and Adam King
1992   At the Center of Peripheries: Late Woodland Persistence in the Interior Coastal Plain of Georgia. Paper presented at the 49th annual Southeastern Archaeological Conference, Little Rock, Ark., October 23.

Stephenson, Robert L.
1975   *An Archaeological Plan for South Carolina*. South Carolina Institute of Archaeology and Anthropology, University of South Carolina. *The Notebook* 7(2–3).

Steponaitis, Vincas P.
1978   Location Theory and Complex Chiefdoms: A Mississippian Example. In *Mississippian Settlement Patterns*, edited by Bruce D. Smith, pp. 417–53. New York: Academic Press.
1981   Settlement Hierarchies and Political Complexity in Nonmarket Societies: The Formative Period of the Valley of Mexico. *American Anthropologist* 83:320–63.
1983   *Ceramics, Chronology, and Community Patterns: An Archaeological Study at Moundville*. New York: Academic Press.
1986   Prehistoric Archaeology in the Southeastern United States, 1970–1985. *Annual Review of Anthropology* 14:363–404.
1991   Contrasting Patterns of Mississippian Development. In *Chiefdoms: Power, Economy, and Ideology*, edited by Timothy K. Earle, pp. 193–228. Cambridge, England: Cambridge University Press.

Stevenson, R.
1968   *Population and Political Systems in Tropical Africa*. New York: Columbia University Press.

Steward, Julian H.
1942   The Direct Historical Approach to Archaeology. *American Antiquity* 7:337–43.

Steward, Julian H. (editor)
1946–50 *Handbook of South American Indians*. Bulletin 143. Washington, D.C.: Bureau of American Ethnology.

Steward, Julian H., and L. Faron
1959   *Native Peoples of South America*. New York: McGraw-Hill.

Stirling, Matthew W.
1938   *Historical and Ethnographic Material on the Jivaro Indians*. Bulletin 117. Washington, D.C.: Bureau of American Ethnology.

Stockton, Charles W., William R. Boggess, and David M. Meko
1985   Climate and Tree Rings. In *Paleoclimate Analysis and Modeling*, edited by Alan D. Hecht, pp. 71–148. New York: John Willey and Sons.

Stoltman, James B.
1974   *Groton Plantation: An Archaeological Study of a South Carolina Locality*. Monographs of the Peabody Museum, no.1. Cambridge, Mass.: Harvard University, Peabody Museum of American Archaeology and Ethnology.

Stout, Sam D.
1972   Osteological Analysis. In The I. C. Few Site (38Pn2), edited by Roger T. Grange, Jr., pp. 193–204. Manuscript on file at the South Carolina Institute of Archaeology and Anthropology, University of South Carolina.

Stuart, George E.
1975   *The Post-Archaic Occupation of Central South Carolina*. Ph.D. dissertation, Department of Anthropology, University of North Carolina. Ann Arbor: University Microfilms.

Stuiver, Minze, and B. Becker
1986   High-precision Calibration of the Radiocarbon Time Scale, A.D. 1950–2500 B.C. *Radiocarbon* 28:863–910.

Stuiver, Minze, and Gordon W. Pearson
1986   High-precision Calibration of the Radiocarbon Time Scale, A.D. 1950–500 B.C. *Radiocarbon* 28:805–38.

Sturtevant, William C.
1983   Tribe and State in the Sixteenth and Twentieth Centuries. In *The Develop-*

ment of Political Organization in Native North America, edited by Elisabeth Tooker, pp. 3–16. Washington, D.C.: American Ethnological Society.

Sullivan, Lynne P.
1987   The Mouse Creek Phase Household. *Southeastern Archaeology* 6:16–29.

Swanton, John R.
1911   *Indian Tribes of the Lower Mississippi Valley and Adjacent Coast of the Gulf of Mexico*. Bulletin 43. Washington, D.C.: Bureau of American Ethnology.
1922   *Early History of the Creek Indians and Their Neighbors*. Bulletin 73. Washington, D.C.: Bureau of American Ethnology.
1928   *Social Organization and Social Usages of the Indians of the Creek Confederacy*. Annual Report 42. Washington, D.C.: Bureau of American Ethnology.
1931   *Source Material for the Social and Ceremonial Life of the Choctaw Indians*. Bulletin 103. Washington, D.C.: Bureau of American Ethnology.
1932   Ethnological Value of the De Soto Narratives. *American Anthropologist* 34(4):570–90.
1939   *Final Report of the United States DeSoto Commission*. House Documents, no. 71, 1st session, 76th Congress, Washington, D.C.
1946   *Indians of the Southeastern United States*. Bulletin 137. Washington, D.C.: Bureau of American Ethnology.

Tainter, Joseph A.
1977   Modeling Change in Prehistoric Social Systems. In *For Theory Building in Archaeology*, edited by Lewis R. Binford, pp. 327–51. New York: Academic Press.
1988   *The Collapse of Complex Societies*. Cambridge, England: Cambridge University Press.

Tatje, Terrence, and Raoul Naroll
1973   Two Measures of Societal Complexity: An Empirical Cross-cultural Comparison. In *A Handbook of Method in Cultural Anthropology*, edited by R. Naroll and R. Cohen. New York: Columbia University Press.

Taylor, Donna
1975   *Some Locational Aspects of Middle Range Societies*. Ph.D. dissertation, Department of Anthropology, City University of New York. Ann Arbor: University Microfilms.

Taylor, Richard L.
1979   *A Synthesis of Archaeological Resources of the South Carolina Piedmont*. Research Manuscript Series, no. 155. Columbia: University of South Carolina, South Carolina Institute of Archaeology and Anthropology.

Taylor, Richard L., and Marion F. Smith (editors)
1978   *The Report of the Intensive Survey of the Richard B. Russell Dam and Lake, Savannah River, Georgia and South Carolina*. Research Manuscript Series, no. 142. Columbia: University of South Carolina, South Carolina Institute of Archaeology and Anthropology.

Teague, George A.
1979   An Assessment of Archeological Resources in the Parr Project Area, South Carolina. Manuscript on file at the South Carolina Institute of Archaeology and Anthropology, University of South Carolina.

Thomas, Cyrus
1891   *Catalogue of Prehistoric Works East of the Rocky Mountains*. Bulletin 12. Washington, D.C.: Bureau of American Ethnology.
1894   *Report of the Mound Explorations of the Bureau of Ethnology*. Annual Report 12. Washington, D.C.: Bureau of American Ethnology.

Thomas, David H., and Clark S. Larsen
1979   *The Anthropology of St. Catherine's Island*, vol. 2: *The Refuge-Deptford Mortu-ary Complex*. Anthropological Papers of the American Museum of Natural History, no. 56(1). New York: The Museum.

Thompson, Timothy A., and William M. Gardner
1983   An Archaeological Survey of Five Islands in the Savannah River: An Impact Assessment for the Richard B. Russell Reservoir Multiple Resource Area. Manuscript on file at the Interagency Archeological Services Division, National Park Service, Atlanta.

Tippitt, V. Ann, and William H. Marquardt (editors)
1984   *Archaeological Investigations at Gregg Shoals, a Deeply Stratified Site on the Savannah River*. Russell Papers. Atlanta: National Park Service, Inter-agency Archeological Services.

Tooker, Elisabeth
1964   *An Ethnography of the Huron Indians, 1615–1649*. Bulletin 190. Washington, D.C.: Bureau of American Ethnology.

Trinkley, Michael B.
1980   *Investigation of the Woodland Period along the South Carolina Coast*. Ph.D. dissertation, Department of Anthropology, University of North Carolina. Ann Arbor: University Microfilms.
1981   *Studies of Three Woodland Period Sites in Beaufort County, South Carolina*. Columbia: South Carolina Department of Highways and Public Transpor-tation.
1983   Ceramics of the Central South Carolina Coast. *South Carolina Antiquities* 15:43–53.
1989   An Archaeological Overview of the South Carolina Woodland Period: It's the Same Old Riddle. In *Studies in South Carolina Archaeology: Papers in Honor of Robert L. Stephenson*, edited by Albert C. Goodyear III and Glen T. Hanson, pp. 73–89. Anthropological Studies, no. 9. Columbia: University of South Carolina, South Carolina Institute of Archaeology and Anthropol-ogy.

Trocolli, Ruth
1993   Women as Chiefs in the Southeast: A Reexamination of the Data. Paper presented at the 50th annual Southeastern Archaeological Conference, Raleigh, N.C., November 5.

Turke, Paul W., and Laura L. Betzig
1985   Those Who Can Do: Wealth, Status, and Reproductive Success on Ifaluk. *Ethology and Sociobiology* 6:79–87.

Turner, E. Randolph, and Robert S. Santley
1979   Deer Skins and Hunting Territories Reconsidered. *American Antiquity* 44:810–16.

Turner, V. W.
1957   *Schism and Continuity in an African Society: A Study of Ndembu Village Life*. Manchester, England: Manchester University Press.

Tyzzer, Robert N., III
1986   Human Skeletal Remains from 38An8 and 38An126. In *Prehistory in the Richard B. Russell Reservoir: The Archaic and Woodland Periods of the Upper Savannah River: The Final Report of the Data Recovery at the Anderson and Elbert County Groups: 38An8, 38An29, 38An126, 9Eb17, 9Eb19 and 9Eb21*, by W. Dean Wood, Dan T. Elliott, Teresa P. Rudolph, and Dennis B. Blanton,

pp. 361–369. Russell Papers. Atlanta: National Park Service, Interagency Archeological Services.

Underwood, E. J.
1977   *Trace Elements in Human and Animal Nutrition.* New York: Academic Press.

Upham, Steadman
1982   *Polities and Power: An Economic and Political History of the Western Pueblo.* New York: Academic Press.
1983   Intensification and Exchange: An Evolutionary Model of Non-egalitarian Socio-political Organization for the Prehistoric Plateau Southwest. In *Ecological Models in Economic Prehistory*, edited by Gordon Bronitsky. Anthropological Research Papers, no. 20. Tempe: Arizona State University.
1987   A Theoretical Consideration of Middle Range Societies. In *Chiefdoms in the Americas*, edited by Robert D.Drennan and Carlos A. Uribe, pp. 345–67. Lanham, Md.: University Press of America.
1990   Analog or Digital?: Toward a Generic Framework for Explaining the Development of Emergent Political Systems. In *The Evolution of Political Systems: Sociopolitics in Small Scale Societies*, edited by Steadman Upham, pp. 87–115. Cambridge, England: Cambridge University Press.

U.S. Geological Survey
1974   *Water Resources Data for Georgia.* Washington, D.C.: U.S. Department of the Interior, Geological Survey.

Van der Merwe, Nikolaas J., and J. C. Vogel
1978   13C Content of Human Collagen as a Measure of Prehistoric Diet in Woodland North America. *Nature* 276:815–16.

Vargas Ugarte, R.
1935   The First Jesuit Mission in Florida. The United States Catholic Historical Society, *Historical Records and Studies* 25:59–148.

Varner, John G., and Jeanette J. Varner
1951   *The Florida of the Inca by Garcilaso de la Vega.* Austin: University of Texas Press.

Vayda, Andrew P.
1960   *Maori Warfare.* Maori Monographs, no. 2. Wellington, New Zealand: Polynesian Society.
1961   Expansion and Warfare among Swidden Agriculturalists. *American Anthropologist* 63:346–58.

Vega, Garcilaso de la (The Inca)
1951   *La Florida del Inca: Historia del Adelantado, Hernando de Soto, Gouernador, y Captan General del Reino de la Florida y de Otros Heroicos Caballeros, Espanoles, e Indios.* Lisbon (2nd ed., Madrid, 1723). Translated by John G. Varner and Jeanette J. Varner. Austin: University of Texas Press.
1993   La Florida by the Inca. History of the Adelantado Hernando De Soto, Governor and Captain General of the Kingdom of La Florida, and of Other Heroic Gentlemen, Spaniards and Indians; Written by the Inca Garcilaso de la Vega, Captain of his Majesty, a Native of the Great City of El Cuzco, Capital of the Kingdoms and Provinces of El Peru. In *The De Soto Chronicles: The Expedition of Hernando De Soto to North America in 1539–1543*, vol. 2, edited by Lawrence A. Clayton, Vernon James Knight, Jr., and Edward C. Moore, pp. 25–559. Tuscaloosa: University of Alabama Press.

Verrazzano, Giovanni da
1600   The Relation of John de Verrazzano, a Florentine, of the Land by Him Discouered in the Name of His Maiestie. Written in Diepe the Eight of Iuly, 1524. In *The Third and Last Collection of the Voyages, Navigations, Traffiques,*

and Discoueries of the English Nation, and in some few places, where they have not been, of strangers, performed within and before the time of these hundred yeeres, to all parts of the Newfound world of America . . . , edited by Richard Hakluyt. London: George Bishop, Ralfe Newberie, and Robert Barker.

Waddell, Eugene
1980   *Indians of the South Carolina Lowcountry 1562–1751.* Spartanburg, S.C.: Reprint Co.

Ward, Trawick
1965   Correlation of Mississippian Soil Types. *Southeastern Archaeological Conference Bulletin* 3:42–48.
1983   A Review of Archaeology in the North Carolina Piedmont: A Study of Change. In *Prehistory of North Carolina: An Archaeological Symposium,* edited by Mark A. Mathis and Jeffery A. Crow, pp. 53–81. Raleigh, N.C.: Department of Cultural Resources, Division of Archives and History.

Waring, Antonio J., Jr.
1968a   The Southern Cult and the Muskhogean Ceremonial: General Considerations. In *The Waring Papers: The Collected Papers of Antonio J. Waring, Jr.,* edited by Stephen Williams, pp. 30–69. Papers of the Peabody Museum of American Archaeology and Ethnology, no. 58. Cambridge, Mass.: Harvard University, The Museum.
1968b   The Indian King's Tomb. In *The Waring Papers: The Collected Papers of Antonio J. Waring, Jr.,* edited by Stephen Williams, pp. 209–15. Papers of the Peabody Museum of American Archaeology and Ethnology, no. 58. Cambridge, Mass.: Harvard University, The Museum.
1968c   A History of Georgia Archaeology. In *The Waring Papers: The Collected Papers of Antonio J. Waring, Jr.,* edited by Stephen Williams, pp. 288–99. Papers of the Peabody Museum of American Archaeology and Ethnology, no. 58. Cambridge, Mass.: Harvard University, The Museum.
1968d   The Cultural Sequence at the Mouth of the Savannah River. In *The Waring Papers: The Collected Papers of Antonio J. Waring, Jr.,* edited by Stephen Williams, pp. 216–21. Papers of the Peabody Museum of American Archaeology and Ethnology, no. 58. Cambridge, Mass.: Harvard University, The Museum.
1968e   The Refuge Site, Jasper County, South Carolina. In *The Waring Papers: The Collected Papers of Antonio J. Waring, Jr.,* edited by Stephen Williams, pp. 198–208. Papers of the Peabody Museum of American Archaeology and Ethnology, no. 58. Cambridge, Mass.: Harvard University, The Museum.

Waring, Antonio J., and Holder, Preston
1945   A Prehistoric Ceremonial Complex in the Southeastern United States. *American Anthropologist* 47:1–34.

Watson, Patty Jo
1976   In Pursuit of Prehistoric Subsistence: A Comparative Account of Some Contemporary Flotation Techniques. *Midcontinental Journal of Archaeology* 1:77–100.

Wauchope, Robert
1948   The Ceramic Sequence in the Etowah Drainage, Northwest Georgia. *American Antiquity* 13:201–9.
1950   The Evolution and Persistence of Ceramic Motifs in Northern Georgia. *American Antiquity* 16:16–22.
1966   *Archaeological Survey of Northern Georgia.* Society for American Archaeology Memoir 21. Salt Lake City: University of Utah Printing Service.

Weaver, David S., Carol Roetzel, David G. Anderson, William R. Culbreth, and David C. Crass

1985 A Survey of Human Skeletal Remains from the Rucker's Bottom Site (9Eb91), Elbert County, Georgia. In *Prehistoric Human Ecology along the Upper Savannah River: Excavations at the Rucker's Bottom, Abbeville, and Bullard Site Groups*, edited by David G. Anderson and Joseph Schuldenrein, pp. 591–638. Russell Papers. Atlanta: National Park Service, Interagency Archeological Services.

Webb, Clarence H.

1977 *The Poverty Point Culture*. Geoscience and Man 17. Baton Rouge: Louisiana State University.

Webb, Robert S.

1987 *Cultural Resource Survey: Proposed Water Treatment Plant Site and Water Line Corridors, Wildwood Park, Columbia County, Georgia*. Marietta, Ga.: Webb Diversified Consulting.

Webb, Robert S., and Patrick H. Garrow

1981 *Archaeological Reconnaissance Survey: Proposed Georgia Kraft Mill, Elbert County, Georgia*. Report ES-1633A. Marietta, Ga.: Soil Systems.

Webster, David

1975 Warfare and the Evolution of the State: A Reconsideration. *American Antiquity* 40:464–70.

Weinland, Marcia K.

1981a *Assessment of Cultural Resources in Skidaway Island State Park*. Carrollton: West Georgia College, Office of the State Archaeologist.

1981b *Assessment of Cultural Resources in Alexander H. Stephens State Park, Taliaferro County, Georgia*. Carrollton, Ga.: West Georgia College, Office of the State Archaeologist.

Weiss, K. M.

1973 *Demographic Models for Anthropology*. Society for American Archaeology, Memoirs, no. 27.

Welch, Paul D.

1986 *Models of Chiefdom Economy: Prehistoric Moundville as a Case Study*. Ph.D. dissertation, Department of Anthropology, University of Michigan. Ann Arbor: University Microfilms.

1990 Mississippian Emergence in West Central Alabama. In *The Mississippian Emergence*, edited by Bruce D. Smith, pp. 197–225. Washington, D.C.: Smithsonian Institution Press.

1991 *Moundville's Economy*. Tuscaloosa: University of Alabama Press.

Wenke, Robert J.

1981 Explaining the Evolution of Cultural Complexity: A Review. *Advances in Archaeological Method and Theory*, edited by Michael B. Schiffer, 4:79–127. New York: Academic Press.

Wheaton, Thomas, Terry H. Klein, Linda Stoutenburg, Beth Gantt, Mark Bracken, and David Babson

1982 *Cultural Resource Survey and Testing of the Proposed Vogtle-Wadley Transmission Line, Burke and Jefferson Counties, Georgia*. Report 476-20056. Marietta, Ga.: Soil Systems.

White, George

1849 *Statistics of the State of Georgia*. Savannah, Ga.: W. Thorne Williams.

White, John

1972 *A Briefe and True Report of the New Found Land of Virginia by Thomas Harriot, the Complete 1590 Theodore De Bry Edition*. New York: Dover.

White, John W.
1982   An Integration of Late Archaic Settlement Patterns for the South Carolina Piedmont. M.A. thesis, Department of Anthropology, University of Arkansas.

Widmer, Randolph J.
1988   *The Evolution of the Calusa: A Non-agricultural Chiefdom on the Southwest Florida Coast.* Tuscaloosa: University of Alabama Press.

Willey, Gordon R.
1937   Notes on Central Georgia Dendrochronology. *Tree-Ring Bulletin* 4(2):6–8.
1949   *Archaeology of the Florida Gulf Coast.* Smithsonian Miscellaneous Collections, no. 113. Washington, D.C.: Smithsonian Institution Press.

Willey, Gordon R., C. DiPeso, William Ritchie, Irving Rouse, John R. Rowe, and Donald Lathrap
1956   An Archaeological Classification of Culture Contact Situations. In *Seminars in Archaeology, 1955*, edited by Robert Wauchope, pp. 1–30. Society for American Archaeology Memoir 11. Salt Lake City: University of Utah Press.

Williams, Mark
1983   *The Joe Bell Site: Seventeenth Century Lifeways on the Oconee River.* Ph.D. dissertation, Department of Anthropology, University of Georgia. Ann Arbor: University Microfilms.
1986   The Origins of Macon Plateau. Paper presented at the Ocmulgee National Monument 50th anniversary conference, Macon, Ga., December 13.
1988   *Scull Shoals Revisited: 1985 Archaeological Excavations at 9Ge4.* Watkinsville, Ga.: Lamar Institute.
1990a   *Archaeological Excavations at Shoulderbone (9Hk1).* Watkinsville, Ga.: Lamar Institute.
1990b   *Archaeological Excavations at Shinholser, 9Bl1.* Watkinsville, Ga.: Lamar Institute.

Williams, Mark, and Gary Shapiro
1986   Shoulderbone Was a 14th Century Frontier Town. Paper presented at the 43rd annual Southeastern Archaeological Conference, Nashville, Tenn., November 7.
1987   The Changing Contexts of Oconee Valley Political Power. Paper presented at the 44th annual Southeastern Archaeological Conference, Charleston, S.C., November 13.
1990a   Paired Towns. In *Lamar Archaeology: Mississippian Chiefdoms in the Deep South*, edited by Mark Williams and Gary Shapiro, pp. 163–174. Tuscaloosa: University of Alabama Press.
1990b   *Archaeological Excavations at the Little River Site (9Mg46).* Watkinsville, Ga.: Lamar Institute.

Williams, Mark, and Marvin T. Smith
1989   Power and Migration. Paper presented at the 46th annual Southeastern Archaeological Conference, Tampa, Fla., November 10.

Williams, Woody, and Carolyn Branch
1978   The Tugalo Site, 9St1. *Early Georgia* 6:32–37.

Williams, Stephen
1982   The Vacant Quarter Hypothesis. Paper presented at the 40th annual Southeastern Archaeological Conference, Memphis, Tenn., October.
1990   The Vacant Quarter and Other Events in the Lower Valley. In *Towns and Temples along the Mississippi*, edited by David H. Dye and Cheryl Anne Cox, pp. 170–80. Tuscaloosa: University of Alabama Press.

Williams, Stephen (editor)
1968   *The Collected Works of Antonio J. Waring, Jr.* Papers of the Peabody Museum of American Archaeology and Ethnology, no. 58. Cambridge, Mass.: Harvard University, The Museum.
Williams, Stephen, and Jeffrey P. Brain
1983   *Excavations at the Lake George Site, Yazoo County, Mississippi, 1958–1960.* Papers of the Peabody Museum of American Archaeology and Ethnology, no. 74. Cambridge, Mass.: Harvard University, The Museum.
Willingham, Charles G.
1983a   *Cultural Resources Survey of the Pounding Mill Creek Timber Sale, Rabun County, Georgia.* Report, no. 83GA05S01. Gainesville, Ga.: U.S.D.A. Forest Service.
1983b   *Cultural Resources Survey of the Ramey Creek Timber Sale, Rabun County, Georgia.* Report, no. 83GA05I04. Gainesville, Ga.: U.S.D.A. Forest Service.
1983c   *Cultural Resources Survey of the Hoojah Branch Timber Sale, Rabun County, Georgia.* Report, no. 83GA05S02. Gainesville, Ga.: U.S.D.A. Forest Service.
1984a   *Cultural Resource Survey of the Worley Ridge Tracts, Rabun County, Georgia.* Report, no. 82GA05I06. Gainesville, Ga.: U.S.D.A. Forest Service.
1984b   *Cultural Resources Survey of Six Wildlife Openings in Warwoman Management Area, Rabun County, Georgia.* Report, no. 84GA05X01. Gainesville, Ga.: U.S.D.A. Forest Service.
1984c   *Phase II Testing of the Hoojah Branch Site, Rabun County, Georgia.* Report, no. 83GA05T07. Gainesville, Ga.: U.S.D.A. Forest Service.
Willingham, Charles G., and Jack T. Wynn
1984   *Cultural Resources Survey of Six Timber Sales Areas in Rabun County, Georgia.* Report, no. 84GA05S06. Gainesville, Ga.: U.S.D.A. Forest Service.
Wilson, David J.
1987   *Prehispanic Settlement Patterns in the Lower Santa Valley, North Coast of Peru: A Regional Perspective on the Origins and Development of Complex Society.* Washington, D.C.: Smithsonian Institution Press.
Wing, Elizabeth S., and Antionette B. Brown
1979   *Paleonutrition and Method and Theory in Prehistoric Foodways.* New York: Academic Press.
Winterhalder, Bruce D., and Eric A. Smith
1981   *Hunter-Gatherer Foraging Strategies: Ethnographic and Archaeological Analyses.* Chicago: University of Chicago Press.
Winters, Howard D.
1968   Value Systems and Trade Cycles of the Late Archaic in the Midwest. In *New Perspectives in Archaeology*, edited by Sally R. Binford and Lewis R. Binford, pp. 175–221. Chicago: Aldine.
Wise, Robert P.
1986   *CRM: Vogtle-Effingham-Thalmann 500 kV Electric Transmission Line: GP-SN-09 Data Recovery.* Atlanta, Ga.: Garrow and Associates.
Wissler, C.
1917   *The American Indian: An Introduction to the Anthropology of the New World.* New York: D. C. McMurtrie.
Wittfogel, Karl A.
1957   *Oriental Despotism: A Comparative Study of Total Power.* New Haven, Conn.: Yale University Press.
Wobst, Martin
1977   Stylistic Behavior and Information Exchange. In *For the Director: Research Essays in Honor of James B. Griffin*, edited by Charles E. Cleland, pp. 311–42.

Anthropological Papers, no. 61. Ann Arbor: University of Michigan, Museum of Anthropology.

Wood, Judy L.
1980   *A Cultural Resources Reconnaissance of the Areas of Proposed Recreational Facilities Development in the Lake Springs Recreation Area, Clarks Hill Lake, Columbia County, Georgia.* Savannah, Ga.: U.S. Army Corps of Engineers.

Wood, Karen G.
1986   Faunal Remains from Feature 160, Simpson's Field. In *Prehistory in the Richard B. Russell Reservoir: The Archaic and Woodland Periods of the Upper Savannah River: The Final Report of the Data Recovery at the Anderson and Elbert County Groups: 38An8, 38An29, 38An126, 9Eb17, 9Eb19 and 9Eb21,* edited by W. Dean Wood, Dan T. Elliott, Teresa P. Rudolph, and Dennis B. Blanton, pp. 371–76. Russell Papers. Atlanta: National Park Service, Interagency Archeological Services.

Wood, W. Dean
1981   *An Analysis of Two Early Woodland Households from the Cane Island Site, 9Pm209.* Wallace Reservoir Project Contribution 4. Athens: University of Georgia, Department of Anthropology.

Wood, W. Dean, and Thomas Gresham
1982   Excavations at 38Lu107 in the Rabon Creek Watershed, Laurens County, South Carolina. *South Carolina Antiquities* 14:31–64.

Wood, W. Dean, and R. Jerald Ledbetter
1988   *Rush: An Early Woodland Period Site in Northwest Georgia.* Athens, Ga.: Southeastern Archaeological Services.

Wood, W. Dean, and Charlotte A. Smith
1988   *An Archaeological Evaluation of the Anthony Shoals Site.* Athens, Ga.: Southeastern Archaeological Services.

Wood, W. Dean, Dan T. Elliott, Teresa P. Rudolph, and Dennis B. Blanton
1986   *Archaeological Data Recovery in the Richard B. Russell Multiple Resource Area: The Anderson and Elbert County Groups: 38An8, 38An29, 38An126, 9Eb17, 9Eb19 and 9Eb21.* Russell Papers. Atlanta: National Park Service, Interagency Archeological Services.

Woodward, Henry
1674   A Faithful Relation of My Westoe Voyage. 1674. In *Narratives of Early Carolina 1650–1708*, edited by Alexander S. Salley, Jr., pp.130–34. New York: Barnes and Noble.

Worth, John E.
1988   Mississippian Occupation on the Middle Flint River. M.A. thesis, Department of Anthropology, University of Georgia.
1993a   Account of the Northern Conquest and Discovery of Hernando De Soto. In *The De Soto Chronicles: The Expedition of Hernando De Soto to North America in 1539–1543*, vol. 1, edited by Lawrence A. Clayton, Vernon James Knight, Jr., and Edward C. Moore, pp. 247–306. Tuscaloosa: University of Alabama Press.
1993b   Relation of the Island of Florida by Luys Hernández de Biedma. In *The De Soto Chronicles: The Expedition of Hernando De Soto to North America in 1539–1543*, vol. 1, edited by Lawrence A. Clayton, Vernon James Knight, Jr., and Edward C. Moore, pp. 221–246. Tuscaloosa: University of Alabama Press.

Worth, John E., and W. Maxwell Duke
1991   Hogcrawl Creek: Early Mississippi Period Occupation in the Middle Flint River Floodplain. *Early Georgia* 19:19–42.

Wright, Henry T.
1969   *The Administration of Rural Production in an Early Mesopotamian Town.*
        Anthropological Papers, no. 38. Ann Arbor: University of Michigan, Mu-
        seum of Anthropology.
1977   Recent Research on the Origin of the State. *Annual Review of Anthropology*
        6:379–97.
1984   Prestate Political Formations. In *On the Evolution of Complex Societies:
        Essays in Honor of Harry Hoijer, 1982*, edited by Timothy K. Earle, pp. 43–77.
        Malibu, Calif.: Undena.
1986   The Evolution of Civilizations. In *American Archaeology Past and Future: A
        Celebration of the Society for American Archaeology 1935–1985*, edited by
        David J. Meltzer, Don D. Fowler, and Jeremy A. Sabloff, pp. 323–65.
        Washington, D.C.: Smithsonian Institution Press.
1987   The Susiana Hinterlands during the Era of Primary State Formation. In *The
        Archaeology of Western Iran: Settlement and Society from Prehistory to the
        Islamic Conquest*, edited by Frank Hole, pp. 141–55. Washington, D.C.:
        Smithsonian Institution Press.
Wright, Henry T., and Gregory A. Johnson
1975   Population, Exchange, and Early State Formation in Southwestern Iran.
        American Anthropologist 77:267–89.
Wynn, Jack T.
1980a   *Cultural Resources Survey of Stamp Creek Road (FS 25) Tallulah Ranger Dis-
        trict, Rabun County, Georgia.* Report, no. 80-Ta-81-R-3. Gainesville, Ga.:
        U.S.D.A. Forest Service.
1980b   *Cultural Resources Survey of Proposed Georgia Power Company Land Exchange,
        Rabun County, Georgia.* Report, no. 80-Ta-65-E-2. Gainesville, Ga.: U.S.D.A.
        Forest Service.
1980c   *Cultural Resources Survey of Darnell Creek Road (FS 150) Tallulah Ranger
        District, Rabun County, Georgia.* Report, no. 80-Ta-15-R-2. Gainesville, Ga.:
        U.S.D.A. Forest Service.
1981a   *Cultural Resources Survey of Stamp Creek Road Extension, Rabun County,
        Georgia.* Report, no. 81-Ta-83-R-1. Gainesville, Ga.: U.S.D.A. Forest Service.
1981b   *Cultural Resources Survey of Walnut Fork Road (FS 155), Rabun County,
        Georgia.* Report, no. 81-Ta-36-R-2. Gainesville, Ga.: U.S.D.A. Forest Service.
1982a   *Cultural Resources Overview for the Chattahoochee-Oconee National Forests.*
        Gainesville, Ga.: U.S.D.A. Forest Service.
1982b   *Cultural Resources Survey Thrift Exchange Tract, Stephens County, Georgia.*
        Report, no. 82-CA-233-E-1. Gainesville, Ga.: U.S.D.A. Forest Service.
1983   *Cultural Resource Surveys on Tullulah District, FY 1986, Rabun County,
        Georgia.* Report, no. 86GA05E01. Gainesville, Ga.: U.S.D.A. Forest Service.
Yoffee, Norman
1993   Too Many Chiefs? (or, Safe Texts for the '90s). In *Archaeological Theory: Who
        Sets the Agenda?* edited by Norman Yoffee and Andrew Sherratt, pp. 60–78.
        Cambridge, England: Cambridge University Press.

Index

Abandonment: of European colonies, 57, 63, 64, 65, 68, 285; of features, 232; of fields, 231, 248; of sites, 81, 86, 93, 102, 103, 136, 138, 143, 145, 164, 174, 192, 213, 214, 237, 240, 242, 249, 253, 267, 286, 287, 291, 293, 294, 296, 297, 299, 300, 302, 304, 306, 309, 310, 311, 312, 316, 319, 325, 342, 372; of structures, 196, 198, 228, 290, 291, 293, 325; territorial, 3, 4, 27, 103, 133, 134, 147, 158, 237, 240, 242, 249, 260, 261, 263, 267, 275, 286, 287, 288, 302, 304, 311, 319, 324, 325, 326–29, 367, 368
Acorns, 69, 203, 225, 226, 231, 300, 317, 319
Adamson mound group, 80
Adelphic succession, 33
Affinal kin, 6, 16, 26
African chiefdoms, 1, 11, 21, 22, 26, 29, 36, 43, 45, 46
Agnathic inheritance, 92
Agricultural shortfall, 21, 38, 79, 275, 276, 280, 281, 283, 285, 286, 287, 288, 319, 321, 324, 327
Alabama River phase, 123, 149
Allatoona Reservoir, 195, 372
Allendale chert quarries, 164, 273
Allendale County, S.C., 161, 164, 187, 270, 271, 336, 368
Alliance networks, 14, 15, 16, 23, 25, 26, 44, 47, 49, 50, 53, 70, 74, 77, 78, 88, 89, 99, 101, 102, 105, 132, 134, 136, 137, 142, 147, 153, 154, 155, 289
Amaranth, 203
American Bottom, 136, 138, 140, 141, 142, 143, 144, 145, 308, 330
American Revolution, 213, 274
Anasazi, 287
Ancestor cults, 79–82
Anderson phase, 375
Anghiera, Pietro Martiere d', 56, 57
Anilco, 81
Anneewakee Creek site, 374
Apalachee, 59, 67, 77, 94, 106, 109, 136
Appalachian Summit, 163, 373
Appalachicola Indians, 372
Arc-angle motif, 370
Arthritis, 203
Atomic absorbtion spectrometry, 224
Auger sampling, 228
Augusta, Ga., 159, 162, 163, 194, 223, 337, 338, 343, 344
Authority structures, 2, 7, 12–20, 22, 26, 35, 39, 43, 45, 46, 47, 48, 50, 136, 323;

centralized, 119; evolution of, 20, 33, 330; ideological, 79; sacred vs. secular, 19
Awls, 181, 183
Azande, 43, 45
Aztalan site, 140

Bald cypress, 277, 289, 336
Bandera, Juan de la, 66, 68, 97
Bantu, 37
Barbacoas, 71, 77, 222, 301
Bark cloth, 77, 78, 135, 191, 352
Barnett phase, 135
Bartram, William, 158, 193, 194, 217, 221, 337, 338, 343, 354, 355, 356, 358, 361
Beads: bone, 347; glass, 58, 164, 372; shell, 164, 173, 181, 183, 191, 196, 217, 218, 221, 224, 294, 304, 333, 342, 352, 353, 358, 372
Beaverdam Creek mound site, 124, 171, 172, 196–205, 227, 228, 232, 235, 237, 240, 286, 290, 296–99, 300, 304, 306, 307, 308, 309, 312, 313, 314, 316, 317, 318, 373, 375
Beaverdam phase, 159, 195, 196, 205, 217, 219, 221, 224, 225, 227, 230, 233, 234, 245, 296, 299, 300, 301, 306, 316, 318, 319, 320, 321, 322, 370, 373, 375, 377; diagnostic ceramics, 375
Beaverdam Site Group, 172, 232
Bell Field site, 128
Bell phase, 258
Bessemer site, 308
Biedma, Luys Hernandez de, 58, 60, 61, 62, 76, 99
Big Generostee Creek site, 172, 232–33, 316
Big-man systems, 16
Bilbo site, 366
Black drink, 57, 183
Black Warrior River, 121, 134, 145, 147, 149
Blair mound site, 267, 287
Blake, Michael, 36, 129
Blanton, Dennis B., 362
Blastomycosis, 203
Blitz, John, 292
Blue Ridge physiographic province, 165, 250, 260, 261, 271
Bogan, Arthur A., 125
Bold incising, 233, 249, 255, 367, 370, 376
Borrow pits, 184, 222, 358
Bottles, ceramic, 181, 183, 190, 191, 348, 350
Boulders, mound, 199, 207, 211, 213, 214, 301, 307
Boundary markers, 41, 259, 270

Killed pots, 191, 350
King site, 219
Kinship, 6, 22, 45, 46, 85, 92, 141
Knight, V. James, Jr., 79, 84, 89, 127
Kolomoki site, 374
Kowalewski, Stephen A., 115
Kuma, 33
Kus, Susan, 111, 112, 113

L-Lake sites, 369
Labor, 6, 13, 14, 16, 20, 21, 27, 30, 41, 44, 53,
    81, 84, 97, 98, 101, 113, 124, 127, 133, 137,
    141, 147, 150, 293, 319, 320, 325, 354, 357
Laboratory of Archaeology, University of
    Georgia, 165
Lake Jackson site, 136
Lake Spring site, 163, 372
La Libertad site, 22
Lamar Bold Incised, 376
Lamar ceramics, 114, 115, 154, 162, 201,
    210, 211, 213, 255, 306, 372, 375, 377;
    design motifs, 365
Lamar Complicated Stamped, 370, 375, 376
Lamar site, 354
Land plats, 194
Langford, James, 151
Larson, Lewis H., 129, 133
Late Woodland, 123, 145, 163, 195, 217,
    230, 233, 235, 250–52, 253, 317, 318, 363,
    366, 368, 369, 371, 373, 374, 375, 376, 377
Laudonnière, René, 55, 64, 65, 89, 101, 103
Lawson, John, 85
Lawton mounds, 161, 171, 172, 187–89, 237,
    240, 249, 252, 253, 270, 286, 309, 310, 311,
    332, 371; description by C. B. Moore,
    336–37
Lawton phase (provisional), 159, 187, 189,
    252, 310, 370, 375; diagnostic ceramics,
    370
Ledford Island site, 219
Lee, Chung Ho, 118
Le Moyne de Morgues, Jacques, 64, 65, 76,
    293
Lenski, Gerhard E., 17, 21, 29, 31, 32, 35, 36,
    43
Lindsey mound site, 162
Line block motif, 362, 367, 368, 370, 376
Lithic raw material sources, 35, 101, 162,
    164, 201, 271–74
Litters, chiefly, 57, 71, 76, 82
Little Egypt, 64, 81, 151, 154
Little Egypt site, 128
Little Tennessee River, 376
Little Tennessee site cluster, 154
Locational analyses, 34, 36–37, 41, 115–18,
    121, 130, 132, 136, 141, 147, 151–53, 155,
    328–29
Lohmann phase, 136, 138, 140, 141, 143,
    144

Lohmann site, 138, 145
Long-distance exchange, 15, 23, 29, 32, 42,
    44, 78, 94, 111, 112, 136, 137, 143, 147,
    149, 201, 271, 296
Looting, 157, 187, 190, 199, 205, 213, 217,
    297, 333, 334, 336, 358, 360
Lower Cherokee Towns, 158, 164, 205, 210,
    213, 217, 218, 270, 273, 274; possible
    origin, 304, 305, 328, 376
Lozi, 21, 37, 45
Lubbub Creek site, 148, 321
Luna y Arellano, Tristan de, 54, 55, 60, 63,
    64, 69, 70, 72, 73, 98, 101, 102, 103, 106,
    117, 151, 153, 154, 155
Lunda, 22, 76
Lunsford-Pulcher site, 138, 144

McCann, Catherine, 183, 184, 314, 362, 370
McDowell mound site, 267, 287
Machiavelli, Niccoló, 103
Macon Plateau, 289, 308, 354, 357, 362, 374,
    375
Madisonville phase, 133
Magnesium, 123, 224, 321
Managerial stress arguments, 12, 13
Mandeville site, 374
Manganese, 123
Mangareva, 19
Marquardt, William H., 86
Martinez, Francisco, 66
Mason's Plantation mound group, 157,
    161, 170, 171, 172, 193–94, 195, 235, 237,
    240, 242, 249, 252, 253, 270, 286, 287, 296,
    309, 332, 370, 371; description by C. B.
    Moore, 343; description by C. C. Jones,
    338, 343; interpretation as Cofitachequi,
    193, 338, 343
Matrilineality, 26, 33, 45, 46, 62, 76, 84–87,
    89, 92, 93, 129
Mauvilla, 62, 67
Maygrass, 203
Maypops, 203, 204, 225, 228, 231
Menéndez de Avilés, Pedro, 65, 66, 284
Men's houses, 140
Mesoamerica, 25, 331
Mesopotamia, 10, 330
Metavolcanics, 271, 272, 273
Mica, 191, 201, 340, 344, 352, 360
Micos, 96, 97, 104, 118
Middle-range theory, 156
Migration, 46, 47, 48, 102, 142, 144, 287,
    296, 307, 311, 328, 329
Miller, Carl F., 163, 195
Milner, George R., 138, 141, 143
Minimum-number-of-individuals, 204, 227
Mississippian: change over time, 136–37;
    definitions, 108–11
Mississippian Burnished Plain, 370
Mississippian Plain, 370
Mississippian triangular points, 157, 184,

About the Author

David G. Anderson is an archaeologist with the National Park Service Regional Office in Atlanta, Georgia. He received his doctorate in anthropology from the University of Michigan in 1990. He is coauthor of more than twenty monographs, seventy published papers, and fifty papers presented at professional meetings.